THE COMPLEXITIE
Integrative Essays in Psych

Nancy J. Kenney
Michelle D. Brot
Karen E. Moe
Kitty Dahl
University of Washington

KENDALL/HUNT PUBLISHING COMPANY
4050 Westmark Drive   Dubuque, Iowa 52002

Cover Art

Eva Isaksen was born in Norway in 1955. She grew up in
Bodo, a city north of the Arctic Circle. She moved to the
United States in 1980, where she earned a Master of Fine Arts
degree. Eva now lives in Seattle. During the last few years she
has concentrated on monotypes, a type of print. She paints
directly onto a plate, and the paint is then transferred to the
paper. The same plate is altered, and the paper then pulled
through the press again. A single print may be pulled through
the press more than 20 times in order to achieve its
deep-toned shading and strong contrasts. Most of Eva's work
carries strong reference to nature and seasonal changes, which
are reiterated by the cyclical nature of the printing process
itself. She uses nature as a metaphor for psychological issues
arising from her own life, which has been deeply inspired by
different cultures and climates. Eva's work is usually abstract,
in contrast to the monotype used here, which she designed
specifically to capture the content and spirit of this book.

Copyright © 1992 by Kendall/Hunt Publishing Company

Library of Congress Catalog Card Number: 91-76825

ISBN 0-8403-8548-X

Printed in the United States of America
10 9 8 7 6 5 4 3

Dedication

To our Mothers, Sisters, Children and Students who have taught us so much.

Figure 1. "Waihines o'Wailea" by Ken Schutt. Photographed and reprinted by permission of the Wailea Four Seasons Resort, Wailea, Maui.

Contents

Chapter 7

Chapter 8

Chapter 9

Chapter 10

Preface

Scientists have long argued that women's bodies are more complex than men's. To some extent, this is true. Women have monthly menstrual cycles during which the levels of numerous hormones vary in a dramatic fashion. And women, unlike men, are equipped for the processes of pregnancy and childbirth which require rapid modification of all of their biological systems—a process which makes even the transitions of puberty pale by comparison.

Traditionally women have been denied access to information related to their biological functioning. Such information is the domain of science. Our tradition tells us that science is complex, it's masculine, it's too hard for women to understand. Spelled out like this, these ideas sound archaic and slightly ridiculous. And yet we can see evidence of their impact on women's lives everywhere. Girls are discouraged, both subtly and directly, from the study of science in high schools and from training for scientific careers. Women are encouraged to seek a physician's (usually male) advice about the normal and abnormal workings of their bodies. Contraceptive and hormone treatments are prescribed, "female" parts of the body removed or manipulated surgically in epidemic proportions. Such events frequently occur with the woman having little if any information about the drugs prescribed, the usual or any unusual side-effects of drugs or surgery. A woman who dares to ask "why" or "what for" all too commonly receives a glib response suggesting that she relax and "trust" her healthcare provider or she is subjected to an outpouring of incomprehensible jargon.

Women are often left to their own devices in discovering the truths about their bodies. They rely on friends, family and the popular media for information. Frequently, their sources of information are no better informed than they are. The information obtained may be inaccurate or lag behind current scientific understanding. Or, in the case of the media, the presentation may be limited to the sensational with little relevance to the everyday functioning of women in general.

The purpose of this book is to provide a source of current scientific knowledge about the biological milestones and issues of women's lives. We have searched the scientific and popular literature for articles which present, in the clearest possible terms, the biological events experienced by women, the psychological or behavioral implications of these events and the latest options provided by medical and biological science which directly affect women's lives. Utilizing previously-published articles made it impossible to avoid jargon entirely. Thus, we have included a comprehensive glossary of the specialty terms used throughout the book. This glossary should not only make it easier to comprehend the articles presented here but should also provide the reader with a "decoder" for future reading and for conversations with those individuals (such as physicians) who speak this language on a regular basis.

For those readers with little or no background in the biology of women and for those who might like a refresher course, we have included a brief overview of the female reproductive system (Chapter 1). Readers already familiar with this topic may want to skip this chapter.

The list of topics which could be included in a book like this is lengthy. The toughest decisions we faced in preparing this book were ones related to the inclusion or exclusion of topics. In making these difficult choices we relied heavily on the comments and questions raised by the approximately 3000 students who have taken our course in Psychobiology of Women at the University of Washington over the past 15 years. We have searched through scholarly publications in the fields of medicine, nursing, social work, biology, psychology, women studies, sociology and ethics as well as numerous popular magazines to find articles which offer clear and accurate presentations of current knowledge. Having selected the best for presentation here, we also included a list of additional sources at the end of each chapter which can be pursued for further information.

The major shortcomings of this book reflect those of the sciences we surveyed. Researchers in these areas rely heavily on young, white, urban, middle- to upper-middle class, highly-educated, heterosexual women as their subjects of study. We searched for studies utilizing women of other ages, races, classes and sexual-orientations only to find that in the relatively few cases where such studies exist, they usually examine extremely specific, often stereotypical, situations and provide no overview of the lives of such women. It is our hope that this book will encourage current and future scientists to include a wider variety of women in their work.

This book represents the first truly interdisciplinary presentation of the major biological issues in women's lives. As such, it can serve as a primary or supplemental text in undergraduate and graduate courses in a variety of disciplines such as psychology, sociology, biology, women studies and nursing. It can function as a resource for all people, both women and men, who want to understand women's experiences of puberty, the monthly cycle, sexuality, contraception, wanted and unwanted pregnancy, infertility, and menopause. It provides a foundation of knowledge which will prepare both women and men to evaluate future scientific and technological discoveries which intimately affect women's lives and the workings of our society.

We would like to extend our special thanks to Eva Isaksen who designed the original artwork for the cover of this book. While the design depicted is not typical of Eva's portfolio, she graciously modified her artistic approach to fit the theme of this book. We cannot thank her enough.

Our thanks also to our families, friends, and colleagues who offered moral support throughout this project, in good times and, especially, in bad. And our special thanks to all the women and men who inspired this book through their active and stimulating participation in our Psychology/Women Studies course, Psychobiology of Women, over the years.

Nancy J. Kenney
Michelle D. Brot
Karen E. Moe
Kitty Dahl
Seattle, Washington

Chapter 1

A Preview/Review of Women's Reproductive Biology

Medicine and the biological sciences have made phenomenal progress in their understanding of the human body. Scientists now know more about how our bodies function, what is good for them and what is bad than at any time in history. This knowledge has increased the ability to cure and to avoid disease. It has also created many ethical questions about the right to life, the economics of curing the sick versus maintaining the healthy, and the relationship between quality and length of life.

Some of the greatest advances of medical science have had a direct impact on the lives of women. Over the last few decades, options for contraception have increased in number and accessibility, allowing more women the option of family planning. Our understanding of genetically-transmitted diseases and our ability to diagnose them prenatally have given women options to determine which problems they can best cope with in their children. Modern reproductive technology has made it possible for women to have healthier babies later in life and for some infertile women to bear children. Numerous other examples could be described.

While medical options and biological understanding of women's bodies have increased dramatically, the knowledge of individual women about their bodies and about the options made available to them by medicine and science has lagged far behind. Traditionally, women have not been expected to understand the biological underpinnings of the major life events they commonly experience. Women today experience the monthly menstrual cycle, practice contraception, get pregnant or undergo infertility treatment, have children, experience menopause and counsel their children in these events, having little more information than did women one, two, and even three generations ago.

Why do women have so little knowledge about events so central to their lives? There is no easy answer to this question. A number of factors may play a role. First, our educational system provides little information for either girls or boys about the normal physiological functioning of their reproductive systems. The controversy over sex education and the still Puritanical view of our society toward sex-related information has had a major influence on the education of our children. While many people argue that these

1

topics should be taught by the parents in the home, very few parents have enough accurate information to pass on to their children. Even those that do often find it hard to believe that their children are old enough to be told or to understand these details. Second, while topics such as menstruation and female sexuality are sensationalized by the media, the publicity has done little or nothing to alleviate society's predominantly negative view toward these normal biological functions. Finally, most people in our society still believe that medicine and science are the province of men. As a result of this stereotype, girls come to believe that the workings of their bodies are too complex for the female mind to understand. While the number of women entering scientifically-based professions has increased, their numbers remain small. Thus, only a tiny percentage of all women have in-depth knowledge of the latest discoveries of science which affect the lives of all women.

Today, many women are finding that this system does not work for them. They have a greater desire to know what is happening in their lives, to know what options are available to them, and to make informed decisions among the myriad of options provided. It is the goal of this book to help women understand their bodies, the unique physiological events that have so much impact on their lives, and the technology that is currently available for dealing with those events.

It is true that a woman's body is complex. A wonderful circuit of intimately interconnected **endocrine** or hormone-producing glands release into her bloodstream an entire orchestra of substances which act together to prepare her body each month for the possibility of pregnancy. The entire circuit can be likened to a symphony with each organ being responsible for the production and release of just the right hormone at just the right time. While the end result might be considered complex, it *is* understandable.

The remainder of this chapter is devoted to an overview of the glands and hormones which control the female reproductive system. Those readers who are already familiar with this material may want to go directly to Chapter 2. Those readers less familiar with the woman's reproductive system should review the following material at this time.

The Monthly Cycle

One of the most common myths about the monthly cycle of women is that each cycle is 28 days long. While this is the average cycle length for all women, many perfectly normal women experience cycles much shorter or much longer than this standard. Cycles as short as 21 days or as long as 35 days are all considered to be within the normal range.

The cycle is traditionally divided into two parts. The first half of the cycle runs from the first day of **menses** or menstrual bleeding to **ovulation** (the release of the **ovum** (egg) from the ovary). This part of the cycle is called the **preovulatory** or **follicular phase**. Interestingly, this is the part of the monthly cycle that varies in length. When two women experience cycles of different lengths or when the cycle of one woman differs in length from month to month, it is typically variation in the length of the preovulatory phase of the cycle that accounts for the differences in cycle length. This is important as many women erroneously believe that they can predict ovulation by simply counting a fixed number of days from the start of menstrual bleeding. If a survey were taken, we would probably find that a large number of us now populating the earth are here due to this simple misconception about the cycle.

The second half of the cycle runs from ovulation to the first day of the next menstrual bleeding. This is the **postovulatory** or **luteal phase** of the cycle. The length of the postovulatory phase of the cycle is relatively fixed at 14 ± 2 days. In other words, for the vast majority of women, menses or menstrual bleeding begins 12 to 16 days after ovulation. Thus, once a woman's period begins, she can count backwards to determine a restricted number of days during which ovulation must have occurred. Since this can only be done after-the-fact, it is not a useful method of contraception.

The Glands and Hormones of the Monthly Cycle

The hormones which work together to determine a woman's monthly cycle come from three major sources: the ovaries, the anterior pituitary and the hypothalamus (see Figure 1).

The Ovaries

Most women have two ovaries. These small glands, each about the size of a flattened walnut, are suspended by ligaments within the pelvic cavity. The ovaries serve two functions. First, they are the site of the maturation of the **ova** or eggs, the female contribution to the development of a baby. Second, they are a major site of hormone production.

When a girl is born, her ovaries already contain all of the ova she will ever produce. Each ovum is enclosed in a layer of cells called the **ovarian follicle**. The ovaries of a newborn baby girl contain approximately 400,000 to 1 million immature ova each surrounded by its own follicle. Between birth and puberty, the number of immature ova decreases. At puberty, only about 50,000 immature ova remain. The reason for this decrease in number (which actually begins before birth) is not known.

The ovaries are relatively inactive prior to puberty. Levels of hormones produced by the ovaries of adult women are very low in prepubescent girls. Although we tend to think of puberty as the time when ovarian-hormone levels begin to cycle (increase and decrease in a regular fashion), the cyclicity of these hormones actually begins years before the first menstrual period (**menarche**). The amplitude of the changes in ovarian hormone levels prior to puberty is very small, however. In other words, there's only a small difference between the highest and the lowest level of the hormones during each month. As puberty progresses, the variation increases until the adult pattern of hormone release is achieved.

At the beginning of each monthly cycle, a number of immature follicles and ova begin the maturation process. Under normal conditions only one of these follicle-ovum units (the **Graafian follicle**) will complete the maturation process. The Graafian follicle

3

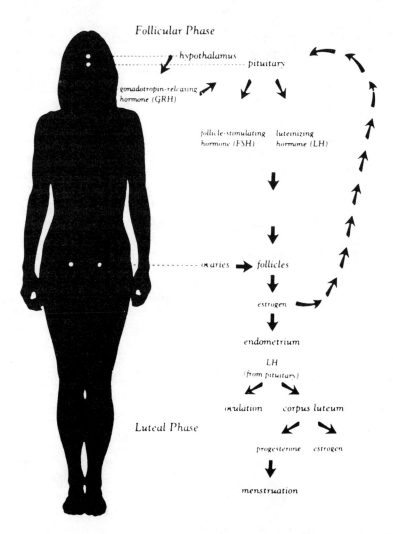

Follicular Phase

hypothalamus
pituitary
gonadotropin-releasing
hormone (GRH)

follicle-stimulating   luteinizing
hormone (FSH)   hormone (LH)

ovaries → follicles

estrogen

endometrium

LH
(from pituitary)

ovulation   corpus luteum

Luteal Phase

progesterone   estrogen

menstruation

Figure 1. This drawing describes hormone activity during the monthly cycle. During the preovulatory phase of the cycle, the hypothalamus produces gonadotropin releasing hormone (GRH) which stimulates the (anterior) pituitary to release the gonadotropins FSH and LH. FSH stimulates the development of the ovarian follicles. LH stimulates the production of estrogens by the developing follicles. During the preovulatory phase, the Graafian follicle becomes dominant and increases its estrogen production. When the ovum contained by the Graafian follicle is mature, a large amount of estrogen is secreted. This high level of estrogen triggers the release of a large amount of GRH and, consequently, LH and FSH. The surge in LH and FSH stimulates ovulation.

    After ovulation, LH transforms the remaining cells of the ruptured follicle into the corpus luteum and stimulates the corpus luteum to produce estrogens. Prolactin (also from the anterior pituitary) stimulates the production of progesterone by the corpus luteum. Progesterone prevents the anterior pituitary from producing FSH, thus halting the development of additional follicles. If the ovum is not fertilized, the corpus luteum dies and estrogen and progesterone levels drop. Menses begins as the cycle begins again. See the text for a more detailed explanation of all of the hormones and glands which regulate the monthly cycle.

contains the ovum which will be released at ovulation. The rest of the follicles that began the maturation process that month die off. While this process may sound extremely wasteful of ova, recall that a woman's ovaries contain over 50,000 immature ova at puberty. Using one ovum per month between puberty and menopause requires only 400–500 ova.

During the first half of the monthly cycle (prior to ovulation), the ovarian follicle is the site of hormone production within the ovary (Figure 1). The major hormone produced by the ovarian follicle is **estrogen**. Scientists once argued that it was the presence of estrogens that made women women. Another class of hormones, the **androgens,** were thought to be the masculinizing influence in men. We now know that the bodies of both women and men make both estrogens and androgens. But women have much more estrogen than men and men have much more androgen than women. Perhaps it is telling that the term androgen is derived from Greek meaning ''to make a man'' whereas the term estrogen is derived from Latin meaning ''to make frenzy.''

Estradiol is the most prevalent estrogen produced by the cycling woman. Frequently the words estradiol and estrogen are used interchangeably when referring to the cycling woman. The major role of estradiol during the monthly cycle is to stimulate the growth and development of the **endometrium** (the lining of the uterus) in preparation for pregnancy. Estradiol's actions are not limited to the reproductive organs, however. Estrogens act at every cell in the woman's body. In addition to its effect on the uterus, estradiol is involved in the regulation of blood pressure, the softening of the skin, and the development of female secondary sex characteristics such as the widening of the hips, the deposition of fat in ''female-appropriate'' sites such as the buttocks and the breasts and many other biological functions.

When the ovum is mature, ovulation takes place. Ovulation consists of the rupturing of the Graafian follicle and the release of its contents including the ovum. Some women can feel ovulation taking place. The sensation can vary from a slight, short-lived twinge to severe pain mimicking that of appendicitis. Pain felt at ovulation is called **Mittelschmerz** and is caused when the blood that is lost as the follicle ruptures irritates the tissue within the peritoneal cavity around the ovary.

After ovulation, the cells remaining from the Graafian follicle regroup to form a new hormone-producing structure called the **corpus luteum** (Figure 1). The corpus luteum produces the hormones **progesterone** and estrogen during the postovulatory or luteal phase of the monthly cycle. Progesterone is one of a class of hormones called the **progestins**. Its major reproductive action is to work with estrogen in preparing the uterus for pregnancy. Like estrogen, progesterone acts at all cells in a woman's body so its actions are not all directly related to reproduction.

If the woman does not become pregnant, the corpus luteum dies within 14 ± 2 days after ovulation took place. The cause of the death of the corpus luteum in women has not been identified. Scientists speculate that the signal may come from the uterus in the form of a yet-unidentified hormone which is referred to as **luteolytic** (luteum killing) **hormone**. Once the corpus luteum dies, the cycle begins again.

The Anterior Pituitary

The functioning of the ovary is directly controlled by hormones produced by the **anterior pituitary**. The anterior pituitary is the front portion of a small pea-like structure which hangs below an area of the brain called the **hypothalamus**. The hormones produced by the anterior pituitary which control the function of the ovaries are called the **gonadotropins** (Greek for turning towards the **gonad;** the gonads are the organs which produce the reproductive cells, i.e., the ovaries in women and the testes in men.) There are three gonadotropins: **LH** (luteinizing hormone), **FSH** (follicle-stimulating hormone) and **prolactin.**

LH has multiple functions which make it an integral part of all aspects of the monthly cycle. During the monthly cycle, **LH:**

1. **stimulates the ovarian follicle to make estrogen**
2. **works with FSH to cause ovulation**
3. **causes the corpus luteum to develop** and
4. **stimulates the corpus luteum to make estrogen.**

FSH stimulates the **growth of the ovarian follicle** and **works with LH to stimulate ovulation**. The actions of prolactin are best understood in terms of breastfeeding. After childbirth, prolactin stimulates the production of milk by the mammary glands of the breast. It also plays an important role in the monthly cycle. **Prolactin stimulates the production and release of progesterone from the corpus luteum during the postovulatory phase of the cycle.** Excessive or reduced levels of prolactin have been implicated in some forms of infertility.

The Hypothalamus

The **hypothalamus** is a small area at the base or bottom of the brain just above the roof of the mouth. This relatively small area of the brain is known to be involved in a variety of basic physiological functions including the control of hunger, thirst, sex-drive, and temperature regulation. In addition to these functions, the hypothalamus produces substances called **releasing hormones** which control the production and release of the gonadotropins by the anterior pituitary (Figure 1).

A single hypothalamic releasing hormone controls the secretion of both LH and FSH. This releasing hormone is called **gonadotropin releasing hormone (GRH or GnRH).** Some older sources (such as the Golub reading in the chapter on puberty) refer to two different releasing hormones controlling LH and FSH production, LRF and FRF. More recent studies have determined that there is only one releasing factor for both of these hormones. While it is chemically identical to what used to be called LRF, it has been renamed GRH.

Hypothalamic control of the production and release of the gonadotropin prolactin is more complicated. The hypothalamus produces two releasing hormones which regulate prolactin. One, **prolactin releasing hormone**, stimulates the production and release of prolactin by the anterior pituitary. The second, **dopamine,** inhibits production and release of prolactin by the anterior pituitary. Although you will read less about these controllers of prolactin than about GRH, the presence of multiple controls suggests that the precise regulation of prolactin levels must be important for normal functioning of the reproductive system.

Hormone Levels Across the Monthly Cycle

The ovary, the anterior pituitary and the hypothalamus work in concert to control the monthly cycle (Figure 1). On Day 1 of the cycle (the first day of menstrual bleeding), the ovary contains no developing follicles and no corpus luteum. As a consequence, a woman's levels of both estrogen and progesterone are very low. The lack of estrogen and progesterone tells the hypothalamus to produce GRH. In turn, GRH tells the anterior pituitary to produce FSH and LH. FSH causes immature follicles (containing immature ova) in the ovary to begin to grow and mature. At the same time, LH stimulates the growing follicles to produce estrogen. Estrogen levels rise gradually through most of the preovulatory phase of the cycle.

When the Graafian follicle along with its ovum reaches maturity, the follicle signals the hypothalamus by releasing a tremendous surge of estrogen. In response, the hypothalamus releases of large amount of GRH. The consequent surge of LH and FSH from the anterior pituitary causes ovulation to take place.

Following ovulation, LH and FSH levels decrease. LH causes the cells remaining from the ruptured follicle to regroup into the corpus luteum. The corpus luteum begins producing estrogen (in response to the presence of LH) and progesterone (in response to the presence of prolactin). The estrogen and progesterone secreted by the corpus luteum act directly on the anterior pituitary to keep FSH in check, thus preventing additional follicle growth. If the ovum that was released at ovulation is not fertilized, the corpus luteum dies within 14 ± 2 days after ovulation took place. Estrogen and progesterone levels drop to very low levels and menstruation begins as the cycle starts over again.

Androgens

There are multiple sources of androgens in a woman's body. Both the ovarian follicle and the corpus luteum secrete small amounts of androgens. Levels of androgens coming from these ovarian structures vary across the monthly cycle following a pattern similar to that of estrogen although at a much attenuated level.

The majority of a woman's androgens come from another endocrine or hormone-producing gland, the **adrenal cortex**. The adrenal cortex is the outer rind of the tiny adrenal gland which sits just above the kidney. This gland produces not only androgens but also estrogens, progesterone and other hormones which are involved in the regulation of metabolism and electrolyte levels. The amounts of estrogens and progesterone produced by the adrenal cortex are relatively insignificant to the cycling woman.

The most prevalent androgen produced in women is **androstenedione**. This form of androgen is much less potent than the better-known androgen, **testosterone**. Testosterone is the most prevalent form of androgen produced in men. Cells in a woman's body which use androstenedione are equipped to convert this androgen to testosterone. Other cells are not. Thus, the woman can have localized androgen effects without risking total masculinization of her body.

Not much is known about the role of androgen in women. It is known to be involved the growth of underarm and pubic hair and to be a cause of acne. Behaviorally, androgen has been suggested to play a role in the control of female sex drive although the specifics of its action and its degree of control are still disputed.

Androgen can also be converted to estrogen. A significant site of conversion of androgen to estrogen is body fat. While this route of estrogen production may not be important during a woman's reproductive years, it may be significant during puberty and after menopause. During puberty, the amount of body fat in girls increases. As more fat becomes available, more androgen is converted to estrogen. Increased estrogen may trigger changes in the functioning of the hypothalamus which are necessary before ovarian-hormone production can reach adult levels.

After menopause, the conversion of androgen to estrogen in **adipose** (fat) tissue may offer some protection against the serious consequences of estrogen loss such as **osteoporosis** (loss of bone tissue). Research has suggested that obese women are less likely than lean women to develop osteoporosis after menopause.

The Uterus

The uterus has been amazingly misunderstood throughout history. At one time, the uterus was blamed for all of the psychological and most of the physical problems a woman experienced. Remnants of these beliefs may underlie the epidemic rate of **hysterectomy** (surgical removal of the uterus) in the U. S. today.

The uterus is a hollow, extremely muscular organ designed to house the fetus during development. Shaped like an upside-down triangle, the uterus is located in the center of the lower pelvic cavity. The upper, wider portion of the uterus is called the **fundus;** its narrow lower section which extends into the vagina is called the **cervix.** The **Fallopian tubes** (the tubes which transport the ovum from the ovary to the uterus) join the uterus at the fundus. At the bottom of the cervix is the **cervical os,** the opening between the vagina and the uterus.

The layer of cells lining the uterus (the **endometrium)** goes through a series of changes during the monthly cycle as the ovarian-hormone levels vary. The best recognized phase of the endometrial cycle is **menses** or menstrual bleeding. During this phase of the cycle, the cells of the endometrium die and are removed from the body with the menstrual fluid. Menstrual fluid is made up of blood coming from blood vessels damaged as the endometrium dies, fluids which had filled the endometrial cells, and tissue fragments from the cells themselves.

As estrogen levels increase during the preovulatory phase, the endometrium is rebuilt. New cells are added to replace those lost during menses. This period of endometrial renewal is called the **proliferative phase.**

After ovulation, progesterone acts with estrogen to further prepare the endometrium for pregnancy. The cells of the endometrium fill with **glycogen** (a stored form of glucose) and fats. The glycogen will provide nutriment for the fertilized ovum as it implants in the uterine wall. The fats, on the other hand, make the endometrium a soft and protective place for implantation to take place. This phase of endometrial development is called the **secretory phase.** As noted above, if the ovum is not fertilized, estrogen and progesterone levels drop as the corpus luteum dies. In absence of estrogen and progesterone, the cells of the endometrium die. The cycle begins again with menses.

The cells lining the cervix of the uterus are also sensitive to the cyclic changes in ovarian-hormone levels. Cervical cells produce a fluid or mucus which varies in consistency as estrogen and progesterone levels change. At midcycle, when ovulation is imminent, the high levels of estrogen cause the cervical mucus to be rather liquid and stringy, very much like raw egg whites. This slippery mucus facilitates conception by making it easier for sperm to swim into the uterus from the vagina. During the luteal phase, when progesterone levels are high, the cervical mucus becomes very thick and pasty. This type of cervical mucus is commonly called a **hostile cervical mucus** because sperm have a hard time penetrating it. Some hormonal contraceptives capitalize on this effect of progesterone on the cervical mucus and rely, partially, on the presence of a thick cervical mucus to prevent sperm from reaching the ovum.

The Fallopian Tubes

The **Fallopian tubes** or **oviducts** are tubes which transport the ovum from the ovary to the uterus. While the Fallopian tubes are physically joined to the uterus, they are not directly attached to the ovaries. Rather, the portion of the Fallopian tube closest to the ovary **(the fimbria),** surrounds the ovary without being physically bound to it. The ruffled ends of the fimbria constantly move over the entire surface of the ovary, ready to pick up the ovulated ovum and sweep it into the Fallopian tube.

Once inside the Fallopian tube, the ovum moves rapidly to the **ampulla-isthmus junction,** a point approximately three-quarters of the way down the length of the tube. The ovum remains at the ampulla-isthmus junction of the Fallopian tube for approximately two days. Fertilization of the ovum typically occurs during this layover. Later the ovum (fertilized or not) continues its journey reaching the uterus three to four days after ovulation.

Near the uterus, the passage through the Fallopian tube is extremely narrow and, thus, easily blocked. Fallopian tubes are most commonly blocked by scar tissue which develops following inflammation as occurs with **pelvic inflammatory disease (PID).** This is a common cause of infertility. If the Fallopian tubes are completely blocked, sperm and ovum cannot meet. If the blockage is only partial, the tiny sperm may be able to reach the larger ovum for fertilization, but the impregnated ovum will be unable to move on to the uterus. The embryo will begin to develop in the confined space of the

Fallopian tube. **Tubal pregnancies** cannot progress to term. If the pregnancy is not halted, the growing embryo will cause the Fallopian tube to rupture. Hemorrhage resulting from the rupturing of the tube can be fatal.

Pregnancy

The physiological changes which take place during pregnancy are so numerous that it is impossible to do justice to them in a brief review. Changes are evident in every part of the woman's body. Changes in the uterus as it expands to accommodate the growing embryo and placenta and in the breasts as the mammary glands mature are apparent and well known. Changes in the digestive system result in one of the most common early signs of pregnancy, **morning sickness.** Fifty to eighty percent of all pregnant women experience this symptom to some degree. The cause of morning sickness remains unknown, though some investigators have speculated that it is due to the extremely high levels of estrogen found during pregnancy. Others attribute morning sickness to the presence of another hormone, **human chorionic gonadotropin (HCG),** which is produced first by the fertilized ovum and then by the placenta during early pregnancy. Progesterone levels are also extremely high during pegnancy. As a consequence, many women report **somnolence** or sleepiness until their bodies adapt to the elevation of progesterone. The volume of blood in the woman's body increases to meet the needs of the developing embryo and the heart must work harder to pump the extra fluid. The skeletal system undergoes changes as the ligaments that hold the sacroiliac and pubic bone in place soften. This allows the pelvic cavity to expand without breaking bones. Softening of the ligaments is a function of a hormone, **relaxin,** which is apparently produced by the corpus luteum.

While the corpus luteum typically remains functional throughout all of pregnancy, much of the hormone production during pregnancy is carried out by the **placenta.** Most of the estrogen and progesterone measurable in the bloodstream of a pregnant woman comes from the placenta. **Estriol** is the most common form of estrogen produced during pregnancy. The placenta produces estriol from androgen provided to it by the adrenal gland of the fetus. Thus, estriol levels can be monitored to assess the viability of the fetus. If the fetus is severely defective or dies, no androgen will be provided to the placenta and estriol levels will drop.

The placenta develops from cells of the fertilized ovum. Genetically it is identical to the fetus. Many people mistakenly believe that the placenta is a tube in which the blood vessels of the mother and fetus are joined. This is not the case. The placenta is a large sac-like organ which, at full development, fills almost half of the uterus. Inside the placenta, blood vessels of the fetus terminate in pools of the mother's blood. In addition to its role in hormone production, the placenta also acts as a transfer station between mother and fetus. Waste products found in high concentrations in the fetus' blood diffuse out of the fetal blood vessels into the mother's blood. Similarly, substances such as nutrients and drugs which are in higher concentration in the mother's blood diffuse into the circulatory system of the fetus.

The mechanisms underlying the initiation of childbirth or **parturition** remain a mystery. It is known that levels of estrogen and progesterone decrease just before labor begins. Levels of both **oxytocin**, a hormone secreted by the **posterior pituitary** (a small gland just behind the anterior pituitary), and **prostaglandins**, substances produced by the uterus as well as other organs, are high during labor. While both oxytocin and prostaglandins can cause contractions of the uterus, it is not clear whether their role is to initiate labor or to maintain it once it has begun.

Breastfeeding requires at least two hormones. **Prolactin** acts at the mammary glands **to stimulate milk production**. Once produced, the milk is stored in the **sinuses**, small sacs near the nipple. When the baby suckles at the breast, the hormone **oxytocin** is released. Oxytocin **stimulates milk letdown** or the release of milk through the nipple. The release of oxytocin is highly conditionable. Although actual suckling at the breast is required to stimulate its release at first, oxytocin release soon occurs in response to the sight or sound of a hungry infant.

Menopause

Menopause marks the last of the major transitions of the reproductive biology of women. At menopause, estrogen production by the ovaries decreases. The rate of decline of ovarian hormone production is highly variable. For some women, it is quite rapid; for others, the process occurs gradually over many years. Even when a woman is officially past menopause, i.e., she has had no menstrual periods for at least twelve months, her ovaries may continue to produce a small amount of estradiol for some, as yet unpredictable, length of time.

Once ovarian estradiol production has ceased, **estrone** becomes the most predominant form of estrogen. Estrone is made when androgen from the adrenal cortex is converted to estrogen in the adipose tissue or fat. As noted above, higher body-fat levels may result in higher postmenopausal estrogen levels and may decrease the risk of symptoms such as osteoporosis which sometimes result from low estrogen.

The most common symptom experienced by women as their estrogen level decreases is the **hot flash**. This is a sudden, intense feeling of warmth which may be accompanied by reddening of the face and sweating. Hot flashes can be treated with **estrogen replacement therapy (ERT),** although they will stop spontaneously as the body adapts to the lower estrogen level. Other consequences of low estrogen which can be halted or eliminated by ERT are reduced vaginal lubrication and osteoporosis. Other symptoms commonly associated with menopause are due to aging itself, and not to the decline of estrogen production. These symptoms include the decrease in the thickness of the skin and the loss of muscle mass. ERT will do nothing to reverse or halt these events. ERT is a drug treatment that should be utilized only if the symptoms warrant it. ERT, in spite of the predictions when it was first introduced, is not a fountain of youth that will prevent the aging process.

Chapter 2

Puberty and Its Pitfalls

Puberty marks the first great transition of the female, the transition from an immature to a mature female body. The exact timing and mechanisms underlying the changes of puberty are not clearly understood. As **Golub,** the author of the first paper in this section points out, various hormone-producing glands including the ovary, the anterior pituitary, the adrenal gland and the hypothalamus are involved in this event. While it is known that levels of estrogen begin to cycle before any outward physical signs of puberty have occurred, the exact timing of the onset of this cycling and its pattern of change from very low amplitude cycles (those with very little difference between the highest and the lowest value of the hormone) to large amplitude cycles is unknown. **Brooks-Gunn** (the second paper in this chapter) concentrates on the psychological effects of the variation of timing of pubertal changes from individual to individual.

Education about puberty and the changes of the body is sorely lacking even in this day of organized sex education in the schools. Golub cites a number of studies from the US and other countries which show that one-quarter to one-third of all girls feel that they were inadequately prepared for menarche. While the studies cited here are relatively old, our own experiences in the classroom indicate that a large percentage of college women remain unaware of the actual physiological changes of puberty as well as the location and function of various parts of the female body involved in the monthly cycle. As **Brooks-Gunn** points out, the younger the age at which a girl undergoes the changes of puberty, the less likely she is to be prepared for those changes. Early maturing girls frequently experience these changes prior to the age when such material is being taught in the classroom. The parents of such girls may be unprepared psychologically to speak to their very young daughters about the physical and psychological changes of puberty or may not have the knowledge to pass on to their child. This leaves early-maturing girls most vulnerable to problems associated with puberty.

Some of the major social and psychological problems associated with puberty and menarche may be due to the confusion that may result from the advanced maturation of the body in contrast to the relatively immature emotional and social state of adolescent girls. As our society has increased in complexity, the length of time required to prepare adolescents for the adult role has increased. The young woman of the 1800s frequently entered into the adult roles of work, marriage and/or household management prior to or shortly after menarche. Today, young women of most western cultures experience menarche at age 12, long before they are fully indoctrinated into the adult female role. We certainly would not recommend that this conflict be resolved by granting more of the adult role to pubescent girls. But we do need to be aware of this conflict and educate girls accordingly. Instead of introducing menarche solely as the onset of fertility and the potential for childbearing (the adult physiological role), we must take the time to recognize the difference between reproductive and cultural maturation and the difficulties this can cause for girls.

The last selection in this chapter, by **Plehn,** deals with one of the major pitfalls which girls face as they go through puberty—the pressure to maintain a low body weight and the consequent risk of developing eating disorders. The contrast between the cultural ideal of extreme thinness and the reality of the greater body weight, higher body-fat level and larger skeletal structure of real women produces conflict for women of all ages. Anorexia nervosa, a syndrome marked by refusal to eat and severe loss of body weight, is most likely to begin during adolescence. The risk of developing bulimia, the binge-purge syndrome, increases during late puberty and young adulthood. The incidence of these eating disorders among white, middle- to upper-middle class girls is increasing at a dramatic rate. The causes of these diseases remain elusive, but they share the common feature of preoccupation with food and markedly distorted body image. Researchers have argued that these syndromes have their basis in everything from a rejection of the adult female role to an excessive response to the pressures for low body weight for women in our society. Very frequently, the onset of eating disorders is marked by what our society accepts as normal dieting. Since the probability of curing both anorexia and bulimia is greatest at the onset of the disease, it is important that we be able to recognize the signals that suggest that these problems are developing. **Plehn's** article, written for health-care workers, offers signs to look for in distinguishing ''normal'' dieting from eating disorders. As Plehn points out, both anorexia and bulimia are serious health problems which can result in death.

Ed. note: One aspect of the hormonal-feedback systems involved in the control of the monthly cycle of women as presented in Figure 1 of the article by Golub has changed since the article was first published. Scientists at that time postulated two separate releasing hormones from the hypothalamus (FSH-RF and LRF) to be involved in the control of FSH and LH secretion by the anterior pituitary. It is now known that the hypothalamus produces only one releasing hormone which controls the production and release of both FSH and LH. This single releasing hormone is most commonly referred to as gonadotropin-releasing hormone (GnRH or GRH).

REFERENCES AND SUGGESTED READINGS

Brooks-Gunn, J. and Warren, M. P. Biological and social contributions to negative affect in young adolescent girls. *Child Development* (1989) 60: 40–55.

Casper, R. C. The pathophysiology of anorexia nervosa and bulimia nervosa. *Annual Review of Nutrition* (1986) 6: 299–316.

Frank, E. S. Shame and guilt in eating disorders. *American Journal of Orthopsychiatry* (1991) 61: 303–306.

Frisch, R. E. Body fat, menarche, fitness and fertility. *Progress in Reproductive Biology and Medicine* (1990) 14: 1–26.

Mukai, T. A call for our language: anorexia from within. *Women Studies International Forum* (1989) 12: 613–638.

Rosenfield, R. L. Puberty and its disorders in girl. *Endocrinology and Metabolism Clinics of North America* (1991) 20: 15–41.

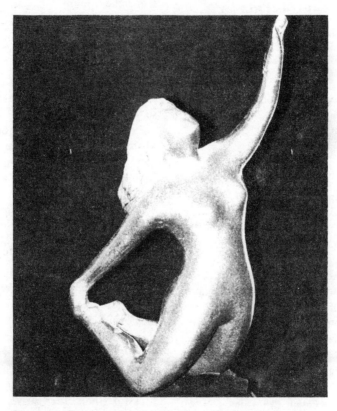

Figure 4. Bronze sculpture by Gary Humiston.
Photographed and reprinted by permission of the sculptor.

Menarche:
The Beginning of Menstrual Life
Sharon Golub, PhD

ABSTRACT. Menarche represents a developmental milestone in a woman's life. This paper reviews current knowledge about the physiological aspects of menarche and its place in the sequence of pubertal development. Hypotheses regarding the mechanisms that trigger menarche are presented, as is our current understanding of the influence of hormones, genetic factors, nutrition, exercise, and illness. Also discussed are the ways in which the changes of puberty and menarche affect the adolescent girl's psychosocial development, the unique problems of the early maturing girl, and the kind of preparation for menarche that is needed.

In "The Curse of an Aching Heart," playwright William Alfred captures the significance of menarche in a woman's life. One of the characters, a woman in her sixties, recalls being frightened and embarrassed when she got her first period. She awoke with stained bed clothes and sheets and didn't understand what was happening to her. Confused, she ran out of the house and after walking for awhile she happened upon a neighbor who recognized that she was upset and invited her in for a cup of tea. The neighbor explained menstruation to the girl and then, in honor of the occasion, the woman gave the girl a brooch. In the play, memory of this event was poignantly related to another woman more than forty years later.

Is this vignette a fluke, a bit of a sentimental whimsy? Probably not. Psychological research confirms the dramatist's intuition that menarche is an important developmental event. In a study of recollections of menarche, Golub and Catalano (1983) found that almost all of the 137 women studied, ranging in age from 18 to 45, remembered their first menstruation. And a majority could describe in detail where they were when it happened, what they were doing, and whom they told. How many events in our lives are so vividly recalled?

It is surprising, therefore, that menarche has received so little research attention until quite recently. Now scientists have begun to look at both the physical and psychological aspects of menarche and at the ways in which they are inextricably linked. It is acknowledged that the changes of puberty do not occur in a psychosocial vacuum. Body changes affect a person psychologically and socially, and the person's life experiences influence the biological processes as well. Nowhere is this seen more clearly than at menarche. For example, what is the relationship between exercise and the onset of menarche? Do menarcheal experiences affect the later development of menstrual distress? What determines whether menarche is a stressful time for girls? What does the menarcheal experience mean to the pubertal girl? How does it affect the way she sees herself? Is there a relationship between menarche and sexual activity? And how soon after menarche is a young woman fertile? Although there is a great deal that we still do

This article first appeared in *Women and Health* (1983) 8 (1): 17–36. Copyright © 1983. Haworth Press, Inc., Binghampton, NY. Reprinted with permission of the publisher.

not know, this paper will address these questions and will review the highlights of what is known about the physiological and psychosocial aspects of menarche.

PHYSIOLOGICAL ASPECTS OF MENARCHE

Sequence of Pubertal Development

Menarche is preceded by characteristic body changes that occur some time between the ages of 9 and 16. Breast development usually, but not always, occurs first. There is an increase in body hair and there is also a weight gain, growth spurt, and a change in body proportions with the hips becoming fuller. Sweat glands become more active and a body odor develops that is thought to be related to an increase in sex hormone secretions from the adrenal gland. The skin becomes oilier, sometimes giving rise to skin problems. And while these external changes are going on there are concomitant changes occurring within the body: the uterus and vagina are growing (Grumbach, Grave, & Mayer, 1974; Katchadourian, 1977).

As noted above, breast development is usually the first sign of puberty with breast buds beginning to form around the age of 11. Breast development is influenced by the secretion of estrogen, particularly estradiol from the ovary, and probably by the secretion of prolactin from the anterior pituitary gland as well (Warren, 1983). There is a slight enlargement of the areolar and elevation of the breast as a small mound. Soon after, pubic hair begins to develop, usually about age 11 1/2. Axillary hair generally appears about two years after the beginning of pubic hair development. On the average, menarche occurs between 12.8 and 13.2 years. (For photographs and a detailed description of the stages of breast and pubic hair growth during puberty see Tanner, 1978.)

Pubertal development may be fast or slow. Some girls pass rapidly through the stages of breast and pubic hair development while others move slowly. On the average, the total time for the overall process of physical transformation from child to adult is about four years (Tanner 1978). However, some girls may take only 1 1/2 years to pass through all the stages while the slower developers may take as long as five years to do so. For those working or living with girls in this age group it is important to keep in mind that there can be great variation in the normal time of onset and completion of pubertal development. It is perfectly normal for a girl to begin to menstruate any time between the ages of 9 and 16 and age mates may be at very different stages of sexual maturation— one 12 year old can look like a woman, another very much like a child.

There is a close relationship between menarche and the pubertal spurt in height. Girls start to menstruate after the growth spurt has peaked, when the rate of increase in height (height velocity) is falling. The growth spurt is nearly over at the time of menarche, with girls on the average growing only about two more inches after the onset of menstruation. However, some girls do grow as much as four inches more (Tanner, 1978).

Menarche marks a mature stage of uterine development but not reproductive maturity. Early cycles are often irregular and between 55 and 82 percent of menstrual cycles during the first two postmenarcheal years are anovulatory. Regular menstruation may not occur for several years. However, it is important to remember that despite the apparent absence of regular monthly ovulation, any individual cycle may be ovulatory and is potentially fertile (Brennock, 1982) as indicated by the fact that there were 30,000 pregnancies among girls under the age of 15 in the United States between 1973 and 1978. These teenagers are at high risk for pregnancy complications such as low birthweight, high infant mortality, and pregnancy induced hypertension (Leppert, 1983), in addition to the stressful social and psychological consequences of having a baby at 13 or 14 years of age.

What Triggers Menarche?

There is some controversy about what triggers menarche. Currently there are two hypotheses which relate menarcheal age to physical growth: one focusing on skeletal growth and the other on the accumulation of fat. The skeletal growth hypothesis is based on the idea that the premenarcheal girl must reach an appropriate stage of skeletal development in order to reproduce and, therefore, the age at which she reaches this structural status (mature height and pelvic dimensions) is closely correlated with menarcheal age (Tanner, 1978). The importance of skeletal maturity is related to the need for a body, specifically a pelvis, that is adequate in size to bear a child. And there is some data to support the idea that pelvic dimensions—an average biiliac diameter of 26.2 cms.—are significantly correlated with menarcheal age (Ellison, 1982). Thus menarcheal age is closely related to skeletal development and bone age can be used as an appropriate measure of developmental age in predicting when menarche will occur (Tanner, 1978). This view attributes the decline in average age at menarche during the last century (referred to in the literature as the secular trend) to the acceleration of skeletal growth during this time, presumably related to better nutrition and health. In contrast, slow skeletal growth, resulting from poor nutrition or high altitude, leads to delay in the onset of menstruation.

An alternative hypothesis, proposed by Frisch (1980), suggests that the onset of menstruation is contingent upon the accumulation of fat and that a critical minimum weight for height is necessary to trigger and maintain ovulation and menstruation. Frisch's explanation of the secular trend in menarcheal age is that girls reach 101 to 103 pounds, the average weight at menarche, sooner now, and therefore menstruation begins earlier. She points out that a late menarche is associated with slower increases in body weight such as that seen in cases of malnutrition, or among twins, because they grow more slowly. Frisch notes that the greatest change during the adolescent growth spurt up to the time of menarche is a 120 percent increase in body fat. At menarche, girls' bodies average about 24 percent fat, not much different from the 28 percent fat found in the average 18 year old woman. In contrast, boys at about 18 years of age are much leaner with 14 percent fat. Frisch theorizes that reproduction requires energy and the function of the stored fat is to provide readily accessible energy should it be needed for pregnancy and lactation.

In a recent study entitled, "Skeletal Growth, Fatness, and Menarcheal Age," Ellison (1982) compared the two hypotheses using factor analysis of longitudinal growth data on 67 middle-class white girls born in 1928 and 1919 and drawn from the Berkeley Guidance Study. Ellison found that height velocity prior to menarche was the strongest independent correlate of menarcheal age, accounting for over 50 percent of the variance. The weight factor made the second largest contribution, accounting for 18 percent of the variance in menarcheal age. Thus while there seems to be a strong relationship between adolescent weight and menarcheal age, its effect is apparently less than that of the skeletal development. Ellison makes the point that since skeletal growth tends to cease soon after menarche, natural selection would delay menarche until the pelvis could handle reproduction.

Hormones

Although incompletely understood, significant hormonal changes occur at puberty. The gonadal, adrenal, and hypothalamic-hypophyseal hormones are of major importance. It is

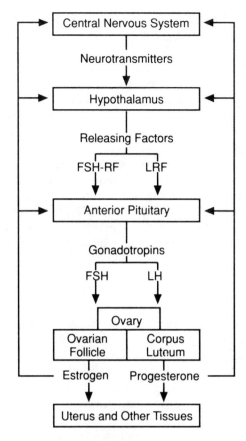

Figure 1.

the interrelationship of these hormones that later controls the female reproductive cycle. However, endocrinologists now believe that the hormonal changes associated with sexual maturation actually begin at the time of conception. By the third trimester of pregnancy, the negative feedback system is established. (See Figure 1.) During infancy the hypothalamic gonadotropin regulating mechanism is "set" at a low level and remains there until around the time of puberty when there is an increase in the secretion of follicle stimulating hormone (FSH) and luteinizing hormone (LH) and a decrease in hypothalamic sensitivity. Put another way, the hypothalamic set

point increases inducing a subsequent increase in the secretion of FSH, LH, and gonadal hormones (Petersen & Taylor, 1980).

The adolescent growth spurt is a result of the joint action of androgens and growth hormone (Tanner, 1978). A progressive increase in plasma dehydroepiandosterone and dehydroepiandosterone sulfate, which are weak androgens, begins at about eight years of age and continues through ages 13 to 15. These hormones, thought to originate from the adrenal gland, are the earliest hormonal changes to take place at puberty (Warren, 1983). They and the more potent androgens—testosterone and dihydrotestosterone—increase significantly as pubertal development progresses (Dupon & Bingel, 1980). Increased secretion of gonadotropins from the pituitary (FSH and LH) and sex steroids from the gonads follow (Warren, 1983).

The main female sex hormone secreted by the ovaries is estradiol which is present in relatively small amounts in the blood until about age eight or nine when it begins to rise. This increase in blood levels of estradiol causes growth of the breasts, uterus, vagina, and parts of the pelvis. When menstruation begins, estradiol levels fluctuate with the various phases of the cycle and are controlled by pituitary FSH (Tanner, 1978).

The two pituitary gonadotropins, follicle simulating hormone (FSH) and luteinizing hormone (LH), are both secreted in small amounts during childhood and increase at puberty. The pubertal rise is first seen as pulses of LH that are released during sleep. This sleep-associated rise in LH is not seen in either the prepubertal child or the adult (Warren, 1983). Gradually LH is released during the daytime too.

Menstruation, as well as earlier pubertal development, is thought to begin with a signal to the hypothalamus from the central nervous system. As noted above, a hypothalamic feedback system does exist before puberty, but the hypothalamus is responsive to low levels of LH in the prepubertal girl. Then around the time of menarche, a gradual change occurs making the hypothalamus less sensitive. Higher levels of estrogen are needed. The hypothalamus then secretes more FSH-releasing hormone. This neurohormone stimulates the pituitary gland to release FSH, which, in turn, triggers the growth of the ovarian follicle. As the follicles grow they secrete estrogen which causes growth of the cells lining the uterus (the endometrium). Increasing levels of estrogen in the blood also signal the pituitary to reduce FSH and secrete LH. LH triggers the release of the ovum from the follicle which then evolves into the corpus luteum and secretes progesterone and a little estrogen. If the ovum is not fertilized, the pituitary stops production of LH, levels of both estrogen and progesterone drop, menstruation begins, and the cycle starts again. (See Figure 1.)

Other Factors Affecting Pubertal Development

Genetics. Genetic factors play an important role in determining rate of growth, pubertal development, and age at menarche. Studies of monozygotic twin sisters growing up together indicate that they reach menarche about two months apart, with the first born twin—for some unknown reason—more likely to menstruate first (Shields, 1962). Dizygotic twins differ by about 12 months (Tanner, 1978). Mother-daughter and sister-sister correlations have also been reported to be significant (Chern, Gatewood, & Anderson, 1980). Kantero and Widholm (1971) found other menstrual similarities between mothers and daughters: significant correlations were found between mothers' and daughters' length of cycle, duration of menstrual flow, and symptoms of dysmenorrhea and premenstrual tension. It is thought that both mother and father exert an equal influence on rate of growth and maturation. Thus a late-maturing girl is as

likely to have a late-maturing father as a late-maturing mother (Tanner, 1978).

Nutrition. There is a well documented link between nutrition and fertility. Famine amenorrhea was reported in both world wars (Menkin, Watkins, & Trussell, Note 1). Young women who are undernourished because of excessive dieting or those with anorexia nervosa often do not have menstrual periods. And it is well known that malnutrition retards growth and will delay menarche (Tanner, 1978). The fall in age at menarche that has occurred between 1830 and 1960 coincides with the increased availability of protein in the diet of developed countries during this time. In some countries, where nutrition has remained inadequate, age of menarche is comparatively high. For example, in contrast with the average age of menarche in the United States, which is now 12.8 years, in Bangladesh it is just under 16, and among certain New Guinea tribes, it is about 18 (Menkin, Watkins, & Trussel, Note 1). A recent study by Goodman, Grove, and Gilbert (1983) in which no differences in age at menarche were found among Caucasian, Japanese, and Chinese women living in Hawaii, suggests that nutrition and environmental factors are responsible for population differences. Tanner (1978) has noted that children in urban, as opposed to rural, areas are more likely to have more rapid growth and an earlier menarche that is probably attributed to better nutrition, health, and sanitation.

Exercise. Exercise also affects menstruation. Women who experience high energy outputs, such as ballet dancers and athletes who train intensively, have a later age at menarche and a high incidence of amenorrhea. This is particularly true when intensive training begins at an early premenarcheal age (Frisch, 1980; Frisch et al., 1981; Frisch, 1983). It is not known whether an altered lean-fat ratio is responsible for the delay in

20

menarche in young athletes, as proposed by Frisch, or if the delay occurs through the direct effects of exercise on hormonal secretion and metabolism (Rebar & Cumming, 1981). Some investigators have questioned whether delays in the age of menarche in athletes occur at all (Malina, 1982). Others have expressed concern about the short-term and long-term effects of exercise on reproductive function (Rebar & Cumming, 1981). Also at this time it is not known whether it is disadvantageous to have a later menarche rather than an early one. However, the consensus seems to be that exercise-related alterations in reproductive function are not serious and are readily reversible.

Climatic and seasonal effects: Climate has no more than a very minor effect on age at menarche. In fact, contrary to earlier beliefs, people who live in tropical countries are somewhat more likely to have a *late* menarche. This is thought to be related to nutrition rather than a climate because children in the higher socioeconomic groups in these countries experience menarche at about the same time as children living in temperate zones.

Season of the year does influence growth velocity, with peak growth seen between March and July, and girls are most likely to have their first menstruation in the late fall or early winter (Science News, 1980; Tanner, 1978).

Acute and chronic illness. There are some conditions where menstruation will not occur. For example, a child with Turner's Syndrome, a chromosomal anomaly in which the second X chromosome is absent, will not menstruate because she lacks ovaries. Ehrhardt and Mayer-Bahlberg (1975) advise that sex hormone administration is crucial in order for these girls to attain psychosocial and psychosexual maturity. Administration of estrogen will cause the breasts to grow and an artificial menstrual cycle may be produced by giving estrogen for three weeks followed

by a week without treatment. This is important because these girls want to look, develop, and be treated like normal female adolescents.

Other illnesses can delay menarche, probably because of their effects on nutrition. This is most likely to be true in cases of uremia, regional enteritis, ulcerative colitis, congenital heart disease, cystic fibrosis, and diabetes mellitus. The timing of the onset of the illness as well as the illness per se seem to be important. For example, if diabetes develops during the initial pubertal period, menarche is delayed, whereas if it develops later, menarche may be unaffected (Warren, 1983).

Conversely, some conditions will advance the age of menarche. These include hypothyroidism, central nervous system tumors, encephalitis, head trauma, and some virilizing disorders. Inactive, retarded, or bedridden children also reach menarche at an earlier age than their more active counterparts. And blind children have a younger age at menarche that may be related in part to their limited activity (Warren, 1983).

Thus menarche occurs after a series of changes in hormone secretion and somatic growth. These processes are in turn influenced by genetic and environmental factors such as nutrition, exercise, and illness which may accelerate or retard the onset of menstruation. We now turn to the psychosocial aspects of menarche and its meaning to the adolescent girl and those around her.

PSYCHOSOCIAL ASPECTS OF MENARCHE

Effects of Menarche on the Early Adolescent Girl

Much of the early writing about the psychology of menarche presented it as a traumatic experience. For example, early psychoanalytic theory postulated a marked increase in sex drive at puberty and an inevitable period of anxiety, worry about impulse control, and increased lability as "a relatively strong id confronts a relatively weak ego" (A. Freud, 1946). Benedek (1959) believed that menarche might evoke fears associated with the anticipation of pain during intercourse and childbirth. Current psychoanalytic views are much more positive. Notman (1983) and others suggest that meeting the developmental tasks of adolescence need not be as tumultuous as was previously believed. True, the early adolescent needs to modify her attachment to her parents and develop the capacity to form relationships with peers; and eventually she must establish her identity as a woman and develop the capacity for intimacy with another person. However, this need not happen overnight and the process should not cause turmoil or disintegration.

Menarche can have an organizing effect for the adolescent girl, helping her to clarify her perception of her own genitals, particularly confirming the existence of the vagina and correcting the confusion she may have had about the female genitalia. Kestenberg (1965) suggests that menarche may serve as a reference point around which girls can organize their pubertal experiences; it is a landmark for feminine identification. This is in keeping with the greater awareness of sexual differentiation between males and females among postmenarcheal girls demonstrated by Koff, Rierdan, and Silverstone (1978).

Knowledge, Attitudes, and Expectations in Anticipation of Menache

What do the girls themselves say? Whisnant and Zegans (1975) interviewed 35 white middle class pre- and postmenarcheal girls at a summer camp. The girls had learned about menstruation from friends, commercial booklets, school, and their parents—especially their mothers. They perceived themselves as being knowledgeable about menstruation and used the appropriate terms. However, when questioned further the interviewer found that they really did not have a good conception of what the internal organs were like or how they functioned and they were even more inept at describing the external genitalia. Thus, despite their access to information about menstruation, they had not assimilated it particularly well. The girls were most concerned about what to do when they got their periods and many had mentally rehearsed what they would do in a variety of situations.

Brooks-Gunn and Ruble (1980) found that both boys and girls in the seventh and eighth grades have similar and mostly negative beliefs about menstruation. For example, most believed that menstruation is accompanied by physical discomfort, increased emotionality, and a disruption of activities. Only a third thought that the onset of menstruation was something to be happy about.

Williams (1983) found more positive attitudes toward menstruation in a group of 9 to 12 year old girls, most of whom were premenarcheal. These girls generally equated menstruation with growing up and being normal. However, about a third of these subjects also believed menstruation to be embarrassing, 28 percent thought it a nuisance, 27 percent found it disgusting, and 23 percent disliked the idea that it is not controllable. The girls in this sample also believed some of the popular menstrual taboos. About half the subjects thought a girl should not swim when menstruating and 22 percent believed she should not be active in sports. Many were influenced by concealment taboos with a majority expressing concern about concealing sanitary pads and menstrual odor. A striking 85 percent thought that a girl should not talk about menstruation to boys and 40 percent did not even think that it was all right to discuss menstruation with their fathers. And, as in the Brooks-Gunn and Ruble study noted above, most believed that girls are more emotional when they menstruate.

Reactions to Menarche

What do girls actually experience at the time of menarche? In several studies menarche has been found to be an anxiety producing or negative event (Brooks-Gunn & Ruble, 1980; Golub & Catalano, 1983; Koff, Rierdan, & Jacobson, 1981; Whisnant & Zegans, 1975) and mixed feelings such as being "excited but scared" or "happy and embarrassed" are common (Petersen, 1983; Woods, Dery, & Most, 1983). Most of these data were collected using interviews and questionnaires, and sometimes were based on recollections of older subjects.

Petersen (1983) in looking at menarche as one part of her study of 400 middle-class suburban boys and girls in the 6th, 7th, and 8th grades, found that the adolescents were remarkably inarticulate in describing their feelings about their changing bodies. Therefore, she decided that projective measures might be more useful than direct questions in exploring girls' feelings about menstruation. The girls were presented with an incomplete story about menarche adapted from Judy Blume's book, *Are You There, God? It's Me, Margaret.* For example:

> "Mom—hey, Mom—come quick!" When Nancy's mother got to the bathroom she said: "What is it? What's the matter?" "I got it," Nancy told her. "Got what?" said her mother.

The girls were then asked, "What happened next?" Some of the girls responded that, "She told her Mom that she had gotten her period;" others said that Mom explained or helped. They were then asked, "How did Nancy feel?" About a third gave negative or fearful responses, about half were positive or pleased, and another five percent were ambivalent.

Maxine Kumin (1982) in a short story entitled "Facts of Life" differentiates between the expectations about menarche and its actual occurrence. She describes a group of twelve-year-old girls as longing to begin to menstruate. "An eager band of little girls, itchy with the work of sprouting, sits expectant. The old reticences, embarrassments, and complaints have given way to progress. Now we have sex education, cartoon films of the reproductive tract, a beltless sanitary napkin, a slender, virginal tampon" (p. 11). Yet, when the first blood does indeed come the girl is described as both terribly happy and terribly sad as mother and daughter celebrate together.

Changes in Body Image

Changes in body image are among the most dramatic reactions to menarche. Although the body changes associated with puberty occur gradually, girls do expect to act differently after menarche and they also see themselves differently. In a clever study of seventh grade girls, Koff (1983) asked the subjects to draw male and female human figures on two occasions, approximately six months apart. Of the 87 girls sampled, 34 were premenarcheal on both test occasions, 23 were postmenarcheal, and 30 changed menarcheal status between the two test sessions. The findings were striking. Postmenarcheal girls produced drawings that were significantly more sexually differentiated than those of their premenarcheal peers and a greater percentage of the postmenarcheal girls drew their own sex first. Most notable was the difference in the drawings done by the girls whose menarcheal status changed during the course of the study. There was a significant increase in the sexual differentiation of their drawings at the time of the second testing with the postmenarcheal girls drawing womanly females with breasts and curves in contrast to their earlier, more childlike, premenarcheal drawings. (Examples of these drawings may be seen in Koff, 1983.)

To further explore girls' beliefs about the change menarche would have on them, Koff, Rierdan, and Jacobson (1981) gave a sentence completion task to seventh and eighth grade girls. In response to the cue sentence "Ann just got her period for the first time," the girls said such things as, "She saw herself in a different way," and "She felt very grown up." In response to another item, "Ann regarded her body as . . . ," postmenarcheal girls were more likely than premenarcheal girls to describe a change in body image. For example, Ann's body was "a women's body" and "more mature than it was."

These studies clearly demonstrate that girls do experience menarche as a turning point in their development and they apparently reorganize their body images in the direction of "greater sexual maturity and feminine differentiation" (Koff, 1983). Postmenarcheal girls are more aware of sexual differentiation between males and females and of themselves as women than are premenarcheal girls of the same age.

The Early Maturing Girl

The age at which a girl experiences menarche does seem to affect her reaction to it. Petersen (1983) found that girls who experience menarche early, in the sixth grade or before, seem to have more difficulty with it. Some of the girls denied that they had begun to menstruate and when Petersen questioned the mothers of her early maturing subjects, over 70 percent of the mothers reported that menarche was very difficult for their daughters. The mothers of five of the six girls who denied having gotten their periods reported the negative aspects of the experience for them. Notman (1983) has suggested that the denial of menstruation may be related to conflicts about accepting the female role or to an attempt to delay adulthood. Certainly one of the girls in Petersen's sample who denied menstruating lends support to that view. In response to a Thematic Apperception Test card showing a middle-aged woman with a girl holding a doll, this subject described the girl in the picture as scared

about growing up and asking her mother when she was going to get her period.

Unlike boys who are eager for their growth spurt and physical signs of maturity, girls would prefer to mature at the same time as everyone else. This may be because of the age difference between the sexes in the onset of puberty—boys normally start later than girls. Girls' attitudes about early development may also be related to the changes in their lives that occur when they develop the breasts and curves characteristic of a woman. There is some evidence that sixth and seventh grade girls who are already pubertal are more likely to be dating and, somewhat paradoxically, these girls also have lower self-esteem, lower school achievement, and more behavioral problems than comparable boys and non-pubertal girls (Simmons, Blyth, Van Cleave, & Bush, 1979). In this study pubertal development per se had little effect on the girls' self-esteem. However, the early maturing girls who had also begun dating were most likely to indicate low self-esteem (50 percent as opposed to 36–40 percent of the other girls). It is interesting that while early dating behavior is disadvantageous for girls, it has no statistically significant impact on boys.

Thus girls' self-esteem was negatively affected by their own physiology (early menarche) and social relationships, while boys' self-esteem was not. Simons et al. (1979) suggest some reasons why this may be so. First, the sexes develop different value systems at this age. For girls, appearance and sociability assume priority, while for boys these values remain secondary. When asked to rank the importance of popularity, competence, and independence, seventh grade girls were more likely to rank popularity first. This places a great deal of importance on other peoples' opinions of oneself. These girls also placed a high value on looks. Moreover, the changes in body image may be qualitatively different for girls than for boys. Pubertal boys are generally happy with their new height and muscle development. Pubertal girls are not sure whether their new figures make them better or worse looking than their peers. Further, pubertal girls' negative reactions to dating may be a result of sexual pressures from their male partners for which these girls are not prepared. In interviews with some of these girls the researchers found them likely to express dislike for "guys trying to touch me." One subject said, "I don't really like to be kissed." It looks as if some of these girls were vulnerable, with their emotional maturity lagging well behind their physical development, causing confusion and contributing to their feelings of low self-esteem. This is in keeping with data from the California Adolescent Study which show that it is the girl with accelerated growth and maturation who is at a disadvantage (Jones, 1958; Jones & Mussen, 1959). However, social class may also play a role. Clausen (1975) found that for middle-class girls early maturation was positively related to self-confidence, whereas working class girls experienced a negative effect. In contrast to early maturation, late maturation, although quite disturbing for boys, does not seem to have the same degree of negative consequences for girls, perhaps because a childlike appearance is part of femininity for some adult women (Friedman, Note 2).

Relationships with Parents

In view of the changes that go on in girls' perceptions of themselves it seems reasonable to ask if menarche affects girls' relationships with other people, particularly family members. On the basis of limited data, the answer seems to be a qualified yes. Danza (1983) compared 48 pre- and postmenarcheal girls in the sixth and seventh grades. She found that although they were no different in age than their premenarcheal peers, the postmenarcheal girls were more likely to wear make-up or a bra, to shave their legs, and to

date. They also slept less on school nights, moving from nine or more hours a night toward the more usual adult eight hour sleep cycle. The postmenarcheal girls were also significantly more uncomfortable in discussing emotionally charged topics such as love, sex, drugs, and alcohol with their parents, and they reported having more conflict with their parents than the premenarcheal girls did.

Effects on Sexual Behavior

Because it marks the onset of reproductive potential, menarche is important to a girl's family and community as well as to herself. This is seen in other cultures when one looks at the different tribal rituals celebrating menarche and at customs, such as purdah, veiling, and virginity tests, which guard girls' reproductive potential. Economics comes into play too. Paige (1983) has suggested that there is a relationship between various methods of controlling girls' chastity and the economic resources of a particular culture. In societies where marriage bargains are important, chastity is crucial to the girls' marriageability and is rigorously controlled.

This is not seen in our culture today. Rather, in the United States the physical transformation from girl to woman and the onset of menstruation are accompanied by changes in social and sexual behavior. And the timing of menarche is important. Several researchers have reported that girls with an early menarche were more likely to date and pet at an earlier age than their later maturing peers (Gagnon, 1983; Presser, 1978; Simons et al., 1979; Udry, 1979). And there is data indicating that women with early menarche begin premarital coitus earlier as well (Gagnon, 1983; Presser, 1978; Udry, 1979). In an extensive study of black and white low income women in 16 American cities, Udry (1979) found that girls with early menarche, as compared to those with late menarche, were more than twice as likely to have had intercourse by age 16. Udry and Cliquet (1982) also examined the relationship between ages at menarche, marriage, and first birth among women in four widely diverse countries (United States, Malay, Belgium, and Pakistan) and concluded that there was a clear behavioral sequence relating age at menarche to age at first intercourse and first birth. Menarche seems to initiate a chain of events. In the United States the pattern is one of dating and other sexual behavior that increase the probability of early intercourse and early childbearing.

Whether this sequence is more readily attributable to hormonal or sociocultural factors is a difficult question to answer. Gagnon (1983) found no significant relationship between the onset of menarche and masturbatory experience. Similarly, in their studies of children with the problem of precocious puberty (beginning at six to eight years of age), Ehrhardt and Mayer-Bahlberg (1975) have found that early puberty does not automatically trigger an early sex life. Masturbation and sex play in childhood did not appear to be enhanced and premarital intercourse did not occur earlier than normally expected. Thus at this time it seems reasonable to conclude that the timing of puberty influences when the girl, her parents, and her peers perceive of her as being someone for whom dating and heterosexual relationships are appropriate and this in turn affects her socio-sexual behavior.

Preparation of Menarche

In view of the ambivalent feelings about menarche expressed by so many adolescent girls and the difficulties experienced by the early maturing girl, it seems reasonable to ask if adequate preparation makes any difference. It probably does. Both Rierdan (1983) and Golub and Catalano (1983) found that subjects who report being adequately prepared have a more positive initial experience with menstruation. There are other studies indicating a need for more and better menstrual education. For example, Logan (1980), in a study of 95 women from 23 foreign countries, found that 28 percent complained about not having enough information. Similarly, in a large study of American women, 39 percent reported that their preparation was inadequate (Weideger, 1976). And Brooks-Gunn and Ruble (1980) reported that the adolescent girls they tested said they had sufficient prior knowledge about menstruation but still felt unprepared for menarche.

What do girls want to know? Reirdan (1983), in a study of 97 college women's recollections of menarche, found that the young women wanted to know about menstrual physiology and menstrual hygiene—the facts that are usually included in menstrual education materials—but they also wanted information about menstruation as a personal event. Subjects said that girls need to know about the normality of menstruation and it must be distinguished from disease, injury, and uncleanliness. They suggested that the feelings of fright and embarrassment girls experience at menarche be acknowledged as normal and the negative aspects of the menstrual experience need to be discussed in order to provide a balanced view of menstruation. The college women emphasized that girls need support and reassurance at the time of menarche and Rierden says, "Many referred specifically to the importance of an informed, understanding, accepting mother" (Rierdan, 1983). Unfortunately, however, interviews with mothers of adolescent girls indicate that the mothers themselves are not prepared to fill this role, suggesting a need to prepare mothers as well as daughters for menarche.

In Support of a New Tradition

Some researchers have suggested that we need a "contemporary tradition for menarche" in order to overcome some of the negative connotations associated with it (Logan, Calder, &

Cohen, 1980). They believe that currently we address the physical needs of the menarcheal girl, teaching her how to take care of herself, but leaving her without the social and emotional support that she needs at this time. In order to explore what the appropriate ritual might be, Logan et al. designed five short stories describing possible responses to a girl's first period and gave them to girls between the ages of eight and seventeen, mothers of girls in this age group, and women psychologists. The most popular response of the mothers and daughters to being told about the onset of menstruation was "Congratulations, our little girl is growing up." However, the psychologist preferred, "Something special has happened," apparently acknowledging the ambivalent and even negative emotions that a girl may have about the beginning of menstruation. As for symbolic gestures, the most popular among the mothers was a toast to the girl from her mother and father, or a meal in her honor. But the daughters had reservations about this, fearing an invasion of privacy and reinforcing feelings that "everyone is watching her." The daughters preferred a hug or a kiss and a material token such as a gift or flowers. It seems dramatists often capture in a few lines what scientists seek in reams of data: William Alfred was right on target with the gift of a brooch.

REFERENCE NOTES

1. Menkin J., Watkins, S. C., & Trussell, J. Nutrition, health, and fertility. Report prepared for The Ford Foundation. December 1980.
2. Freedman, R. Personal Communication. December, 1983.

REFERENCES

Benedek, T. Sexual functions in women and their disturbance. In S. Arieti (Ed.) *American handbook of psychiatry*. New York: Basic Books, 1959.

Blume, J. *Are you there, God? It's me, Margaret*. New York: Dell, 1970.

Brennock, W. E. Fertility at menarche. *Medical Aspects of Human Sexuality*. 1982, 16, 21–30.

Brooks-Gunn, J. & Ruble, D. Menarche, In A. J. Dan, E. A. Graham, & C. P. Beecher (Eds.) *The menstrual cycle. Vol. 1*. New York: Springer, 1980.

Chern, M. M., Gatewood, L. C., & Anderson, V. E. The inheritance of menstrual traits. In A. J. Dan, E. A. Graham, & C. P. Beecher (Eds.) *The menstrual cycle. Vol. 1*. New York: Springer, 1980.

Clausen, J. A. The social meaning of differential physical and sexual maturation. In S. E. Dragastin, & G. H. Elder, Jr. (Eds.) *Adolescence in the life cycle*. New York: Halsted, 1975.

Danza, R. Menarche: Its effects on mother-daughter and father-daughter interactions. In S. Golub (Ed.) *Menarche*. Lexington, Massachusetts: D. C. Heath, 1983.

Dupon, C. & Bingel, A. S. Endocrinologic changes associated with puberty in girls. In A. J. Dan, E. A. Graham, & C. P. Beecher (Eds.) *The menstrual cycle. Vol. 1*. New York: Springer, 1980.

Ehrhardt, A. E., & Meyer-Bahlberg, H. F. L. Psychological correlates of abnormal pubertal development. *Clinics in Endocrinology and Metabolism*. 1975, 4, 207–222.

Ellison, P. T. Skeletal growth, fatness, and menarcheal age: A comparison of two hypotheses. *Human Biology*, 1982, 54, 269–281

Freud, A. *The ego and the mechanisms of defense*. New York: International Universities Press, 1946.

Frisch, R. E. Fatness, puberty and fertility. *Natural History*. 1980, 89, 16–27.

Frisch, R E. What's below the surface. *New England Journal of Medicine*. 1981, 305, 1019–1020.

Frisch, R. E., Gotz-Welbergen, A. V., McArthur, J. W., Albright, T., Witschi, J., Bullen, B., Birnholz, J., Reed, R. B., & Hermann, H. Delayed menarche and amenorrhea of college athletes in relation to age of onset of training. *Journal of the American Medical Association*. 1981, 246, 1559–1563.

Frisch, R. E., Fatness, menarche, and fertility. In S. Golub (Ed.) *Menarche*. Lexington, Massachusetts: D. C. Heath, 1983.

Gagnon, J. H. Age at menarche and sexual conduct in adolescence and young adulthood. In S. Golub (Ed.) *Menarche*. Lexington, Massachusetts: D. C. Heath, 1983

Golub, S., & Catalano, J. Recollections of menarche and women's subsequent experiences with menstruation. *Women & Health*. 1983, 8, 49–61.

Goodman, M. J., Grave, J. S., & Gilbert, R. I. Age at menarche and year of birth in relation to adult height and weight among Caucasian, Japanese and Chinese women living in Hawaii. In S. Golub (Ed.) *Menarche*. Lexington, Massachusetts, D. C. Heath, 1983.

Grumbach, M. M., Grave, G. D., & Mayer, F. E. (Eds.) *Control of the onset of puberty*, New York: Wiley 1974.

Jones, M. C. A study of socialization patterns at the high school level. *Journal of Genetic Psychology*, 1958, *93*, 87–111.

Jones, M. C., & Mussen, P. H. Self conceptions, motivations, and interpersonal attitudes of early and late maturing girls. *Child Development*, 1958, *29*, 491–501.

Kantero, R. L., & Widholm, O. Correlation of menstrual traits between adolescent girls and their mothers. *Acta Obstetricia et Gynecologica Scandinavica, Supplement*, 1971, *14*, 30–36.

Katchadourian, H. The biology of adolescence. San Francisco: W. H. Freeman & Co., 1977

Kestenberg, J. S. Menarche. In S. Lorand, & H. Schneer (Eds.) *Adolescents*. New York: Dell, 1965

Koff, E., Rierdan, J., & Silverstone, E. Changes in representation of body image as a function of menarcheal status. *Developmental Psychology*, 1978, *14*, 635-642.

Koff, E., Rierdan, J. & Jacobson, S. The personal and interpersonal significance of menarche. *Journal of the American Academy of Child Psychiatry*, 1981, *20*, 148–158.

Koff, E. Through the looking glass of menarche: What the adolescent girl sees. In S. Golub (Ed.) *Menarche*. Lexington, Massachusetts, D. C. Heath, 1983.

Kumin, M. *Why can't we live together like civilized human beings?* New York: Viking Press, 1982.

Leppert, P. Menarche and adolescent pregnancy. In S. Golub (Ed.) *Menarche*. Lexington, Massachusetts: D. C. Heath, 1983.

Logan, D. D. The menarche experience in twenty-three foreign countries. *Adolescence*, 1980, *15*, 247–256.

Malina, R. M. Delayed age of menarche of athletes. *Journal of the American Medical Association*, 1982, *247*, 3312.

Notman, M. Menarche: A psychoanalytic perspective. In S. Golub (Ed.) *Menarche*. Lexington, Massachusetts: D. C. Heath, 1983.

Paige, K. E. Virginity rituals and chastity control during puberty: Cross-cultural patterns. In S. Golub (Ed.) *Menarche*. Lexington, Massachusetts: D. C. Heath, 1983.

Petersen, A. C., & Taylor, B. The biological approach to adolescence. In J. Adelson (Ed.) *Handbook of adolescent psychology*. New York: Wiley, 1980.

Petersen, A. E. Menarche: Meaning of measures and measuring meaning. In S. Golub (Ed.) *Menarche*. Lexington, Massachusetts: D. C. Heath, 1983.

Presser, H. B. Age at menarche, socio-sexual behavior, and fertility. *Social Biology*, 1978, *25*, 94–101.

Rebar, R. W., & Cumming, D. C. Reproductive function in women athletes. *Journal of the American Medical Association*, 1981, *246*, 1590.

Rierdan, J. Variations in the experience of menarche as a function of preparedness, In S. Golub (Ed.) *Menarche*. Lexington, Massachusetts: D. C. Heath, 1983.

Rosenbaum, M. B. The changing body image of the adolescent girl. In M. Sugar (Ed.) *Female adolescent development*. New York: Brunner/Mazel, 1979.

Shields, J. *Monozygotic twins*. London: Oxford University Press, 1962.

Simmons, R. G., Blyth, D. A., Van Cleave, E. F., & Bush, D. M. Entry into early adolescence: The impact of school structure, puberty, and early dating on self esteem. *American Sociological Review*, 1979, *44*, 948–967.

Tanner, J. M. *Foetus into man*. Cambridge, Massachusetts: Harvard University Press, 1978.

To everything there is a season. *Science News*, 1980, *118*, 150.

Udry, J. R. Age at menarche, at first intercourse, and at first pregnancy. *Journal of Biosocial Science*, 1979, *11*, 433–441.

Udry, J. R., & Cliquet, R. L. A cross-cultural examination of the relationship between ages at menarche, marriage, and first birth. *Demography*, 1982, *19*, 53–63.

Warren, M. P. Clinical aspects of menarche: Normal variations and common disorders. In S. Golub (Ed.) *Menarche*. Lexington, Massachusetts: D. C. Heath, 1983.

Weideger, P. *Menstruation and menopause*. New York: Knopf, 1976.

Whisnant, L., & Zegans, L. A study of attitudes toward menarche in white middle class American adolescent girls. *American Journal of Psychiatry*, 1975, *132*, 809–814.

Williams, L. R. Beliefs and attitudes of young girls regarding menstruation. In S. Golub (Ed.) *Menarche*. Lexington, Massachusetts: D. C. Heath, 1983.

Woods, N. F., Dery, G. K., & Most, A. Recollections of menarche, current menstrual attitudes, and perimenstrual symptoms. In S. Golub (Ed.) *Menarche*. Lexington, Massachusetts: D. C. Heath, 1983.

Antecedents and Consequences of Variations in Girls' Maturational Timing
J. Brooks-Gunn, Ph.D.

The antecedents and consequences of variations in girls' physical development are reviewed. Girls' development is highlighted because research on antecedents addresses genetic and environmental influences on menarcheal age variations, and because findings on the behavioral consequences of tempo variations have been less consistent for girls than for boys. Implications for adolescent health care are considered, particularly for the early maturing girl.

Early adolescence is the period when a young girl is physically transformed from a child into an adult and when she is expected to exhibit at least some behaviors indicative of her new status. The rise in hypothalamic-pituitary hormones occurring prior to secondary sexual development is not typically used as a marker of the entrance into the new life phase. Developmentalists are concerned with a young person's responses to physical changes, such as alterations in self-definition, choice of different activities and peer groups, or experimentation with new behavior, as well as others' reactions to the adolescent's changing body, such as expectations for more socially mature behavior, alterations of family relations, or inclusion in more mature peer groups (1). Early adolescence is typically defined as 11–14 years of age (2,3). However, given the normal variations in the onset of physical growth, studies of girls' psychologic adaptation to puberty may need to focus on 10 year olds, and perhaps 9 year olds. Likewise, most girls do not complete their physical growth by age 14 years, especially the relatively long period of breast growth and body fat accumulation. Thus, when the effects of pubertal change on girls' behavior are studied, the period from 10 to 15 years of age may be appropriate; when responses to tempo variations in development are of interest, the time period may need to be expanded to include 9 and 16 year olds.

This article focuses on the antecedents and consequences of the variations in girls' physical development. Early research results on behavioral effects have not been consistent for girls, as they have been for boys. Early maturing boys have an advantage relative to late maturers in many aspects of social-emotional functioning (4–7). Early maturation does not seem to be a social advantage for girls. In Berkeley and Oakland growth studies, effects of being an early maturer did not persist, were mediated by social class, and only occurred at certain ages (8–10). Findings from current research address the hypothesis that early maturation has negative psychosocial effects for girls.

Individual Variation in Pubertal Development

Variability is the rule, rather than the exception, for all pubertal processes. Three points need to be emphasized: the individual varia-

Reprinted with permission of Elsevier Science Publishing Company, Inc., from "The antecedents and consequences of variations in girls' maturational timing" by J. Brooks-Gunn, *Journal of Adolescent Health Care*, vol. 9, pp. 365–373. Copyright © 1988 by the Society for Adolescent Medicine.

tion in timing seen in all pubertal processes; the variability in sequence of pubertal events; and the rate at which girls pass through puberty. First, individual variation occurs in all of the changes associated with puberty. For example, while the "average" age of the onset of breast buds (Tanner stage 2) is 11 years in American girls, the range is from 8 to 13 years of age ($\pm$ 2 SD) (11,12). Completion of breast development usually occurs between 12 and 18 years of age. Second, the "typical" sequence of pubertal events is not as standard as is often implied. For example, although the breast bud is usually the first event, with pubic hair following shortly thereafter, in about one fourth of all girls studied, pubic hair occurs before breast buds (11,12). Breast and pubic hair growth are somewhat independent, which might be expected as each is controlled by different hormones (13). Third, the speed with which girls pass through puberty varies. For example, the "average" girl will take 4 years to develop mature breasts (Tanner breast stage 2 through stage 5). However, some girls may go through the entire sequence in 1.5 years (11,12,14). Thus, variability occurs in duration, or rate, of secondary sexual development as well as in the onset and completion of linear and weight growth. Possible consequences of such variations have only been studied for timing, or what Tanner has termed "tempo," even though duration and sequence also may influence behavior. These topics have not been investigated (15).

When considering the effects of maturation timing on the young woman, it is important to remember that girls' and boys' progression through puberty is different, with girls typically having their growth spurt and onset of secondary sexual development earlier and the peak height velocity occurring at different points in the process (girls prior to menarche and Tanner breast stage 4 and boys after Tanner genital stage 4). Hypothetically, early maturing girls and late-maturing boys

may be at greater risk for adjustment problems than others with more "normal" maturation timing (1).

Defining Early and Late Maturation

Timing of maturation is a relative concept, referring to an individual's status vis-à-vis a specific reference group or a set of norms. To define maturation group, behavioral and developmental researchers have a variety of decisions to make: which pubertal event must be used; whether age or grade distributions of the event will be examined; how much of the sample will be defined as early or late; and whether classifications will be normative or criterion based.

Many different pubertal status measures have been used in timing research, such as bone age, menarche, age at peak height velocity, Tanner stage, and hormone levels. Age at peak height velocity is used in several studies (16,17), but is more often used for boys than for girls. Menarche is the most widely used measure for girls, in part because of the problems in obtaining height data prior to adolescence and in part because menarche is a measure that may be obtained relatively reliably by self-report. Menarche cannot be used to define groups of girls prior to the age of 14, however. A 13 year old who has not reached menarche may be an on-time or late maturer.

Girls may also be defined as early, on time, or late using the Tanner stage norms from the National Health Survey (18). An advantage of this procedure is that classifications may be made for girls aged 9 to 14 years. However, it may be less appropriate for older girls because by age 15 years most girls are in Tanner stage 4 or 5. Because Tanner staging data have only been collected in hospital- or clinic-based behavioral studies, few examples of this approach are found in the behavioral literature (19, 20). However, the demonstrations of high convergent validity between early adolescent reports of Tanner stages using schematic drawings and physician ratings make it more likely that this procedure will gain in popularity (21, 22). Finally, hormone status may also be used as a marker of maturation timing. Given the difficulty of obtaining blood samples and accuracy problems with detecting small concentrations of hormones using saliva samples (especially in Tanner stages 1 and 2), few maturation studies have used hormone levels as markers (23).

The decision must be made whether to identify more or less extreme groups of "off-time" maturers. Typically, extreme group analyses focus on clinical disorders such as precocious puberty (24, 25). From a developmental perspective, adolescents who are very early or very late (i.e., 2 SD from the mean, comprising about 1% of the population), by virtue of the large disparity between themselves and others in maturation status, may be in a very different set of circumstances than adolescents who are less off time (i.e., 1 SD from the mean, comprising about 4–5% of the population). Thus, the more deviant groups of off-time maturers may be psychologically different from the less deviant groups. This hypothesis, however, has not been tested.

Many cross-sectional studies are unable to include all stages of pubertal development at any one age point or several age groups. For example, if one is interested in studying the 9–10 year olds, only a few girls will be in Tanner breast stages 4 and 5. Typically, samples are split into three groups whereby 20–30% of the sample is defined as early, 40–60% as on-time, and 20–30% as late. When menarcheal age is used, 14 years is typically used as the cutoff for late maturation and 11.5 years as the cutoff for early maturation [based on the population mean of 12.7–12.8 years and an SD of 1.2 (26)].

Antecedents of Maturation Timing

What accounts for the individual variation in menarcheal age? Clearly, genetic factors play a role. Menarcheal age of mothers and daughters is related, with correlations typically ranging from 0.30 to 0.45 (26–28). Nutrition and leanness are relevant environmental factors (29–32). Nutrition and weight early in life (the fetal and infancy periods) as well as nutrition and weight at puberty may influence menarcheal age (33). Weight does not account for all menarcheal variations. Earlier debate focused on whether a critical body weight [47–48 kg (34)] or a critical body composition of relative fatness [17% (35)] was necessary for the onset of menstrual cycle. However, current data do not suggest that a specific level of fatness is critical for menarche (32). Problems exist with the formula used to derive estimates of body composition (36,37), and reduced variability in skinfold thickness following menarche has not been found (36,38). Variations in the weight at which menarche is attained have been seen (31,37).

In some instances, illnesses influence maturation timing. Hypothyroidism and thyrotoxicosis may retard menarche (39,40). The number of children in the family is another predictor of menarcheal age. In families with more children, menarcheal age appears to be delayed by about 0.11 to 0.22 years per additional sibling (41). The mechanism underlying this association is not known. Also, populations of women living at high altitudes are more likely to have delayed menarche than those at low altitudes (41); again, the reasons for this are not fully understood.

Another approach to the study of "tempo-variation" antecedents focuses on groups who are likely to have delayed menarche, such as elite athletes or young adolescents with anorexia nervosa. In both instances, menarcheal age occurs later than population norms would predict. Delayed

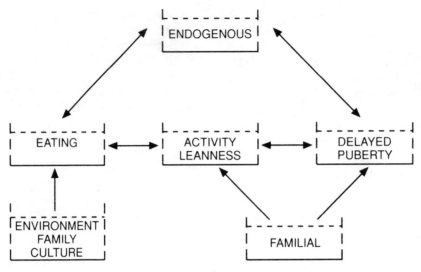

Figure 1. Model showing delayed menarche.

menarche is a common characteristic of many groups of female athletes. Delays of 1–2 years have been reported for gymnasts, figure skaters, dancers, volleyball players, and runners (42–44). The stringent selection process for elite athletes may make it more likely that late maturers will become athletes. The physical characteristics associated with delayed menarche—relatively narrow hips, long legs, and lower weight for height (45,46)—may render an individual girl more suited for most competitive athletics. Early maturers may be at a special disadvantage in sports, although few studies have directly examined this issue (42).

As found in samples of athletes, environmental factors possibly associated with delayed menarche include weight and body mass, intensity and duration of exercise, and restricted food intake (42,47). However, it is difficult to assess the relative effects of such factors because they are often interrelated. The challenge is to disentangle the contribution of each factor and to develop a multidimensional model, such as that shown in Figure 1.

Comparing the characteristics of adolescents in different athletic groups may help explain variations in menarcheal age across different sports. In one study, adolescents were compared who were engaged in three sports that varied on two dimensions—energy expended and weight demands. Dancing requires low weight and has a low caloric expenditure; figure skating requires low weight but has a high caloric expenditure; and swimming does not require a particular weight and has a relatively high caloric expenditure per hour of exercise. Menarche delays are more common and weight for height is lower for figure skaters and ballet dancers than for swimmers (48). In addition, dancers engage in more dieting behavior to maintain their low weight than do figure skaters, perhaps reflecting the low energy expenditure of the former group (48).

Entering athletics prepubertally rather than postpubertally has been associated with menarcheal delays in some but not all studies of athletic groups (43,49,50). Duration of current training may also be a factor in menarcheal age. Training and loss of body weight have been shown to suppress the secretion of gonadotropins and cause secondary hypoestrogenism in postmenarcheal girls and women (51–54). Similar processes may occur in the premenarcheal athlete.

While dieting behavior seems to be associated with delayed menarche and secondary amenorrhea (47), less is known about actual nutrition intake and delayed menarche. In a study of adult dancers, high eating problem scores (indicative of dieting and bulimia) are related to lower levels of reported protein and fat intake (55). In addition, several studies of adult dancers and gymnasts suggest that overall caloric intake and nutrients (e.g., calcium, iron, niacin) are below the Minimum Daily Requirement even before controlling for the energy expenditure (55–57). In a small study of college athletes, premenarcheally trained women consumed fewer calories (specifically, less fat and protein) than the postmenarcheally trained athletes (43).

Antecedents of tempo variations appear to include genetic and environmental components. What is of interest to the developmental psychologist is that a girl's behavior might alter the genetic time-table for tempo. This may be best illustrated by the athlete who has chosen a sport for which very low weights are required or who has begun training at a very early age.

Consequences of Being an Early or Late Maturer

Until recently, not much was known about the psychologic consequences of girls being early or late maturers, in part due to the disparities in measuring tempo and the findings of earlier studies (8–10). It has been hypothesized that being on time is more advantageous than being off time, and that early maturing girls are at more of a disadvantage than late maturers because the former are more deviant compared to their male and female classmates. Most current research suggests that most timing effects have to do with being early, not late (1). Maturation-timing influences can be seen in physical development, preparation for and feelings about menarche, body image and self-image, deviant behavior, and relationships with parents and peers, as discussed below.

Summary of Current Research

Early maturers weigh more and are slightly shorter than late maturers when pubertal growth is complete. These differences remain throughout life (31). Early maturers may not be as prepared for pubertal change as late maturers. Approximately 10–15% of white adolescent girls report not being prepared for menarche (i.e., not given information and not having parents discuss it) (58). The early maturer may not receive as much factual information as the late maturer because health education classes typically occur at the end of fifth grade or in the sixth grade, after the early maturer has already had menarche. In addition, mothers, who are a girl's most likely primary source of information about puberty and menarche, may be less likely to discuss changes with their early maturing daughters (59). Perhaps mothers are uncomfortable with their daughters' early development or were unprepared for menarche themselves. Early maturers are less likely to report that their fathers know about their menarche and are less likely to directly tell their fathers about it (60). Because girls in part seem to choose close girlfriends on the basis of physical status (61), early maturing girls may have a smaller network of intimate friends. All of these potential influences may affect the early maturers' attitudes about menstruation, which continue to be more negative, and their menstrual symptoms more severe, even in later adolescence (59).

Early maturers seem to have a poorer body image than on-time or late maturers, at least when global measures of body image and weight-related measures are used (6,62). This is true of girls in elementary, junior, and senior high school (63–65). In addition, higher eating problem scores are found among early maturing girls compared to on-time and late maturers, and this lasts throughout the adolescent years (62). In part, such differences are because body build appears to be related to peer evaluations and prestige; being thin is a desirable condition for almost all adolescent girls, and dieting is a common response to the current cultural demands for thinness (66–68). Early maturers, by virtue of being somewhat heavier, do not conform to the cultural values that promote thinness. Thus, it is not surprising that they may have a less positive body image (related to weight) and are thus more concerned about dieting than are late maturers.

Maturation status by itself, however, does not seem to affect overall self-esteem. Instead, self-esteem appears to be affected simultaneously by the occurrence of physical and social changes. Girls who are developing at the time when they are making the transition to middle school have lower self-esteem than girls not developing at the time of the school change (65). Early maturing sixth graders find the transition to middle school more difficult than on-time or late-maturing sixth-grade girls or than early maturing sixth graders not moving to middle school.

Early maturers may engage in "adult behaviors" (such as smoking, drinking, and intercourse) at a younger age than late maturers, as reported in the large prospective Swedish study of Magnusson and colleagues (69). This may be due, in part, to the fact that early maturers tend to associate with older peers. Perhaps by virtue of their physical appearance, some early maturers seek out (or are sought out by) older peers, who are more likely to engage in such behaviors. Whether or not there are any long-term consequences of engaging in such behaviors at young ages is currently being studied by

Magnusson (70) as a function of pubertal status.

Early maturers seem to be somewhat more advanced with respect to dating than are on-time or late maturers, at least in middle school (69,71). However, pubertal status does not seem to be associated with dating behavior (20,69,71,72), suggesting that maturation vis-à-vis one's peers plays a larger role than the actual maturation status.

Few studies have examined the relation between parent-child interaction and timing of maturation (73,74,77). Much has been written about how both parents and young adolescents negotiate the pubertal transition (75,76). Currently, a number of investigators are pursuing the issue of family adaptation to early adolescence, but only one group has focused on maturation timing (77). Observation of family interactions and self-report measures have been collected on seventh-grade girls and their parents, divided into four groups: menarche more than 12 months ago; menarche 6–11 months ago; menarche within the last 6 months; and premenarcheal. Results suggest that "perturbations," to borrow a term used by Hill, occur immediately following menarche, as compared to premenarcheal and more postmenarcheal girls. Mothers in the immediate postmenarcheal group are perceived as less accepting and the family as more controlling than in the premenarcheal and more postmenarcheal groups. Of particular interest are the results of those girls who reached menarche over a year ago. They resemble the immediate postmenarche group in terms of reporting strain in parent-child relations. The authors hypothesize that these findings may be due to the early maturation status of the girls in the group reaching menarche a year ago (i.e., menarche in the sixth grade or earlier). Longitudinal analyses or cross-sectional studies of eighth graders will be necessary to see whether early maturation or length of time since menarche is a more influential determinant of family relations.

Finally, a few studies have examined emotional function and adjustment as related to maturation timing. Early maturers may exhibit more psychopathology than on-time or late maturers, as found in two studies (16,62). They may also exhibit less impulse control and poorer emotional tone (i.e., more depressive affect). In the study that used hormone status to define early and late maturation, earlier maturing girls, as defined by follicle-stimulating hormone levels, had higher psychopathology and depressive affect scores than on-time or late-maturing girls. However, no relations were found between emotional function and other hormones (23). In another study measuring hormones, the most rapid rises in estradiol hormone were associated with relatively high levels of depressive affect, irrespective of maturational timing (78). Thus, psychopathology and poor emotional tone (which may be indicative of a mild depressive affect) may be associated with early maturation in young adolescent girls. Additionally, early maturing girls who experience negative family and school events are more likely to exhibit depressive affect than later maturing girls who experience negative events (79). In brief, early maturation is not an advantage for girls, and in some it is a disadvantage.

Significance of Results on Timing of Maturation

Although early maturation may be a risk factor, several caveats are in order. First, the effects appear to be small. Not all early maturers will have a poor body image or will date, smoke, or drink earlier. Indeed, the effects of grade in school are often stronger than maturation timing effects (16). Because the adolescent's social world is organized by their grade in school rather than by pubertal development, the primacy of the former is not surprising. On the other hand, this does not mean that maturation has no influence on behavior, but it suggests the need to embed pubertal timing effects within a larger framework.

Second, our understanding of maturation timing effects is greatly enhanced by the notion of on-time and off-time events. Neugarten (80), in particular, discussed how the life cycle is perceived in terms of a set of norms about what events should occur and when. The "social clock," which is internalized by individuals, identifies life phases and expected life transitions. Events that are off-time, occurring earlier or later than anticipated, may result in a crisis for the individual. Critical to this notion is the individual's perception of timeliness, as well as actual timing. That is, an event may be perceived to be on-time or off-time depending on a variety of factors, such as one's reference group, the cohort in which one finds oneself, the importance to the individual of being in the "correct" phase, and an individual's perception of the on-time range (1,62).

Third, an early maturer may be at most risk when the requirements of a particular social context and a girl's physical and behavioral characteristics are mismatched. On-time dancers are a case in point. With regard to the general peer group, they are on-time and should not exhibit any particular problems; however, they do not have the characteristics deemed ideal by the dance world. That they do look quite different physically from late maturers is probably a consequence of having higher weights and less control over eating than the profession demands (62).

Fourth, only certain behaviors seem to be affected by timing of maturation. Cultural standards seem to play a role. Of all of the psychologic factors studied, body image is most affected by early maturation. Clearly, the demand for thinness, to the point of desiring to be below one's supposed ideal weight for height, contributes to the potential difficulties an early maturing girl may face

(81). At the same time, the entire repertoire of adolescent behaviors have not been examined vis-à-vis the timing of maturation. Therefore, other behaviors may also be influenced.

Implications for Health Care

What might be done to identify the off-time maturer and help those at risk for problems? Girls who are extremely early or late are likely to come to the attention of a physician, such as the girl who begins to menstruate before age 8 years or after age 15 years. Girls who are early or late maturers but well within the normal range are less likely to be taken to a physician because of their maturation status. However, these girls may also have concerns about normalcy. These concerns may not be raised by the girls unless the physician takes the initiative. A brief discussion outlining the sequence and timing of events and the large variations may be all that is needed to reassure many off-time maturers.

What might be done to help the off-time maturer? Health care providers could target the daughter, the mother, or both. If early maturers are less likely to receive information from their mothers than later maturers, mothers may need more information so they can discuss puberty with their daughters at the appropriate time. Both mothers and daughters could potentially benefit from facts concerning the psychologic effects of being an early developer. Especially helpful might be information on potential peer pressures to date and to engage in adultlike behavior at early ages. Also, the transition to junior high school may be more difficult for the girl who is developing physically than for the girl who is not. Parents who are cognizant of this can be particularly sensitive to the needs of their emerging middle school daughter. Most early maturers easily negotiate their puberty. For those who do not, advance preparation and ongoing discussions with physicians and parents may help.

This work was supported by the W. T. Grant Foundation and the National Institutes of Health. Dr. Michelle Warren's collaboration in the research is greatly appreciated.

REFERENCES

1. Brooks-Gunn J, Petersen A C, Eichor, D, eds. Time of maturation and psychosocial functioning in adolescence. J Youth Adolesc 1985;14(3/4).
2. Brooks-Gunn J, Petersen A C. Problems in studying and defining pubertal events. J Youth Adolesc 1984;13:181–96.
3. Brooks-Gun, J, Petersen A C, eds. Girls at puberty: Biological and psychosocial perspectives. New York: Plenum Press, 1983.
4. Clausen J A. The social meaning of differential physical and sexual maturation. In: Dragastin S E, Elder Jr, G H, eds. Adolescence in the life cycle: Psychological change and the social context. New York: Halstead, 1975.
5. Jones M C. Psychological correlates of somatic development. Child Dev 1965;36:899–911.
6. Jones M C, Bayley N. Physical maturing among boys as related to behavior. J Educ Psychol 1950;41:129–48.
7. Peskin H. Pubertal onset and ego functioning. J Abnorm Psychol 1967;72:1–15.
8. Faust M S. Developmental maturity as a determinant in prestige of adolescent girls. Child Dev 1986;31:173–86.
9. Mussen P H, Jones M C. Self-conceptions, motivations, and interpersonal attitudes of late- and early-maturing boys. Child Dev 1957;28:243–56.
10. Peskin H. Influence of the developmental schedule of puberty on learning and ego functioning. J Youth Adolesc 1973;2:273–90.
11. Harlan W R, Harlan E A, Grill, G P. Secondary sex characteristics of girls 12 to 17 years of age: The U. S. Health Examination Survey. J Pediatr 1980;96:1074–8.
12. Marshall W A, Tanner J M. Variations in pattern of pubertal changes in girls. Arch Dis Child 1969;44:291–303.
13. Grumbach M M, Richards H E, Conte, F A, et al. Clinical disorders of adrenal function and puberty: An assessment of the role of

the adrenal cortex in normal and abnormal puberty in man and evidence for an ACTH-like pituitary adrenal androgen stimulating hormone. In: Serio M. ed., The endocrine function of the human adrenal cortex, Serono Symposium. New York: Academic Press, 1977.

14. Lee P. A. Normal ages of pubertal events among American males and females. J Adolesc Health Care 1980;1:26–9.

15. Brooks-Gunn J, Warren M P. Measuring physical status and timing in early adolescence: A developmental perspective. J. Youth Adolesc 1985;14:163–89.

16. Petersen, A C, Crockett L. Pubertal timing and grade effects on adjustment. J Youth Adolesc 1985;14:191–206.

17. Simmons R G, Blyth D A. Moving into adolescence: The impact of pubertal change and school context. New York, Aldine Press, 1987.

18. Gross R T. Patterns of maturation: Their effects on behavior and development. In: Levine M D, Satz P, eds. Middle childhood: Development and dysfunction. Baltimore: University Park Press, 1984:47–62.

19. Dornbusch S M, Carlsmith J M, Gross R T, et al. Sexual development, age, and dating: A comparison of biological and social influences upon one set of behaviors. Child Dev. 1981;52:179–185.

20. Gargiulo J, Attie I, Brooks-Gunn J, et al. Dating in middle school girls: Effects of social context, maturation, and grade. Dev. Psychol 1987;23:730–7.

21. Brooks-Gunn J, Warren M P, Rosso J, et al. Validity of self-report measures of girls' pubertal status. Child Dev 1987;58:829–41.

22. Duk, P M, Litt I F, Gross R T. Adolescents' self-assessment of sexual maturation. Pediatrics 1980;66:918–20.

23. Susman E J, Nottelmann E D, Inoff-Germain, G. E., et al. The relation of relative hormonal levels and physical development and social-emotional behavior in young adolescents. J Youth Adolesc 1985;14:245–64.

24. Cutler Jr, G B, Comite F, Rivier J, et al. Pituitary desensitization with a long-acting luteinizing-hormone-releasing hormone analog: A potential new treatment for idiopathic precocious puberty. In: Brooks-Gunn J, Petersen A C, eds. Girls at puberty: Biological and psychosocial perspectives. New York: Plenum Press, 1983;89–102.

25. Meyer-Bahlburg H F L, Ehrhardt A A, Bell J J, et al. Idiopathic precocious puberty in girls: Psychosexual development. J Youth Adolesc 1985;14:339–53.

26. Zacharias L, Wurtma, R J. Age at menarche: Genetic and environmental influences. N Engl J Med 1969;280:868–75.

27. Brooks-Gunn J, Warren M P. Genetic and environmental influences: Contributions to delayed puberty. Ann Hum Biol 1988;15:35–43.

28. Damo, A, Damo, S T, Reed R B, et al. Age at menarche of mothers and daughters, with a note on accuracy of recall. Hum Biol 1969;41:161–75.

29. Brooks-Gunn J, Warren M P. The psychological significance of secondary sexual characteristics in 9- to 11-year-old girls. Child Dev, in press.

30. Frisch, R. E. Fatness, puberty, and physical training on menarche and ovulation. In: Brooks-Gunn, J., Petersen, A. C., eds. Girls at puberty: Biological and psychosocial perspectives. New York: Plenum Press 1983:29–49.

31. Garn S M. Continuities and change in maturational timing. In: Brim O, Kage, J, eds. Constancy and change in human development. Cambridge: Harvard University Press. 1980:113–62.

32. Malina R M. Adolescent growth and maturation: Selected aspects of current research. Yearbook of Physical Anthropology 1978;21:63–94.

33. Liestol K. Social conditions and menarcheal age: The importance of early years of life. Ann Hum Biol 1982;9:521.

34. Frisch R E, Revell R. Height and weight at menarche and a hypothesis of menarche. Arch Dis Child 1971;46:695–701.

35. Frisch R E. Fatness of girls from menarche to age 18 years, with a nomogram. Hum Biol 1976;48:353–9.

36. Billewicz W Z, Fellowes H M, Hytten C A. Comments on the critical metabolic-mass and the age of menarche. Ann Hum Biol 1976;3:51–9

37. Johnston F E, Borden M, MacVea, R B. The effect of genetic and environmental factors upon growth of children in Guatamala City. In: Watts E S, Johnston F E, Lasker G W, eds. Mouton, The Hague, 1975:377–88.

38. Cameron N. Weight and skinfold variation at menarche and critical body weight hypotheses. Ann Hum Biol 1976;3:279–82.

37

39. Barnes N D, Hayles A B, Rya, F J. Sexual maturation in juvenile hypothyroidism. May Clin Proc 1972;48:849–56.

40. Osler D.C, Crawford J D. Examination of the hypothesis of a critical weight at menarche in ambulatory and bedridden mentally retarded girls. Pediatrics 1973;51:674–9.

41. Malina R M. The adolescent growth spurt and sexual maturation. In: Shangold M, Mirkin G. eds. Women and exercise. Philadelphia: F A Davis Co:1988:121–28.

42. Malina R. Menarche in athletes: A synthesis and hypothesis. Ann Hum Biol 1983;10:1–24.

43. Frisch R E, Gotz-Welbergen A V, McArthur J W, et al. Delayed menarche and amenorrhea of college athletes in relation to age of onset of training. JAMA 1981;246:1559–90.

44. Warren M P, Brooks-Gunn J, Hamilto, L H, et al. Scoliosis and fractures in young ballet dancers: Relationship to delayed menarcheal age and secondary amenorrhea. N Engl J Med 1986;314:1348–53.

45. Tanner J M. Growth at adolescence: With a general consideration of the effects of hereditary and environmental factors upon growth and maturation from birth to maturity. 2nd edition. Oxford: Blackwell Scientific Publications, 1962.

46. McNeil, D, Livson N. Maturation rate and body build in women. Child Dev 1963;34:25–32.

47. Brooks-Gunn J, Warren M P, Hamilton L H. The relationship of eating disorders to amenorrhea in ballet dancers. Med Sci Sports Exerc 1987;19:41–4.

48. Brooks-Gunn J, Burrow C, Warren M P. Menarcheal age in different athletic groups: Associations with weight, eating behavior, and energy expenditure. Int J Eating Dis 1988.

49. Sidhu L S, Grewal, R. Age of menarche in various categories of Indian sportswomen. Br J Sports Med 1980;14:199–203.

50. Stager J M, Robertshaw D, Miescher E. Delayed menarche in swimmers in relation to age at onset of training and athletic performance. Med Sci Sports Exerc 1984;16:550–5.

51. Warren M P, Vande Wiele R L. Clinical and metabolic features of anorexia nervosa. Am J Obstet Gynecol 1973;117:435–49.

52. Bonen A, Keizer H A. Athletic menstrual cycle irregularity: Endocrine response to exercise and training. Phys Sports Med 1984;12:78–94.

53. Bullen B A, Skrinar G S, Beitin, I Z, et al. Induction of menstrual disorders by strenuous exercise in untrained women. N Engl J Med 1985;312:1349–53.

54. Jurkowski et al. Ovarian hormonal responses to exercise. J Appl Physiol 1978;44:109–14.

55. Hamilton L H, Brooks-Gunn J, Warren M P. Nutritional intake of female dancers: A reflection of eating problems. Int J Eating Dis 1986;5:925–34.

56. Cohen J L, Potosnak L, Frank O, et al. A nutritional and hematologic assessment of elite ballet dancers. Phys Sports Med 1985;13:43–54.

57. Calabrese L H. Nutritional and medical aspects of gymnastics. Clin Sports Med 1985;4:23–30.

58. Ruble D N, Brooks-Gunn J. The experience of menarche. Child Dev 1982;53:1557–66.

59. Brooks-Gunn J, Ruble D N. The development of menstrual-related beliefs and behaviors during early adolescence. Child Dev 1982;53:1567–77.

60. Brooks-Gunn J. Pubertal processes and girls' psychological adaptation. In: Lerner R, Foch T T, eds. Biological-psychosocial interactions in early adolescence: A life-span perspective. Hillsdale, NJ: Lawrence Erlbaum Associates, 1987:123–53.

61. Brooks-Gunn J, Samelson M, Warren M P, et al. Physical similarity of and disclosure of menarcheal status to friends: Effects of age and pubertal status. J Early Adolesc 1986;6:3–14.

62. Brooks-Gunn J, Warren M P. Effects of delayed menarche in different contexts: Dance and nondance students. J Youth Adolesc 1985;14:285–300.

63. Blyth D A, Simmons R G, Zakin D F. Satisfaction with body image for early adolescent females: The impact of pubertal timing within different school environments. J Youth Adolesc 1985;14:207–25.

64. Duncan P D, Ritter P L, Dornbusch S M, et al. The effects of pubertal timing on body image, school behavior, and deviance. J Youth Adolesc 1985;14:227–35.

65. Simmons R G, Blyth D A, Van Cleave E F, et al. Entry into early adolescence: The impact of school structure, puberty, and early dating on self-esteem. Am Sociol Rev 1979;44:948–67.

66. Lerner R M. Adolescent maturational changes and psychosocial development: A

dynamic interactional perspective. J Youth Adolesc 1985;14:355–72.

67. Thornberry O T, Wilson R W, Golden P. Health promotion and disease prevention provisional data from the National Health Interview Survey: United States, January–June 1985. Vital and Health Statistics of the National Center for Health Statistics 1986;119:1–16.

68. Wooley S C, Wooley O W. Intensive outpatient and residential treatment for bulimia. In: Garner D M, Garfinkel P E, eds. Handbook of psychotherapy for anorexia nervosa and bulimia. New York: Guilford Press, 1985:391–430.

69. Magnusson D, Stattin H, Allan V L. Biological maturation and social development: A longitudinal study of some adjustment processes from mid-adolescence to adulthood. J Youth Adolesc 1985;14:267–83.

70. Magnusson D. Long term effects of early maturation in girls. Paper presented at the International Society for the Study of Behavioral Development, Japan 1987 (July).

71. Simmons R, Blyth D, McKinney K. The social and psychological effects of puberty of white females. In: Brooks-Gunn J, Petersen A C, eds. Girls at puberty: Biological and psychosocial perspectives. New York: Plenum Press, 1983:229–72.

72. Tobin-Richards H. Sex differences and similarities in heterosocial activity in early adolescence. Paper presented in a symposium on Love and Sex in Early and Middle Adolescence at the Biennial Meeting of the Society of Research in Child Development, Toronto, 1985 (April).

73. Brooks-Gunn J. Zahaykevich, M. Developmental trajectories in adolescence: Family and environmental influences. In: Kreppner K, Lerner R M. eds. Family systems and life-span development. Hillsdale, NJ: Erlbaum, 1988.

74. Hill J P. Adapting to menarche: Familial control and conflict. In: Gunnar M, ed. Development during the transition to adolescence. Vol 21. Hillsdale, NJ: Erlbaum, 1988:43–77.

75. Blos P. The adolescent passage. New York: International Universities Press, 1979.

76. Erikson E H. Identity: Youth and crisis. New York: WW Norton, 1968.

77. Hill J P, Holmbeck G N, Marlow L, et al. Menarcheal status and parent-child relations in families of seventh-grade girls. J Youth Adolesc 1985;14:301–16.

78. Brooks-Gunn J, Warren M P. Biological contributions to affective expression in young adolescent girls. Child Dev (in press).

79. Brooks-Gunn J, Warren M P, Rosso J T. The impact of pubertal and social events upon girls' problem behavior. J Youth Adolesc (in press).

80. Neugarten B L. Time, age, and life cycle. Am J Psychiatry 1979;136:887–94.

81. Attie I, Brooks-Gunn J, Petersen A C. The emergence of eating problems: A developmental perspective. J Child Psychol Psychiatry (in press).

Anorexia Nervosa and Bulimia: Incidence and Diagnosis

Kathleen Winters Plehn, R.N., M.S.N., C.R.N.P.

ABSTRACT. The incidence of eating disorders is increasing at an alarming rate. The clinician who sees many female teenagers and young women in the course of practice is a prime candidate for identifying and providing early diagnosis and communication with the anorexic or bulimic client. Vigilance when assessing the client's physical, psychological, personal and family-history status will increase case-finding for eating disorders at an earlier point in the disease.

The clinician who sees many female teenagers and young women in the course of practice is a prime candidate for identifying women with possible eating disorders. The ideal image of a woman's body is thinner than 20 years ago. Miss America candidates and winners are less curvy and weigh less than they did 17 years ago.[1] The teenager looking for an ideal appearance sees a thin Miss America and very thin top fashion models. In spite of the increasing amount of information about eating disorders in the lay literature, identifying and informing a client about the advanced signs, symptoms and subclinical clues of eating disorders still is necessary, so that early treatment and possible prevention may be promoted.

Incidence

Although females comprise approximately 95 percent of the eating-disorder population, attention to male clients, particularly athletes, should not be forgotten. The number of patients with anorexia and bulimia is on the rise.[2-3] Even more disturbing is the prevalence of preanorectic and/or prebulimic behaviors among teenagers and young women of all backgrounds. Jane Fonda's lifetime practice of bulimia was a surprise to many. Adolescent desires for personal autonomy, achievement and physical attractiveness along with cultural pressures toward thinness may contribute to eating disorders.[4]

Holding a distorted body image is common. Rosen and Gross studied 1,373 adolescents (geographically, racially and economically mixed females and males) and found 63 percent of the females and 16.2 percent of the males to be on diets and/or weight-reducing regimens. The majority of these adolescents were within normal weight ranges. Although most of the methods for weight control used were exercise and calorie restriction, a significant number used fasting, vomiting, laxatives or appetite suppressants.[5] Feldman et al. discovered that out of 170 female high school students, 50.6 percent believed they were overweight and 68 percent believed they should lose weight. Fifty-five percent had binges and felt out of control in their behaviors, with 15 percent vomiting and 13.5 percent fasting. Only eight of the 170 students were above the normal weight-chart limits.[6] Greenfield studied private preparatory students (age range of 13 to 19 years) and found 11.6 percent females and 5 percent males reporting self-induced vomiting; in addition, a sizeable number of women reported amenorrhea secondary to weight loss.[7] Pope surveyed 300 female shoppers in a suburban

This article first appeared in *The Nurse Practitioner: The American Journal of Primary Health Care* (1990) 15: 22–31. Copyright © 1990, *The Nurse Practitioner: The American Journal of Primary Health Care*.

shopping mall with a one-page eating behavior questionnaire. The female subjects were divided into two age groups. The group aged 13 to 20 reported the highest incidence of bulimic-like behavior (17.7 percent), while among the 21- to 30-year-olds, 10.3 percent reported bulimic behavior.[8] These studies support the contention that a striking number of young women think they are fat when they are not, and use potentially dangerous methods to reduce their weights.

The incidence of anorexia nervosa in the female population has been found to be approximately 1 percent.[8-9] Bulimia incidence rates vary from 4 percent, 8 percent and 10.3 percent, depending on the population, method and criteria used.[2-3,8] Some of the variance in these incidence figures may be due to the American Psychiatric Association's DSM III 1982 definition for bulimia, which did not include the frequency of food binges or the amount of food consumed. The 1987 revised edition defines the frequency as a minimum of two binges per week.

Definition

The usual criteria used to define anorexia nervosa and bulimia are derived from the 1987 DSM III (R) (See Tables 1 and 2 in the accompanying article, "Anorexia Nervosa, Bulimia Nervosa: Causal Theories and Treatment," p. 14).[10] According to the DSM III (R), all of the criteria must be present in order to make a diagnosis. In individuals with anorexia, amenorrhea is often an early sign before weight loss occurs. Loss of appetite is usually rare until late in the illness. Although the anorexic eats very little or low-caloric food, she or he feels fat even when emaciated. Other signs of anorexia may include delayed psychosexual development in the adolescent or a decreased interest in sex in the adult. Although 50 percent of anorectic patients may exhibit bulimic behavior along with the anorectic condition, the main differentiating factor in anorexia is the severe weight loss.[10-11]

Subjective Symptoms and Clues for Diagnosis

The primary health care clinician frequently comes in contact with the population at risk for an eating disorder (e.g., through annual physical exams, contraceptive-information counseling, pregnancy, and sports or camp physicals). Patients rarely volunteer information about their eating patterns—either from embarrassment, lack of concern or denial. Asking the client to complete a past medical history form (see Table 1) may give the clinician a quick look at the client's lifestyle and thereby save time. Kolodny's book *When Food's a Foe* also contains useful questions for the discovery of eating disorders.[12] A helpful open-ended question is "Do you have any questions or desire any other information or resources that we may be able to help you with?"

Other clues pointing toward an eating disorder may arise from questions the patient may ask (e.g., asking for advice on a good diet to lose weight when the patient is already thin, or seeking advice or prescriptions for laxatives or diuretics). Visiting several health care providers to acquire the needed prescriptions is common. Family or friends may also provide clues by describing a diet that started out sensibly and now is out of control. Family members may allude to frequent trips to the bathroom after a meal, with the sound of running water and their suspicions of the patient vomiting. Excessive exercise of from three to five hours daily may also be described by the patient's family.

Binge eating is expensive. Binge eating may be reported as "She is eating us out of house and home," or "She leaves nothing for the rest of the family to eat." On a fixed income this may add a considerable financial burden, since a single binge can include from 1,000 to 25,000 calories. The foods chosen are usually high-carbohydrate, easily digested junk foods, which can cost from $8 to $50 for a single binge. The bulimic may steal money to get the food, steal the laxatives used to purge, go to several different stores to pick up supplies and/or find a secret place to binge.

For the bulimic, secretive binges are followed by a depressed mood and self-deprecating thoughts. Most bulimics fall within normal weight guidelines, but frequent weight fluctuations of 10 pounds are not unusual. Food becomes the narcotic fix that temporarily reduces the feelings of loneliness, boredom, frustration, lack of self-worth and perceived rejection.[13] The eating process

---

Table 1. Brief Health History Form to Help Alert the Primary Health Care Provider to a Potential Eating Disorder in the Client

---

Date:

Name:

Reason for visit:

Age menstrual periods started:

Frequency and length of periods:

Any change in the last year?

Please circle yes or no.
Change in physical or emotional health since last year? Yes No

Change in weight of 10 lb in last year? Yes No

Are you on a diet? Yes No

Do you exercise? Yes No
If yes, type and amount per week:

Are there current stresses in your life? Yes No

Change in family health since last visit? Yes No

Do you use alcohol? Yes No
How much per week?

Do you use drugs?
How much per week?

Family history of drug or alcohol abuse? Yes No

Episodes of depression: Self Family

---

of biting, chewing and swallowing can have an emotionally soothing effect;[14] however, some gobble quickly with little chewing.[10] Some bulimics have described getting a high from the binge and vomiting, but later they know they have failed again in what they had promised themselves never again to do.

Depression is a common finding in both anorexia and bulimia. Whether depression causes eating disorders or results from them is uncertain.[9] Depression may be evidenced by lowered self-esteem, noted by the presence of self-deprecating remarks. The clinician needs to evaluate these patients for suicidal tendencies. For the bulimic client, high-risk personality behaviors include alcohol or drug abuse, and an inability to handle anger. High-risk traits for both the bulimic and anorexic include a perfectionistic attitude, a low frustration level, passive behavior, exaggerated guilt feelings, an unidentified or confused sexual role, lack of control over one's life, and compulsive behaviors toward food and weight control.[15] In addition, high-risk anorexic occupations or avocations include modeling, acting, ballet and athletics.[9]

Objective Symptoms

Eating-disorder symptoms are often subclinical until the disease is advanced. Clinicians should compare a patient's height and weight with a current chart; weight 15 percent below the midpoint weight of that person's body frame is considered serious. For example, using the current Metropolitan Life Insurance tables, a woman with a small body frame and a height of 5 feet 7 inches has a normal weight range of 123 to 136 pounds. Using 129 as the midpoint, weight below 109 pounds should be considered seriously underweight even for the weight-conscious teenager. Anorexia nervosa clients may lose up to 40 percent of their body weight, in contrast to bulimic clients who fall within or slightly above their weight ranges.

Common observations that may be associated with an eating disorder include weight fluctuations, a hoarse voice, hemoptysis, swollen but not tender parotid glands, and calluses or abrasions on the fingers, especially on the index and second fingers (from forced vomiting). With very frequent vomiting, conjunctival hemorrhages and small broken blood vessels on the cheeks may be noted, as well as dental enamel erosion. A sore tongue and erythematous buccal mucosa may result from poor nutrition. Hair loss, dry skin, slower reflex response and cold intolerance can result from inadequate nutrition, fat-insulation loss and lowered thyroid function. The body's metabolism slows down to accommodate the low level of food intake and nutrition. Lanugo, a fine downy hair, may be seen covering the arms, legs and face of the anorexic. In addition, the blood pressure and temperature are often low, with a compensating rapid pulse.

Changes in weight also affect the hormonal levels in the body. Hormonal changes may manifest themselves in amenorrhea or irregular menstrual periods. Amenorrhea has been seen in female athletes when the fat stores fall below 22 percent; the consequential insufficient hormonal production inhibits menstruation. When low-weight women are given a progestin challenge, no withdrawal bleeding occurs. Amenorrhea may also be associated with a reduced gonadotropin secretion to prepubertal levels. With adequate weight gain, this usually reverses itself. It is important to note that amenorrhea occurs in 20 percent of anorexics *before* low weight levels are attained, and can be a cardinal symptom of an eating disorder. Although the bulimic client is frequently at the right weight ratio for her height or slightly above, 40 percent may also have problems with menstrual irregularity.[9] If the estrogen level is very low, breast and vaginal atrophy may occur.

As severe weight loss occurs, the anorexic is at increasingly high risk for developing osteoporosis and incurring fractures, since calcium intake is insufficient and estrogen level is lowered. One mitigating factor is that the anorexic often engages in vigorous physical exercise to help lose more weight; exercise helps reduce the amount of bone-mass loss.[16] This may explain why more fractures are not seen in the severe anorexic.

Gastrointestinal complaints are also common; complaints can include bloating, heartburn, abdominal pain, ulcer-like symptoms and constipation. One side effect of constant laxative use is an atonic colon, resulting in constipation. Many teenagers are notorious for their lack of fruit, vegetable and roughage intake, so the health care provider must differentiate between inadequate-intake constipation and laxative-abuse constipation. Specific questions about laxative use will be helpful. It is not unusual for an eating-disorder client to take from 10 to 100 laxative or diuretic tablets per day or per binge. Taking large amounts of laxatives means that 4 to 6 liters of fluid may be lost, resulting in an enormous loss of electrolytes. Laxative use is a very ineffective way of reducing calories. Tests show that if 2,100 calories are consumed followed by 50 laxative tablets, the net calorie savings is only 252 calories.[17] Thus, laxative use is a very inefficient way of purging; the eating-disorder client needs to become aware of this information.

Weight loss and fluid and electrolyte imbalance also affect the central nervous system. Central nervous system complaints present as headaches, syncope, fainting during or after exercise, muscle weakness or cramping, irritability, insomnia and fatigue. These symptoms usually are traced to inadequate nutrition, dehydration and electrolyte imbalance arising from the abuse of cathartics and diuretics, and self-induced vomiting. Sodium, potassium and magnesium are some of the electrolytes that become seriously affected. Cardiac arrhythmias also occur from these imbalances and may lead to death.

As muscle mass reduces, the heart is also affected; the left ventricular wall becomes thin and the cardiac chamber size decreases.[9] Physical stamina at this point is reduced. The emetic Ipecac®, if used continuously, is absorbed into the body and causes cardiac arrhythmias that can lead to death.[11]

Lab values help in defining an eating disorder. Urine dipsticks test positive for ketones and protein if there is deficient carbohydrate metabolism. Specific gravity is elevated with dehydration or lowered if patient is water-loading to temporarily increase weight gain. Blood studies (e.g., CBC) can assess anemia as a result of malnutrition. A blood chemistry panel is important for the electrolyte values. Hypokalemia, hypocalcemia, hypomagnesemia, hypochloremia and hyponatremia may be noted, as well as an elevated BUN. The most critical value is the potassium level (normal = 3.5 to 5.0 mEq), since low levels cause cardiac arrhythmias that can result in death. Oral replacement of 20 mEq of potassium chloride once or twice daily can be effective for values of 2.8 or above, with a recheck of the potassium level in 24 to 48 hours. Values under 2.8 should be considered for parenteral treatment or hospitalization.[9,18]

Differential Diagnosis

The health care provider must differentiate between the young adult's self-consciousness/body preoccupation and an eating disorder. An important key to this differentiation is the anorexic's and bulimic's intense fear of becoming fat. "While the anorectic deals with this fear by not eating or by eating very little, the bulimic often tries to restrain eating; this triggers binging and leads to self-induced vomiting, hyperexercise and/or abuse (of) laxatives or diuretics to control weight. Abnormal, obsessive-compulsive efforts toward weight reduction are key early signs of eating disorders."[19] The following questions will help the health care provider diagnose a potential eating disorder: 1) Determine whether the client's choice for an ideal weight is realistic; 2) determine whether the client has a distorted body image; 3) ask whether the client believes his/her problems will disappear when the magical weight occurs; and 4) find out how the client plans to attain and maintain the weight goal. Ascertain the truthfulness of the answers with family, friends or spouse, with the permission of the client.

44

Conclusion

The incidence of eating disorders and distorted eating behaviors in teens and young women is increasing at an alarming rate. Early diagnosis provides the best prognosis for both anorexia and bulimia. Vigilance when assessing the client's physical, psychological, personal and family-history status will increase case-finding for eating disorders at an earlier point in the disease.

REFERENCES

1. Chernin, K.: The Obsession: Reflections on the Tyranny of Slenderness, New York, Harper & Row, 1981.
2. Zukerman, D. et al.: "Prevalence of Bulimia Among College Students," American Journal of Public Health, 1986, 76:9, pp. 1135–7.
3. Maceyko, S. J. and Nagelberg, D. B.: "The Assessment of Bulimia in High School Students," Journal of School Health, 1985, 55:4, pp. 135–7.
4. Harding, S. E.: "Anorexia Nervosa," Pediatric Nursing, 1985, 4, pp. 275–7.
5. Rosen, D. and Gross, M.: "Prevalence of Weight Reducing and Weight Gaining in Adolescent Girls and Boys," Health Psychology, 1987, 6:2, pp. 131–47.
6. Feldman, W. et al.: "Adolescents' Pursuit of Thinness," American Journal of Diseases of Children, 1986, 140, p. 294.
7. Greenfeld, D. et al.: "Eating Behavior in an Adolescent Population," International Journal of Eating Disorders, 1987 6:1 pp. 99–111.
8. Pope, H. et al.: "Anorexia and Bulimia Among 300 Female Suburban Shoppers." American Journal of Psychiatry, 1984, 141, pp. 292–4.
9. Herzog, D. B. and Copeland, P. M.: "Eating Disorders," New England Journal of Medicine, 1985, 313:5, pp. 295–301.
10. American Psychiatric Association: Diagnostic and Statistical Manual of Mental Disorders, 3rd Ed. (Revised), Washington, D. C., 1987.
11. Lipscomb, P. A.: "Bulimia Diagnosis and Management in the Primary Care Setting," Journal of Family Practice, 1987, 24:2, pp. 187–94.
12. Kolodny, N.: When Food's a Foe, Boston, Little Brown, 1987.
13. Cerrato, P.: "Helping Food Addicts Kick the Habit," RN, 1987, 50:8, pp. 75–7.
14. Fairburn, C.: "A Cognitive Behavioral Approach to the Treatment of Bulimia," Psychological Medicine, 1981, 11, pp. 707–11.
15. Lane, C. K.: "Pragmatic Information on Bulimia," Occupational Health Nursing, 1985, 33:11, pp. 572–5.
16. Torrance, C.: "Boning Up on Exercise," Nursing Times, 1985, 81:43, p.38.
17. Bo-Linn, G. et al.: "Purging and Caloric Absorption in Bulimic Patients and Normal Women," Annals of Internal Medicine, 1983, 99, pp. 14–17.
18. Williams, J. et al.: "Hand Lesions Characteristic of Bulimia," American Journal of Diseases of Children, 1986, 140, p. 28.
19. Crawshaw, J.: "Anorexia and Bulimia: The Earliest Clues," Patient Care, 1985, 19:18, pp. 80–3, 86–90, 93–5.

Chapter 3

The Monthly Cycle: Do Those Hormones Really Rage?

Menstruation has come "out of the closet." It is now mentioned publicly in magazine, television, and radio reports and advertising for menstruation related products from tampons to pills used to quiet jittery premenstrual nerves are rampant. Still menstruation remains one of the most misunderstood of our biological functions. As **Ouellette** points out in the first selection of this chapter, more open discussion about menstruation does not give it a positive or even a normal image. Advertisements encourage women to hide the fact that they are menstruating with an array of costly and often unnecessary products. At the same time, the popular press has introduced premenstrual syndrome (PMS) to the general public. Article after article suggest that PMS underlies any and every negative event or emotion in women's lives during at least one-quarter of each month.

Negative attitudes towards menstruation and menstruating women are not a modern invention. Throughout all of recorded history, references to the physical and spiritual uncleanliness of menstruation and to the negative or fear-inducing status of menstruating women can be found (See Delaney, et al., 1988 in Suggested Readings for a historical review of the menstrual taboo). These ideas may have been quite rational prior to our understanding of the biological underpinnings of menstrual bleeding. Clearly, our ancestors, having no concept of reproductive endocrinology, could easily look at menstrual bleeding with awe and fear. It was bleeding that occurred on a regular basis, with no apparent physical injury. To suppose spiritual injury provided a much-needed explanation of the phenomenon. And, at times, the monthly cycle of bleeding ceased, only to begin again following the birth of a child. If one does not understand reproduction or the role of sexual intercourse in providing the necessary conditions for conception, such a phenomenon must be truly frightening.

We've come a long way in our scientific understanding of menstruation, pregnancy, and childbirth. Today, very few people in technologically-advanced cultures refer to menses as a sign of spiritual injury. But, the remnants of the old fears remain. In keeping with the language of technology menses (menstrual bleeding) is no longer a sign of increased spiritual power or punishment by the gods. It is now an illness—a time of the month when women are debilitated in their functioning and incapable of positive action in the world of men.

A number of studies have shown that our beliefs about menstruation affect the symptoms women report experiencing across the monthly cycle. The second selection in this chapter (**Ruble**) is a classic example of such a study. **Ruble** used a clever technique to convince some women who are not truly premenstrual that their periods were imminent. Women who were led to believe that they were premenstrual reported increased water retention and pain compared to women in the same actual cycle phase but convinced that their periods were still a long way off.

In the third selection in this chapter, **McFarlane, Martin, and Williams** tackle the societal stereotypes about the influence of menstrual, weekly and lunar cycles on our moods and behaviors. The societal stereotypes of depressed mood during the premenstruum for women and increased energy and positive mood on weekends for both women and men were supported when the subjects in this study were asked to recall moods experienced in the past. These stereotypes were not supported, however, when the subjects were asked to record mood and arousal on a daily basis. The lack of agreement between mood records collected on a daily basis and those based on recall and the similarity between recalled moods and societal stereotypes suggests that our recollections of moods may be strongly influenced by our culturally-determined expectations. Unfortunately, these researchers collected only daily mood reports for the lunar cycle. The results indicate no increase in strange behaviors or irritability during the full moon. Without recall data, it is impossible to know whether the subjects in this study believed in the stereotypical negative effect of full moon on behavior.

While studies of randomly-selected groups of women show little if any evidence of PMS when moods and behaviors are recorded on a daily basis, a small subset of women do suffer from PMS. In 1987, the American Psychiatric Association proposed criteria for the diagnosis of Late Luteal Phase Dysphoric Disorder in the appendix of its Diagnostic and Statistical Manual of Mental Disorders, Third Edition, Revised (DSM-III-R).

Table 1. Symptoms for the diagnosis of Late Luteal Phase Dysphoric Disorder as outlined in the appendix of the DSM-III-R (APA, 1987).

1. marked mood lability
2. anger and irritability
3. anxiety
4. depressed mood or hopelessness
5. decreased interest in usual activities
6. easy fatigability or marked lack of energy
7. subjective sense of difficulty concentrating
8. change in appetite, overeating, or specific food cravings
9. hypersomnia or insomnia
10. other physical symptoms

The name change from PMS was instituted to minimize the emotional or political impact of inclusion of this disorder (Amchin, 1991).

The symptoms of Late Luteal Phase Dysphoric Disorder as indicated in the DSM-III-R are listed in Table 1. Special emphasis is given to the first four symptoms. These events must occur during the week immediately preceding and during the first few days of menses and their existence and pattern of occurrence is to be confirmed through daily records. **Rivera-Tovar and Frank,** in the fourth article in this chapter, utilized the DSM-III-R symptoms to determine the prevalence of PMS in a large group of college women. Their analyses indicate that less than 5% of the women studied displayed these symptoms in sufficient number and with the timing and the regularity required by the DSM-III-R. Although these numbers are far lower than estimates provided by earlier, less cautious studies, the actual incidence of PMS may still be overestimated. The DSM-III-R criteria for the diagnosis of Late Luteal Phase Dysphoric Disorder also indicate that the disturbance must interfere with the normal occupational or social functioning of the woman. It is not clear that any of the subjects of this study actually met this criterion. The bottom line is that PMS is a reality for some women. Perhaps by concentrating their efforts on women who clearly have PMS, researchers will soon be able to identify the cause(s) and develop effective treatment programs for this disorder.

When we think about the interactions between our physiology and behavior we most commonly think of the ways in which our behavior is controlled by our physical condition as in the case of PMS. The last two articles in this chapter are classic ones which refer to the opposite condition—the effect of behavior and/or environment on physiological functioning. **McClintock's** article presents the first scientific evidence that women who live together have their menstrual periods at or near the same time. After considering a number of possible mechanisms underlying menstrual synchrony, **McClintock** suggests that women who live together communicate their menstrual status to other women through pheromones or chemical communicators. **Russell, Switz, and Thompson,** in the last paper in this chapter, devised a specific test of this chemical—or pheromonal-communication hypothesis. They report that the menstrual cycles of women who are exposed to the underarm perspiration (a pheromone loaded secretion) of a donor woman with whom they have no other contact become synchronous with the cycle of the donor woman. Whether this phenomenon is an evolutionary relic or plays an active function in reproductive behaviors of women today remains to be determined.

Finally, McClintock reports a second example of behaviors effect on physiology. Contact with men can affect the length of a woman's monthly cycle. Women in her study who had more frequent contact with men (greater than three times per week) had shorter cycles than did women who had less frequent contact with men. Although this phenomenon has been reproduced in later work by other researchers (e.g., Jarret, 1988), the mechanism underlying this effect remains unknown.

References and Suggested Readings

Amchin, J. (1991). *A Biopsychosocial approach to Using the DSM-III-R* Washington, D.C.: American Psychiatric Association Press.

American Psychiatric Association (1987). *Diagnostic and Statistical Manual of Mental Disorders,* 3rd ed. (Revised). Washington, D. C.: American Psychiatric Association Press.

Delaney, J., Lupton, M. J., and Toth, E. (1988). *The Curse: A Cultural History of Menstruation,* revised edition. Urbana: University of Illinois Press.

Gise, L. H., Lebovits, A. H., Paddison, P. L., and Strain, J. J. (1990). Issues in the identification of premenstrual syndromes. *The Journal of Nervous and Mental Disease,* 178, 228–234.

Jarett, L. R. Psychosocial and biological influences on menstruation: Synchrony, cycle length, and regularity. *Psychoneuroendocrinology* (1984) 9: 21–28.

McFarland, C., Ross, M. and DeCourville, N. Women's theories of menstruation and biases in recall of menstrual symptoms. *Journal of Personality and Social Psychology* (1989) 57: 522–531.

Parlee, M. B. (1973). The Premenstrual Syndrome. *Psychological Bulletin* 80: 454–465.

That Time of the Month
Laurie Ouellette

Taboos about menstruation deny the power of women's natural cycles.

Imagine a world where menstruation is revered as a sign of female fertility and life; where women proudly celebrate their monthly menses with rituals and bright red clothing; where they take time off during their menses to maximize the special powers that come with menstruation.

But back in the real world, menstruation is still far from being treated like the natural, healthy process that it is, much less being honored. While virtually every other "forbidden" topic is now openly debated, menstruation is still taboo. One more generation of women is being socialized to view their periods as embarrassments. Females are ever vigilant against the telltale stain and the dreaded accusation that they're acting like they're "on the rag." It's not surprising that—if they had a choice—69 percent would prefer not to menstruate at all.

While patriarchal society has always defined menstruation as bad, the multi-billion-dollar feminine "protection" industry reinforces the stigma, says Ann Treneman in her essay on menstruation and advertising in the book *The Female Gaze: Women as Viewers of Popular Culture* (Real Comet Press, 1989). The huge array of feminine products—ranging from "deodorant" tampons and pads that obliterate natural odors to decorative pouches that disguise the purpose of these products—give women a dual message: Menstruation is not only shameful, it should be hidden at all costs. Ironically, advertising for menstrual products—with oblique scripts that never mention words like *menstruation* or *blood*—uses a feminist rhetoric to suggest that women can hide menstruation so effectively that they can be "liberated" from it. Images of women who have careers, are active in sports, and turn heads at the beach sell the idea that, with the help of modern products, today's women can be free from all evidence of menstruation.

Downplayed by the sanitary product industry is the fact that these products carry health risks and create what some say is unnecessary environmental waste. The FDA is lax when it comes to regulating the tampon industry, even though dozens of chemicals (waxes, acids, and alcohols) may leach from tampons and high-absorbency tampons are linked to the deadly toxic shock syndrome, warns Hannah Holmes in the environmental magazine **Garbage** (Nov./Dec. 1990). She also notes that the average woman throws away 250 to 300 pounds of tampons, pads, and applicators in her lifetime.

Though not often found on drugstore shelves, there are alternatives to disposable products. **Garbage** details the pros and cons of various ways to catch the menstrual flow, including natural sea sponges, rubber cups similar to diaphragms, and reusable cotton pads. **Mothering** magazine (Winter 1991) features a guide to making your own cloth pads and belts. Although society's predominantly negative view of menstruation may be a psychological obstacle to trying alternative methods, Homes reminds us that "over the generations, women have stemmed the tide

Reprinted with permission from the *Utne Reader*, July/August, 1991, pp. 34–36.

with everything from papyrus to wool, commercial tampons and quartered kitchen sponges—and lived to tell the tale.''

The recent hype over PMS—a catchall phrase for more than three dozen psychological and physical ''symptoms'' of the ''female problem''—may also reinforce negative attitudes about menstruation, writes Marcy O'Koon in the quarterly **Special Report on Health** (Feb./April 1991). While it's natural for women to experience physical and emotional changes during their periods, overdiagnosis and classification of PMS as an ''illness'' feeds stereotypes of women as irrational, incompetent creatures who are hostages to their menstrual cycles.

While the PMS debate has spurred sales of over-the-counter medicines to cure menstrual ''ills,'' the positive aspects of menstruation have been virtually ignored. The California-based Menstrual Health Foundation asserts that high spirits, increased insight, creativity, vivid dreams, increased sexual desire, and feelings of power are positive attributes of menstruation. As reported in the feminist pagan journal **Snake Power** (Vol. 1, No. 2), the group encourages women to accept and embrace the built-in healing and recharging mechanism of the menstrual cycle by celebrating, going on retreats, and turning inward instead of denying the time they feel most like women. Comedian Roseanne Barr puts that sentiment in her own words: Her premenstrual days ''are the three days of the month I get to be myself.''

Dena Taylor, author of *Red Flower: Rethinking Menstruation* (The Crossing Press, 1988), explains in *Mothering* that seclusion, or time away from the demands of everyday routines, is a natural response to menstruation. ''It has long been a custom of women in various cultures to seclude themselves—either singly or in groups—during menstruation. Most often, the purpose has been to rest, heal, receive visions, and gather ideas.''

In ancient matriarchal cultures, menstrual blood was revered and honored as a sign of fertility. As Taylor notes, Navajo and Apache menstruation ceremonies are important religious rites; celebrations elevate the menarcheal girl to a position of great respect in the society. Taylor suggests that celebrations be held in our culture for first-time menses to present a clear message that menstruation is natural and healthy. In the absence of traditional rites, some families celebrate with special baths, ceremonial meals, and gifts.

Taylor says the menstrual taboo persists in modern culture because of various fears related to the cyclical nature of menstruation and its relation to the moon, the association of blood with birth and death, and the fact that men don't menstruate. *The Curse—A Cultural History of Menstruation* (University of Illinois Press, 1988) gives an extensive history of the menstrual taboo.

What if men were the ones who menstruated? Gloria Steinem once explored the possibilities in **Ms.** magazine (Oct. 1978): ''Menstruation would become an enviable, boast-worthy event. Men would brag about how long and how much. Boys would mark the onset of the menses, that longed-for proof of manhood, with religious rituals and stag parties. Congress would fund a National Institute of Dysmenorrhea to help stamp out monthly discomforts.''

It's time for women to reclaim the positive power of the female fertility cycle. In addition to celebrating their menses with rituals, choosing alternative products, and being more open about menstruation, some women are demanding flexible work schedules to take advantage of the special powers of menstruation while minimizing the discomforts.

Premenstrual Symptoms: A Reinterpretation
Diane N. Ruble

Abstract. Conclusions regarding the physiological basis and disruptive effects of premenstrual symptoms may be biased because of the reliance of self-report questionnaires as a source of data. In order to examine this possible bias, women's perceptions on their cycle phase were separated experimentally from actual cycle phase. Women who were led to believe that they were premenstrual reported experiencing a significantly higher degree of several physical symptoms, such as water retention, than did women who were led to believe they were intermenstrual. Thus, because of these psychosocial influences on symptom reports, it seems necessary to reexamine previous conclusions regarding the magnitude of menstrual-related changes as well as their physiological basis.

A variety of physical and psychological symptoms, such as cramps, painful breasts, irritability, and depression have been associated with the premenstrual and menstrual phases of women's reproductive cycles (1–4). These uncomfortable symptoms have generally been interpreted as reflecting underlying physiological changes which accompany the menstrual cycle (2,3). However, a major source of evidence regarding cyclic changes has been women's self-reports of symptoms experienced at various phases of the menstrual cycle (1). The data presented in this report suggest that self-report studies may have led to exaggerated conclusions regarding the kinds of symptoms experienced, the magnitude of cyclic changes, and the physiological basis of premenstrual symptoms.

Although studies based on women's self-reports of symptoms have found cyclic differences, studies based on less subjective measures have frequently found no differences. For example, in spite of strong beliefs that women gain weight and retain water premenstrually (4), carefully controlled observations have shown little cyclic variation in these symptoms (5). Furthermore, investigators who find a premenstrual increase in these variables usually also report a midcycle peak (5,6). In addition, according to a recent review (7), most objective measures of performance (such as athletics or tests of reasoning) fail to show an impairment associated with the menstrual cycle, even though 8 to 16 percent of the women themselves believed that their performances are affected negatively by their cycles.

In view of the inconsistent findings regarding menstrual-related symptoms, it becomes necessary to question the validity of self-report studies. That is, self-report measures are susceptible to various kinds of biases and may reflect cultural beliefs concerning the kinds of symptoms women experience at various phases of the cycle. This report presents a study in which a woman's actual cycle phase was separated experimentally from her belief concerning her cycle phase. Women were told that it was possible, through new scientific techniques, to predict the expected date of menstruation. In this way, it was possible to assign them to "pre-

This article first appeared in *Science* (1977) 197: 291–292. Copyright © 1977, the American Association for the Advancement of Science.

Table 1. Mean ratings on MDQ ± the standard error of the means. The ratings ranged from 1 (not at all) to 6 (extremely).

Variable	Experimental condition			P*
	Premenstrual (N = 15)	Intermenstrual (N = 14)	Control (N = 15)	
Scales				
Water retention	2.62 ± 0.29	1.54 ± 0.12	2.35 ± 0.31	<.01†
Pain	2.32 ± 0.17	1.88 ± 0.17	2.12 ± 0.21	<.05†
Negative affect	3.13 ± 0.32	3.10 ± 0.30	2.44 ± 0.25	
Concentration	2.51 ± 0.27	2.20 ± 0.19	2.39 ± 0.24	
Behavioral change	2.57 ± 0.38	2.23 ± 0.23	2.92 ± 0.27	
Autonomic reactions	1.45 ± 0.18	1.27 ± 0.08	1.18 ± 0.07	
Arousal	3.35 ± 0.31	3.06 ± 0.22	3.09 ± 0.30	
Control	1.56 ± 0.19	1.41 ± 0.14	1.57 ± 0.15	
Individual items				
Change in eating habits	2.93 ± 0.51	1.57 ± 0.27	2.93 ± 0.44	<.025†
Sexual arousal	3.60 ± 0.42	2.50 ± 0.40	3.20 ± 0.48	.05‡

*Levels of significance for *t*-tests between premenstrual and intermenstrual groups. †One-tailed test. ‡Two-tailed test.

menstrual'' and ''intermenstrual'' groups on a random basis. It was hypothesized that the different groups of women would report experiencing different levels of menstrual-related symptoms even though they were all tested at about a week before the onset of menstruation.

Subjects were 44 women under-graduates at Princeton University, aged 18 to 24, who were not taking oral contraceptives at the time of the study nor had taken them within the previous 3 months. Variability in the length of their cycles did not exceed 2 weeks. Upon initial telephone contact, subjects were told they were participating in contraception-related research in which a new technique for predicting the expected date of menstruation from an electroencephalogram (EEG) was being surveyed on young women, having been successfully tested with older women. Brief menstrual histories were also obtained. Later, subjects were telephoned to arrange an appointment. Unknown to the subject, the scheduled day of testing was chosen specifically to correspond to the

sixth or seventh day (as estimated from her menstrual history) before her next menses.

The research was conducted in the university infirmary in two connecting rooms, one of which contained an examining table and a large oscilloscope with EEG electrodes attached to it. Subjects were greeted by the first experimenter, given a sheet explaining the purpose of the study, and asked to complete a short medical history. The experimenter then took the temperature and blood pressure of the subject and explained the EEG procedure. Electrodes were attached to the subject's forehead with beautician's tape, and the experimenter proceeded to ''run'' the simulated EEG machine. After 4 minutes, the electrodes were removed, and the experimenter pretended to read the output. She then informed the subject, according to the experimental group to which she had been randomly assigned, that (i) the subject was ''premenstrual'' and her period was due in 1 or 2 days (premenstrual group), or that (ii) she was ''intermenstrual'' and her period was not expected for at least a week to 10 days (intermenstrual group), or (iii) she was given no information at all about the expected date of menstruation (control group). The subject was then instructed to go into an adjoining room, where a second experimenter, who did not know to which experimental group the subject belonged, administered the Moos (2) Menstrual Distress Questionnaire (MDQ), consisting of 48 items, 46 of which form eight clusters of symptoms (8). Subjects were asked to rate the extent to which they had experienced any of the symptoms in the last day or two. Immediately afterward, subjects were given information describing the true intent of the experiment and were questioned concerning any suspicions they might have about the manipulations (9). They were also contacted later to find out the actual day of onset of menstruation, which did not differ across groups (P >.25).

The MDQ was selected as the dependent variable because it is one of the most frequently used instruments in self-report studies and has yielded reasonably consistent results. Previous research has shown that water retention, pain, and negative affect are the scales that show the greatest premenstrual as compared to intermenstrual differences (2–4, 10, 11). In addition, one of the individual items, "change in eating habits," has also shown a very strong association with the premenstrual phase in a sample very similar to that described here (11). Thus, it was predicted that women who thought they were premenstrual would report experiencing a higher level of water retention, pain, negative affect, and change in eating habits, as compared to women who thought that they were intermenstrual.

Scale scores were created for each subject by summing the items in each of the eight scales identified by Moos and dividing by the number of completed items in each scale (12). An examination of the means for these eight scales plus the two individual items (Table 1) reveals a pattern consistent with the predictions; that is, symptom ratings

of "premenstrual" women were higher than those of "intermenstrual" women. Statistical analyses revealed that these differences attained significance for three of the four predicted variables: water retention, pain, and change in eating habits. Furthermore, the magnitude of the mean differences for most scales was very similar to that reported in previous research (2, 4, 10, 11). The means for the control group either generally fell in between the two other groups or were closer to the premenstrual group's means. Possibly, the women given no information about their cycle phase perceived themselves as premenstrual at 6 or 7 days before the onset of their next period. One other comparison reached significance—sexual arousal. This result, while not specifically predicted, is consistent with some previous reports of cyclic changes in sexual interest (13). Contrary to predictions, ratings for negative affect did not approach significance.

Although one might argue that the results of this study are partly due to implicit demands for the women to report symptoms consistent with their cycle phase, similar "demands" are present in previous self-report studies. That is, subjects are asked to respond to a series of items identified as possible menstrual symptoms. Indeed, demand characteristics represent a major problem affecting the validity of self-report measures.

These results question previous accounts of menstrual cycle-symptoms associations in two respects. First, it may be misleading to assume that responses on a self-report scale accurately represent the nature and extent of changes accompanying the menstrual cycle. Second, previous physiological interpretations of premenstrual symptoms must be reevaluated, since cyclic differences in symptoms were found for women who only believed they were premenstrual or intermenstrual. The results reported here do not suggest that women never experience pain or water retention nor that such symptoms never accompany the premenstrual phase. Instead, it appears that learned associations or beliefs might lead a woman either to overstate what she is actually experiencing or to perceive an exaggeration of naturally fluctuating bodily states (for example, pain and weight changes) when she believes she is premenstrual. This interpretation is consistent with suggestions in other research concerning the importance of psychosocial factors in women's experience of menstruation (4, 11, 14).

In conclusion, these results show that psychosocial factors can influence reports of menstrual-related symptoms. In conjunction with inconsistent results from other kinds of studies, these data suggest that the extent to which psychologically or physiologically based changes (or both) accompany the premenstrual phase must remain an open question.

References and Notes

1. M. B. Parlee, *Psych. Bull.* 80, 454 (1973).
2. R. H. Moos, *Psychosom. Med.* 30, 853 (1968).
3. S. Silbergeld *et al., ibid.* 33, 411 (1971).
4. M. B. Parlee, *ibid.* 36, 229, (1974).
5. J. Bruce and G. F. M. Russell, *Lancet* 1962-II, 267 (1962); P. E. Watson and M. F. Robinson, *Br. J. Nutr.* 19, 237 (1965).
6. D. S. Janowsky, S. C. Berens, J. M. Davis, *Psychosom. Med.* 35, 143 (1973).
7. B. Sommer, *ibid.* p. 515.
8. The two items not grouped were "change in eating habits" and "sexual arousal." The latter was not part of the original scale but was included in a later publication (3).
9. Only one subject questioned the use of the EEG manipulation. Two others expressed general suspiciousness about psychology experiments. Eliminating these subjects from the analyses made no difference in the results.
10. G. H. Gruba and M. Rohrbaugh, *Psychosom. Med.* 37, 265 (1975); L. A. Wilcoxon, S. L. Schrader, C. W. Sherif, *ibid,* 38, 399 (1976).
11. J. Brooks, D. Ruble, A. Clarke, *ibid.,* in press.
12. Previous research with the MDQ has typically presented mean total scores for the MDQ scales. Mean item scores were used in the present analyses because this procedure allows for comparisons across the scales, which vary in the number of items included.
13. M. Ivey and J. M. Barowick, *Psychosom. Med.* 30, 336 (1968); G. S. Seward, *Psychol. Bull.* 31, 153 (1934).
14. R. K. Koeske and G. F. Koeske, *J. Pers. Soc. Psychol.* 31, 474 (1975); K. E. Paige, *Psychosom. Med.* 33, 515 (1971); J. Rodin, *J. Pers. Soc. Psychol.* 33, 345 (1976).
15. Supported by NIMH biomedical support grant and by NSF (SOC 76-02137). I thank M. C. Kamin for technical assistance; J. Brooks, N. S. Feldman, B. L. Jacobs, and T. L. Ruble for reading the manuscript; and A. Clarke for help in all phases of the research.
13. October 1976; revised 16 March 1977.

Mood Fluctuations: Women Versus Men and Menstrual Versus Other Cycles

Jessica McFarlane, Carol Lynn Martin, and Tannis MacBeth Williams
University of British Columbia

Mood fluctuations in women and men were studied both prospectively and retrospectively to determine whether cyclic changes occur over phases of the menstrual cycle, lunar cycle, and/or days of the week. The participants (15 women using oral contraceptives, 12 normally cycling women, and 15 men), who did not know the purpose of the study, recorded the pleasantness, arousal, and stability of their moods daily for 70 days (concurrent data). Later they recalled (retrospective data) their average mood for each day of the week and phase of the menstrual cycle (women only). The only evidence of mood fluctuation over the menstrual cycle in the concurrent reports was that normally cycling women reported more pleasant moods in the follicular and menstrual phase than did men and women on oral contraceptives. Women's moods fluctuated less over the menstrual cycle than over days of the week. Recollections of menstrual mood changes differed from actual changes: Women recalled more pleasant moods in the follicular phase and more unpleasant moods in the premenstrual and menstrual phases than they had reported concurrently. Bias also was evident in recollections of weekday mood fluctuations: Weekend highs were exaggerated and Monday blues were reported even though they were not reported concurrently. There was no evidence of mood fluctuations over the lunar cycle and the groups did not differ in mood stability. The retrospective reporting bias for both the menstrual cycle and days of week suggests the influence of stereotypes about moods. Implications for research and practice are discussed.

The belief that the day of the week influences human behavior is widespread, but the empirical evidence is sparse. Rossi and Rossi (1977) found support for the stereotype: Moods were less positive at the beginning of the week and more positive on Fridays and Saturdays. Results obtained by Stone, Hedges, Neale, and Satin (1985) were more complex. Weekends were experienced as happier than weekdays. Monday moods were believed to be lowest, but actually were experienced as similar to moods on Tuesdays, Wednesdays, and Thursdays. One purpose of our study was to confirm weekday mood fluctuations and to compare their magnitude with mood changes over the menstrual cycle.

The influence of the lunar cycle on behavior has been studied more extensively. Some researchers have found that behavior varies with phases of the moon (e.g., Lieber & Sherin, 1972; Tasso & Miller, 1976) but the evidence that the moon does not affect behavior is more convincing (e.g., Frey, Rotton, & Barry, 1979; Michelson, Wilson, & Michelson, 1979). Nevertheless, belief in a *Transylvania Effect* is widespread, particularly among those who work in institutions (e.g., the medical community, police). To our

This article first appeared in *Psychology of Women Quarterly* (1988) 12: 201–223. Copyright © 1988, Division 35, American Psychological Association. Reprinted with the permission of Cambridge University Press.

knowledge there have been no studies of mood fluctuations over the lunar cycle. This study was designed in part to obtain such data and to compare lunar, weekday, and menstrual mood fluctuations.

The scientific and popular literature on menstrual mood fluctuations is more voluminous and more complex than that for weekday and lunar cycles. Up to the mid-1970s, researchers found what has come to be known as the "classic" menstrual mood pattern (Altman, Knowles, & Bull, 1941; Benedek & Rubenstein, 1939a, 1939b; Golub, 1976; Ivey & Bardwick, 1968; Janowsky, Berens, & Davis, 1973; Luschen & Pierce, 1972; Moos et al., 1969; Patkai, Johannson, & Post, 1974; Rossi & Rossi, 1977). It is characterized by pleasant affect in the ovulatory phase (when ovarian hormones are typically high), followed by negative affect in the premenstrual phase (when ovarian hormone concentrations are dropping) and menstrual phase (when hormones are at their lowest).

Over the past 15 years, however, it has become increasingly common for researchers to fail to find the classic menstrual mood pattern (Golub & Harrington, 1981; Lahmeyer, Miller, & DeLeon-Jones, 1982; Little & Zahn, 1974; O'Neil, Lancee, & Freeman, 1984; Sommer, 1973; Swandby, 1981; Wilcoxon, Schrader, & Sherif, 1976; Zimmerman & Parlee, 1973). Discrepancies in results seem to be due to methodological inconsistencies among the studies, and in particular to a number of flaws in the design of most of the earlier and some of the later studies. These have been discussed at length by others (e.g., Parlee, 1973, 1974; Ruble, 1977; Ruble & Brooks-Gunn, 1979) but because they are central to the design of this study, we shall briefly review them.

The first problem is bias due to expectations. There is some evidence that women who know they are in a study of the influence of the menstrual cycle on moods report

mood variations, but when the purpose is concealed, changes are reported less often (Parlee, 1974). Ruble (1977) found that women who merely believed they were "premenstrual" (on the basis of incorrect information provided by the experimenter) reported more symptoms than women who believed they were "intermenstrual."

The second set of problems is mood checklists that consist mainly or entirely of negative moods or "symptoms." The four most common ones are: the Thayer Activation-Deactivation Adjective Checklist (AD-ACL; Thayer, 1967), the Profile of Mood States (POMS; McNair, Lorr, & Droppleman, 1971), the Multiple Affect Adjective Check List (MMACL; Zuckerman, 1960; Zuckerman, Lubin, Vogel, & Valerius, 1964), and the Menstrual Distress Questionnaire (MDQ; Moos, 1968; Moos et al., 1969). With the exception of the AD-ACL and one of six scales in the POMS (vigor), all measure only socially undesirable moods. When faced with only negative items, people may respond more negatively than they would if positive options were included. It also is impossible to detect fluctuations in positive moods (see Rossi & Rossi, 1977). In addition, as the number of items increases, the likelihood of error arising from idiosyncratic interpretations of the labels increases. Moreover, the longer the scale, the more likely participants are to drop out, or become less conscientious. Because prospective longitudinal studies over several menstrual cycles are crucial to understanding mood patterns, it is important to devise accurate but brief scales that economically use participants' time.

The third problem is reliance on retrospective reports. Women often are asked to recall their moods over the phases of their most recent menstrual cycle and check off symptoms (e.g., Coppen & Kessel, 1963; Jensen, 1982; Moos, 1968; Moos et al., 1969). There is growing evidence that retrospective reports differ from concurrent daily reports obtained in prospective studies (e.g., Ascher-Svanum, 1984; May, 1976; McCance, Luff, & Widdowson, 1937; Parlee, 1974; Slade, 1984). Retrospective reports may be more likely to reflect participants' attitudes or stereotypes than their recall of actual experiences (e.g., Parlee, 1974; Ruble, 1977; Ruble & Brooks-Gunn, 1979; Slade, 1984).

The fourth problem is failure to use appropriate comparison groups. For example, normally cycling women could be compared with women taking oral contraceptives and with men to assess the extent to which endogenous hormones affect emotionality.[1] Some evidence has suggested that women taking oral contraceptives (OCs) experience less menstrual mood fluctuation than normally cycling women (Morris & Udry, 1972; Paige, 1971; Rossi & Rossi, 1977). Glick and Bennett (1982) contended that OCs may stabilize moods but further research is required to establish this effect firmly. Men, whose endogenous hormonal patterns are quite different from women's patterns, have in two studies reported more stable moods than women (Swandby, 1981; Wilcoxon et al., 1976).

Finally, if a woman's moods do fluctuate over her menstrual cycle it is important to determine whether the fluctuations fall within a normal and healthy range of emotionality, or whether treatment may be warranted. Comparison with other groups (e.g., men) provides one approach to this issue but comparison with the woman's mood fluctuations over other cycles (e.g., days of the week) also would help place menstrual experiences in a broader context.

Recent findings have indicated that menstrual mood fluctuations are not a problem for most women (Golub & Harrington, 1981; Lahmeyer et al., 1982; O'Neil et al., 1984; Sommer, 1973; Swandby, 1981; Wilcoxon et al., 1976; Zimmerman & Parlee, 1973), yet the belief that most women are "victims of their raging hormones" is still widespread. Indeed, the number of articles in

the popular literature describing the "classic" mood pattern and suggesting how it can be treated is increasing; premenstrual syndrome (PMS) has become a household phrase and is said to be widespread.

Why are popular beliefs about moods and the menstrual cycle so discrepant from the scientific evidence? One possibility is that methodological problems have resulted in failure to find consistent evidence of menstrual cycle effects. Although each flaw outlined earlier has been corrected in one or more studies, no one study has corrected them all. Another possibility is that individual women may believe they have menstrual moods when they really do not, or do so only rarely (Ruble, 1977; Ruble & Brooks-Gunn, 1979; Slade, 1984). For instance, women who occasionally or randomly experience negative moods during their premenstrual phase may look for a biological explanation (Asso, 1983; Koeske & Koeske, 1975; Slade, 1980). They usually know they will be menstruating shortly, so they may label their symptoms PMS. During other premenstrual phases they may not notice the absence of symptoms or consider positive moods to be evidence contradicting PMS. In this way, belief in PMS could be maintained with little or no systematic support.

Ruble (1977) and Rubel and Brooks-Gunn (1979) contended that the widespread belief in PMS is consistent with social-cognitive schematic models. According to schematic processing theories (e.g., Taylor & Crocker, 1979), individuals' perceptions and experiences are filtered through their schemata. Information consistent with a schema is likely to be noticed and remembered whereas inconsistent information is likely to be forgotten, ignored, or changed to better fit the stereotype (see Martin & Halverson, 1981; 1983, for a discussion in the context of gender schemata). A schema-based explanation could account for the discrepancy between the beliefs and experiences about

Monday moods (Stone et al., 1985) and belief in the Transylvania Effect as well as the classic menstrual mood pattern.

This research was designed to minimize the methodological problems associated with menstrual cycle research, and to assess how beliefs about moods may contribute to perception of mood fluctuations. Data were obtained daily over 70 days to ensure the inclusion of at least two menstrual cycles (Parlee, 1982). Three groups were studied: women who were normally cycling (womenNC), women taking oral contraceptives (womenOC), and men. To avoid biasing participants' reports, interest in the menstrual cycle was camouflaged (Parlee, 1974). Mood data were obtained both prospectively (concurrently) to assess actual mood changes and retrospectively to assess possible reporting biases. To avoid labeling problems and decrease the likelihood of participant attrition, a simple bipolar mood scale was used. Menstrual mood fluctuations were studied in the context of the weekday and lunar cycles. Finally, positive as well as neutral and negative moods were assessed.

Two aspects of mood fluctuations were of interest. First was the stereotype that most women experience the classic menstrual mood pattern. This was addressed by comparing women's mean reports of arousal and pleasantness at different phases of the menstrual cycle and by comparing the mean reports of women and men (who were randomly assigned to pseudocycles). Second was the stereotype that women's moods are changeable. This was addressed in two ways. The participants provided daily reports of mood stability, which indicated how moods fluctuated *within* a day. In addition, the standard deviations for the pleasantness and arousal reports were analyzed to indicate the range of variations in moods from *day-to-day*. For both within-day and day-to-day variability, women's reports were compared with men's reports across the phases of the menstrual cycle, days of the week, and lunar phases.

METHOD

Subjects

A sample of 20 men, 21 womenOC, and 21 womenNC was recruited from the volunteer subject pool comprising first and second year undergraduates in psychology courses. After attrition,[2] the final sample consisted of 15 men, 15 womenOC, and 12 womenNC with a mean age of 21 years (range 19 to 26).

Procedure

Potential participants were identified and then recruited by a telephone call during which the general purpose and length of the study were described. To conceal our interest in the menstrual cycle, participants were told the investigation concerned emotional, behavioral, and physical patterns.

In an initial 30-minute interview, demographic and other general information was obtained. Participants were asked about typical patterns of exercise, sleep, health, diet, menstrual cycle flow and discomfort (women only), complexion problems, libido, weight, and future plans for career and/or family.[3] They were asked to complete a one-page chart each day over the next 70 days, and were instructed to fill out this daily chart at approximately the same time each day. The first section of the chart indicated the time and date of completion. Participants were instructed to be sure to fill out a chart every day, but if they forgot, to "catch-up" by filling in two charts the next day and indicating which one was for the missed day. For forgotten days, they were asked to provide only information about which they were reasonably sure and to leave a question blank rather than to guess. The second section, which dealt with body awareness, was designed to distract

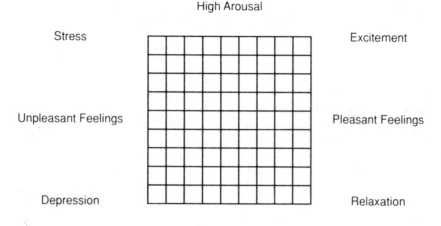

High Arousal

Stress

Excitement

Unpleasant Feelings

Pleasant Feelings

Depression

Relaxation

Sleepiness

Figure 1. The *Mood Grid*, Russell, et al. (1987)

from interest in the menstrual cycle. A question asking women whether or not they were menstruating that day was embedded in several other questions about general health.

The third section contained the Mood Grid (Figure 1), (Russell, Weiss, & Mendelsohn, 1987). Pleasantness is measured along the horizontal axis, arousal along the vertical axis, and intensity is measured from the center (no or low intensity) to the circumference (high intensity). Participants describe their mood by placing an "X" in the one box which best indicates their emotional state for that day. A bipolar scale similar to the Mood Grid has been found to be highly correlated with other mood measures including the AD-ACL, POMS, and MAACL (Russell & Mehrabian, 1977). Pleasantness and arousal accounted for almost all the reliable mood variance in 42 commonly used scales of affect.[4] After marking the Mood Grid, participants rated the stability of their moods on a 4-point scale ranging from *very changeable* to *very stable*. The completed daily charts were returned about every two weeks. The actual length of participation ranged from 60 to 70 days.

At the end of the investigation, participants returned for an interview. They first completed the final questionnaire in privacy. Some questions were designed to ascertain whether participants had guessed the purpose of the study. Others asked about significant life events, employment, willingness to continue in study, religion, and changes in birth control. Participants then provided retrospective data by recalling their moods since the study began. On a series of Mood Grids, one labelled for each day of the week, they indicated their average mood over the past two months on Sunday, Monday, and so on. Women also were given five Mood grids and asked to indicate their average mood over the last two months during menstruation, the next 7 days, ovulation (the middle 5 days), the next 7 days after ovulation, and premenstrually (the 4 days before flow).

Scoring

Menstrual cycle. The menstrual cycle was divided into the five phases used by Rossi and Rossi (1977): Menstrual=Day 1–5 (Day 1=the first day of menstruation); Follicular=Day 6–12; Ovulatory=Day 13–17; Luteal=Day 18–24; and Premenstrual=Day 25–28. Since not all women have a 28-day cycle, cycles were adjusted to a standard length. The procedure recommended by Rossi and Rossi (1977) was used.

Men were randomly assigned to 28-day pseudo-menstrual cycles. Day 1 varied so that the men's "cycles" began on different dates and simulated the starting date variations of women's cycles. Men were assigned to cycles so they could be included in the analyses of concurrent reports.

The means for the concurrent analyses were calculated by averaging for each individual across the days within each menstrual phase for all menstrual cycles. For example, the mean for premenstrual arousal was based on the arousal scores for the four days in each of (usually) two premenstrual phases (eight days total). Means were calculated for each menstrual phase for arousal, pleasantness, and stability. The women's retrospective menstrual cycle scores were the single arousal and pleasantness scores recalled for each menstrual phase. Women were not asked retrospectively about the stability of their moods, and, of course, retrospective menstrual cycle data could not be obtained from men.

Weekday cycle. For each measure, the concurrent means were calculated by averaging across all observed Sundays (for Sunday's mean), and so on for each day of the week. The retrospective scores were the single arousal and pleasantness scores recalled for each day of the week.

Lunar cycle. The lunar cycle was divided into four phases (new moon, first quarter, full moon, last quarter), based on newspaper data. For each measure, the means for the concurrent analyses were calculated by averaging across all days of each lunar phase. Recollec-

tions regarding the lunar cycle were not obtained.

Standard deviation analyses. The procedures used for means were followed except that standard deviations were calculated.

RESULTS

Mood Grid

The Pearson correlation for more than 3,000 pairs of arousal and pleasantness scores was .25, $p<.03$. The fact that only 6% of the variance in the two dimensions was shared indicated they are more independent than related and provides further evidence of the validity of this measure.

Knowledge of the Menstrual Purpose of the Experiment

Only four participants (two womenOC and two womenNC) guessed the purpose of the study. In multivariate analyses of variance (MANOVAs) there were no significant differences for arousal, pleasantness, or mood stability means or standard deviations between the women who did and did not guess the purpose. The data from women who guessed correctly therefore were included in the analyses. The women who guessed correctly also anecdotally reported during the interview that their menstrual cycles did not influence their moods.

Remembered vs. Forgotten Days

The forgotten days constituted 19.2% of the total data.[5] The mean arousal score for forgotten days (5.49) was lower than the mean (5.83) for remembered days, $t(3021)=4.15$, $p<.001$. The differences for pleasantness and stability were not statistically significant. The pattern of results for arousal, pleasantness, and stability was the same whether or not forgotten days were included, so they were included.

Demographic Results

A MANOVA revealed that men, womenOC, and womenNC did not differ overall in age, years of post-secondary education, or willingness to continue in the study for one or two months. Chi-square analyses revealed the groups did not differ in type of university program (e.g., Arts versus Science).

Overview of Major Analyses

Three similar sets of analyses were performed, one for each cycle (menstrual, weekday, lunar). In the interest of brevity, the complete set of analyses for the menstrual cycle will be outlined in this overview. The necessary changes for analyses of the weekday and lunar cycles will then be noted.

First, a set of repeated-measures, unweighted means analyses of variance (ANOVA) was used to compare the concurrent reports of the three groups, that is, men (who were assigned to pseudo-menstrual cycles), womenOC, and womenNC, across the five cycle phases (menstrual, follicular, ovulatory, luteal, and premenstrual) using the means for each measure (arousal, pleasantness, mood stability). Then similar sets of analyses were performed on standard deviations and on the retrospective menstrual data from the two groups of women for arousal and pleasantness. Finally, the women's mean concurrent and retrospective scores were compared in ANOVAs for arousal and pleasantness.[6] Type I error was controlled by using Bonferroni criteria to establish the alpha levels for statistical significance within each set of ANOVAs. The Bonferroni alpha level for main effects and interactions in ANOVAs on only concurrent data (three dependent variables) was $p < .017$. For analyses that included retrospective data it was $p < .025$, since stability reports were not obtained retrospectively and there were only two dependent variables. Except where specifically noted, findings that had been statistically significant using the original alpha level of $p < .05$ did not drop to a non-significant level.[7] The source of any significant interactions was assessed with simple main effects analyses. Differences among pairs of means were tested with the Tukey B range test. Only the major findings are reported in this article.

The analyses were repeated for the weekday cycle using the seven days and for the lunar cycle using the four phases. The major difference between these analyses and those for the menstrual cycle is that men were included in the retrospective weekday analyses. Unfortunately, recollections of lunar moods were not obtained, so only concurrent reports could be analyzed.

Mood Stability

There were no significant findings for groups or cycles for concurrent reports of stability or range (standard deviation) of daily mood scores, with one exception. The concurrent reports of stability yielded a group by menstrual phase interaction, $F (8, 156)=2.37$, $p=.02$, but it did not meet the Bonferroni criterion of $p < .017$. Moreover, simple main effects analyses yielded no significant differences among the groups at any phase of the menstrual cycle and no significant changes over the menstrual cycle for any group. The pattern of means (in absolute terms) did not indicate even a trend in the direction of the stereotypes.

The failure to find sex differences in mood stability indicates that young men and women experience similar mood changes within a day and from day-to-day. In addition, young women did not report more or less variability in moods during different phases of their menstrual cycle. These findings contradict the stereotype that women are "more changeable" or experience more "mood swings" than men, especially premenstrually or menstrually.

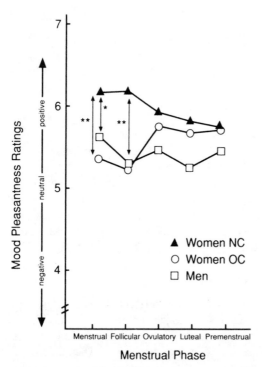

Figure 2. Mood pleasantness ratings for women who were normally cycling (womenNC), women taking oral contraceptives (womenOC), and men, for each phase of the menstrual cycle (*p<.05, **p<.01).

Concurrent Menstrual Cycle Reports

Pleasantness. As can be seen in Figure 2, the groups differed in only two phases of the menstrual cycle, $F (8, 156)=2.69$, $p <.01$, and neither result supported the stereotypes. In both the follicular phase, $F (2, 39)=6.00$, $p<.01$, and the menstrual phase, $F (2, 39)=3.43$, $p<.05$, womenNC reported feeling more pleasant than did both men and womenOC.

Arousal. Arousal did not vary over phases of the menstrual cycle (see Figure 3).

Retrospective Menstrual Cycle Reports

Arousal. Both groups of women recalled that their arousal varied over the menstrual phases, $F (4, 100)=3.15$, $p <.05$, but not enough to reach the Bonferroni criterion for significance (.025). There was a trend for arousal to be recalled as significantly higher in the follicular phase than in the premenstrual and menstrual phases ($p <.10$ for both).

Pleasantness. Whereas prospectively obtained reports indicated these women did not experience the classic menstrual mood pattern, they recalled that they had. Moreover, whereas womenNC and womenOC reported different mood patterns prospectively, they reported the same (classic) mood pattern retrospectively. They both recalled, $F (4, 100)=14.41$, $p <.001$, that the menstrual phase was significantly less pleasant than the follicular phase ($p<.05$) and the premenstrual phase was less pleasant than every other phase ($p <.01$). The average mood recalled during the premenstrual phase (3.93) was the only instance in the concurrent or retrospective menstrual data of a mean on the negative side of the midpoint of the pleasantness or arousal scales.

Direct Comparison of Concurrent and Retrospective Menstrual Reports

Arousal. As can be seen in Figure 3, the pattern of concurrent-retrospective reporting differences varied over the menstrual cycle, $F (4, 100)=4.24$, $p <.01$. Both womenNC and womenOC recalled their arousal in the follicular phase as higher than they had reported it concurrently, $F (1, 25)=6.13$, $p <.05$.

Pleasantness. As illustrated in Figure 4, the pattern of similarities and differences between concurrent and retrospective reports varied over the menstrual cycle, $F (4,$

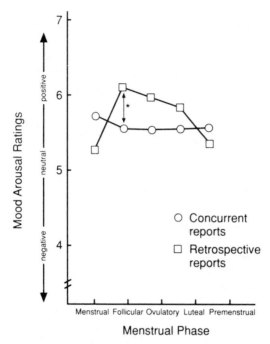

Figure 3. Comparison of concurrent and retrospective reports of mood arousal averaged across both groups of women for each phase of the menstrual cycle (*p<.05).

100)=11.84, p <.001. Both womenOC and womenNC overestimated the pleasantness they had experienced in the follicular phase, F (1, 25)=7.80, p <.01, and underestimated their pleasantness in the premenstrual phase, F (1, 25)=44.71, p <.001. There also was a trend, F (1, 26)=4.18, p=.051, to underestimate pleasantness in the menstrual phase.

Summary of Menstrual Cycle Results

Contrary to the stereotypes, neither concurrently reported pleasantness nor arousal was more negative in the menstrual or premenstrual phases and women were not more changeable than men. Instead, womenNC reported more pleasantness in both the follicu-

lar phase and the menstrual phase than did men who had been randomly assigned to pseudo-cycles and womenOC. The women's recollections differed from their concurrent reports and were consistent with stereotypes about women's mood fluctuations, in particular, beliefs about premenstrual syndrome (PMS).

Concurrent and Retrospective Weekday Cycle Reports

The same mood variations over days of the week were reported by all three groups, but the pattern varied depending on whether reports were made concurrently or retrospectively and for arousal or pleasantness. Concurrently reported arousal, F (6, 234)=4.47, p <.001, was higher on Friday than on Sunday (p <.01), Monday, Tuesday, and Wednesday (p <.05 for the latter three comparisons), and higher on Saturday than on Sunday (p <.05). Concurrently reported pleasantness, F (6, 234)=6.96, p<.001, was higher on Saturday than on Monday, Tuesday (p<.01) for both), Wednesday, and Thursday (p<.05 for both), and higher on Friday than Monday and Tuesday (p<.01 for both). The retrospective patterns were similar to the prospective ones, but exaggerated. Arousal, F (6, 228)=9.08, p<.001, was recalled as higher on Saturdays than on Sundays, Mondays, Tuesdays, Wednesdays, and Thursdays (p <.01 for all five comparisons), and higher on Fridays than on Sundays, Mondays, Wednesdays (p<.01 for all three comparisons), and Thursdays (p <.05). Pleasantness, F (6, 228)=9.08, p<.001, was recalled as greater on Fridays than on Sundays, Mondays, Tuesdays, Wednesdays, and Thursdays (p <.01 for all five comparisons); greater on Saturdays than on Sundays (p <.05), Mondays (p <.01), Tuesdays, and Wednesdays, (p<.05 for both); and greater on Thursdays than Mondays (p <.05).

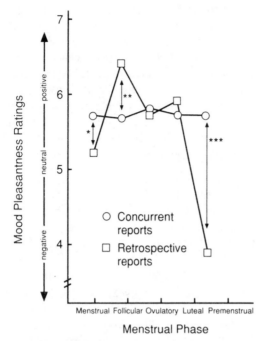

7 — positive

6 —

5 — neutral

4 — negative

Mood Pleasantness Ratings

○ Concurrent reports
□ Retrospective reports

Menstrual Follicular Ovulatory Luteal Premenstrual

Menstrual Phase

Figure 4. Comparison of concurrent and retrospective reports of mood pleasantness averaged across both groups of women for each phase of the menstrual cycle ($^+p=.05$, $^{**}p<.01$, $^{***}p<.001$).

Direct Comparison of Concurrent and Retrospective Weekday Reports

Arousal. The prospective and retrospective reports of arousal for days of the week were significantly different, $F(6, 228)=4.89$, $p<.001$. Both men and women retrospectively underestimated arousal they had experienced on Sundays, $F(1, 38)=4.58$, $p<.05$, and overestimated their arousal on Fridays, $F(1, 38)=4.66$, $p<.05$, and Saturdays, $F(1, 38)=13.15$, $p<.01$ (see Figure 5).

Pleasantness. Recollections of pleasantness (5.76) were more positive, on average, than concurrent reports (5.47), $F(1, 38)=12.70$, $p<.001$. The patterns of concurrent and retro-

spective reports also differed significantly according to day of the week, $F(6, 228)=7.42$, $p<.001$ (see Figure 6). Both women and men retrospectively overestimated pleasantness for Fridays, $F(1, 40)=51.19$, $p<.001$, and Saturdays, $F(1, 40)=11.25$, $p<.002$.

Summary of Weekday Results

There was considerable variation in concurrent reports of arousal and pleasantness over days of the week, indeed, more than over phases of the menstrual cycle. The pattern was the same for men and women. The highest levels of both arousal and pleasantness were reported on Friday and Saturday, but arousal peaked Friday and was at its lowest Sunday, whereas pleasantness peaked and ebbed a day later. The results provide much less support for the stereotype of Monday blues than for Friday-Saturday highs. Both arousal and pleasantness were higher on Friday and Saturday than most other days of the week. In both the concurrent and retrospective reports, pleasantness and arousal means were lowest for Monday, but they were only significantly lower than Friday's mean for arousal and only significantly lower than Friday's and Saturday's means for pleasantness. Participants seem to have been influenced not only by the positive stereotype associated with weekends but also by the apparently less well-founded negative stereotype associated with Mondays. Monday's arousal was recalled as lower than Saturday's and Friday's arousal. Monday's pleasantness was recalled as lower than Thursday's, Friday's, and Saturday's pleasantness. A similar pattern of results was obtained by Stone et al. (1985), that is, an increase in positive mood on Friday, Saturday, and Sunday but no decrease in pleasantness on Monday even though their participants believed they had Monday blues feelings.

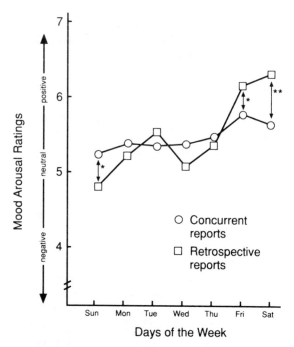

Figure 5. Comparison of concurrent and retrospective reports of mood arousal averaged across the three groups for each day of the week (*p<.05, **p<.01).

Lunar Cycle

There were no significant mood fluctuations according to phases of the lunar cycle in any of the analyses on the concurrent reports. These results contradict the Transylvania Effect, at least with respect to mood, and suggest that belief in this alleged phenomenon may be an ill-founded cultural stereotype. Unfortunately, participants were not asked to recall their moods according to phases of the lunar cycle, so it is not clear whether they held this stereotype.

DISCUSSION

Our results indicate that the women in this study did not actually experience the classic menstrual mood pattern but when they were asked to recall their moods, they reported

that pattern. The evidence regarding their actual moods suggests that the stereotype that most women are victims of their raging hormones is wrong; the university women in this study were relatively unaffected emotionally by menstrual hormonal fluctuations. Our groups were small, and it is possible that larger samples would have yielded different results. Data were obtained for two cycles, however, which increased the likelihood of finding the classic mood pattern. Moreover, although the nature and size of the samples limit the generalizability of the results, they were large enough to detect significant mood fluctuations. Epidemiological studies of much larger samples over at least three and preferably more menstrual cycles are badly needed, but they are expensive and it is difficult to find people willing to keep daily records over long periods.

Demonstrating that the university women in this study did not have menstrual mood fluctuations does not contradict the possibility that *some* women do experience the "classic" menstrual mood pattern (e.g., PMS). It may be more common among older women. Some women may infrequently experience cyclic mood changes so the changes are not picked up in studies of only two menstrual cycles. Other women may have mood fluctuations with sufficiently unique patterns that they are not apparent when averaged across individuals. All three possibilities nevertheless contradict the stereotypes regarding moods and the menstrual cycle, which emphasize that most women have similar mood cycles, not different ones.[8]

We found that young women's moods fluctuated more over days of the week than across the menstrual cycle, and young men also experienced emotional fluctuations over days of the week. The women were not "moodier" than the men; their moods were not less stable within a day or from day-to-day. Evidence of weekday mood cycles in both sexes suggests that treating emotional

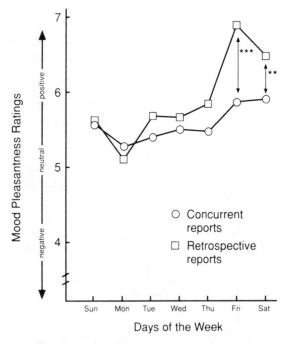

Figure 6. Comparison of concurrent and retrospective reports of mood pleasantness averaged across the three groups for each day of the week (**$p<.01$, ***$p<.001$).

fluctuations as unhealthy symptoms, and assuming that only women usually manifest them, is misleading.

We considered several alternative explanations for our results. Perhaps the measures were not sensitive enough to detect premenstrual mood fluctuations. This is unlikely because the same measures detected significant group differences in concurrent reports for the follicular and menstrual phases, several fluctuations in the retrospective menstrual phase reports, and fluctuations over days of the week in both the concurrent and retrospective reports.

A second possibility is that the concurrent data were biased. For example, women may have been describing their moods after filtering out some menstrually-related changes. If they filtered for menstrual phase,

however, day-of-week filtering also would be expected. Positive moods on Fridays and Saturdays were reported concurrently as well as retrospectively, which suggests this did not happen. Perhaps social stigma associated with the menstrual cycle but not the weekday cycle could account for hypothetical differential filtering of concurrent reports. Recall, however, that normally cycling women concurrently reported more positive moods in the follicular and menstrual phases than did women on oral contraceptives and men. A filtering hypothesis thus becomes very complicated; it would have to be made specific to some phases of the menstrual cycle and to some women. The explanation we favor, that retrospective reports differed from concurrent reports because they were biased by stereotypes, is more parsimonious. It also is consistent with all of the results for both positive moods (follicular phase, weekend highs) and negative moods (premenstrual, menstrual, Mondays) for both the menstrual cycle and days of the week.

Are self-reports the best way to measure moods? There are few, if any, alternatives, because moods are internal. Asking others to rate participants' moods raises many new problems, such as the possibility that the observer is biased, etc.

Might retrospective reports provide a better indication of moods than daily reports? In other areas concurrent self-reports (e.g., of childrearing practices) are more accurate indicators of observed behavior than are retrospective reports so it is widespread practice to collect concurrent data whenever possible. It would not make sense to change to a different paradigm for mood assessments.

In sum, although several alternative explanations of these results are possible, the most parsimonious and plausible one is that concurrent reports of moods are more valid than retrospective reports, and that stereotypes about weekday and menstrual moods influence memory for moods and subsequent reports.

Perhaps some sort of contrast effect has contributed to stereotypes about moods and the menstrual cycle and Monday blues. Recall that normally cycling women prospectively reported more pleasant feelings during the follicular phase of their cycle than did women taking oral contraceptives and men assigned to pseudo-cycles (see Figure 2). And both groups of women recalled higher levels of arousal and pleasantness in the follicular phase than they had reported prospectively (see Figures 3 and 4). The moods of women who are normally cycling apparently peak in the follicular phase and even women who are not normally cycling apparently have this expectation. It may be that women (and perhaps men) think women's increased follicular pleasantness is normal and that during the premenstrual phase their mood is depressed below normal. For the women in this study, however, and perhaps for other normally cycling young women, their relatively increased pleasantness in the follicular phase is unique, not their moods at other times. The contrast between those women who do experience negative premenstrual moods either regularly or occasionally and women who experience relatively positive moods in the follicular phase (e.g., womenNC in this study) could contribute to the belief that most women experience negative moods in their premenstrual phase. Women's exaggerated recall of their positive mood in the follicular phase also may provide an enhanced contrast with the premenstrual and menstrual phases. In a similar vein, perhaps participants in our study and in the Stone et al. (1985) study recalled their Monday moods as negative because although Monday moods are not low relative to the weekday moods which follow, they are low when contrasted with the preceding weekend's moods. Moreover, because weekend moods are recalled as even more positive than they are experienced, the contrast with Mondays may seem even greater.

The sources of the stereotypes that most women experience menstrually-related mood difficulties are probably subtle and complex. It seems unlikely that women are complete dupes of socially-produced expectations. Perhaps most women do not usually experience mood problems, but occasionally, if a number of other factors converge (and those factors may vary for individual women), they feel or behave in ways that are out of character. For example, if they are very tired, *and* some things have gone wrong at home or on the job or both, *and* they are in the premenstrual or menstrual phase of their cycle, *and* they then encounter an unfair or frustrating situation, they may cry more readily or become angrier than usual. The "straw that breaks the camel's back" may surprise both the woman herself and others because her response is uncharacteristic, and all involved may come to believe she has PMS. "Out-of-character" experiences that occur rarely would not be picked up in studies covering only one or a few menstrual cycles. This idea was prompted by our own and others' "yes, but" reactions to these and other research findings that do not yield evidence of the classic menstrual mood pattern. It raises several questions. How common are "out-of-character-for-me" experiences? That is, how many women experience them, and how often do they occur? Do similar experiences occur for days of the week, e.g., blue Mondays, or the lunar cycle? Do men have "out-of-character-for-me" experiences when certain factors converge? What attributions do people make for such experiences when the menstrual cycle is not salient?

Once established, stereotypes are very resistant to change, in part because people selectively attend to information congruent with their stereotypes. They also may be more likely to notice their negative moods than their positive ones, or to seek an explanation for their negative moods. People almost always know what day it is, and women typically know when they are or will be menstruating, so if their mood is negative and they seek an explanation, they may conclude they have "Monday blues" or the "classic" menstrual mood pattern. Because women will be in the premenstrual or menstrual phase of their cycle 25–35% of the time, only an occasional negative mood coinciding with that phase may be sufficient to maintain the belief they have PMS. Stereotypes also are resistant to change because contradictory evidence tends to be ignored or processed as an exception (Martin & Halverson, 1981; 1983). Thus, even if women's moods during the premenstrual and menstrual phases are predominantly positive, or Mondays usually are pleasant, negative moods may be recalled.

An interesting question for future research is *how* stereotypes bias recollections. Perhaps asking participants about days of the week or the menstrual cycle sets up demand characteristics, perhaps it evokes memories of a younger age when menstrual experiences were more negative (e.g., more cramps; Asso, 1983), or perhaps it makes the menstrual cycle or weekends more salient than usual. One puzzling question about the reporting bias is why it occurs even when participants are asked to recall their experiences over a very specific time period (in this case the preceding two months). Research comparing the relationship of menstrual stereotypes and early menstrual experiences to degree of biased retrospective reporting might help to answer such questions.

With the exception of recollections of pleasantness during the premenstrual phase and low arousal on Sundays, all mean mood scores were neutral or positive, so use of a measure with a negative bias would have yielded misleading data. It also would have precluded the detection of exaggerated recall of positive moods for the follicular phase and weekends. Diagnostic measures must assess positive moods and experiences as well as

negative moods or "symptoms." The results also highlight the importance of evaluating mood fluctuations in broad context. Are the individual's mood swings significantly greater over one cycle (e.g., menstrual) than another (e.g., days of the week)? They also illustrate the importance of basing diagnoses of mood abnormalities on evidence obtained prospectively rather than on retrospective reports, especially when there is reason to believe that recollection may be biased by stereotypes. Unfortunately, it would be difficult or impossible to conceal the purpose of monitoring daily moods from people who have sought treatment for mood problems. Perhaps the best solution is to explain that expectations affect most people's reports, and thus underscore the importance of trying to assess and report one's experiences as precisely as possible. This is not to imply the problem is all "in the head" (as women often were told in the past about menstrual difficulties), but to give the client credit for seeking and helping to produce the best diagnosis possible.

In the case of PMS, substantial advances have been made in empirically defining it as a clinical syndrome covering several diversified subtypes, and distinguishing it from psychological concomitants of normal menstrual cycles (e.g., Halbreich, Endicott, & Nee, 1983). The data reported in this study were obtained in the hope that they would add to those advances and help in understanding the discrepancy between the scientific evidence and popular beliefs concerning mood fluctuations over the menstrual, lunar, and weekday cycles.

NOTES

1. Women may be taking different oral contraceptives (e.g., low dose, triphasic, etc.), but to determine overall differences among the three broadly defined endogenous hormonal environments, studying specific oral contraceptives is not necessary.

2. Attrition occurred for several reasons: Three men, one womenOC, and three womenNC did not complete the study. One man, one womanOC, and two womenNC had more than seven missing days of data. Four womenOC changed their method of birth control. Four womenNC had menstrual cycles longer than 38 days. One man was dropped from the study because of prolonged illness.

3. Questions about family and career were added because Rossi and Rossi (1977) found that family-oriented women were more likely to have menstrual problems. In this study, however, all participants wanted a career and almost all a family, so there was insufficient variation to analyze differences.

4. These results and others described in Russell et al. (1987) provide strong evidence for the validity of the Affect Grid. Indicators of temporal stability are inappropriate for mood checklists because moods have been shown in this and other studies to vary across days and within days (Hedges, Jandorf, & Stone, 1985).

5. The number of forgotten days did not vary significantly across phases of the menstrual or lunar cycles. There were more forgotten days, however, on Fridays and Saturdays than on any other day of the week, $x^2(6)=89.20$, $p<.0001$. What implications does this have for the results? Parametric tests comparing forgotten and remembered days for arousal, pleasantness, and stability yielded a significant difference only for arousal. Specifically, arousal reported prospectively was lower on forgotten days than on recommended days. Since arousal on Friday and Saturday was significantly higher than on other days of the week in our major analyses for both the concurrent and retrospective reports, inclusion of the increased number of forgotten days on Fridays and Saturdays produced a conservative test. That is, if these days had not been forgotten, the means for arousal would have been even higher on Friday and Saturday.

6. At first glance the most succinct way of describing the results would be to conduct one overarching analysis for the concurrent and retrospective menstrual cycle data, and another for days of the week. This was not possible for the menstrual cycle because men could not provide retrospective data. It would have been possible for days of the week but one man did not provide retrospec-

tive data. It seemed best to use all the data possible and to avoid confusion by analyzing the data for the two cycles in the same way.

7. Findings which were statistically significant using standard alpha levels but not after Bonferroni criteria were applied have been so identified. They have been included rather than omitted because although it is in general important to control Type I error, many readers may wish to use a less stringent criterion in evaluating results that contradict or fail to support widely held hypothesis that have received inconsistent support in previous research. Bonferroni criteria were applied to each sets of ANOVAs but not to simple main effects or Tukey B analyses used to break down results from the ANOVAs.

8. In this context it is informative to note that the "classic" pattern of hormonal fluctuations graphed in textbooks for estrogen and progesterone applies to few individual women and is widely acknowledged to be an artifact of averaging across many women (B. Gorzalka, personal communication, July 24, 1985).

REFERENCES

Altman, M., Knowles, E., & Bull, H. D. (1941). A psychosomatic study of the sex cycle in women. *Psychosomatic Medicine, 3,* 199–225.

Anderson, E. I. (1972). Cognitive performance and mood change as they relate to the menstrual cycle and estrogen level. *Dissertation Abstracts International, 32,* 1758.

Ascher-Svanum, H. (1984, August). *Biased recollections of menstrual discomfort.* Paper presented at the meetings of the American Psychological Association, APA, Toronto.

Asso, D. (1983). The menstrual cycle. In D. Asso (Ed.), *The real menstrual cycle* (pp. 15–29). Toronto: Wiley.

Benedek, T., & Rubenstein, B. B. (1939a). The correlations between ovarian activity and psychodynamic processes: I. The ovulative phase. *Psychosomatic Medicine, 1,* 245–270.

Benedek, T., & Rubenstein, B. B. (1939b). The correlations between ovarian activity and psychodynamic processes: II. The menstrual phase. *Psychosomatic Medicine, 1,* 461–485.

Coppen, A., & Kessel, N. (1963). Menstruation and personality. *British Journal of Psychiatry,* 109, 711.

Frey, J., Rotton, J., & Barry, T. (1979). The effects of the full moon on human behavior: Yet another failure to replicate. *Journal of Psychology, 103,* 159–162.

Glick, I. D., & Bennett, S. E. (1982). Oral contraceptives and the menstrual cycle. In R. C. Friedman (Ed.), *Behavior and the menstrual cycle* (pp. 345–365). New York: Dekker.

Golub, S. (1976). The magnitude of premenstrual anxiety and depression. *Psychosomatic Medicine, 38,* 4–12.

Golub, S., & Harrington, D. M. (1981). Premenstrual and menstrual mood changes in adolescent women. *Journal of Personality and Social Psychology, 41,* 961–965.

Halbreich, U., Endicott, J., & Nee, J. (1983). Premenstrual depressive changes: Value of differentiation. *Archives of General Psychology, 40,* 535–542.

Hedges, S. M., Jandorf, L., & Stone, A. A. (1985). Meaning of daily mood assessments. *Journal of Personality and Social Psychology, 48,* 428–434.

Ivey, M., & Bardwick, J. (1968). Patterns of affective fluctuations in the menstrual cycle. *Psychosomatic Medicine, 30,* 336–345.

Janowsky, D. S., Berens, S. C., & Davis, J. M. (1973). Correlations between mood, weight, and electrolytes during the menstrual cycle: A renin-angiotensin hypothesis of premenstrual tension. *Psychosomatic Medicine, 35,* 143–152.

Jensen, B. K. (1982). The menstrual cycle effects on task performance examined in the context of stress research. *Acta Psychologica, 50,* 159–178.

Koeske, R. K., & Keoske, G. F. (1975). An attributional approach to moods and the menstrual cycle. *Journal of Personality and Social Psychology, 31,* 473–478.

Lahmeyer, H. M., Miller, M., & DeLeon-Jones, F. (1982). Anxiety and mood fluctuation during the normal menstrual cycle. *Psychosomatic Medicine, 44,* 183–193.

Leiber, A. L., & Sherin, C. R. (1972). Homicides and the lunar influence on human emotional disturbance. *American Journal of Psychiatry, 129,* 101–105.

Little, B. C., & Zahn, T. P. (1974). Changes in mood and autonomic functioning during the menstrual cycle. *Psychophysiology, 11,* 579–590.

Luschen, M. E., & Peirce, D. M. (1972). Effect of the menstrual cycle on mood and sexual arousal. *Journal of Sexual Research, 1,* 41–47.

Martin, C. L., & Halverson, C. F. (1981). A schematic processing model of sex-typing and stereotyping in children. *Child Development, 52,* 1119–1134.

Martin, C. L., & Halverson, C. F. (1983). The effects of sex-typing schemas on young children's memory. *Child Development, 54,* 563–574.

May, R. R. (1976). Mood shifts and the menstrual cycle. *Journal of Psychosomatic Research, 20,* 125–130.

McCance, R. A., Luff, M. C., & Widdowson, E. E. (1937). Physical and emotional periodicity in women. *Journal of Hygiene, 37,* 571–605.

McNair, D. M., Lorr, M., & Droppleman, L. F. (1971). *Profile of mood states.* San Diego: Educational & Industrial Testing Service.

Michelson, L., Wilson, J., & Michelson, J. (1979). Investigation of periodicity in crisis intervention calls over an 8-year span. *Psychological Reports, 45,* 420–422.

Moos, R. H. (1968). Development of a Menstrual Distress Questionnaire. *Psychosomatic Medicine, 30,* 853–867.

Moos, R. H., Kopell, B. S., Melges, F. T., Yalom, I. D., Lunde, D. T., Clayton, R. B. & Hamburg, D. A. (1969). Fluctuations in symptoms and moods during the menstrual cycle. *Journal of Psychosomatic Research, 13,* 37–44.

Morris, M. M., & Udry, J. R. (1972). Contraceptive pills and day-by-day feelings of well-being. *American Journal of Obstetrics and Gynecology, 113,* 763–765.

O'Neil, M. K., Lancee, W. J., & Freeman, S. J. J. (1984). Fluctuations in mood and psychological distress during the menstrual cycle. *Canadian Journal of Psychiatry, 29,* 373–378.

Paige, K. E. (1971). Effects of oral contraceptives on affective fluctuations associated with the menstrual cycle. *Psychosomatic Medicine, 33,* 515–537.

Parlee, M. B. (1973). The premenstrual syndrome. *Psychological Bulletin, 83,* 454–465.

Parlee, M. B. (1974). Stereotypic beliefs about menstruation: A methodological note on the MDQ and some new data. *Psychosomatic Medicine, 36,* 229-240.

Parlee, M. B. (1982). Changes in moods and activation levels during the menstrual cycle in experimentally naive subjects. *Psychology of Women Quarterly, 7,* 119–131.

Patkai, P., Johannson, G., & Post, B. (1974). Mood, alertness and sympathetic-adrenal medullary activity during the menstrual cycle. *Psychosomatic Medicine, 36,* 503–512.

Rossi, A. S., & Rossi, P. E. (1977). Body time and social time: Mood patterns by menstrual cycle phase and day of week. *Social Science Research, 6,* 273–308.

Ruble, D. N. (1977). Premenstrual symptoms: A reinterpretation. *Science, 197,* 291–292.

Ruble, D. N., & Brooks-Gunn, J. (1979). Menstrual symptoms: A social cognition analysis. *Journal of Behavioral Medicine, 2,* 171–193.

Russell, J. A. (1979). Affective space is bipolar. *Journal of Personality and Social Psychology, 37,* 345–356.

Russell, J., Weiss, A., & Mendelsohn, G. (1987). *The Mood Grid: A single-item scale of affect.* Unpublished manuscript available from J. Russell, Department of Psychology, University of B. C., Vancouver, Canada V6T 1Y7.

Russell, J. A., & Mehrabian, A. (1977). Evidence for a three-factor theory of emotions. *Journal of Research in Personality, 11,* 273–294.

Slade, P. (1984). Premenstrual emotional changes in normal women: Fact or fiction? *Journal of Psychosomatic Research, 28,* 1–7.

Sommer, B. A. (1973). Behavioral and affective correlations of the menstrual cycle. *Dissertation Abstracts International, 33,* 5003.

Stone, A. A., Hedges, S. M., Neale, J. M., & Satin, M. S. (1985). Prospective and cross-sectional mood reports offer no evidence of a "Blue Monday" phenomenon. *Journal of Personality and Social Psychology, 49,* 129–134.

Swandby, J. R. (1981). A longitudinal study of daily mood self-reports and their relationship to the menstrual cycle. In P. Komnenich, M.

McSweeney, J. A. Noack, & N. Elder (Eds.), *The menstrual cycle (Vol. 2): Research and implications for women's health* (pp. 93–103). New York: Springer.

Tasso, J., & Miller, E. (1976). The effects of the full moon on human behavior. *Journal of Psychology, 93,* 81–83.

Taylor, S. E., & Crocker, J. (1979). Schematic bases of social information processing. In E. T. Higgins, P. Herman, & M. P. Zanna (Eds.), *The Ontario Symposium in Personality and Social Psychology* (Vol 1), pp. 89–134. Hillsdale, NJ: Erlbaum.

Thayer, R. E. (1967). Measurement of activation through self-report. *Psychological Reports, 20,* 663–678.

Wilcoxon, L. A., Schader, S. L., & Sherif, C. W. (1976). Daily self-reports on activities, life events, moods, and somatic changes during the menstrual cycle. *Psychosomatic Medicine, 38,* 399–417.

Zimmerman, E., & Parlee, M. B. (1973). Behavioral changes associated with the menstrual cycle: An experimental investigation. *Journal of Applied Social Psychology, 3,* 335–344.

Zuckerman, M. (1960). The development of an Affect Adjective Check List for the measurement of anxiety. *Journal of Consulting Psychology, 24,* 457–462.

Zuckerman, M., Lubin, B., Vogel, L., & Valerius, E. (1964). Measurement of experimentally induced affects. *Journal of Consulting Psychology, 28,* 418–425.

Late Luteal Phase Dysphoric Disorder in Young Women

Ana D. Rivera-Tovar, Ph.D.,
and Ellen Frank, Ph.D.

The authors determined the prevalence of late luteal phase dysphoric disorder in 217 university women aged 17–29 years. Unaware of the focus on premenstrual syndrome (PMS), the participants rated DSM-III-R symptoms of late luteal phase dysphoric disorder over 90 days. Using a 30% or greater premenstrual change as an index of luteal variation, the authors found that 10 women (4.6%) met the symptom criteria during two menstrual cycles. Compared to 25 young women seeking treatment for PMS who met the same diagnostic criteria, the 10 women from the university sample reported significantly less fatigue and impaired concentration and somewhat less severe depression and overall symptoms.

Establishing the prevalence of premenstrual syndrome (PMS) on the basis of existing data is difficult because of the 1) lack of agreement on the syndrome's definition, 2) failure to differentiate premenstrual symptoms from a syndromal condition, and 3) past reliance on retrospective diagnoses in estimating prevalence rates. While depression and irritability are among the most common emotional manifestations of the condition (1, 2), researchers have not always focused on a similar subset of symptoms, and the lack of a common definition of PMS has led to disparate estimates of its occurrence, ranging from 20% (3) to 50% (4) of women. The recent inclusion of diagnostic criteria in the appendix to *DSM-III-R,* under the heading of Late Luteal Phase Dysphoric Disorder, has established guidelines for clinicians and researchers that can further systematic research in this area.

Prevalence rates based on retrospective data are highly questionable, since approximately 50% of women who report histories of premenstrual changes fail to confirm these reports when they complete prospective daily ratings over several months (5). Only Haskett has used prospective ratings and a rigorous application of the *DSM-III-R* criteria in a community survey (R. F. Haskett, unpublished data, 1987). He found that late luteal phase dysphoric disorder occurred in only 3.4% of women of reproductive age. This estimate is quite different from earlier figures based on retrospective self-reports and needs to be substantiated by additional prospective epidemiological data.

The average age at onset of the syndrome has also been subject to speculation, as PMS was once thought to be an affliction of women over 30. Older women did in fact predominate in many study settings, such as gynecological outpatient clinics, which led to the belief that PMS was more common in mature women (6), despite studies that found no relationship between prevalence and age (7, Haskett). As yet, however, no prospective study has specifically examined the extent or nature of late luteal phase dysphoric disorder in younger women. In our investigation we evaluated this research question in a non-clinical sample, using a design intended to overcome several of the limitations of previous studies.

Method

The subjects were 217 female university students fulfilling a research participation requirement for an introductory psychology course in which they were enrolled. Pregnant women, women taking oral contraceptives or any medication on a daily basis, and those with chronic health problems were excluded. The women ranged in age from 17 to 29 years (mean ±SD=18.5±1.8), were predominantly Caucasian (94%, N=205), and were regularly menstruating (cycles=21–35 days). Although an initial sample of 335 participated in symptom monitoring, the 84 women who supplied data on only one menstrual cycle and the 34 whose cycles were irregular (<21 or >35 days) were not included in the final sample. Those women did not differ from the final sample on any demographic variable.

The subjects were informed that the study was investigating the occurrence of emotional and physical changes in relation to life events in young women. Our interest in premenstrual symptoms was not disclosed at recruitment in order to 1) prevent biasing the sample toward women who believed they suffered menstrually related problems and 2) reduce the possible tendency to respond according to stereotypic beliefs about the deleterious effects of menstruation on mood and performance (8). Eligible participants were asked to rate the occurrence of 33 physical and emotional symptoms (including *DSM-III-R* symptoms of late luteal phase dysphoric disorder) daily over 90 days using a 6-point rating scale, ranging from 1 (no symptom or change) to 6 (extreme change). The 90-day rating period was used to ensure the collection of data on at least two menstrual cycles. The self-report instrument (Daily Assessment Form) also asked the participants to indicate any significant life events, the use of alcohol or medication, and whether or not they were menstruating.

The diagnosis of late luteal phase dysphoric disorder was determined by applying a rigorous percent-change criterion. Scores on the items on the Daily Assessment Form that corresponded to each of the 10 symptoms of the *DSM-III-R* criteria were summed and averaged over the 7 days before menses (premenstrual week) and the 7 days after the cessation of menses (postmenstrual week). For each symptom, the difference between the premenstrual average and the postmenstrual average (premenstrual minus postmenstrual) was divided by the postmenstrual average and expressed as percent change. A subject met the diagnostic criteria for a given cycle if the averages for at least five of the 10 symptom areas showed a 30% or greater premenstrual increase in severity and if all postmenstrual averages were less than 3. In an attempt to exclude cases of chronic symptoms that were heightened premenstrually (premenstrual magnification), symptoms with a postmenstrual average score higher than or equal to 3 (signifying "mild" distress) were excluded. A positive diagnosis also required that at least one of the five symptoms be one of the first four symptoms listed in the *DSM-III-R* criteria (mood lability, irritability, anxiety, or depressed mood) and that the subject meet the criteria during at least two menstrual cycles.

To determine the differences between women who do and do not seek treatment for PMS, we compared the symptoms of the undergraduates who met our syndrome criteria with those of a clinic sample of 25 women under age 30 with prospectively confirmed late luteal phase dysphoric disorder. Although similar in age range, the clinic women were significantly older than the undergraduate sample (mean±SD=25.4±3.2 versus 18.5±1.8; z=2.74, p=0.006, Mann-Whitney U test). The diagnoses for the clinic sample were derived with the same rating instrument and symptom criteria as those just outlined. Mann-Whitney U tests were used to compare the distributions and evaluate whether the treatment seekers' symptoms were more severe than those of the undergraduate sample.

Table 1. Symptom Severity in Young Women With Late Luteal Phase Dysphoric Disorder Who Did or Did Not Seek Treatment

| Premenstrual Symptom | Score on Daily Assessment Form[a] | | | | Mann-Whitney U Test | |
| | Treatment Seekers (N=25) | | University Sample (N=10) | | | |
	Mean	SD	Mean	SD	z	p
Physical discomfort	2.52	0.9	2.17	0.7	—	—
Depression	2.76	1.1	2.15	0.7	−1.55	0.06
Social withdrawal	2.00	1.0	1.98	0.8	—	—
Irritability	3.13	1.2	2.65	1.0	—	—
Fatigue	3.10	1.2	2.35	0.7	−1.75	0.04
Mood swings	3.15	1.3	2.82	1.0	—	—
Anxiety	2.89	1.2	2.62	0.9	—	—
Concentration difficulties	3.00	1.2	2.15	0.7	−1.83	0.03
Increased appetite	2.78	1.4	2.33	0.9	—	—
Decreased sleep	2.07	1.3	2.33	1.2	—	—
Increased sleep	2.50	1.2	1.94	1.0	−1.28	0.10
Total	2.58	0.7	2.22	0.6	−1.38	0.08

[a]1=no symptom or change, 6=extreme change.

Results

In our sample of 217 female undergraduates, 10 women (4.6%) met all the criteria for the diagnosis of late luteal phase dysphoric disorder. The mean age of these 10 women was 20.3±4.5 years. Nine reported mild premenstrual symptoms, and only one woman's symptoms fell in the moderate-to-severe category (average premenstrual total of 4 on a 6-point scale).

The premenstrual symptom severity ratings for the undergraduates and clinic sample are displayed in table 1. The young college women reported significantly less fatigue and concentration difficulties than the clinic women. In addition, there were nearly significant differences in depression, increased sleep, and overall premenstrual symptoms.

Discussion

Our results indicate that late luteal phase dysphoric disorder, when strictly and carefully defined, is relatively rare; it was found in only 4.6% of the young college women we studied. This modest estimate is consistent with the 3.4% found by Haskett in a prospective epidemiological study of premenstrual changes among women of reproductive age in a community sample. This finding underscores the importance of using specific criteria to differentiate between premenstrual symptoms and the less common premenstrual syndrome. While isolated or minor premenstrual changes are reported by at least 75% of women (9–12), such cases do not signal the presence of a syndromal condition that may disrupt daily activities. Although college women may not be completely representative of the population of late adolescent and young adult women, our large sample, prospective ratings, rigorous diagnostic criteria, and blinding of subjects to our focus on the menstrual cycle reduced the bias inherent in earlier studies. The present findings, therefore, contradict previous indications that late luteal phase dysphoric disorder is primarily an affliction of women over 30 and suggest that when strict criteria are used, the rate of PMS is quite low.

The finding that women seeking help for late luteal phase dysphoric disorder had more severe depression, fatigue, impaired concentration, and overall symptoms than undergraduates who met the symptom criteria may be a direct result of selection factors, since help seekers would tend to be more debilitated by symptoms. An alternative hypothesis, however, is that the severity of symptoms increases over time, thus accounting for more severe symptoms in the somewhat older clinic sample. Longitudinal studies may be able to answer questions about the natural course of this cyclical disorder and examine whether women with a milder syndrome in late adolescence and early adulthood are at risk for increased distress in the future. If this pattern were demonstrated, early identification of the syndrome and prompt initiation of effective preventive strategies would be warranted.

REFERENCES

1. Haskett, R. F., Steiner, M., Osmun, J. N., et al: Severe premenstrual tension: delineation of the syndrome. Biol Psychiatry, 1980; 15: 121–139.
2. Haskett, R. F., Abplanalp, J. M.: Premenstrual tension syndrome: diagnostic criteria and selection of research subjects. Psychiatry Res 1983; 9:125–138
3. Kashiwagi, T., McClure, J. N., Wetzel, R. D.: Premenstrual affective syndrome and psychiatric disorder. Dis Nerv Syst 1976; 37:116–119
4. Hargrove, J. T., Abraham, G. E.: The incidence of premenstrual tension in a gynacological clinic. J Reprod Med 1982; 27:721–724
5. Rubinow, D. R., Roy-Byrne, P.: Premenstrual syndromes: overview from a methodologic perspective. Am J Psychiatry 1984; 141: 163–172
6. Reid, R. L.: Premenstrual syndrome, in Current Problems in Obstetrics, Gynecology and Fertility. Edited by Leventhal, J. M., Hoffman, J. J., Keith, L. G., Taylor, P. J. Chicago, Year Book Medical Publishers, 1985
7. Kessel, N., Coppen, A.: The prevalence of common menstrual symptoms. Lancet 1963; 2:61–64
8. AuBuchon, P., Calhoun, K. S.: Menstrual cycle symptomatology: the role of social expectancy and experimental demand characteristics. Psychosom Med 1985; 47:35–45
9. Wood, C., Larsen, L., Williams, R.: Menstrual characteristics of 2,343 women attending the Shepard Foundation. Aust NZ J Obstet Gynaecol 1979; 19:107–110
10. Lamb, W. M., Ulett, G. A., Masters, W. H., et al: Premenstrual tension: EEG, hormonal, and psychiatric evaluation. Am J Psychiatry 1953; 109:840–848
11. Friedman, D., Jaffe, A.: Influence of lifestyle on the premenstrual syndrome: analysis of a questionnaire survey. J Reprod Med 1985; 30:715–719
12. Johnson, S. R., McChesney, C., Bean, J. A.: Epidemiology of premenstrual symptoms in a non-clinical sample, I: prevalence, natural history and help-seeking behavior. J Reprod Med 1988; 33: 340–346

Menstrual Synchrony and Suppression
Martha K. McClintock

Synchrony and suppression among a group of women living together in a college dormitory suggest that social interaction can have a strong effect on the menstrual cycle.

Studies of the influence of pheromones on the oestrous cycles of mice[1-4], and of crowding on variables such as adrenalin production in mice and other species[5] have suggested that social grouping can influence the balance of the endocrine system. Although there has been little direct investigation with humans, anecdotal and indirect observations have indicated that social groupings influence some aspects of the menstrual cycle. Menstrual synchrony is often reported by all-female living groups and by mothers, daughters and sisters who are living together. For example, the distribution of onsets of seven female lifeguards was scattered at the beginning of the summer, but after 3 months spent together the onset of all seven cycles fell within a 4 day period.

Indirect support is given by the investigation of Collet *et al.*[6] on the effect of age on menstrual cycle patterning. A higher percentage of anovulatory cycles were reported for college age women than for older women. Although Collet *et al.* attributed this to a maturational factor, it is interesting that most of the college aged women attended all female schools. Considering the parallel with the Lee-Boot effect in mice[1] (groups consisting only of females become pseudopregnant or anoestrous), it seems possible that an interpersonal factor is operating together with the maturational factor.

Subjects were 135 females aged 17–22 yr—all residents of a dormitory in a suburban women's college. The dormitory in which they resided has four main corridors each with approximately twenty-five girls living in single and double rooms. Six smaller living areas, separated from the main corridors by at least one door, each house approximately eight girls in single rooms.

Three times during the academic year, each subject was asked when her last and second to last menstrual periods had begun; thus the date of onset was determined for all cycles between late September and early April. The average duration of menstruation and presence of dysmenorrhoea were noted. In addition, subjects estimated how many times each week they were in the company of males and listed by room number the girls ($N \leq 10$) with whom they spent the most time, indicating which two of these they saw most often.

The date of menstrual onset was compared for room mates and closest friends, for close friend groups and for living groups. Two people qualified as "closest friends" only if both had indicated that they saw each other most often. While menstrual cycle timing in women using birth control pills is individually invariant, these women were still included in the analysis, because their influence on the menstrual cycles of the others was unknown. For room mates and closest friends, the difference between the date of onset in October for one arbitrarily chosen member of the pair and the closest date of onset for the other was calculated. This difference was compared with a difference for March calculated in a similar way, but with one change: instead of choosing the closest onset dates for the pair, both onsets for March were chosen to follow the initial October onset by an equal number of cycles. For example, if onset 6 occurred on March 10 for the first member of the pair, and onsets 5 and 6 for the other member occurred on March 1 and March 29 respectively, then the March 10 and March 29 dates were used to calculate the differences in onset. This procedure was used to minimize chance coincidences that did not result from a trend towards synchrony.

The Wilcoxon matched-pairs signed-ranks test[7] was used to test for a significant decrease in the difference between onset dates of room mates and closest friends. This test utilizes both the direction and magnitude of change in differences and is therefore a relatively powerful test.

There was a significant increase in synchronization (that is, a decrease in the difference between onset dates) among room mates ($P \leq 0.0007$), among closest friends ($P \leq 0.003$) and among room mates and closest friends combined ($P \leq 0.0003$). The increase in synchrony for room mates did not differ significantly from the increase for closest friends. The increase in synchrony was further substantiated by non-overlapping confidence intervals, calculated for the median difference on onset dates[8] (Table 1).

This synchrony might be due to some factor other than time spent with an individual; Koford[9] has attributed synchrony of the breeding season in *Macaca mulata* on Cayo Santiago to common seasonal changes in available food. The fact that the subjects generally eat as a dormitory group in a common dining room might be a significant factor in creating synchrony. A similar life pattern and common, repeated stress periods might also effect synchrony. Subjects were therefore randomly paired and tested for synchrony

Table 1. Confidence Intervals (>0.99, in days) for the Median Difference in Onset Date between Members of the Pair

	October	March
Close friends and room mates N=66	7<M<10	3<M<7
Random pairs N=33	6<M<14	5<M<15

within the dormitory as a whole, but no significant trend (N.S., ($P \leq 0.8$)) was found, and the confidence intervals for the median difference in onset date overlapped completely.

Group synchrony was also investigated and the data were analysed to verify that the decrease in difference between onset dates was a true measure of synchrony. All subjects were divided into fifteen groups of close friends ($5 \leq N \leq 10$), using the lists of close friends made by each subject. During the interview, it was stressed to each subject that her list of "close friends" should include the people she saw most often and with whom she spent the most time, not necessarily those with whom she felt the closest. But because there is usually some overlap, the term "close friends" was adopted. Only subjects who mutually listed each other were included in a group.

A mean onset date (μ_t) was determined for each group in October, late November, January, late February and April. As before, the onset dates (X_t) being compared, each followed the October onset (X_1) by an equal number of cycles. The mean individual difference from the group onset mean

$$\frac{\sum\limits^{n} (X_t - \mu_t)}{n}$$

was determined for each group and compared across time in two ways. First, a linear rank method, designed by Page[10] to test ordered hypotheses for multiple treatments, showed a significant decrease in individual differences from the group onset mean for close friend groups ($P \leq 0.001$). Second, a graph of this de-

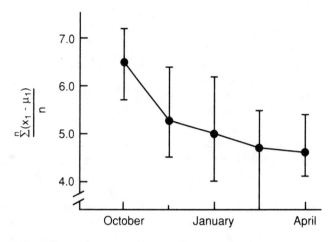

Figure 1. The median individual mean difference from the group onset mean $\left(\dfrac{((\overset{n}{\Sigma} X_t - \mu_t)}{n} \text{ days}\right)$ as a function of time. The asymptotic relation and non-overlapping confidence intervals[8] for the medians in October and late February, and October and April (>0.99), indicate an increase in synchrony for close friend groups.

crease as a function of time (Fig. 1) indicated that the greatest decrease occurred in the first 4 months with little subsequent change. This asymptotic relation indicated that the decrease in difference between onset dates was indeed an increase in synchrony for close friend groups.

Usually those who considered themselves close friends lived together. Because this was not always the case, however, subjects were divided into thirteen living groups ($5 \leq N \leq 12$), solely on the basis of arrangement of rooms, to test the importance of geographic location. When grouped in this way, there was no significant increase in synchrony within groups.

Dewan[11] has suggested that the menstrual cycles of monkeys around the equator are synchronized because each cycle is locked in phase with the Moon. As the production by the pineal gland of a substance which inhibits the action of luteinizing hor-

mone is suppressed by light, the continuous light of nights with a full Moon would facilitate ovulation across a group of monkeys and induce synchrony. This suggests that the synchrony in close friend groups and among room mates comes from a common light-dark pattern, perhaps with common stress periods in which the subjects may stay up for a large part of the night. It would be expected that if synchrony arose from common light-dark cycles, room mates would exhibit a more significant amount of synchrony than do closest friends. The opposite trend was found, however, although it was not significant (room mates, $P \leq 0.007$; closest friends, $P \leq 0.003$). It does not seem likely therefore that a photoperiodic effect is a significant cause of synchrony. This is further supported by the lack of significant synchrony in random pairings in the dormitory.

Paralleling the Whitten effect in mice[3] (in which suppression of oestrus in groups of females can be released by the introduction of a male pheromone) synchrony may result from a pheromonal interaction of suppression among close friend groups, followed by a periodic release due to the presence of males on the weekend. However, this would be insufficient to explain the synchrony which occurred among room mates and close friends, but did not occur throughout the dormitory. Some additional pheromonal effect among individuals of the group of females would be necessary. Perhaps at least one female pheromone affects the timing of other female menstrual cycles.

Another possible source of synchrony might be the awareness of menstrual cycles among friends. A sample taken from the dormitory, however, indicated that 47% were not conscious of their friends' menstrual cycles, and, of the 53% who were, 48% (25% of the total) were only vaguely aware.

The significant factor in synchrony, then, is that the individuals of the group spend time together. Whether the mechanism underlying this phenomenon is pheromonal, mediated by awareness or some other process is a question which still remains open for speculation and investigation.

Subjects were divided into two groups: those who estimated that they spent time with males, once, twice or no times per week (N=42), and those who estimated that they spent time with males three or more times per week (N=33). Borderline cases and those taking birth control pills were discarded. After testing for homogeneity of variance, the mean cycle length and duration of menstruation was compared using Student's t test. Those who estimated seeing males less than three times per week experienced significantly ($P \geq 0.03$) longer cycles than those of the other group whose mean cycle length corresponded with national norms (approximately 28 days)[12]. There was no significant difference in duration of menstruation itself ($P \geq 0.2$, Table 2).

Table 2. Mean Cycle Lengths and Duration of Menstruation

Estimated exposure to male (days/week)	Length of cycle (days)	Duration (days)
0–2 N=56	30.0±3.9	5.0±1.1
3–7 N=31	28.5±2.9	4.8±1.2
P	≤0.03	N.S.≤0.2

The possibility that the results were confounded by a maturational factor was tested, as subjects included members of the freshman, sophomore, junior and senior classes. The subjects were regrouped and compared according to class: underclassmen were compared with upperclassmen. There was no significant difference in cycle length (underclassmen 29.6 ± 5.6 days; upperclassmen 29.9 ± 5.7 days).

Exposure to males may not be the significant factor. It may be, for example, that those with longer cycles are less likely to spend time with males. However, many subjects spontaneously indicated that they became more regular and had shorter cycles when they dated more often. For example, one subject reported that she had a cycle length of 6 months until she began to see males more frequently. Her cycle length then shortened to 4.5 weeks. Then, when she stopped seeing males as often, her cycle lengthened again. Whether this is due to a pheromone mechanism similar to the Lee-Boot effect in mice[1] has yet to be determined.

Although this is a preliminary study, the evidence for synchrony and suppression of the menstrual cycle is quite strong, indicating that in humans there is some interpersonal physiological process which affects the menstrual cycle.

I thank Professor Patricia Sampson and Monty Slatkin for help in preparing the manuscript.
Received July 28, 1970.

NOTES

1. Van der Lee, S., and Boot, L. M., *Acta Physiol. Pharmacol. Neerl.*, 5, 213 (1956).
2. Whitten, W. K., *Endocrinol.*, 18, 102 (1959).
3. Whitten, W. K., *Science*, **16,** 584 (1968).
4. Parkes, A. S., and Bruce, H. M., *J. Reprod. Fertil.*, 4, 303 (1962).
5. Thiessen, D., *Texas Rep. Biol. Med.*, 22, 266 (1964); Leiderman, P. H., and Shapiro, D., *Psychobiological Approaches to Social Behavior* (Stanford University Press, 1964).
6. Collet, M. E., Wertenberger, G. E., and Fiske, V. M., *Fertil. Steril.*, 5, 437 (1954).
7. Siegal, S., *Nonparametric Statistics for the Behavioral Sciences* (McGraw-Hill, New York, 1956).
8. Nair, K. R., *Indian J. Statistics,* 4, 551 (1940).
9. Koford, C. B., in *Primate Behavior; Field Studies of Monkeys and Apes* (edit. by Devore, I.) (Holt, Rinehart and Winston, New York, 1965).
10. Page, E. B., *Amer. Stat. Assoc. J.,* 58, 216 (1963).
11. Dewan, E. M., *Science Tech.,* 20 (1969).
12. Turner, C. D., *General Endocrinology* (Saunders, Philadelphia, 1965).

Olfactory Influences on the Human Menstrual Cycle
Michael J. Russell, Genevieve M. Switz, and Kate Thompson

Two groups of women were compared for the timing of the onset of their menstrual cycles. One group was rubbed on the upper lip (directly beneath the nose) with a mixture of alcohol and underarm perspiration collected from a single female donor. The other group was rubbed with plain alcohol. The group which received the perspiration showed a significant shift in the timing of their menstrual cycles which conformed closely with the donor's monthly cycle. This is a preliminary study which supports the hypothesis that the time of menstrual onset may be modified by olfactory cues.

That olfactory cues have a significant influence on the endocrine and reproductive systems of a wide variety of mammals including primates is well established; a number of reviews have been written on the subject [1, 2, 6, 8, 9]. Recently, three laboratories working independently have shown that some rudimentary form of olfactory communication also occurs in humans [3, 4, 7]. These studies demonstrated that odors can be used: by breast feeding infants in identifying their mothers, by adults in recognizing specific individuals and by adults and children in determining the sex of strangers. In our present study we wished to determine if olfactory cues might also influence the hormonal or reproductive status of humans in a manner similar to that found in other mammals. Women who live in close proximity experience synchronization of the onset of their menstruation; McClintock [5] has demonstrated that this menstrual synchrony is not due to changes in food, awareness of menstrual timing or lunar cycles and suggested that the only significant factors seem to be the amount of time the women spend together and the length of their cycles. We

Reprinted with permission from *Pharmacology, Biochemistry, and Behavior*, vol. 13, pp. 737–738. Copyright © 1980, Pergamon Press plc.

wished to determine if olfactory cues of one woman could influence the timing of menstrual onset in other women.

Method

For this purpose 16 women were recruited to act as volunteer subjects. None of these women were taking oral contraceptives and none were accepted who were having sexual relations with other women. Their mean age was 28.5 years (range 19–39). The purpose of the experiment was explained to each subject and then we asked them to allow us to place an odor on their upper lip, just below the nose three times a week for a period of four months. The odor for each presentation was collected from the axillary region of a female donor subject. This donor was selected according to a number of criteria: she had a history of a very regular menstrual cycle of 28 days and no significant history of menstrual problems. She had demonstrated a previous experience of "driving" another woman's menstrual cycle on three separate occasions, over three consecutive years, i.e. a friend had become synchronous with her when they roomed together in summer and dissynchronous when they moved apart in the fall. She did not use underarm deodorant nor shave under her arms. During the experiment she was not allowed to use a deodorizing or perfumed soap, and was not allowed to wash under the arms during the odor collection period.

The odorants were collected by having the donor wear square 4×4 in. cotton pads under each arm for a period of twenty-four hours. The pads were then removed and each was cut up into four equal pieces and four drops of 70% alcohol were placed on each piece. The pieces of pad were then put in individual glass vials and frozen in dry ice. When the subject arrived, her sample was taken from the dry ice and allowed to thaw for two minutes and rubbed on her upper lip. The subjects were then allowed to go about

their normal business, but asked not to wash their faces for the next six hours.

The subjects in the control group received the same treatment, but did not receive the odor. Because of subject attrition the final number of subjects was eleven, with five in the experimental group and six in the control group. The study ran for a total of five months, with a one-month pretreatment period and a four-month treatment period. The subjects did not know in which group they had been placed. The date of the subject's menstrual onset was determined by questioning her when she came to the laboratory.

Results and Discussion

The individual results from this experiment are shown in Fig. 1. The mean difference in days (Fig. 2) from onset of the menstrual cycle of the subjects from the donor was 9.3 days in the pre-treatment month and 3.4 days post treatment for the experimental group and 8.0 days for the pre-treatment month and 9.2 days post treatment in the control group. Analysis of variance for repeated measures showed statistical significance of $p < 0.01$ (F at 3.81). Four subjects synchronized to within one day of the donor's onset.

The data indicate that odors from one woman may influence the menstrual cycle of another and that these odors can be collected from the underarm area, stored as frozen samples, for at least short periods, and placed on another woman. Further, the experiment supports the theory that odor is a communicative element in human menstrual synchrony, and that at least a rudimentary form of olfactory control of the hormonal system is occurring in humans in a similar fashion to that found in other mammals.

While this study has been conducted in the context of olfaction, it is also possible that volatile substances were being transferred to the nose that the subject had no awareness of and therefore cannot properly

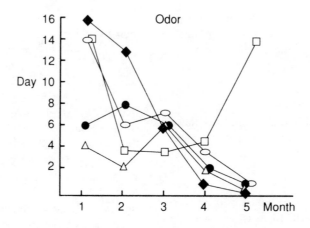

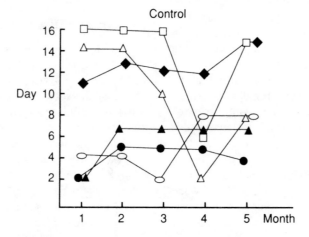

Figure 1. The difference (in days) between each subject and the donor's onset of menstruation are plotted for the experimental and control groups. Each line represents one individual.

be considered odors. It is also possible that the mechanism of transfer did not involve the nose at all, but diffusion of chemical compounds through the skin which may occur when the sample was placed on the subject's upper lip. We hope that these questions and others will be answered with further studies in this area of research.

REFERENCES

1. Birch, R. L. *Mammalian Olfaction Reproductive Processes and Behavior*. New York: Academic, 1976.
2. Cheal, M. L. and R. L. Sprott. Social Olfaction: A review of the role of olfaction in a variety of animal behaviors. *Psychol. Rep.* **29:** 195–243, 1971.
3. Hold, B. and M. Schleidt. The importance of Human Odour in Non-Verbal Communication. *2 Tierpsychol.* **43:** 225–238, 1977.
4. Macfarlane, A. The Human Neonate in Parent-Infant Interaction. *Ciba Found. Symp., Amsterdam* **33:** 103–117, 1975.
5. McClintock, M. K. Menstrual Synchrony and Suppression. *Nature* **229:** 244–245, 1971.
6. Muller-Schwarze, D. and M. Mozell. *Chemical Signals in Vertebrates*. New York: Plenum Press, 1976.
7. Russell, M. J. Human Olfactory Communication. *Nature* **260:** 244–245, 1971.
8. Shorey, H. H. (ed.) *Animal Communication by Pheromones*. New York: Academic Press, 1976.
9. Thiessen, D. and M. Rice. Mammalian Scent Gland Marking and Social Behavior. *Psychol. Bull.* **83:** 505–539, 1976.

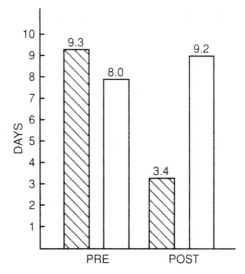

Figure 2. The mean difference of the onset of the menstrual cycle of the donor and the menstrual cycles of the subjects before and after treatment with the odorant. The hatched bar is the experimental group and the open bar is the control group. The post score is the mean of the individual values in the fifth month.

Chapter 4

Sexuality

Social stereotypes about women's sexuality stand in marked contrast with stereotypes about women's moods. As was noted in Chapter 2, most people believe that a woman's emotional state varies widely across the monthly cycle and that those swings are biologically controlled. She is believed, in spite of evidence to the contrary, to be at the mercy of her "raging hormones". Men's moods, on the other hand, are believed to be intentionally controlled and not influenced by their biology. Consequently, one of men's socially-proscribed roles is to act as a moderating, steadying, influence on women and their moods. The opposite stereotypes exist for sexuality. In this case, it is men's—not women's—behavior which is controlled by biology. The women are to provide the rational controlling influence.

These stereotypes have had a huge impact on the study of female sexuality. Because of the presumed lack of sexual drive in women, female sexuality was largely ignored for a long time. The few studies that were conducted measured a woman's desire for sexual contact with such telling questions as, "Did your husband have intercourse with you last night?" Unmarried heterosexual women and lesbian women were not considered appropriate subjects. Lesbians, post-menopausal women and women of many racial/ethnic groups were all but non-existent in sexuality research.

The first significant step toward understanding women's sexuality came with Kinsey's pioneering work in the 1950s, which showed that the range of women's sexual experience and behavior was much wider than previously realized. The biological basis of that sexuality began to be explored in the 1960s with the description of the sexual response cycle by Masters and Johnson. The first article in this chapter (**Langmyhr**) summarizes that work. Though the article is nearly two decades old, the information it contains remains quite current and deserves reiteration.

One possible biological influence on women's sexuality is described in the article by **Harvey.** She reports that heterosexual women initiate and engage in more sexual activity around the time of ovulation than at other times of the menstrual cycle. A similar midcycle increase in self-initiated sexual behaviors has been reported for lesbians (Matteo and Rissman, 1984). This cycling of sexual activity (expressed by both women and men) could be the consequence of the common reluctance to engage in sex during the menstrual flow and of the physical and psychological changes that some women experience premenstrually. However, given that the sexual behavior of many animal species is confined to or increases at ovulation, the midcycle increase of sexual behaviors by women may have a hormonal basis. Although no one has been able to demonstrate the tight hormonal control over the sexual behavior of women as has been shown for other species, researchers have speculated that either estrogen or androgen or a combination of the two may influence sex drive and sexual behavior of women.

A biological influence on sexual preference has been the subject of much speculation. A recent study by LeVay (1991) suggested that the brains of homosexual and heterosexual men differ with respect to the size of a small area of the brain known to be involved in sexual behavior. Lesbians were not included in the study, however. This omission is typical of both research on homosexuality and research on female sexuality in general. Lesbians continue to be an "invisible" group in sexuality research. As the article by **Barrett** describes, lesbians are "invisible" not only to science but to society as a whole. Based on personal accounts, Barrett's article eloquently describes the weighty effects of prevalent negative stereotypes about lesbians on their lives.

Leigh's work is somewhat unusual in that she studied both heterosexual and homosexual women and men. Her work supports the notion that women and men have different motivations for sex, regardless of sexual preference. She also found some differences between homosexuals and heterosexuals, regardless of gender, in the importance of some motivations for sex. However, as she cautions, none of these differences is large. She does not speculate about the possible cause(s) of these gender differences.

Though biological factors may influence sexuality, social norms and expectations clearly play a very important role. Consider, for example, Freud's declaration that vaginally-centered orgasms are the expression of mature female sexuality while clitoris-centered orgasms are the expression of a neurotic and immature sexuality. For decades, many heterosexual women believed that vaginal intercourse was the only appropriate expression of their sexuality and they felt inadequate if they were unable to achieve orgasm through it. Since then, the nature, quantity and quality of women's orgasms has received much attention. And the role of culture in shaping a woman's sexual experience, including orgasm, has been increasingly recognized. **Lightfoot-Klein** gives an anecdotal account of women's sexuality in a culture where female "circumcision" is practiced. This centuries-old rite of passage has been undergone by more than 80 million African women. The form described by Lightfoot-Klein, infibulation (also called Pharonic circumcision), is the most extreme form. In other cultures, the procedure consists of either removing the tip of the clitoris or removing the entire clitoris and labia minora. As the clitoris and the penis develop from the same embryological tissue in a fetus, consider what the equivalent procedure would be in a man! Many prefer to describe this practice as genital mutilation rather than circumcision, because the term "circumcision" medically refers to removal of part or all of the foreskin from the penis. The analogous operation in women would be to remove part of the hood surrounding the clitoris. Though female "circumcision" is illegal in many African countries and is not mandated by any religion, it remains a powerfully entrenched tradition. Westerners often react with horror to this particular procedure, but not to the plastic surgery and implants that many women in this country are willing to undergo in pursuit of the socially-defined sexy and "perfect" body, despite the documented health risks of such procedures.

References and Suggested Reading

Alzate, H. (1985). Vaginal eroticism: A replication study. *Archives of Sexual Behavior, 14*, 529–537.

Bressler, L. C., & Lavender, D. L. (1986). Sexual fulfillment of heterosexual, bisexual and homosexual women. *Journal of Homosexuality, 12*, 109–122.

Forrest, J. D. & Singh, S. (1990). The sexual and reproductive behavior of American women, 1982–1988. *Family Planning Perspectives, 22*, 206–214.

Kinsey, A., Pomeroy, W. B., Martin, C. E., & Gebhard, P. H. (1953). *Sexual behavior in the human female.* New York: Saunders.

Leiblum, S. R. (1990). Sexuality and the midlife woman. *Psychology of Women Quarterly, 14*, 495–508.

LeVay, S. (1991). A difference in hypothalamic structure between heterosexual and homosexual men. *Science, 253*, 1034–1037.

Lightfoot-Klein, H. (1989). *Prisoners of ritual: An odyssey into female genital circumcision in Africa.* New York: Harrington Park.

Masters, W. H., & Johnson, V. E. (1966). *Human sexual response.* Boston: Little, Brown.

Matteo, S., & Rissman, E. F. (1984). Increased sexual activity during the midcycle portion of the human menstrual cycle. *Hormones and Behavior, 18*, 249–255.

Physical Signs of Sexual Response and Orgasm in Women
George J. Langmyhr, M.D.,

It is estimated that 10% of sexually active American women have never experienced orgasm. Another 10% to 15% report that they are unable to achieve full sexual responsivity as frequently and/or as easily as they would like. Thus it is understandable that physicians will be asked many questions about the physical signs of the female sexual response cycle. It is important to have clear and accurate information, particulary about the advanced stages of sexual response, plateau and orgasm, since the physician will be cast in the role of an educator as well as a therapist.

1. The sexual response cycle. Masters and Johnson delineated four stages: (1) excitation; (2) plateau; (3) orgasm; (4) resolution. While there are specific anatomical and physiological changes which occur during each, the stages may merge or overlap to a certain degree. Of what use are the various signs? For the woman and her partner, as well as the physician, they are indicators of the level and degree of her sexual responsivity. However, it is essential to emphasize that some signs or physiologic changes may be minimal or absent in some individuals who nonetheless do have physiologic orgasm as well as the corresponding psychologic experience.

2. Physical signs of plateau. Plateau is the advanced stage of sexual arousal which follows the initial excitement stage (marked by vaginal lubrication and initial swelling of the clitoris and pelvic organs) and precedes orgasm. After sexual stimulation has begun, the pla-

teau stage prepares the body for orgasm. The tissues are further engorged with blood and muscle tension increases.

A. The most dramatic change is the engorgement and swelling of the tissues surrounding the outer third of the vagina, which reduces its diameter by as much as 50% (creating the *orgasmic platform*, as described by Masters and Johnson). The vagina actually grips the penis, further exciting the man. The uterus is elevated still more and becomes larger. In women who have had children, it may double in size. There is increased ballooning of the inner two-thirds of the vagina, minimizing its contact with the penis.

B. The clitoris rises from its normal position overhanging the pubic bone, draws farther away from the vaginal entrance, and seems to become retracted. The clitoral shaft is shortened by as much as 50%. Thus the clitoris is harder to locate. This important physiological change should be understood by the woman and her partner, who previously may have thought that continued *direct* stimulation of the clitoris was all-important. Despite its retraction, the clitoris continues to respond to stimulation either applied directly to the mons veneris or indirectly through penile thrusting in the vagina.

C. The labia majora of women who have had children become more engorged; less swelling may be observed in nulliparous women.

D. If coitus is prolonged, a few drops of moisture may emerge from the Bartholin's glands in the labia majora. Late in the plateau stage, the labia minora change to a bright red or deep wine color. This color change is a sure sign that orgasm will occur in a minute to a minute and a half if effective sexual stimulation is continued.

E. There is further swelling of the areolae surrounding the nipples. While this tends to mask the swelling of the nipples, they continue to erect.

F. Other signs: The rate of breathing increases, and there is a further rise in the pulse rate and blood pressure. At this point the sex flush—a rash-like reddening of the face and chest—may appear or become more marked and widespread if it has appeared during excitation. Voluntary and involuntary muscles become more tense. There may be contractions of a spastic nature in some muscles of the face, ribs, and abdomen. The rectal sphincter may tighten; some women contract this muscle and the muscles of the buttocks to heighten sexual tension.

3. Physical signs of orgasm. Orgasm is an intensely pleasurable and gratifying response involving both mind and body. When orgasm becomes imminent, women feel increased sensuality and eroticism. Sexual tension reaches a peak with pelvic thrusting often becoming more rapid and urgent. As orgasm begins, the pelvic and genital areas are flooded with an extremely thrilling and satisfying sensation. There may be a profound sense of release and the senses in general often seem to be heightened. This subjective response coincides with the following physical signs:

A. The major physical sign is a series of rhythmic muscular contractions. Following an initial spasm, there are rhythmic contractions of the orgasmic platform, which is the outer third of the vaginal barrel, and the en-gorged tissues surrounding it. These contractions occur at intervals of 0.8 seconds initially, then become less intense and occur at longer intervals. A mild orgasm may be accompanied by only three to five contractions; an intense orgasm will be accompanied by eight to twelve contractions. Other muscles, particularly the anal sphincter, may undergo similar contractions.

B. The uterus contracts rhythmically in the same way it does during childbirth. Contractions begin at the upper end of the uterus and move toward the cervix. They are more severe when orgasm is more intense. Women are generally not aware of these uterine contractions. However, there may be a vague feeling deep in the woman's pelvis which may add to her pleasure. (Contrary to myth, there is no release or discharge of any sort of fluid.)

C. General changes: As in the man, the pulse rate, blood pressure, and breathing rate reach a peak. The sex flush is at its most pronounced. Muscles of the face, arms, legs, and elsewhere contract. These contractions are particularly pronounced in the hands and feet, where there may be spastic contractions known as carpopedal spasms. In general women, like men, are unaware of these extreme muscular contractions.

Summary

As has been emphasized, no one physical sign, during either plateau or orgasm, should be taken out of context. However, it may be clinically useful to analyze the various physical signs manifested by the woman and observed or felt by her partner. This analysis can be particularly useful to delineate the degree of responsivity in women complaining of sexual dysfunction.

Female Sexual Behavior:
Fluctuations During the Menstrual Cycle
S. Marie Harvey

Abstract—This longitudinal prospective study was designed to examine the influence of menstrual cycle phase on female sexuality. Sixty-nine normally cycling women monitored their sexual behavior including both heterosexual and autosexual activities and their basal body temperature daily over two or three consecutive menstrual cycles. Temperature charts were used to ascertain five cycle phases (menstrual, postmenstrual, ovulatory, luteal and premenstrual) and data were analyzed using analyses of variance with repeated measures. The results supported a significant cyclic fluctuation in sexual behavior with both female-initiated and male-initiated sexual activities peaking in the ovulatory phase. Moreover, the findings indicated that women experienced increased sexual arousal and sexual pleasure as they progressed from the menses to the premenstruum. These data suggest that human sexual behavior may be influenced by hormonal fluctuations and cognitive factors associated with the menstrual cycle.

INTRODUCTION

Periodicity is characteristic of the sexual behavior of lower mammals. In animals with estrus patterns the female will accept the male only when she is 'in heat', a condition corresponding temporally to ovulation and the presence of certain gonadal hormones [1,2]. In contrast, primates, including humans, do not show well defined periods of estrus and will copulate throughout the female's menstrual cycle. Laboratory studies of several species of primates indicate, however, that a sexual rhythm does persist in higher primates and that increased frequency of copulation occurs near the expected period of ovulation [3–5].

The influence of the menstrual cycle on human sexual behavior has been a subject of interest and controversy for over fifty years. Although research efforts have been extensive, the data remain inconclusive. In a recent review of the literature Schreiner-Engel listed 32 such studies [6]. Only eight studies found increased sexuality around the time of ovulation; whereas in seventeen investigations increases were observed premenstrually, 18 postmenstrually and four during menstruation. In addition, when female sexual arousibility is measured in a laboratory setting, midcycle increases are not found [7]. However, laboratory induction of arousal may reflect a different phenomenon than self-report data of naturally occurring fluctuations in sexual interest over the menstrual cycle.

The inconsistencies reported in the literature may in part stem from three methodological short-comings: (1) the use of retrospective interviews or questionnaires for collecting data; (2) the inadequate measurement of female sexual behavior; and (3) the use of unreliable methods for determining midcycle ovulation.

Early research efforts relied heavily on retrospective data for identifying cyclic changes in sexual desire and behavior over the menstrual cycle. However, retrospective studies aimed at obtaining information on daily changes in feeling states and activities have many inherent problems. For instance, many women may have difficulties accurately remembering the specific time of sexual activity. Furthermore, their memories may be clouded by cultural beliefs regarding sexuality and the menstrual cycle. It is noteworthy that retrospective data consistently found that heightened sexual desire occurred just before or after menstruation. The menstrual flow is a convenient marker during the menstrual cycle and events occurring near this time may be more easily remembered. In contrast, ovulation has no external manifestations. Therefore, since this phase is less likely to be noticed associated events may be less easily remembered.

Research on female sexuality has traditionally focused on measures of coital rate which are heavily influenced by the male partner. Most studies failed to distinguish between sexual intercourse and other types of sexual activities (e.g. masturbation), to identify subjective feelings of sexual desire or to establish whether sexual activity was initiated by the woman or her partner. An innovative study by Adams, Gold and Burt did adequately measure female sexuality by separating female-initiated, joint-initiated and male-initiated sexual activities and by considering autosexual experiences as well as heterosexual activities [8]. Moreover, they used daily recordings of sexual behavior for the collection of data. The findings from this study indicate that women not on oral contraceptives exhibit peaks of female-initiated sexual behavior during the ovulatory phase. However, time of ovulation was estimated by reverse cycle day 14 (the fourteenth day counting backwards from the succeeding menses). This mode of determining day of ovulation has been criticized as an unreliable method and has been estimated to be correct only 48 to 75% of the time [9, 10].

The present study attempted to overcome the limitations of previous investigations through the use of daily logs of sexual behavior as the primary data source, the recording of autosexual as well as heterosexual activities that distinguished between female and male-initiated behaviors, and the use of basal body temperature as the primary method for determining time of ovulation. The overall objective of this study was, therefore, to investigate the relationship between menstrual cycle phase and female sexuality. Specifically, the following research questions were examined: (1) Does the frequency of female-initiated autosexual and heterosexual activities vary over menstrual phases? (2) Does the frequency of male-initiated heterosexual activities vary over menstrual phases? (3) Are women less receptive to male sexual advances at various menstrual phases? (4) Do women feel more sexually aroused and experience more sexual pleasure and orgasms during different menstrual phases?

METHODS

Subjects

The study population was composed of 69 normally menstruating volunteers aged 18 to 34 who were recruited from among the women affiliated with the University of California, Los Angeles. Because of the sensitive nature of the data gathered, a random sample of female participants was impossible to obtain. Subjects were, therefore, recruited through announcements in university classes and an advertisement in the university paper. All women who indicated an interest in participating in the project were screened in a telephone interview. Volunteers were excluded from participation if they (1) indicated menstrual cycle irregularities (defined as having at least one menstrual cycle during the previous six months that was less than 21 days or more than 35 days in length) or other medical problems that might affect sexual activity or menstrual cyclicity; (2) reported use of hormonal medications or oral contraceptives during the previous six months; (3) were using the pill, IUD, tubal ligation or vasectomy as contraceptive methods; (4) were pregnant or trying to become pregnant; and (5) reported a history of emotional problems or mental illness. The study was further limited to sexually active women, defined as those who engaged in sexual intercourse at least once a week. In an attempt to control for the effect of the availability of a sexual partner on frequency of heterosexual activity, all subjects were involved in stable heterosexual relationships. However, the majority of women were single (65.2%) with 17.4% married and 17.4% cohabitating with their sexual partners. Chance factors may have affected the opportunities for heterosexual activity more for the single woman than the married or cohabitating subjects.

The sample was predominantly white (87%), fairly young (mean age of 24) and highly educated (81% with more than two years of college education). Sixty percent of the sample were undergraduate students, 36% were graduate students and 4% were employees of the University. The average frequency of intercourse, as measured during the study, was 2.58 episodes per week. With respect to current contraceptive choice 83% used the diaphragm, 13% used condoms and the remaining 4% used the cervical cap.

Data Collection

As part of a larger study of the interrelationships among the menstrual cycle, female sexuality and alcohol use, subjects monitored sexual experiences, contraceptive use and basal body temperature (BBT) daily over two or three consecutive menstrual cycles. Materials and detailed instructions for recording responses were provided in a 30 min training session. BBTs were taken each morning upon awakening and prior to getting out of bed or any physical activity. Participants recorded oral temperatures to the nearest tenth of a degree fahrenheit on a temperature log. Days of the menstrual flow and pertinent physical variations such as illness, medication, sleepless nights, etc. were also noted on the BBT chart. Sexual activity was recorded by date and time of occurrence on a sexual behavior log that distinguished between intercourse, heterosexual stimulation that did not result in intercourse (e.g. oral sex), and autosexual activities (e.g. sexual desire, fantasy, masturbation). The initiator of each heterosexual session was indicated (i.e. mutual, self, partner) as was whether the initiator's invitation was accepted or rejected by the partner. For each instance of intercourse, women indicated whether contraception was used and, when used, the type of contraception. For each instance of sexual activity, (1) self-rating of overall arousal, (2) self-rating of sexual pleasure, and (3) occurrence of orgasm were recorded. Subjects rated their sexual arousal and sexual pleasure for each activity on a five-point scale, zero representing no arousal/pleasure and five indicating very intense arousal/pleasure. Participants deposited completed logs with the researcher at the end of each week and were contacted by telephone if they missed their weekly appointment. For practical reasons, hormonal levels were not determined, because regular assays over such a long period would have been an unreasonable burden for subjects.

Although the research variables were difficult to blind, an attempt to mask the true purpose of the study from the subjects was made. Thus, the research project was presented to the participants as an investigation of the factors affecting time of ovulation.

The 69 women completed data for 191 menstrual cycles. The mean number of cycles completed per subject was 2.8 with a mode of three. Although all women gave a verbal commitment to a minimum of three months participation in the study, one participant became pregnant during her second menstrual cycle and was, therefore, unable to continue with the research. Fourteen subjects discontinued after two months participation because spring quarter ended at the university and they moved from the Los Angeles area. Upon conclusion of the daily log recording, participants completed a questionnaire that assessed personal beliefs regarding sexual behavior and received US $50.00 for their participation in the study.

Data Analysis

A menstrual cycle included the period from the first day of menstruation to the day preceding the onset of the next menstrual bleeding. Based on days of menstruation and estimated time of ovulation five menstrual phases were distinguished: menstrual, postmenstrual, ovulatory, luteal and premenstrual. Time of ovulation was determined from basal body temperature charts for 154 (81%) of the 191 cycles completed. Since ovulation typically occurs 6–36 hr following a 0.3 to 0.5°F drop in BBT, the four day ovulatory period included the day characterized by a BBT drop and the following three days. A nurse practitioner who teaches natural family planning and fertility awareness at the Los Angeles Regional Family Planning Council evaluated the charts and designated a four day ovulatory phase of each cycle. Ten cycles (5%) were excluded from analysis because they exceeded 35 days in length and were, therefore, thought to be anovulatory.

Since the remaining 27 cycles (14%) failed to show a biphasic BBT pattern, time of ovulation was estimated by reverse cycle day 14 (the fourteenth day when counting backwards from the succeeding menstruation). Based on the two-week life span of the corpus luteum, ovulation is thought to occur the fourteenth day prior to the next menstrual flow [11]. Thus, the four-day ovulatory phase for these cycles was designated by reverse

cycle days 13–16. According to Moghissi monophasic BBT charts can and do occur during ovulatory cycles: his results indicated that in approximately 20% of ovulation cycles as determined by hormonal patterns, the BBT failed to demonstrate ovulation [12].

A comparison of cycle lengths for those showing a biphastic BBT pattern with those failing to exhibit this pattern, indicated that the cycles were exceedingly similar. The cycle lengths ranged from 22 to 35 days for both categories and mean cycle length for those with a biphasic BBT pattern was 28.5 days compared to 28.8 days for those without this pattern. Moreover, the mean length of menstruation (4.9 days) was exactly the same for both groups.

With the ovulatory phase pinpointed the remaining four cycle divisions were distinguished as follows: the menstrual period was the actual days recorded by subjects on their BBT charts; the premenstrual period consisted of the three days preceding menstruation; the postmenstrual and luteal periods were bounded by the menstrual and ovulatory periods and by the ovulatory and premenstrual periods respectively.

The mean scores for eight variables of sexual behavior were calculated for each of the five menstrual cycle phases and included the following: (1) mean number of female-initiated heterosexual activities per day: this measure included all female-initiated and mutually-initiated sessions of intercourse and sex play, and female advances rejected by the partner; (2) mean number of autosexual activities per day including sessions of masturbation, sexually arousing fantasies and sexual desire; (3) mean number of all female-initiated sexual activities per day including both heterosexual and autosexual experiences; (4) mean number of male-initiated heterosexual activities per day: this measure included all male-initiated and mutually-initiated sessions of intercourse and sex play, and male advances rejected by the partner; (5) pro-

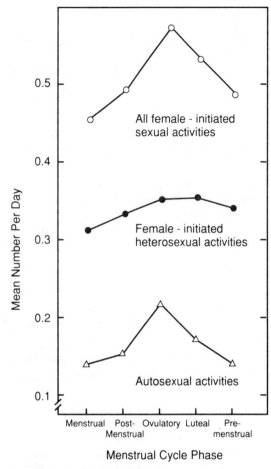

Figure 1. Cyclic fluctuation in mean number of female-initiated sexual activities.

portions of female rejections of male-initiated heterosexual activities per total number of male-initiated activities; (6) mean rating of sexual arousal; (7) mean rating of sexual pleasure; and (8) proportion of sexual activities in which orgasm occurred. In calculating each of these sexuality measures, data for all available menstrual cycles were used to compute an average per subject for each of the five phases.

With these eight variables of sexual behavior, cyclic fluctuations were tested using single-group analyses of variance with repeated measures. This procedure tested for a significant trend over time; the total variation was subdivided into linear, quadratic (U-shaped curve) and cubic (S-shaped curve) trend components through the use of orthogonal polynominals. The analysis, therefore, provided information regarding the best-fitting curve or shape of the sexuality variables across menstrual phases.

Two separate analyses were performed for each of the sexuality variables. Whereas the first analysis included data from all menstrual cycles except those thought to be anovulatory, the second used data from only those cycles showing a biphasic BBT pattern. While the analysis using all cycle data found a significant trend for sexual arousal, the analysis excluding reverse cycle day 14 data showed a similar trend but it was not significant. However, there were no other significant differences in the findings. Therefore, the results from the analyses using all cycle data are presented.

RESULTS

Female-Initiated Sexual Activity

A significant cyclic fluctuation was found for two of the three variables that examined frequency of female-initiated sexual activities (Table I). Autosexual activity was significantly related to a quadratic trend ($F = 6.17$, df = 1,66, $p<0.05$) with the mean frequency per day rising at mid-cycle (0.22). Similarly, total female-initiated sexual activity (heterosexual and autosexual) showed a statistically significant quadratic trend ($F = 5.35$, df = 1,66, $p<0.05$) with mean frequency again peaking in the ovulatory phase (0.57). As seen in Fig. 1, the shapes of the curves were similar for both variables: rates were lowest during menstruation, increased in the post-menstrual phase, peaked during ovulation, and progressively declined during the luteal and premenstrual phases. Thus, women initiated 1.6 times the number of autosexual ac-

Table 1. Means Standard Deviations and Repeated Measures Analysis of Variance Results for Variables Related to Sexuality According to Menstrual Phase

	Menstrual	Postmenstrual	Ovulatory	Luteal	Premenstrual	Overall
Female-initiated heterosexual activities‡	0.314 (0.330)	0.337 (0.282)	0.353 (0.267)	0.359 (0.243)	0.344 (0.274)	0.341
Autosexual activities†‡	0.141 (0.171)	0.155 (0.196)	0.220 (0.267)	0.175 (0.243)	0.145 (0.166)	0.167
All female-initiated sexual activities†‡	0.455 (0.405)	0.492 (0.374)	0.573 (0.394)	0.533 (0.376)	0.489 (0.361)	0.509
Male-initiated heterosexual activities†‡	0.343 (0.336)	0.376 (0.265)	0.426 (0.284)	0.417 (0.253)	0.376 (0.319)	0.388
% of rejections of male advances	0.052 (0.123)	0.045 (0.129)	0.030 (0.092)	0.086 (0.174)	0.039 (0.105)	0.050
Self-rating of sexual arousal*	3.47 (0.923)	3.67 (0.677)	3.79 (0.766)	3.70 (0.581)	3.78 (0.722)	3.68
Self-rating of sexual pleasure*	3.68 (0.649)	3.74 (0.651)	3.81 (0.724)	3.79 (0.540)	3.90 (0.724)	3.78
% of sexual activities resulting in orgasm	0.630 (0.310)	0.655 (0.295)	0.676 (0.290)	0.676 (0.256)	0.703 (0.318)	0.668

*Linear trend $p<0.05$.
†Quadratic trend $p<0.05$.
‡Values represent mean number of sexual activities per day.

tivities and 1.3 times the number of total sexual activities in the ovulatory phase of their cycle as compared to menstruation.

Furthermore, despite the findings that no significant cyclic variation occurred, female-initiated heterosexual activity displayed a similar tendency and curve (Fig. 1) with increased frequency in the ovulatory and luteal phases. In general, women initiated twice as many heterosexual activities as autosexual (0.34 and 0.17 respectively).

These findings suggest that women initiate and engage in more sexual activities during midcycle, the time of maximum fecundity. Moreover, premenstrual and postmenstrual peaks in female sexual behavior are not supported by the data.

Sexual Arousal, Sexual Pleasure and Orgasm

Subjects rated their sexual arousal and sexual pleasure for each activity on a five-point scale, zero representing no arousal/pleasure and five indicating very intense arousal/pleasure. The mean self-ratings of both arousal and pleasure significantly fluctuated over the five menstrual cycle phases (Table 1). A statistically significant linear trend of increased sexual arousal ($F = 5.84$, df = 1,66, $p<0.05$) and increased sexual pleasure ($F = 6.55$, df = 1,66, $p<0.05$) emerged. The mean rating of arousal was lowest during menstruation (3.47) and highest in the ovulatory and premenstrual periods (3.79 and 3.78 respectively). Similarly, the mean rating of pleasure was lowest in the menstrual phase (3.68), progressively increased over the cycle phases and peaked in the premenstruum (3.90). The second highest rating for pleasure was, however, at ovulation (3.81).

Although not statistically significant, frequency of female orgasm showed a similar linear trend (Table 1). Overall, these data indicate the women experience increased sexual responsiveness as they progress from menstruation to premenstruum.

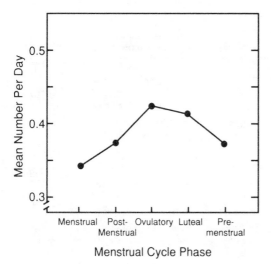

Figure 2. Cyclic fluctuation in mean number of male-initiated heterosexual activities.

Male Initiated Sexual Activity

Overall men initiated more heterosexual activities than did women (0.39 and 0.34 respectively). Of considerable interest is the statistically significant relationship between male sexual behavior and the female menstrual cycle. A significant quadratic trend ($F = 4.38$, df = 1,66, $p<0.05$) of male-initiated heterosexual activity over the menstrual cycle was found (Fig. 2). Men initiated 1.3 times the number of sexual activities during the woman's ovulatory phase (0.43), the period of maximum fecundity, as compared to her menstrual phase (0.34). The mean number of female rejections of male advances was also lowest during the ovulatory phase but this difference failed to achieve statistical significance (Table I).

Questionnaire Data

The post-study questionnaire collected data on the attitudes and personal beliefs regarding the menstrual cycle and female sexual behavior. Women were asked the following five questions: (1) Is there a particular time of the month when you feel more sexual and desire sexual activity more? If yes, when? (2) Is there a particular time of the month when you feel sexually turned off? If yes, when? (3) Do you object to sexual activity when you are menstruating? (4) Does your partner object to sexual activity when you are menstruating? (5) At what time of the month is conception most likely to occur?

The majority of women (71.7%) replied that they did feel more sexual at a particular time during the menstrual cycle. Interestingly, more women reported the premenstruum (20.9%) or this phase in combination with other phases (38.8%) as the period of maximum sexual desire. Nevertheless, 14.9% of the subjects attributed peak sexual desire to the ovulatory phase of the cycle.

Nearly one-half (46.2%) of the sample population replied that there was not a particular time during the month when they felt sexually turned off. However, of the 36 women responding positively to the questions one half (26.9% of the total subjects) attributed decrease in desire to the menstrual phase (Table II). In addition, 37.3% of the participants stated that they objected to sexual activity during menstruation and 28.4% reported that their partners objected or occasionally objected.

The sample population appeared to be knowledgeable regarding fertility and risk of pregnancy with 86.6% associating conception with the ovulatory phase or midcycle; 4.4% linked conception with the premenstruum and the remaining 9.0% stated they did not know when conception was most likely to occur.

DISCUSSION

Female-initiated sexual behavior displayed a significant cyclic pattern and peaked in the ovulatory phase. This finding partially corroborates the data from the study of Adams *et al.* which found an ovulatory peak in both female-initiated heterosexual and autosexual activity among nonpill-using subjects [8]. In the present study, however, only autosexual

Table II. Percentage of Women Feeling More Sexual and Feeling Sexually Turned Off According to Menstrual Cycle Phase.

	Feel more sexual	Feel sexually turned off
No particular phase	28.3	46.2
Menstrual	4.5	26.9
Postmenstrual	4.5	1.5
Ovulatory	14.9	6.0
Luteal	4.5	4.5
Premenstrual	20.9	8.9
Premenstrual and menstrual	7.4	3.0
Premenstrual and postmenstrual	6.0	0.0
Premenstrual and ovulatory	4.5	0.0
Premenstrual and luteal	0.0	1.5
Ovulatory and postmenstrual	4.5	1.5

and, thus, total female-initiated sexual activity peaked during midcycle. Female-initiated heterosexual activity did not significantly fluctuate over the menstrual cycle. According to the survey data, nearly 87% of the subjects were aware of the increased probability of conception at midcycle. It is plausible, therefore, that women initiated proportionately more autosexual than heterosexual activities during the fertile phase of the cycle in response to a fear of pregnancy. This finding, however, may be less related to female sexual desire or fear of pregnancy and more indicative of male dominance in heterosexual encounters. In support of this supposition previous research data indicate that males usually take the lead in both initiating and controlling heterosexual interactions [13, 14].

The presence of an ovulatory peak in female and male sexual activity is not surprising. That humans would desire and engage in more sexual activity at the time of maximum fecundity seems logical from an evolutionary viewpoint. Furthermore, it is unlikely that a mechanism such as estrus, which has played such an important role in the sexual behavior of animals phylogenetically related to humans, would be totally absent from human sexual behavior. It is conceivable, therefore, that biological factors may still be important in human sexuality. In particular, increased female sexual activity at

midcycle may be mediated by rising hormonal levels associated with ovulation.

Women reported heightened sexual arousal and sexual pleasure during the premenstruum. Vasocongestion of the genitals, characteristics of many premenstrual women and usually present in sexually excited women, could possibly provoke feelings of sexual arousal and increase sexual pleasure. Moreover, women may find sexual contact more pleasurable and arousing during this 'safe' period because of decreased fears of pregnancy.

Women's perceptions of their sexual feelings and activities as reported in the post-study questionnaire, were partially compatible with their daily log data. The participants reported that they felt more sexual and desired sexual activity most during the premenstrual and ovulatory phases. As previously mentioned, women initiated more sexual activities during ovulation and experienced increased sexual arousal and sexual pleasure in the premenstruum. However, although more women reported the premenstruum or this phase in combination with other phases as the period of maximum sexual desire, they did not initiate significantly more sexual activities during this period. Since the menstrual flow is a convenient marker during the menstrual cycle, sexual feelings and activities occurring near this time may have been more easily remembered. In addition, many women experience feelings of discomfort, anxiety and unattractiveness during their premenstrual period. These feelings could inhibit sexual initiation and activity.

Of the women responding positively to the question that there was a time they felt sexually turned off, one half attributed decrease in desire to the menstrual phase. Furthermore, over one third of the participants stated that they objected to sexual activity during menstruation and nearly one third reported that their partners objected. The daily log data corroborate these perceptions: during the menstrual phase women initiated fewest sexual activities in all categories and rated sexual arousal and sexual pleasure the lowest. Moreover, men initiated substantially fewer heterosexual activities at menstruation. These data support the societal custom of abstinence from heterosexual relations during the menstrual flow [15, 16].

Despite the decrease in sexual behavior during the menstrual phase, premenstrual and postmenstrual peaks in sexual activity were not supported by this research. For this study population increased sexual desire and activity appeared to be unrelated to the anticipation of or actual abstinence from intercourse during menstruation.

Of potential significance is the relationship between male sexual behavior and the female menstrual cycle. Contrary to the study by Adams *et al.* [8] which reported a drop in male-initiated heterosexuality at ovulation, the present research found a rise in male initiation during the ovulatory phase. Adams and his colleagues speculated that fears about impregnation reduced male heterosexual initiation at ovulation. Worthy of note is the midcycle increase in male initiation found in the present study despite the higher probability of conception.

It is tempting to attribute this rise to an increase secretion of pheromones at midcycle. There is ample evidence from multiple animal species that ovulation is associated with production of pheromones. These chemical substances transmit messages through the sense of smell and elicit sexual desire in the male. Although researchers have isolated sex-related pheromones in the human female and have found that they peak at ovulation [17], the role of olfactory factors in human sexual behavior is still largely unknown. There is, however, preliminary evidence that male exposure to vaginal secretions increased the frequency of sexual intercourse in married couples [18].

The dyadic interaction of male sexual initiation and the female menstrual cycle may, however, be due to interpersonal factors. Persky and colleagues found that sexual 'initiation' scores for individuals were significantly correlated with their partner's 'responsivity' scores [19]. In other words, initiation by one partner was positively related to the responsiveness by the other. The results of the present study are compatible with these data. The period of increased male initiation correspond to the phase of increased female initiation. Thus, in response to their partners' heightened sexual interest, men may enjoy and initiate more sexual encounters.

In summary, the findings from the present study indicate that various expressions of human sexual behavior fluctuate over the female menstrual cycle. The ovulatory peak in both female and male sexual activity suggests that biological factors such as fluctuating hormonal levels may be operant in human sexuality. However, further research on women followed for several menstrual cycles using hormonal measurements and concurrent assessment of multiple expressions of female sexuality is needed before the possible mediating factors underlying cyclic fluctuation can be determined.

REFERENCES

1. Ford CS, Beach FA. *Patterns of Sexual Behavior*. New York: Harper and Row, 1951.
2. Feder HH. Estrous cyclicity in mammals. In: *Neuroendocrinology of Reproduction* (Edited by Adler NT). New York: Plenum, 1981.
3. Beach FA, Hormonal control of sex-related behavior. In: *Human Sexuality in Four Perspectives* (Edited by Beach FA), Baltimore: The Johns Hopkins University Press, 1976.
4. Michael RP, Zumpe D. Rhythmic changes in the copulatory frequency of rhesus monkeys (*Macaca mulatta*) in relation to the menstrual cycle and a comparison with the human cycle. *J. Reproduct Fertility* 1970; **21**: 199.
5. Gordon TP. Reproductive behavior in the rhesus monkey: social and endocrine variables. *Am Zool* 1981; **21**: 185.
6. Schreiner-Engel P. Female sexual arousability: its relation to gonadal hormones and the menstrual cycle. *Dis Abst Int* 1980; **41**: 527.
7. Schreiner-Engel P, Schiavi RC, Smith H, White D. Sexual arousability and the menstrual cycle. *Psychosom Med* 1981; **43**: 199.
8. Adams DB, Gold AR, Burt AD. Rise in female-initiated sexual activity at ovulation and its suppression by oral contraceptives. *N Engl J Med* 1978; **299**: 1145.
9. Kolodny RC, Bauman JE. Comments on female sexual activity at ovulation. *N Engl J Med* 1979; **300**: 626.
10. Rose RM: Psychoendocrinology of the menstrual cycle. *N Engl J Med* 1978; **299**: 1186.
11. Speroff L, Glass RH, Kase NG. *Clinical Gynecologic Endocrinology and Infertility* Baltimore: Williams and Wilkins, 1983.
12. Moghissi KS. Accuracy of basal body temperature for ovulation detection. *Fertil Steril* 1976; **27**: 1415.
13. Gagnon JH, Simon W. *Sexual Conduct: The Social Sources of Human Sexuality*. Chicago: Aldine, 1973.
14. Peplau LA, Rubin A, Hill CT. Sexual intimacy in dating relationships. *J Soc Iss* 1977; **33**: 86.
15. Delaney J, Lupton MJ, Toth E. *The Curse: A Cultural History of Menstruation*. New York, New American Library, 1977.
16. Paige KE. Women learn to sing the menstrual blues. *Psychol Today* 1973; **7**: 41.
17. Michael RP, Bonsall RW, Warner P. Human vaginal secretions: volative fatty acid content. *Science* 1974; **186**: 1217.
18. Morris NM, Udry JR. An experimental search for pheromonal influences on human sexual behavior. Eastern Conference on Reproductive Behavior, Nags Head, North Carolina, May 1975 (Abstract).
19. Persky H, Lief HI, Strauss D, Miller WR, O'Brien CP. Plasma testosterone level and sexual behavior of couples. *Arch Sex Behav* 1978; **7**: 157.

Double Lives:
What It's Like to Be Lesbian Today
Martha Barron Barrett

- Homosexual women are huge and terrifying.
- They inhabit inner cities and drink to hide their sadness and the shame they have brought to their families.
- At the first sign of lesbianism, good parents should send their children to a psychiatrist to be cured.
- Women who associate with homosexuals are latent ones themselves.
- Because adult lesbian couplings are against the natural order of things, they cannot last.

There are many myths and negative stereotypes about lesbians. And whether these attitudes are subtle or overt, they not only can shape the way lesbians are seen and treated by others, they often affect the way homosexual women themselves live. In order to lead full lives—to maintain relationships with their families, their co-workers and their communities—many feel they must hide their sexual preference and lead double lives.

But a double life is a double-edged sword. While it protects a woman from hostility, prejudice, ridicule, and sometimes rape and hatred, it allows others to retain their stereotypic misconceptions. Many people insist that they do not know any lesbians when one is, in fact, occupying the next desk at work, living in the house across the street, sitting at the family Christmas table.

Why don't gay women speak up? And what is life really like for them?

SEPARATE LIVES:
"Sometimes I Just Feel Ripped Off"

Taylor,* six feet tall with an athlete's body, a competent manner and a gentle voice, has lived in the conservative city of Spokane, Washington, all of her adult life. Short, dusty-blonde hair curls around her face and glasses frame her blue eyes. "The straight world just doesn't understand," she says. "If I had the guts I could help, but there's that part of me that doesn't want to shed my blood to be the sacrificial lamb for those women in the year 2040 who want to come out. I'm ashamed of that. But I have to live.

> "It's a rush for me to be around lesbians, because I spend over half my life pretending not to be who I am. That is sad to me. I have a heterosexual life and I have a lesbian life."

"The secretary that I had for eight years when I was teaching watched an ABC documentary on homosexuality one night, and when I came in the next day she asked me if I'd seen it. I said, 'Yeah, I did,' and I was about to say I thought parts of it were really good when she said, 'I turned it right off. It made me nauseous.' I almost said, 'Lou, I'm one of them.'

"I kept thinking. 'You're so ignorant. I'm right here. I'm in the flesh. You go out

* Names in personal stories have been changed.
This excerpt is from Ms. Barrett's book, *Invisible Lives: The Truth about Millions of Women-Loving Women*, New York: William Morrow, 1989 and appeared in *Glamour*, September, 1989, p. 316+.

drinking with me. We once shared a room together on a trip.' ''

For the past twelve years, Taylor, who is thirty-seven, has lived in a suburban neighborhood of modest houses. On this July night, she sits in the private backyard world that she created by building a deck, an enclosure for a hot tub and a high fence around the yard. Kate,* her partner of three years, sits nearby, her hazel eyes alert, her long black hair loose around her shoulders. Their friends Tara* and Lisa*, a couple who have been together less than a year, share a lounge chair. Tara is twenty-five, Kate and Lisa twenty-nine; all three are natives of Spokane.

The women exchange stories about the raw edges where the lesbian and heterosexual worlds meet. One tells about a woman she knows, a straight woman who was traveling with longtime lesbian friends, who heard the motel maid apologize for forgetting to put extra blankets for both beds in their room. With surprise and anger, she realized that her friends pretend to sleep in separate beds.

Taylor nods and says, "When Kate and I were in Hawaii, we got up every morning and jumped around on the beds to make it look like they had both been slept in." Tara, a delicate and bubbly woman, leans forward. "It wasn't like that when I traveled with Lisa. She made all the reservations by phone and I heard her say, 'No. Two women. One bed.' Lisa, what are you doing! I yelled. She's determined."

Lisa only acknowledged her lesbian sexuality eight months ago, and is fighting not to lose self-respect, not to treat or be treated by the world any differently. She describes feeling assaulted and invaded by the assumption of heterosexuality that pervades store windows, billboards and movies, then adds, "Tara will say, 'God, sometimes I just feel ripped off.' ''

Kate was married for three-and-a-half years and Taylor is the first woman she has been with. Her entire family lives in Spokane. "Ever since Taylor and I have

been together, there's been a distance between my mother and me," she says. "We used to be very, very close and I'd talk to her about my relationships. I never pretend I'm interested in guys—that's just not happening. I can't lie to my mother, but I can't just go up and tell her. I'm too afraid."

The pretense of having separate bedrooms angers Kate. "But," she explains, "at this point, it's something I need to do in order to stay in this relationship, and to stay on the same terms that I want to with my family." She is sad about the wall between herself and her parents. "It feels like they don't really know who I am. There's a big part of me that's not connecting with them. I'd like them to see that part of me—to know that I'm healthy and everything is okay with me."

"The most important person in my world," Taylor says, "is Kate. And not to be able to share the most important thing in the world with your family hurts. I apologized once to my father, told him the only reason I was sad I wasn't married was because I couldn't give him a grandchild. 'You don't have to worry about that,' he said. 'But your mother and I are very happy and our happiness in our life has been our marriage and that's why we want you to be married.' I say, 'I am happy,' and he says, 'That's fine then.' But there's this piece of them that is always waiting for me to call and say, 'Sit down, I've got something to tell you,' and tell them I'm going to get married."

COMING OUT:
"My Closet Has a Revolving Door"

"Throughout life there is the decision of whether to come out or not come out," says Boston therapist Sarah Pearlman about her lesbian clients. "And that is always a crisis, either major or minor."

Heterosexuals who are not part of a minority have difficulty understanding the cultural pressure that makes coming out a crisis.

When asked, "When did you know you were gay?" many gays and lesbians answer with "When did you know you were heterosexual?" That reply, however, begs the question. Boys and girls are so thoroughly gender-imprinted from the time of their birth, and so thoroughly schooled in compulsory heterosexuality, that heterosexuals never find out their sexual identity. They simply *are*. A boy. A girl. Lesbians *discover* they are different. So, if they wish to separate themselves from the assumption of their heterosexuality, they must tell their therapist, doctor, employment counselor, visiting nephew or any of the scores of people with whom they interact. And unless the statement is a purely political one, the telling imparts this information: "I enjoy intimate physical relations with a person of the same sex."

Lisa believes that in her first enthusiasm of coming out she told too many people, and she feels that they now have a weapon if they choose to use it. Kate once confided in a man, only to get a sexual response: "Hey, will you teach me how you do it?" Taylor said, "If I had been born lavender then my parents could have said, 'Oh look, we got one of those.' Then they could have kept me or thrown me away. I would never have had to tell them."

"Our society determines how 'out' one is able to be," says Pearlman, who has helped edit two books on lesbian psychology. "There is an ongoing fear of detection. Will I lose my job? Will I lose my house? Will I lose my children? Will I be attacked? I've *seen* people lose a job. And even if you don't lose it, you become marginal, excluded either actively or through uncomfortable vibes."

Kate talks about her former boss, whose attitude toward her and two of her lesbian co-workers was "Damn it, you have a right to be what you want to be!" He once told her something that he'd said to a man who worked for the state in child protective services, "There're three lesbians out there and they're just doing a fine job."

Kate's back is very straight as she says, "I felt he had no right to reveal information that we did not give him permission to. We're talking about a state worker who can make decisions about our jobs. My boss didn't see the risks that living this life actually poses. What he saw was 'Well, everybody out there ought to feel okay about it and I'm going to see that they know that I feel okay about it.' I believe it's my personal life and it's up to me to tell people."

Taylor agrees. "It's easy to go spouting off about other people, showing how cool you are."

Heterosexuals haven't developed the lesbian's antenna that constantly scans for subtle prejudice, so in blurting out statements designed to portray themselves as good liberals, they sometimes endanger those they would befriend. Their courage is often glib. "Well, sue them if you get fired!" is a statement void of imagining what it would be like to have their own sexual lives described on the front page of the local paper. "Ignore the adolescents, the drunks, the homophobes—they're just ignorant," implies that lesbians can stride through the world, so secure that ridicule has no effect on their self-esteem.

Lesbians are aware that a very personal confidence can become a careless, "Oh yeah, she's gay," said to a crowd in a lounge, or at a party, or at the water cooler at work. The information becomes common gossip and then the lesbian, realizing her cover is blown, braces herself for what she knows has happened to others. A high school student shouting, "Dirty lesbian!"; a parent screaming, "I won't have you touching my daughter!" as she drags her child from a day-care center; a drunk male acquaintance slurring, "Why does a pretty girl like you want to eat pussy?"

The fact that there is no simple definition of the phrase "coming out" is one of the problems. It may mean one thing to the listener, another to the speaker. When lesbian and straight attempt to communicate, bewilderment may result. The definitions are even different among lesbians. Dougal Haggart, a resident of Toronto said, "The first time you have sex with a woman is when you 'come out,' " Liz Pierce, a Minneapolis lawyer, referred to "coming out to myself" after she had lived with a woman for ten years. A New Hampshire woman said, "I come out constantly, every day. And I'm tired of it."

A lesbian's degree of openness ranges from keeping it a secret and being scared to death others will find out, to observing a lifetime of caution, to informing a select few, to never discussing it yet feeling that it is generally known, to openly acknowledging it. And each woman may be on a different place on the scale with regard to her neighborhood, her workplace, her parents, her siblings, heterosexual social groups, and her own children. One woman expressed this complicated scenario by simply saying, "My closet has a revolving door"; another said, "The door to my closet is open, but my hand is always on the knob."

"The main reason I don't tell my parents," Taylor says, "is fear of rejection, like them saying, 'I just won't acknowledge your presence.' Like you're dead. Every time I go home, except toward the end of my visit, I lie in bed at night questioning, 'Why am I lesbian?' " There is a murmur of "Mmhmms" from the others. "Maybe I should . . . maybe if I was . . . maybe if I tried harder . . ." "And I shake my head and I say, 'No, you don't have to try harder, you're fine.'

"Because at home I lose my identity, question myself, I only visit for short periods. But when I'm home—back here—there is no question in my mind that I'm happy. It always shakes me up because I am so at ease, so happy with who I am, but all I have to do is go home without another lesbian person around. Five days and I'm frantic."

"There is a tension that is not present for heterosexuals," says Pearlman. "You talk about it as ongoing stress. You can talk about it as heartbreak when your mother won't see you. You can talk about it as anger when you go out and can't hold your partner's hand. You can be depressed about the sodomy laws." In some cases, Pearlman believes, being closeted is the best choice. "But where there's a secret, there's a guard and there's a selection," she says. "There is also counterfeit secrecy: They know you know, you know they know, but you don't talk about it. You go through life with this monitor sitting on your shoulder. It's right there editing you. Editing your pronouns, your activities. It's got to have an effect."

SEXUALITY: "I Don't Find Beauty In Men's Bodies"

Lisa is a writer; before she realized her attraction to women, it was evident to others who read the manuscript of her first novel. "The first-person narrator's descriptions of another woman were really, really erotic. I had no idea. It's like I was totally blind. When I finally came out to a writer friend who had read it, she said, 'Yeah. I saw it all over your book and I was wondering when you'd become aware of it.' I was so embarrassed. How come I didn't see it?"

Kate had a different signal. "I loved the guy I was married to and I was happy, but a part of me was dissatisfied. We mutually decided we were happier apart. After that, I began to talk to my counselor about my feelings for women. The idea of a relationship with a woman in this town just freaked me out, but I went to a dinner of professional women who were lesbians because I had heard about"—blushing, she motions toward Taylor—"her."

For a long time, the two women played an approach/avoidance game. They would go out and drive and talk until two or three in the morning, not wanting to say good night, yet not acknowledging their sexual attraction. Taylor admits, "In a lot of things I'm really assertive, but when it comes to women I'm not.

"Sexually, I'm just not attracted to men at all," she continues. "I don't find any beauty in men's bodies. I'm madly in love with my boss—I'd do almost anything for him—but that's an emotional love and respect. And I have other men I really love, so it's not a hate thing. Yet I don't get turned on when I look at women either."

Kate says, "When you first came out, didn't you do the little adolescent thing, you know, everybody is a possible. . ."

"Yes!" Tara shouts. "And I thought, 'No wonder men look at women like that! And it just hit me, 'I'm a pervert, too!' "

Lisa murmurs, "Yeah. No wonder men like it. God. . ."

"Yeah, The lust. . . ."

Taylor interrupts Kate. "But that's faded away for me. I *look* at the real beauties, the 10's, but I'm *attracted* to women who are the 3's and 2's. But sexual doesn't happen for me until I know them."

That a women could be sexually fulfilled by another woman is a concept that many consider laughable, bewildering, or too threatening to contemplate. A lack of anatomical knowledge may account for some of this—certainly the clitoris has been so ignored, or slighted by being defined as a miniature penis, that even some grown women do not understand its existence or function.

The occasions for and techniques of lesbian lovemaking are as varied or as monotonous as between a male and female, and the results just as satisfying, exciting or banal. The difference is that a woman-loving woman, like a woman-loving man, experiences a sensual/erotic admiration for a female's carriage, her breasts, the flow of her hair. Because the lesbian shares the eroticism of the male and because she partakes of both the lesbian and heterosexual worlds, her culture might best be described as a bridge, a transculture. Lesbians travel this bridge every day, but to heterosexuals, that far end is shrouded in mystery and myth.

In their sexual appetites, heterosexual women run the gamut from highly active to "if he gets it once a month, he should consider himself lucky," but seldom are sexual differences celebrated. Heterosexual women are often nervous or afraid that they are not doing it right, enjoy it too much, have the wrong partner, or aren't measuring up to what surveys deem to be satisfying and proper. In this sexually oriented century, blame and change are the bywords.

Society, however, is more likely to be flexible and tolerant of heterosexual women's sexuality than it is of lesbians'. Because they are perceived as deviant, it is often assumed that they are all alike in their deviancy, their "sexual appetites." But lesbians aren't any different from heterosexual women in this regard: Some lesbians say they are highly sexual, and some say they aren't.

In commenting on a study that portrayed lesbians as less sexually active than gay men and heterosexual couples, therapist Sarah Pearlman explains why she thinks that might be so. "Lesbians don't typically have a female partner who is insistent on having sex," she says, "so that leaves room for cycles of nonsexual behavior. Women are also very responsive to each other, and if they see their partner is not interested, they will back off. A heterosexual woman may have sex because she fears losing the man. Many men see intercourse as their right."

Pearlman believes mechanical sex may be less common between lesbians than heterosexual couples. "There is some expectation of reciprocity," she says. "It's hard to be totally passive."

Two women are much more attuned to emotional withdrawal and relational distance/closeness cues of a partner than a heterosexual couple, where the woman tunes in to the man. The good side of this is responsiveness, but there is a lot of guesswork, and women behave as though they know their partner's feelings and compulsively respond.

They will, for example, sense distraction and translate it into emotional distance. You see women in heterosexual couples doing this, but you don't see it with men.

"I think men are overwhelmed by too much female emotion and too much closeness after the initial falling in love," adds Pearlman. "For the most part, the men create a distance in heterosexual couples. They create it with their jobs, with their secretiveness, and—I'll be biased—with their obnoxious behavior. In the classic heterosexual couple, if there is such a thing, you see a woman dying for intimacy and communication and togetherness, and he doesn't know what she is talking about.

"With two women, what seems to happen is that one woman takes on the distancing role. It would seem logical to assume that this is a person who needs more space, needs more distance, but shuffle the couple into a new relationship and lots of times the one who in the past has created distance is the first to want closeness. It's as though someone has to distance or both people will be crazy with too much intimacy."

One aspect of lesbian sexual relationships that would baffle an outsider is the close friendships maintained with former lovers. These are not situations where ties are close because of mutual children or property; they are genuine continuations of adult friendships. There are bitter breakups among lesbian couples, of course, and acts of dramatic anger, physical harm done, suicide attempts, grudges nursed. But there is a factor at work which is less frequently found among heterosexuals. Julie, who has enjoyed lesbian love for over thirty years, explains: "Sex is one of life's premier experiences, but a relationship should be multifaceted. If it is founded on the attributes of friendship, including similar basic values, that will remain after the passion diminishes."

BEING INVISIBLE:
"I'm a Pro at This Double Life"

Taylor recalls the deep excitement and validation she felt the first time she was with a group of lesbians and heard their coming out stories. "The most support we have in Spokane is ourselves, sitting and talking. It's a rush for me to be around lesbians, because I spend over half my life pretending not to be who I am. That is something that is sad to me. I have a heterosexual life and I have a lesbian life. When I'm at work I talk hetero and when I come home I love to walk through that door because then I can relax. I'm a pro at this double life."

Lisa tells of coming out to a straight friend at work who talked constantly about her boyfriend. "The woman looked blank and said, 'What do you want from me?' " Lisa lowers her voice, "I want your body." After the laughter subsides she continues. "No. I said, 'I want you to be as understanding of my relationship with Tara as I have been of yours.' And she got tears in her eyes. She was thinking that she couldn't be. She realized that she did not have the capacity and she felt badly. So she doesn't talk about him anymore. Not much at all is left. It's sad."

"When the weekend comes," Taylor says, "I'm exhausted. I've spent a whole week being a hetero and I want to be able to sit and touch this person if I want to and not be playing that game. This separates lesbians, it makes us more a minority, but it is unifying for us.

"I would choose this life and whatever you want to call it—oppression, living a double life—fifty times over trying to live a straight life, which would certainly be easier in some ways," Taylor continues. "I would never get married to a man. I couldn't do it, just to do it. So my choices are to be single and not have a relationship with a woman and be okay to talk about anything I want to, or to live like this.

"It's like what Lisa said and Tara said about things fitting. When I finally realized that I was gay, everything came together for me. I've certainly had my ups and downs since then, but I am terribly happy. I feel fulfilled. What was missing is there."

The strong message from society is "keep it quiet," and many lesbians do that by becoming invisible. Because it's not socially acceptable to be women-loving women, they leave their lesbian persona at home when they go to work on Monday morning. On Friday they don it again. That weekend at home, the opposite side of the double life, is what most of heterosexual society never sees.

"I don't realize how much I need validation until I get it," Lisa says. I don't go to bars and I'm not in any of these lesbian circles—these are my only two lesbian friends. But when I am at a lesbian party, there is something special and empowering about being able to express your love and your relationship in public. I feel myself beaming and I'm proud and I'm happy. I don't miss the affirmation until I have it and then there I am in the middle and I want it all the time. That's what I wish the world understood."

Reasons for Having and Avoiding Sex: Gender, Sexual Orientation, and Relationship to Sexual Behavior
Barbara Critchlow Leigh, Ph.D.

Traditional sex-role stereotypes suggest that men and women engage in sex for different reasons. Previous studies have supported the notion that women are more motivated by emotional expression in having sex, and men are more concerned with physical gratification. In a survey of sexual behavior, heterosexual and homosexual respondents were asked to rate the importance of a variety of reasons for having sex and not having sex. The results showed that men and women differed in the importance attached to emotional and physical motives, with gender differences appearing in both heterosexuals and homosexuals. Certain practical motives (e.g., to reproduce, fear of AIDS, fear of pregnancy) differentiated between homosexuals and heterosexuals. Motivations predicting frequency of sexual behavior in the last month depended on the relationship status of the respondent. These findings, although suggesting that gender differences in motivations for sex persist in all kinds of relationships, point to many similarities among gay and straight men and women in reasons for having sex and limiting sexual activity.

Conventional wisdom and sex-role stereotypes tell us that men and women differ in their reasons for engaging in sexual activity. While men allegedly pursue sex largely out of lust and the quest for physical pleasure,

This article first appeared in *The Journal of Sex Research* (1989) 26: 199–209. Published with permission of the Journal of Sex Research, a publication of The Society for the Scientific Study of Sex.

women are instead motivated by the desire to express love or emotional commitment to their sexual partners. These differences in motivation may stem from cultural scripts that describe and prescribe appropriate sexual activity for men and women (e.g., DeLamater, 1987; Gagnon & Simon, 1973; Laws & Schwartz, 1977), or from the expression of individual sex-role self-concepts (e.g., Bem, 1981).

Much of the available data on reasons for having sex does not address the issue directly. Twice as many women as men say that they were in love with their first sexual partner (see DeLamater, 1987); men are more likely to initiate sexual activities within a dating relationship (DeLamater & MacCorquodale, 1979; Peplau, Rubin, & Hill, 1977); and women report a desire for more affection from their partners during sex (Hatfield, n.d., in DeLamater, 1987; Hite, 1976). Carroll, Volk, and Hyde (1985) found that 95% of their sample of college women, as compared to 40% of men, stated that emotional involvement was "always" or "most of the time" a prerequisite for having sex. These data are consistent with the notion that the expression of love is a more important motivator of sexual activity in women than in men.

Studies that have asked respondents specifically about their reasons for having sex show a similar pattern. Carroll et al.'s (1985) study included an open-ended question asking "What would be your motives for having sexual intercourse?" Women typically gave love-related reasons, while typical answers for men focused on physical pleasure (actual frequencies are not given by the authors). Whitley (1988) asked subjects to answer the question "What was your most important reason for having sexual intercourse on the most recent occasion?," and reports that 51% of women and 24% of men gave love/emotion reasons, 9% of women and 51% of men gave lust/pleasure reasons.

Two studies that quizzed respondents about their reasons for not having sex yielded similar findings. Peplau et al. (1977) found that for dating couples, the most common reason given for not having sex in the relationship was the woman's resistance (64% of men gave this reason), followed by fear of pregnancy (given by 46% of both sexes). In Carroll et al.'s (1985) study, the most frequent response given by women to the question "What would be your primary reason for refusing to have sexual intercourse with someone?" was "not enough love/commitment," and the most frequent reason given by men was "never neglect an opportunity."

In these studies, reasons given for *not* having sex seem to be in large part the flip side of reasons *for* having sex. However, both studies provided respondents only four reasons from which to choose, and in Carroll et al.'s (1985) study, the given alternatives all related to emotional involvement (e.g., did not know partner well enough, too soon in relationship, not enough love/commitment). Reasons for limiting one's sexual activity are many, and these include emotional (e.g., not enough love), practical (unavailability of partners) and avoidance (fear of AIDS or pregnancy) motives, most of which are not tapped by existing studies.

Also not examined in previous studies is the relationship of sexual orientation to motivations for sexual intercourse. Gay men and lesbians have, by definition, stepped out of traditional sex roles by engaging in sex with same-sex partners. However, most researchers have noted that women's feelings about sexual relationships differ from men's, regardless of their sexual orientation. Peplau and her colleagues (Peplau, 1981; Peplau & Gordon, 1983) report that lesbians place more value on emotional expressiveness in their close relationships than do gay men, and sex is more closely tied to love and emotional involvement for lesbians. Additionally, various studies have shown that lesbians, in comparison with gay men, are much less likely to have sex with strangers (or those for whom they felt no affection) and are more likely to be in a close committed relationship (e.g., Bell & Weinberg, 1978; Peplau & Gordon, 1983). Thus, it has been suggested that gender exerts a stronger influence on people's feelings about relationships than does sexual orientation (Basow, 1986; Peplau, 1981; Tavris & Offir, 1977).

This paper describes reasons for having and not having sex, and examines differences between heterosexual men and women, gay men, and lesbians. Where most previous studies have used open-ended responses, asking respondents for the one most important reason for having sex (e.g., Whitley, 1988), this study used a rating scale asking about reasons in general, thus enabling an analysis of the relative importance of different reasons.

In addition, a measure of frequency of sexual activity was gathered, in order to examine whether the importance of various reasons is related to actual behavior. This measure is significant because behavior does not always correspond to cognitions, attitudes, and feelings (as is seen, for example, in literature on attitude-behavior relations; e.g., Ajzen & Fishbein, 1977). Moreover, sexual behavior is influenced by a number of factors (in addition to individual desires), many of which depend on conditions not under personal control. For example, the availability of a suitable partner and the existence of dangerous consequences such as contracting AIDS might be factors that limit sexual activity despite the motivations of the individual.

Based on previous work on sex roles and sexual behavior, it was hypothesized that men and women would differ on the importance attached to emotional involvement as a prerequisite for sex, regardless of sexual orientation. It was also predicted that the importance attached to reasons for not having sex would differ with gender and sexual orientation, especially fear of pregnancy and fear of AIDS.

METHOD

Subjects, Materials and Procedure

In conjunction with a larger study of sexual behavior and AIDS risk, a systematic random sample of 4,000 households was drawn from a household directory covering the San Francisco City area. Respondents were mailed a questionnaire that contained a business reply envelope and cover letter soliciting their participation. Second and third mailings were sent to those who failed to respond to the first mailings. The questionnaire included a modified respondent selection table (Kish, 1965) that designated, randomly, the person in the household who was asked to fill out the questionnaire.

The questionnaire included sections focusing on sexual behavior, attitudes and beliefs. Measures included marital/relationship status, sexual orientation, and frequency of having sex in the past 30 days. A series of five-point scales asked respondents to indicate the importance of various reasons for having sex and not having sex (endpoints *not at all important* and *very important*; see Tables 1 and 2 for items).

Because not all addresses were legitimate, approximately 400 questionnaires were undeliverable. Completed questionnaires were received from 844 respondents, for a response rate of 24%. This response rate, although low, is not unusual for mail surveys, especially considering the length of the questionnaire (20 pages) and the sensitivity of the items.

Of the final sample, 80% were white, 10% Asian, 4% Hispanic, and 3% black. The sample included 445 women (48%) and 477 men (52%), with a median age of 35 (range 18–76). Seventy-six percent described themselves as exclusively or primarily heterosexual, with the remaining 24% bisexual or homosexual. Among the heterosexuals, 61% of the men and 54% of the women described

Table 1. Reasons for Having Sex by Gender and Sexual Orientation.

	Heterosexuals		Homosexuals		All Hetero-sexual	All Homo-sexual	All Men	All Women
	Men (n = 262)	Women (n = 318)	Men (n = 150)	Women (n = 52)				
For pure pleasure	3.7	3.1	3.3	3.1	3.2	3.2	3.5	3.1**
To express emotional closeness	3.5	3.6	3.3	3.5	3.6	3.4+	3.4	3.6**
To reproduce	1.2	1.2	.2	.2	1.2	.2***	.8	1.0
Because your partner wants to	2.8	2.5	2.3	2.2	2.7	2.3***	2.7	2.5*
To please your partner	3.2	2.7	2.7	2.6	2.9	2.6***	3.0	2.7***
For conquest	.6	.3	.8	.6	.5	.7***	.7	.4**
To relieve sexual tension	2.5	2.0	2.8	2.1	2.2	2.6***	2.6	2.0***

Note: 0 = not at all important; 4 = extremely important.
+p < .10. *p < .05. **p < .01. ***p < .001.

themselves as being in a primary relationship (married or living with a lover); these percentages were 36% for gay men and 56% for lesbians. The sample as a whole was well educated, with 70% college graduates or better.

RESULTS

Reasons for Having Sex

The seven reasons for having sex were analyzed with a two-factor multivariate analysis of variance, with between-subjects factors of gender and sexual orientation. Significant multivariate effects were followed with univariate tests. Because of unequal cell sizes, resulting in nonorthogonal main effects, a procedure (SPSS-X MANOVA) that adjusts each effect for the contribution of all other effects in the design was used. The MANOVA yielded significant main effects for gender ($F = 7.8$, $p < .001$) and sexual orientation ($F = 14.4$, $p < .001$). As seen in Table 1, men attached more importance to pleasure, pleasing one's partner, conquest, and relief of tension than did women, while women rated expressing emotional closeness more important than did men. Heterosexuals rated reproduction, emotional closeness, and pleasing one's partner as more important than did homosexuals, and homosexuals rated conquest

and relief of sexual tension more highly than did heterosexuals.

Reasons for Not Having Sex

The eight reasons for limiting sexual activity were analyzed with a multivariate analysis of variance with between-subjects factors of gender and sexual orientation, again adjusting each effect for the contribution of all other effects. Significant main effects were found for gender ($F = 7.4$, $p < 0.01$) and sexual orientation ($F = 15.9$, $p < .001$), as well as a significant gender X sexual orientation interaction ($F = 4.8$, $p < .001$). Table 2 presents the means for these items. Men rated fear of AIDS and fear of rejection as more important than did women, and women rated fear of pregnancy, lack of interest, and lack of enjoyment more highly than did men. Heterosexuals attached more importance to fear of sexually transmitted diseases (STDs), fear of pregnancy, and dislike of contraception than did homosexuals.

The significant gender X sexual orientation interaction appearing in the MANOVA resulted from two items: fear of AIDS and fear of pregnancy. Heterosexual men and women were equivalent in the importance attached to fear of AIDS as a barrier to sex, while among

Table 2. Reasons for Not Having Sex by Gender and Sexual Orientation.

	Heterosexuals		Homosexuals		All Hetero-sexual	All Homo-sexual	All Men	All Women
	Men (n = 262)	Women (n = 318)	Men (n = 150)	Women (n = 52)				
Fear of VD	2.3	2.1	1.8	1.5	2.1	1.7***	2.1	2.0
Fear of AIDS	2.6a,b	2.5b	3.1a	1.9b	2.5	2.8	2.8	2.4***
Fear of pregnancyb	1.7a	1.6a	.2b	.8c	1.7	.4***	1.2	1.5*
Don't like using contraceptive	1.0	.85	.6	.4	.9	.5***	.9	.8
Not interested	1.2	1.6	1.2	1.7	1.4	1.3	1.2	1.6**
No opportunity/can't find anyone I like enough	1.5	1.8	1.7	1.8	1.7	1.7	1.6	1.8
Fear of rejection	1.2	.8	1.4	1.2	1.0	1.3*	1.2	.9+
I don't enjoy sex	.4	.6	.3	.6	.5	.4	.4	.6**

Note: 0 = not at all important; 4 = extremely important. Means with different subscripts differ at the .05 level of significance by Scheffe tests.
aInteraction significant at $p < .01$.
bInteraction significant at $p < .05$.
+$p < .10$. *$p < .05$. **$p < .01$. ***$p < .001$.

homosexuals, men rated AIDS fear much more highly than did women. Male and female heterosexuals also rated fear of pregnancy approximately equally, but lesbians rated it as more important than did gay men.

Relationship of Reasons to Sexual Behavior

Multiple regression analyses were performed with frequency of sex in the last 30 days as the outcome variable. In these analyses, predictor variables were: the importance ratings for the seven reasons for having sex and the eight reasons for not having sex. A stepwise selection procedure selected only those predictors that contributed significantly to explained variability in frequency of sex. Analyses were performed for heterosexual men and women, gay men, and lesbians separately. In addition, analyses were performed separately for those in primary relationships, and not in relationships, because it was expected that different considerations would influence frequency of sexual activity for those with and without loved partners (for example, fear of AIDS and lack of opportunity).

The results of these analyses indicate that not all of these reasons are significantly related to actual frequency of sex. Among people in a primary relationship, pleasure was the strongest predictor of frequency, with fear of pregnancy and partner wishes adding a small amount of variance in men only. For people not in a primary relationship, sexual frequency was related to lack of opportunity or desirable partners, pleasure of the partner, and fear of AIDS and rejection.

DISCUSSION

The results of this study echo many of those from previous work on motivations for sex. In general, men attached more importance than did women to sexual pleasure, conquest, and the relief of sexual tension as reasons for sex, while women saw emotional closeness as more important than did men. These sex differences appeared in both heterosexuals and homosexuals, lending credence to the notion that men's and women's motivations for sex are different, no matter what the sex of their partners. Men also more strongly endorsed items (not described here) measuring

Table 3. Prediction of Frequency of Sex from Reasons for Having and Not Having Sex, by Gender, Sexual Orientation, and Relationship Status

In a Primary Relationship

Heterosexual Men (n = 143)		Heterosexual Women (n = 149)		Gay Men (n = 49)		Lesbian (n = 30)	
	Beta		*Beta*		*Beta*		*Beta*
Partner wants	.21**	Pleasure	.24**	Pleasure	.36**	Please partner	.49**
Not interested	−.17*						

Not in a Primary Relationship

Heterosexual Men (n = 82)		Heterosexual Women (n = 128)		Gay Men (n = 81)		Lesbian (n = 22)	
	Beta		*Beta*		*Beta*		*Beta*
Please partner	.28**	No opportunity	−.31****	Fear AIDS	−.32**	No opportunity	−.50*
No opportunity	−.28**	Pleasure	.19*	Pleasure	.29**		
		Please partner	.16*				

Note: "In Primary Relationship" includes respondents reporting themselves married or living with someone; "Not in Primary Relationship" includes separated, divorced, widowed, and never married respondents.
* R^2 change $p < .05$.
** R^2 change $p < .01$.
*** R^2 change $p < .001$.

attitudes toward casual sex (sex without love), and sex just "for fun." However, there were also differences between gays and straights independent of gender: conquest and relief of sexual tension were rated more highly by gay men and lesbians than by heterosexuals, and reproduction was rated much lower by homosexuals. Note, however, that for the most part, these differences are small. It is not the case that women think sexual pleasure is unimportant, or that men don't care about emotional closeness; rather, it would appear that these reasons are slightly different in level of importance.

The finding that men rated pleasing one's partner as more important than did women is somewhat paradoxical, given findings from other, earlier studies. For example, Christensen and Gregg (1970) report that 23% of the women, but only 2.5% of the men in their college sample, said that their first intercourse was the result of force, or a sense of obligation, rather than personal desire. Similarly, many respondents in Bard-

wick's (1971) interviews stated that they engaged in intercourse because they feared losing their partner, or because their partner wanted to. However, the 1970s was a decade in which women were encouraged to experience and enjoy their sexuality to the fullest, and men were encouraged to help them do so; thus, male performance in ensuring women's sexual pleasure was emphasized. The attitudes of the respondents in this study may then reflect this increased pressure on men to ensure that their female partners enjoy themselves. Note that the gender differences in these items were larger in heterosexuals than in homosexuals, and that the sexual orientation difference was larger in men than in women. Concern with partner's pleasure and desire seems then to be concentrated in heterosexual couples.

Gender differences in reasons for not having sex also followed sex-role differentiations. Men saw fear of rejection as a more important obstacle to sex than did women, in accordance with cultural scripts that mandate

113

that men initiate sexual activity and women limit it by saying no (e.g., DeLamater, 1987; Peplau et al., 1977). Again, this difference was larger in heterosexuals than in homosexuals, among whom initiation/rejection roles are not gender-specific. Women indicated lack of interest and enjoyment as more important reasons than did men, although the means for all groups were low; this finding (at least superficially) conforms to the usually-discredited stereotype of women having a weaker sex drive than men (Basow, 1986).

Pregnancy and contraception issues were more important in avoiding sex for heterosexuals; this is an unsurprising finding, given that only heterosexual sex can lead to pregnancy. Fear of AIDS as a motivation for avoiding sex was, as expected, particularly high in gay men and low in lesbians, the groups at highest and lowest risk for contracting AIDS through sexual behavior. Interestingly, fear of STDs was rated as more important by heterosexuals than by homosexuals. Lesbians may (correctly) assume themselves to be at low risk for contracting STDs, and gay men may be experienced and/or knowledgeable enough about STDs (common in San Francisco's gay community) to be less fearful.

The various reasons for having and limiting sex were related to actual frequency of sex differently, depending upon the gender and relationship status of the respondent. Pleasure was the major predictor of frequency among those in primary relationships, while for single people, lack of opportunity was the most important predictor. Although some differences were found by gender and sexual orientation in the reasons most predictive of sexual frequency, relationship status was the more striking mediator. For those in steady relationships, many of the barriers to sexual activity experienced by single people (no available partners, fear of rejection, fear of AIDS) are either nonexistent or much less salient. The amount of variance in sexual fre-

quency explained by reasons, although small in both "attached" and "unattached" respondents, is larger for singles ($R^2 = .18$) than for those in relationships ($R^2 = .09$; $Z = .10$, two-tailed), suggesting that sexual frequency for people in primary relationships is influenced greatly by factors unique to a partnered situation.

Despite the prevalence of a variety of significant findings, several cautionary remarks are also warranted. For example, it should be noted that the sampling methodology of this study leads to serious problems of generalizability. Most existing studies on motivations for sex have used college students as subjects, a group that may be atypical with regard to sex, due to their youth and social situation. Thus, an attempt was made in this study to recruit a more representative sample, but this was compromised by a low response rate (a problem inherent in mail surveys). Additionally, San Francisco is not a typical city, especially in regard to AIDS, and data from this study may not accurately reflect the sexual behavior of people in other parts of the country.

To summarize, the findings of this study point up several differences between men and women, gay and straight, in motivations for engaging in or avoiding sex. Reasons for having and not having sex may be emotional (e.g., expressing closeness, fear of rejection) or practical (e.g., to reproduce, fear of AIDS or pregnancy). In general, sex differences in this study were larger between heterosexual men and women than between gay men and lesbians, and larger between gay and straight men than between lesbians and straight women, suggesting that they are more concentrated in cross-sex relationships. Obviously, traditional sex roles are blurred in gay and lesbian relationships (Peplau, 1981) (and necessarily so), since cultural sex-role scripts are based on relationships between men and women.

Some of the emotional aspects of these roles, however, seem to persist in all types of relationships: Gender differences, when found, appeared in both straights and gays, lending credence to the notion that "one's experience and feelings during a sexual interlude seem to have less to do with whether one is gay or straight than with whether one is a man or a woman" (Tavris & Offir, 1977, p.72). However, none of these differences was large, and many were not significant predictors of actual frequency of sexual activity. Therefore, perhaps we should concentrate on the many similarities in motivations among the groups, rather than on their small differences.

REFERENCES

Ajzen, I., & Fishbein, M. (1977). Attitude-behavior relations: A theoretical analysis and review of empirical research. *Psychological Bulletin*, 84, 888–918.

Bardwick, J.M. (1971). *Psychology of women: A study of bio-cultural conflicts*. New York: Harper & Row.

Basow, S. A. (1986). *Gender stereotypes: Traditions and alternatives*. Monterey, CA: Brooks/Cole.

Bell, A. P., & Weinberg, M. S. (1978). *Homosexualities: A study of diversity among men and women*. New York: Simon and Schuster.

Bem, S. L. (1981). Gender schema theory: A cognitive account of sex typing. *Psychological Bulletin*, 88, 354–364.

Carroll, J. L., Volk, K. D., & Hyde, J. S. (1985). Differences between males and females in motives for engaging in sexual intercourse. *Archives of Sexual Behavior*, 14, 131–139.

Christenson, H. T., & Gregg, C. F. (1970). Changing sex norms in America and Scandinavia. *Journal of Marriage and the Family*, 32, 616–627.

DeLamater, J. (1987). Gender differences in sexual scenarios. In K. Kelley (Ed.), *Females, Males, and Sexuality*. Albany: SUNY Press.

DeLamater, J. D., & MacCorquodale, P. (1979). *Premarital sexuality: Attitudes, relationships, behaviors*. Madison, WI: University of Wisconsin Press.

Gagnon, J. H., & Simon, W. (1973). *Sexual conduct: The social sources of human sexuality*. Chicago: Aldine.

Hite, S. (1976). *The Hite report*. New York: MacMillan.

Kish, L. (1965). *Survey Sampling*. New York: John Wiley.

Laws, J. L., & Schwartz, P. (1977). *Sexual scripts: The social construction of female sexuality*. Hinsdale, IL: Dryden Press.

Peplau, L. A. (1981). What homosexuals want in relationships. *Psychology Today*, 15(3), 28–37.

Peplau, L. A., & Gordon, S. L. (1983). The intimate relationships of lesbians and gay men. In E. R. Allgeir & N. B. McCormick (Eds.), *Changing boundaries: Gender roles and sexual behavior*. Palo Alto, CA: Mayfield.

Peplau, L. A., Rubin, Z., & Hill, C. T. (1977). Sexual intimacy in dating relationships. *Journal of Social Issues*, 33(2), 86–109.

Tavris, C., & Offir, C. (1977). *The longest war: Sex differences in perspective*. New York: Harcourt Brace Jovanovich.

Whitley, B. E. (1988, August). College students' reasons for sexual intercourse: A sex role perspective. Paper presented at the 96th Annual Meeting of the American Psychological Association, Atlanta.

The Sexual Experience and Marital Adjustment of Genitally Circumcised and Infibulated Females in the Sudan

Hanny Lightfoot-Klein, M.A.

In a study conducted over a 5-year period, the author interviewed over 300 Sudanese women and 100 Sudanese men on the sexual experience of circumcised and infibulated women. Sudanese circumcision involves excision of the clitoris, the labia minora and the inner layers of the labia majora, and fusion or infibulation of the bilateral wound. The findings of this study indicate that sexual desire, pleasure, and orgasm are experienced by the majority of women who have been subjected to this extreme sexual mutilation, in spite of their also being culturally bound to hide these experiences. These findings also seriously question the importance of the clitoris as an organ that must be stimulated in order to produce female orgasm, as is often maintained in Western sexological literature.

BACKGROUND

Pharaonic circumcision in the Nile Valley is as old as recorded history. To this date, it distinguishes "decent" and respectable women from unprotected prostitutes and slaves, and it carries with it the only honorable, dignified, and protected status that is possible for a woman there. Like other Arab cultures, Sudanese society is characteristically patriarchial and patrilineal. In such a society, an unmarried woman has virtually no rights, no status in the society, and severely limited, if any, economic recourse. Without circumcision, a girl can not marry and is thereby unable to fulfill her intended role, i.e., to produce legitimate sons to carry on her husband's patrilineage.

The greatest measure of a family's honor is the sexual purity of its women. Any transgression on the part of the woman disgraces the whole family, and only the most extreme measures will restore this honor. This may take the form of divorce, casting the woman out, or putting her to death.

Under British colonial occupation, several unsuccessful attempts were made to abolish Pharaonic circumcision. It has since been declared illegal under a Sudanese law, with the inception of an independent state in 1956. However, this law has never been implemented.

The northern, Islamic part of Sudan consists largely of desert areas. Sudan is considered to be the second least developed country in the world. Only Chad, bordering it to the west, is more acutely poverty-stricken, barren, bleak, disease-ridden, and impervious to repeated attempts at technological development. In the entire country, there are virtually no paved roads, and travel modes are extremely primitive and arduous. Except in the capital, Khartoum, Sudan is still largely untouched by Western influences. The way of life is profoundly traditional and continues to be ruled by age-old custom. Pharaonic circumcision is practiced virtually without exception, even among the educated class in the capital, to this day. It is celebrated with great festivity by the families, and the day of

This article first appeared in *The Journal of Sex Research* (1989) 26: 375–392. Published with permission of The Journal of Sex Research, a publication of The Society for the Scientific Study of Sex.

circumcision is considered to be the most important day in a woman's life, far more important than her wedding day.

METHODOLOGY

The bulk of the body of knowledge discussed herein was obtained by the author during three separate six-month overland journeys through the Sudan, within a time span of five years. During this period, she traveled alone among the native population and at every opportunity that presented itself discussed the practice of female circumcision with the people she got to know. Many of these interviews were arranged by letters of introduction obtained along the way. The total number of people interviewed in this fashion came to more than 100 men and more than 300 women. These people came from all walks of life. Representative among them were gynecologists, pediatricians, psychiatrists, nurses, midwives, pharmacists, paramedics, teachers, college professors, college and high school students, obstetrical patients, mothers of pediatric patients, brides, bridegrooms, homemakers, merchants, historians, religious leaders, grandmothers, village women and men.

Among those people highly sympathetic to the author's research was the director of a small gynecological hospital, Dr. Salah Abu Bakr, who put his entire staff, his patients, the use of a private room and two excellent translators at her disposal. The translators were Sudanese nurses who had been trained in London. Both were pharaonically circumcised, and both carried on a flourishing circumcision practice on the side, as did all other nurses and midwives at the hospital. They were able to translate not only linguistically but could interpret the finer nuances of what took place in the interviews. The major part of the information that was obtained on sexual intercourse and orgasm came from the series of interviews conducted at this hospital, and also at Ahfat College and Khartoom University, among students, professors and other intellectuals that the author befriended. This more formalized project included 97 women and 34 men.

Discussing the subject with intellectual friends was relatively easy since there is no taboo regarding an exchange of information on the subject between women, nor is there one between Sudanese men and a woman from a Western culture. Both sexes among this group seemed to welcome the opportunity to discuss a subject that generally does not bear discussion.

The hospital staff and patient body interviewed consisted mostly of women with little or no education. When questioned, these women usually professed a total absence of sexual desire and sexual enjoyment. However, when it became evident to the author that she was receiving "institutional answers" to her questions, she consulted with the translators about how to overcome this.

The translators suggested that the questions on sexual desire and enjoyment be preceded by a question on whether the woman employed the "smoke ceremony." (The significance of this will be explained later in this paper.) This almost invariably solved the problem. Once a woman had admitted to using the ceremony, which nearly all did, and when it became evident that the author understood its significance, communication tended to flow and was enjoyed by all four participants in the interview. The author's expressed willingness to answer whatever questions interviewees might have about her own culture and personal experiences was also found to be extremely disarming and tended to promote an animated exchange of information. Their interest rarely, if ever, extended beyond whether the author herself was circumcised or not. The revelation that neither she, nor her daughters, nor any of the women of her family were circumcised was virtually incomprehensible to them. At the end of each hospital interview, there was a three-way conference between the author and the Sudanese nurse-translators regarding the validity of the information obtained. It did not, in essence, differ from the information obtained from other sources.

FINDINGS

Pharaonic circumcision of girls, as it is practiced in Sudan, involves the excision of the clitoris, the labia minora and the inner, fleshy layers of the labia majora. The remaining outer edges of the labia majora are then brought together so that when the wound has healed they are fused so as to leave only a pinhole-sized opening. The resultant infibulation is, in effect, an artificially created chastity belt of thick, fibrous scar tissue. Urination and menstruation must thereafter be accomplished through this remaining pinhole-sized aperture.

This surgical procedure has for thousands of years been performed ritually but is, at present, often performed routinely in a clinic-like setting in the urban centers on all small girls, most frequently between the ages of 4 and 8, regardless of their social standing in the society. In the outlying areas, the procedures are conducted in the age-old fashion, by medically untrained midwives, without anesthesia or antiseptic. The struggling child is simply held immobile throughout the operation, and it is obvious that under such conditions the likelihood of hemorrhage, infection, trauma to adjacent structures, shock from pain, urinary retention due to sepsis, edema or scarring, and psychic trauma is extremely high.

The infibulation, even among girls who are circumcised by trained midwives or nurses in a clinic-like setting, under only slightly more antiseptic conditions with a locally injected analgesic to mitigate the pain, presents tremendous health problems to the girl later on in life, if she survives the initial trauma of the operation. Various degrees and types of urinary obstruction are a frequent result of infibulation, and concomitant urinary tract infections are very common in pharaonically circumcised women (Abdallah, 1982; Cook, 1979; Dareer, 1983; Huber, 1969; Laycock, 1950; Sami, 1986; Shandall, 1967; Verzin, 1975).

The onset of menstruation generally creates a tremendous problem for the girl as the vaginal aperture is inadequate for menstrual flow, and an infibulated virgin suffers protracted and painful periods of menstruation, with a great deal of blockage, retention and buildup of clots behind the infibulation. Adolescence is not a happy time for the Sudanese girl, and depression is said by doctors to be common at this time. Girls are often married soon after menstruation commences.

Sudan, as an Afro-Arab Islamic culture, measures the all-important honor of its families largely by the virtue and chastity of its women. Women are assumed to be (by nature) sexually voracious, promiscuous and unbridled creatures, morally too weak to be entrusted with the sacred honor of the family. Pharaonic circumcision is believed to insure this honor by not only decreasing an excessive sexual sensitivity in them but by considerably dampening their sex drive. Furthermore, the actual physical barrier of the infibulation is believed to prevent rape. In small girls at least, this is not always the case, as they are sometimes brought into medical installations for repair of tears resulting from sexual assault. Another widely held belief, even among the educated, is that if the clitoris is not cropped in a young girl, it will grow to enormous size and dangle between the legs, like a man's penis, a belief which carries with it great revulsion. Without circumcision, a girl is simply not marriageable, and the tighter her infibulation, the higher the bride price that can be obtained.

The role of the woman in the society is one of total submission to the man, and her behavior must at all times reflect extreme modesty, unassailable chastity, and a virtual withdrawal from the world outside of the home. Even when educated women in the metropolitan areas now occasionally hold jobs, they are not able to go out into society except under the strictest supervision of either their husbands or some other dominant family member.

Marriages are arranged by the families, although a certain amount of leeway is presently allowed among the more modern and educated class, so that a young man may decide for himself which girl he wishes to marry. And if his choice is an acceptable one to both families, the arrangements are then made. Even without this, arranged marriages are often remarkably successful, as measured by the satisfaction expressed by both partners. One of the main conditions for the girl's happiness is that she is not located away from her extended family (or clan) by marriage. In other words, she remains in a familiar and supportive environment.

Both the bridegroom and the bride are required to play rigidly assigned roles at the marriage ceremony. He must appear relaxed, smiling, supremely confident, totally in control, while she must be unsmiling and present the abjectly submissive picture of maidenly modesty. His role is the more difficult to maintain because it masks an anxiety that he may not be able to penetrate her infibulation, that he will cause her to hemorrhage in the attempt (and perhaps even see her die), or that his anxiety will cause erectile dysfunction, which would be so devastating to his manhood that he may actually commit suicide as a consequence.

Her withdrawn, unresponsive expression is far closer to the truth and hides an abject terror of what is in store for her. The penetration of the bride's infibulation takes anywhere from 3 or 4 days to several months. Some men are unable to penetrate their wives at all (in my study over 15%),

and the task is often accomplished by a midwife under conditions of great secrecy, since this reflects negatively on the man's potency. Some who are unable to penetrate their wives manage to get them pregnant in spite of the infibulation, and the woman's vaginal passage is then cut open to allow birth to take place. A great deal of marital anal intercourse takes place in cases where the wife can not be penetrated—quite logically in a culture where homosexual anal intercourse is a commonly accepted premarital recourse among men—but this is not readily discussed. Those men who do manage to penetrate their wives do so often, or perhaps always, with the help of the "little knife." This creates a tear which they gradually rip more and more until the opening is sufficient to admit the penis. In some women, the scar tissue is so hardened and overgrown with keloidal formations that it can only be cut with very strong surgical scissors, as is reported by doctors who relate cases where they broke scalpels in the attempt.

Clearly, the Sudanese bride undergoes conditions of tremendous pain, as well as physical and psychic trauma. These were always readily spoken of by women, generally with a great deal of easily expressed affect, when they were speaking to a female interviewer. Paradoxically, most women related that their husbands were considerate and loving throughout the ordeal, and that they are sensitive and tender lovers. A far smaller number of women said that their husbands had been brutal.

Sudanese couples tend to bond quite strongly, by and large, in spite of the trauma the woman undergoes. Most women give the appearance of being very proud of their husbands. They often express great satisfaction with their marriages and their lives. Nonetheless, when they are asked whether they would have preferred to have been men, rather than women, they say without any exception that if only Allah had willed it, they would very much have preferred to have been created men.

The Sudanese, in general, are a remarkably open, friendly, peaceable, mutually supportive, generous, deeply devout people, who, to the Western mind, are inexplicably happy in their desperately poor, monotonously barren, harsh and bleakly desertized land. Their emotional lives, from childhood on, are quite remarkably rich, as Sudanese psychiatrists will also verify, and loving relationships are plentiful in their widely extended families. They are deeply convinced of the infinite goodness and mercy of Allah, and they practice the obligations imposed by their religion fervently and with great joy. The rule of custom is powerful and all-pervading and is accepted by the populace without question.

The rigidly defined roles for men and women instill the belief that in order to fulfill the masculine role, the bridegroom must inflict pain, and the woman in her role must suffer it. With this in mind, it is not inconsistent for a strong bonding to take place, in spite of the pain that is inflicted on a bride by her bridegroom, since it is seen as their lot in life. In talking about this part of their marital lives, women often said that their penetration was terrible, agonizingly painful, and frequently resulted in hemorrhage or prolonged infection, but that when it was finally over, the wife forgave her husband, and they were happy together.

Although the consequences of Pharaonic circumcision render many women sterile, it is far more common for them to give birth to a large number of children. Since no infibulated woman, even after she has been penetrated for sexual intercourse, can dilate the necessary 10 centimeters to permit birth to take place, her infibulation scar must be cut anteriorly before the baby can be expelled. The necessary incision generally measures 2 ½–3 inches and is repaired after birth occurs.

In recent years, a curious modification of this procedure has occurred. Instead of the vaginal opening being resutured to the size that it was before the infibulation was incised for birth to take place, women are now being resewn to a pinhole-sized opening. This "repair" is called "recircumcision." The practice was unknown in Sudan only 50 years ago, and among the interviewed women who were over 65 years of age, it has never been performed. The author assumes that the practice is a bastardization of the Western vaginal tuck procedure, since it was first practiced by educated upper-class women with exposure to the West and has gradually filtered down from the capital into more and more remote areas and to women who have little or no education (Dareer, 1982, p. 58).

Although Dareer (1982), a Sudanese researcher who interviewed an extensive cross-section of the Sudanese population, also reports that it is now performed on the greater majority of Sudanese women, it is difficult to get accurate information on the real impetus behind it. Midwives, who profitably tout and perform the procedure, tend to say that it is men who pay generously for it, and women concur that it is all done for the pleasure of the man. Some educated women, however, frankly admit that the procedure makes the most of what is left of their damaged genital musculature and facilitates their own pleasure as well, once the pain of the then-necessary penetration is over. There is also the characteristically Sudanese notion of renewable virginity and a reassertion of the husband's role of male dominance which requires him to inflict pain on his bride. Behind it all, there is the irrefutable fact that without a tight repair, the condition of the woman's sex organs (sooner or later) makes her an ostensibly inadequate sex partner. This is a source of great anxiety to all women, as multiple marriage is permitted to the Islamic man, and a wife fears having to share with another wife not only her husband, but also his very limited economic resources. The reconstitution of a pinhole-sized vaginal opening is thought to insure the wife's position by providing her husband with a "virginal" vagina once more. After a six-week period of abstinence following birth prescribed by the religion, the women submits once more to a period of repenetration.

Circumcised women, in general, and uneducated village women, in particular, give every indication (also often reported by non-Sudanese men) of being enviably intact in terms of sexual "lustiness," in spite of their mutilation, quite contrary to the intent of circumcision to reduce their sexual drive. Sudanese women are culturally bound to hide their "lustiness," and so they skillfully navigate between the demands of custom and their husbands and the demands of their own sexuality. They do so by means of a series of maneuvers and sex signals. Custom places severe penalties on a woman's initiation or even show of interest in sexual intercourse. However, the use of the "smoke ceremony" is known to every Sudanese woman, and to every Sudanese man as well. Practically every woman uses this ceremony. She signals her desire and receptivity by permeating her skin with the smoke of burning spices, sandalwood, frankincense and myrrh. She squats naked over the embers, wrapped in a tentlike robe, so that her skin absorbs the volatile oils, and afterwards rubs generous quantities of fat into her skin to fix them. Moorehead (1962, p. 234) quotes Baker (the 19th-Century explorer) as commenting that he could smell a woman who had performed this ceremony a hundred yards away, and my own experiences bear this out.

The intent of the signal is clearly understood by every Sudanese husband, and he acts upon it with no verbalization or other act of agreement being needed. The wife can now behave in a way that totally negates her intent. She can act out the role of the ravaged one while he acts out the role of the ravisher, or she can be dutifully acquiescent to her husband's sexual demands while giving the appearance of having no interest or pleasure whatsoever herself.

Other covert sexual initiatives are also permitted. I was told by several women that if their husbands did not respond to their signals, or if the sexual activity was desired by them during the night, they would bang pots and pans around to wake their husbands. After this had had the desired effect, the husband would be able to resume his sleep.

Custom decrees that a Sudanese woman remain totally passive during the sex act. She must lie like a block of wood and participate in no way whatsoever. She must exhibit this unnatural immobility, for her being sexually active would be regarded as "being like an animal." Only such immobility will enable her to manifest the demands of modesty imposed on her.

If the woman has an orgasm she hides it, and if she is unable to control the intensity of her reaction, she denies that it was brought on as sexual ecstacy. One woman, who told me she had frequent, intense orgasms, commented that she "moved about a great deal during intercourse" and that she had given her husband to understand that this was the case because she liked to change position frequently.

Even though women generally do not admit to their husbands that they experience sexual pleasure and orgasm (in spite of the fact that some men tell them they would like them to do so), most men say they know when their wife's orgasm takes place. Nonetheless, the wife's outright initiation of or active participation in the sex act is grounds for immediate and incontestable divorce. Many women are able to relate at least one case where they know of such an outcome. Thus, the possibility is much feared. A woman who gives herself away by showing interest and pleasure openly is condemned as being licentious, lewd, and of easy virtue, and she is dealt with accordingly.

How is orgasm possible at all under such conditions? Contrary to expectations, nearly 90% of all women interviewed said that they experienced orgasm (climax) or had at various periods of their marriage experienced it. Frequency ranged from always to rarely. Some women said that they had intense, prolonged orgasms, and this was verified by their happy and highly animated demeanor as they described it. Other women said that their orgasms were weak or difficult to achieve. Frequently, intractable pain, a residual of the circumcision, prevented orgasm altogether. Sometimes, anorgasmia was the probable result of an unhappy marriage. Among the anorgasmic women, some were educated upper-class women who had become aware of orgasmic uncircumcised women in other parts of the world. They were full of rage at what had been done to them. They said that, although they loved their husbands as human beings, they could feel no sexual desire for them or any other man.

Sudanese men of the upper strata who have had sexual experiences with Western women (or with women from African countries where less drastic or no circumcision procedures are practiced) are of the opinion that "Sudanese women lose a lot." They concur that orgasm in Sudanese women, as they perceive it, is weaker, less frequent, and takes longer to elicit. The delay in arousal time is believed by Bakr (1982) to be the result of the vulval nerve destruction. The perception that orgasm occurs less frequently and is less intense must, however, be interpreted cautiously in the context of the culture in which it occurs, where women need to hide their sexual response. While the orgasm of a woman may be detected by her partner, the purity of the experience itself is subjective, and its intensity can be perceived only by the woman herself.

Among doctors interviewed, several reported having had patients, especially among the educated, who expressed the fear that they were not sexually adequate for their husband's needs. Many of these women paradoxically suffered guilt that they were not able to function better sexually. It is a point of honor for men to have a child born within a year of marriage. Gynecologists report that there is an increasing number of women who come to the clinics in the capital with sexual and marital problems related to fertility. They are concerned with their lack of sensation and response and are afraid that this will prevent them from becoming pregnant. They are aware, in any event, that "things are not as they should be."

The subject of orgasm among circumcised African women has been discussed in a number of studies (Karim & Ammar, 1965; Megafu, 1983; Shandall, 1967). Although only 27% of Dareer's 2,375 Sudanese women (1982, p. 48) admitted to having "sexual pleasure," Assaad's study (1982) in Egypt found that 94% of the 54 circumcised women interviewed by her reported that they enjoyed sex and were happy with their husbands. Giorgis (1981, p. 31) comments that the correlation between female circumcision and *lack* of sexual satisfaction has been grossly exaggerated. She quotes Verzin (1975, p. 167) as a representative of the *misconceptions* that are common on this score: "Lack of sexual gratification appears to be common, the absence of the clitoris probably playing a part in this. The information is never volunteered and very rarely admitted. A blank expression, an enigmatic smile or at most an evasive reply towards a curious question, and this is irrespective of color, creed or sex of the questioner. In such a society, the woman is regarded as a vassal for man's pleasure and subsequently the bearer of his offspring. It is probable that many are not even aware that there should be reciprocal enjoyment."

The behavior described herein is typical of women who hide their sexual enjoyment, especially from a male interviewer. Sami (1986), in discussing his study of female circumcision in Sudan, also complains that "people's reluctance to discuss the subject makes the task of collecting reliable information extremely difficult."

My own facility in collecting more accurate data came about through the use of a number of devices. I preceded my question on sexual enjoyment with the question on whether a woman used the smoke and oil ceremony. She nearly always readily admitted to this, and once it had become clear that I understood its meaning, communication between us generally became easy, especially when I offered to reciprocate by answering whatever questions she had about my own personal life. This offer, coming from a woman who obviously lived a different (and no doubt fascinating) lifestyle to the Sudanese nearly always proved to be irresistible. Sudanese women also appeared to feel that I posed no threat.

I suggest, therefore, that the differences in findings of the various studies are, in part, a function of the differences in the interview situations. Primarily, the interviewer's gender, approach, and ease with which sexual matters could be discussed all play a part.

Sudanese psychiatrists theorized that the various crippling effects of Pharaonic circumcision can be counteracted only by an unusually strong bonding between marriage partners. In the opinion of most, the sexual response of Sudanese women is largely nothing more than a kind of stereotypic response. However, Sudanese psychiatrists (who are male) also admit they are in a poor position to judge because of their gender and because female patients are rarely brought to them. They do think, however, that since orgasm entails both cerebral as well as muscular responses, and involves also respiratory and vascular reactions, the physiological phenomena are present but damaged or lessened in circumcised women. In compensation, they suggest that the cerebral component may be heightened.

In the literature, orgasm in clitoridectomized females is mentioned by Money et al. (1955) and by Verkauf (1975). Megafu (1983) observed that, whereas the clitoris tends to be reported as the most erotically sensitive organ in uncircumcised women, other sensitive parts of the body, such as the labia minora, the breasts and the lips take over this erotic function in clitoridectomized females. Perhaps as Otto (1988) suggests, women are capable of experiencing 7 distinct types of orgasm: the clitoral, vaginal/cervical, breast, oral, G-spot, anal and mental orgasm. Similarly, Ogden (1988) reports on extragenital stimulation, emotional involvement and spiritual connection in easily orgasmic women, whereas orgasms have also long been reported by practitioners of tantric yoga.

When asked to name the most sensitive parts of their body, Sudanese women tended to name their lips, neck, breasts, bellies, thighs or hips. The genitalia were never spontaneously mentioned. This is due, at least in part, to the fact that a virtuous and modest Sudanese woman is required to never speak of that part of her body. When the genitalia were addressed directly by the question "What about the area of your scar?," and following that, "What about inside?," erogeneity of one or the other (or of both areas) was admitted, or even glowingly described by many women. Others had little or no erogeneity and said things like: "With the Pharaonic, you can not really feel your man. Everything is closed," or more drastically: "It is as if your husband comes with a stick to leather."

In the interviews, women were able to talk freely and lucidly about their orgasms. To the question: "How often do you experience orgasm?" (to be used interchangeably here with "climax," which was more readily understood), the following responses were representative:

> "We have intercourse every two or three days. I never have orgasm during the first time, even though my husband maintains an erection for 45 minutes or an hour. When we have intercourse a second time, about an hour later, I am able to reach orgasm."

> "With my first husband, I almost never had any pleasure, and I had orgasm only a handful of times over the years. It was an arranged marriage, and although he was a kind man and good to me, I did not have any passion for him. My second marriage is a love match and I always have strong orgasm with him, except on rare occasions, when I am too tired or one of the children is sick."

> "When I was younger, I used to have it happen 9 times out of 10. Now there are so many children and grandchildren in the house that we can have intercourse only every second or third week. We have so little privacy, and we have to be very quiet about it. Also, I have had frequent problems with urinary infections. When we have intercourse, I am able to come to orgasm once in a while now, perhaps 1 time in 10."

> "I have never had any pleasure from my husband. I try to avoid sex with him whenever I can. It is not that he is brutal or that we do not love one another. It would be the same no matter whom I was married to. The only thing I ever feel there is pain. I am happy when he lets me go to sleep and does not bother me."

Descriptions of orgasm were clearly recognizable and often quite vivid.

> "I feel as if I am trembling in my belly. It feels like shock going around my body, very sweet and pleasurable. When it finishes, I feel as if I would faint."

> "All my body begins to tingle. Then I have a shock to my pelvis and my legs. It gets very tight in my vagina. I have a tremendous feeling of pleasure, and I can not move at all. I seem to be flying far, far up. Then my whole body relaxes and I go completely limp."

> "I feel as if I am losing all consciousness, and I love him most intensely at that moment. I tremble all over. My vagina contracts strongly and I have a feeling of great joy. Then I relax all over, and I am so happy to be alive and to be married to my husband."

> "I feel shivery and want to swallow him inside my body. Then a very sweet feeling spreads all over my entire body, and I feel as if I am melting. I float higher and higher, far, far away. Then I drift off to sleep."

> "I feel as if I am losing all consciousness, it is such a strong feeling. I hold my husband very, very tightly, and if the baby fell out of the bed, I would not be able to pick it up."

A primary factor in orgasm appears to be the bonding between couples. This is dramatically illustrated by the accounts given by a few women who have been married twice and whose experiences in the two separate marriages have been significantly different. Some of these histories are presented herein.

History #1:

This 24-year-old practical nurse comes from a village in western Sudan, where circumcision practices are at their most extreme. She has had 5 years of education. Her Pharaonic circumcision was performed at the age of 4, and she remembers very little of the experience except that she cried a great deal. However, she began to menstruate at the age of 12, and her periods were consistently very difficult and painful for ten days each month until her arranged marriage at 16.

In the village where she lived, custom demanded that the bridegroom penetrate his bride in one night, and a great deal of peer pressure was placed on him. The experience was so brutal that she was terrified of him for half a year afterward. Then, as he was quite gentle with her following this initial trauma, she adapted to a degree. She was never able to enjoy sex with this husband, however, and continually implored her family to arrange a divorce for her. This was done after the birth of a son, when she was 17. She was "recircumcised" to make her ready for a second marriage, but this time a 1–2 centimeter opening was left.

She was remarried to a man she had loved since childhood. There was only one day of moderate pain in repenetrating her. He is patient and gentle, she says, and she feels secure and loved with him. Also, she has a strong orgasm with him about one-third of the time. She enjoys being kissed and has a highly pleasurable feeling of "shock" in her lips. She also enjoys having her scar stroked. The strongest sensation is experienced at the contact of his penis with her cervix, and her orgasm, when it occurs, is precipitated by his ejaculation. She has strong vaginal pulsations and says she feels as if she were under sedation. Orgasm occurs after about 20 minutes of intercourse. The other two-thirds of the time she is unable to climax, even when intercourse is prolonged or repeated. Her body is simply too tired on these occasions, she states. Still, she feels happy and relaxed afterwards just from the contact with his body. There is "a slight feeling of disappointment," but she realizes that "it has to be that way," that her body "simply can not respond more often than it does."

Even though communication is very open between her and her husband, and he cares deeply about keeping her sexually happy (and happy in all other ways), she is too shy to initiate intercourse directly. She has been strongly indoctrinated that this would be extremely shameful, and so she resorts to the use of smoke and perfumed oil when she wants to let him know that she is receptive.

Unfortunately, this woman has recently been forced to separate from her husband because of an intractable conflict with her mother-in-law. She now lives with her own family again, and she and her husband miss one another acutely. They meet at her sister's house, but no privacy is possible there. Her mother-in-law is adamant that her husband divorce her, but he has refused to do this so far.

History #2:

This 32-year-old practical nurse has had 9 years of education. Her Pharaonic circumcision occurred at the age of twelve and was performed with the use of local analgesic by a medically trained midwife in the capital. She says that she was able to urinate almost immediately after the operation, a fairly unusual occurrence (due to the rawness of the wounded area), and that she remembers only two hours of severe pain after the operation. She resumed her normal activities after 10 days.

She began to menstruate at 16 and suffered a great deal of pain from obstruction of her menstrual flow until she was married at 17. On the fourth day of her marriage, her husband succeeded in creating a tear in her infibulation which bled profusely. Two days later, he enlarged this tear, which by that time bled so much that she had to be taken to a dispensary for treatment. The bleeding was stopped, but her husband was told to continue in his attempt to penetrate her so that she would not heal shut again. After two more weeks, he succeeded in penetrating her completely, and after 15 more days of pain, she said, "Things were normal."

She did not love this husband. He was a distant relative, and the marriage had been arranged without her consent. He drank a great deal (an extremely rare occurrence among Islamic men) and was often abusive. She did not enjoy sexual relations with him because he was rough and entered her without any preparation. He was involved in subversive politics and spent much of the ten years that she was married to him as a political prisoner. Finally, he left Sudan for Saudi

Arabia and was not permitted to return. Subsequently, her family obtained a divorce for her. She did not miss him at all, she says. She feels that he had treated her very badly.

Her marriage to her present husband took place a few months after her divorce. As is customary with every new marriage, she was once more infibulated. Penetration took two months to achieve, and her husband was patient, loving, considerate and supportive throughout. She says that she is extremely happy in this marriage. They love one another passionately, and she has an extremely enjoyable sex life. She absolutely glows with happiness as she speaks about it. She also has strong orgasm every time they have intercourse, and her breasts, mouth, inner thighs, and scar area are very sensitive. Greatest sensitivity is inside her vagina. She never directly initiates intercourse but signals receptivity almost every night with smoke and perfumed oil.

History #3:

This 39-year-old medically trained midwife has had seven years of education. She was circumcised at the age of 3. She remembers nothing about the event but has been told that she bled massively. This may be the reason that her outer labia were left intact. Her clitoris and inner labia were excised and she was infibulated to a pin-hole. She had the "usual difficulties with menstruation" from its onset at the age of 12 until her first delivery.

She was married at 13. Her husband was unable to penetrate her and only after three years succeeded in impregnating her. When she gave birth, her infibulation was cut open by the midwife. She loved her husband very much. The sexual adjustment between them was excellent, she recalls wistfully. They had intercourse almost daily, and she consistently enjoyed strong orgasm with him. The marriage lasted for 20 years. Then economic pressures forced him to take a job

in Saudi Arabia, and there he simply disappeared without a trace. After two years, and a fruitless search for him, her family divorced her from him through the courts. She continued to wait for him, but he was never heard from again and is presumed to have died.

Her husband had cared very much about her feelings and her sexual happiness. She had strong sensation inside her vagina, and also some sensation in the area of her scar, although it was less there because of the circumcision, but it was still pleasant. Whereas he never gave her a chance to initiate sex because he wanted her constantly, she felt so secure with him that she might possibly have done so. She laughed happily as she recalled this. She hardly ever refused his advances, only when she was really sick. She played her role of being shy and having intercourse only for his pleasure, but she loved it, and he saw through her pretense completely and loved her for it.

After some years, her family arranged a second marriage to an older, widowed neighbor. She was reinfibulated to a 1-centimeter opening, and repenetration was accomplished in three weeks. After another three weeks, she had no further pain. He is a gentle man and very good to her and her children, but "Sex does not matter one way or the other." She has intercourse only because it is her duty, almost never reaches orgasm, and "Then it is only a shadow."

DISCUSSION

As reported herein, sexual pleasure and orgasm are experienced by most Sudanese women who have been subjected to the extreme sexual mutilation known as Pharaonic circumcision. This is true, in spite of the repeated trauma to which their sex organs are subjected during their adult lives and in spite of the fact they are culturally bound to hide sexual interest and pleasure from their husbands.

There are a number of factors that make it possible for them to experience orgasm in spite of these seemingly overwhelming handicaps. Perhaps primary among these is the fact that nearly all of them are unaware that other options exist for women in the world. They are, with only a handful of exceptions, unaware that the hardships inflicted on them (which they perceive as "normal") need not be a part of a woman's experience. Perhaps, women in Sudan, where pain is endemic, develop a level of adaptability which enables them to persist despite physical pain and psychic trauma. Presumably, Pharaonic circumcision also facilitates the enhancement of remaining erogenous zones, and possibly the development of others.

Emotionally secure childhoods, within strongly cohesive extended families, and strong bonding in marriage are characteristic of Sudanese women. The role and code of behavior for these women are rigidly defined in the society, and they adhere to them with security. Finally, Sudanese women have access to a limited series of covert but clearly defined and easily communicated sex signals and behaviors, which they are able to use successfully and without penalty. This finding suggests that mental and emotional factors play a primary role in eliciting orgasm in these clitoridectomized women.

REFERENCES

Abdalla, R. M. D. (1982). *Sisters in Affliction: Circumcision and Infibulation of Women in Africa.* London: Zed Press.

Bakr, S. A. (1982). Circumcision and Infibulation in the Sudan. *WHO/EMRO Technical Publication: Seminar on Traditional Practices Affecting the Health of Women and Children in Africa.* Alexandria, 138–144.

Cook, R. (1979). Damage to Physical Health from Pharaonic Circumcision (Infibulation): A Review of the Medical Literature. *Background Document for the Seminar on Traditional Practices Affecting the Health of Woman and Children.* Khartoum, 53–69.

Dareer, Asma El. (1982). *Woman, Why Do You Weep?* London: Zed Press.

Dareer, Asma El. (1983). Epidemiology of Female Circumcision in the Sudan. *Trop. Doctor,* 1, 41–45.

Huber, A. (1969). Die Weibliche Beschneidung (Female Circumcision). *Zeitschrift fur Tropenmedizin und Parasitologie,* 20, 1–9.

Karim, M., & Ammar, R. (1965). *Female Circumcision and Sexual Desire.* Cairo: Ain Shams University Press.

Laycock, H. T. (1950). Surgical Aspects of Female Circumcision in Somaliland. *East Afr. Med. J.,* 27, 445–450.

Megafu, U. (1983). Female Ritual Circumcision in Africa: An Investigation of the Presumed Benefits Among Ibos of Nigeria. *East Africa Med. Journal,* 40(11), 793–800.

Money, J., et al. (1955). Hermaphroditism: Recommendations Concerning Assignment of Sex and Psychologic Management. *Bulletin of Johns Hopkins Hospital,* 97(4), 284–300.

Moorehead, A. (1962). *The Blue Nile.* New York: Harper and Row.

Ogden, G. (Nov. 10–13, 1988). Women and Sexual Ecstasy. Paper presented at the *31st Annual Meeting of the Society for the Scientific Study of Sex,* San Francisco.

Otto, H. A. (Nov. 10–13, 1988). The Extended Orgasm: New Perspectives. Paper presented at the *31st Annual Meeting of the Society for the Scientific Study of Sex,* San Francisco.

Sami, I. R. (1986). Female Circumcision with Special Reference to the Sudan. *Annals of Trop. Paediatrics,* 6, 99–115.

Shandall, A. A. (1967). Circumcision and Infibulation of Females. *Sudan Medical Journal,* 5, 178–212.

Verkauf, B. S. (1975). Acquired Clitoral Enlargement. *Medical Aspects of Human Sexuality,* 9(4), 134.

Verzin, J. A. (1975). Sequelae of Female Circumcision. *Trop. Doctor,* 5, 163–169.

Chapter 5

Contraception

Decisions, decisions, decisions!! Having numerous methods of contraception to choose among is definitely advantageous. It allows a woman to choose the method best suited to her life style, personality and medical condition. But the availability of often poorly-understood alternatives makes the lives of heterosexual women more complicated. At one time, childbearing was a mandatory part of a woman's life. Women in intimate heterosexual relationships expected and were expected by society to have children. Although women have used a variety of methods to regulate and time the birth of their children throughout history (some of which are discussed in the article by **Eichhorst** in this chapter), the reliability of the methods was poor.

Family planning, delayed childbearing, child spacing and contraception are major issues in heterosexual women's lives. Most women, no matter how many children they desire, spend a large portion of their lives not wanting to be pregnant *right now*. Modern medical science has provided a number of reliable and highly effective forms of contraception for women to choose among. While we still need more effective, less risky contraceptives for women and effective contraceptives for men, the array of currently-available contraceptives can seem mind-boggling to the uninitiated. There are hormonal contraceptives in the form of pills of various types, injections, and implants. There are IUDs and barrier methods such as the diaphragm, condom, cervical cap and sponge. There are natural methods which utilize body temperature, cervical mucus and cervical position to determine the time of fertility which can be paired with the use of barrier contraceptives or abstinence to prevent unwanted pregnancy. For those who are certain that they do not want to have any or any additional children, sterilization is an option. Only total abstinence is 100% effective in preventing unwanted pregnancy. Each mode of contraception has its advantages and disadvantages. The methods vary in effectiveness, in risk of minor or serious side-effects and in potential to prevent the transmission of sexually-transmitted diseases.

Since only two of the currently-available methods (the condom and vasectomy) are for use by men, the major burden of contraceptive choice and use is carried by women. Often contraceptive choice is made with too little information, is based solely on the advice of friends and relatives or is dictated for the woman by her medical practitioner who may or may not understand her lifestyle and needs.

The choice of a contraceptive method takes careful consideration and knowledge of the methods available, their mechanisms of action, the way in which they are used and their risks as well as benefits. Consideration must be given to the woman's medical condition, her lifestyle and her attitude towards unwanted pregnancy. The woman must play an active role in selecting the contraceptive best for her. And it's not a once-in-a-lifetime choice. Women's lives change. Their sexual behavior changes. Their attitude towards the risk of unplanned pregnancy changes. Their medical condition changes. In the opening selection of this chapter **Eichhorst** describes the contraceptive methods currently available in the U.S. along with the effectiveness, risks and benefits of each of these choices. While this article was originally intended to help physicians assist women in their choice of contraceptives, it provides information that all women should have in making well-grounded decisions regarding contraceptive use.

The second selection in this chapter discusses Norplant, the long-acting, hormonal contraceptive made available in the U.S. in 1991. This is not a new contraceptive *per se,* but rather a new way of administering an old hormonal contraceptive. It provides women in the U.S. with their first alternative to the IUD for long-term but reversible contraception. While its ease of use may be attractive to many women, the up-front costs puts Norplant ''out of arms reach'' for large numbers of women.

In the final selection of this chapter **Norris** proposes an answer to the question, ''Why don't sexually-active women who don't want to have children use contraception?'' The failure to use contraception is particularly noted among adolescents but is seen among women of all ages to some extent. Many researchers have cited lack of information and reduced availability of contraceptives as an answer to this question. Others have cited the extreme pressure on women to not admit sexual activity to themselves or others as the reason underlying so many unwanted pregnancies. It is more in keeping with our image of ''good'' girls and women to face unplanned pregnancy after being swept off our feet in the heat of passion than it is to face up to our sexuality and be prepared for sex when it does occur.

Norris's theory of cognitive awareness provides a framework which can account for the failure to use contraceptives by women of all ages and educational levels. More importantly, it suggests some ways in which the cognitive barrier to effective contraceptive use can be overcome.

References and Suggested Readings

Archer, D. F. (1990, February). Cardiovascular disease and oral contraceptives. *Medical Aspects of Human Sexuality,* pp. 26–33.

Brown, K. H., and Hammond, C. B. (1989). The risks and benefits of oral contraceptives. *Advances in Internal Medicine* 34: 285–306.

Connell, E. B. (1991, April). Contraceptive options for the woman over 40. *Medical Aspects of Human Sexuality,* pp. 20–24.

Hatcher, R. A. et al. (1990). *Contraceptive Technology 1990–1992* (15th Revised Edition). New York: Irvington Publishers, Inc.

Hughes, C. B., and Torre, C. (1987, September). Predicting effective contraceptive behavior in college females. *Nurse Practitioner* 12: pp. 44–54.

Ponzetti, J. J., Jr., and Hoefler, S. (1988). Natural family planning: A review and assessment. *Family and Community Health, 11,* 36–48.

Wilcox, L. S., Chu, S. Y., Eaker, E. D., Zeger, S. L., and Peterson, H. B. (1991). Risk factors for regret after tubal sterilization: 5 years of follow-up in a prospective study. *Fertility and Sterility* 55: 927–933.

Contraception
Bradley C. Eichhorst, M.D.

The primary care of women of reproductive age often includes helping them to avoid or properly time pregnancy. Fertility control, whether mechanical or hormonal, has important implications for the health and medical management of these women as well as for society as a whole. The effects of frequent pregnancies and short birth intervals are averted, decreasing maternal morbidity and infant mortality. With reproductive freedom come opportunities for women to participate in affairs of family and society that might otherwise be closed to them.

Approximately 33 million fertile American couples practice some form of contraception. Too often, choices of a contraceptive method are based on prejudices, rumors, or fears rather than fact. Provision of complete, accurate, and timely contraceptive advice is an integral part of the clinician's job. The risks, benefits, and implications of each contraceptive option must be clearly understood by the physician to best aid the patient in making the most appropriate choice for her particular situation. Although, discussions of contraception often revolve around the woman, the active participation of both partners in the selection and use of a contraceptive method is vitally important.

Although no new contraceptive chemicals have been introduced in the United States for nearly 20 years, there have been major advances in formulation, safety, patient acceptance, and convenience. In this article, the current status of contraceptive technology will be reviewed, highlighting recent developments and important clinical aspects of each contraceptive technique.

HISTORICAL PERSPECTIVE

Contraception has existed in some form for at least several thousand years. The desire for reliable contraception has been characteristic of many societies widely separated in time and place—even those societies dominated by mores and religious codes demanding that people multiply. Humans have always longed for both sterility and fertility, each at its appointed time.

Primitive societies used magical rites, formulae, and potions concocted by medicine men; but they have also used coitus interruptus, vaginal tampons, prolonged suckling, and avoidance of intercourse during the 9 days following cessation of menstruation (the first example of the rhythm method, probably discovered quite accidentally and with little comprehension of the underlying physiology).

The Petri Papyrus, dating to the Twelfth Dynasty of the Egyptians (c. 1850 B.C.), presents one of the oldest medical prescriptions for contraception. The papyrus contains references to vaginal pessaries of crocodile dung and irrigation of the vagina with honey and sodium carbonate. The Bible makes reference to coitus interruptus in Genesis 38:7–10. Throughout history, literature makes reference to various contraceptive practices with many allusions to coitus interruptus, vaginal sponges moistened with many different substances, vaginal pessaries, and removal of semen from the vagina by violent body movements (e.g., coughing, sneezing, or douching). Casanova is said to have used the juice of a lemon to detect venereal disease and to have used half of a small lemon from which the juice is removed as a cervical cap. Some of the most popular practices, such as the use of a sponge soaked in lemon juice, may have been quite efficacious, as citric acid is an effective spermicidal agent.

The development and widespread use of the condom was an important step in contraceptive technology. The first description of the condom dates back to 1564 when Fallopius described a linen sheath to protect the wearer from syphilis, and other early condoms were probably fashioned from the intestines of animals. A revolution occurred with the vulcanization of rubber in the 1840's and again with the development of latex in the early 1900's.[14]

Contraceptive technology has made dramatic strides in the last three decades. With the development of oral contraceptives in 1960 and the modern intrauterine device shortly thereafter, a new era in contraception began. For the first time, couples were provided with effective, reversible contraception. Exciting new possibilities lie on the horizon as contraceptive technology continues to make dramatic advances.

SELECTION OF A CONTRACEPTIVE METHOD

The selection of a contraceptive method for an individual patient is a complex decision that often involves social, religious, cultural, psychologic, and monetary factors, as well as medical considerations.

The first step in contraceptive counseling must be a careful history and physical exam. The history should include an assessment of sexual function and patterns of sexual expression, as well as uncovering any underlying medical conditions that may influence selection of a contraceptive method.

Physical factors or limitations may make a given method impractical or ineffective.

It is important that the physician be as objective as possible while aiding the patient in making contraceptive choices. The advice rendered may be influenced by the physician's own moral or religious perspective, thereby distorting the facts. Accurate assessment of the patient's contraceptive needs requires that physicians be able to accept in a nonjudgmental fashion information about a life that may be very different than their own. The physician's task is to integrate the patient's desires and lifestyle, identify the risks and benefits of each method, and assist patient and partner in making their contraceptive choice.

Effectiveness and Safety

Effectiveness. In the consideration of contraceptive techniques, two principal factors are vital to both patient and physician: effectiveness and safety. To answer questions regarding effectiveness, the clinician must know the definitions of contraceptive effectiveness and the techniques used to measure it. Theoretic effectiveness refers to the maximal effectiveness of a particular contraceptive method when used precisely as prescribed or advised by the manufacturer and is approximated by lowest observed failure rates. Use effectiveness refers to the success of a sample of patients actually using the method to prevent pregnancy and is reflected by typical user failure rates. The difference between these two rates reflects human error or lack of compliance and will vary from sample population to population.

The magnitude of the difference between theoretic and use effectiveness will vary with the contraceptive method. The oral contraceptive requires a high degree of patient compliance in taking the pill every day, whereas the IUD requires only an occasional check. Thus the gap between theoretic and

Table 1. Failure Rates of Birth Control Methods

Method	Lowest Observed Failure Rate (%)	Typical User Failure Rate (%)
Sterilization	0.4	0.4
Injectable progestin	0.25	0.25
Combined birth control pills	0.5	2
Progestin only pill	1	2.5
IUD	1.5	5
Condom	2	10
Diaphram	2	19
Contraceptive sponge	9–11	10–20
Cervical cap	2	13
Vaginal spermicides	3–5	18
Fertility awareness techniques	2–20	24
None	90	90

Adapted from Hatcher RA, Guest F, Stewart F, et al: Contraceptive Technology 1986–1987. New York, Irvington Publishers, Inc., 1986.

use effectiveness will be much greater for the oral contraceptive. In counseling patients, use effectiveness is probably a more helpful indicator for selecting a contraceptive method. However, the clinician must remember that use effectiveness rates depend greatly on characteristics of the population being studied, size of the population, method of data collection, and method of computation of results.

Two methods of calculating pregnancy rates have been widely used in studies of contraceptive effectiveness. The earlier is known as the Pearl pregnancy rate; it is expressed as failures per 100 women-years of exposure. This technique is deficient in that the longer a study is run, the lower the failure rate will be as women gain experience in using the technique or as less effective users drop out of the study. The second method, life table analysis failure rates, applies only to the first year of use of a given contraceptive method and is designed to answer the following question: "Of 100 women who start and continue to use a method, how many will become pregnant in the first year of usage?" Again, the physician must be aware that even with life table analysis, the results of a given study will be dependent on the population being studied.

Table 1 lists lowest observed (theoretic) and typical failure rates of commonly used contraceptive methods using life table analysis studies.

Safety. An equally important consideration in the selection of a contraceptive method is safety. Risks include both those inherent in the method itself, as well as the risk of pregnancy and childbirth should the method fail. Assessment of risk must also include possible impairment of future fertility. The physician must also be aware of risks in terms of inconvenience, dissatisfaction, embarrassment, or discomfort. Because of the risks inherent in pregnancy itself, the use of any contraceptive method is safer than none at all for most sexually active women. Any assessment of risk must also weigh the benefits of the method, including noncontraceptive benefits such as treatment of dysmenorrhea, acne, dysfunctional bleeding, and functional ovarian cysts with oral contraceptive agents.

When discussing the risk of various contraceptive methods, it is often useful to view risk in the perspective of other activities of daily life. Table 2 lists some of the voluntary risks to which we commonly expose ourselves.

Table 2. Voluntary Risks to Which We Commonly Expose Ourselves

Activitiy	Chance of Death in One Year
Smoking	1 in 200
Motorcycling	1 in 1,000
Driving automobile	1 in 6,000
Playing football	1 in 25,000
Sexual intercourse (PID)	1 in 50,000
Using tampons (toxic shock)	1 in 350,000
Oral contraception—nonsmoker	1 in 63,000
Oral contraception—smoker	1 in 16,000
IUD	1 in 100,000
Barrier methods	None
Fertility awareness	None
Laparoscopic tubal ligation	1 in 20,000
Vasectomy	None
Pregnancy	1 in 10,000

Adapted from Hatcher RA, Guest F, Stewart F, et al: Contraceptive Technology 1986–1987. New York, Irvington Publishers, Inc. 1986.

FERTILITY AWARENESS TECHNIQUES

Fertility awareness methods or natural family planning are based on abstinence from intercourse during a woman's fertile period. These methods include the following: calendar or rhythm method; basal body temperature; mucus method; and symptothermal methods. These methods have the advantage of being safe, inexpensive, acceptable by major religious and cultural groups, and they encourage couples to learn more about the menstrual cycle and communicate about family planning.[12]

Calendar Method

The calendar method calculates the fertile period of the woman by way of the following assumptions: ovulation occurs on day 14 before the next menses, sperm remain viable for 2–3 days; and the ovum survives for only 24 hours. The woman carefully records her menstrual cycles and calculates the first day of her fertile period by subtracting 18 from the length of her shortest cycle, and the last day of her fertile period by subtracting 11 days from the length of her longest cycle. For

example, if a woman experienced 28–30 day cycles, her fertile period would be days 10–19. The couple would either abstain or use backup contraception during the fertile period.

Basal Body Temperature

Basal body temperature methods are based on the fact that many women show a drop in their basal body temperature immediately before ovulation, followed by a slight rise in their basal body temperature 24–72 hours after ovulation. By recording basal body temperature carefully for 3–4 cycles, a woman can determine her time of ovulation and more accurately predict her fertile period. In practice, it should be noted that basal body temperature graphs are often difficult to interpret and often require the physician's assistance.

Mucus Method

Mucus methods employ observation of changes in cervical mucus that many women experience at the time of ovulation, as well as the awareness of ovulatory pain or mittelschmerz. At the time of ovulation, cervical secretions increase, become clear, and exhibit spinnbarkeit (can be stretched out into a thin strand). This is in contrast to the cloudy, viscous mucus present in the pre- and postovulatory phases. Care must be taken to ensure that it is only vaginal secretions that are being assessed and not semen, lubricants, spermicides, or infectious discharge.

Symptothermal Method

Symptothermal method refers to simultaneous monitoring of physical symptoms of mucous changes, ovulation discomfort, and changes in the cervical os, along with thermal changes of the basal body temperature.

Effectiveness

The effectiveness of fertility awareness techniques is controversial, with many different rates being reported. Effectiveness rates generally range from 70 to 85 per cent. The effectiveness of these methods is increased if intercourse is restricted to the postovulatory phase of the cycle.

Risks

There are essentially no risks to the use of these methods themselves, but there have been reports of an increased incidence of birth defects when pregnancy does occur in couples using these methods. It is hypothesized this may be caused by fertilization of an over-ripe ovum. However, the data are inconclusive, and any increase in risk is felt to be small.

Contraindications

There are no absolute contraindications to use of these methods, although irregular cycles, temperature charts that are difficult to interpret, and an unwillingness to do the necessary recordkeeping will render these techniques ineffective. Because of their relatively low effectiveness, these methods would not be suitable for a patient in whom pregnancy is strongly contraindicated.

Noncontraceptive Benefits

The keen awareness of the menstrual cycle fostered by these methods will be useful to couples when they decide to attempt conception and pregnancy, as well as enhancing communication and cooperation in family planning.

CONDOMS

Condoms consist of a rubber or processed collagenous tissue sheath that is placed over the erect penis and prevents release of semen into the vagina. Condoms are all approximately the same size but are available in different shapes, differing textures, with or without lubricants, and with or without spermicides. Lubricants are available both as wet jellies or dry powders. The presence of spermicide has been shown to be highly effective at killing sperm within the condom.

Effectiveness

Typical use failure rate is approximately 10 pregnancies per 100 women per year. Most condom failures are the result of vaginal penetration before the condom is placed or spillage during withdrawal. Optimal efficacy is obtained by using the condom in conjunction with a vaginal spermicide such as foam.

Risks

There are no significant medical risks to the use of condoms. The major concerns related to their use are decreased sensitivity and spontaneity. This is a significant problem for some men, making them unable to enjoy intercourse or hold an erection. Rarely, patients may be allergic to the rubber, or one of the lubricant or spermicidal components.

Contraindications

Contraindications include inability to sexually function while wearing a condom, or sensitivity to the rubber, lubricants, or spermicides found in condoms. Patients who are allergic to rubber can usually use the lambskin condoms.

Noncontraceptive Benefits

The list of noncontraceptive benefits of condoms is substantial. Chief among these benefits is the prevention of transmission of sexually transmitted diseases, including HIV (the causative agent of AIDS). This protection against infection leads to consequent decreases in the risks of infertility, complications of pregnancy, and cervical intraepithelial neoplasia.[23] Condoms are occasionally beneficial in the treatment of premature ejaculation, infertility caused by sperm antibodies, and in women allergic to semen.

CONTRACEPTIVE SPONGE

The contraceptive sponge (Today—VLI Corporation) is a 6 cm by 2 cm polyurethane sponge impregnated with 1.15 gm of the spermicide nonoxynol 9. The sponge has a concavity on one side, which fits against the cervix, and a woven loop on the other to facilitate removal. It was approved by the FDA in 1983 and is available over the counter. The sponge is moistened with a small amount of water and inserted deeply into the vagina prior to intercourse. It provides protection for a 24 hour period and must be left in place at least 6 hours after intercourse.

The contraceptive sponge works by releasing spermicide contained within the sponge, by providing a mechanical barrier between sperm and the cervical os, and by absorbing and trapping sperm within the sponge.

Effectiveness

Use effectiveness of the contraceptive sponge typically ranges from 80 to 90 percent. A comparative trial of the sponge with the diaphragm showed parous sponge users were twice as likely to conceive as were diaphragm users (28 per cent versus 13 per cent), but there was no difference in pregnancy rates in nulliparous women (13 per cent for both groups).[9] Other studies have generally found the sponge to be slightly less effective than the diaphragm.

Risks

The most serious risk associated with the use of the contraceptive sponge is that of toxic shock syndrome.[10] The risk is estimated to be 10 per 100,000 users per year, similar to that for tampon users.[11] To minimize this risk, it is recommended that the sponge not be used during menstruation, the puerperium, or after termination of pregnancy. Local irritation, difficulty removing the sponge, and vaginal dryness have also been reported. No systemic effects related to absorption of spermicide have been reported.

Contraindications

Women who have a history of toxic shock syndrome or colonization of the vagina with *Staphylococcus aureus,* allergy to sponge components, inability to insert or remove, or anatomic abnormalities that would prevent proper placement or retention of the sponge should not use the contraceptive sponge.

Noncontraceptive Benefits

In addition to providing contraception, there is evidence that the contraceptive sponge decreases the risk of acquiring sexually transmitted diseases. A recent comparative trial in high-risk women demonstrated a decreased risk of chlamydia and gonorrhea in women using the sponge compared with women using no vaginal contraception. Sponge users were more likely to become infected with Candida.[24]

DIAPHRAGM

The diaphragm consists of a dome-shaped rubber cap with a flexible rim. In use, it rests between the posterior fornix and the posterior aspect of the symphysis pubis. It is available in a variety of sizes and in different rim constructions. The arcing spring diaphragm has a sturdy rim with a firm spring. It folds into a curved shape to facilitate insertion. Most women can use the arcing spring diaphragm comfortably, and it can usually be retained even by women with a cystocele/rectocele or poor vaginal muscle tone. The coil spring also has a sturdy rim with a firm spring. It folds flat and can be used with a diaphragm introducer. The flat spring diaphragm has a thin rim with gentle spring. It folds flat for insertion and can be used with a diaphragm introducer. The flat spring diaphragm is useful in a patient with very firm vaginal muscle tone or a shallow notch behind the pubic arch.

The most recent development in diaphragms, the wide seal rim, was introduced in 1983. This diaphragm has a soft latex flange attached to the inner rim of the diaphragm designed to create a seal with the vaginal wall. The wide seal rim diaphragm comes in both an arcing and coil spring model.

All diaphragms are used in a similar fashion. A dose of spermicide is placed in the dome of the diaphragm, and the diaphragm is placed inside the vagina, covering the cervical os and holding the spermicide in contact with the cervix. The diaphragm must be left in place for at least 6 hours after intercourse.

Effectiveness

Widely disparate rates for effectiveness have been reported for the diaphragm as with many other of the barrier methods. Factors that may possibly alter the demonstrated effectiveness of a method include the fre-quency of intercourse, motivation, consistency in usage, ability to master proper use, fertility of the couple, as well as the product or method itself. Failure rate of the diaphragm in typical usage is 19 pregnancies per 100 women per year.

Risks

The risks associated with the use of the diaphragm are minimal when used correctly. There has been a reported association with toxic shock syndrome and recurrent cystitis. Allergic reactions to the rubber or the spermicide and local irritation have also occurred. Vaginal ulceration and pelvic discomfort can result from an improper fit or prolonged usage.

Contraindications

The diaphragm is contraindicated in women with a history of toxic shock syndrome or vaginal colonization with *Staphylococcus aureus*. It should also be avoided in patients with recurrent urinary tract infections, anatomical abnormalities of the vagina preventing proper placement or retention, inability of patient or partner to correctly insert the diaphragm, pelvic pain, and in the first 6 weeks following vaginal delivery.

Noncontraceptive Benefits

The diaphragm and vaginal spermicide also provide some protection against sexually transmitted diseases, including herpes, gonorrhea, trichomonas, and chlamydia. As a secondary benefit of this protection, women are also protected against PID and subsequent infertility.[5] There is also some evidence that diaphragm users are at decreased risk for cervical intraepithelial neoplasia, probably also a result of the anti-viral properties of vaginal spermicides.[26]

CERVICAL CAP

The cervical cap is a cup-shaped device with a tall rubber dome and a firm flexible rim. Spermicide is placed in the cap, and it is placed in the vagina over the cervix prior to intercourse. The length of time the cervical cap may safely be left in place is not known, and current recommendations are that the cap should not be left in place longer than 24 hours. Cervical caps are not currently approved for marketing as a contraceptive in the United States but are widely available in Europe and can be acquired through various sources in the United States. The cap is available in four sizes, and fitting is empirical. The contraceptive effect of the cap is similar to that of the diaphragm, providing a mechanical barrier to sperm and acting as a reservoir for spermicide to kill any sperm that are able to cross the mechanical barrier.

Effectiveness

Limited data are available on the effectiveness of the cervical cap, but preliminary studies suggest a failure rate in typical users of 8 to 20 per 100 women per year, with 13 pregnancies per 100 women per year being a representative figure.[26,17]

Risks

Data on the risks associated with the cervical cap are few. Clinicians have noted the development of acute pelvic infections, cervicitis, vaginal lacerations and abrasions, and abnormal Pap smears.

Contraindications

Contraindications to the use of the cervical cap include a history of toxic shock syndrome or vaginal colonization with *Staphylococcus aureus*, allergy to rubber or spermicide, anatomic abnormalities that preclude a proper fit of the cap over the cervix, inability of patient and partner to perform proper insertion, or cervicitis, vaginitis, abnormal Pap smear, cervical surgery, delivery in the past 6 weeks, or unavailability of medical personnel qualified to fit the cap.

Noncontraceptive Benefits

Noncontraceptive benefits of the cervical cap probably mirror those of the diaphragm, although no data are available to confirm this theory.

VAGINAL SPERMICIDES

Vaginal spermicides have been used for 5,000 years but only two are available on the market today—nonoxynol-9 and octoxynol-9. These agents are available in a variety of different bases and dosage forms including foam, jelly, cream, suppositories, and tablets. The spermicide, whatever its dosage form, is placed in the vagina next to the cervix prior to intercourse. The effectiveness of spermicides is markedly enhanced by concurrent usage of a barrier method. Jellies and creams are slightly less effective than foam or suppositories when used alone and are best used in conjunction with a diaphragm or cervical cap.

Effectiveness

The reported effectiveness for vaginal spermicides varies widely. Failure rates ranging from 1.55 to 29 pregnancies per 100 women per year have been reported. A failure rate of 18 per 100 women per year, as presented in Table 1, is a representative figure and useful for discussions with patients.

Risks

There have been suggestions that the use of vaginal spermicides may result in an increased risk of birth defects should a pregnancy result.[15,16] However, most authorities

139

do not feel there is a significant association between use of vaginal spermicides and risk of birth defects.[18]

Contraindications

Vaginal spermicides are contraindicated in patients with an allergy to the products, and in patients who are unable to properly insert them.

Noncontraceptive Benefits

There is evidence that vaginal spermicides may be effective in vivo at killing agents of sexually transmitted diseases, including HIV.[13]

INTRAUTERINE DEVICE

The intrauterine device consists of a small plastic device with associated exposed copper or a slow release system for progesterone. The exact mechanism of action of the IUD is not known, but several possibilities have been suggested. The presence of the IUD in the uterus stimulates a local foreign body inflammatory response that may act to inhibit implantation. Copper increases the inflammatory reaction, decreases the viability of sperm, impairs ovum transport, and may interfere with estrogen uptake and utilization by the endometrium. Progestin causes changes in the cervical mucus, making it less penetrable by sperm. Most experts now believe that the IUD interferes with fertilization of the ovum rather than simply preventing implantation.[21]

There is currently only one IUD available in the United States—the Progestasert (Alza), a progesterone-releasing IUD. However, a new copper-bearing IUD will soon be released, the copper T 380A (ParaGard-GynoPharma). Two previously popular copper-bearing IUDs, the Cu-7 and the Tatum-T, were withdrawn from the market in 1986. The T 380A has nearly twice as much exposed copper as previous copper-bearing

IUDs and has been shown to be effective for 4 years, or possibly even longer. The most popular IUD worldwide is probably a tailless stainless steel ring used in China.

Effectiveness

Theoretic effectiveness of most IUDs is 97 to 99 per cent, whereas use effectiveness is approximately 95 per cent. Trials of the copper T 380A have demonstrated a 1-year pregnancy rate of ≤ 1.1 (lower than that of most other IUDs) but the T 380A has a slightly higher spontaneous expulsion rate, and its discontinuation rate is higher, usually because of pain or bleeding.

Risks

The most serious risk of IUD usage is that of pelvic inflammatory disease, accounting for the majority of IUD-related deaths, hospitalization, and morbidity. The relative PID hospitalization risk for women using IUDs was 1.6 compared to women using no contraception, most of which occurred in the first 4 months after insertion. Tubal damage and infertility are long-term complications of IUD use, primarily related to infection.

Once infection occurs, the IUD should be removed and appropriate antibiotic therapy instituted. Treatment of the infection with the IUD in place should usually not be attempted. Once infection has occurred, one should wait 3 months before inserting another IUD. Careful consideration of the risk of infection and subsequent infertility should be given in any patient who desires future fertility, and the IUD may be the least attractive option in this patient group.

Other potential risks of the IUD include spotting, bleeding, or pain leading to removal in 10 to 15 per cent of patients. Increased menstrual blood loss leading to anemia may occur. Spontaneous expulsion occurs in 5 to 20 per cent of users in the first year, and patients should be counseled to check their IUD string regularly. IUD strings may occasionally be lost or migrate into the uterine cavity. Localization and removal of the IUD may then require anesthesia. Uterine perforation occasionally occurs with migration of the device into the peritoneal cavity, usually within the first few days after insertion. Extrauterine copper-bearing IUDs should be removed because of the local inflammatory response they induce.

If pregnancy occurs with an IUD in place, the risk of spontaneous abortion is increased to approximately 50 per cent, the likelihood of ectopic pregnancy is increased to about 5 per cent, and the risk of septic abortion is dramatically increased. If the string is visible, the IUD should be removed and the patient should be informed there is an approximately 25 per cent chance of spontaneous abortion occurring following the removal. The combination of pregnancy and infection in the IUD user is potentially fatal, and the possibility of sepsis in any pregnant patient with an IUD and flu-like symptoms should be considered.

Contraindications

Absolute contraindications to IUD insertion include active pelvic infection, pregnancy, and cervical or uterine malignancy. Strong relative contraindications include multiple sexual partners, nulliparity, desire for future fertility, recent pelvic infection, cervicitis, bleeding diathesis, history of ectopic pregnancy, and chronic disease. Other conditions that may contraindicate IUD use include valvular heart disease, uterine malignancy, cervical stenosis, endometriosis, small uterus, fibroids, uterine or cervical polyps, severe dysmenorrhea, menorrhagia, impaired ability to recognize symptoms of concern or check string, history of gonorrhea, and chronic disease.

COMBINATION ORAL CONTRACEPTIVES

Combination oral contraceptives consist of tablets containing estrogen and a progestin. The tablet is taken daily for 21 days, followed by 7 days on which no tablet or an inert tablet is taken. During the 7 days off of the hormonal preparation, the patient will usually experience withdrawal bleeding.

The mechanisms of action include both effects of the estrogen and of the progestin. Estrogen acts to inhibit ovulation by its effect on the hypothalamic gonadotropin-releasing hormone and consequent suppression of secretion of FSH and LH by the pituitary. Oral contraceptives containing ≤ 50 μg of estrogen are probably 95 to 98 per cent effective at suppressing ovulation, but the addition of the strong contraceptive effect of the progestin make them nearly 100 per cent effective in preventing pregnancy in practice.

Progestins cause the cervical mucus to become scanty, thick, and cellular, thereby inhibiting the transport of sperm and decreasing their ability to penetrate the cervical mucus. There is also some evidence that progestins inhibit the capacitation of sperm, but the significance of that action in humans remains uncertain. Progestins may inhibit ovum transport in the fallopian tubes and may inhibit implantation of the fertilized ovum.

The FDA first approved these agents for use as contraceptives in 1960. Early birth control pills contained 50 to 150 μg of estrogen and 1 to 10 mg of a progestin in contrast to modern oral contraceptives containing 30 to 50 μg of estrogen and ≤ 1 mg of a progestational agent. It is important to recognize this fact, as many of the side effects commonly attributed to the pill were described using the early, relatively high-dose pill and are absent or markedly diminished in the preparations currently being used.

Table 3. Biologic Activity of Progestation Agents

Agent	Progestational Activity	Estrogenic Activity	Androgenic Activity	Endometrial Activity
Norethindrone	1.0	1.0	1.0	1.0
Norethindrone acetate	1.16	1.52	1.60	0.45
Ethynodiol diacetate	1.40	3.44	0.63	0.45
Norethynodrel	0.26	8.32	0	NA
Levonorgestrel	5.26	0	9.4	5.1
dl-Norgestrel	2.63	0	4.7	2.6

Adapted from Dickey RP: Managing contraceptive pill patients, Fifth ed. Durant, Oklahoma, Creative Infomatics, Inc., 1987.

The estrogen present in currently available oral contraceptives is one of only two agents, mestranol or ethinyl estradiol. Mestranol is converted to ethinyl estradiol, the form in which the estrogenic effects are exerted. However, mestranol has only 67 per cent of the biologic estrogenic activity of ethinyl estradiol, and thus pill potency cannot be compared on a milligram for milligram basis.[8] Most authorities believe use of a pill containing more than 50 μg of estrogen is rarely if ever indicated for contraceptive purposes.

There are five progestins commonly used in currently available oral contraceptives. The biologic activity of these agents is listed in Table 3.[8]

Recently biphasic (1982) and triphasic (1984) combination oral contraceptives have been introduced. These agents are used in the same fashion and contain varying amounts of estrogen and progestin to more closely approximate the hormonal pattern of a normal menstrual cycle. This also allows a lower total dose of progestin per cycle and helps to minimize metabolic changes and side effects. They also reportedly decrease the incidence of such minor side effects as breakthrough bleeding and amenorrhea.

Effectiveness

Oral contraceptives have the lowest failure rate of any nonsurgical method available in the United States, a typical first year failure rate being 2 per 100 women, with the rate somewhat higher in users under the age of 22. A large proportion of failures occur when women discontinue the pill, usually for nonmedical reasons, and fail to use alternative contraception. Drop-out rates in the first year of usage typically range from 30 to 50 per cent.[11]

Risks

The major risk associated with oral contraceptives has been the association with thromboembolic disease, stroke, and heart attack. Epidemiologic studies of deep-vein thrombosis were based on clinical diagnoses that have been shown to have a false-positive rate of approximately 50 per cent. When this correction factor is introduced, statistical associations between deep-vein thrombosis and oral contraceptive use disappear. Similarly, epidemiologic studies of stroke and myocardial infarction are flawed in that they failed to consider the variables of age and smoking. Recalculation has shown the risk in a 35-year-old nonsmoker to be no greater than a nonsmoker nonuser.[4,22]

The effect of contraceptive steroids on plasma lipids continues to be an area of concern. It is possible that some of the adverse cardiovascular effects of oral contraceptives may be mediated through their effects on plasma lipids. The introduction of modern low-dose contraceptives has reduced adverse effects on plasma lipoproteins and decreased concern about their risk.[28] However, it is recommended that lipid screening be per-

Table 4. Contraindications to Oral Contraceptives

Absolute Contraindications

Thromboembolic disease or history of same
Cerebrovascular disease or history of same
Myocardial infarction or known coronary artery disease
Liver tumors—benign or malignant
Carcinoma of the breast
Estrogen-dependent neoplasia
Known or suspected pregnancy
Liver disease

Strong Relative Contraindications

Smokers over age 35
Nonsmokers over age 40 with second risk factor
Nonsmokers over age 45
Hypertension (systolic > 140, diastolic > 90)
Undiagnosed abnormal vaginal bleeding
Diabetes mellitus
Hyperlipidemia
Severe vascular headaches
Gallbladder disease
Cervical dysplasia
Surgery, injury, or casting requiring immobilization
Sickle cell disease

Other Relative Contraindications

Gestational diabetes
Coagulopathies
Systemic lupus erythematosus
Porphyria
Cholestatic jaundice of pregnancy
Chloasma of preganancy
Irregular menses, oligomenorrhea
Leiomyomata uteri
Family history of breast disease
Urinary tract infections
Epilepsy
Depression
Asthma
Marked varicosities
Cardiac or renal disease
Conditions likely to make patient unreliable at pill usage
Family history of myocardial infarction prior to age 50

formed prior to beginning oral contraceptives and that other contraceptive methods be considered in hyperlipidemic patients.

The effect of combined oral contraceptives on the incidence of cancer, particularly breast cancer, has been debated. There is no currently accepted evidence that oral contraceptives increase the incidence of any cancer regardless of the age at which the pill was started, the duration of usage, or the composition of the pill.[25]

Contraindications

The contraindications to the use of oral contraceptives are summarized in Table 4.[4,8,11]

Noncontraceptive Benefits

The use of oral contraceptives has substantial noncontraceptive benefits. There is a significant decrease in the incidence of endometrial and ovarian cancer, and this protection seems to persist following discontinuation of the pill.[3] The decreased number of hospitalizations and surgical procedures that results from this decrease comprises a substantial public health benefit. Oral contraceptives markedly decrease benign breast disease, such as fibroadenomas and fibrocystic changes, thus decreasing the need for breast biopsies by as much as 50 per cent in users as compared to nonusers.

Oral contraceptives also provide significant benefits for such conditions as primary dysmenorrhea, menorrhagia, iron deficiency, and irregular menstruation.[6] There is evidence suggesting that oral contraceptives reduce the risk of PID probably through changes in cervical mucus,[29] as well as decreasing the incidence of ectopic pregnancy to 1/10 that of sexually active women using no contraception. Acne is often improved in women while they are taking oral contraceptives.

PROGESTIN-ONLY ORAL CONTRACEPTIVES

Progestin-only oral contraceptives, also termed the mini-pill, have been available in the United States since 1973. These tablets contain the same progestins found in combined oral contraceptives but in smaller doses, and they contain no estrogens. Progestin-only pills are taken every day without regard to menstrual periods. The mechanism of action of these pills is felt to relate primarily to changes in cervical mucus as described above. Forty per cent of patients taking progestin-only oral contraceptives will continue to have regular ovulatory cycles, while another twenty per cent will have intermittent ovulatory cycles.

Effectiveness

Theoretical effectiveness of the progestin-only pill is lower than that of combined oral contraceptives. Typical user failure rates range from 1.1 to 3.75 pregnancies per 100 women per year of usage, with a representative figure of 2.5. These agents are more effective in women who are switching over from a combined oral contraceptive than in those women who have not used oral contraceptives before. Failure rates are highest in the first 6 months of use, and consideration should be given to use of a backup method during the first few months of use and thereafter at midcycle.

Progestin-only oral contraceptives may be a way of avoiding estrogen-related side effects (e.g., headaches, hypertension, weight gain, and nausea) of combined pills. Even those side effects related to progestin excess may be improved on the mini-pill, as it contains a lower dosage of progestin than combined agents. Irregular menstruation, spotting, and amenorrhea are the most commonly reported side effects.

Risks

Many of the risks associated with combined oral contraceptives are thought to be caused by the estrogen component of those preparations. Because the mini-pill contains only progestin, it is theoretically safer, but this has not yet been proven. For the present, the clinician must consider the risks to be similar to those of the combined oral contraceptives.

Contraindications

The same absolute contraindications that apply to the combined oral contraceptives may be applied to the progestin-only pill, because it is unknown whether there is an increased risk of cardiovascular disease with the mini-pill. Progestin-only pills may promote irregular menstrual bleeding, and thus it is extremely important to avoid its use in undiagnosed abnormal vaginal bleeding.

Noncontraceptive Benefits

Dysmenorrhea and total menstrual blood loss are diminished in some users of the progestin-only pill. It is likely that it also provides some protection from PID through its influence on cervical mucus.

ALTERNATIVE HORMONAL DELIVERY SYSTEMS

Several alternative methods of hormonal delivery are currently in use in other countries and may soon be available in the United States.

Injectable Steroids

A long-acting synthetic progesterone, medroxyprogesterone acetate (Depo-Provera), can be administered by IM injection every 3 months and is nearly as effective as combined oral contraceptives. It is currently in use in nearly 80 countries and appears to provide nearly 100 per cent protection against pregnancy. Side effects include irregular menses or amenorrhea and some delay in return of fertility following discontinuation. Medroxyprogesterone is approved by the FDA for treatment of endometriosis and certain cancers and is not approved for use as a contraceptive agent.

Implantable Steroids

Implantable steroid capsules provide highly effective contraception for as long as 5 years, with rapid return of fertility upon removal of the capsules. One such device, Norplant, consists of several Silastic rods that slowly release levonorgestrel. These rods can be implanted subdermally in the office using local anesthesia and can be removed in a similar fashion with prompt return of fertility. This device is in use in several countries and has been shown to have high rates of effectiveness (0.7

pregnancies per 100 women per year), user satisfaction, and safety, but it has not yet been approved by the FDA for use in this country.

Vaginal Contraceptive Rings

Vaginal contraceptive rings made of Silastic that release an estrogen and progestin and are left in place for 3 weeks out of 4 will probably be available in the near future. The hormones are absorbed systemically and provide contraception by way of a mechanism similar to oral contraceptives. There may also be a vaginal analogue of the mini-pill consisting of a small ring that slowly releases a progestin, such as levonorgestrel, and may be left in place for as long as 6 months.[27]

STERILIZATION

Sterilization currently provides the highest degree of contraceptive protection short of complete abstinence cf any method currently available. It is rapidly gaining in popularity and availability, now representing the most popular method of birth control in the United States. It is now available to nearly all segments of our society, which is a significant change from the past. It is estimated that one quarter of all American couples will use sterilization within 2 years of the birth of their last child, and that by 10 years after their last child, more than one half of the couples will undergo sterilization.

It is crucial that the physician stress that sterilization procedures are permanent. Although reversal procedures are available, subsequent pregnancy rates are only 70 to 80 per cent, and these procedures are rarely covered by insurance. Informed consent must be obtained prior to proceeding with any sterilization procedure. Although there is no legal requirement for consent of partner or spouse, many physicians view this to be an ethical and practical necessity. For patients using federal or state funds, a waiting period between the signing of the consent form and the procedure is mandatory.

Vasectomy

Vasectomy is a simple procedure involving interruption of the vas deferens, usually by removal of a small segment of that structure. It is accomplished by way of a small incision in the scrotum and can be performed in the office under local anesthesia. Vasectomy is the safest method of sterilization available and serious complications are extremely rare. The failure rate for the procedure is 0.4 per cent, and the incidence of such complications as infection, hematoma, epididymitis, and sperm granuloma totals less than 5 per cent. No long-term health risks to vasectomy have been identified in humans.[19]

Tubal Sterilization

Tubal sterilization involves disruption of the continuity of the fallopian tubes by ligation, electrocoagulation, mechanical occlusion with clips or rings, or some combination of these. This can be accomplished either through the abdominal or the vaginal wall. Abdominally, the procedure can be done through laparoscopy or by mini-laparotomy. Both of these procedures can be performed on an outpatient basis under local anesthesia although many are done under general anesthesia. The fatality rate for tubal sterilization is 3.8 per 100,000 cases, most occurring from anesthetic complication, infection, and hemorrhage. Complications include infection, bleeding, bowel trauma, bladder trauma, and uterine perforation, but in the hands of a skilled surgeon total less than 5 per cent. Failure rates are dependent on the exact technique used. Current failure rate for laparoscopic tubal sterilization is 3 to 5 per 1000.[2,7]

Tubal sterilization can also be accomplished by way of culpotomy. This approach is generally considered less attractive because of higher rate of complications, principally infection and hemorrhage.

Hysterectomy

Hysterectomy was once the most common method of permanent sterilization for women. However, it is not now generally felt justified to perform a hysterectomy when the primary indication for surgery is sterilization. The morbidity and mortality of hysterectomy is 10 to 100 times greater than tubal ligation, the cost is larger, and the potential psychological impact greater.

LACTATION

Breastfeeding has a contraceptive effect, although it is far from reliable. Postpartum amenorrhea lasts longer in nursing women, often lasting as long as 4 to 24 months, while nonlactating women will usually resume menstruating in 2 to 3 months following delivery. The more frequently an infant nurses, the more likely return of menses will be delayed. A change from breastfeeding only to supplementation with other food sources is likely to cause the menstrual cycle to resume. The longer a woman breastfeeds, the more likely menstruation will resume while she is nursing.

Women should be counseled regarding the unreliability of nursing as a contraceptive method and the need for some other backup method to avoid possibility of pregnancy. Approximately 80 per cent of lactating women will ovulate before their first menstrual period following delivery, and 3 to 7 per cent of women will become pregnant before having their first menstrual period. Thus other methods of contraception need to be employed even prior to the first menstrual period.

Conversely, contraception can have an important effect on breastfeeding. Effective contraception ensures that the infant will have an adequate source of nutrition for sufficient period of time by preventing another pregnancy from occurring too soon after childbirth.

Contraception should be employed as soon as the woman resumes sexual activity, although the risk of pregnancy is slight in the first 6 weeks postpartum. Several contraceptive options exist for nursing women. Spermicides and barrier methods have no effect on breastfeeding and may safely be used in the immediate postpartum period. IUDs, both copper and progestin-containing, have not been shown to have any effect on quality or quantity of breast milk, but extreme care must be taken in the insertion of these devices into the postpartum uterus. Sterilization, either by tubal ligation or by vasectomy, is an excellent method for those couples who have completed their families.

Oral contraceptives may safely be used in breastfeeding women, and the American Academy of Pediatrics has issued a policy statement approving the use of combined oral contraceptives in nursing mothers.[1] Levels of estradiol secreted in the milk from a 50 μg dose pill do not exceed those that occur during physiologic cycling once the woman has resumed ovulation. The primary concern with the use of oral contraceptives in lactating mothers is that the pill may suppress lactation and decrease milk supply. However, most clinicians believe that lower dose estrogen pills cause fewer problems, provided they are given only after lactation is well established. The patient should be warned of the possible adverse effect on her milk supply.

Progestin-only contraceptive pills probably have little or no effect on milk supply and may be the best hormonal choice for many lactating women. The mini-pill may be started in the immediate postpartum period or at the 6-week postpartum exam.

POSTCOITAL CONTRACEPTION

Although there is no FDA approved method of postcoital contraception, physicians in the United States have used postcoital contraception for nearly a decade, particularly for the treatment of rape victims. Postcoital contraception is a controversial issue, as many view it as an abortifacient, and thus is a delicate political issue as well.

The most common regimen used is a postcoital pill containing 50 μg of ethinyl estradiol and 0.5 mg of dl-norgestrel (Ovral). Two tablets are taken within 72 hours of intercourse (preferably 12 to 24 hours) and two more tablets are taken 12 hours later. The failure rate of this method of postcoital contraception is 21.6 per cent, and the side effects are primarily those of nausea and vomiting.

High-dose oral estrogens and progestins have also been used for postcoital contraception, and danazol is also currently being studied. Postcoital placement of copper-bearing IUDs, has been shown to be effective in preventing pregnancy.

PSYCHOLOGY OF CONTRACEPTION

In any discussion of contraceptive techniques, we must not ignore the impact of psychological factors on use or misuse of these techniques. Many couples who do not want a pregnancy still avoid the use of contraception or misuse a method. Inadequate knowledge is one factor and the primary care physician must ensure that the couple has knowledge and training sufficient for effective use of the chosen method.

Not using contraception may be a sign of personal embarrassment about sexuality or about a given method. Many patients, particularly adolescents, are afraid to divulge that they plan to be or are currently sexually active. Some feel that "planning" for sexual intercourse makes it mechanical, unromantic, or immoral. Hostility, power struggles, and differences in the reproductive goals of sexual partners may lead to disuse or misuse of contraceptive techniques. Sexual difficulties in a relationship may lead to less careful employment of birth control methods.[20]

The primary care physician must be aware of these psychological factors and attempt to anticipate their effect on the contraceptive effectiveness of a given method. Careful patient education remains the mainstay of maximizing effectiveness of any given birth control method.

FUTURE TRENDS IN CONTRACEPTION

Many exciting new possibilities lie on the horizon of contraception. Oral contraceptives continue to evolve with lower and lower dosages providing safer, yet effective contraception. IUDs are becoming smaller, safer, more flexible, and some release chemicals or hormones. A disposable diaphragm that will release a spermicide is being considered.[11]

Long-acting steroid injections utilizing microspheres that gradually release norethisterone are currently being studied and will provide 30 to 180 day protection against pregnancy.

Improved ovulation detection and prediction methods may make it easier for a woman to avoid intercourse or use back-up methods during her fertile period.

There is also a study under way of a luteinizing hormone-releasing hormone analogue that when given as an oral pill inhibits ovulation. Nasal sprays are also being investigated as a means of delivering LHRH agonists or antagonists.

RU 3486, a progesterone-inhibiting steroid, has also undergone clinical studies and can be used to induce menses at the expected time of menstruation or as an early abortifacient if a women misses her period.

There has been intense interest in the development of male contraceptives. Such agents may interfere with sperm production, maturation, transport, or capacitation. There have been reports from China of a cottonseed oil derivative called gossypol that suppresses sperm production. A synthetic form of inhibin, the hormone that suppresses production of FSH, has recently been developed. FSH controls sperm production without having any effects on sexual function.

Nonsurgical methods of female sterilization involving blockage of the fallopian tubes with a variety of substances are being developed. These blocks are placed by way of hysteroscopy and do not require an incision or general anesthesia. Percutaneous injection into the vas deferens may also provide a nonsurgical alternative to vasectomy.

Many other possibilities exist for the more distant future. These include antifertility vaccines, antisperm drugs, simpler and more easily reversible sterilization techniques, and pharmacologic or immunologic sterilization techniques.

SUMMARY

The technology of fertility control has made dramatic strides in the past 25 years, offering a wider variety of safe, effective contraceptive choices than ever before. Lower dose oral contraceptives, new barrier techniques, and improved IUDs have been important recent advances, and new methods of hormonal delivery offer promise for the future. However, the search for safer, more effective, and more convenient contraceptive options must continue as a high research priority.

REFERENCES

1. American Academy of Pediatrics. Breast-feeding and contraception. Pediatrics 68:138–140, 1981
2. Centers for Disease Control: Surgical sterilization surveillance: Tubal sterilization, 1976–1978, March 1981

3. Centers for Disease Control/NIH: Combination oral contraceptive use and the risk of endometrial cancer. JAMA 257:796–800, 1987

4. Connell EB: Oral contraceptives: The benefits and the cardiovascular risks. Postgrad Med 81:46–58, 1987

5. Cramer DW, Goldman MB, Schiff I, et al: The relationship of tubal infertility to barrier method and oral contraceptive use. JAMA 257:2446–2450, 1987

6. Derman R: Oral contraceptives, assessment of benefits. J Reprod Med 31:879–886, 1986

7. Destefano F, Greenspan J, Dicker R, et al: Complications of interval laparoscopic tubal sterilization. Obstet Gynecol 61:153–158, 1983

8. Dickey RP: Managing contraceptive pill patients. 5th Ed. Durant, Oklahoma, Creative Infomatics, Inc., 1987

9. Edelman DA, McIntyre SL, Harper J: A comparative trial of the Today contraceptive sponge and diaphragm. Am J Obstet Gynecol 150:869–876, 1984

10. Faich G, Pearson K, Fleming D, et al: Toxic shock syndrome and the vaginal contraceptive sponge. JAMA 255:215, 1986

11. Hatcher RA, Guest F, Stewart F, et al: Contraceptive Technology 1986–1987. New York, Irvington Publishers, Inc., 1986

12. Hatcher RA, Stewart GK, Stewart FH, et al. Fertility awareness methods. *In* Sciarra JW (ed): Gynecology and Obstetrics. Philadelphia, Harper & Row, 1984

13. Hick DR, Martin LS, Getcje JP, et al: Inactivation of HTLV-III/LAV-infected cultures of normal human lymphocytes by nonoxynol-9 in vitro. Lancet 2:1422, 1985

14. Himes NE: Medical History of Contraception. Baltimore, Williams & Wilkins Co., 1936

15. Huggins G, et al: Vaginal spermicides and outcome of pregnancy: Findings in a large cohort study. Contraception 25:219–230, 1982

16. Jick H, et al: Vaginal spermicides and congenital disorders. JAMA 245:1329–1332, 1981

17. Johnson JM: The cervical cap: A retrospective study of an alternative contraceptive technique. Am J Obstet Gynecol 148:604–608, 1984

18. Kowal, D: Study raises question of spermicide safety. Contraceptive Technol Update 1:49–51, 1981

19. Massey FJ, Bernstein GS, O'Fallon WM, et al: Vasectomy and health: Results from a large cohort study. JAMA 252:1023–1029, 1984

20. Masters WH, Johnson VE, Kolodny RC: Masters and Johnson on sex and human loving. Boston, Little, Brown and Co., 1986

21. Abramowicz M (ed): New copper IUD. The Medical Letter on Drugs and Therapeutics 30:25–26, 1988

22. Realini J, Goldzieher J: Oral contraception and cardiovascular disease: A critique of the epidemiologic studies. Am J Obstet Gynecol 152:729–749, 1985

23. Richardson AC, Lyon JB: The effect of condom use on squamous cell cervical intraepithelial neoplasia. Am J Obstet Gynecol 140:909–913, 1981

24. Rosenberg MJ, Rojanapithayakorn W, Feldblum PJ, et al: Effect of the contraceptive sponge on chlamydial infection, gonorrhea, and candidiasis: A comparative clinical trial. JAMA 257:2308–2312, 1987

25. Sattin RW, Rubin GL, Wingo PA, et al: Oral contraceptive use and the risk of breast cancer. N Engl J Med 315:405, 1986

26. Sherris JD: New developments in vaginal contraception. Pop Reports Series H, Number 7, 1984

27. Speidel JJ: Steroidal contraception in the 1980's: The role of current and new products. J Reprod Med 28:759, 1983

28. Tikkanen MJ, Nikkila EA: Oral contraceptives and lipoprotein metabolism. J Reprod Med 31:898–905, 1986

29. Wolner-Hanssen P, Svensson L, Mardh P-A: Laparoscopic findings and contraceptive use in women with signs and symptoms suggestive of acute salpingitis. Obstet Gynecol 66:233, 1985

Norplant: Birth Control at Arm's Reach
Marian Segal

The newest birth control option for women is literally at arm's reach. The Norplant contraceptive, approved by the Food and Drug Administration last December and marketed since February, is implanted just under the skin of the inner arm, right above the elbow. Developed by the Population Council of New York, this birth control alternative is distinctly different from methods previously available.

New Form, Old Content

Norplant consists of a familiar ingredient in a new package. Six silicone rubber capsules about the size of matchsticks contain a synthetic progestin hormone long used in birth control pills. The flexible tubes are inserted in a fan-like arrangement and can be felt but not easily seen.

Once in place, they steadily release a low dose of hormone into the bloodstream. Effective within 24 hours after insertion, Norplant can continue to prevent pregnancy for up to five years.

The hormone usually inhibits ovulation so that eggs are not produced regularly, and causes the mucus of the cervix to thicken, making it more difficult for sperm to reach the egg. Other ways that Norplant may provide contraceptive effects have been proposed but not proven.

Experimental Attitude

Jennifer Collier, a 28-year-old New York law student, entered a study of Norplant at the Robert Wood Johnson Institute in New Bruns-

wick, N.J., in the spring of 1984 and is now on her second implant, inserted last June.

"It sounded like a really neat invention, so I decided to try it," says Collier. She had been dissatisfied with the weight gain and irritability she experienced using oral contraceptives. With Norplant, she says, she isn't troubled with either of those side effects. Collier describes the implant as visible, "but not terribly obvious. No one has noticed it unless they were looking for it, probably partly because of where it's inserted."

Each Norplant capsule is 2.4 millimeters (about one-tenth of an inch) in diameter and 34 millimeters (just under one-and-a-half inches) long, and holds 36 milligrams of powdered crystals of the progestin levonorgestrel. The tubes are made of Silastic, a silicone material long used in surgical implants such as heart valves and hip joints.

The hormone seeps through the permeable tubes into the bloodstream, initially at a rate of about 85 micrograms a day. The amount declines gradually to about 50 micrograms by nine months, 35 by 18 months, and about 30 micrograms at the end of five years. In comparison, birth control pills that contain levonorgestrel provide about 50 to 150 micrograms of the progestin a day, plus estrogen. (The only progestin-only contraceptive available in the United States contains 75 micrograms of norgestrel, a progestin similar to levonorgestrel.)

When the hormone supply dwindles, usually in about five years, a new implant can be inserted if desired. On the other hand, if a woman wishes to become pregnant ear-

This article first appeared in the *FDA Consumer*, May, 1991.

Effectiveness Rates of Contraceptive Methods

(Shown are the number of pregnancies for every 100 women during the first year of use)

Method	Lowest Expected	Typical
Male sterilization	0.1	0.15
Norplant	0.2	0.2
Female sterilization	0.2	0.4
Oral contraceptives		3
Combined	0.1	*
Progestin only	0.5	*
IUD	<1	3
Condom without spermicide	2	12
Cervical cap	6	18
Diaphragm with spermicide cream or jelly	6	18
Vaginal sponge		
women who haven't borne children	6	18
women who have borne children	9	28
Spermicides alone (foams, creams, jellies, and vaginal suppositories)	3	21
Periodic abstinence (all methods)	1–9	20
No contraception (planned pregnancy)	85	85

* = not available

(Source: Adapted from Table 1 in *Studies in Family Planning*, 1990, by J. Tussell et al.)

lier, she can have the implants removed at any time, and fertility is restored very soon. Blood levels of the progestin are undetectable within 5 to 14 days.

Population Council Project

Norplant has been marketed in other countries for several years. According to the Population Council, more than half a million women in 46 countries have used the implant since it was first approved in Finland—where it is manufactured—in 1983. It now has regulatory approval in 17 other countries as well, including Sweden, Indonesia, the Dominican Republic, Thailand, China, Peru, and the United States. Norplant's U.S. distributor is the Philadelphia-based pharmaceutical firm Wyeth-Ayerst Laboratories.

"The first implants were tested in 1968," says Population Council vice president Wayne Bardin, M.D., "and then the council began to develop and test implants that released a whole variety of progestins. By 1974, we came up with what is now the Nor-

plant implant, using levonorgestrel. The first clinical trial of that was begun in 1975."

FDA approval of the implant was based on the results of clinical studies involving 2,400 women in the United States, Finland, Sweden, Denmark, Jamaica, Brazil, Chile, and the Dominican Republic.

In the studies, the contraceptive's effectiveness approached that of sterilization in the first year. (See chart above.)

Pregnancy rates were slightly higher in heavier women, increasing after the third year of use in those who weighed more than 69 kilograms (153 pounds). Nevertheless, the protection is still quite good. For example, among 100 women of all weights using the implant for five years, it is expected that four would become pregnant during that time. By contrast, of 100 women using the pill for the same time, at least 15 might be expected to become pregnant.

Norplant's effectiveness does not depend on patient compliance—a feature shared by only one other type of reversible contraceptive—the intrauterine device, or IUD. This particularly appeals to Collier for the convenience it affords. "Unlike the pill, you don't have to remember to take it every day, and, unlike the diaphragm, there's no problem with spontaneity," she says.

Because Norplant is not a barrier contraceptive, however, it offers no protection against sexually transmitted diseases such as AIDS, herpes, chlamydia, and gonorrhea. For optimum protection from both disease and pregnancy, couples may choose to use both Norplant and a condom.

The Drawbacks

As with virtually any drug or medical device, Norplant isn't entirely trouble-free. Side effects that women have reported with the implant during the first year include irregular menstrual bleeding, headache, nervousness, depression, nausea, dizziness, skin rash, acne, change of appetite, breast tenderness, weight gain, enlargement of the ovaries, and excessive growth of body or facial hair.

Some Norplant users have also reported breast discharge, vaginal discharge, inflammation of the cervix, abdominal discomfort, and muscle and skeletal pain. These effects, however, cannot be linked to use of the implant because the complaints are common among the general population and could stem from many other causes. There is no known biological reason to link the complaints specifically to use of the contraceptive.

By far, the most common side effect is menstrual cycle irregularity. "To give the percentage of women with menstrual irregularities is complex," says Bardin, "because it changes with time." He says that over a five-year period of use, about 45 percent of women will have irregular periods and another 45 percent will have normal periods. The remaining 10 percent will have long periods of time—three to four months—with no bleeding. "That's an average," says Bardin. "Basically what happens is you have more women with irregular periods in

the first year and that tends to diminish with continuing use."

The bleeding irregularities result from the continuous hormone release. "With the oral contraceptive pills, estrogen and progestin are taken for three weeks and withdrawn for one week, causing regular bleeding," explains Lisa Rarick, M.D., a medical officer in FDA's division of endocrine and metabolism drug products. "Norplant, on the other hand," says Rarick, "provides no cyclic withdrawal, and thus each individual creates her own bleeding pattern."

In the multi-center trials, more women had increases in their hemoglobin concentrations than decreases, indicating that they lost less menstrual blood when using Norplant. (Hemoglobin is the oxygen-carrying pigment of red blood cells that gives them their red color and serves to transport oxygen to tissues.) Bardin says that this is because, on average, even if the number of bleeding days increases in the first year of use, the total amount of blood lost may be less than would be lost without hormonal contraception.

He says that most women who use Norplant don't perceive bleeding as a problem. "To illustrate," he says, "if you say, 'What is the biggest complaint that women have about Norplant,' it's bleeding irregularities. But if you ask all women if bleeding irregularities bother them, something like 60 percent say 'no.'"

Collier says she has spotting and a lighter flow with Norplant. "Sometimes, I have no discernible cycle at all," she says, but maintains that "although of course I'd rather have regular periods, the effects are not that bad."

Nevertheless, the major reason women give for discontinuing Norplant is bleeding problems, accounting for about 9 percent of those who stop in the first year, according to FDA's Rarick. Another 5 percent stop for other medical reasons, from headaches to dizziness, and perhaps another 5 percent stop for other reasons, including to have a baby. She estimates that about 60 to 65 percent of women continue with the implant longer than two years.

Not for Everyone

More serious complications are possible as well, and Norplant is not recommended for everyone. As with oral contraceptives, women with acute liver disease or liver tumors—whether malignant or benign—unexplained vaginal bleeding, breast cancer, or blood clots in the legs, lungs or eyes should not use the implant.

Norplant contains only progestin, whereas most oral contraceptives contain both progestin and estrogen. Some side effects of the pill, such as eye disorders and increased risk of cardiovascular problems among women who smoke, are believed to be related to the estrogen component. Nevertheless, FDA advises physicians to "consider the possible increased risks associated with oral contraceptives, including elevated blood pressure, thromboembolic disorders [blood clots obstructing blood vessels], and other vascular problems that might occur with use of the contraceptive implant."

Bardin suggests that Norplant will be most attractive to women who:

- wish to use highly effective low-dose hormone contraception
- want long-term contraception after completing their family, but don't want sterilization
- want to delay childbearing for an extended period of time
- cannot use estrogens
- are unhappy with other forms of contraception.

On the flip side, Bardin expects the implant to be less popular among women who:

- are happy with their present form of contraception
- cannot or do not want to pay the upfront cost of Norplant

- will not tolerate irregular menstrual bleeding if it should occur
- do not want to use a method that requires a visit to a health-care professional to discontinue. ("Some women feel that puts them at the mercy of the clinic and they want to be able to stop it any time they want," says Bardin. "That's why they like pills and barrier methods—it's under their control," he says.)

Surgical Insertion

Successful use of the Norplant system depends on careful insertion of the capsules. Wyeth-Ayerst markets the implant as a kit with detailed instructions for insertion and removal, and, through the Association of Reproductive Health Professionals, offers physician training programs as well.

The firm describes the insertion as a minor, outpatient surgical procedure requiring only 10 to 15 minutes. The area is numbed with a local anesthetic, and a small incision, less than an eighth of an inch long, is made. Using a special instrument called a trocar, the physician places the six capsules just under the skin. The incision is then covered with protective gauze and a small adhesive bandage. Stitches are not required.

When the anesthetic wears off, there may be some tenderness or itching, and perhaps some temporary discoloration, bruising and swelling. Infection at the site of insertion has also been reported.

It takes a bit longer to remove the implant than to insert it—usually from 15 to 20 minutes, according to the distributor. As with insertion, a small incision is made under a local anesthetic. Then the physician removes the capsules and, again, the incision is covered with an adhesive bandage. Sometimes, some capsules may be more difficult to remove than others. When this happens, the woman may have to return a second time, after the area has healed, for removal of the remaining capsules.

The reason for suggesting the second visit, Bardin says, is to let the physician know that "if you have trouble removing, don't cut a big hole in the woman's arm and go fishing around looking for it [the capsule]." If the anesthetic has caused the area to puff up, for example, it may be difficult to feel the implant. "Wait until the next week or whenever she can come in again," says Bardin, "and you'll be able to see it and take it out with minimal trauma."

If desired, a new set of implants can be inserted at the same time the old set is removed, either in the same arm and through the same incision, or in the other arm.

The price to the medical professional for a single Norplant system, which includes all the necessary apparatus for insertion and removal as well as the set of six capsules, has been set at $350. Fees for insertion and related costs, such as counseling and removal, vary, depending on the physician.

Collier says that this will probably be the last Norplant she'll have, at least for a while, as she plans to get pregnant eventually. She's not sure if she would come back to the implant later. "Hormone therapy and the risks associated with it—more with the pill and estrogen than with Norplant—concern me," she says. "I'll just have to see what else might be available when that time comes." For now, Collier is pleased with Norplant and would recommend it to any woman, "especially," she says, "if they're going to be on hormone therapy anyway."∎

Cognitive Analysis of Contraceptive Behavior
Anne E. Norris

This paper presents a new approach to contraceptive behavior—an approach that draws on research and theory in the areas of memory and information processing. The approach generates a model for predicting both pregnancy risk taking and risk-avoidance behaviors. This model integrates descriptive findings in the contraceptive literature and is supported by a preliminary laboratory study.

Several authors have argued that adolescents risk pregnancy because the use of contraceptives involves planning (Cobliner, 1974; Cvetkovich & Grote, 1981; Diamond, Steinhoff, Palmore & Smith, 1973; Sachs, 1985; Tauer, 1983). The ability to anticipate and prepare for intercourse is thought to be contingent on the ability to perceive cause and effect relationships. Adolescent beliefs regarding insusceptibility to pregnancy are believed to arise from this inability to perceive causal relations (Cobliner; Cvetkovich & Grote; Marcy, Brown, & Danielson, 1983).

Several findings challenge a developmental explanation for risking pregnancy. First, successful professional women in their 20s also regard themselves as being insusceptible to pregnancy and engage in pregnancy

This article first appeared in *IMAGE: The Journal of Nursing Scholarship* (1988) 20: 135–140. Copyright © 1988, Sigma Theta Tau, International. Reprinted with permission.

risk-taking behavior, even though these women, by this point in their lives, would seem to have developed the ability to perceive causal relations (Luker, 1975; Span, 1986). In addition, two recent studies have found no correspondence between cognitive maturity and the use of contraceptives (Hughes & Torre, 1987; White, 1984). Moreover, several psychological studies have demonstrated that individuals generally perceive negative events such as an accident or illness as being more likely to happen to others than to themselves (Perloff & Fetzer, 1986; Tversky & Kahneman, 1973). Thus statements of insusceptibility and pregnancy risk-taking behavior may not be unique to the adolescent age group and do not necessarily appear to be linked to the cognitive ability to perceive causal relations.

Perhaps a better explanation of why teenage and adult women risk pregnancy can be provided by a cognitive approach that emphasizes the role of memory structure and information processing. Indeed, one could argue that the ability to anticipate and prepare for intercourse is contingent on the ability to think about sexual intercourse, contraception, and the negative impact on one's life of an unplanned pregnancy. Actual pregnancy risk taking or risk avoidance might arise as a function of the thoughts on a woman's mind at the time that she is presented with an opportunity to engage in intercourse. Thoughts about the negative impact of an unplanned pregnancy on one's goals and life circumstances would be likely to motivate risk-avoidance behaviors. Pregnancy risk-taking behaviors, on the other hand, might be motivated by thoughts about the positive impact of intercourse on the relationship (e.g., pleasing partner, validating a commitment, increasing intimacy) or thoughts about the pleasurable physical and emotional feelings associated with intercourse (e.g., feeling cared about).

A variety of factors could influence what thoughts are on a woman's mind in both intimate and nonintimate situations (e.g., recent conversation with her partner, observing difficulties that a peer experiences with an unplanned pregnancy). To understand how a cognitive approach could explain the influence of such factors, it is necessary to consider how thoughts are represented in the memory and how thoughts in the memory become active and thus capable of influencing judgment, perception and behavior.

Thoughts Represented in Memory

According to a network model of memory, thoughts are represented by nodes that correspond to concepts, and associative pathways that link concepts together forming networks (Collins & Loftus, 1975). The associative pathways represent properties of or information about the concept and may include semantic relations with other concepts. For example, thoughts about sex might be represented by a structure such as the one depicted in **Figure 1**. The concept "sex" might be linked to other nodes corresponding to concepts about genitals and components of sexual behaviors, producing a network that represents thoughts about sex.

Memory structures (nodes, networks) vary in terms of availability and accessibility (Tulving & Pearlstone, 1966). A structure is considered to be available when it is stored in the memory but is currently not in an active or accessible state. Information represented by an accessible structure is present in the working memory (Powell & Fazio, 1984). It is important to note that only a small portion of one's available memories are accessible to the working memory at any one point in time. Information represented by an available structure cannot influence perception, judgment or behavior. Because accessible structures are present in the working memory, such structures can influence perception,

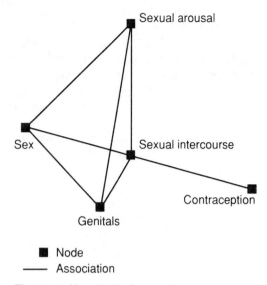

Figure 1. Hypothetical memory representation for sex-related constructs.

judgment and behavior (Bargh, 1984; Higgins & King, 1981).

In the contraception literature, the relationship between knowledge and the use of contraceptives demonstrates the importance of and the difference between availability and accessibility. The absence of knowledge about reproduction and contraception is associated with an increased risk for unwanted pregnancy (Hayes, 1987). Yet, as Hayes points out, possessing this knowledge does not predict the use of contraceptives or the avoidance of unprotected intercourse to those who view pregnancy as being undesirable. Stated differently, the person who lacks knowledge about reproduction and contraception does not have this information available in the memory, and so the knowledge cannot be made accessible. However, neither does having knowledge available in the memory ensure that the knowledge will influence behavior. Rather, the impact of this knowledge is contingent on factors that make the knowledge accessible.

Active Thoughts in Memory

A variety of social, psychological and contextual factors may increase the accessibility of an available structure in any of three ways (Bargh, 1984; Higgins & King, 1981). First, structures can become chronically accessible when they are used frequently. For example, students attending a school with a school-based clinic frequently use structures in the memory that correspond to thoughts about contraception as they observe signs and notices referring to the clinic and its services and note the uproar concerning the propriety of providing contraceptive services to minors. Frequent use of these structures may then increase the use of contraceptives because thoughts about contraception are in the working memory (i.e., "on a person's mind").

Second, recent use of the memory structures will also render the structures accessible. A sexually active woman attending a lecture on reproduction and contraception will have temporarily accessible in memory structures corresponding to sex, contraception and pregnancy. Consequently she may immediately decide to forgo unprotected intercourse or to make an appointment with Planned Parenthood. Yet a few days later she may engage in unprotected intercourse without even thinking about pregnancy, or she may forget to keep the appointment.

Last, memory structures may become accessible through the phenomenon of spreading activation (Bargh, 1984; Collins & Loftus, 1975). Activation spreads along the associations joining nodes and networks. Hence a given memory structure can become accessible when activation spreads from a structure with which it is associated. The strength of the association increases the likelihood and the rapidity with which the activation will spread. The more associations and the stronger the association, the more likely the structure will be accessible at any point in time.

Several studies in the psychological literature have demonstrated the effects of accessibility but are not reviewed here (e.g., Bargh & Pietromonaco, 1982; Fazio & Williams, 1986). Suffice it to say, by predetermining or manipulating the accessibility of a particular structure, these researchers have been able to demonstrate the influence that that particular structure has on perception, judgment or behavior. Fazio and his colleagues (Fazio, Chen, McDonel, & Sherman, 1982; Fazio & Williams, 1986; Powell & Fazio, 1984) have done research that is particularly exciting since they found that attitudes are good predictors of behavior when accessibility of the attitude is taken into account. By generalizing findings such as these to contraception, we may be able to determine when and where attitudes on contraception will be good predictors of contraceptive behavior.

A Cognitive Model

The basic premise of this cognitive model is that a woman's contraceptive behavior is a function of the thoughts that are accessible at the time that she is presented with an opportunity to engage in sexual intercourse. It is hypothesized that (a) thoughts about relationships tend to encourage risking pregnancy, and (b) thoughts about the impact of an unwanted pregnancy tend to discourage risking pregnancy and encourage contraceptive use. The impact of an unwanted pregnancy is defined as the negative consequences of a pregnancy on one's immediate and near future life circumstances and goals.

Two classes of factors are thought to influence the accessibility of the memory structures in intimate situations. First, situational factors make it difficult for the woman to think broadly or clearly about her behavior and its consequences (Easterbrook, 1959; Nemeth, 1986; Steele, Critchlow, & Liu, 1985; Steele & Southwick, 1985; Zajonc, 1965;

Zeichner & Pihl, 1979). These factors place demands on attentional resources, increasing the likelihood that chronically accessible structures will have the greatest impact on judgment and behavior. Situational factors include the partner, alcohol (the effects of social or moderate drinking as well as intoxication), and arousal.

A second class of factors are those that are independent of or external to the intimate situation. These factors include the sex and contraceptive experiences of self and others, educational and career goals, relationship goals, and culture. Unlike situational factors, external factors may influence both the structure and accessibility of the memory. For example, a peer's unwanted pregnancy or a newly acquired career interest might stimulate thinking about the impact of a pregnancy on one's life. This thinking could generate new structures concerning pregnancy and/or career interests, create new or stronger associations among the existing memory structures or make available structures accessible.

As a class, external factors may promote either risking pregnancy or the avoidance of pregnancy. Sex and contraceptive experiences of self and others could generate taking more risks if, for example, individuals have unprotected intercourse but do not get pregnant or experience positive benefits associated with an unplanned pregnancy. Conversely, negative experiences of pregnancy or social acceptance for avoiding unprotected intercourse might generate more avoidance behavior. Educational or professional goals might foster more avoidance behavior since a pregnancy may interfere with achieving such goals.

Relationship goals, on the other hand, could be impeded by the use of contraceptives. Luker (1975) reported that women believe that using contraceptives could turn a partner off since this might imply that sex was premeditated or that the woman is too experienced sexually. Luker's work also sug-

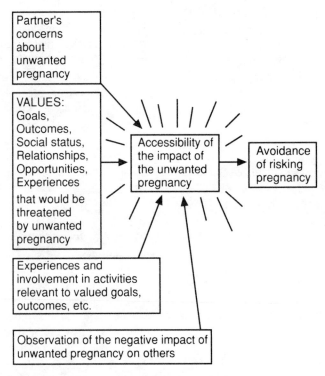

Figure 2. Factors hypothesized to increase the accessibility of concepts relevant to the impact of an unwanted pregnancy.

gests that the U.S. culture may encourage more risking of pregnancy because this culture views sex as being spontaneous and women who plan for sexual encounters as being loose or "bad." Abramson and Mechanic (1983) found that the U.S. media (best-selling books and major motion pictures) depict sex as spontaneous and do not associate sex with the use of contraceptives or pregnancy.

Both the situation and external factors can have a varied effect on behavior. Moreover, only some of the factors in either class are likely to increase the accessibility of concerns about the impact of a pregnancy. These factors are diagrammed in **Figure 2.**

Yet this diagram is incomplete. It ignores the contribution of spreading activation as well as the importance of preexisting associations between various memory structures. Anecdotal evidence obtained from interviews with college women (Norris, 1987) shows the importance of these preexisting associations.

> Mary Smith is thinking about a fraternity party while making plans to attend one. She believes that some of the men at these parties try to get women drunk so that they can have sex with them. Mary does not want to get pregnant because an unwanted pregnancy would interfere with school. She decides to tell her friends they must look out for her while at the party and not let her wander off alone with any man.

In this example, thinking about a fraternity party increases the accessibility of concerns about the impact of an unwanted pregnancy and generates preventive behaviors.

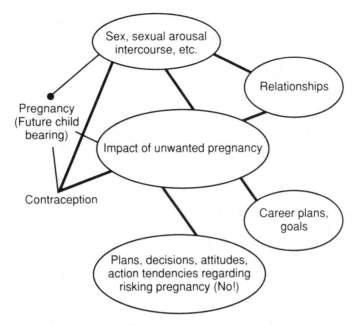

a. Memory structure of someone who does not risk pregnancy

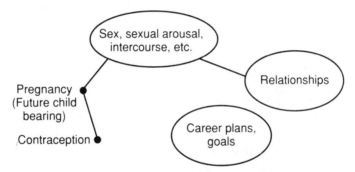

b. Memory structure of someone who does risk pregnancy

Figure 3. Possible memory structures for women who (a) avoid risking pregnancy or (b) risk pregnancy. Heavier lines indicate stronger associations; circles identify networks. For simplicity, nodes and associations within networks are not diagrammed.

In general, the more experiences and the more thinking a woman does about the impact of an unwanted pregnancy, the more likely it is that strong associations will develop between thoughts about the impact of pregnancy and other thoughts represented in the memory. This increases the likelihood that thoughts about pregnancy will be activated by spreading activation. Therefore a more complete understanding of how thoughts about the impact of an unwanted pregnancy become accessible requires consideration of how the memory of women who avoid risking pregnancy might be structured.

As can be seen from **Figure 3,** the potential associations are many and differ from that which would be predicted for women who do not think about the impact of unwanted pregnancy. Concerns about unwanted pregnancy may integrate structures related to such factors as relationships, sex and contraception (plans and attitudinal positions regarding the use of contraception and the risk of pregnancy). The web of interconnecting associations that results from an active concern about unwanted pregnancy increases the likelihood that this concern as well as plans for coping with this concern will remain accessible.

Obviously, considerations of memory structure could make this cognitive model quite complex. Yet, this complexity enables the prediction of changes in pregnancy risk taking and risk avoidance behaviors. For example, Span (1986) interviewed successful career women in their late 20s and early and mid-30s. These women had always planned to be married and viewed a long-term relationship as being very important. Unlike relationship goals, career goals were being realized and were now less important. What was of paramount concern to these women was the establishment of a satisfying, enduring, intimate relationship. Once careful, these women were now risking pregnancy.

Linking Literature and Model

Three sets of findings are relevant to the fit of the model with contraceptive behavior and unwanted pregnancy: intervention programs, interview studies and anecdotal reports, and descriptive research.

Few intervention programs have succeeded in decreasing the incidence of unwanted pregnancy (Hayes, 1987). Interestingly, programs that have succeeded (e.g.,

school-based clinics) incorporate interventions that may strengthen associations between sex and contraception and may create the memory structures needed for coping with intimate situations and for considering pregnancy as a real, important and avoidable consequence.

School based clinic programs have decreased the incidence of pregnancy and delayed the initiation of intercourse (Edwards, Steinman, Arnold & Hakanson, 1980; Zabin, Hirsch, Smith, Steett, & Hardy, 1986). These programs involved homeroom presentations, clinic-run discussion groups, individual counseling, announcements, signs and, as mentioned earlier, a great deal of attention from the media. It seems likely that such programs increase the strength of associations between sex and contraception and keep thoughts about contraception accessible.

The Teen Outreach Project (Philliber, 1985) appears to have decreased the incidence of pregnancy through an after-school program intended to improve self-esteem, decrease dropout rate and prevent unwanted pregnancy through structured discussion groups and involvement in community service. Since the Outreach Project was designed to decrease both dropout and pregnancy rates, discussion group participation may have created or increased the accessibility of concerns about unwanted pregnancy.

Marcy et al. (1983) used a ''developmentally appropriate'' counselling strategy in a clinic setting and observed a decrease in the incidence of pregnancy, which lasted a full year following a brief counselling session. This strategy entailed a personalized discussion of the meaning of using contraceptives, partners' responses to contraceptives and one's ability and responsibility to make decisions concerning the use of contraceptives. Such a strategy should generate or increase accessibility of the memory structures representing the impact of unwanted pregnancy and plans for coping with the use of contraceptives.

Interview studies and anecdotal reports also provide support for this model. Relationship goals seem to be linked to risking pregnancy (Luker, 1975; Rogel, Zuehlke, Petersen, Tobin-Richards, & Shelton, 1980; Span, 1986). Women who have a strong need for a relationship seem not to think about pregnancy at all or to focus only on its likelihood or desirability and not its impact (Finkel & Finkel, 1975; Luker, 1975; Nadelson, Notman, & Gillon, 1980; Rogel et al.; Ryan & Sweeney, 1980; Sherline & A-Davidson, 1978; Smith, Weinman, & Mumford, 1982).

In contrast, descriptive research identifies variables related positively to pregnancy risk avoidance—variables that are capable of increasing the likelihood that thoughts about the impact of pregnancy or about sex and contraception are accessible. For example, frequency of intercourse is related positively to use of contraceptives (Anderson, McPherson, Beeching, Weinberg & Vessey, 1978; Cvetkovich & Grote, 1981; Geis & Gerrard, 1984). Perceived susceptibility to pregnancy is correlated with risk-avoidance behavior, while perceived insusceptibility is positively associated with pregnancy risk taking in both males and females (Finkel & Finkel, 1975; Jaccard, 1987; Kantner & Zelnik, 1973; Klein, 1983; Sorenson, 1973; White, 1984).

Eisen and Zelman (1986) observed that adolescents who saw themselves as being more susceptible to pregnancy had more knowledge, independent of sex education and previous sexual experiences, about the effectiveness of contraceptive methods. This finding is particularly interesting since it can be interpreted as an example of the effects of accessibility; that is, an awareness of one's vulnerability to pregnancy may be associated with an increased likelihood that the memory structures corresponding to pregnancy are accessible. If these structures are accessible,

then information regarding pregnancy is more likely to be perceived and remembered.

Other variables such as age (Devaney & Hubley, 1981; Kantner & Zelnik, 1972; Zabin & Clark, 1981) and academic goals or achievement also correspond to an increase in pregnancy risk avoidance. One interpretation of these findings is that as women grow older they have more valued opportunities and activities that could be threatened by an unplanned pregnancy. Consistent with this interpretation, Kantner & Zelnik and Zelnik, Kantner and Ford (1981) have observed that older women are more likely to use an effective method of birth control.

Several findings in the literature on contraceptives highlight the importance of educational goals. What remains unclear is whether goals are important in and of themselves or whether it is the possession of a goal that would be impeded by an unwanted pregnancy that makes the difference.

Devaney and Hubley (1981) reported that both black and white adolescents with clear goals and expectations are more likely to use contraceptives. These and other researchers found that initiation of intercourse at a young age is less likely for males and females who score high on intelligence tests or are academically motivated and doing well in school (Devaney & Hubley; Durant, Jay, Linder, Shoffitt, & Litt, 1984; Jessor, Costa, Jessor, & Donovan, 1983).

In contrast, Davies, Beck, Smith and Angelo (1987) note that poor contraception users tend to discontinue school and view vocational training as their goal. Furstenberg & Brooks-Gunn (1985) observed that the academic performance of young pregnancy teens was below the age-appropriate grade level at the time these teens became pregnant. Ensminger (1987) found black inner-city mothers with low expectations for their child's academic success had children who were more likely to be involved in sexual activity, particularly at a younger age. Interest-

Table 1. Number of Subjects Who Described the Couple in the Story as Risking or Not Risking Pregnancy as a Function of the Three Priming Conditions.

Choice	Career goal	Neutral	Relationship goal
Risks pregnancy	0	2	6
Does not risk pregnancy	10	8	4

Note: $X^2 = 9.5$, p<.01.

ingly, the expectations of mothers did not predict involvement in drugs or criminal acts.

A Test of the Model

A laboratory study was designed to assess the effects of manipulating the accessibility of relationship and career goal-related structures on the decisions of college students to engage in or avoid unprotected intercourse, as revealed by a story completion task. Thirty female subjects were randomly assigned to one of three conditions—relationship goal, career goal, and neutral—and were asked to read a story describing an enjoyable date between two college students and write an ending for it. In this story, the two characters were alone in the female's dorm room at the end of the evening. Neither character had any contraceptives. The female roommate was out of town for the weekend. The male character had just verbalized his positive feelings and regard for the female character and his desire to engage in intercourse. The female character had thought about (but not verbalized) her own desires to engage in intercourse.

The first paragraph of the story, designed to increase the accessibility of particular memory structures, varied across conditions. In the first condition, the paragraph described the advantages of being in a satisfying relationship. In the second condition, the paragraph described the importance of school and career goals. A third condition, included as a control, described doing laundry in a college dorm. It was predicted that when thoughts about relationships were ac-

cessible, the subjects would write an ending in which the characters risked pregnancy. When thoughts about school and career were accessible, it was predicted that subjects would write an ending in which the risk of pregnancy was avoided.

Content analyses of story endings (see **Table 1**) supported both predictions. Particularly striking was the finding that no subject in the career condition wrote an ending in which pregnancy was risked. Alternative explanations such as demand characteristics (the subjects guessed the hypothesis and wrote an ending consistent with this guess), demographic or attitudinal differences or differences in sexual experiences failed to explain this pattern of findings. These results are viewed as preliminary support for this cognitive model.

Research is in progress to assess predictions for contraceptive behavior based on this model and to test assumptions made regarding differences in memory structure such as those depicted in Figure 3. Should this and other research generate more support for the model, the door will be opened to a variety of new interventions that draw on an understanding of memory structure and information processing. In addition, the model may provide a means for understanding and predicting the effectiveness of current interventions and thereby provide for more efficient application of these interventions.

REFERENCES

Abramson, P., & Mechanic M. (1983). Sex and the media: Three decades of best-selling books and major motion pictures. *Archives of Sexual Behavior, 12*, 185–206.

Anderson, P., McPherson, K., Beeching, N., Weinberg, J., & Vessey, M. (1978) Sexual behavior and contraceptive practice of undergraduates at Oxford University. *Journal of Biosocial Science, 10*, 277–286.

Bargh, J. (1984). Automatic and conscious processing of social information. In R. Wyer & S. Srull (Eds.), *Handbook of social cognition* (Vol. 3). Hillsdale, NJ: Erlbaum.

Bargh, J., & Pietromonaco, P. (1982). Automatic information processing and social perception: The influence of trait information presented outside of conscious awareness on impression formation. *Journal of Social and Personality Psychology, 43*, 437–439.

Cobliner, W. (1974). Pregnancy in the single adolescent girl: The role of cognitive functions. *Journal of Youth and Adolescence, 3*, 17–29.

Collins, A. M., & Loftus, E. F. (1975). A spreading activation theory of semantic processing. *Psychological Review, 82*, 407–428.

Cvetkovich, G., & Grote, B. (1981). Psychosocial maturity and teenage contraceptive use: An investigation of decision-making and communication skills. *Population and Environment, 4*, 211–226.

Davies, D., Beck, J., Smith, P., & Angelo, A. (1987, August). *Good and poor contraceptors: Who are the teens at risk?* Paper presented at the American Psychological Association Meeting, New York City.

Devaney, B., & Hubley, K. (1981). *The determinants of adolescent pregnancy and childbearing*. Final report to the National Institute of Child Health and Human Development. Washington, D.C.: Mathematica Policy Research.

Diamond, M., Steinhoff, P., Palmore, J., & Smith, R. (1973). Sexuality, birth control and abortion. A decision-making sequence. *Journal of Biosocial Science, 5*, 347–361.

Durant, R., Jay, M., Linder, C., Shoffitt, T., & Litt, I. (1984). Influence of psychosocial factors on adolescent compliance with oral contraceptives. *Journal of Adolescent Health Care, 5*, 1–6.

Easterbrook, J. (1959). The effect of emotion on the utilization and organization of behavior. *Psychological Review, 66*, 183–201.

Edwards, L., Steinman, M., Arnold, K., & Hakanson, E. (1980). Adolescent pregnancy prevention services in high school clinics. *Family Planning Perspectives, 12*, 6–14.

Eisen, M., & Zelman, G. (1986). The role of health belief attitudes, sex education, and demographics in predicting adolescents' sexuality knowledge. *Health Education Quarterly, 13*, 9–22.

Ensminger (1987, August). *Patterns of adolescent delinquency, drug use, and sexual activity.* Paper presented at the American Psychological Association Meeting, New York City.

Fazio, R., Chen, J., McDonel, E., & Sherman, S. (1982). Attitude accessibility, attitude-behavior consistency, and the strength of the object-evaluation association. *Journal of Experimental Social Psychology, 18*, 339–357.

Fazio, R., & Williams, C. (1986). Attitude accessibility as a moderator of the attitude-perception and attitude-behavior relations: An investigation of the 1984 Presidential election. *Journal of Social and Personality Psychology, 51*, 505–514.

Finkel, M., & Finkel, D. (1975). Sexual and contraceptive knowledge, attitudes and behavior of male adolescents. *Family Planning Perspectives, 7*, 256–260.

Furstenberg, F., & Brooks-Gunn, J. (1985). Adolescent fertility: Causes, consequences and remedies. In L. Aiken & D. Mechanic (Eds.), *Applications of social science to clinical medicine and health policy.* New Brunswick, NJ: Rutgers University Press.

Geis, B., & Gerrard, M. (1984). Predicting male and female contraceptive behavior: A descriminant analysis of groups high, moderate, and low in contraceptive effectiveness. *Journal of Personality and Social Psychology, 46*, 669–680.

Hayes, C. (1987). *Risking the future* (Vol. 1). Washington, D.C.: National Academy Press.

Higgins, E., & King, G., (1981). Accessibility of social constructs: Information processing consequences of individual and contextual variability. In N. Cantor & J. Kihlstrom (Eds.), *Personality, cognition, and social interaction.* Hillsdale, NJ: Erlbaum.

Hughes, C., & Torre, C. (1987). Predicting effective contraceptive behavior in college females. *Nurse Practitioner, 12*, 45–54.

Jaccard, J. (1987, August). *When attitudes aren't enough: Issues in understanding consistent contraceptive use.* Paper presented at the American Psychological Association Meeting, New York City.

Jessor, R., Costa, F., Jessor, S. & Donovan, J. (1983). The time of first intercourse: A prospective. *Journal of Personality and Social Psychology, 44*, 608–626.

Kantner, J., & Zelnik, M. (1973). Contraception and pregnancy: Experience of young unmarried women in the United States. *Family Planning Perspectives, 5*, 23–35.

Kantner, J., & Zelnik, M. (1972). Sexual experience of young unmarried women in the United States. *Family Planning Perspectives, 4,* 9–18.

Klein, P. (1983). Contraceptive use and perceptions of chance and ability of conceiving in women electing abortion. *Journal of Obstetrical and Gynecological Nursing, 12,* 167–171.

Luker, K. (1975). *Taking chances: Abortion and the decision not to contracept.* Berkeley: University of California Press.

Marcy, S., Brown, J., & Danielson, R. (1983). Contraceptive use by adolescent females in relation to knowledge, and to time and method of contraceptive counseling. *Research in Nursing and Health, 6,* 175–182.

Nadelson, C., Notman, M., & Gillon, J. (1980). Sexual knowledge and attitudes of adolescents: Relationship to contraceptive use. *Obstetrics & Gynecology, 55,* 340–345.

Norris, A. (1987). Taped interviews with 70 female undergraduates conducted at the University of Wisconsin-Madison.

Nemeth, C. (1986). Differential contributions of majority and minority influence. *Journal of Personality and Social Psychology, 93,* 23–32.

Perloff, L., & Fetzer, B. (1986). Self-other judgments and perceived vulnerability to victimization. *Journal of Personality and Social Psychology, 50,* 502–510.

Philliber, S. (1985). *Teen outreach: Results of the first year of a national replication.* Unpublished report. The Charles Stewart Mott Foundation, Flint, Michigan.

Powell, M., & Fazio, R. (1984). Attitude accessibility as a function of repeated attitude expression. *Personality and Social Psychology Bulletin, 10,* 139–148.

Rogel, M., Zuehlke, M., Petersen, A., Tobin-Richards, M., & Shelton, M. (1980). Contraceptive behavior in adolescence: A decision-making perspective. *Journal of Youth and Adolescence, 9,* 491–506.

Ryan, G., & Sweeney, P. (1980). Attitudes of adolescents toward pregnancy and contraception. *American Journal of Obstetrics and Gynecology, 137,* 358–366.

Sachs, B. (1985). Contraceptive decision making in urban female adolescents: Its relationship to cognitive development. International Journal of Nursing Studies, 22, 117–126.

Sherline, D., & A-Davidson, R. (1978). Adolescent pregnancy: The Jackson, Mississippi experience. *American Journal of Obstetrics and Gynecology, 132,* 245.

Smith, P., Weinman, M., & Mumford, D. (1982) Social and affective factors associated with adolescent pregnancy. *Journal of School Health, 52,* 90–93.

Sorenson, R. (1973). *Adolescent sexuality in contemporary America.* New York: World Publishing.

Span, P. (1986). Why smart women are stupid about birth control, *Glamour,* November, 252, 321–324.

Steele, C., Critchlow, B., & Liu, T. (1985). Alcohol and social behavior II: The helpful drunkard. *Journal of Personality and Social Psychology, 48,* 35–46.

Steele, C., & Southwick, L. (1985). Alcohol and social behavior I: The psychology of drunken excess. *Journal of Personality and Social Psychology, 48,* 18–34.

Tauer, K. (1983). Promoting effective decision-making in sexually active adolescents. *Nursing Clinics of North America, 18,* 275–292.

Tulving, E., & Pearlstone, Z. (1966). Availability versus accessibility of information in memory for words. *Journal of Verbal Learning and Verbal Behavior, 5,* 381–391.

Tversky, A., & Kahneman, D. (1973). Availability: A heuristic for judging frequency and probability. *Cognitive Psychology, 5,* 207–232.

White, J. (1984). Initiating contraceptive use: How do young women decide? *Pediatric Nursing, 10,* 347–352.

Zabin, L., & Clark, S. (1981). Why they delay: A study of teenage family planning clinic patients. *Family Planning Perspectives, 13,* 205–217.

Zabin, L., Hirsch, M., Smith, E., Street, R., & Hardy, J. (1986) Evaluation of a pregnancy prevention program for urban teenagers. *Family Planning Perspectives, 18,* 119–126.

Zajonc, R. (1965). Social facilitation. *Science, 149,* 269–274.

Zeichner, A., & Pihl, R. (1979). Effects of alcohol and behavior contingencies on human aggression. *Journal of Abnormal Psychology, 88,* 153–160.

Zelnik, M., Kantner, J., & Ford, K. (1981). *Sex and pregnancy among adolescents.* Beverly Hills, CA: Sage Publications.

Chapter 6

Choices Related to Pregnancy and Motherhood

Of the basic sex differences, the one that has the biggest impact on women's lives is the ability to bear children. No matter how far reproductive technology has come and no matter how the social roles of women and men change in regard to family life, the fact remains that women, not men, bear children. Although some have argued that the only way women can achieve full equality with men is for women to give up the childbearing role, this option remains a technological impossibility and women, in general, have expressed little interest in urging science to find a replacement for the womb.

Pregnancy and motherhood are seen by many as the epitome of the female role. Most societies expect all women to desire children. As the old school yard rhyme says, marriage is to be followed by the baby carriage. This expectation exists side-by-side with our society's highly valued emphasis on individual freedom and choice. Nonetheless, women in our society face at least three important choices related to pregnancy and motherhood.

The first choice is whether or not to become a mother. This choice exists largely because of widely available and effective contraception (Chapter 5) and because of recent advances in reproductive technology (Chapter 8). Women who do not want children do not have to have them, and most women who want children can.

The entry of large numbers of women into the work force during the last few decades was accompanied by dire predictions of the demise of the family. Many feared that women pursuing careers would not want to be mothers. However, **Baber and Monaghan** found that the majority of the college women they surveyed expect to have a career, a marriage, *and* a family. (Note: the sexual orientation of the subjects was not addressed.) While childbearing may be delayed until their careers are established, most women expected to have children and expressed a desire to remain at home and/or work part-time until their children reached preschool age. Although the women they surveyed strongly believed that they could ''have it all'', Baber and Monaghan point out that social roles and gender bias will make their paths difficult.

A small percentage of women voluntarily choose to not have children. **Joseph** describes how she arrived at that decision. She also describes the difficulty in defending

165

this choice to others. As motherhood has historically been perceived to be the ultimate expression of femininity, women who choose to remain childless are sometimes criticized as "unnatural" and less than fully feminine.

Pregnant women, having achieved the ultimate in femininity, are presumed to feel serene and fulfilled, with no second thoughts. Believing this myth can have traumatic consequences. As **Robinson and Stewart** point out, most pregnant women vacillate between excitement and pleasure and fear and trepidation. Having second thoughts about the life-long commitment to a child, fears about their own health and that of their baby, and discomfort with the physical changes of pregnancy are perfectly normal. This article also describes the impact of various motivations for becoming pregnant on the actual experience of pregnancy.

Pregnancy is not free of risk for either the mother or her fetus. These risks are greater for some women than for others. **Chez** emphasizes the importance of preconception counseling for identifying such women. Being tested for all sexually-transmitted diseases (STDs) is an essential component of that counseling, as STDs are a major cause of infertility. It can provide valuable information that will help them maximize the chances of a healthy pregnancy or that may guide them to ultimately decide against having children.

The second major choice that women face with regard to pregnancy is whether or not to continue the pregnancy. This decision is especially important for women whose pregnancies were not planned or are high risk. High risk pregnancies typically occur when the woman has a serious medical problem (see **Chez**), when there is a greater than average chance of genetic defects, or when the mother has used drugs while pregnant. **Zamula** describes some unfortunately common problems, such as fetal alcohol syndrome, that result from drug use during pregnancy. The increasing public awareness of the impact of drugs during pregnancy has led to some thorny ethical dilemmas. For example, should the employees of a restaurant or tavern refuse to serve alcoholic beverages to women who are clearly pregnant?

Many women are delaying childbearing until they reach their thirties or even forties. One of their biggest concerns is that the risk of many genetic disorders (such as Down Syndrome) increases with maternal age. Prenatal testing for genetic disorders is highly recommended for women over 35 years of age and for younger women with a family history of such problems. Until recently, amniocentesis was the only such prenatal test available. Though it remains an important and frequently-used source of information about the genetic characteristics of the developing fetus, it cannot be performed until relatively late in the pregnancy (generally after 16 weeks). This is highly undesirable. Between the time a woman discovers she is pregnant and the time she receives the results of amniocentesis, she may feel she should hide the pregnancy from others and prevent herself from becoming attached to a fetus she may later choose to abort. More recently, chorionic villus sampling (CVS) has been offered as an alternative to amniocentesis. This procedure, and its advantages and disadvantages, are described by **Kolker.** While providing an opportunity for identification of genetic and chromosomal disorders during the first trimester of pregnancy CVS does not eliminate all of the problems associated with amniocentesis and it creates its own set of ethical dilemmas.

A variety of factors may cause a pregnant woman to decide that she does not want or cannot assume the responsibilities of parenting. She then has two options. She may elect to have an abortion, although the legality of this option is under constant challenge, or she may carry the pregnancy to term and relinquish the child for adoption. Regardless of which option she chooses, it is important that she understand the potential psychological consequences of her decision.

Adler and her co-authors review and critique the literature on the psychological consequences of abortion for U.S. women. They conclude that although the timing of the abortion and the reasons for it influence a woman's psychological response to the procedure, severe negative reactions after abortions are generally rare. They also point out that there have been no truly longterm followup studies of the psychological adaptation of women who have had legal abortions.

The experience of a woman who has chosen to carry her pregnancy to term but does not want to raise the child herself is addressed in the last article in this chapter, by **Deykin** and co-authors. They interviewed mothers (and fathers) who had no contact with the child after relinquishment and no information about the child's placement or well-being. In other words, it was as if the child had died. They found that, under these conditions, relinquishing a child for adoption has long-term negative consequences. The intensely negative psychological consequences of relinquishment described by Deykin stand in stark contrast to the relatively mild, positive, reactions to first trimester abortion described by Adler et al. It is important to note that, unlike the majority of women having first trimester abortions, the majority of women relinquishing children are doing so in response to external pressures from family and health care professionals. Additionally, most of the subjects in Deykin's study were members of an organization of birthparents and were involved in searches for their relinquished children. These characteristics may set them apart from other relinquishing parents. Finally, the subjects of this study had relinquished their children under strictly followed closed-adoption rules. In response to studies such as Deykin's, many agencies and private sources have modified or loosened their adoption rules. Today, it is very common for the birthmother to play an active role in choosing the adoptive family. And a woman contemplating relinquishing a child for adoption can often choose among varying degrees of contact with the child and the adoptive parents. Such "open" adoption can be limited to communication between the birthmother and adoptive parents through an intermediary such as an agency or lawyer or it can involve regular direct participation of the birthmother in the daily life of the child and adoptive family. No research has yet assessed the psychological and social adaptation of relinquishing mothers in the case of open adoption.

REFERENCES AND SUGGESTED READING

Bailey, L. A., and Hailey, B. J. (1986–87). The psychological experience of pregnancy. *International Journal of Psychiatry in Medicine, 16*, 263–274.

Berkowitz, G. S., Skovron, J. L., Lapinski, R. H., and Berkowitz, R. L. (1990). Delayed childbearing and the outcome of pregnancy. *New England Journal of Medicine, 322,* 659–664.

McLaughlin, S. D., Manninen, D. L., and Winges, L. D. (1988). Do adolescents who relinquish their children fare better or worse than those who raise them? *Family Planning Perspectives, 20,* 25–32.

Meilaender, G. (1989, November/December). Abortion: The right to an argument. *Hastings Center Report,* pp. 13–16.

Rothman, B. K. (1986). *The tentative pregnancy. Prenatal diagnosis and the future of motherhood.* New York: Penguin Books.

Solimini, C. (1991, January). The career woman's guide to fertility. *Working Woman,* pp. 90–97.

Torres, A., and Forrest, J. D. (1988). Why do women have abortions? *Family Planning Perspectives, 20,* 169–176.

Wertz, D. C., and Fletcher, J. C. (1989, May/June). Fatal knowledge? Prenatal diagnosis and sex selection. *Hastings Center Report,* pp. 21–27.

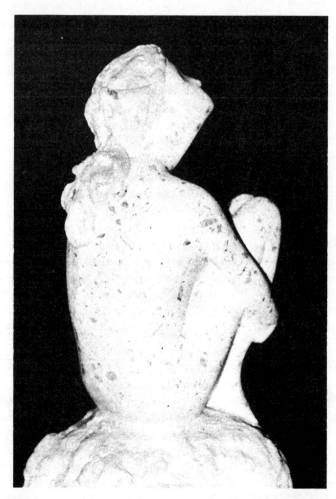

Alabaster scuplture by Gary Humiston. Photographed and reprinted by permission of the sculptor.

College Women's Career and Motherhood Expectations: New Options, Old Dilemmas

Kristine M. Baber and Patricia Monaghan

Women who desire to both work and parent are faced with the dilemma of how to integrate potentially conflicting roles and responsibilities. This study explores 250 college women's thinking about careers and childbearing. The results suggest that although these young women have been rethinking their career options and expanding their career choices into areas that have been traditionally male dominated, there is little indication of a reciprocal change in thinking about the primacy of mothering. All of the women expected to have careers, but few planned to be child free or have only one child. Women pursuing innovative careers were, however, less child oriented than those planning careers moderately innovative or traditional for women. The findings are discussed in the context of these women's proposed strategies for managing conflicting demands of work and family roles. These strategies include delayed childbearing, egalitarian marriages, and part-time work.

It is commonly believed our society is experiencing widespread and dramatic change in traditional sex roles. However, empirical evidence indicates that the major sex role change has been the increased labor force participation of young women, which in turn has influenced age at marriage and childbearing decisions (Leuptow, 1984). A majority of young women now expect to work after completion of their education, and the more highly educated a woman is, the more likely she is to be employed. The employment rate for single, college-educated women, for example, reached 85% in 1980 (Bianchi and Spain, 1983).

Young women face a critical conflict regarding employment because the early period of their career development usually coincides with prime childbearing years. Most young women internalize a system of beliefs about the primacy of childbearing and integrate the mothering role into their sense of self (Burroughs, Turner, and Turner, 1984; Houseknecht, 1982; Russo, 1979). If women desire to both work out of the home and parent, the dilemma that they generally face is whether to sequence career and parental roles, or try to integrate responsibilities and pursue both roles simultaneously. Daniels and Weingarten's (1982) work on the timing of parenthood explored the trade-offs of these different approaches to "shifting and varying the balance between parenthood and work in the world."

Contingency Orientation

Historically, a common solution to the career/family dilemma involved women adopting a contingency approach—opting for one of a few traditionally female professions and fitting one's work life around family responsibilities (Angrist, 1969; Angrist and Almquist, 1975). Angrist proposed that women in our society are socialized to prepare for and adjust to contingencies, the most important of which is the marriage and parenting

This article first appeared in *Sex Roles* (1988) 19: 189–203. Copyright ©, Plenum Publishing Corporation. Reprinted with permission.

role. She further suggested that this contingency orientation is reflected in women's personality development, in their belief systems, and in their life choices. Young women have been encouraged to accept traditionally feminine roles and expectations, thereby maximizing their complementarity with a potential spouse and ensuring their availability for maternal responsibilities.

One of the correlates of a contingency orientation is a limited perception of occupational options. In the late 1960s, over 70% of employed American women were clustered in four fields: teaching, nursing, secretarial work, and social work (Tangri, 1972). Although women's employment options are expanding, the majority of women still work in traditional female occupations (U.S. Department of Commerce, 1986). These occupations have been perceived to allow reasonable flexibility in terms of movement into and out of the work force. They have also been perceived to be integrated more easily with parenting responsibilities than most other types of work. Among the trade-offs made in selecting these occupations, however, are the relatively low prestige and financial rewards that accompany them.

Research exploring the career and marriage plans of unmarried college students, a group that would be expected to include a large number of career-oriented women, provides evidence of the persistence of this contingency orientation and the primacy of the mothering role. Greenglass and Devins' (1982) data collected in 1977 from female undergraduates indicated that although 67% of the sample saw their careers as very important, only 10% planned to work full time while they had preschool children. The majority of the women did not expect to work more than half time regardless of the age of their children.

However, there is also evidence that women's career preferences might be moving away from a contingency orientation. Burroughs et al. (1984) examined social-psychological influences on sex typing of occupational expectations and preferences. They used a system delineated by Tangri (1972) to categorize occupational choices. Occupations in which fewer than 30% of the workers were women were coded innovative, those with 30–50% women were coded as moderate, and those composed of more than 50% women were coded as traditional. They found that, of the females they surveyed, only 40% preferred traditionally feminine occupations, 32% preferred moderate, and 28% preferred those that usually employed few women and were categorized as innovative. However, 57% of the women *expected* to have traditional occupations, while only 17% expected to have those that could be considered innovative. The discrepancies between preferred and expected occupational choices were explored by Burroughs and colleagues in relationship to a variable they referred to as *sex role contingency orientation*. This referred to an orientation that reflected a primary and explicit concern with marriage and the family. The majority of women with high or intermediate sex role contingency orientations expected a traditional occupation, while women with low contingency orientation scores expected innovative or moderately innovative occupations.

Educational attainment and career orientation generally correlate negatively with the number of children that women prefer, expect, and actually have. Therefore, it seems likely that as women become more highly educated and committed to demanding careers, more women will choose to forgo motherhood and remain voluntarily childless.

Voluntary Childlessness

Generally, about 6% of wives between 18 and 34 years of age have expected to remain voluntarily childless or child free. According to Census Bureau data, the rate of 1979 varied from 3.6 to 9.5%, depending on education level. Women with more education were more likely to choose to have no children.

Based on current trends, demographers speculate that for women in their mid-20s in 1980, the rate of childlessness could climb to 25 or 30%, which would be the highest rate experienced since records have been kept (Bloom and Trussell, 1984). In 1985, the percentage of 30–34-year-old white women who were childless (for any reason) stood at about 26%, while for those 35–39 years of age, the rate was approximately 17% (U.S. Bureau of Census, 1986). However, because there has been a trend toward postponed childbearing among educated white women since the early 1970s, it is important when making fertility predictions to consider women's fertility preferences for their entire reproductive lifetime. For example, Census Bureau data for 1983 indicated that 47% of women 18–34 years old in June 1983 expected two children, 14% expected one child, and only 11% expected to be childless (U.S. Bureau of the Census, 1984).

Houseknecht (1982), in a review of the research on voluntary childlessness, noted that demographic variables such as education and career commitment have had unpredictable effects on the rate of women choosing to remain voluntarily child free. Even though women's educational and occupational options have greatly expanded, there has not been as great an increase in the number of women planning to forgo motherhood as had been expected. Most college women, even those from elite women's colleges, expect to have children (Hare-Mustin, Bennett, and Broderick, 1983; Komarovsky, 1985; Zuckerman, 1983).

Houseknecht suggested that demographic variables such as education and career commitment may be necessary, but not sufficient, to predict fertility trends. She proposed that a critical missing link in understanding the relationship between fertility decisions and these variables may be the degree of social support for a nonnormative lifestyle. Another relatively unexplored variable in the decision-making process is the influence of a woman's spouse or partner. Because most women make childbearing decisions within the context of a relationship, the direct and indirect effects of their partners' desire may be considerable. Therefore, even though career orientation in women may become more common and commitment to nontraditional careers more prevalent, the effect on fertility plans, and particularly the rate of voluntary childlessness, may be difficult to predict.

Delayed Childbearing

Many women of the baby boom era responded to the dilemma of conflicting roles by postponing childbearing until their late 20s and 30s. The most recent statistics from the U.S. Current Population Survey indicated that between 1975 and 1984 the fertility rate for 30–34-year-old women increased by 27% and that of 35–39-year-old women rose 17% while the fertility rates of all other age groups declined or remained constant (U.S. Bureau of the Census, 1986). However, this pattern of delayed childbearing and the accompanying "boomlet" may have been the result of particular economic and social events affecting those in the postwar baby boom generation, and there is some question as to whether it is a trend that will continue. Baldwin and Nord's (1984) monograph on delayed childbearing, for example, reviews theories of population dynamics that suggest that the post baby boom cohort's smaller number will boost job and earning opportunities of young men, encourage early marriage and childbearing, and result in women staying home with their children (p. 23).

Because demographer's label 1964 the last year of the baby boom, young women now in college represent the first of the post baby boom cohorts. Their expectations and attitudes should be a primary source of information for predicting future fertility trends, and also for investigating young women's thinking about balancing career and family roles.

This study, then, attempts to determine whether there is evidence of a continuing trend away from a contingency approach in women's career planning and, if so, whether there are reciprocal changes in their expectations regarding the mothering role. It investigates the types of occupations college women are planning to pursue and their thinking about whether they will have children, the timing of the birth of their first child, and how they plan to integrate paid work and family roles.

METHOD

Sample

The sample consisted of 250 unmarried females enrolled in a public university in New England in 1985. Participation was solicited in diverse classes in an attempt to reach students with a variety of majors. The mean age of the participants was 19.8 years (range 18–25). Twenty percent of the subjects were majoring in humanities, 20% in business and communications, 21% in physical and biological sciences, and 26% in child and family studies. The remainder of the participants had more specialized or undeclared majors.

Procedure

All participants completed the Career and Family Questionnaire (CFQ) developed for this study. This questionnaire includes questions about marriage and childbearing expectations, career expectations and attitudes, and orientations toward work and family roles.

Marriage and Childbearing. Participants provided basic demographic data, and responded to a series of questions about their expectations regarding marriage and childbearing. They indicated whether they planned

to marry, the age at which they planned to marry, and estimated the probability of having children. If they planned to have children, they were asked at what age they expected to have their first child and the number of children they thought they would have. They also indicated whether there was a critical age by which they would feel compelled to have their first child.

Career. Participants responded to a series of questions about work expectations such as whether they planned to work after graduation and, if so, what type of work they planned to do. To allow for comparisons with previous research, occupational preferences were later coded using the system employed by Tangri (1972) and Burroughs et al. (1984). Occupations were categorized based on the percentage of women in them according to detailed occupational data from the 1970 census (U.S. Department of Commerce, 1973). Innovative occupations were those employing fewer than 30% women; moderate, 30–50% women; and traditional, employing over 50% women.

Work and Family. To determine the relationship between career development and the timing of the first child, participants indicated whether they would have their child first and then establish a career, establish their career first and then have a child, do both simultaneously, or whether they saw no relationship between the two. They estimated how long they would plan to take off after their first child was born and whether they would return to work after that.

Contingency Orientation. A final section of the Career and Family Questionnaire consisted of 25 items tapping attitudes and orientations toward work and family roles, and was used as a measure of contingency orientation. Because the literature suggests that

Table I. Factors Derived from the Attitudes and Orientation Items Using Equimax Rotation

Factor items	Loadings
Child orientation	
4. I would look for a spouse who considers having children a normal part of life.	.82
10. I always thought I would have children; I never thought that I wouldn't.	.66
11. Having children is a normal part of being a woman.	.60
16. I personally could not be psychologically fulfilled if I did not have children.	.66
25. I often envision what life will be like when I am married and have children.	.41
Traditional orientation	
3. I would consider the husband's career more important after the birth of the first child.	.51
17. Women should retain primary responsibility for domestic chores.	.73
19. A woman's most important role is in the home.	.69
Career orientation	
2. I would consider my spouse's career and my career equally important.	.73
4. I would look for a spouse who considers my career and his career equally important.	.60
18. Having a challenging career is as important as being a wife and mother.	.52
Contemporary orientation	
1. I am committed to having a life-long career.	.43
5. I want it all—to be a parent, spouse, have a career.	.69
14. I think it is perfectly natural for a person not to have children.	.43

this may not be a unidimensional concept, items focused on what might be seen as different aspects of such an orientation. These included degree of career commitment, perception of relative importance of own and spouse's career, belief in traditional roles, and importance of having children and mothering in relationship to pursuing one's own career. Participants were asked to indicate the extent of their agreement with each statement on a scale from 0 to 100%. (The scale was presented in 10% increments, i.e., 0, 10, 20, etc.). Factor analysis using an orthogonal rotation confirmed six primary factors. Two factors having to do with perceptions of mother and perceptions of father were not central to the focus of this study and will not be discussed further. The items and factor loadings for the four factors used in this study are presented in Table I.

Factor scores were calculated and analyses of variance used to compare the three occupational groups. Scheffé's test was used to determine the means between which significant differences existed. Factor one was labeled Child Orientation and the possible range of scores was 0–50, with a higher score indicating greater perceived importance of children and mothering to one's sense of self. The other three factors—Traditional Role Orientation, Career Orientation, and Contemporary Orientation—each had a possible range of 0–30. Higher scores on the Traditional Orientation scale reflect greater acceptance of the belief that a woman's primary responsibility is the traditional domestic role and that her career should be secondary. Items on the Career Orientation scale focused on the importance of a woman's career in relationship to that of her potential spouse, and in relationship to the roles of wife and mother. Therefore, higher scores would indicate greater career importance and less of a tendency to see career as contingent on family roles. Contemporary Orientation items reflected the expectation of "doing it all," being a parent, spouse, and career person, but accepting the idea of childlessness as perfectly natural. Higher scores would indicate more agreement with contemporary ideas about work and family integration.

Table II. Means and Standard Deviations of Expectation Variables

	Occupational category			
	Traditional (n = 71)	Moderate (n = 47)	Innovative (n = 90)	
Age at marriage	24.47^{ab} (2.12)	26.10^b (3.48)	25.63^a (2.53)	F = 6.19^c
Age at first child	26.76^{ab} (2.05)	28.02^b (2.54)	28.28^a (2.55)	F = 8.00^d
Probability of having a child	93.42^a (16.61)	89.95 (18.00)	82.41^a (24.84)	F = 5.83^c
Number of children desired	3.07 (1.36)	2.91 (1.18)	2.72 (1.25)	F = 1.48

^{a,b}Groups significantly different at .05 level based on Scheffé test.
$^c p < .01.$
$^d p < .001.$

FINDINGS

Marriage and Childbearing Expectations

Only 3 (1.2%) of the women planned to remain single. The average age at which the participants expected to marry was 25.4. Table II provides a comparison of means and standard deviations for women in each of the occupational groups. Innovators and moderates were significantly more likely to expect to marry at a later age than were traditionals.

Only 6 (2.5%) of the participants planned to remain child free and another 6 (2.5%) planned to have only one child. The mean number of children desired was 2.9 (range 0–8). While the modal number of children desired was 2, over half of the subjects planned to have 3 or more children. A comparison of the mean number of children expected by women planning innovative, moderate, or traditional careers revealed no significant differences. Of those planning to remain child free, 3 were planning innovative careers, 2 traditional careers, and 1 was undecided regarding her career choice.

The mean age at which participants expected to have their first child was 27.7 years, approximately 5 years later than the mean age of their own mothers' first birth.

Those planning to have innovative or moderately innovative careers were significantly more likely than those planning traditional careers to delay the birth of their first child.

Career Expectations

All of the women in the sample planned to work after graduation and indicated occupational choices that would be considered careers rather than jobs. Innovative careers were planned by 90 (36%) of the women. These included choices such as electrical engineer, agribusiness woman, military intelligence, and regional planner. Moderately innovative careers such as journalist, veterinary assistant, and realtor were chosen by 47 (19%) of the participants. Traditional choices such as teacher, day care worker, and social worker were listed by 71 (28%). Seventy-one different occupational preferences were mentioned. Seventeen percent of the participants were undecided about what career they would pursue or gave uncodable responses.

Integration of Work and Family

There were no significant differences among innovators, moderates, or traditionals regarding the timing of their first birth in relationship to the establishment of their career [$\chi^2(6, N = 208) = 6.45, p = .37$]. Seventy-

Table III. Means and Standard Deviations of Orientation Variables

	Occupational category			
	Traditional (n = 71)	Moderate (n = 47)	Innovative (n = 90)	
Child orientation	39.51[a] (10.10)	34.62 (10.85)	32.43[a] (12.63)	$F = 7.72^c$
Career orientation	23.23[a] (6.08)	24.13 (6.27)	25.58[a] (4.76)	$F = 3.61^b$
Traditional role orientation	12.93 (7.30)	11.04 (8.35)	10.04 (7.48)	$F = 2.83$
Contemporary orientation	20.01 (5.80)	18.96 (6.79)	21.60 (6.00)	$F = 3.12$

[a]Groups significantly different at .05 level based on Scheffé test.
[b]$p < .05$.
[c]$p < .001$.

one percent of all participants planned to establish their career before having a child.

Only 36% of the participants indicated that there was a critical age by which they felt compelled to have a first child. Sixty-three percent of this group thought that they should have their first child by age 30. An additional 29% felt the first birth should occur by age 35. However, 7 women gave ages higher than this, with 40 being the oldest anyone responding thought they would wait to have a first birth. Generally, the more career oriented a woman was, regardless of the type of career she expected to have, the higher the age she considered the cutoff point for a first birth $(r = .29, p = .003)$.

Even though all of the women in the sample planned to have careers, only 6% planned to be back at work 6 weeks after their children were born. Only 26% planned to be back at the end of 6 months and a total of 46% indicated that they would return by the end of 1 year. There were no significant differences by occupational groups regarding the length of time the women planned to take off after their first birth.

When asked whether they would work full or part time if they did return to work, only 30% of the participants indicated that they would work full time. The majority indicated they preferred to work part time, at least until their children were old enough for preschool. There was a significant difference among the occupational groups in regard to these plans $[\chi^2(4, N = 208) = 14.14, p = .007]$. Forty-five percent of the innovators planned to return to work full time, while only 16% of the moderates and 32% of the traditionals planned to do so.

Contingency Orientation

Table III presents the results of comparisons by occupational group on the various factors of the attitudes and orientations section of the CFQ. The greatest difference among the groups occurs in regard to Child Orientation. Women who planned traditional occupations were significantly more child oriented than those planning innovative careers.

Even though there was a significant difference among the groups on Child Orientation and innovators were less sure than traditionals that they would have children, there was no significant difference in the mean number of children these women wanted to have (see Table II). Innovators did expect to have a first child at a significantly later age than did traditionals.

A comparison of mean scores on the Career Orientation scale indicated significant differences among innovators, moderates, and

Table IV. Intercorrelations of Orientation Factors with Key Variables

Key variable	Orientation factor						
	1	2	3	4	5	6	7
1. Probability of having children							
2. Age at marriage	$-.37^b$						
3. Age at first child	$.26^b$	$.80^b$					
4. No. of children desired	$.40^b$	$.05$	$-.14$				
5. Child orientation	$.72^b$	$-.36^b$	$-.31^b$	$.42^b$			
6. Career orientation	$-.14$	$.12$	$.16^a$	$-.18^a$	$-.18^a$		
7. Traditional orientation	$.19^a$	$-.23^b$	$-.18^a$	$.17^a$	$.16^a$	$-.31^b$	
8. Contemporary orientation	$-.14$	$-.01$	$.07$	$-.21^b$	$-.01$	$.14$	$-.09$

$^a p < .01.$
$^b p < .001.$

traditionals. Innovators had significantly higher scores than did traditionals. However, means for all three groups were quite high, suggesting that the majority of the participants, but particularly the innovators, expected their own career to be as important as a potential spouse's career and to be as important as their roles as wife and mother.

There were no significant differences among the groups on Traditional Role Orientation or Contemporary Orientation. It should be noted that all three groups had relatively low means on Traditional Orientation.

Table IV provides product-moment correlations between the orientation factors and other key variables. Scores on the Child Orientation scale are highly correlated with the probability of having children and the number of children expected. There is also a moderate negative correlation between Career Orientation and the number of children desired and Child Orientation. Other than a low negative correlation with the number of children desired, there is little relationship between Career Orientation and marriage and childbearing variables.

DISCUSSION

The results of this study provide information about the career and parenthood expectations of a group of women at a public university in New England. Care must be taken when in-terpreting results of research using such nonrandom samples. In addition, only longitudinal research could reveal to what extent these expectations will be realized. However, longitudinal studies (Rexroat and Shehan, 1984; Tangri and Jenkins, 1986) have indicated remarkable consistency between expectations and outcomes for young women who plan careers. Tangri and Jenkins reported that of 117 women involved in their 14-year longitudinal study begun in 1967, 81% of the original innovators and 69% of the original traditionals were actually working in careers so classified in 1981. In 1967, only one-fifth of the sample felt marriage and career or children and career were in conflict. By 1981, half of the women felt this way and only 14% had had the number of children they had intended.

There is little indication of a contingency orientation in the current sample of college women. The majority of the women expect to have careers that are nontraditional for women. They plan to delay marrying and having children while they establish themselves in their work life. Although innovators are significantly more likely than traditionals to be career oriented, the relatively high means for each group on the Career Orientation scale suggest that the majority of these women are not expecting to subjugate their career goals to those of a partner.

If a contingency orientation persists at all in these women's thinking about career planning, it appears in relationship to the integration of work and parenting. Although all participants indicated career plans, surprisingly few of the women plan to remain child free or have only one child. The percentage of women who plan to remain child free is less than one-third the generally reported rate. The average number of children that participants, even the innovators, plan to have is higher than the average of 2.1 that women now in their 30s expect to have by the end of their childbearing years (U.S. Bureau of the Census, 1986).

It cannot be determined from the existing data what particular factors are leading these young women to expect to be able to combine demanding careers and the mothering of several children. Gimenez (1984) proposes that contemporary thinking in our society, including that of many feminists, advocates "the do-both syndrome." Motherhood and careers are not seen as alternatives, but rather as a combination to which all women should aspire. There were no significant differences among the mean scores of innovators, moderates, or traditionals on the Contemporary Orientation scale, which reflects this perspective. The high degree of participant agreement *(M* = 73%, *SD* = 28) with the statement, "I want it all, to be a parent, spouse, and career person, and am determined to manage it all and do it well," indicates the adherence of these college women to this ideology. However, young women today have few role models and little institutional support to make this a realistic undertaking.

In their responses to open-ended questions, some of the women voiced concerns about dealing with the combination of roles because, as one participant stated, "Each of them is a full-time job and I want all of them (career, parenthood, and marriage) at once." Yet many of the women seem to believe if they somehow manage effectively, they will have no particular problems. Their personal sense of responsibility for making it work is reflected in their responses to being asked whether they expect to encounter any special problems in having children, a career, and being married. They expressed the belief that if they handled their responsibilities properly, could stay on top of things, and were organized and flexible enough, they should have little difficulty.

Strategies for Managing Conflicting Demands

A number of strategies for managing the conflicting demands of work and family roles are implicit in the pattern of these women's responses. Like the generation of college-educated women before them, they plan to postpone the birth of their first child. They plan to establish their careers and then have children.

However, while the dynamics of integrating work and family responsibilities later in their adult lives will be different, the task will not be without its own set of challenges. These women may be more financially secure, have a firmer sense of self, a matured marital relationship, and an established career; they also may have more difficulty conceiving when they want to, may be involved in commuter marriages, and feel more conflict between established career and parenting roles. Women choosing this pattern of adaptation should have a realistic understanding of the trade-offs involved.

One advantage of postponing the birth of the first child until after establishing a career is that these women may be financially able to accommodate their plans to work only part time. However, women who see this as even a short-term solution to the problem must accept the fact that they will undoubtedly fall behind their male and child-free peers in terms of advancement, salaries, and expertise in their field. In some professions, these differences may never be made up.

These women's thinking about how long they will take off from work after becoming a parent does not seem to be informed by current policies and procedures regarding maternity and parenting leaves. Only half of the participants expected to be back in the work force one year after their children were born. Although the 1978 Pregnancy Disability Act protects pregnant women's rights, there is no national policy specifying the leave time employers must allow for childbirth and, in the United States, the typical maternity leave is only 6 weeks (Bohen, 1984). Less than 40% of the labor force is entitled to a paid maternity leave covering even the first 6 weeks after childbirth (Kamerman, 1985). If women take off longer than 6 weeks, U.S. law does not require employers to hold their jobs for their return. When companies do guarantee the same or a comparable job upon return to work, such covered leaves are usually only for 2 or 3 months (Bohen, 1984; Kamerman, 1985). Currently proposed federal legislation covering parental leave would mandate, at most, a 10-week unpaid leave.

Another approach to dealing with the combination of work and family responsibilities implicit in these women's thinking relies upon a spouse who assumes equal responsibility for parenting and domestic chores. This expectation is reflected in the high degree of agreement with such statements as "A husband and wife should spend equal time in raising children" $(M = 88\%, SD = 18.4)$, "Parental authority and responsibility for discipline of the children should be equally divided between husband and wife" $(M = 92\%, SD = 16.6)$, and "I would look for a spouse who considers his career and my career equally important" $(M = 84\%, SD = 21.8)$.

Although men have assumed more responsibility for parenting and household work, family work continues to fall more heavily on women's shoulders (Gilbert, 1985; Pleck, 1979; Smith and Reid, 1986). Even in delayed childbearing couples, although men express egalitarian beliefs, these values are not reflected in their day-to-day participation in family work (Baber and Dreyer, 1986).

The results of the current study suggest that while these young women have been rethinking their career options and expanding their occupational horizons, there has not been a reciprocal rethinking of their childbearing expectations. Their career orientation seems to exist in a separate sphere from marriage and fertility expectations. This supports Russo's (1979) contention that motherhood is on a qualitatively different plane than other sex roles for women in our society. While the separation of career and family life traditionally has been workable for males in our society, such an expectation may not be as realistic for women who generally still expect, and are expected, to assume primary responsibility for young children.

College women in our society now receive formal preparation, advisement, and counseling regarding their occupational choices. No such attention is given to choices regarding parenting or the combination of career and parenting roles. How do we best advise young women? How do we empower them to make informed choices and develop workable plans for themselves?

The combination of career and mothering, particularly the mothering of very young children, is a dilemma. Even among feminists there is no consensus regarding the role of motherhood in women's lives, how it affects efforts to achieve gender equality, or the most effective strategies for addressing the responsibilities of mothering (see Trebilcot, 1984). It is clear that the diversity of women's thinking about these issues makes it difficult to formulate social policy or advocate social action that will reduce, rather than exacerbate, the problem (Gerson, 1985). This study suggests that we need much more information about mothering and young women's perceptions of its role in their lives. Only then can we assist them in developing functional life plans that anticipate the career/childbearing conflicts they are likely to encounter and help them knowledgeably choose effective coping strategies.

REFERENCES

Angrist, S. S. The study of sex roles. *Journal of Social Issues,* 1969, 25, 215–232.

Angrist, S. S., and Almquist, E. M. *Careers and Contingencies.* New York: University Press of Cambridge, MA, 1975.

Baber, K. M., and Dreyer, A. S. Gender-role orientations in older child-free and expectant couples. *Sex Roles,* 1986, 14, 501–502.

Baldwin, W. H., and Nord, C. W. *Delayed childbearing in the U.S.: Facts or fiction.* Population Reference Bureau Bulletin, 39, 1984.

Bianchi, S. M., and Spain, D. *American women: Three decades of change* (Document No. C 3.261:80–8). Bureau of the Census, Department of Congress, 1983.

Bloom, D. E., and Trussell, J. What are the determinants of delayed childbearing and permanent childlessness in the United States? *Demography,* 1984, 21, 591–611.

Bohen, H. H. Gender equality in work and family: An elusive goal. *Journal of Family Issues.* 1984, 5, 254–272.

Burroughs, L. R., Turner, B. F., and Turner, C. B. Careers, contingencies, and locus of control among white college women. *Sex Roles,* 1984, 11, 289–302.

Daniels, P., and Weingarten, K. *Sooner or Later: The Timing of Parenthood in Adult Lives.* Norton, 1982.

Gerson, K. *Hard choices: How women decide about work, career, and motherhood.* Berkeley: University of California Press, 1985.

Gilbert, L. A. *Men in dual-career families: Current realities and future prospects.* Hillsdale, NJ: Lawrence Erlbaum Associates, 1985.

Gimenez, M. E. Feminism, pronatalism, and motherhood. In J. Trebilcot (Ed.), *Mothering: Essays in feminist theory.* Totowa, NJ: Littlefield, Adams, and Company, 1984.

Greenglass, E. R., and Devins, R. Factors related to marriage and career plans in unmarried women. *Sex Roles,* 1982, 8, 57–71.

Hare-Mustin, R. T., Bennett, S. K., and Broderick, P. C. Attitude toward motherhood: Gender, generational, and religious comparisons. *Sex Roles,* 1983, 9, 643–661.

Houseknecht, S. K. Voluntary childlessness: Toward a theoretical integration. *Journal of Family Issues,* 1982, 3, 459–471.

Kamerman, S. B. Child care services: An issue for gender equity and women's solidarity. *Child Welfare,* 1985, 64, 259–271.

Komarovsky, M. *Women in college: Shaping new feminine identities.* New York: Basic Books, 1985.

Leuptow, L. B. *Adolescent sex roles and social change.* New York: Columbia University Press, 1984.

Pleck, J. H. Men's family work: three perspectives and some new data. *The Family Coordinator,* 1979, 28, 481–488.

Rexroat, C., and Shehan, C. Expected versus actual work roles of women. *American Sociological Review,* 1984, 49, 349–358.

Russo, N. F. Notes on the motherhood mandate. *Psychology of Women Quarterly,* 1979, 4, 7–15.

Smith, A. D., and Reid, W. J. *Role-sharing marriages.* New York: Columbia University Press, 1986.

Tangri, S. S. Determinants of occupational role innovation among college women. *Journal of Social Issues,* 1972, 28, 177–199.

Tangri, S. S., and Jenkins, S. R. Stability and change in role innovation and life plans. *Sex Roles,* 1986, 14, 647–662.

Trebilcot, J. (Ed.) *Mothering: Essays in feminist theory.* Totowa, NJ: Rowman and Allanheld, 1984.

U.S. Bureau of the Census. Fertility of American women: June 1983. *Current Population Reports.* Series P-20, No. 395, 1984.

U.S. Bureau of the Census. Fertility of American women: June 1985, *Current Population Reports,* Series P-20, No. 406, 1986.

U.S. Department of Commerce. *Detailed Occupation of Employed Persons by Race and Sex for the United States: 1970.* Document C 3.223/12:970/32, 1973.

U.S. Department of Commerce, Bureau of the Census. Taeuber, C. M., and Valdisera, V. *Women in the American Economy.* Current Population Reports, Series P-23, No. 146, 1986.

Zuckerman, D. M. Women's studies, self-esteem, and college women's plans for the future. *Sex Roles,* 1983, 9, 633–642.

Deciding against Motherhood:
One Woman's Story

Roberta Joseph

With strollers, diapers, and toddlers everywhere, there's no denying it: The baby boomlet is on. Although the media makes it seem as if every child-less woman is resorting to adoption or test tubes, there are still plenty of women around who are choosing childlessness. Whether they do so for personal or political reasons, these women remind us that not every female is traumatized by her biological clock. Some are answering its insistent ticking with a silence they call peace.

Nobody will ever send me a Mother's Day Card—one of those Crayola creations made by dedicated small hands. I will never search my newborn's face for hints of my khaki eyes or my husband's aquamarine ones, or sing a lullaby. No child of mine will ever smile at me, or graduate, or marry. I will leave no heir when I die.

Now that infertility has reached epidemic proportions this is an increasingly familiar litany. But there is a difference in my case: I chose this fate. I have made a conscious decision not to have a child.

There is still time, my gynecologist assures me, to join the ranks of the wannabe "elderly primigravidas" even as I reach my 42nd birthday. I could still enter the company of Bette Midler, Cybill Shepherd, and my own delighted friends, some of whom have endured humiliating invasive procedures, or paid upwards of $10,000 for the privilege. But finally, with reluctance, regret, and not a little anguish, I have come to realize that motherhood is simply not for me.

Most major life decisions have come easily to me—I picked my profession as a psychoanalyst at age 10. But not this one. I have always been ambivalent about motherhood. I never categorically ruled it out (sterilization would have foreclosed the possibility of changing my mind), but I never felt a longing for children either. My husband knew my doubts when we married. Since I am not the kind of person to leave something so momentous to chance, a child would have to be planned. In my mid-30s, when I was finally in the position to give it serious consideration, I found myself postponing pregnancy every time I contemplated it. I'll try after we get back from Bali, I thought, or next semester when I don't have to teach at 8 A.M.

Pregnancy itself never appealed to me, but I knew I would tolerate it if necessary. The biggest obstacle turned out to be how I felt about such an enormous upheaval in my life, and the intrusion and interference it represented. On the most overt level, I dreaded the ordeal of moving, reorganizing my complex schedule, interviewing housekeepers. No more midnight suppers, I thought, or spontaneous jaunts, or concert series without elaborate planning, for 20 years. My time would never again be fully my own. My resistance to all the necessary changes and conditions a child would bring always seemed more compelling than any gratification I could anticipate.

I thrive on being able to do what I want when I want unimpeded. I saw that it simply would not be possible to continue to live my way and be a responsible parent—or

This article previously appeared in the *Utne Reader*, January/February, 1990. Reprinted with permission of the author.

a happy one. I spent years making my life the way it is, and I knew I wanted to keep it. Despite what the women's magazines say, I couldn't really see a way to have it all.

But I wanted to be as certain as I could be. At 40, just to be sure I wasn't agonizing for nothing, my husband and I were checked medically. The verdict: Conception was problematic but possible. The choice was still mine to make, and I saw that my feelings were no different. Now, two years later, it is increasingly clear to me that I am not moving toward maternity. Deciding to maintain the status quo of one's life is a less dramatic choice than to change it radically, but a profound choice nonetheless, and for me a painfully conscious one.

Probably the hardest thing about making the decision not to have a child is that biology precludes reconsidering it; very soon the opportunity will be lost forever. If I find at 50 that something fundamental is missing from my life because of my choice, I can't fix it. I couldn't even adopt then. In my experience, nothing has ever felt as final, as irrevocable, as this. You can get divorced, change professions, or leave town, but not having children takes you down a road where you can see that there's no going back.

Making a will (as I did recently) with no child to leave your possessions to is a graphic reminder of mortality. My life, my world, everything I value ends with me. I will never have as direct an impact on anyone as a parent has on a child; my patients, if I do my job right, go their own way. Without the rationalization or the consolation of a biological legacy, whatever I achieve is solely my responsibility.

Every time I watch the sidewalk parade of Snuglis and strollers I feel like an outsider to the main preoccupation of my generation. People my age seem obsessed with the accoutrements and activities of parenthood, and my life seems radically different from theirs. There are times when I feel painfully alienated from even my dearest friends, who now as parents inhabit a world I do not want to share. They don't appear to be oppressed by its constraints, or they deny or suppress it. They get up early and go to bed early, and of necessity have less time for me.

In my own as well as other people's eyes, my action brands me as different, forces me into a particularly threatening form of nonconformity, which derives not from a wish to rebel but from a realization that my prerequisites for happiness are outside the norm.

Because of me, the course of my husband's life changes as well. He, too, feels a sense of lost possibilities, although he says it is less wrenching. He would have had children if we both wanted them, and acknowledges his own mixed feelings. As a man, his concern is more that this choice is irresponsible or immature than it is unnatural.

Childlessness naturally affects a woman more than a man. A man can eschew fatherhood without any threat to his masculinity, but motherhood has always defined a woman's purpose and value. There is no male equivalent of the word "barren," with its connotations of empty lifelessness.

More than my personal psychology is involved here. The current baby boom that I am declining to join in part reflects a backlash from the more confident and expansive '70s, when women seemed finally to be disencumbering themselves of sex-role stereotypes. In this more conservative era, an untraditional life once again becomes harder to justify and sustain.

Still, despite feminism and common sense, I find it difficult not to feel defective and ashamed about not wanting to be a mother, or to feel fully feminine just as I am. What real woman voluntarily turns her back on reproduction or does not naturally want to take care of a baby? How can she put her own life first? I struggle to accept as valid and sufficient alternative ways of nurturing outside the literal maternal role—the relationships with my husband, my friends, my students, and the suffering children within my patients. Only slowly do I see that I feel relief that only one of them actually lives with me.

The deciding factor is that my history and personality make me require (for my own well-being) a certain freedom from constraint. Being my own mother's daughter has made this inevitable. I was the focus of her ambition and energy, the bearer of her destiny. She could not consistently tolerate my emotional autonomy. Fundamental needs of mine conflicted with hers, so that along with all the gifts for living that I received from her came an extreme sensitivity to intrusion, virtually instinctive now.

I don't feel—and I spend most of my waking hours helping others realize—that a woman is doomed to repeat her mother's life or her own childhood, or that parents are to blame for one's fate. I also know that family relationships have effects that cannot always be undone. Because of who I am, I must forgo certain experiences to assure that I have what I need most. This means that things others tolerate I do not, that I would be too bothered by constant arrangements and impingements, by the responses demanded by a child, things that would seem less disruptive to someone with a different past.

Many people gain maturity by becoming parents; I hope to achieve it by choosing not to. This demands self-reliance; when there is no one to live through you must seek meaning within yourself. I won't have the excuse of parenthood as a substitute for personal accomplishment. I know everything depends on me. It really does for everybody, but children can permit parents to avoid this awareness for long stretches. I wish I could say with confidence that all my doubts are resolved and that I live serenely with my choice—or even that I am sure I won't change my mind. Will my house someday feel too terribly quiet, or my interests insufficient? Perhaps full acceptance of this choice is impossible now. It may be only in retrospect that I will finally attain a sense of peace about it and know as much as one ever can that what I did was right for me, that I succeeded in having an empty womb but a full life.

Motivation for Motherhood and the Experience of Pregnancy

Gail Erlick Robinson, M.D. and Donna E. Stewart, M.D.

It is frequently assumed that becoming a mother is an essential step in the development of female identity. Although female hormones may increase a woman's readiness to care for an infant, there is no clear cut evidence of a hormonal basis for maternal feelings. A woman's desire to have and raise children is affected by cultural expectations and opportunities. Current analytical thinking, while viewing reproductive choice as being an important component of feminine identity, does not emphasize the necessity of having a child to feel feminine. Once pregnant, the woman works through issues related to body image, relationship with mother and husband, concerns for the fetus, fears about the future and her new vision of herself.

Because women are physiologically equipped to bear children and nourish them, it is frequently assumed that becoming a mother is an essential component of being a woman. Motherhood has been seen as being critical to the development of gender identity, femininity, and self-esteem. As women now have more choices about reproduction and lifestyle, the question of the importance of motherhood to a woman's sense of identity and maturity becomes a key one (1). In order to examine this issue, the biological, sociocultural, and psychological motivations for becoming a mother must be considered.

Because women give birth to children, an assumption has been made that there must be a chromosomal or hormonal basis for the wish to mother. However, researchers on genetic abnormalities have noted that androgen insensitive chromosomal males, born with female-looking genitalia and reared and raised as girls, play with dolls, desire children and are nurturant towards infants (2). As well, Turner's Syndrome females (XO females who do not have ovaries or produce any gonadal hormones) are no different than normal women in their wish to have children and in their nurturant behavior. There is, therefore, no clear cut evidence for a purely genetic or hormonal basis for maternal feelings in human females (3).

Animal studies seem to indicate some hormonal role in maternal behaviour. Blood plasma taken from female rats that have recently delivered, and administered to virgin rats speeds up their development of maternal behaviour (4). However, "maternal behaviour" has also been demonstrated by virgin females and males who have been sufficiently exposed to newborn pups (4). It is possible, therefore, that the hormones associated with pregnancy and childbirth may contribute to a "readiness" to care for infants.

However, as this behaviour is not unique to parturient females it can not be only hormonally based (5).

Women have been described as having a maternal instinct (6). Instinct, defined as an unlearned, patterned, goal directed behaviour characteristic of the species, seems to function very strongly in lower animals, but as one moves up the evolutionary ladder, cultural and environmental factors play a more important role (5). It can be noted that first time mothers, without previous child-care experience, have to be taught how to feed and look after an infant (6). It is also clear that men who have experience with babies are equally capable of infant care (7). Indeed, it appears that infants have ways of eliciting care taking behaviour from whomever is dealing with them (8). All of these biological and instinctual theories, therefore, have neglected the impact of learning and experience.

Researchers have also postulated sociocultural explanations for the urge to mother. Anthropologists have noted the sexual division of labour witnessed in early man (9). In these primitive societies, the men would hunt whereas the women would gather and rear children. Rossi (10) has theorized that this early sexual division of labour was essential to the groups' survival and, therefore, became built into physiology. Nancy Chodorow (3) has pointed out that there is no evidence that such adaptive practices automatically become genetically programmed. She concludes that the bioevolutionary argument stands as an argument concerning the division of labour in gatherer/hunter societies given the specifically incompatible requirements of child-care and hunting, and not as an argument concerning maternal instinct.

The role of cultural expectations in the maternal role cannot be overlooked. Margaret Mead (11) found no anthropological evidence

This article first appeared in the *Canadian Journal of Psychiatry* (1989) 34: 861–865. Reprinted with the permission of the Canadian Psychiatric Association.

to give support to the value of accentuation of the tie between the mother and the child. She felt that conscious care of the infant is a cultural, not a biological, invention and that it is very hard to separate a woman's desire to have children from society's expectation of her role as chief caretaker. Adrienne Rich (12) noted that most women in history have become mothers without choice. When motherhood is the only acceptable role, birth rates increase. When there are greater options and effective birth control, birth rates decrease and the number of childless women increase (5). Therefore, a woman's desire to have and raise children is very much influenced by the expectancies and opportunities existing in her environment.

Lerner (13) has looked at the development of women's roles in a historical context. According to her, the traditionalists view motherhood as a woman's chief goal and the natural result of biological differences created by God or nature. In their view, a woman who does not become a mother is deviant. The feminists argue that although women bear children due to sex, they nurture them because of gender which is culturally defined. Lerner hypothesized that in hunter/gatherer societies, women's mothering and nurturing activities associated with many life essential skills were experienced as sources of strength and magic powers by both men and women (14). The development of agriculture brought with it the "commodification" of women whereby their sexuality and reproductive capacities became the property of men. In her opinion, women cooperated with the development of this patriarchal system because of their limited power. As "respectable" women (i.e., women who carried out their expected functions) acquired some of the class privileges of their men, the role of mother became established and valued (15).

The early psychoanalysts clearly thought motherhood to be crucial to the development of female identity. Freud spoke of the resolu-

tion of the Oedipal complex leading to giving up the wish for a penis and substituting the wish for a baby. Deutsch (16) spoke about the "essential feminine quality of receptiveness," a biopsychological concept which she saw as the basis of femininity and motherhood. She described motherhood as being the fulfillment of the woman's most powerful and guiding wish. Benedek (17) believed that the biological basis for feelings about motherhood were rooted in the fluctuation of the female endocrine cycle. She described motherhood as being the manifestation of the all prevailing instinct for survival in the child that is the primary organizer of the woman's sexual drive. Erickson (18) spoke of ego identity being developed beginning in puberty and adolescence. He believed this achievement of identity was harder for girls who looked forward to a reduction in status and felt their identity was connected with the development of intimacy with another. Although his stage of generativity encompassed more than just child bearing, he persistently identified women with being mothers and emphasized achievement of identity through motherhood. His work has been criticized as applying more accurately to men and failing to pay sufficient attention to the role of socialization, instead emphasizing biological determinism and anatomical bases for his proposed differences between men and women (19,20).

While Freudians viewed motherhood as compensatory, Karen Horney emphasized the primary gratifications inherent in a woman's biological role (21). She believed that childbirth and motherhood has a value for its own sake and can bring a woman joy and happiness. Clara Thompson (22) pointed out the interaction between biology and culture. Although the biological event of bearing children influences a woman's personality development, she is also very much influenced by the cultural pressures and expectations on her. In her view, tradition and prejudice lead many women to believe that adequate sexual fulfillment, including children, and adequate self-development are mutually exclusive (22).

Kohut (23) also disagreed with the idea that a woman's wish for a baby was a substitute for her wish for a penis. He, too, emphasized the interaction of biological and cultural factors. He described a woman's wish for a child as a manifestation of her nuclear self, central ambitions and ideals that can occur when biological and cultural factors are supportive (24).

Nancy Chodorow (3) represents the more modern psychoanalytic view of women's roles as mothers. She stated that it is "women who reproduce mothers." According to her, the early experience of being cared for by a woman produces a fundamental structure of expectations in women and men concerning mother's lack of separate interest from their infants and total concern with their infants' welfare. Daughters grow up identifying with their mothers and generalizing this set of expectations to the assumption that women naturally take care of children of all ages. Although Chodorow's theories have been criticized for being largely applicable to middle class women in industrialized societies (25), she does provide a theory of development which considers both psychological processes and societal expectations.

Whereas the classical psychoanalytic theories stated that pregnancy and motherhood were essential to feminine identity, the more modern view is that, although reproductive capacity and choice seem to be important components of femininity and self-esteem, it is not vital for a woman to have a baby in order to be feminine. Hare-Mustin (26) studied attitudes toward motherhood comparing young men and younger and older women. It was the young men who believed in the "sanctity" of motherhood and the "moral/normative rightness of maternity." In their eyes, the mother-child relationship was seen as more essential than that between males and females. Among older women, she found the experience of motherhood affected their attitude towards it. Although the older women had a more highly elaborated and powerful image of the maternal role, both younger and older women rejected the idea that motherhood is necessarily "natural" and central to a woman's choice. Betty Friedan (27) states "The right to choose is crucial to the personhood of woman. The right to choose has to mean not only the right to choose not to bring a child into the world against one's will, but also the right to have a child, joyously, responsibly, without paying a terrible price of isolation from the world and its rewarded occupations, its decisions and actions."

Individual women have varied and mixed motivations concerning motherhood. A woman may become pregnant to confirm to herself or others her status as a woman and an adult (28). The pregnancy may make her feel fulfilled and creative and solidify her self-esteem (28, 29). It may also be used to get her out of a difficult situation, keep a boyfriend or unconsciously replace a recently lost loved one (29). Women who are insecure about their intellectual and creative abilities and who feel most feminine and fulfilled when pregnant, may have repeated planned or "accidental" pregnancies (29).

The actual birth of a child may be seen as the culmination of a woman's socialization process and a sign that she is correctly following the life course society expects of her (28). Spousal, family, religious or cultural approval may all enhance her feeling of having achieved a major life goal with a concomitant enhancement of self. Having a child by someone she loves may be a joyous event, and marital satisfaction may be increased by sharing the bonds of parenthood. On the other hand, a woman may feel forced by her spouse or environment to have a child she does not want or is not ready for. She may passively accede to her husband's wishes rather than risk dissent (29). A woman in an unhappy marriage may want a child as someone to love and to love her.

These varied motivations help explain why women might choose to overcome numerous obstacles in order to have a child. A career woman who becomes a mother faces increased tasks, role conflict, possible career limitations and guilt over not being a "good" mother (30), and yet may not want to miss out on the unique experience of raising a child. Despite career success, she may feel unfulfilled as a woman. Indeed, her wish for success may make her question her femininity (31), whereas becoming pregnant confirms she is a woman.

In a similar fashion, a single woman may need to confirm her femininity by having a child. The woman who fears she may not marry, may decide she wants to at least have a child to love, if not a husband. The woman who has chosen to remain single may disdain what she perceives as the burden of a relationship, but still not want to forgo the experience of motherhood. A woman who suffers a chronic physical illness may feel inadequate and defective and be willing to risk her physical health by becoming pregnant in order to feel whole. The pregnancy may be seen as a triumph, a sign of hope, and a protest against the ravages of her chronic illness (32).

Once pregnant, whatever the reason, the woman undergoes a series of psychological changes and adjustments. Bibring (33) described pregnancy as a maturational crisis leading to a new position not identical to that previously felt. Not only does the woman have to cope with a multitude of physical changes, she must also deal with the accompanying emotional upheavals. Unresolved past conflicts related to her own mother, her husband and her marriage, and general issues of femininity and dependence are reactivated during this period of time (34). She may also have concerns about the developing fetus, her upcoming change in life role and her future relationship with her spouse. These internal conflicts may appear in the form of anxiety, depression or severe and persistent physical complaints. Bibring (35) has stated that this period offers the potential of a neurotic outcome or maturation and growth.

This type and level of conflict change throughout pregnancy. During the first trimester, the woman is often preoccupied with the physical changes and symptoms. Some, such as increased breast size, may seem positive while others, such as thickening of the waist or nausea, may be upsetting. As well, she may notice some fluctuations in her mood. It is not clear whether this is related to hormonal changes or to the emotional consequences of discovering she is pregnant. Even if the pregnancy is a planned one, most women experience some ambivalence when it is actually confirmed. Especially in a first pregnancy, they may wonder about whether they should have embarked upon this seemingly irrevocable course. At the same time, they may feel guilty over any negative thoughts, and fear that somehow this will harm the baby. They may also feel the beginning of increased dependency needs and wishes to be loved and looked after.

The second trimester is usually a time of increased sense of accomplishment and physical well-being for the woman. She may also, however, have increased dependency and introversion and her behaviour may at times appear somewhat regressed (35). During this trimester, she is reworking her relationships with her mother and her spouse. She is beginning to identify with the idea of being a maternal figure. This leads her to a reevaluation of her relationship with her own mother. She also begins to wonder how a child will affect the relationship with her husband and whether he will be an adequate father. The experience of quickening makes the baby more real for the woman. She begins to move away from the symbiotic closeness she had in the first trimester and instead starts to visualize the baby as a separate being.

The third trimester brings about an increase in anxiety. As labour and delivery become imminent, the woman may have fantasies about being destroyed or ripped apart. She may also have concerns that she will not behave in an appropriate manner during the delivery. She thinks more about the fetus and worries about its health and safety. Her increased physical discomfort makes her begin to long for the end of the pregnancy. This also assists with the ongoing process of separation from the fetus. At the same time that she is looking forward to the birth, she also may experience ambivalence about the loss of this very special relationship.

The presence of a high risk or complicated pregnancy may lead to an interference with, or an intensification or modification of, the usual reactions to pregnancy (32). The woman who is at high risk because of a previously diagnosed illness, such as diabetes or heart disease, may put special value on her pregnancy. She may already have risked her health to become pregnant and this might be the only pregnancy she will be able to have. This, in turn, may lead to intense fear of loss. These fears may lead to an interference with the normal attachment to the fetus; the woman may try to protect herself against future sadness by remaining distant. There is, therefore, a conflict between this fear of attachment on the one hand and special investment in the pregnancy on the other.

Other women may have become pregnant without any extra risk, but during the pregnancy became exposed to some adverse influence, for example drugs or rubella, leading to increased concerns about the safety of the fetus. The woman may feel guilty and angry at herself and others for not protecting her. She may have a heightened ambivalence about her ability to mother. On the other hand, she feels attached to this baby whom she may have harmed, or she may have fears about giving birth to an ill child who will then become a burden.

The prenatal diagnostic tests used to try to detect possible abnormalities may, in themselves, lead to concerns (36). The woman may be anxious about the test procedure. She may also be ambivalent about the test, knowing a negative outcome may force her to consider the option of an abortion. She may delay attachment to the fetus until the test results are known.

The woman who develops complications during her pregnancy may have to deal with a number of environmental stresses including confinement to bed, prolonged hospitalization, or the need for medication which may put the fetus at risk. She may feel angry at women who are having normal pregnancies and guilty at her inability to ''do it right.'' She may see herself as inadequate and unwomanly. Again, she may delay attachment or distance herself from the fetus as a defensive measure.

Conclusion

In summary, a woman can feel like a complete female and an adult without experiencing pregnancy or motherhood. Motivation for pregnancy varies greatly among women, especially when other satisfying roles are available to them. The ability to become pregnant, however, is extremely important for most women.

For the woman who becomes pregnant, many issues arise and old conflicts are reawakened. The popular image of a pregnant woman, blissfully contented from conception to delivery is a myth. Even ''normal'' pregnancies are a time of emotional turbulence for most women. High-risk pregnancies can generate more complicated reactions. Resolution of these conflicts acts as a developmental stepping stone. As with all such milestones, stress can be created causing deterioration in the woman's psychological functioning, or progress can be made towards a more mature consolidated identity.

References

1. Freud, S. Femininity, new introductory lectures. In: London JS, ed. Standard edition of the complete works of Sigmund Freud. London: Hogarth Press, 1933.
2. Money, J., Ehrhardt,, A. A.. Man and woman, boy and girl. Baltimore: Johns Hopkins University Press, 1972.
3. Chodorow, N. The reproduction of mothering. Los Angeles: University of California Press, 1978.
4. Rosenblatt, J. S. The development of maternal responsiveness in the rat. Am J Orthopsychiatry 1969; 39: 36–56.
5. Greenglass, E. R. A world of difference. Gender roles in perspective. Toronto: John Wiley and Sons, 1982.
6. Wortis, R. P. The acceptance of the concept of the maternal role by behavioural scientists: its effects on women. Am J Orthopsychiatry 1971; 41(5): 733–746.
7. Parke, R. D, O'Leary, S. E. Family interaction in the newborn period: some findings, some observations and some unresolved issues. In: Riegal K., Meacham J, eds. The developing individual in a changing world. Vol. 2. The Hague: Moulton, 1976.
8. Thomas, A., Chess, S., Birch, H. G, et al. Behavioral individuality in early childhood. New York: University Press, 1963.
9. Tiger, L. Men in groups. New York: Random House, 1969.
10. Rossi, A. A biosocial perspective on parenting. Daedalus 1977; 106(2): 1–31.
11. Mead, M. A cultural anthropologist's approach to maternal deprivation in deprivation of maternal care. A reassessment of its effects. Public Health Papers #14, World Health Org., Geneva, 1962.
12. Rich, A. A woman born. New York: W.W. Norton, 1976.
13. Lerner, G. The creation of patriarchy. New York: Oxford University Press, 1986; 15–35.
14. Ibid, 36–53.
15. Ibid, 212–229.
16. Deutsch, H. Psychology of women, Vol. II. New York: Grune and Stratton, 1945.
17. Benedek, T. Psychosocial functions in women. New York: Ronald Press, 1952.
18. Erikson, E. Womanhood and the inner space. In: Erikson E, ed. Identity, youth and crisis. New York: Norton, 1968.
19. Notman, M. Feminine development: changes in psychoanalytic theory. In: Nadelson C. Notman M, eds. The woman patient Vol II. New York: Plenum Press, 1982; 3–30.
20. Gilligan, C. Women's place in man's life cycle. Harv Ed Rev 1979; 49(4): 431–446.
21. Menaker, E. Female identity in a psychosocial perspective. Psychoanal Rev 1982; 69(1): 75–83.
22. Thompson, C. Cultural pressures in the psychology of women. In: Miller JB, ed. Psychoanalysis and women. New York: Brunner/Mazel, 1973; 49–64.
23. Kohut, H. The search for the self. New York: International Universities Press, 1978.
24. Chessick, R. Was Freud wrong about feminine psychology. Am J Psychoanal 1984; 44(4): 355–367.
25. Lerner, G. The creation of patriarchy. New York: Oxford University Press, 1986; 252.
26. Hare-Mustin, R. T., Bennett, S. K., Broderick, P. C. Attitude toward motherhood: gender, generational, and religious comparisons. Sex Roles 1983; 9(5): 643–661.
27. Friedan, B. The second stage. New York: Summit Books, 1981; Chapt. 3.
28. Leiffer, M. Psychological effects of motherhood. New York: Praeger, 1980.
29. Ledz, R. W. Conflicts between fertility and infertility. In: Notman M, Nadelson C, eds. The woman patient. Vol 1. New York: Plenum Press, 1978; 131–136.
30. Robinson, G. Helping women cope with a career and a family. Can Med Assoc J 1980; 123: 712–713.
31. Greenglass, E. R. A world of difference: gender roles in perspective. Toronto: John Wiley and Sons, 1982: 94–106.
32. Wohlreich, M. M. Psychiatric aspects of high-risk pregnancy. Psychiatr Clin North Am 1986; 10(1): 53–68.
33. Bibring, G., Valenstein, A. Psychological aspects of pregnancy. Clin Obstet Gynecol 1976; 19: 357–371.
34. Ballou, J. The significance of reconciliative themes in the psychology of pregnancy. Bull Menniger Clin 1978; 42(5): 383–413.
35. Bibring, G. Some considerations of the psychological processes in pregnancy. Psychoanal Study Child 1959; 14: 113–121.
36. Silvestre, D., Fresco, N. Reactions to prenatal diagnosis. Am J Orthopsychiatry 1980; 50: 610–617.

Identifying Maternal/Fetal Risks Before Pregnancy
Ronald A. Chez, MD

A woman's general health and life-style may affect her infant even before she knows she is pregnant. This preconception workup can minimize the risks and maximize control of preexisting genetic and medical conditions.

Too many women who suspect or even know that they are pregnant postpone their first visit to a physician until the end of the first trimester or the middle of the second trimester. Since the fetus is most vulnerable to environmental influences between the 17th and 56th day after conception, this means the initial prenatal visit would not occur until this period is well underway. By this time, fetal organogenesis is complete, and the mother may find it difficult to modify unhealthy habits.

By contrast, the concept of preventive health care perceives life as a continuum in which antecedent events affect current and future well being. This is particularly true during pregnancy, since a woman's preconception health can influence not only her ability to conceive but also pregnancy maintenance and outcome.

Preconception counseling can contribute to optimum maternal-fetal health. Its primary goals are to identify risk factors a woman or her partner may have that could negatively affect her pregnancy; provide nonjudgmental education tailored to the patient's needs and lifestyle; and, if necessary, refer patients for services such as genetic counseling, nutrition planning, and behavior modification programs.

Format

Preconception health assessment should be performed within the framework of day-to-day office or clinic practice. Therefore, it is useful to take a critical look at specific content, tools, and forms that will facilitate assessment and management of subsequent follow-up.

The major areas covered by preconception assessment mirror those evaluated at the initial prenatal visit—ie, the patient's medical, social, nutritional, infectious disease, medication, reproductive, and family histories. A preconceptional health appraisal form designed by M. K. Moos and R. C. Cefalo can be used to obtain this information. It lists potential areas of risk during pregnancy, and the patient simply checks off information that pertains to her. The check marks also appear on an undersheet containing suggestions for actions the woman might take to reduce or learn more about a potential risk. Thus, potential problems and probable solutions are identified in the same visit.

Another helpful tool is the antepartum form published by the American College of Obstetricians and Gynecologists. Because it emphasizes overall risk assessment—including genetic, infectious disease, and premature labor screening—it is also an excellent tool for preconception assessment.

A physical examination is recommended, but may not be necessary if the physician is already familiar with the patient. The need for and selection of laboratory tests should be determined according to the pa-

This article first appeared in *Medical Aspects of Human Sexuality*, April, 1991, pp. 45–59. Copyright © 1991, Reed Publishing USA. Reprinted with permission.

tient's history. Routine studies may include hemoglobin or hematocrit levels, Rh factor, rubella titer, serum glucose, and, when indicated, tests for chlamydia, herpes, syphilis, gonorrhea, and hepatitis B antigen (discussed below). A Pap smear is recommended if the patient has not had one within the past year, since treating cervical dysplasia may be problematic during pregnancy.

General Workup

Lifestyle. This involves assessment of the home environment, employment, habits, and hobbies of both the woman and her partner. Information about exposure to lead and other chemicals should be sought and counseling given. The controversial issue of exposure to electromagnetic fields from high-tension cables and computer terminals may be discussed as well, although the physician should stress that there are no current data indicating potential harm to the fetus.

Beneficial lifestyle changes such as weight loss, smoking cessation, and refraining from the use of alcohol are best undertaken by both the woman and her partner. It is much easier to change negative behaviors when partners can motivate each other.

The known danger of fetal alcohol syndrome should be reviewed. Although few data are available on the influence of passive smoking on the fetus, the woman's partner should refrain from smoking as well. The use of illicit drugs should be discussed, although routine preconception drug screening is not usually recommended. Alcohol- or drug-abusing couples are obvious candidates for counseling.

Reproductive History. Reproductive organ abnormalities and the possibility of diethylstilbestrol (DES) exposure should be explored, as well as previous poor pregnancy outcomes. A history of recurrent miscarriage may indicate a maternal or paternal genetic

defect, and preconception evaluation by a specialist may be needed. Prepregnancy hysterosalpingography or water contrast vaginal ultrasound may reveal a contributing anomaly.

Family History. This should attempt to pinpoint genetic problems such as hereditary diseases (eg, Tay-Sachs, alpha-thalassemia), mental retardation, and birth defects. Appropriate screening tests and genetic counseling may reassure the couple at risk. Furthermore, the woman with a strong family history of hypertension can be advised about how to maintain optimum blood pressure during pregnancy.

Nutrition. As most authorities still agree that weight loss during pregnancy is inadvisable, the time for dieting is before conception. This is also the time to identify the patient with an eating disorder such as anorexia nervosa or bulimia. A balanced diet is vital, as damage to the embryo from poor nutrition is generally irreparable.

Medication. This involves assessing both prescription and nonprescription drug use, including vitamin supplementation. Ideally, consumption of nonprescription drugs should stop completely prior to conception except as advised by the physician, and prescription drugs should be reviewed for their safety. Special attention should be given to women taking teratogenic medications, such as isotretinoin. Advise these patients to continue to use contraception for at least 30 days after stopping the drug.

Chronic Diseases

The woman who wishes to become pregnant and who has a preexisting medical condition—eg, lupus, cardiac problem, renal disorder—should be fully advised about the maternal and fetal risks she faces. Her medication may need reevaluation, possibly allowing for a therapeutic trial of an agent that is safe during pregnancy before conception is attempted. The possibility that pregnancy may impose additional psychological strain under such circumstances should be discussed with the woman and her partner. Beyond this, a number of specific medical problems discussed below merit special attention prior to conception.

Diabetes. It is now widely recognized that women with diabetes mellitus can substantially reduce the risk of poor pregnancy outcome by achieving optimum serum glucose control before conception. This involves consultation with specialists and probably use of home glucose monitoring, and perhaps an insulin pump. This regimen of intensive diabetes management should be well-established before conception is attempted.

Epilepsy. Due to improved seizure control through medication and subsequent improvement in the quality of life, there are no contraindications to epileptic women becoming pregnant. However, although more than 90% of epileptic women who become pregnant have excellent outcomes, maternal epilepsy is nonetheless a high-risk situation. This is primarily because of the teratogenic properties of anticonvulsant drugs, which can produce craniofacial, cardiac, skeletal, neural tube, and other fetal defects.

Teratogenic dosages of epileptic medications have not been established, forcing the woman to choose between risking birth defects or halting medication and thereby risking seizures with possible maternal-fetal hypoxia and loss of her job and driver's license.

Preconception counseling is especially important for the epileptic woman because most of the medication-induced fetal damage occurs in the first trimester. If the patient has been seizure-free for three to five years, it may be possible to gradually withdraw medication—provided adequate time is allowed for

this process before conception. Other recommendations for the epileptic patient include switching from a combination to a monotherapy regimen if possible, dividing doses to maintain a more consistent serum level of medication, and using folic acid supplementation.

Phenylketonuria. Women with phenylketonuria (PKU) should be encouraged to undertake measures to decrease their serum phenylalanine level prior to conception, as this has been shown to reduce the risk of fetal microcephaly and congenital heart disease.

Infectious diseases. Rubella is still a significant hazard in early pregnancy, as 15% to 20% of American adults lack immunity. Women should be routinely evaluated and vaccinated before conception. Vaccination should also be considered for women who are at risk for hepatitis B.

Sexually transmitted diseases (STDs). These infectious diseases demand a specific, targeted workup due to their soaring prevalence and the significant, even fatal, hazard they pose to the fetus. Screening for the major STDs (syphilis, gonorrhea, chlamydia, herpes, and HIV) is strongly recommended for both partners, especially if either has a high-risk profile—eg, early onset of sexual activity, previous multiple partners (particularly if condoms were not used), bisexuality, history of STDs and/or pelvic inflammatory disease (PID), or intravenous drug use.

Syphilis. The incidence of syphilis in the United States rose by 34% during the past decade to a rate of 18.4 cases per 100,000 people—the highest since 1949. Its prevalence is sharply divided along racial lines, with a rate of 121.8 cases per 100,000 among blacks, for a black-to-white ratio of 47:8. This increase has occurred primarily among heterosexuals, particularly black women.

As might be expected, this epidemic has been accompanied by a similar rise in the number of babies with congenital syphilis. Syphilis can be transmitted to the fetus at any time during gestation, so it is crucial that the disease be detected before conception. Unfortunately, the symptoms of primary infection are often missed in women. Penicillin remains the treatment of choice, to the extent that some authorities recommend serologic retesting to check for treatment failure when other drugs are used. And, as syphilis and other ulcerative STDs appear to substantially magnify the risk of HIV transmission, it is imperative that couples be counseled and screened accordingly, with aggressive treatment provided as needed.

Gonorrhea. The main problem posed by gonorrhea today is not so much the risk of ophthalmic damage to the infant, which is handled routinely at birth, as the potential for treatment resistance in the mother and/or her partner. In addition to penicillin-resistant strains, there is a growing prevalence of gonorrhea strains that are also resistant to tetracycline, cefoxitin, and spectinomycin. Ceftriaxone is recommended as the first-line therapeutic agent for patients with gonorrhea.

Chlamydia. Each year, some 4.5 million American women are infected with *Chlamydia trachomatis,* of whom 45% may also have gonorrhea; indeed, it has been theorized that the infections may have a symbiotic relationship. Chlamydia constitutes a risk both to pregnancy and to the newborn. There also can be an impact on long-term maternal fertility. Because chlamydia is virtually asymptomatic, patients who are planning to become pregnant should be screened with an antibody assay.

Herpes. As herpes episodes may sometimes be "silent"—ie, without genital ulceration and pain—all women who are considering pregnancy should be evaluated for infection. The risks of neonatal infection at the time of delivery are well-recognized. It is no longer recommended that routine cultures be done in the third trimester to detect asymptomatic viral shedding. Approximately 1.5% of these patients will have an active lesion at the time of labor.

Human immunodeficiency virus. All pregnant women and new mothers should receive information about the HIV epidemic and the availability of testing. As mentioned earlier, the risk of HIV transmission is greatly increased by the presence of vesiculoulcerative genital diseases such as syphilis and herpes. Therefore, if either partner has an ulcerative STD, the couple should be strongly advised to avoid high-risk sexual behavior. Screening for HIV should be offered to these patients.

Many questions remain unanswered regarding HIV and pregnancy, including how the virus is transmitted to the fetus, whether pregnancy accelerates its progression, and what treatment regimens should be used by pregnant women. Despite potentially deadly consequences for the infant, however, many women may not appear for prenatal/preconception testing—especially women who engage in high-risk sexual practices.

Experts acknowledge that HIV testing currently offers few direct benefits for these women, and a positive test result brings a myriad of negative consequences. Furthermore, it has also been shown that many women who are HIV-positive decide to conceive anyway and "take their chances." Despite these impediments, the physician should ensure that every high-risk couple has adequate counseling about HIV.

Follow-up

At the end of the initial visit, the physician may have an indication to schedule follow-up visits. These can merely reinforce the current health practices of the patient/couple, or they can help encourage and monitor lifestyle modifications. The physician can also obtain further information required to coordinate care with consultants if necessary. Any difficulties conceiving can be discussed. Importantly, these comprehensive preconception records can provide the basis for the first prenatal visit after conception.

There can be confusion about conceiving once oral contraceptives are stopped. The original recommendation was to wait three months or so. Fundamentally, this was to help determine the estimated due date from an established regular menstrual cycle. This is not as important today with the use of ultrasonography for gestational age dating. More important, conception within the first month of stopping oral contraceptives is not associated with an increase in anomalies or abortion.

Conclusion

Preconception testing is predicated on identifying risk factors. It is increasingly appropriate to integrate preconception care into services offered at family-planning clinics, free clinics, drug and alcohol abuse treatment centers, detention houses, and women's shelters. This will diminish the number of high-risk patients who remain grossly underserved. In this manner, preconception care can be more closely coordinated with social services to ensure an integrated approach to women with multiple problems. As a corollary, because medical insurers do not cover screening tests, the financial barriers must be removed.

There is some concern that preconception counseling may lead to unrealistic expectations of a "perfect" pregnancy outcome—ie, that preventive and remedial action prior to conception will guarantee a healthy newborn. This inappropriate expectation should be reviewed specifically with the patient and her partner at the end of the assessment. This can also be used as an opportunity to reinforce the idea that the patient is directly responsible for her own health practices, and that knowledge is the best basis for wise and appropriate choices.

BIBLIOGRAPHY

Cefalo, R. C., Moos, M. K. *Preconception Health Promotion*. Rockville, MD, Aspen Publications, 1988.

Gindoff, P. R, Jewelewicz, R. Reproductive potential in the older woman. *Fertil Steril* 46:989, 1986.

Handsfield, H. H. Old enemies: Combatting syphilis and gonorrhea in the 1990s. *JAMA* 264:1451, 1990.

Hobel, C. J., Younkeles, L., Forsythe, A. Prenatal and intrapartum high-risk screening: II. Risk factors reassessed. *Am J Obstet Gynecol* 135:1051, 1979.

Jack, B. W., Culpepper, L. Preconception care: Risk reduction and health promotion in preparation for pregnancy. *JAMA* 264:1147, 1990.

Mehta, L., Young, I. D. Recurrence risks for common complications of pregnancy—A review. *Obstet Gynecol Surv* 42:218, 1987.

Molfese, V. J., Thomson, B. K., Beadnell, B., et al: Perinatal risk screening and infant outcome. *J Reprod Med* 32:569, 1987.

Rolfs, R. T., Nakashima, A. K. Epidemiology of primary and secondary syphilis in the United States, 1981 through 1989. *JAMA* 264:1432, 1990.

Schwarcz, S. K., Zenilman, J. M., Schnell, D., et al: National surveillance of antimicrobial resistance in *Neisseria gonorrhoeae*. *JAMA* 264:1413, 1990.

Drugs and Pregnancy: Often the Two Don't Mix

Evelyn Zamula

In the summer of 1986, a group of scientists gathered in Boston to discuss—and to commemorate—an event that ruined lives, tore families apart, and left thousands of women with unbearable feelings of anguish and guilt. The occasion was the 25th anniversary of the recognition that the drug thalidomide was a potent producer of birth defects.

One of the speakers at the conference was a young Canadian scientist who had first-hand knowledge of the effects of the drug. Because his mother took the sedative during her pregnancy, he was born with no feet and was missing fingers on both hands. He once asked his parents a disturbing question: If prenatal diagnosis had been available at the time of his birth and could have detected his malformations in the womb, would they have chosen abortion? They answered, "yes," that based on doctors' opinions at that time, they would have aborted. But now they were glad they hadn't because, besides their love for him and pride in his accomplishments, they had gained an empathy with those less fortunate than he.

If that was a bright note in the thalidomide epidemic, there were few others. Although U.S. babies were almost entirely spared thalidomide's devastating effects—FDA drug reviewer Frances O. Kelsey, M.D., did not approve the manufacturer's application to market the drug here—in some countries deformed children were abandoned by their families to be raised in institutions, and it is believed that some were even left to die. About 40 percent of the nearly 6,000 known

cases of thalidomide children—born between 1956 and 1963—have already died.

Birth Defects Long Connected to Drugs

The unusual deformities caused by thalidomide generated worldwide publicity and focused attention on the fact that certain drugs taken at a critical time in pregnancy had the potential for damaging the unborn baby.

Before thalidomide, most birth defects were thought to be genetic, even though observers in the long-ago past had noticed the connection between drug-taking and birth abnormalities. Some of these ancient men of medicine were also aware that though drugs were most dangerous in the early months of pregnancy, the fetus could be affected later, too.

The Greek physician Hippocrates wrote almost 2,500 years ago that for the safety of the fetus, drugs should be administered to pregnant women only from the fourth to the seventh months. In the second century A.D., the Greek physician Soranus of Ephesus warned women not to take drugs at *any* time during pregnancy, but especially during the first trimester. In particular, he maintained that when drugs taken to cause abortion did not produce the desired result, "let no one assume that the fetus has not been injured at all. For it has been harmed: It is weakened, becomes retarded in growth, less well nourished, and in general, more easily injured and susceptible to harmful agents; it becomes misshapen and of ignoble soul." (For an interesting fictional account of just such a case, read Robertson Davies' *What's Bred in the Bone*.)

Reprinted from the *FDA Consumer*, June, 1989.

According to the March of Dimes Foundation, each year more than a quarter of a million U.S. babies—or about 1 out of every 14—are born with birth defects. About one-third of the abnormalities are life-threatening, making birth defects—including low birth weight—the leading cause of infant mortality. A half million more potential lives are lost through miscarriage and stillbirth, usually because of faulty fetal development. About 1.2 million infants, children and adults are hospitalized each year for treatment of birth defects. Birth defects contribute to the death of more than 60,000 Americans of all ages annually.

The causes of birth defects are unknown in about 65 percent to 70 percent of the cases; about 20 percent of the defects are genetic, or inherited. (Infections account for 2 percent to 3 percent of congenital malformations, maternal health problems for 1 percent to 2 percent, and chromosomal aberrations for 3 percent to 5 percent.) It is estimated that 2 percent to 3 percent of birth defects are due to chemicals or drugs, although it is suspected that the percentage may be higher since many women can't recall all the drugs they took during pregnancy. American women take an average of four prescription or over-the-counter drugs during pregnancy, plus vitamin and mineral supplements.

The effects a drug has on an embryo or fetus (the unborn baby is called an embryo up to eight weeks after conception and a fetus from then until birth) depend mainly on whether a drug has the ability to produce abnormalities, how much of it is taken, and at what point in the pregnancy it is taken.

A drug taken by an expectant mother enters her bloodstream and in most instances passes through the placenta to her unborn child. The drug then passes back through the placenta into the mother's circulatory system and is eventually eliminated. The placenta's normal function is to supply oxygen and nutrients to the fetus and to remove its waste products.

Timing Is Important

If a teratogenic (ter-ah-to-JEN-ik) drug—a chemical that can produce birth deformities—is taken in the earliest part of pregnancy (from conception until about 20 days), it will either cause the death of the embryo and subsequent miscarriage, or not affect it at all.

The possibility of harm to normal embryonic development is greatest from the third to eighth weeks, when the organs are forming. In the third week, the brain, heart and blood vessels start to develop and the spine begins to form; the arms and legs appear as tiny buds. By the fourth week, the heart starts to beat, even though the embryo is only a quarter-inch long. At five weeks, the first signs of hands and feet appear. At eight weeks, the arms and legs are separated into upper arm and forearm, thigh and lower leg; the two halves of the hard palate (roof of the mouth) unite.

From then on, the fetus grows and its systems mature. Teratogenic drugs taken after this period usually don't cause major structural defects, but they can affect growth and organ function. Particularly vulnerable is the unborn baby's nervous system, which continues to develop throughout pregnancy and in infancy. For example, the antibiotic streptomycin taken at even late stages in pregnancy may cause hearing damage in the baby. Other systems can also be affected. Tetracycline, another antibiotic, taken during the second or third trimester, when the fetus' teeth begin to calcify, will cause permanent staining of the baby teeth.

In some cases, drugs can have delayed effects. Diethylstilbestrol (DES), a synthetic estrogen widely prescribed in the 1940s to prevent miscarriage and other problems, came to be seen as a time bomb in the children of some of the 4 million to 6 million women who took it during pregnancy. Hundreds of young women who had been exposed to this drug as fetuses developed vaginal cancer after puberty. And a greater inci-

PREGNANT?

THAT'S TWO GOOD REASONS TO QUIT SMOKING.

U.S. DEPARTMENT OF HEALTH & HUMAN SERVICES.

dence of reproductive system abnormalities, such as undescended testes, also occurred in male offspring.

FDA requires that every new drug that may be used by women of childbearing potential be tested in pregnant laboratory animals before it can be marketed. (Because any untested drug presents a risk of harm to the fetus, pregnant women cannot participate in the human drug studies that are also required for pre-market approval.) But animal testing alone is by no means foolproof; drugs in animals cannot be guaranteed to act the same way in humans. Drugs that cause birth defects in animals may not cause them in people. Conversely, a drug that may be harmful to the unborn baby may not affect animals, or may not affect them to the same degree. For example, humans are 100 times more sensitive to thalidomide than are rats, and 50 times more sensitive than are rabbits. If a drug causes defects in a wide variety of animal species, however, it's almost certain that it will cause them in people, too. (See "The Beginnings: Laboratory and Animal Studies" and "Testing in 'Real People' " in the November 1987 *FDA Consumer.*)

Post-Market Surveillance

After an approved drug is marketed, FDA continues to gather information about adverse effects from a number of sources. Drug manufacturers are required to report to the agency any adverse drug reactions they learn of; doctors do so voluntarily. The U.S. Centers for Disease Control collects reports from hospitals; and large monitoring studies both here and abroad—such as the Finnish Register of Congenital Malformations—gather and analyze information on birth defects. From this data, epidemiologists (scientists who study disease frequency and distribution) can detect a pattern between use of a certain drug and birth defects.

To date, this system has worked so well since its inception that nothing on the scale of the thalidomide tragedy has occurred in the United States, even though potent teratogens do exist. Isotretinoin (Accutane), for example, is an extremely effective treatment for severe cystic acne, but a known teratogen as well. Women are warned not to take the drug if they are pregnant or intend to become pregnant while undergoing treatment. They run a risk of spontaneous abortion and have at least a 25 percent chance of bearing a baby with birth defects, including outer ear malformations, heart and central nervous system abnormalities, and cleft palate.

Since its approval in 1982, Accutane has been labeled in pregnancy category X, meaning it should not be used during pregnancy. (FDA classifies prescription drugs in five pregnancy categories—A, B, C, D and X—based on teratogenic risk. Drugs in category A appear to be least harmful, while those in category X have risks that clearly outweigh the benefits.) Because FDA, CDC, and the manufacturer continued to receive reports of birth defects, warnings against using Accutane in pregnancy were considerably strengthened in 1988. Patients are now required to have a negative pregnancy test before starting therapy and are given a leaflet that contains a drawing of a baby with the birth deformities associated with Accutane.

Fetal Alcohol Syndrome

One drug—alcohol—is so commonly used that some people don't even think of it as a drug. But many experts consider it the most common teratogen in humans. Since more women and teenage girls than ever are drinking now—about 60 percent—and about a quarter of them drink heavily, this has ominous public health implications.

One to three out of every 1,000 newborns, or about 5,000 babies per year, are born with fetal alcohol syndrome (FAS). (A syndrome is a set of symptoms or characteristics that occur together with reasonable consistency.) The syndrome was first described in France in 1967 by a physician who noticed that children of alcoholic mothers shared such distinct characteristics that a diagnosis of maternal alcoholism could be made by just looking at them.

In 1970, in the United States, a young pediatric resident at the University of Washington Health Sciences Center in Seattle had a similar experience. In reviewing newborns' medical records, she noticed that four babies of alcoholic mothers had abnormally low birth weights. Further search revealed seven more cases. When the 11 children were brought together to the Health Sciences Center for examination, researchers in the birth defects unit were struck by their resemblance to each other. Their heads were abnormally small, and they all had small narrow eyes, drooping eyelids, short upturned noses, and wider upper lips in which the normal center groove was reduced or missing. All were small for their age and all were mentally retarded.

Since FAS children do not usually improve in intelligence even when placed in foster homes, the damage points to alcohol rather than the family environment, which is usually poor. As many as 20 studies in various western countries indicate that FAS surpasses Down's syndrome and spina bifida (a birth defect in which part of the vertebral column is missing) as a cause of mental retardation. FAS children may also have defects of the heart and genital and urinary organs and may have poor coordination, short attention span, and behavioral problems.

Women who drink the equivalent of three ounces of pure alcohol daily—six average mixed drinks or six cans of beer—frequently give birth to babies with the full range of FAS defects. They are also more likely to miscarry or have stillborn children or children who die in early infancy. Those who drink less but still heavily (more than two drinks a day, according to the U.S. Surgeon General) may give birth to babies who have some, but not all, fetal alcohol effects. A new study points out that even two or three drinks a week may trigger spontaneous abortion. Since no one knows at which point in the pregnancy alcohol does the greatest damage or what amount can be consumed safely, pregnant women should drink no alcoholic beverages.

Cigarette Smoking

Among the warnings on packages of cigarettes is a statement that smoking may complicate pregnancy. Still, of the approximately 32 percent of women who smoke cigarettes before pregnancy, 25 percent continue to smoke while pregnant. While no specific malformations are connected with smoking, birth weight of babies born to smokers averages a half pound less than that of babies of nonsmokers. Low-birth-weight babies are 40 times more likely to die in infancy than those of normal weight. It is thought that nicotine, which constricts blood vessels, may reduce placental blood flow, and thus the amounts of nutrients and oxygen to the unborn baby. The March of Dimes states that some research has shown that chest breathing motion in an unborn baby temporarily decreases sharply after its mother has smoked only two cigarettes. Smoking may also increase the risk of miscarriage, stillbirth and death in newborns.

Drug Abuse

And then there are drugs of abuse. Paula Crews, a licensed clinical social worker associated with Sharp Memorial Hospital in San Diego, Calif., works with new mothers and their babies. "About 2 percent of the pregnant women in this area are abusing drugs," she says, "which isn't bad compared to some big city hospitals where it's as high as 30 percent or more.

"Cocaine, 'crystal' [methamphetamine], and heroin are the most popular, in that order, and marijuana is used in conjunction with all of them. Many drug abusers haven't had any prenatal care and walk in off the street to deliver. Some of them are high or drunk during labor and delivery. I feel sorry for their babies. The minute the umbilical cord is cut, the baby is on its own. It must clear that drug out of its system. The most pitiful cases are the poor heroin babies, who have classic withdrawal symptoms after they're born. They have feeding problems, sneeze, are irritable, and sometimes have seizures. That's a terrible way to start life.''

But the baby's problems are just beginning. ''Cocaine users don't have much appetite and are malnourished,'' continues Crews, ''so their babies have low birth weight. These mothers are so skinny that they hardly look pregnant even at term. Some don't make it to term, because cocaine users are at high risk for premature delivery. As far as birth defects go, we don't notice any more overt structural abnormalities among cocaine-exposed babies than usual, but they can sustain neurological damage, which is not apparent at birth, but which we pick up later in infancy and childhood. I've been told that some babies exposed to cocaine late in pregnancy have strokes *in utero* [in the womb] that can lead to retardation. When we *do* see malformations, we wouldn't have any idea if a drug is responsible, or which drug is responsible, because many of these women are multiple drug abusers, plus they drink and they smoke, and are often malnourished.''

Medicines and Pregnancy

Women who *must* take known teratogens to treat a chronic underlying physical condition present a difficult case for their doctors. Drugs such as anticonvulsants used to treat epilepsy, antibiotics for tuberculosis, oral anticoagulants to prevent blood clots, anti-cancer drugs, drugs to treat an overactive thyroid, and lithium for manic depression are some substances that cannot always be avoided completely. Doctors must advise women taking these drugs—before they be-

come pregnant—of the risk to the unborn baby and how that risk can be reduced. In some cases, it may be possible to withhold the drugs, if only for the first trimester.

For the best outcome, a little prevention is worth a pound of cure. Women who are pregnant or who think they may be pregnant should let their doctors know about their condition when drugs are being prescribed for them. They should take no over-the-counter (OTC) drugs (or prescription drugs left over from another illness) without consulting their doctors. OTC drugs, which look harmless sitting between the candy and housewares departments in drugstores, may not be harmless. Even a drug as commonly used as aspirin can prolong labor and alter bleeding and clotting time if taken in the last three months of pregnancy. Many OTC labels warn: *As with any drug, if you are pregnant or nursing a baby, seek the advice of a health professional before using this product.* It's worth paying attention to those words.

It's often true that the critical period for the development of most organs in the unborn baby is over by the time a woman is sure she is pregnant. Nevertheless, it is comforting to know that even women who have taken a known teratogen during the first trimester have given birth to healthy babies free from deformities. Probably a majority of fetuses whose mothers took thalidomide—one of the most potent teratogens known—resisted the effects of the drug. (A recent British survey reported that babies born to women who had thalidomide-caused birth defects are having normal babies, which was expected.) Timing of exposure to a drug is crucial, of course, but some experts think that other factors yet unknown—though perhaps genetic—appear to determine a fetus' vulnerability to a drug's effects.

For the safest pregnancy, the most sensible course is not to drink or smoke, and to take drugs only if necessary and only on the doctor's advice.

Advances in Prenatal Diagnosis:
Social-Psychological and Policy Issues
Aliza Kolker

Abstract

Chorionic villus sampling (CVS), a new technique for prenatally diagnosing chromosomal and genetic disorders, may soon replace amniocentesis. This procedure, performed by inserting a catheter through the pregnant woman's cervix or through the abdomen and removing cells from the placenta, has the advantages of being available earlier in the pregnancy than amniocentesis (at 9 to 11 weeks gestational age) and of yielding results in a shorter time. Although the medical aspects of the procedure are being investigated, its psychosocial and policy implications have not been studied systematically. These issues include the subjective assessment of risk that prompts women to choose or to reject CVS, the implications of earlier diagnosis for feelings about abortion, the potential of negative findings (i.e., the absence of the designated disorder) for well-being during the remainder of the pregnancy, the ramifications of first trimester identification of fetal sex, equity of access to prenatal diagnosis, and the possible overutilization of these procedures. Drawing on previous research regarding amniocentesis and more recent research concerning CVS, this article discusses the potential implications of CVS.

Technologies affecting pregnancy and childbirth are changing rapidly (84). Chorionic villus sampling (CVS), a new technique for first trimester prenatal diagnosis, may soon revolutionize prenatal care by replacing am-

niocentesis as the method of choice for diagnosing chromosomal abnormalities. The implications of CVS have not been studied systematically by social scientists. The existing literature on CVS is predominantly medical, concentrating on the physical aspects of the procedure. Drawing on the medical literature on CVS, earlier social-scientific literature on amniocentesis, and our ongoing research on CVS, this article describes the benefits and risks of the new technique and offers some speculations regarding the psychosocial and policy issues that CVS raises.

The disadvantages of amniocentesis have been well documented. Because of the late timing of the procedure (between 14 and 19 weeks gestational age) and the lengthy waiting period for the results (between 10 days and 6 weeks), abortions following amniocentesis entail major medical risks and financial costs. Such abortions also present ethical and legal concerns because the fetus is approaching the threshold of viability and the pregnancy is advancing toward the legal limit on abortion (24 weeks in the United States). Prospective parents considering amniocentesis may therefore experience considerable emotional anguish (1;4;9;22;26;32;74;77). Even when the ultimate results are normal, parents may experience stress in the interim because of uncertainty about keeping the pregnancy at a time when the pregnancy is publicly "showing," signs of life (quickening or fetal movement) are perceptible, and their own emotional investment is frequently high. As Jean

This article first appeared in *The International Journal of Technology Assessment in Health Care* (1989) 5: 601–617. Copyright © 1989, Cambridge University Press. Reprinted with permission of the publisher.

Ashton (2,5) points out, "It is one thing to contemplate the abortion of a defective or unwanted fetus when the only signs of pregnancy are frequent urination and sleepiness, symptoms that seem to belong only to your own body. . . . Once the fetus has quickened, however, the situation seems radically different." Another woman put it more vividly: "[Initially I thought that] if I were carrying a retarded child I would admit myself to a hospital immediately [for an abortion]. However, by the time the results came in (the 24th week) the baby had been leaping in my womb for a month. Pride of authorship and female hormones took over. During one of the sleepless nights before the results were in I decided I would raise that child even if it looked like E.T." (54,105).

By contrast, CVS is performed in the 9th to 11th week of the pregnancy and the results can be known within 3 to 14 days. The advantages of this procedure are obvious. However, CVS raises new issues, both medical and psychosocial, that must be addressed if the technique is to replace amniocentesis and perhaps increase the use of prenatal diagnosis in general.

THE CVS PROCEDURE

CVS is performed with the woman lying down. The physician inserts a catheter through her cervix, or in a few cases through the abdominal wall, and using syringe suction, removes some cells from the placenta (6;7;19;27;42;43;57;58). The procedure is done under the guidance of ultrasound, an imaging technique used to verify the viability of the pregnancy, to confirm fetal age and to determine the precise location of the placenta. The cells removed are part of the chorionic villi, hairlike projections of the membrane that surrounds the fetus early in the pregnancy and is beginning to develop into the placenta. The placenta consists largely of extraembryonic cells.

Because the chorionic villi have the same composition as fetal cells and divide rapidly, the sample may be analyzed immediately for chromosomal and biochemical defects. The sex of the fetus may be determined at the same time. Women who have CVS may later undergo maternal serum alphafetoprotein testing (MSAFP), a blood test performed at approximately the 16th to 18th week in the pregnancy to screen for neural tube defects such as spina bifida and anencephaly. This may be followed by ultrasound and amniocentesis if a possible abnormality is detected. For most women no further tests are necessary beyond CVS and MSAFP (19;48;83).

THE HISTORY OF CVS

Although investigators have attempted since the 1960s to develop a safe, reliable method of prenatal diagnosis that may be used in the first trimester of the pregnancy, CVS has become available only recently. Several recent developments have made this procedure possible, including the availability of high-resolution ultrasound, highly sophisticated technology for DNA analysis, and cytogenetic analysis of embryonic tissue (44;58;71).

Research on CVS began at approximately the same time as the first clinical tests of amniocentesis. Between 1968 and 1975, Swedish and Danish geneticists performed the procedure on pregnant women shortly before elective termination of the pregnancy. They encountered several major difficulties: inability to determine the exact location of the placenta, contamination of the sample with maternal cells (decidua), and maternal infection. In the early trials chorionic samples were obtained successfully in only a small number of the procedures, and several of the samples could not be analyzed because of contamination (19;42;43).

Meanwhile, amniocentesis gained international acceptance as the technique of choice for prenatal diagnosis. Amniocentesis had a higher accuracy record than CVS; its risks to mother and fetus were judged acceptably low; and it did not entail experimentation with complicated instruments as did CVS.

In 1975 a group of Chinese investigators successfully obtained fetal placental tissues by suction without the use of optical guidance. As they did not have tissue culturing facilities, they could not look for chromosomal or biochemical abnormalities. They were, however, able to determine the fetal sex in almost all cases. The biopsies were eventually discontinued because no medically useful information was obtained and because the information concerning fetal sex was often used for the selective abortion of female fetuses (19;42;43). Similar attempts were made in the Soviet Union, but with an important advance: the use of ultrasound guidance of the biopsy catheter. This significantly increased the rate of successful samplings (19;42;43).

By the late 1970s, growing dissatisfaction with amniocentesis prompted a renewed interest in CVS in Europe and North America. Investigators in the United States, Great Britain, and Italy soon recognized that the key to successful sampling was the use of simultaneous ultrasound guidance. Other breakthroughs included the development of cytogenetic techniques for direct observation of the chorionic villi without the lengthy process of cell culturing, which permitted almost immediate analysis of the sample, and the use of effective techniques for disinfecting the cervical canal, which minimized the risk of infection (19;42;43;57;58;83;84).

THE RISKS OF CVS

Although the use of CVS for prenatal diagnosis is steadily gaining acceptance, the procedure is still quite new, and its risks have not been identified fully. The principal risk is the possibility of spontaneous abortion; miscarriages may be precipitated by vaginal bleeding, puncture of the amniotic sac, leakage of the amniotic fluid, or maternal infection.

Infection may occur from the introduction of micro-organisms into the uterus. In one case early in the history of the widespread use of the procedure (44), a woman who underwent CVS developed an acute infection which necessitated an abortion by suction curettage; this procedure was performed incompletely and had to be followed a day later by uterine evacuation to remove retained fetal skeletal parts. When the symptoms did not abate, the woman's uterus, ovaries, and fallopian tubes had to be removed under general anesthesia. The price paid by this woman was not only the loss of her fetus and a grave danger to her own life, but the permanent loss of her ability to bear children.

Acute maternal infection following CVS is rare; very few cases have been reported in the literature. Infection usually can be avoided by the application of a new, sterile catheter for each insertion, if more than one transcervical insertion is needed to obtain a sampling, or by the use of transabdominal insertion (45;57;58).

The precise risk of miscarriage due to CVS is hard to establish. Researchers have not been able to determine exactly what proportion of miscarriages following CVS are caused by the procedure and what proportion would have occurred spontaneously, as the rate of natural loss at each gestational age is not known. Allen Wilcox et al. (90) have found that 22% of all pregnancies result in miscarriage very soon after implantation, before the pregnancy can be recognized clinically, whereas an additional 9% to 12% miscarry subsequently. When a miscarriage occurs in a clinically recognized pregnancy, the fetus may have been dead for several weeks.

In approximately 10% of the women who present for CVS the ultrasound performed prior to the procedure reveals a nonviable pregnancy, that is, an empty gestational sac or a dead fetus (30;45). The appropriate comparison for evaluating the safety of CVS would be the rate of pregnancy loss among women who, at 8 or 10 weeks' gestational age, have an ultrasonographically normal fetus, yet who do not have CVS. Several recent studies (30;39;45) have compared the rate of loss for women who have CVS with those who present for the procedure yet decline to have it, either because they consider its risks too high or because another condition, such as the presence of twins, precludes the test. These studies have estimated that the true risk of miscarriage *due to the CVS procedure* varies from less than 1% to 2%. This figure compares with a chance of approximately 0.5% to 1% of miscarriages following amniocentesis. Definitive determination of this risk, however, must await randomized clinical trials comparing CVS, amniocentesis, and unscreened pregnancies.

Additional medical concerns about CVS include the possibility of intrauterine growth retardation, prematurity, and developmental problems after birth. Although no systematic follow-up studies exist of infants and children born to women who had CVS, worldwide experience has failed to document such abnormalities (7;8;20;39;45;63).

Another risk is diagnostic error. W. Allen Hogge et al. (39) report, on the basis of 1000 CVS procedures performed at the University of California at San Francisco, an overall error rate of 1.7%. This includes both false-positive and false-negative results. Alice Martin et al. (63) have found, on the basis of 103 procedures performed at Northwestern Memorial Hospital in Chicago, that half of the abnormalities diagnosed by CVS are subsequently not confirmed. One couple whose fetus was diagnosed by CVS as having Turner's syndrome mosaic chose to have an abortion, only to find out on subsequent examination that the fetus was normal. (Females with Turner's syndrome mosaic have a missing X chromosome in some, but not all, of the cells; full-blown Turner's syndrome results in the failure of the female sexual or-

gans to mature, whereas Turner's syndrome mosaic may not result in any apparent abnormality.) In other cases abnormalities were not confirmed by follow-up amniocentesis or after the birth of a normal baby.

The incidence of diagnostic error with CVS may be attributable to the small number of cells available for analysis, to contamination of the sample with maternal or other extraneous cells, to incorrect interpretation of the results, or to the early gestational age at which the procedure is performed. Some abnormalities found in placental cells, particularly mosaicisms (abnormalities that affect some but not all of the cells), are not present in the fetus or found by amniocentesis (63). These "abnormalities" are actually examples of trophoblastic mosaicism (the trophoblast is a layer of extraembryonic tissue that functions to attach the ovum to the uterine wall and to supply nutrition to the embryo). It is now recognized that when a mosaicism is detected by CVS, appropriate treatment requires follow-up amniocentesis. Such confirmation will avoid errors in essentially all cases.

It should be emphasized that CVS is generally accurate, and false or exaggerated positive diagnoses are rare. Risks generally decline as physicians gain more experience. But when errors do occur, even if they do not lead to the abortion of a healthy fetus, they may cause parental anxiety, unnecessary surgery for the baby or the mother, or maternal rejection of the newborn (31).

PSYCHOSOCIAL ISSUES IN CVS

Although the physical concerns surrounding CVS are being systematically investigated, there are many unanswered questions about the social-psychological and policy implications of the procedure. Social-psychological questions include the factors influencing the subjective assessment of risks that prompts women to choose or to reject CVS, the implications of earlier diagnosis for feelings about abortion, the potential of negative findings (i.e., the absence of the disorders) for well-being during the remainder of the pregnancy, and the ethical and pragmatic ramifications of first trimester identification of fetal sex. Issues at the policy level include equity of access to CVS and its possible overutilization. It is these factors, in addition to the considerations of safety and accuracy, that will determine the acceptability of CVS as a replacement for amniocentesis and the future course of prenatal diagnosis. Because little social-scientific research on CVS is available, the following discussion of these issues must draw on earlier research about amniocentesis as well as on our own ongoing research about CVS.

Subjective-Risk Assessment of CVS

CVS is a medical innovation that carries considerable benefits but entails risks, albeit statistically small ones. Potential users must decide, in the absence of precise information, whether the possible danger of the procedure to the fetus or to themselves is outweighed by the hazard and implications of having a child affected by a detectable condition.

One factor in the decision on risk taking is the subjective assessment of the probability of a given outcome. Previous studies of risk interpretation (23;47;59;60;86;87) suggest that the *availability* or salience of an event is correlated with a "pessimistic" interpretation of the chance of occurrence of that event. Those who have had previous experience with birth defects will interpret a given genetic risk as higher than will those who have had no such experience. The severity of the risked disorder and the perceived burden of caring for a child with the disorder also contribute to a pessimistic interpretation. Generally mental disorders are rightly or wrongly perceived as more severe and "burdensome" than physical ones (55). Another factor influencing parents in the direction of a more "pessimistic" risk assessment is discussion with a genetic counselor of the implications for their lives and the lives of their existing children of having an affected child (87).

The availability of the disorder is somewhat independent of the known "objective" or numerical odds of its occurrence. In other words, not only parents who are carriers of a genetic disorder and therefore known to be at higher risk, but others who have had children or siblings with birth defects or who have known or cared for such children are likely to assess their own risk to be higher. These parents may be reacting to the perceived seriousness or burden of the disorder rather than to the numeric probability of its occurrence (87). Such parents may be more willing to accept the risks of CVS to avert the birth of an affected child. Hence there may be an association between prior experience with birth defects, perceived genetic risk, and the choice of CVS.

A major drawback of amniocentesis, of course, is the late gestational age at which it is performed. In the past women who would not countenance a midtrimester abortion have tended to shun prenatal diagnosis altogether (17). CVS changes the dynamics of the decision to abort for chromosomal abnormalities (although not for neural tube defects) by making the diagnosis available in the first trimester of the pregnancy. The ramifications of this change are still unfolding.

CVS and Abortion

The promise of prenatal diagnosis rests on the view that some genetic disorders can be "prevented" before birth. As the only "treatment" for most prenatally diagnosed disorders is abortion, abortion is sometimes viewed as "preventive medicine" by physicians and genetic ethicists as well as by the general public (24;65;71). Abortion, however, neither prevents nor cures birth defects. It is the choice of one tragic alternative over another.

204

The physical and emotional hardships of a second trimester abortion are well documented. First trimester abortions, usually performed by vacuum aspiration, may take place in clinics on an outpatient basis. They are considered safer than childbirth or even tonsillectomy. Second trimester abortions, by contrast, often take place in hospital maternity wards and resemble term deliveries, but with the anguish of loss replacing the joy of childbirth. The proximity of women undergoing normal deliveries and of healthy babies adds to the anguish.

Second trimester abortions may be done by one of three methods or by a combination of methods: saline or urea injection, prostaglandin induction, or dilatation and evacuation (D & E). The first method involves injecting saline solution or urea into the amniotic fluid, which causes the death of the fetus. The woman then goes into labor and delivers the dead fetus. In the second method a drug, prostaglandin, is used to induce labor. In the third method, D & E, the cervix is dilated, the woman is sedated, and the fetus is removed in pieces (4;37).

Each of these methods has drawbacks. The saline solution is toxic to the woman as well as to the fetus and if inadvertently injected into her bloodstream may kill her as well. Further, saline instillation cannot be performed until the amniotic sac is sufficiently large, which in some cases entails an additional wait after the diagnosis. Prostaglandins may cause unpleasant side effects including severe nausea, vomiting, and diarrhea. They may also cause contractions not only in the uterus but, in rare cases, in respiratory and other organs. A further disadvantage of prostaglandins is that unless toxic substances are introduced the fetus may show signs of life. The possibility that the fetus may be born alive, like the deliberate killing of the fetus with toxic substances, deeply stresses both the woman and the hospital staff.

D & E is believed by some to be safer than either saline injection or prostaglandins and easier on the woman because she does not need to confront the dead fetus (33;37). It is more repugnant to physicians, however. Saline and prostaglandin abortions allow the doctor to inject the substance and then depart, leaving the woman and the nurse to cope with the hours or days of painful labor and with the expulsion of the dead fetus. The D & E procedure, by contrast, places complete responsibility for performing the abortion on the physician. In the words of a doctor who has performed many such procedures: "We have reached a point in this particular technology where there is no possibility of denying an act of destruction. It is before one's eyes. The sensations of dismemberment flow through the forceps like an electric current" (38,7). D & E abortions are less common than either saline or prostaglandin abortions because physicians are reluctant to perform them. As Barbara Rothman (77) points out, there is simply no "good" way to perform second trimester abortions.

After the abortion women usually find themselves alone in their grief. Whereas a baby is real to anyone who sees it, a fetus is real only to the woman who carries it. The loss experienced by the mother is not socially recognized or shared (77;78). Medical authorities, society at large, family members, and even husbands tend to trivialize this loss (24;66). Others, however, report that the father's pain gets even less recognition from society than does the mother's.

It is important to realize that although abortion following CVS is physically safer and easier than one following amniocentesis, it may still be very painful emotionally. In both cases the abortion involves not a way of correcting for contraceptive failure but the termination of a wanted pregnancy. Selective abortion of a wanted pregnancy at any gestational age is experienced as the loss of a child that one will never have and to whom one is already attached. These feelings are present in the first trimester as they are in the second. The reality of the baby is reinforced by the ultrasound performed before the CVS, which enables the parents to "see" the fetus for the first time (53).

In one sense aborting a fetus with a genetic defect, especially a defect that would have been fatal in utero such as trisomy 16, relieves the parents of the guilt accompanying spontaneous abortion. When no cause for a miscarriage has been found women often blame themselves for having "done something" to cause it. When a genetic cause has been established there is little sense in self-blame. At another level, however, there may be guilt for having participated in "killing" the baby (5). As many fetal abnormalities discovered through CVS normally abort spontaneously without intervention, Rothman (77,184) believes that "shouldering responsibility for a decision that God or nature might have made" adds an unnecessary burden of guilt.

CVS sometimes involves another unanticipated tragic consequence. In some cases the ultrasound reveals a nonviable pregnancy. Although these pregnancies also would abort spontaneously if allowed to continue, they are often terminated because women find it intolerable to carry a nonviable fetus. As with the diagnosis of a genetic defect, the discovery of a nonviable pregnancy avoids the bewilderment accompanying an unexplained spontaneous abortion but at the same time creates new patterns of grief, the grief of confronting a loss without prior warning. The discovery of a nonviable pregnancy is less frequent at amniocentesis because most spontaneous abortions occur during the first trimester.

CVS and Emotional Well-Being in Pregnancy

As with amniocentesis, the CVS results usually bring relief, not anguish. In 95% of the cases (and a higher percentage for amniocen-

tesis) no abnormality is found and the pregnancy is allowed to continue to term. One woman describes the euphoria and confidence that followed the postamniocentesis notification of "Everything is O.K.—you have a little girl": "It was great to find out everything was fine. From then on I didn't worry about losing the pregnancy. I had confidence in the doctor and confidence in myself. I was doing everything right" (54, 112). Another said, "It's a feeling that . . . I have done all I can do that is medically feasible and advisable, at my age, to ensure that any baby I have will be fine. There still may be defects . . . indeterminable ones. But . . . I have done what I can . . . and I can't blame myself for what I couldn't have done" (54,112–113).

Many parents, although aware that prenatal diagnosis does not rule out all birth defects, derive more reassurance from it than objectively it has to give. Some women cite the search for reassurance as the major motive for having amniocentesis. Others report that they would not have gotten pregnant "at their age" if amniocentesis had not been available: "This was a totally elective baby. I had deliberately chosen to have this baby partly because the amniocentesis was available. . . . We didn't 'have to have' this baby. It was not our first and only baby. . . . We didn't want a defective baby, not just because of the care involved but because of the harmful effects on the other children" (Personal interview).

Although the grief is real, prenatal diagnostic procedures merely alleviate the anxiety that they first accentuate. Women about to have amniocentesis or CVS dread the possibility of Down syndrome, the most common defect diagnosed; those about to have MSAFP dread neural tube defects (Brenda Seals, personal communication). The test's availability sharpens what might otherwise be low-level, diffuse concerns that surface only, as one woman put it, "on bad days," and turns them into real and dreaded possibilities. In both amniocentesis and MSAFP the anxiety is exacerbated by the lateness of the procedure. It is further exacerbated by the lengthy waiting period for the results with amniocentesis and by the relatively high instance of ambiguous results with MSAFP. When the result is normal the relief is all the more palpable because of the stress that preceded it.

CVS usually causes less anxiety if only because there is less time to worry before the procedure, the waiting period for the diagnosis is shorter, and abortion is easier to contemplate at 10 weeks' gestational age than at 20. However, because CVS does not test for neural tube defects, women who have had this procedure still must wait until the 16th to 18th week to have MSAFP screening, with a possible diagnosis of abnormality reopening the question of abortion. Additionally, women who have had ambiguous results based on CVS (3%–5% of all cases) must undergo more testing—usually amniocentesis—to confirm the diagnosis. Thus, even with CVS, the possibility of a late abortion for abnormality still looms. The parental stress may not end with the CVS results but continue into the second trimester.

CVS and Gender Identification

Aside from uncovering certain fetal abnormalities, both amniocentesis and CVS also disclose the fetus' sex. The identification of fetal sex has potentially far-reaching consequences, already unfolding with amniocentesis but likely to become more pervasive and more controversial with CVS. The most serious consequence is the possibility of selecting the sex of one's offspring through abortion of a fetus of the "wrong" sex. This practice, although rare in industrialized countries, is relatively common in developing countries (46). The potential uses of CVS for sex selection must be understood in the context of the nearly universal preference for

male children. In Western societies the mild but persistent preference for boys is well documented. Most American studies show a preference for a sex-balanced completed family combined with a preference for a male first child. When only one child is desired it is usually a son; when an odd number of children is wanted ideally the number of sons exceeds the number of daughters. Gerald Markle and Charles Nam's study of American college students (62) shows that 122 male children are desired for every 100 female children, a ratio of 6:5 for the sample as whole. The preference for sons is stronger among blacks than among whites and among Catholics and Jews than among Protestants and those with no religious affiliation. It is roughly the same among men and women, including women with feminist convictions (13;16;28;61;89).

Until recently the only way to have a given number of offspring of the desired sex was to continue having children until this goal was achieved. Evidence of the effect of sex preference on actual fertility behavior, however, is inconclusive (13;62). Studies using the parity progression ratio (that is, the likelihood of having an additional child at each family size and sex composition) have found that families whose children are of one gender are more likely to have an additional child than mixed-gender families. The likelihood of having another child is the same whether the existing composition is all female or all male. A recent study by Richard Dixon and Diane Levy (16), however, indicates that the desire for small families outweighs the desire for a child of a specific sex. That is, most families will not have more children than they want in order to have a child of the desired sex. Dixon and Levy (16,263) conclude that "sex preferences are virtually unimportant factors in actual or intended fertility behavior in a low fertility population."

If technology enabled people to have children of the sex that they want and only when they wanted them, would they take advantage of this technology to achieve the desired sex and birth order composition of their families? The controversy over abortion illustrates that although the technological capability exists to avoid having a child at an inopportune time, people may not use it. The ability to predetermine not only the number and timing, but the sex of future children, may encounter even more serious ethical and pragmatic opposition. Nancy Williamson (93), citing technical, cultural, and moral barriers, predicts a low use of such techniques in both developing and industrialized countries. In the United States, Dixon and Levy (16) have found that only one-quarter to one-third of their respondents favor using *preconceptive* sex-selection methods such as separating the X- and Y-sperm. The proportion drops to 11% to 13% when the proposed method is abortion following amniocentesis.

Contrary to earlier fears, amniocentesis has not resulted in a wave of abortions for sex selection in the United States. John Fletcher (25) estimates that the number of amnioceneses done in this country between 1970 and 1983 for sex determination alone (not involving sex-linked disease) did not exceed 50. This figure probably underestimates the true incidence of such amnioceneses. Women over 35 or with an actual or fabricated family history of genetic defects may request amniocentesis for "legitimate" reasons and hide their intent to use it for sex selection. Because both genetic counselors and society at large strongly disapprove of amniocentesis for sex determination alone, the motivation to persist in such a request differs radically from the typical desire for a sex-balanced family. This motivation is likely to come from considerable anguish and despair following multiple births of the same gender or from a strong cultural preference for a son, particularly among foreign-born couples from traditional societies. Haig Kazazian (49,18) reports that at one medical center nearly all the couples seeking amniocentesis for sex choice were of Asian extraction, frequently Indians desperate for a son after the birth of one or more daughters. Warren Hern (37,85), by contrast, reports the case of a highly educated, professional woman with healthy children who had amniocentesis for genetic diagnosis and who subsequently requested an abortion because the fetus, although normal, was male. She succeeded in persuading the abortion clinic staff that she was so disappointed and resentful over having a boy that she would not be able to nurture the child properly and would be miserable for the rest of her life. She was given the abortion for the sake of her own mental health as well as her family's welfare. Such incidents, however, have been rare in western societies.

Aborting a fetus of the "wrong" sex may become more common with CVS. At the gestational age of 2 or 3 months the pregnancy can still be private; neither the pregnancy nor the abortion need be known to anyone other than the woman. A woman can easily find out if the fetus is of the "right" or "wrong" sex and, based on that knowledge, decide whether to keep or abort the pregnancy. The decision to abort may be made ostensibly for other reasons, such as timing or parity; yet it may be consciously or subconsciously, openly or secretly influenced by the knowledge of the sex of the fetus (77).

Abortion for sex selection is a more salient issue in developing countries. In many countries the preference for sons is very strong. The ideal sex ratio—the preferred number of boys divided by the preferred number of girls—goes as high as three to five boys for every girl among some segments of the population in India and North Africa. Paradoxically, the pressure to have a son often intensifies with modernization. This happens because governments apply disincentives against large families and couples become less willing to accept large families but still hope to have a desired number of sons. Some couples move toward this goal either through the neglect of "surplus" girls, which leads to higher rates of mortality among them, or through the selective abortion of female fetuses. Roger Jeffery, Patricia Jeffery, and Andrew Lyon (46) quote an Indian hospital leaflet that advertises amniocentesis as a means of helping couples to have sons without unduly increasing the population and aggravating economic pressures on the family by giving birth to more daughters. Although governments in China, India, Singapore, and other countries frown on preference for sons and try to promote the notion that daughters are equally desirable, the cultural preference for sons remains strong. So do the practices of female neglect and abortion of female fetuses (91;92). Although no data are available yet, CVS will probably lead to the abortion of more female fetuses in developing countries.

The potential social and demographic consequences of the use of abortion for sex selection in developing countries are controversial. Williamson (93) and Nathan Keyfitz (51) speculate that this practice may have positive consequences, including a slowing down in the rate of population increase because couples would be guaranteed the desired number of sons. A further decline in the birth rate would occur in the long run because a lower female ratio at birth means that fewer women would be available to bear children in the future. Another possible consequence is an improvement in the situation of women, both mothers and daughters. Women who could be sure of producing desired sons would have more security in their marriages and more prestige in their husbands' families. Further, the decrease in the number of unwanted girls born may result in an improved treatment for those already alive, lowering the rate of female neglect and female mortality. In addition, to the extent that women are viewed as an economic com-

modity, scarcity may enhance their value and eventually eliminate gender inequality.

Such speculation may be overly optimistic, however. At present there is no evidence that gender inequality has lessened as a result of the existing sporadic shortages of women in societies in which female infanticide, female neglect, or selective abortion have been practiced. Rather, in those societies women's status remains low and patriarchal values remain well entrenched. Population growth, too, has not lessened significantly as a result of such practices. There appears to be little reason to expect that the wider use of abortion for sex selection, made possible through CVS, will have desirable consequences (46;72;73;77).

In industrialized societies the effect on both fertility and the sex ratio of the use of CVS for sex selection would be slight. The major impact would be on birth order, with more first-born and only sons and more second-born and subsequent daughters (16;35;89).

Changes in the birth order of boys and girls, however, may have important implications. Research shows that birth order influences personality traits. First-born children are believed to be more assertive, independent, and achievement-oriented and more likely to achieve highly than subsequent children. Highly achieving women tend to be disproportionately first-born children whose socialization compensated for the disadvantages of gender stereotypes with the advantages of birth order. A society in which most boys were first born and most girls second born would perpetuate and lend greater credence to the stereotyped view of women as more passive, weaker, and less achievement-oriented than men (11;72;73).

CVS may also aggravate sex discrimination in more subtle ways. In most cases, of course, fetal sex identification does not lead to selective abortion for sex. In continuing pregnancies the knowledge of the fetus' sex may affect the way the pregnancy is experienced. The knowledge of sex implies more than chromosomal or anatomical differences. It implies gender, and with it images of personality and social role expectations: "not only what the fetus is, but what we expect the child to become" (77,127). The ramifications of gender stereotyping in infancy have been documented by Jeffrey Rubin et al. (79) and others. With CVS, even more than with amniocentesis, socialization into culturally prescribed gender roles may start in utero.

Thus CVS, by making knowledge of the fetus' sex available in the first trimester, raises new and troublesome issues. As information about the fetal sex is of some pragmatic and emotional value, few would wish to deny it to parents who request it. Nevertheless, some may wish to establish guidelines forbidding the use of prenatal diagnosis explicitly for the purpose of sex determination (11;72;73) or forbidding the disclosure of gender information before the third trimester (a practice currently in effect in some Canadian provinces). Others advocate continued freedom of choice to use prenatal diagnosis for sex selection on the grounds that interference with a woman's right to have an abortion for *any* reason would establish a dangerous precedent and that the positive value of freedom of choice outweighs the possible negative consequences of sex selection (25). Clearly, further investigation and more debate on this issue are needed.

EQUITY OF ACCESS AND OVERUTILIZATION OF PRENATAL DIAGNOSIS

Which demographic groups are most likely to use—or abuse—CVS? The literature on the diffusion of innovations suggests the potential correlates of CVS use. As earlier studies indicate, over a period of time adoption follows a bell-shaped curve as knowledge about the innovation accumulates and access to it becomes easier. Individual adopters, accord-

ing to Everett Rogers and F. Floyd Shoemaker (75,176–96), may be divided into five categories: innovators, early adopters, early majority, late majority, and laggards. Early adopters have a higher socioeconomic status than late adopters as measured by education, income, and occupational prestige. They are better informed, with more access to both formal and informal communications. This leads us to expect that when actual and perceived genetic risk is controlled, white, upper- and middle-class women who live in metropolitan areas will be more likely than lower-class, rural, and minority group women to use prenatal diagnosis. Although no data are currently available, there is reason to believe this would apply particularly to the latest technique, CVS.

In the United States the inequality of access to CVS results from the cost of health care. Here, in contrast with other industrialized countries, access depends on ability to pay or on the level of insurance coverage rather than on need as determined by genetic risk. Aside from Medicaid, which covers only a small proportion of the medically needy, the American health care system offers the means for avoiding tragedy and improving the quality of life only to those who can afford them and who are knowledgeable enough to seek them (36;48;64;81).

Although prenatal diagnosis is unavailable to some women with high-risk pregnancies, it is increasingly used in many low-risk pregnancies. As the techniques become cheaper, safer, and easier to administer, pressures increase to lower the minimum age at which they are offered. Consumer demand is one source of such pressure. The demand is especially high among middle- and upper-class women, who are more likely than working- and lower-class women to worry about the impact of a handicapped child on their lives and careers and to have either insurance coverage or money to pay for such tests (67). Additional pressures come from medical and health finance sectors. As with other sophisticated and expensive health technologies, availability creates pressures for use to justify the initial investment. Pressures also arise from societal concerns about containing the costs of health care. Clearly, the "prevention" of birth defects through prenatal screening and selective abortion is cheaper than providing medical and social services for handicapped children and adults. Much of the impetus for routine screening, for example, the recommended use of MSAFP for all pregnancies in the United States and England, is fueled by societal cost-benefit considerations rather than by concern for the well-being of women and their children. Thus, the technological innovations originally developed for the benefit of women with high risks of fetal abnormalities are increasingly influencing the pregnancy and childbirth experiences of women with low risks, whereas elsewhere many women with high risk are denied access to these technologies (22).

The tendency to expand the use of CVS and other reproductive technologies to cover low-risk pregnancies is seen by some as a further step in the medicalization and dehumanization of pregnancy and childbirth (14;50;76;88). "The primary characteristic of the modern medical model of health and illness in general is that it is based on the ideology of technology . . . with its values of efficiency, . . . rationality, . . . and controlling. . . . [Pregnant] women are thus objects on whom certain procedures must be done" (76,34). Yet technological interventions, despite the risks they entail, have not always spelled better results. The medical literature is replete with studies of obstetric interventions that carry definite risks but show little evidence of effectiveness, that is, of resulting in lower morbidity and mortality for babies and mothers (10;12;34;40;56;69;70). Seen in this light, CVS is another technological intrusion in a process that has turned women into reproductive machines.

CONCLUSIONS AND IMPLICATIONS

Clearly, few would wish to turn the clock back on prenatal diagnosis. The potential benefits of CVS, the latest frontier, are undisputed. By making possible direct observation of fetal cells, CVS may make prenatal screening both cheaper and more easily available. By avoiding the major drawback of amniocentesis, the late gestational age at which it must be performed, it may make genetic screening more attractive to women at risk for chromosomal disorders. Expanding the use of prenatal diagnosis, in turn, may avert tragedies and enhance reproductive choices for many women. However, CVS carries some risks, both physical and emotional, that need to be studied further, and guidelines governing proper and improper use must be developed.

Although the physical risks of CVS—principally those of miscarriage and of incorrect or ambiguous diagnosis—are being investigated, research is needed on the social-psychological and policy issues that must be resolved if CVS is to be more widely used. One issue is equity of access for members of minority groups and lower socioeconomic strata. Access includes not only physical proximity and financial affordability but also information that enables potential users to make informed choices. Such information must include an understanding of the procedure and of its emotional as well as physical risks and benefits. At the same time we must guard against the tendency to expand the use of prenatal diagnosis to cover more low-risk pregnancies for reasons arising from societal pressures rather than individual reproductive freedom.

The implications of first trimester identification of fetal sex must be explored and debated. In particular, studies are needed on the demographic and ethical implications of the potential use of CVS in conjunction with abortion for sex selection and on the effects of sex identification on the perpetuation of gender stereotypes.

Research is needed also on the social-psychological and emotional implications of CVS-related fetal loss, whether through selective abortion or through the sonographic disclosure of a nonviable pregnancy. Additionally, the implications of CVS for emotional well-being in continuing pregnancies must be explored.

REFERENCES

1. Adler, B., and Kushnick, T. Genetic counseling in prenatally diagnosed trisomy 18 and 21: Psychosocial aspects. *Pediatrics,* 1982, 69, 94–99.
2. Ashton, J. Amniocentesis: Safe but still ambiguous. *Hastings Center Report,* 1976, 6(February), 5–6.
3. Bennett, N. G. (ed.) *Sex selection of children.* New York: Academic, 1983.
4. Benderly, B. L. *Thinking about abortion.* Garden City, NY: Doubleday, 1984.
5. Borg, S., and Lasker, J. *When pregnancy fails.* Boston: Beacon, 1981.
6. Brambati, B., Simoni, G., and Fabro, S. (eds.). *Chorionic villus biopsy.* New York: Marcel Dekker, 1986.
7. Cadkin, A. V., Ginsberg, N. A., Pergament, E., and Verlinkski, Y. Chorionic villi sampling: A new technique for detection of genetic abnormalities in the first trimester. *Radiology,* 1984, 151, 159–62.
8. Carpenter, R. Comments on Elias, et al. "Chorionic villus sampling. . ." *American Journal of Obstetrics and Gynecology,* 1985, 152, 211–13.
9. Chervin, A., et al. Amniocentesis for prenatal diagnosis: Subjective patient response. *New York State Journal of Medicine,* 1977, 77, 1406–08.
10. Chiswick, M. L., and James, D. K. Kielland's forceps: Association with neonatal morbidity and mortality. *British Medical Journal,* 1979, 1, 7–9.
11. Clark, L. R. Sex preselection: The advent of the made-to-order child. *The Pharos,* Fall, 1985, 2–7.
12. Cohen, W. R. Influence of the duration of second stage labor on perinatal outcome and puerperal morbidity. *Obstetrics and Gynecology,* 1977, 49, 266–69.
13. Coombs, C. The preference for sex of children among U.S. couples. *Family Planning Perspective,* 1977, 9, 259–65.
14. Corea, G. *The mother machine: Reproductive technologies from artificial insemination to artificial wombs.* New York: Harper & Row, 1985.
15. Davies, B. L., and Doran, T. A. Factors in a woman's decision to undergo genetic amniocentesis for advanced maternal age. *Nursing Research,* 1982, 31, 56–59.
16. Dixon, R. D., and Levy, D. E. Sex of children: A community analysis of preferences and predetermination attitudes. *Sociological Quarterly,* 1985, 26, 251–71.
17. Ekwo, E. E., et al. *Factors which influence subjects' acceptance or rejection of amniocentesis.* Research proposal submitted to the National Institute of Child Health and Human Development (NIH), Grant #NCJ 190457-03-0, 1981.
18. Ekwo, E. E., et al. Factors influencing maternal estimates of genetic risk. *American Journal of Medical Genetics,* 1985, 20, 497–504.
19. Elias, S., Simpson, J. L., Martin, A. O., et al. Chorionic villus sampling for first-trimester prenatal diagnosis: Northwestern University program. *American Journal of Obstetrics and Gynecology,* 1985, 152, 204–13.
20. Elias, S., Simpson, J. L., Martin, A. O., et al. Chorionic villus sampling in continuing pregnancies: Low fetal loss rates in initial 109 cases. *American Journal of Obstetrics and Gynecology,* 1986, 154, 1349–52.
21. Etzioni, A. *Genetic fix.* New York: Harper & Row, 1973.
22. Farrant, W. Who's for amniocentesis? The politics of prenatal screening. In H. Homans (ed.), *The sexual politics of reproduction.* England: Gower Publishing, 1985, 96–123.
23. Fischhoff, B., Lichtenstein, S., Slovic, P., et al. *Acceptable risk.* Cambridge: Cambridge University Press, 1981.
24. Fletcher, J. C. *Coping with genetic disorders.* New York: Harper & Row, 1982.
25. Fletcher, J. C. Ethics and public policy: Should sex choice be discouraged? In N. G. Bennett (ed.), *Sex selection of children.* New York: Academic, 1983, 213–52.
26. Fletcher, J. C., and Schulman, J. D. Fetal research: The state of the question. *Hastings Center Report,* 1985, 15(April), 2, 6–12.
27. Fraccaro, M., Simoni, G., and Brambati, B. (eds.). *First trimester fetal diagnosis.* Berlin: Springer-Verlag, 1985.

28. Gilroy, F., and Steibacher, R. Preselection of child's sex: Technological utilization and feminism. *Psychological Reports,* 1983, 53, 671–76.

29. Golbus, M. S., et al. Prenatal diagnosis in 3000 amniocenteses. *The New England Journal of Medicine,* 1979, 300, 157–63.

30. Green, J. E., Dorfmann, A., Jones, S. L., et al. Chorionic villus biopsy: Experience with an initial 940 cases. *Obstetrics and Gynecology,* 1988, 71, 208–12.

31. Griffiths, D. M., and Gough, M. Dilemmas after ultrasonic diagnosis of fetal abnormality. *Lancet,* 1985, 623–25.

32. Grimes, D. A. Second-trimester abortions in the United States. *Family Planning Perspectives,* 1984, 16(Nov.–Dec.), 260–65.

33. Grimes, D. A., and Schulz, K. F. The comparative safety of second-trimester abortion methods. In Ciba Foundation Symposium 115, *Abortion: Medical progress and social implications.* London: Pitman, 1985, 83–102.

34. Harris, R. E. An evaluation of the median episiotomy. *American Journal of Obstetrics and Gynecology,* 1970, 106, 660–65.

35. Hartley, S. F., and Petraczyk, L. M. Preselecting the sex of offspring: Technologies, attitudes, and implications. *Social Biology,* 1979, 26, 232–46.

36. Hayward, R. A., Shapiro, M. F., Freeman, H. E., and Corey, C. R. Inequities in health services among insured Americans. *The New England Journal of Medicine,* 1988, 318, 1507–12.

37. Hern, W. M. *Abortion practice.* Philadelphia, PA: J. B. Lippincott, 1984.

38. Hern, W. M., and Corrigan, B. What about us? Staff reactions to D & E. *Advances in Planned Parenthood,* vol. 15. Rpt. in *Excerpta Medica,* 1980.

39. Hogge, W. A., Schonberg, S. A., and Golbus, M. S. Chorionic villus sampling: Experience of the first 1000 cases. *American Journal of Obstetrics and Gynecology,* 1986, 154, 1249–52.

40. Hughey, M. J., McElin, T. W., and Lussky, R. Forceps operations in perspective. *Journal of Reproductive Medicine,* 1978, 20, 253–59.

41. Hutson, J. M., McNay, M. B., MacKenzie, J. R., et al. Antenatal diagnosis of surgical disorders by ultrasonography. *Lancet,* 1985, 621–22.

42. Jackson, L. G. First-trimester diagnosis of fetal genetic disorders. *Hospital Practice,* 1985, 39–48.

43. Jackson, L. G. Chorion villus sampling. *Jefferson Alumni Bulletin,* 1985 (Spring), 2–7.

44. Jackson, L. G. *CVS Newsletter:* July 26, 1985.

45. Jackson, L. G., and Warner, R. J. Risks of chorion villus sampling. *Bailliere's Clinical Obstetrics and Gynaecology,* 1987, 1, 513–31.

46. Jeffery, R., Jeffery, P., and Lyon, A. Female infanticide and amniocentesis. *Social Science and Medicine,* 1984, 19, 1207–12.

47. Kahneman, D., and Tversky, A. The psychology of preference. *Scientific American,* 1982, 246, 160–71.

48. Kasper, A. S. Maternal serum alpha fetoprotein testing: Some public policy considerations. *Women and Health,* 1981, 6, 147–53.

49. Kazazian, H. H. Prenatal diagnosis for sex choice: A medical review. *Hastings Center Report,* 1980, 10, 17–18.

50. Kitzinger, S. *Women as mothers.* Fontana, 1978.

51. Keyfitz, N. Foreword. In N. G. Bennett (ed.), *Sex selection of children.* New York: Academic, 1983, xi–xiii.

52. Kolata, G. First trimester prenatal diagnosis. *Science,* 1983, 221, 1031–32.

53. Kolker, A. *Abortion following a finding of abnormality with prenatal diagnosis: What difference does timing make?* Paper presented at the Meetings of the Eastern Sociological Society, March, 1988.

54. Kolker, A., and Burke, B. M. Amniocentesis and the social construction of pregnancy. *Journal of Marriage and Family Review,* 1987, 11, 95–116.

55. Kolker, A., Phillips, J., Jones, S., and Schulman, J. *CVS: Preliminary findings.* Paper presented at the Meetings of the Society for the Study of Social Problems, August, 1988.

56. *Lancet.* A time to be born [editorial]. 1974, ii, 1183–84.

57. Lilford, R. J. Chorion villus biopsy. *Archives of Disease in Childhood.* 1985, 60, 897–99.

58. Lindsten, J., Marsk, L., and Mikkelsen, M. Role of chorion villi biopsy in prenatal diagnosis of genetic disorders. In K. Berg (ed.) *Medical genetics: Past, present, future.* New York: A. R. Liss, 1985, 195–212.

59. Lippman-Hand, A., and Fraser, F. C. Genetic counseling—the post-counseling period: Parents' perceptions of uncertainty. *American Journal of Medical Genetics,* 1979, 4, 51–71.

60. Luker, K. *Taking chances: Abortion and the decision not to contracept.* Berkeley: The University of California Press, 1976.

61. Markle, G. E. Sex ratio at birth: Values, variance and some determinants. *Demography*, 1974, 11, 131–42.

62. Markle, G. E., and Nam, C. B. Sex predetermination: Its impact on fertility. *Social Biology*, 1971, 18, 73–83.

63. Martin, A. O., Simpson, J. L., Rosinsky, B. J., and Elias, S. Chorionic villus sampling in continuing pregnancies: Cytogenic reliability. *American Journal of Obstetrics and Gynecology*, 1986, 154, 1353–62.

64. Mechanic, D. *From advocacy to allocation: The evolving American health care system.* New York: Free Press, 1986.

65. Milunski, A. *Know your genes.* Boston: Houghton-Mifflin, 1977.

66. Milunski, A. (ed.). *Genetic disorders and the fetus: Diagnosis, prevention, and treatment.* New York: Plenum, 1979.

67. Mittenthal, S. Amniocentesis: On the increase. *The New York Times.* August 22, 1984, p. C1.

68. Oakley, A. *Women confined: Toward a sociology of childbirth.* New York: Schocken Books, 1980.

69. O'Sullivan, M. J., Fumia, F., Holsinger, K., and McLeod, A. G. Vaginal delivery after cesarean section. *Clinics in Perinatology*, 1981, 8, 131–43.

70. Ott, W. J. Primary cesarean section: Factors related to postpartum infection. *Obstetrics and Gynecology*, 1981, 57, 171–76.

71. Perry, T. B, Vekemans, M. J. J., Lippman, A., et al. Chorionic villi sampling: Clinical experience, immediate complications, and patient attitudes. *American Journal of Obstetrics and Gynecology*, 1985, 151, 161–66.

72. Powledge, T. M. Toward a moral policy for sex choice. In N. G. Bennett (ed.), *Sex Selection of Children,* New York: Academic, 1983, 201–13.

73. Powledge, T. M. *The last taboo: Genetic manipulation and eugenics.* Boston: Houghton-Mifflin, 1984.

74. Rice, N., and Doherty, R. Reflections on prenatal diagnosis: The consumers' views. *Social Work in Health Care,* 1982, 8, 47–57.

75. Rogers, E. M., and Shoemaker, F. F. *Communication of innovations.* New York: Free Press, 1971.

76. Rothman, B. K. *In labor: Women and power in the birthplace.* New York: W. W. Norton, 1982.

77. Rothman, B. K. *The tentative pregnancy.* New York: Viking, 1986.

78. Rothman, B. K. Reflections: On hard work. *Qualitative Sociology.* 1986, 9, 48–53.

79. Rubin, J., Provenzano, F., and Luria, Z. The eye of the beholder: Parents' views on sex of newborns. *American Journal of Orthopsychiatry*, 1974, 44, 47–55.

80. Schulman, J. D. Prenatal treatment of biochemical disorders. *Seminars in Perinatology,* July, 1985, 9, 75–77.

81. Schwartz, H. D. *Dominant issues in medical sociology,* 2nd edition. New York: Random House, 1987.

82. Seals, B., Williamson, R., Hanson, J., and Ekwo, E. Moral and religious influences on the amniocentesis decision. *Social Biology,* 1985, 32, 12, 13–20.

83. Seals, B., et al. *State-wide evaluation of MSAFP screening.* Research proposal submitted to the National Institute of Child Health and Human Development, NIH, 1985.

84. Seibel, M. M. A new era in reproductive technology. *The New England Journal of Medicine,* 1988, 318, 828–34.

85. Simoni, G., Brambati, B., Danesino, C., et al. Diagnostic applications of first trimester trophoblast sampling in 100 pregnancies. *Human Genetics,* 1984, 66, 252.

86. Wertz, D. C., and Sorenson, J. R. Genetic counseling and reproductive uncertainty. *American Journal of Medical Genetics,* 1984, 18, 79–88.

87. Wertz, D. C., Sorenson, J. R., and Heeren, T. C. Clients' interpretation of risks provided in genetic counseling. *American Journal of Human Genetics,* 1986, 39, 253–64.

88. Wertz, D. C., and Wertz, R. W. *Lying-in: A history of childbirth in America.* New York: The Free Press, 1977.

89. Westoff, C. F., and Rindfuss, R. R. Sex preselection in the United States: Some implications. *Science,* 1974, 184, 633–36.

90. Wilcox, A. J., Weinberg, C. R., O'Connor, J. F., et al. Incidence of early loss of pregnancy. *The New England Journal of Medicine,* 1988, 319, 189–94.

91. Williamson, N. E. *Sons or daughters: A cross-cultural survey of parental preferences.* Beverly Hills, CA: Sage, 1976.

92. Williamson, N. E., Lean, T. H., and Vendgadasalam, D. Evaluation of an unsuccessful sex preselection clinic in Singapore. *Journal of Biosocial Science,* 1978, 10, 375–88.

93. Williamson, N. E. Parental sex preferences and sex selection. In N. G. Bennett (ed.), *Sex selection of children.* New York: Academic, 1983, 129–151.

Psychological Responses After Abortion

Nancy E. Adler, Henry P. David, Brenda N. Major,
Susan H. Roth, Nancy F. Russo, Gail E. Wyatt

A review of methodologically sound
studies of the psychological responses
of U.S. women after they obtained
legal, nonrestrictive abortions indicates that distress is generally greatest
before the abortion and that the incidence of severe negative responses is
low. Factors associated with increased
risk of negative response are consistent with those reported in research on
other stressful life events.

Abortion has been a legal medical procedure
throughout the United States since the 1973
Supreme Court decision in *Roe v. Wade,* with
1.5 million to 1.6 million procedures performed annually. U.S. abortion patients reflect all segments of the population. In 1987,
almost 60% of abortion patients were under
25 years of age. Most (82%) were not married, and half had no prior births. Nearly
69% of women obtaining abortions were
white (*1*). Abortions are most often performed in the first trimester; the median gestational age is 9.2 weeks; 97% of abortions
are performed by instrumental evacuation (*2*).

Although much literature exists on the
psychological consequences of abortion, contradictory conclusions have been reached.
Disparate interpretations are due in part to
limitations of the research methods and in
part to political, value, or moral influences.
In this review of studies with the most rigorous research designs, we report consistent
findings on the psychological status of
women who have had legal abortions under
nonrestrictive circumstances (*3*). This article

is limited to U.S. studies; however, results
from a study in Denmark are also relevant
because of the existence of a uniform national population registration system not
available in the United States (*4*).

Responses After Abortion

Responses after abortion reflect the entire
course of experiencing and resolving an unwanted pregnancy. Although there may be
sensations of regret, sadness, or guilt, the
weight of the evidence from scientific studies
(*3*) indicates that legal abortion of an unwanted
pregnancy in the first trimester does not pose a
psychological hazard for most women.

Descriptive studies have shown the incidence of severe negative responses after
abortion to be low (*5–10*). After first-
trimester abortion, women most frequently
report feeling relief and happiness. In a study
by Lazarus (*5*), 2 weeks after first-trimester
abortions, 76% of women reported feeling relief, while the most common negative emotion, guilt, was reported by only 17%. Negative emotions reflecting internal concerns,
such as loss, or social concerns, such as social disapproval, typically are not experienced as strongly as positive emotions after
abortion (*5–8*). For example, Adler (*6*) obtained ratings of feelings over a 2- to 3-
month period after abortion on Likert-type
scales, with 5 representing strongest intensity. Mean ratings were 3.96 for positive
emotions, 2.26 for internally based negative

This article first appeared in *Science* (1990) 248: 41–44. Copyright © 1990, the American Association for the Advancement of Science. Reprinted with permission.

emotions, and 1.89 for socially based negative emotions.

Women show little evidence of psychopathology after abortion. For example, on the short form of the Beck Depression Inventory, scores below 5 are considered nondepressed (11). In a sample of first-trimester patients, Major et al. (9) obtained mean scores of 4.17 (SD = 3.92) immediately after the abortion and 1.97 (SD = 2.93) 3 weeks later.

Measures used in most studies were not designed to assess psychopathology, but, rather, emotional distress within normal populations. These indicators show significant (12) decreases in distress from before abortion to immediately after and from before abortion or immediately after to several weeks later (9, 10). For example, Cohen and Roth (10) found a drop in the depression subscale of the Symptom Checklist 90 (SCL-90) from a mean of 24.1 (SD = 11.8) at the time of arrival at a clinic to a mean of 18.4 (SD = 12.2) in the recovery room. Similar drops were shown on the anxiety scale of the SCL-90 and on the Impact of Events scale, an indicator of distress.

Only two studies compared responses after abortion with those after birth. Athanasiou et al. (13) studied women after early (suction) abortion, late (saline) abortion, and term birth. Starting with 373 women, researchers matched 38 patients in each group for ethnicity, age, parity, and marital and socioeconomic status. Thirteen to sixteen months after abortion or delivery, women completed the Minnesota Multiphasic Personality Inventory (MMPI) and the SCL. None of the groups had a mean score on any subscales of the MMPI above 70, the cutoff indicating psychopathology. Few differences among groups were shown (14), and the authors concluded that the three groups were "startlingly similar."

Zabin et al. (15) interviewed 360 adolescents seeking pregnancy tests and compared those who had negative results, those who were pregnant and carried to term, and those who were pregnant and aborted. All three groups showed higher levels of state (transient) anxiety at base line than they did 1 or 2 years later (for example, for the abortion group X = 74.6 at base line versus 45.6 and 43.6 at 1 and 2 years later). Two years after the initial interview, the abortion group showed, if anything, a more positive psychological profile than either of the other two groups. There were no differences on state anxiety, but the abortion group was significantly lower on trait anxiety than either of the other two groups, was higher on self-esteem than the negative pregnancy group, and had a greater sense of internal control than the childbearing group.

Factors Relating to Psychological Responses

Although most women do not experience negative psychological responses after abortion, case studies document some negative experiences. Various aspects of the abortion experience may contribute to distress. Ambivalence about the wantedness of the pregnancy may engender a sense of loss. Conflict about the meaning of abortion and its relation to deeply held values or beliefs, perceived social stigma, or lack of support may also induce negative reactions.

The Decision Process. The greater the difficulty of deciding to terminate a pregnancy, the more likely there will be negative responses after abortion (6–8, 16). For example, Adler (6) found that the difficulty of deciding to abort, reported several days before abortion, was positively associated with the experience of negative emotions reflecting loss 2 to 3 months after abortion (r = 0.37), but was not related to a statistically significant extent to the experience of positive emotions or of negative emotions reflecting social disapproval.

Although most women do not find the decision to abort difficult, some do (*16*), and it appears to be more difficult for women seeking termination later in pregnancy. Whereas only 7% of 100 first-trimester patients studied by Osofsky *et al.* (*17*) reported initial indecision and 12% reported difficulty in deciding about abortion, corresponding figures among 200 second-trimester patients were 36 and 51%. Women undergoing second-trimester abortions also report more emotional distress after abortion than do those terminating first-trimester pregnancies (*17–19*).

Women who perceive more support for the decision to abort are more satisfied with their decision (*7, 20*). Those with fewer conflicts over abortion are also more satisfied; in a sample of adolescents, Eisen and Zellman (*21*) found that satisfaction with the decision 6 months after an abortion was associated with a favorable opinion of abortion in general as well as for themselves.

The more a pregnancy is wanted and is viewed as personally meaningful by the woman, the more difficult abortion may be. Major *et al.* (*9*) found that among 247 first-trimester abortion patients, women who described their pregnancy as being "highly meaningful" compared to those who found their pregnancy to be less personally meaningful reported more physical complaints immediately after the abortion and anticipated more negative consequences. Three weeks after the abortion, women who had indicated having had no intention to become pregnant scored significantly lower on the Beck Depression Inventory ($X = 1.68$, SD $= 2.33$) than did the minority of women who had at least some intention to become pregnant ($X = 3.71$, SD $= 5.03$).

In summary, women who report little difficulty in making their decision, who are more satisfied with their choice, and who are terminating pregnancies that were unintended and hold little personal meaning for them show more positive responses after abortion.

Women with negative attitudes toward abortion and who perceive little support for their decision have more difficulty deciding about abortion. These factors may also contribute to delay in obtaining abortions (*19*), potentially subjecting women to the greater stress of second-trimester procedures (*17–19*).

Perceived Social Support. Perceived social support can buffer some adverse effects of stressful life events (*22*). However, social support is complex. Support for having the abortion needs to be differentiated from support in general; the former is associated with more favorable outcomes; the latter may not be.

Women with greater support for their abortion from parents and the male partner generally show more positive responses after abortion (*8, 23, 24*). Intimacy with and involvement of the male partner was a significant predictor of emotional reaction in two samples (*8*). Together with satisfaction with the decision and the woman's initial emotional response to becoming pregnant, partner support accounted for almost 40% of the variance in psychological response 2 to 3 weeks after abortion. Moseley *et al.* (*24*) found that having negative feelings toward one's partner, making the abortion decision alone, and experiencing opposition from parents were associated with greater emotional distress on the Multiple Affective Adjective Check List both before a first-trimester abortion and immediately after. However, Robbins (*25*) found that single women who maintained a strong relationship with their partner reported more negative change on the MMPI 6 weeks after abortion and more regret 1 year later than those whose relationships deteriorated.

In a study of actual social support, Major *et al.* (*9*) recorded whether women were accompanied to the clinic by a male partner. Out of 247 women, 83 were accompanied. Compared to unaccompanied women, those with partners were younger and expected to cope less well beforehand; women who were more distressed about the abortion may have expressed a greater need for their partners to accompany them. Accompanied women were significantly more depressed and reported more physical complaints immediately after abortion than unaccompanied women. Differences in depression after abortion remained after controlling for age and coping expectations, but they did not remain in a 3-week follow-up of a subset of women.

Coping Processes and Expectancies. Generalized positive outcome expectancies and situation-specific coping expectancies and processes have been linked to a variety of health-relevant outcomes (*26*). Major *et al.* (*9*) found that among abortion patients, those who expected to cope well scored lower on the Beck Depression Inventory than those with more negative expectations (X = 2.98, SD = 3.04 versus X = 5.93, SD = 4.41, respectively). Those expecting to cope well also showed more positive mood, anticipated fewer negative consequences, and had fewer physical complaints both immediately after abortion and 3 weeks later.

Cohen and Roth (*10*) examined coping styles and levels of anxiety and depression before and immediately after abortion. As noted earlier, anxiety and depression decreased significantly from before the abortion to afterwards for all women, but those who used approach strategies (for example, thinking about the procedure, talking about it) showed a greater decrease in anxiety from before to after abortion than those not using these strategies. Women who used denial scored significantly higher in depression and anxiety than did those who did not deny.

Limitations of Research and Future Directions

Although each study has methodological shortcomings and limitations, the diversity of methods used provides strength in drawing general conclusions. Despite the diversity, the studies are consistent in their findings of relatively rare instances of negative responses after abortion and of decreases in psychological distress after abortion compared to before abortion. However, weaknesses and gaps found among studies provide challenges for future research.

First, samples of well-defined populations and information on subjects who choose not to participate are needed. Studies have sampled women from specific clinics or hospitals. Both public and private clinics have been used, and samples have varied in their ethnic and socioeconomic character. Women whose abortions are performed by private physicians are not represented; they are estimated to be about 4% of women having abortions (*27*).

Of more concern is the necessary use of volunteers, which can introduce bias if women who agree to participate in research differ from those who do not on characteristics linked to more positive or negative outcomes. An analysis of studies that provide data on characteristics of research participants versus the population from which the sample was drawn suggests that women who are more likely to find the abortion experience stressful may be underrepresented in volunteer samples. However, the amount of bias introduced by this underrepresentation appears to be minor and unlikely to influence the general conclusions (*28*).

Second, the timing of measurement has been limited. Many studies lack base-line data from before the abortion. We know of no studies with data collected before the pregnancy, making it impossible to control for variables that may be associated with the initial occurrence of the pregnancy and which could influence responses after abortion. One of the best predictors of a woman's psychological status after abortion is likely to be her functioning before the occurrence of the unwanted pregnancy (*29*). Former Surgeon General C. Everett Koop has called for a prospective study of a nationally representative sample of women of childbearing age (30). Such a study would address both issues of representativeness and of base-line measurement.

Timing of assessment after abortion has also been limited. Some studies obtained measures within a few hours after the procedure, while the woman was still in the clinic. Responses at this time may not be indicative of longer term response. A few studies have obtained measures a few weeks or months after abortion; the longest follow-up is 2 years. Therefore, no definitive conclusions can be drawn about longer term effects. Although individual case studies have identified instances in which individuals develop severe problems that they attribute to an earlier abortion experience (31), the number of such cases is comparatively small. Moreover, research on other life stresses suggests that women who do not experience severe negative responses within a few months after the event are unlikely to develop future significant psychological problems related to the event (32). Longer term studies are needed to confirm this observation and to ascertain the influence of other life events attributed retrospectively to the abortion experience.

Finally, in studying psychological responses after abortion, it is important to separate the experience of abortion from the characteristics of women seeking abortion and from the context of resolving an unwanted pregnancy. A useful comparison would be women who carry an unwanted pregnancy to term and surrender the child for adoption; this would control both for the unwantedness of the pregnancy and the experience of loss. The study by Athanasiou et al. (13) matched women who were terminating pregnancies with those carrying to term on key demographic variables, but they were not matched on ''wantedness'' of the pregnancy. Similarly, the comparison used in the Danish study (4) for women aborting their pregnancies was women carrying to term, most of whom were likely to be delivering wanted pregnancies. One would expect more adverse outcomes for women carrying unwanted pregnancies to term (33).

A number of questions can be addressed without a comparison group. Theoretically grounded studies testing conditional hypotheses about factors that may put women at relatively greater risk for negative responses are particularly important. Such studies can address critical questions about the nature of the abortion experience and its aftermath, and can point the way to interventions if needed.

Conclusion

Scientific studies on psychological responses to legal, nonrestrictive abortion in the United States suggest that severe negative reactions are infrequent in the immediate and short-term aftermath, particularly for first-trimester abortions. Women who are terminating pregnancies that are wanted and personally meaningful, who lack support from their partner or parents for the abortion, or who have more conflicting feelings or are less sure of their decision beforehand may be at relatively higher risk for negative consequences.

Case studies have established that some women experience severe distress or psychopathology after abortion and require sympathetic care. As former Surgeon General C. Everett Koop testified before Congress regarding his review of research on psychological effects of abortion, such responses can be overwhelming to a given individual, but the development of significant psychological problems related to abortion is ''minuscule from a public health perspective'' (34).

Despite methodological shortcomings of any single study, in the aggregate, research with diverse samples, different measures of response, and different times of assessment have come to similar conclusions. The time of greatest distress is likely to be before the abortion. Severe negative reactions after abortions are rare and can best be understood in the framework of coping with a normal life stress.

REFERENCES AND NOTES

1. S. K. Henshaw and J. Silverman, *Fam. Plann. Perspect.* 20, 158 (1988).
2. S. Henshaw, *ibid.* 19, 5 (1987); C. Tietze and S. K. Henshaw, *Induced Abortion: A World Review* (Alan Guttmacher Institute, New York, 1986); E. Powell-Griner, *Mon. Vital Stat.* 36 (no. 5), 1 (1987).
3. Studies included in this article had to meet the following three criteria: (i) the research was empirical and based on a definable sample; (ii) the sample was drawn from the United States; and (iii) the women studied had undergone abortions under legal and nonrestrictive conditions (for example, women did not have to qualify for the procedure on the basis of threat to physical or mental health). These criteria allow for maximal generalizability to U.S. women under current conditions.
4. Through the use of computer linkages to national abortion and birth registers, the admissions register to psychiatric hospitals was tracked for women 3 months after abortion (n = 27,234) or delivery (n = 71,370) and for all women 15 to 49 years of age residing in Denmark (n = 1,169,819). To determine incidence rates, only first admissions to psychiatric hospitals were recorded, excluding women who had been admitted within the 15 previous months. The key finding was that for both never-married women and currently married women, the psychiatric admission rate after pregnancy was roughly the same for abortions or deliveries—about 12 per 10,000 compared to 7 per 10,000 for all women of reproductive age. Among the much smaller group of separated, divorced, or widowed women, those who had terminated pregnancies (which perhaps were originally intended) experienced a fourfold higher admissions rate (64 per 10,000) than the group of separated, divorced, or widowed women who delivered (17 per 10,000). However, because there may be a bias against hospitalizing a new mother, particu-

larly if she is nursing, the relative psychological risk of delivery may be underestimated [H. P. David, N. Rasmussen, E. Holst, *Fam. Plann. Perspect.* 13, 88 (1981)].
5. A. Lazarus, *J. Psychosom. Obstet. Gynaecol.* 4, 141 (1985).
6. N. E. Adler, *Am. J. Orthopsychiatry* 45, 446 (1975).
7. J. D. Osofsky and H. Osofsky, *ibid.* 42, 48 (1972).
8. L. R. Shusterman, *Soc. Sci. Med.* 13A, 683 (1979).
9. B. Major, P. Mueller, K. Hildebrandt, *J. Pers. Soc. Psychol.* 48, 585 (1985). Means for 3-week follow-up interviews reported here do not match means published in the original article. Due to an error in the original publication, standard deviations were reported instead of means, but all tests of significance were accurate. The correct means are reported here.
10. L. Cohen and S. Roth, *J. Hum. Stress.* 10, 140 (1984).
11. A. T. Beck and R. W. Beck, *Postgrad. Med.* 52, 81 (1972).
12. In this article, significance is used in terms of statistical significance and may not represent clinically significant changes or associations.
13. R. Athanasiou, W. Oppel, L. Michaelson, T. Unger, M. Yager, *Fam. Plann. Perspect.* 5, 227 (1973).
14. The only statistically significant differences found were as follows: (i) women who had experienced term birth scored higher on the paranoia subscale of the MMPI (X = 61.7, SD = 14.6) than did women in either abortion group (X = 58.9, SD = 12.2 for suction patients and X = 54.6, SD = 9.4 for saline patients) and (ii) suction abortion patients reported fewer somatic complaints on the SCL (X = 10.6, SD = 8.0) than either the saline abortion or delivery patients (X = *14.7, SD = 8.1* and X = *14.8, SD = 9.3, respectively*).
15. L. S. Zabin, M. B. Hirsch, M. R. Emerson, *Fam. Plann. Perspect.* 21, 248 (1989).
16. M. B. Bracken, *Soc. Psychiatry* 13, 135 (1978).
17. J. D. Osofsky, H. J. Osofsky, R. Rajan, D. Spitz, *Mt. Sinai J. Med.* 42, 456 (1975).
18. J. B. Rooks and W. Cates, Jr., *Fam. Plann. Perspect.* 9, 276 (1977): N. B. Kaltreider, S. Goldsmith, A. Margolis, *Am. J. Obstet. Gynecol.* 135, 235 (1979).

19. M. Bracken and S. Kasl, *ibid.* 121, 1008 (1975).
20. M. B. Bracken, L. V. Klerman, M. Bracken, *ibid.* 130, 251 (1978).
21. M. Eisen and G. L. Zellman, *J. Gen. Psychol.* 145, 231 (1984).
22. S. Cohen and T. A. Wills, *Psychol. Bull.* 98, 310 (1985); R. C. Kessler and J. D. McLeod, *Social Support and Health,* S. Cohen and S. L. Syme, Eds. (Academic Press, Orlando, FL, 1985), pp. 219–240.
23. M. B. Bracken, M. Hachamovitch, G. Grossman, *J. Nerv. Ment. Dis.* 158, 154 (1974).
24. D. T. Moseley *et al., J. Clin. Psychol.* 37, 276 (1981).
25. J. M. Robbins, *Soc. Probl.* 31, 334 (1984).
26. M. F. Scheier and C. S. Carver, *J. Pers.* 55, 169 (1987); A. Bandura, *Psychol. Rev.* 84, 191 (1977).
27. S. K. Henshaw, J. D. Forrest, J. Van Vort, *Fam. Plann. Perspect.* 19, 63 (1987).
28. N. E. Adler, *J. Appl. Soc. Psychol.* 6, 240 (1976); E. W. Freeman, *Am. J. Orthopsychiatry* 47, 503 (1977).
29. E. C. Payne, A. R. Kravitz, M. T. Notman, J. V. Anderson, *Arch. Gen. Psychiatry* 33, 725 (1976): E. M. Belsey, H. S. Greer, S. Lal, S. C.

Lewis, R. W. Beard. *Soc. Sci. Med.* 11, 71 (1977).
30. C. E. Koop, letter to R. W. Reagan, 9 January 1989.
31. A. C. Speckhard, *The Psycho-Social Aspects of Stress Following Abortion* (Sheed and Ward, Kansas City, MO 1987).
32. C. B. Wortman and R. C. Silver, *J. Consult. Clin. Psychol.* 57, 349 (1989).
33. One may also find more adverse consequences for the children born as a result of unwanted pregnancy [H. P. David, Z. Dytrych, Z. Matejcek, V. Schuller, *Born Unwanted: Developmental Effects of Denied Abortion* (Springer, New York, 1988)].
34. Committee on Government Operations, House of Representatives, *The Federal Role in Determining the Medical and Psychological Impact of Abortions on Women,* 101st Cong., 2d sess., 11 December 1989, House Report 101-392, p. 14.
35. This article is based on a review conducted by a panel convened by the American Psychological Association. The authors were members of the panel. We thank J. Gentry and B. Wilcox for contributions to the manuscript and G. Markman and A. Schlagel for manuscript preparation.

The Postadoption Experience of Surrendering Parents

Eva Y. Deykin, Dr. P.H., Lee Campbell, M.Ed., Patricia Patti, B.S.N.

In order to ascertain the effects on subsequent life adjustment of having relinquished a child for adoption, a survey was conducted among 334 individuals, most of whom are members of Concerned United Birthparents. Findings indicate that having surrendered a child is perceived by these respondents as having a protracted negative influence on their lives in the areas of marriage, fertility, and parenting. Implications for adoption work and policy are discussed.

This investigation describes the current life adjustment of parents who surrendered a child for adoption and evaluates selected variables as determinants of present adjustment. An understanding of the extended impact of adoption on this group of parents is important since it is possible that both the number of children born to single women and the proportion of such children adopted will grow as a result of complicated access to abortion, reduced welfare benefits, and a public policy which stresses adoption as the best option for young single mothers.

During the past 20 years, increasing numbers of single mothers have chosen to raise their children. Fifteen years ago, 80% of out-of-wedlock newborn babies were placed for adoption; last year only 4% of such children were surrendered.[1, 12] A less moralistic view of premarital sexual activity, a high divorce rate making single parenthood commonplace, and the rise of the women's rights movement may all have played a role in affording single women the opportunity to raise their children. Nonetheless, such a major societal change could not have taken place without the coexistence of adequate social services and income maintenance programs.

Recently, eligibility for and benefits of welfare programs (food stamps, Medicaid, and Aid to Families with Dependent Children) have been severely curtailed. Concurrently, several bills have been proposed which seek to outlaw abortion, prevent federal court interference in local anti-abortion rulings, and define the beginning of life as the moment of conception.[11, 13] The Adolescent Family Life Act, enacted by the 96th Congress, requires that grantees of funds appropriated under the Act notify parents when unemancipated minors seek prescribed contraceptives, promote adoption for adolescent parents, and refuse abortion counseling or referral. The combination of current fiscal cutbacks and proposed "right to life" legislation poses the prospect of a high percentage of young single mothers relinquishing children for adoption.

The traditional view of adoption is that it simultaneously meets the needs of the mother, the child, and the prospective adoptive couple. As three distinct clients are served at the same time, the potential for conflict of interest exists. Since an irrevocable decision on the part of the mother is considered essential, there is little incentive to encourage her to verbalize grief. Conversely, the focus of work has been to help the mother reconstitute her life quickly by bolstering the defenses of denial and repression at the cost of other emotional needs. The validity of such a stance is now challenged by increasing numbers of parents seeking data on their surrendered children.

In an attempt to deal with some of these emotional conflicts, a small number of people joined together in the mid 1970s to form a discussion and support group that formed the nucleus of Concerned United Birthparents (CUB), now a nationwide organization with a membership of 1500. The availability of this group as a unique study population, coupled with projected adoption trends, has sparked the current investigation. The results of this study may be useful in formulating adoption policy or law, in structuring family support programs, and in the design of mental health services.

Despite the recognized importance of natural parents in the adoption process, relatively little is known of the impact of adoption on their subsequent life. The results of three recent studies indicate that child surrender remains an issue of conflict and intrapersonal difficulty even years after the adoption. Pannor et al[7] studied 38 natural parents and found that the majority still experienced mourning and feelings of loss. While not specifically designed to assess the impact of adoption on subsequent adjustment, this study suggested that the parents involved continue to carry a considerable emotional burden. Burnell and Norfleet[3] followed up 300 women, members of the Kaiser-Permanente prepaid medical plan, who in the previous three years had placed a child for adoption. The subjects' medical and maternity status and their perceptions of child surrender were ascertained by means of a mailed questionnaire. Based on a 26% response rate, the authors reported that gynecological, medical, and psychiatric problems were each present in about 60% of the subjects. Depression, reported by 40% of the sample, was the most common emotional disorder. Rynearson,[9] in a study of 20 women in psychotherapy who had given up children for adoption, found that fantasies of restitution were common, and that subsequent parenting behavior was characterized by intense attachment and overprotection. The lack of a control group makes it impossible to assess whether the past experience of this group constitutes a risk factor for psychiatric difficulties.

In the study presented here, we attempt to relate various aspects of current functioning to personal and demographic characteristics and to variables related to the process of surrender. This study is not designed to assess the overall impact of adoption on the subsequent life adjustment of surrendering parents. No comparable control group was available for study. Furthermore, since the membership of CUB is a self-selected group composed of individuals who might differ from nonmembers on a number of personal characteristics (age, education, social class, personality type, etc.), the findings of this survey may not be applicable to all parents who have given up children for adoption.

METHODOLOGY

A questionnaire designed to elicit information on members' current life status and adjustment, as well as on the process which had led to the surrender of the child for adoption, was published in the August 1980 issue of the *Communicator*, the official newsletter of CUB. The purpose of the study was explained in an accompanying article, which encouraged participation. Readers who were willing to be contacted at a later date could so indicate by signing the questionnaire and by providing their address and telephone number. Data from the questionnaires were coded, and frequency distributions were run for all variables. Associations between variables were assessed and statistically tested by chi-square analysis satisfying SPSS computer programming.

A total of 364 natural parents completed questionnaires, 339 of whom indicated that they were CUB members. Responders constituted 40% of the membership at that time. Respondents who had relinquished more than one child were excluded from the sample on the assumption that issues attending multiple surrenders might be different. The final sample consisted of 334 respondents (321 mothers and 13 fathers). Characteristics of the sample are summarized in TABLE 1. The educational attainment of the sample was surprisingly high, perhaps reflecting the self-selected nature of the respondents. To assess adjustment, we investigated four areas of life functioning: search activity, marital interaction, subsequent reproduction, and parenting behavior. We hypothesized that life functioning having to do with spousal relationships, reproduction, and parenting would be the most likely affected since these areas are at the very core of every birth experience.

FINDINGS

Characteristics of the Adoption Process

The majority of respondents (76.3%) had held, or at least seen, their child prior to surrender, although for most the adoption of the child had occurred within the first month of the child's life. External factors, including family opposition, pressure from physicians or social workers, and financial constraints,

Table 1. Demographic and Personal Characteristics of Study Sample

Characteristics	Mean	Range	N(%)
Current Age	35.5 yrs	19–76	
Age at Child's Birth	19.8 yrs	13–44	
Education (yrs)	14.0 yrs	10–20	
Marital Status			
Never married			43 (13.1%)
Married			226 (68.3)
Divorced/Separated			50 (15.0)
Widowed			9 (2.6)
Subsequent Children			
None			125 (37.9)
One			44 (13.3)
Two or more			161 (48.8)

were cited by 69% of the sample as the primary reasons for surrender. Only 14% of the respondents identified personal factors such as age, uncompleted education, unpreparedness for parenthood, or shame as the major reasons for adoption, while the remaining 17% cited other factors. For 85% of the sample, adoption had been arranged through a social service agency; for 7% by lawyers or physicians; and for the remainder it was implemented privately. Pregnancy and subsequent child surrender took place for most respondents at an early age when they were in the midst of their education. Yet, a high proportion of the study subjects continued their education through high school or beyond.

Determinants of Search Activity

To ascertain whether the surrender of a child continued to be an issue of importance, we asked respondents to indicate whether at any time they had considered searching for their surrendered child. The vast majority (96%) responded affirmatively, and 65% indicated that they had actually initiated a search. Since the desire to search for a surrendered child was almost universal among the respondents, and was thus a nondiscriminating variable, we grouped those respondents who had never thought of searching with those who had considered it but had not actively

searched. This combined group of 118 "non-searchers" was then compared to the group of 215 respondents who had undertaken an active search.

We evaluated several personal, demographic, and historical variables relevant to the surrendering parent, the surrendered child, and the process of surrender, to determine whether any were associated with subsequent search activity. TABLE 2 lists the variables assessed, and displays their chi-square values. Only the primary reason for surrender and the elapsed time since surrender were significantly related to subsequent search activity. Those individuals who reported that adoption was the result of external pressure (family, social workers, or money) were significantly more likely to have searched than were those who invoked personal reasons such as youthful age, unpreparedness for parenthood, or a desire to complete schooling. Elapsed time since surrender was also associated with search activity. Parents who had surrendered children more than 12 years ago were more likely to have searched than those who surrendered children recently. A direct time relationship was evident. Among parents who had surrendered a child within the past seven years, only 37% had actively searched; the corresponding percentages of searchers among those who relinquished children 8–12, 13–17, or 18 or more years ago, were 43%, 69% and 81%, respectively.

Table 2. Characteristics of Study Sample by Search Activity

Characteristics	Searchers	Nonsearchers	Chi Square
Marital Experience			
Ever married	190	97	3.685 (df=1)
Never married	22	21	
Education			
Less than high school	15	8	0.8111 (df=3)
High school graduate	131	73	
College graduate	50	30	
Beyond college	16	6	
Age at Surrender of Child			
≤ 17 years	65	30	0.864 (df=1)
≥ 18 years	150	88	
Sex of Child			
Male	106	51	1.1043 (df=1)
Female	108	67	
Contact With Child Before Surrender			
Saw child	167	87	0.6632 (df=1)
Did not see child	48	31	
Desire for Child			
Wants to repossess	82	46	3.291 (df=1)
Does not want to repossess	122	67	
Primary Reason for Surrender			
External pressure	148	64	9.623* (df=2)
Own preference	19	23	
Other	32	20	
Time Elapsed Since Surrender			
≤ 7 years	12	20	37.766** (df=3)
8–12 years	31	40	
13–17 years	89	39	
≥ 18 years	83	19	

*p<.01; **p<.001.

Several variables were not associated to search activity. Present desire to retrieve the child, educational attainment, age at surrender, contact with infant prior to adoption, subsequent marriage, other births, and adoption facilitator were not predictive of searches. Written comments by respondents indicated that search activity was both emotionally taxing and rewarding:

> After ten long painful years, it gives me peace of mind that I am making every possible effort to locate my daughter. It's scary though, not knowing what the outcome will be.

> The disappointments are so devastating. Each time a new lead fails, I am so depressed. However, it's so exciting every time I can find out something new.

For other respondents, searching had become a consuming activity, eroding other aspects of their life. The pressing, obsessional nature of searching is seen in this comment:

> It's very hard to be brief. I have had one letdown after another. I can't find out anything. It's almost as if it (the birth) never happened. I am very frustrated. I have become obsessed with finding her. I've lost a lot of sleep and have headaches all the time. I think of her every minute of the day.

Subsequent Marriage

Of the 280 subjects who had been married subsequent to the surrender of the child, and who also provided information on marital interaction, 71% stated that their earlier birth experience had colored their marital interaction. Subjects who had attained a high level of education or those who were married to the other parent (17% of all respondents) were most likely to regard their past experience as a negative influence on marriage. Examples of extreme stress among couples who had surrendered their child are evident in the following statements:

> My husband was the birthfather and had made me feel guilty about the adoption. We could never talk about our daughter without feeling guilty and miserable. I felt so bad when I sent our children (subsequent births) to visit their grandparents in another state. I didn't want them to go but my husband insisted.

> I am bitter against my wife and her parents for giving away the child. I was bitterly opposed from the start, but was allowed no say in the matter. My first attempt to attend college after my son's birth was a disaster. I had to drop out. It was a very difficult period. I even considered suicide.

Yet, for other couples, the shared loss became the cement of a fragmented relationship. Despite unhappy marriages, they seemed to stay together because their common bereavement was a stronger bond than the forces pulling them apart:

> It's been hard to forgive him for pressuring to give up our baby. We have no other children and in a way that has brought us closer together because now he cares too. We continue to fear that our marriage would not last if we had another child.

Or:

> We have clung to each other through the most terrible times. Neither one of us could bear to have us end in divorce.

While surrendering parents married to each other bear an especially high risk of marital difficulty, other subjects also attributed their marital problems to issues of allegiance, commitment, and jealousy resulting from their prior experience of childbirth and surrender.

Subsequent Fertility

Interest in the subsequent fertility of parents who have given up children for adoption was sparked by the common but unsubstantiated impression that such individuals hold complicated attitudes toward subsequent reproduction and may be at elevated risk of secondary infertility. Among the 334 survey respondents, 308 provided information on their subsequent fertility and reproductive attempts. In this subgroup, 208 (64%) had been successful in having at least one live-born child following the surrender of the index child: 45 subjects (14%) reported that they had tried but been unable to produce another child: and 55 respondents (17%) stated that they had chosen to remain childless. Eliminating from consideration the 55 subjects who had not wanted other children, the rate of secondary infertility among the study sample is thus 16.2%. This rate is statistically significantly higher ($p < .001$) than the 6% general population rate of secondary infertility among couples who have had one child and desire another.[6] This rate is also somewhat, but not significantly, higher than the 15% rate of primary infertility for the U.S. population.[2, 6] While it appears that parents in our sample may experience about a 170% increase in secondary infertility over the general population, both the stability of this estimate and its possible causes require further study.

Our survey found no significant relationships among social and personal characteristics of the respondents, adoption process variables, and subsequent fertility. The lack of association between personal and process variables and fertility status provides little information regarding the possible causes of infertility in this sample. Comments provided by the 55 respondents who had elected to remain childless cannot serve as explanations for the involuntary childlessness of those respondents who identified themselves as infer-

Table 3. Impact of Child Surrender on Subsequent Marriage

Subject	Impact on Marriage				Chi Square
	None	Mixed	Positive	Negative	
Age at Time of Surrender					
≤17	25	10	9	39	5.492
≥18	49	47	16	81	(df=3)
No. of Years Since Surrender					
≤7	5	3	0	7	9.19
8–12	14	10	10	25	(df=9)
13–17	27	25	9	54	
≥18	28	19	6	34	
Education					
Less than high school	12	1	1	6	21.3*
High school graduate	45	42	14	68	(df=9)
College graduate	14	11	5	34	
Beyond college	3	2	4	10	
Primary Reason for Surrender					
External pressure	42	37	19	79	8.626
Own preference	12	5	2	13	(df=6)
Other	13	10	3	20	
Marriage to Other Biological Parent					
Yes	9	18	2	27	10.210*
No	65	39	23	93	(df=3)

*p<.02.

tile. Nevertheless, the following remarks shed light on the complex attitudes regarding subsequent reproductive activity and appear to reflect a devalued self-esteem, as well as an idealization of the surrendered child:

> Desired not to have children: I did not want to be unfaithful to her (the child).

> Always felt unfit to become a mother again (even though I loved children) after signing adoption papers. I have not been able to even hold a baby since the surrender.

> I do not want children. My husband agrees and is very understanding. I want my daughter's birth fresh in my mind.

Subsequent Parenting

Nearly 80% of the 219 subjects who responded to the questions on parenting stated that their earlier surrender of a child had exerted a powerful impact on their subsequent parenting practices. Almost all reported both positive and negative consequences. Overprotectiveness, compulsive worry about the children's health, and difficulty in accepting growing children's independence were the most frequent negative features cited by the subjects. At the same time, many of these respondents also stated that they felt closer to their children and were more involved in their lives and activities than are most parents. It was clear that, for many of the subjects, children constituted their most important source of emotional gratification. The words "precious," "valuable," and "irreplaceable'" were frequently used to describe subsequent children. However, these valued children were rarely seen as substitutes for the adopted child, and in a few instances the advent of other children triggered renewed anguish over the surrender. One woman wrote:

> I regret the joy my children give me when they do something special because I cannot share the event with the son I gave up.

A more extreme and pathologic process is seen in the two following comments:

I can't seem to get close to anyone. I fear their (the children) leaving me. I cannot believe that anyone could really accept me when I haven't yet. So I dump on them. Sometimes I think they would be better off with someone else.

I have had absolutely no patience with my children, and when frustrated with two toddlers, I've manifested an awful rage much greater than the situation called for. I feel this rage is over my birthparenthood past—a rage that has been suppressed for years!

No personal, demographic, or adoption process variables differentiated subjects who felt their adoption experience affected their subsequent parenting behavior from subjects who did not. Respondents who were married to the other natural parent were no different in this respect from subjects who had gone on to marry others.

DISCUSSION

The results of this survey indicate that, for some individuals, the experience of relinquishing a child to adoption has a prolonged effect on subsequent life functioning. It should be noted that the applicability of our findings may be limited, since the study sample consisted of a volunteer subset of an already self-selected population. Participation in a support organization such as CUB may be more likely for those who experience continuing conflicts over the surrender of a child or who have a particular interest in searching. In addition, recollection of prior events can be colored by present attitudes: thus, the reported associations between variables may be specific to surrendering parents who are members of support groups.

While the results of the present investigation may be generalizable only to a subset of natural parents, the rapid and continuous growth of CUB suggests that membership is not limited to a small or unusually vulnerable group of parents who have surrendered their children. Rather, the appeal of the organization may reflect society's current acceptance of single parenthood, which has both made it easier for unwed parents to declare themselves and has diminished a major reason for relinquishing a child to adoption. Placing a child for adoption was once the price expected from the single mother for the shame and trouble she had caused. For many, society's softened stance may have paradoxically served to trigger the reemergence of suppressed but unresolvable conflicts.

The data on the determinants of search activity do not support the commonly proposed idea that natural parents initiate searches in an attempt to retrieve the surrendered child. On the contrary, the evidence from this study indicates that search activity is closely related to adoption process variables and to the time elapsed since surrender. If retrieval were the primary reason for searches, subsequently childless parents would be over-represented among those who had initiated searches. In fact, the majority of searching parents had had other children.

It is possible that search activity represents an attempt to resolve a significant loss. Unlike other permanent losses, for which society has constructed supportive rituals, there is no recognizable support following the loss of the child to adoption. Psychodynamic theory has proposed, and clinical experience confirmed, that losses inadequately grieved may produce feelings of unworthiness, diminished self-esteem, and depression. Evidence of low self-esteem and severe mood disorder was clear in the comments made by searching respondents. Search activity may thus be a means of achieving restitution not of the surrendered child, but of the self.

Although marital disharmony was reported by a majority of the sample, the 15% prevalence of divorce was less than the 40% rate of divorce in the general population,[4, 5] implying either that the disharmony was not as severe in this group as in the general population, or that the respondents were more willing to withstand an unhappy marriage. The source of disharmony appeared to be different for study subjects who married the other parent of the surrendered child than for subjects who did not. Those whose mates were not partners in the earlier childbirth indicated that their marital difficulty stemmed primarily from their search activity and its resulting drain on their time and emotional energy. Among couples who had shared the adoption experience, conflict involved many areas of interaction. Comments by such couples suggested that they were united by shared pain rather than by commonality of interest or spirit. A study by Plomin *et al*[8] tended to support this observation. Their investigation of assortive mating among married and unmarried parents showed that both groups shared high intracouple correlations for physical attributes but only married parents displayed high intracouple correlations for behavioral attributes. This suggests that unwed parents may have less in common with one another than married parents at the time of mating and may thus be at higher risk of marital conflict should they marry after relinquishing their child.

The observed high occurrence of reproductive failure among respondents is difficult to evaluate since it is not known what proportion of secondary infertility might be due to deficiencies in the spouse rather than the subject. Furthermore this finding may simply be the result of selection bias since infertile individuals may be more likely to join a support organization such as CUB than would those without reproductive problems. Nevertheless, the estimated 170% excess of secondary infertility in the sample is sizable, and should be studied further.

The reported difficulties in parenting appear to reflect unresolved sadness over past loss and lack of self-confidence rather than active deleterious parenting. Overprotection, overindulgence and overinvolvement may well have a negative impact on a child's development but clearly are not as damaging as abuse and neglect. It is possible that those subjects who felt very unsure of their ability to parent subsequent children were the ones who opted not to bear more children. While we have no objective measures of parenting skills, there is considerable evidence suggesting generalized anxiety in interactions.

The results of this study indicate the need to consider the biological parent more fully both at the time of adoption and subsequent to the signing of adoption papers. Specifically, adoption workers should facilitate, rather than discourage, parental mourning for the surrendered child. Innovative techniques, based on a clearer understanding of the magnitude of this loss, its difficult resolution, and its possible long-range consequences, will have to be developed. Since grief over a surrendered child appears to remain undimmed with time, present knowledge of the dynamics of mourning may only partially apply to this situation.

Finally, our results suggest that adoption does not always fulfill the needs of three distinct clients. The inherent conflict of interest should be recognized and appropriate changes instituted in the administration and services of adoption agencies. This is of particular importance in light of the current trend of social policy toward hindering access to abortion for young women, promoting adoption as the option of choice, and severely limiting social services and financial aid. Implementation of such policies is likely to increase both the numbers of children born to younger single mothers and the proportion of such children surrendered for adoption.

REFERENCES

1. ALAN GUTTMACHER INSTITUTE. 1981. Teenage Pregnancy: The Problem That Hasn't Gone Away. Alan Guttmacher Institute, New York.

2. AMELAR, R. AND DUBIN, L. 1977. Male Infertility. Saunders, Philadelphia.

3. BURNELL, G. AND NORFLEET, M. 1979. Women who place their infant for adoption: a pilot study. Patient Couns. Hlth Ed. 1:169–172.

4. EDITORIAL RESEARCH REPORTS. 1979. The changing American family. Congressional Quart., Washington, D.C.

5. KAPLAN, H., FREEDMAN, A. AND SADOCK, B. 1980. Comprehensive Textbook of Psychiatry, Vol. 2. Williams and Wilkins, Baltimore.

6. NATIONAL CENTER FOR HEALTH STATISTICS. 1980. Reproductive Impairment Among Currently Married Couples. Advance Data No. 55, Dept. of Health, Education and Welfare, Washington, D.C.

7. PANNOR, R., BARON, P. AND SOROSKY, A. 1978. Birthparents who relinquished babies for adoption revisited. Fam. Child Placement Pract. 17:329–337.

8. PLOMIN, R., DEFRIES, J. AND ROBERTS, M. 1977. Assortive mating by unwed biological parents of adopted children. Science 196:449–450.

9. RYNEARSON, E. 1982. Relinquishment and its maternal complications: a preliminary study. Amer. J. Psychiat. 139:338–340.

10. SILVERMAN, P. 1981. Helping Women Cope With Grief. Sage Publications, Beverly Hills, Calif.

11. United States House of Representatives, 97th Congress. 1981. Bill #900. Sponsor, Rep. Hyde.

12. United States Senate, 94th Congress. 1976. School Age Mother and Child Health Act, 1975. Hearings Before the Subcommittee on Labor and Public Welfare, November 4, 1975.

13. United States Senate, 97th Congress. 1981. Bill #158. Sponsor, Sen. Helms.

Chapter 7

Childbirth and Early Motherhood

Historically, childbirth was women's work. Women not only had the babies, but female midwives helped deliver them. As medical practice became more established and masculinized, the control over childbirth was removed from women and placed in the hands of men. As medical technology advanced, the physical and psychological needs of pregnant women were largely ignored. The resurgence of the feminist movement and the rebellion against technology in the late 1960s and early 1970s was marked, in part, by women's demand for more control over their bodies. Nowhere was this more apparent than with regard to childbirth. In a remarkable example of consumer influence on medical practice, the entire process of childbirth was revolutionized. Childbirth preparation courses were soon offered in almost every community. The use of general anesthetics during delivery declined. And, although doctors had argued vigorously that the presence of partners and family members in the delivery room would be disastrous, consumer demand soon made this practice common. The predictions of disaster were never realized.

The experience of childbirth today is a far cry from what it was for our mothers and grandmothers. Women are better prepared for the experience, and choices about types of health-care providers and sites of delivery abound. **McCall** describes and discusses many of these options. The existence of so many options and the pregnant woman's right to choose the options that best fit her own situation are an important step forward in women's health care.

However, carefully made plans for labor and delivery are all too often set aside at the last minute so that a ''C'' section can be performed. In a **Cesarean section** delivery, the baby is delivered surgically, from an opening made through the woman's abdomen and uterus. The timing of it as the last part of an emotionally intense and physically draining process (i.e., labor) combined with its frequency obscure the fact that it *is* a major surgical procedure, with accompanying risks, long recovery, and high cost. The article by **Kaplan** discusses the disturbingly high incidence of Cesarean section deliveries in this country.

One aspect of Cesarean section delivery that pregnant women dislike is the feeling of losing control and becoming a passive rather than active participant in labor and delivery. The third article, by **Crowe and von Baeyer,** focuses on this and other factors that affect how positive the childbirth experience is for the mother.

The central theme of the first three articles in this chapter is the importance of information and control on the part of the mother. No single option is the best for all women. Each woman should be informed of all options and should select those best suited to her personality, beliefs, and medical condition. As not all health care providers are comfortable with every option, it is important for the woman to select a provider whose philosophy and practice meet her requirements.

Major post-pregnancy concerns for new mothers include breast feeding and postpartum depression. In keeping with the increased visibility of women's health issues, public mention and/or performance of breast feeding is no longer taboo, though many people remain uncomfortable with it. Moreover, women who choose to bottle-feed rather than breast-feed are more likely now to have to contend with open and emotional criticism of their choice. The article by **Stehlin** discusses this important decision.

As with PMS (premenstrual syndrome), the nature, incidence and cause(s) of postpartum depression remain controversial. While a small percentage of women experience a psychotic depressive episode following childbirth (postpartum depression), a milder form of depression sometimes called the "baby blues" is more common. **Richman** and her co-authors examine the influence of gender roles and social support on the "baby blues". Their work suggests that depressed mood is a common occurrence for both new mothers and new fathers.

REFERENCES AND SUGGESTED READING

Garel, M., Lelong, H., Marchand, A., & Kaminski, M. (1990). Psychosocial consequences of caesarean childbirth: a four-year follow-up study. *Early Human Development, 21,* 105–114.

Jordan, B. (1983). *Birth in Four Cultures,* 3rd edition. Montreal: Eden Press.

Milner, I. (1986). Choosing a natural or an active childbirth. *Balliere Tinadall's Nursing, 2,* 39–45.

Oates, M. (1989). Normal emotional changes in pregnancy and the puerperium. *Bailliere's Clinical Obstetrics and Gynaecology, 3,* 791–804.

Palmer, G. (1988). *The politics of breast feeding.* London: Pandora Press.

Romiton, P. (1988). Mothers' experience of breastfeeding. *Journal of Reproductive and Infant Psychology, 6,* 89–99.

Too many Caesareans. (1991, February). *Consumer Reports,* pp. 120–126.

Childbirth in America
Robert B. McCall

"What should have been the most exalting of experiences," complained one newly-delivered mother, "was riddled with horrors at the hospital. I felt I was going to the Bastille, never to be seen again. . . . They handled me like a watermelon; stuck a needle in my arm without asking me if I wanted any medication or telling me what it was for. Throughout labor I had about fourteen interns looking up me before they finally had me curl up for a caudal anesthesia which left me feeling completely paralyzed after the birth. . . . The delivery room . . . seemed like a butcher shop, and I was in the middle of it like a trussed-up turkey. . . . Once out of the delivery room and into bed, this Valkyrie right out of a Wagnerian opera came in and punched my stomach back down."

In contrast, a mother who delivered at home had different memories:

"Wows and phews," she said of the birth. "Tears and laughter. Popping of champagne corks. They put Joshua on my stomach and he stayed there for two days."

The Rights of Women and Children

Extremely different experiences such as these formed the basis of a popular uprising of American women who were dissatisfied with traditional birth practices and worked to get them changed.

"The young women," observed George Silver, M.D., professor emeritus of public health at Yale University School of Medicine, "who have fought the battles for economic equality, for abortion, contraception, and sex education are asking why they cannot have pregnancy restored to them, too."

At root, the issue was control, and in the extreme, some women took the matter into their own hands—almost literally—by having their babies at home. "Home birth," said one lay midwife, "is a civil rights issue. It's a woman's civil right to give birth where she chooses to give birth."

As in every social movement, not everyone agreed. "The dangers are so great with a home birth," countered one physician, "that one wonders whether a woman has the right to make that decision for the unborn baby. . . . We do not have the right to expose our children to undue hazard."

While hospital versus home birth were the poles of the argument, the focal issue of control was more typically bound up in mother-doctor relationships.

"I just wasn't satisfied with my obstetrician," reported one mother a few years ago, "and he 'discharged' me. . . . He felt my requests were above and beyond the call of duty. . . . I wanted my husband to stay with me before the baby was born and after. . . . He thought that was a little severe. . . . He said, 'I'm not going to be strait-jacketed by a patient.' I just wanted somebody I could talk to. . . . I waited 30 years to have a baby . . . if somebody says 'do this' I'm not going to say 'yes' without questioning it."

Another woman put it succinctly. "I wasn't going to be told what I was going to *get*. I knew what I *wanted* . . . a doctor who would take my desires into consideration. . . . I just didn't want to be pushed around."

Today, the dust has settled somewhat after the bitter arguments of a few years ago. There are more alternatives available and more research to help parents choose a birth-style and setting that meets their requirements.

Birth Through the Ages

Before this century babies were generally born at home. The health of the mother and child—even their survival—was a problem, however. As sanitation, blood banks, anesthesia, and technology improved, it seemed only sensible for women to have their babies in hospitals, where both mother and child could take advantage of these developments.

With these developments, though, came procedures that grew to be routine. Typically, sedatives were given during labor, enemas administered, pubic hair shaved, labor induced, anesthetics and sometimes labor-inducing drugs (e.g., oxytocin) were given, fetal monitors were applied, and episiotomies performed. The father was excluded entirely, and the baby whisked away from the mother who had just delivered it.

Today some of these procedures are coming under scrutiny. For example, an episiotomy is done because a straight cut is easier to stitch than a jagged tear, but some argue that tearing is less likely if birth positions other than lying on the back are used.

Shaving pubic hair is presumably a precaution against germs and prevents hair from getting in the way of stitching the episiotomy. But some claim shaving can bring up germs from hair follicles, antibacterial solutions are just as effective as shaving, and relatively little hair grows where the episiotomy is actually made.

These measures can have positive effects, though. For example, an enema emp-

ties the bowel leaving more room for the baby and prevents contamination of the baby if feces are expelled during birth. Similarly, the labor-regulating drug oxytocin can transform labor that proceeds slowly into a normal one, and the fetal monitor can often detect problems early enough to prompt a cesarean delivery that could save a baby who might otherwise die. But some argue that such complications and deaths are too rare to require routine use of many of these procedures.

"It's the old 'what if syndrome,'" complained one mother. "It's always 'what if this or that happens,' but 'this' or 'that' really doesn't happen very often."

The facts show, however, that the introduction of such procedures was accompanied by a marked decline in the mortality of mothers and babies. But it is not clear that any or most of these procedures were actually responsible in a major way for the improved safety of childbirth. Instead, Kenneth J. Ryan, M.D., professor of obstetrics and gynecology at Harvard Medical School, believes that "the better mortality rates are probably due to improved prenatal care, better general health of the population, and availability of blood and blood products for transfusion as well as antibiotics to fight infection."

Dr. Ryan also feels that these preventative procedures occasionally create risks of their own. "Mother or infant might be injured by an unnecessary procedure or medication. Induction of labor has occasionally resulted in a forced, premature birth. Infections have been spread in hospitals—sometimes by physicians themselves.

Rigid Hospital Regulations

But, these risks were secondary to the fact that the prevention procedures became rigid policy in almost all hospitals; women were given few if any choices and often were not even told what each precaution was for. Deviation from the medical standard was definitely discouraged.

"In some hospitals," one mother remarked, "you have the feeling that you are in the way—that if they could have the baby without you, they would."

"I felt that they were taking over my baby," said another. "If they wanted to do something, they just did it. It didn't seem like it was my baby anymore."

The Advent of Prepared Childbirth

Resistance to such practices initially came from Europe. As early as the 1930's, the English obstetrician Grantly Dick-Read advocated non-medicated childbirth and coined the phrase "natural childbirth," and the French obstetrician Fernand Lamaze introduced his now-famous approach in the early 1950's.

Lamaze preparation for childbirth, now widely practiced in the United States, usually consists of five elements: information about anatomy, physiology, and the birth process so parents know what is happening and why; breathing procedures that contribute to a balanced level of carbon dioxide and oxygen in the system; relaxation techniques that make a labor contraction become a signal to relax and begin work rather than to become tense; activities (e.g., sucking on hard candies, ice chips) that provide sugar, water, and distractions from discomfort; and social support from a "coach," usually the husband. These techniques are supposed to facilitate the birth process, reduce pain and discomfort, and increase the parents' emotional enjoyment of delivery.

Does Lamaze preparation work? Depending on the study, length of labor may or may not be shortened and the frequency of complications may or may not be reduced. What does seem clear is that Lamaze-prepared women are calmer, more relaxed,

maintain better control during delivery, seem to experience less pain, and fewer of them ask for an anesthetic. Some scientists argue, however, that Lamaze women probably perceive as much pain as others, but they are more controlled and tolerate it better.

There is perhaps a disadvantage to Lamaze preparation, though. It is occasionally advertised as being "natural" and "painless." One psychologist observed that there is nothing "natural" about Lamaze. "It is a deliberate attempt to teach relaxation in the face of natural tension and pain."

And one mother advised, "Don't ever tell a pregnant woman it won't hurt. It's a volcanic eruption. But it's finite, it's fruitful—and you *can* do something about it."

Complicating the matter is the fact that women differ in how painful childbirth is for them, partly as a function of their size and other factors not under their control. But, unfortunately, psychological damage can occur when, after hearing so much about the alleged perils of anesthetics and how delivery can be done without any drugs, a woman becomes guilt-ridden because she asks for something to relieve the pain. "I have a beautiful son," said one mother who asked for an anesthetic, "but I feel like a failure."

One doctor asserted that there is nothing wrong with wanting painkillers, but he also understood the desire of some women to conquer the pain of childbirth. "It's part of reaching a goal," he said. "Mastery of tolerable pain can be a very positive experience."

Leboyer and the Gentle Birth

While Lamaze was focusing on the mother's ordeal of childbirth, French obstetrician Frederick Leboyer concentrated on the baby's experience in his famous book, *Birth Without Violence.* Leboyer argued that traditional hospital environments and practices were cruel to the newborn. He advocated dim lights, whispered communications, placing the newborn on the mother's abdomen until the cord stops pulsating, giving the baby a warm bath, and then allowing mother and infant to get acquainted through skin-to-skin contact. These procedures were intended to reduce the stress, shock, and pain inflicted on infants as they entered the world.

Leboyer described his approach with phrases calculated to evoke the maximum emotional response, and argued that the "evidence" for his approach was the smiles of a thousand babies. The first scientific-sounding study of Leboyer procedures did seem quite positive. Psychologist Danielle Rapoport of the French National Center for Scientific Research reported that Leboyer babies were more advanced physically, adroit with both hands, walked earlier, had less difficulty being toilet-trained and learning to feed themselves, and were less likely to get colic and shortness of breath. The problem with the study was that no group of infants born with other procedures was evaluated in comparison. So it was not clear that Leboyer babies were "better" or who they were "better than."

More recently, in one of the scientifically best studies, Nancy M. Nelson, Ph.D., and her colleagues at the McMaster University Medical Centre in Hamilton, Ontario, randomly assigned 28 mothers to have Leboyer births and 26 mothers to have a relatively modern delivery but one lacking Leboyer's lighting, room temperature, draping of the infant with a sheet, timing of cord clamping, and opportunity and timing of skin-to-skin contact between infant and mother. The researchers then thoroughly assessed the mother's subjective experience of labor and delivery and psychological adjustment six weeks after birth and the baby's physical, mental, and temperamental development at three days, six weeks, and eight months of life. While first stage labor was shorter for the Leboyer mothers (for unexplained reasons), no other differences were found. Other studies have been slightly more positive, indicating that Leboyer babies are more relaxed shortly after birth.

At present, the Leboyer approach appears safe and may make the babies more relaxed, but the particular procedures do not have obvious and enduring benefits over the contemporary practices of hospital birthing.

The Home-Birth Movement

While Lamaze and Leboyer contributed early to the consumer movement in American birth practices, changes on a broad scale did not occur until the middle 1970's. As a group, home-birth advocates argued that hospital practices were rigid and physicians were authoritarian and impersonal, treating childbirth as a disease. They also objected to having no control over routine practices from anesthesia to episiotomy, most of which they did not want. Instead, they believed that childbirth was a normal bodily function that usually did not require hospital trappings. They argued that home births restored control over the event to the woman and her husband and conferred significant psychological advantages to the parents, infants, and siblings who could attend the birth of the new baby in a familiar and supportive environment.

The medical community was horrified. A past director of the American College of Obstetrics and Gynecology called home births "in utero child abuse." Another obstetrician said home birthers are "kooks, the lunatic fringe, people who have emotional problems."

Home-birth advocates accused physicians of being crassly profit motivated, afraid of losing business, and feeling threatened that midwives might take over birth and the treatment of other female problems as well. Physicians rebutted that the risks at home were too high. "All you need to see is one baby die that could have been saved," said one doctor, "and you do whatever you can to prevent that from happening again."

The home birthers countered with results from studies that showed home births to be as safe as hospital births. They pointed to the fact that several countries having substantial numbers of home births—Sweden, Denmark, Holland, and England, for example—have better infant mortality rates than the United States. And studies conducted by Lewis E. Mehl, M.D., Ph.D., and his colleagues at the University of Wisconsin seemed to show that home deliveries in California in the middle 1970's were at least as safe as hospital births.

But medical critics complained that the women in Mehl's studies were screened for possible risks, and then they were compared to all women giving birth in California regardless of risk status. The latter group would be expected to have more problems than the home-birth mothers who were selected to be risk free.

The Opposition

The main opposition to home births, says G. David Adamson, M.D., an obstetrician-gynecologist in Palo Alto, California, who has studied the homebirth movement, comes from physicians who manage complicated pregnancies. They argue that home births are fine *if no complications occur.* But the time involved in getting a problem delivery from home to a hospital can literally mean the difference between life and death or between a normal and less than normal life for the baby.

The crucial issue, then, is being able to predict complications and screen out in advance women who are likely to need hospital services. While some problems can usually be identified before birth, other complications cannot be predicted very accurately. And the potential risks to the baby are greater than to the mother, contends Dr. Adamson. Approximately 20 percent of the preventable newborn deaths and 30 percent of circumstances that produce abnormalities occur in *low-risk women* and are not apparent before labor. Indeed, 15 percent to 30 percent of women who have been screened for delivery at home or in an alternative birth center are transferred to a hospital.

Critics of home birth also argue that while birth is a normal process and the vast majority of deliveries occur without problems, birth is not as safe or as uncomplicated as some people believe. Specifically, the number of newborn deaths occurring at or shortly after birth equals the number of deaths from all causes for the next forty years of life.

But some home-birth advocates are unimpressed by that statistic. They are still willing to deliver at home, citing great psychological and emotional benefits.

"The bonding was unbelievable," said one mother.

"Bonding" is the attachment that presumably is created by close contact between parent and infant during the first few minutes or hours following birth. Great claims have been made for the long-lasting effects of such early and extended contact. But not much scientific evidence is available to justify such claims, and most of the evidence on early contact and bonding in particular suggests that its effects are limited. The ongoing parent-child relationship seems to have broader effects, even though early contact can create superb memories and may have some positive influence on attachment for some families. Moreover, what effects may occur are thought to be associated with the physical contact and early social interaction between parent and infant, not whether such contact occurs at home or in a hospital, where it is now routinely practiced.

What Everyone Agrees on

Despite the disagreements, certain principles in the home-versus-hospital debate are clear, according to Drs. Adamson and Ryan. They stress that thorough prenatal care is essential, regardless of where birth will take place. In addition, whoever attends the birth—nurse-midwife or physician—should be well-trained and experienced.

Some form of medical backup for home or out-of-hospital births also should be arranged before the birth. It's also important that families planning a home birth be aware of the risks involved and contemplate how they would react to a problem that might have been minimized had the birth occurred in a hospital.

Birthing Alternatives

The most prevalent alternatives that attempt to combine the psychological advantages of home delivery with the medical safeguards of a hospital are the birthing room, a special room in the obstetrics ward of a hospital, and an alternative birthing center—or ABC—which may be either a separate section of a hospital or freestanding but has a relationship with a hospital.

While centers do vary, labor and birth in an ABC or birthing room typically take place in the same room, eliminating the need to change locations at a time of substantial excitement and discomfort.

The room's decor is similar to that of a living room or bedroom, and husband—and sometimes relatives, siblings, and friends—are encouraged to attend the birth, providing a familiar, comfortable, and socially supportive environment for the mother and family, who are permitted to get acquainted with their infant immediately after birth.

Some choice is also given the woman regarding birth procedures (e.g., anesthetic, episiotomy), although the range of alternatives varies greatly between centers and physicians.

Finally, of course, some provision is made for emergencies by having most necessary emergency equipment and personnel in the room, in an adjacent room, or in a nearby hospital.

Has the ABC ended the controversy? In large part it may have. It usually includes many of the features originally desired by opponents of the traditional delivery room—presence of husband and others, a single comfortable environment for both labor and delivery, some choice about birth procedures, and early-contact with the newborn.

"It was great," said one mother. "It was like giving birth at home but with a feeling of safety because you're at the hospital."

But not everyone agrees. "Too hospitally," said a staunch home-birth advocate. "The vibes are still there."

The fact that most ABC's and birthing rooms are in hospitals riles home-birth advocates who feel the medical community has taken over their movement. Some physicians even admit it. "I'm running the show," one physician said, "in the ABC more than anywhere else. . . . I *permit* them the opportunity to run the show . . . but they understand that I'm the boss."

The issue, then, is how much choice and control will a mother actually have? Expecting parents should investigate this carefully before the birth, because policies and procedures of ABC's and obstetricians vary greatly.

Freestanding ABC's, for example, are often more flexible than hospital units and certified nurse-midwives may be the principal professionals and provide extensive prenatal, delivery, and even postnatal physical and psychological care.

In contrast to these benefits, emergency care at a freestanding ABC is more difficult. Most, but not all, have an arrangement with a nearby hospital, and from 15 to 30 percent of women are transferred to hospitals, where they may be treated by a doctor they have never met. "What baffles me," one obstetrician wondered, "is why this is considered by some to be a great leap forward in birth care?"

Apparently many women agree. While birthing rooms, bonding, and rooming-in may be all the rage in many quarters, some families do not want them. In one study of two hospitals, for example, women were asked within the first three days of their delivery if they wanted "standard" contact with their infants or daytime or 24-hour rooming-in. One quarter of the mothers in one hospital and two-thirds in the other did *not* want to room-in with their infants.

Then, too, some modern practices have become trendy, pushing some families toward procedures they really do not want or creating expectancies that may not be fulfilled. One husband, for example, was not comfortable attending the birth of his child. He was criticized by his friends for not being present at the delivery, even though his wife was relieved that he was not there.

In addition, some women have the usual expectancy of a beautiful birth, but then have complications and require a cesarean section. In such cases, a woman may view herself as a failure, and the birth experience becomes a major source of disappointment and depression.

"Some couples," remarked a nurse-midwife, "will just not find hospitals suitable to them in any way, shape, or form and are willing to take the risk and gamble that everything will go well. And some women will want the most expensive obstetrician and the most expensive hospital they can find and insist on being knocked out cold so they won't know a thing about it."

Today, couples are free to make these extreme choices as well as a great many more in between. Each family must make their own decisions, balancing their desires and hopes for the type of birth experience they want, cost and convenience, and safety for women and their babies.

Weighing the Choices

If you are a prospective parent, get thorough prenatal care. At the same time, talk with physicians, nurses, midwives, hospital personnel, and other parents who have recently given birth to discover the options available in your community. Expect to make trade-offs—you may want a specific physician but prefer the options available at a hospital where he or she does not practice. Check on the training, experience, and certification of people you expect to assist you at the birth, and weigh your own perceptions of risk in light of the information presented here. And if you are considering an out-of-hospital birth, check whether insurance will cover the birth *and* any complications.

Finally, think ahead about unexpected changes that might alter your perfect birth scheme. Work out with your physician or attendants how decisions will be made concerning complications, anesthesia, or the need for a cesarean. In addition, prepare yourself mentally for such events, so if they do occur, you will not feel that you have failed because the birth did not happen precisely as planned.

Do Cesareans Save Lives?
Janice Kaplan

Like many couples, Ginny and Peter planned for a natural delivery of their first baby. They took Lamaze classes and thought about the first happy moment they would share as a family. But it didn't quite work out the way they'd planned. Ginny started feeling contractions on a Thursday, went to the hospital imediately, and labored there for 24 hours. At eight o'clock on Friday night, her doctor decided that he wanted to do a cesarean section. "He said, 'This baby is never going to come out,' " remembers Ginny. "We asked for more time, but he said it might be risking the baby's health."

Exhausted and discouraged, Ginny tearfully agreed to the surgery. "Peter was there, stroking my back and keeping me calm," says Ginny. "Then the doctor announced that hospital policy didn't allow husbands in the delivery room during a cesarean. I started crying, but they wheeled me away and wouldn't let Peter come with me. I'll never forget how scared and alone I felt during the surgery. It seemed that once the decision was made to do a cesarean, nobody cared about our feelings anymore."

For increasing numbers of couples across the country, the joy of a natural, family-centered birth will dissolve into the tension and medical protocols of cesarean delivery. In the past twenty years, the national cesarean section rate has *quintupled*—from roughly 5 percent in 1967 to nearly 25 percent today. In many teaching hospitals, the rate is even higher. What's shocking is that virtually nobody believes that number of cesareans is really necessary—but there is also no indication that the trend will be reversed.

Reasons for the Increase

"In the late 1800's, the general feeling among medical practitioners was that it was safer to be gored by a bull than to have a cesarean," says Mortimer Rosen, M.D., chairman of the department of obstetrics and gynecology at the College of Physicians and Surgeons at Columbia University in New York City. "Now it's extremely safe—and it's become the single most common surgical procedure for women."

That doesn't mean though, that there are no unpleasant consequences of having a cesarean delivery. Dr. Rosen points out that a woman typically loses two units of blood during the surgery. Instead of staying in the hospital two or three days, as you would for a vaginal delivery, you usually remain five to seven days and have a more painful recovery. There are also risks from anesthesia—the most common cause of cesarean related deaths.

Given the drawbacks, why are more and more cesareans being performed every year? "It's a complex problem," says Norbert Gleicher, M.D., chairman of the department of obstetrics and gynecology at Mt. Sinai Medical Center in Chicago. "The first issue is that doctors are hesitant to change their practice patterns—even when it's been shown that what they're doing is wrong. The second problem is a fear of malpractice. Doctors believe that if something goes wrong and they get sued, the best defense is being able to say, 'I did a cesarean as soon as possible.' "

Cesareans Aren't Cure-Alls

Parents have come to expect that their babies will be healthy and well—and they blame the obstetrician for any less-than-perfect outcome. Unfortunately, the vast majority of defects can't be avoided by a cesarean birth. For example, most experts now believe that cerebral palsy and mental retardation are only rarely the result of birth trauma. They usually develop *in utero* and are beyond the control of either parents or doctor. It's telling that the percentage of babies born with cerebral palsy has remained constant in the last twenty years, even while cesarean rates have soared.

"We shouldn't go to the other extreme and say that every cesarean is unnecessary," says Dr. Gleicher. There are times when a cesarean delivery can be a life-saving process for mother or baby. For example, a cesarean is vital in cases in which there's a prolapsed cord, hemorrhaging, severe toxemia, or placenta previa (a condition in which the placenta blocks the entrance to the cervix). "I'd suggest a cesarean section rate of 6 to 10 percent would be about right to maintain a decreasing perinatal mortality," says Dr. Gleicher.

Making the Decision

Delivering a baby is more art than science, and during labor, parents have to rely on the instincts of their obstetrician (or midwife). So, for example, when Ginny's doctor suggested that delaying a cesarean might be risky to the baby, she was in no position to argue. "At that point, you're telling yourself, What difference does it make? All I want is a healthy baby," she says. "It's only afterward that you start resenting it and wondering if the surgery was really necessary."

Ginny's diagnosis was dystocia, or difficult labor—a common reason for having a cesarean. "Often, that doesn't really mean anything," says Beth Shearer, a childbirth educator and codirector of C/SEC, a cesarean support and education group. "A doctor may do a cesarean for 'prolonged labor' when a woman is only three or four centimeters dilated. It's often a misinterpretation to say labor has gone on too long. Progress may vary for different women, and time shouldn't be a factor." While the American College of Obstetrics and Gynecology defines prolonged labor as lasting over twenty hours with only four centimeters' dilation, they recognize the difficulty of determining precisely where the twenty hours begins and ends. But some doctors have a blanket policy that a woman can't labor for more than 24 hours; others base their decision to do a cesarean on whether a woman follows the Friedman curve, which shows a median of dilation rates and which many doctors use as a guide.

Similarly, doctors differ in how long they allow a woman to push before deciding that the baby won't appear, and they may fail to try out or consider the possible advantages of different birth positions. "What frequently happens is that a woman pushes for two hours, flat on her back, and then has a cesarean," says Beth Shearer. "Later, she's angry when she learns that if she had squatted, the pelvis would get bigger. This is a natural consequence of squatting. Also, hormones released during pregnancy cause a softening of connective tissue between the pelvic bones. Real cephalopelvic disproportion (when the pelvis is too small for the baby's head) is rare—it's usually more a question of position and angle."

In hospitals that use constant electronic fetal monitoring, false positives may increase the number of cesareans performed. Many doctors feel that's an example of technology hurting more than it helps. "Fetal distress is being overdiagnosed," says Dr. Rosen. "You have to understand that a fetal monitor doesn't tell you anything about brain damage; it measures the heart rate. Just because there's a wiggle on the monitor, or the heart rate is up, doesn't mean the baby is sick. If we all walked around wearing heart monitors, I'm afraid there'd be a lot of unnecessary heart surgery, too." Many doctors now use an additional test called fetal scalp sampling, whenever there's a question of fetal distress. In fetal scalp sampling, the fetal heart rate is monitored through an internal monitor implanted into the fetal scalp. Interestingly, a consensus panel from the National Institutes of Health found no particular advantage to electronic monitoring over intermittent auscultation (listening to the fetal heart rate with a stethoscope), except in some very high-risk cases, but it did find a greater likelihood of cesarean delivery.

The most common reason for having a cesarean is simply that you've had one before. Across the country, about 94 percent of women who have had one cesarean now deliver all their children the same way. Consider Sandy, a 27-year-old mother who had her first cesarean because of fetal distress. "When I was pregnant the second time, I thought vaguely about having a vaginal delivery," says Sandy. "I asked my doctor for his advice, and he said, 'It's up to you, but if it were my wife, I'd tell her to have a cesarean. Pick a day, go into the hospital, and get it done safely.' "

While that's common advice, it's not necessarily good advice. Dozens of recent studies show that as many as 80 percent of women who have had one cesarean can successfully deliver vaginally the next time. That's true even if it's a large baby and the first surgery was done for dystocia or cephalopelvic disproportion. "Your pelvis changes and the fetus is different in each pregnancy," says Richard Porreco, M.D., director of the perinatal program at St. Luke's/Children's Hospital in Denver. "What happened once won't necessarily happen again." If your first cesarean was for breech presentation or fetal distress, your chance of delivering vaginally the second time is even better.

Virtually the only reason *not* to try a vaginal birth after cesarean (VBAC) is if you had a vertical uterine incision the first time, because of the risks of rupture. If you had a low transverse scar, the risk of rupture is extremely low. According to Dr. Porreco, with a VBAC, you have the same risks, and same likelihood of needing a cesarean, as any woman in labor who is pregnant for the first time.

"We've known for years that a large majority of women don't need repeat cesareans," says Dr. Gleicher. "Yet nationwide, only a very small number of women are even given the *chance* at a VBAC. It's beyond me how that's possible. What's going on is simply bad medicine."

Some doctors try to shift the responsibility, arguing that women who have had one cesarean don't want to try labor a second time. "I have a philosophical problem with that," says Dr. Gleicher. "We can't let patients dictate incorrect medical practice." It's also unlikely that a woman would choose surgery without subtle pressure from her doctor, who may find a scheduled cesarean easier than the close monitoring necessary for a VBAC.

A woman opting for a cesarean the second time may do so for various reasons, including the possibility that she may have lost faith in her own body. "In most cases, she's not chosing a second operation over a vaginal birth," says Beth Shearer. "She chooses scheduled surgery over what she assumes will be another miserable labor that ends in a cesarean." If more women realized that they had a very strong chance of avoiding a repeat cesarean—and that trying was extremely safe for them and the baby—they might make a different decision.

Strength from the struggle

A planned cesarean may fit everyone's schedule—except the baby's. It's impossible to judge exactly when a baby will be ready to be born, and there's always the risk of removing the baby prematurely. There's also new evidence that babies benefit from the actual process of labor. Researchers in Sweden have found that babies born after labor have higher levels of stress hormones in their blood than babies born by elective cesarean. These hormones—called catecholamines—help a baby's lungs mature, regulate body temperature, and send blood to the brain and heart. This may partially explain why cesarean babies are at far greater risk of suffering from symptoms of respiratory distress than babies who are born vaginally.

Not only does the normal stress of labor help the baby, but the physical process of moving through the birth canal squeezes fluid from the baby's lungs and helps it prepare for life outside the womb. "There's a higher mortality at all birthweights for infants delivered by a cesarean, and far more respiratory complications except for those infants three pounds and under," says Albert Haverkamp, M.D., clinical professor of obstetrics and gynecology and preventive medicine at the University of Colorado Health Science Center. He points out that Denver General Hospital has a very low cesarean rate—about 13 percent—and one of the lowest rates of perinatal mortality in Colorado. "Those facts aren't directly related," he says, "but it does show that after a certain point, doing a lot of cesareans doesn't mean you're saving babies."

Even if you think you'll need to have a repeat cesarean, you'll be helping the baby and possibly yourself if you wait until you go into labor. "I think just about every woman should have a trial of labor, unless there are serious medical complications," says Dr. Rosen. "A scheduled repeat cesarean should be an uncommon occurrence."

Allowing fathers to attend birth

When a cesarean *is* necessary, it's important to remember that it's surgery—but it's also a way of giving birth. While many hospitals are changing their policies, fathers still often aren't allowed into the delivery room during a cesarean, and even a healthy baby is immediately whisked off for observation.

"Being without my husband during the delivery was the worst part of having a cesarean," says Katherine Smith, a young accountant who delivered her first child at Lenox Hill Hospital in New York City. "I had never planned to have a cesarean, so I didn't even think of checking hospital policy. I was shocked to discover that family-centered deliveries stop at the operating-room door."

Hugh Barber, M.D., director of obstetrics and gynecology at the hospital, refuses to make exceptions to the policy and defends this two-class system. "A surgical team functions better when there's nobody in the way," he says. He worries that fathers present during a cesarean might faint or need to leave the room, requiring an extra nurse or other medical personnel to monitor the father, and that's not always possible. If this sounds curiously like the arguments used in the 1960's to keep all fathers uninvolved and anxiously pacing in waiting rooms, it's even more foolish when you realize that a sheet is drawn during a cesarean so neither the father nor the mother can see the surgery. The father is there, after all, to support the mother and share the first exciting moments after birth.

Some hospitals allow fathers to be present only during elective cesareans—a policy that Dr. Barber is considering for his hospital. The problem is obvious. "We shouldn't be having elective cesareans at all—and now we're thinking of a policy that would, in effect, encourage them," says one doctor who practices there. "It's truly outrageous."

Getting the necessary information

A law in Massachusetts now requires hospitals to reveal to patients their rates of cesarean sections and VBACs. "It's hard for parents to take responsibility for childbirth if they don't have good information,'' says Beth Shearer, who initiated the legislation. Parents need to choose an obstetrician and hospital carefully and to do their research well before labor starts. ''There are certain red flags that should go up,'' says Dr. Gleicher. ''Beware of hospitals and doctors that automatically do cesareans for breech presentation or when there are twins. There's no evidence that infants in either situation do better if they're born surgically, but some young doctors have never even seen a vaginal breech delivery. Also, patients should find out how many women deliver vaginally after a cesarean. It should be an overall rate of about 60 percent.''

Changing the trend

Many experts feel that the trend toward more and more cesareans won't change until the malpractice crisis eases or there are dramatic changes in how insurance companies reimburse obstetricians. Right now, most doctors charge—and insurance companies pay—far more for a surgical delivery than they do for a vaginal delivery. Would the cesarean rate change if doctors collected only one flat fee no matter how the baby was delivered? Some have suggested that doctors should not be able to collect for a repeat cesarean unless there's a good medical reason for doing it.

On the positive side, having a cesarean is a way of having a baby. If a woman is confident that her cesarean was done for a good reason, and that she herself did everything possible to avoid it, she's less likely to feel angry or disappointed. Ultimately, it's the baby, not the method of delivery, that matters.

Predictors of a Positive Childbirth Experience
Kathryn Crowe, B.A.(Hon.), and Carl von Baeyer, Ph.D.

ABSTRACT: *Knowledge of childbirth, fears regarding pregnancy, locus of control, state anxiety, expectation of pain, and confidence in ability to control pain were examined as possible predictors of positive childbirth experience. Self-reports of these variables were collected from 30 primiparous women enrolled in prenatal courses, on three occasions: before the first class, after the last class, and 24 to 48 hours after delivery. The number of women completing postdelivery measures was 21. It was found that those who demonstrated greater knowledge of childbirth and higher confidence after classes subsequently reported a less painful childbirth. Of interest, those with higher levels of childbirth-related fear before classes reported experiencing less anxiety during labor and delivery. It was suggested that these women may have recognized and dealt with their concerns earlier. Psychologic factors that appear to be most predictive of a positive childbirth experience include knowledge, confidence, and anxiety. The present findings support the current emphasis in prenatal education on imparting knowledge, instilling confidence, and providing a forum for dealing with childbirth-related fears.*

INTRODUCTION

Childbirth is an emotional as well as a physical experience. What determines whether the experience will be joyful or terrifying? While it is partly determined by physiologic factors such as length of labor and the baby's position, psychologic factors also play an important role. It has been suggested that the attitudes, expectations, and beliefs of an expectant couple may prove to be the most important determinants of their experience of childbirth (1).

Psychologic variables identified as predictive of positive childbirth outcome include a sense of personal control (2,3), confidence in preparation (4), and low levels of anxiety (5). Bradley (6) found that positive feelings were influenced by type of birth. Women who had spontaneous vaginal deliveries rated their experience as "easy" and significantly more satisfying, and rated themselves as having a greater degree of control, than did those who had forceps or cesarean delivery. The responses were consistent both in the hospital and at one month postpartum.

Women's confidence level also appears to be influential. Knowledge of practical labor and delivery skills acquired in prenatal classes was significantly associated with confidence in ability to cope (7). In a study of 98 primiparous women recruited from prenatal classes, women who indicated that their birth experience was not "as expected" were likely to rate it as unpleasant (8). Anxiety emerged as one of the strongest predictors of labor pain, as measured on the McGill Pain Questionnaire's total, sensory, affective, and evaluative scales (5).

Thus, psychologic factors that appear to influence women's perception of their own experience as positive or negative include knowledge of childbirth, anxiety, fears regarding pregnancy, locus of control, expectations of anticipated pain, and confidence in ability to control pain. We examined these variables as possible predictors of positive or negative childbirth experience as perceived by the women.

Methods

All first-time mothers enrolled in prenatal classes through three urban health agencies during a five-month period were approached as potential subjects. Thirty agreed to take part in our study. Nine subjects dropped out due to premature delivery and other factors, leaving 21 mothers after delivery.

Procedure

The measures were compiled into a questionnaire packet that subjects completed on three occasions: immediately before the first prenatal class, immediately after the last class, and 24 to 48 hours after delivery. On the first two occasions the women were instructed to fill out the 10-cm visual analog scales (pain and confidence in ability to control pain) to reflect how they expected to feel at the most difficult point in their labor. On the third occasion, the women completed the same measures indicating their actual experiences during the most difficult point in their labor. Subjects received the final packet of questionnaires and a stamped, addressed envelope at their last prenatal class to take with them to the hospital. A telephone call was made shortly before their due date to remind subjects to complete and mail the final set of measures after delivery.

All women enrolled in the prenatal classes were in the last trimester of pregnancy. The classes were not of the same length; one agency held classes for four consecutive weeks while the other two programs ran for six consecutive weeks. In two of the agencies nurses were instructors and in one,

Reprinted with the permission of Blackwell Scientific Publications, Inc. from K. Crowe and C. von Baeyer, Predictors of a positive childbirth experience, *Birth* (1989) 16 (2): 59–63.

mothers were. The investigators had no other involvement with the agencies providing prenatal education, or with the content of the classes. All classes provided information on anatomy, nutrition, normal labor and delivery, and common interventions. The average number of days from the last class to delivery was 40.

Measures

The McGill pain questionnaire (MPQ) (9,10) consists of 20 groups of pain descriptors from which subjects choose one word. It was adapted to obtain women's description of the pain they expected to experience as well as reports of the pain they did experience. The MPQ has frequently been used to measure pain associated with childbirth and is regarded as a reliable indicator of labor pain (11).

The State-Trait Anxiety Inventory (STAI) (12) separately measures anxiety as an enduring personality trait and anxiety states brought on by specific stressful situations. The importance of including measures of situational anxiety to record changes in anxiety level in childbirth is emphasized in the literature (13). Although the subjects completed both the state and trait anxiety scales, only data from the former are reported. For the purposes of this study, anxiety was of more interest as a means of detecting each woman's changing anxiety levels during pregnancy.

The childbirth education review, constructed and pilot tested for this study, is a 26-item measure of women's knowledge of the labor and delivery process and other areas covered in prenatal courses (e.g., nutrition, anatomy, laboring skills). The following are sample items: "Describe two functions of the placenta" and, "Describe two breathing techniques."

The pregnancy research questionnaire (PRQ) (14) contains scales to assess fears for self and fears for baby. Internal consistency reliabilities of 0.83 and 0.67 are reported for the two scales, respectively (14).

The pregnancy attitude index (PAI) (15), a locus of control scale specific to pregnancy, classifies women according to their expectations that their experience of pregnancy will be determined by their own behavior (Internal control), by that of their physician or hospital (Powerful others' control), or by luck or fate (Chance control). The PAI contains eight statements in each of the I, P, and C scales.

The expectations form was made up of two 10-cm visual analog scales (VAS) (16) measuring pain during labor and delivery ("no pain" to "pain as bad as it could possibly be") and confidence in ability to control pain ("no confidence" to "complete confidence").

The obstetric checklist was completed by a nurse after delivery. Length of labor, medical interventions, description of complications, type and amount of medication, presence of labor support, and condition of the newborn were among the information collected.

RESULTS

Respondents' Birth Experience

Within 48 hours after delivery, the attending nurses completed the obstetric checklist for 17 of the 21 subjects. Fifteen women had spontaneous vaginal deliveries and two had cesarean sections. Four women received epidurals. Labor was induced in five women. Forceps were used in one delivery and vacuum extraction in three. Episiotomies were reported for 10 women. Two women showed increased blood pressure postpartum. Oxytocin was the most frequently administered medication: 10 women received this, with the most common dose being 10 units.

Measures of length of labor (mean 11.3 hrs), weight of baby (mean 3244 g), and medical interventions suggested that our sample was an average group of primiparae. In each case, the husband was present in the delivery room.

Table 1. Significant Regression Coefficients for Prediction of Childbirth Experience from Measures Taken Before and After Prenatal Classes

Criterion Variables Measured After Delivery	Knowledge of Childbirth	Fears Concerning Childbirth	State Anxiety	Expectation of Pain	Confidence in Pain Control	Chance Locus of Control
	(betas for predictor variables measured before/after prenatal classes)					
Pain						
MPQ total	__/−0.52*	__/__	__/−0.41†	__/−0.35†	−0.52†/−0.37†	__/
VAS	__/−0.79*	__/__	__/−0.49†	__/__	__/−0.53	__/−0.52†
Confidence in pain control	__/	__/	__/	__/	0.51†/	__/
Anxiety	__/__	−0.47†/__	__/	__/	__/	__/

*Betas significant at $P<0.01$
†Betas significant at $P<0.05$.

Overview of Analysis

It was assumed that a more favorable childbirth experience would be characterized by lower anxiety, lower pain, and greater confidence and self-control. Therefore, the following four variables, measured after delivery, made up the criteria for a positive experience: 1) MPQ total score measuring actual pain in labor and delivery, 2) VAS score measuring actual pain, 3) VAS score measuring amount of confidence in ability to control pain, 4) STAI score measuring state anxiety.

Stepwise multiple regression with forward inclusion was used to determine whether the preclass and postclass measures significantly predicted the postdelivery criteria. Multiple regression previously was used in the same fashion to identify predictors of birth experience from prenatal questionnaires (8). One set of regression equations each was constructed to identify preclass and postclass predictors. The limited sample size did not permit inclusion in the regression equations of birth-related variables such as length of labor and use of medications, although these factors would also be important determinants of the psychologic outcome of labor and delivery. Instead, the focus in this analysis was on psychologic predictors.

The significant regression coefficients are shown in Table 1 and are interpreted below.

Preclass Predictors

Women who had greater confidence in their own ability to control pain before beginning prenatal classes did subsequently report that they had less pain, and remained more confident during labor and delivery. Of interest, those who reported more fears concerning childbirth before beginning classes subsequently reported actually experiencing less anxiety.

Postclass Predictors

Significant predictions from postclass measures were found for the postdelivery MPQ and VAS measures of pain, but not as expected for postdelivery confidence and anxiety. Women whose childbirth education review scores showed greater knowledge of childbirth (nutrition, anatomy, physiology, labor skills) after classes reported less pain during labor and delivery on both measures.

To illustrate the nature of the relationship between the postclass predictors and actual reported pain (MPQ total). Figure 1 shows the means on the MPQ for subjects above and below the median on three significant predictors. In each comparison, a mean difference of 7 to 10 points on the MPQ was found between groups. These mean differences are notable in light of one report of 5.7

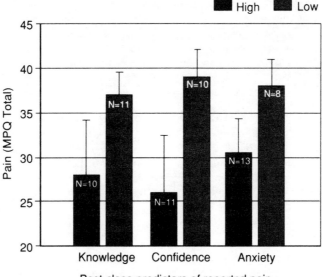

Figure 1. Mean pain measured on the MPQ after delivery for subjects scoring above (high) and below (low) the median on three postclass predictor variables.

points mean difference in MPQ total scores between women who had attended prenatal classes and those who had not (10). In that study, the mean pain rating by prepared women was 32.9, while for unprepared women it was 37.2. In the present study, the overall MPQ total mean was 33.0, almost identical to that reported by Melzack et al. for their prepared sample. However, the mean difference of 7 to 10 points associated with individual differences in postclass knowledge, confidence, and anxiety in the present study was greater than the difference attributed to attending childbirth classes by those authors.

The following two unexpected results were found in the regression analysis for only one of the two measures of pain in each case. Women who after classes said they expected more pain actually experienced less pain during labor and delivery.

The same was true for women whose PAI scores indicated a high chance locus of control for pregnancy.

DISCUSSION

Anxiety and Reported Pain

An unexpected finding was the inverse relationship between state anxiety and reported pain; that is, the higher a woman's anxiety after classes, the less pain she reported experiencing during labor and delivery. Two groups (17, 18) found that high anxiety is associated with greater levels of pain, supporting the accepted view that anxiety augments the experience of it. Two possible mediating variables were investigated in this study. First, epidural rates were analyzed for women with high and low levels of anxiety, since epidural anesthesia would affect reported pain; however, women with high levels of anxiety did not receive epidurals with greater frequency. A second possible mediating mechanism was that highly anxious women gained more knowledge to assuage their anxiety than did those with low levels of anxiety. This was also not substantiated. The most plausible explanation is that those with high levels of anxiety tend to expect more pain and are relieved when labor is not as painful as anticipated. An insignificant negative correlation also existed between postclass expectation and actual pain ($r(21) = -0.18$), which suggests that women's expectations are neither accurate nor realistic. It is likely that those with low levels of anxiety experience surprise or shock at the intensity of the pain. A useful inclusion in future studies would be brief, open-ended interviews with subjects shortly after delivery. This would afford researchers the opportunity to ask questions like, "How was your actual labor and delivery different from what you had expected?"

Chance Locus of Control

Another unexpected predictor of pain was chance locus of control as measured after class. This suggested that women who expressed the belief that much of labor and delivery was controlled by chance and not themselves or powerful others experienced less pain. It was expected that those who held this belief would see less reason to apply pain-control strategies learned in class and thereby experience more pain. These women may have used the techniques they were taught, however, regardless of their belief that such methods may or may not be beneficial. It would be useful to determine which women applied the learned pain-control strategies when in labor.

Knowledge, Confidence, and Anxiety

Significant predictors of pain in childbirth, as measured on the MPQ total shortly after delivery, included preclass and postclass expectation of confidence in ability to control pain as well as postclass knowledge, anxiety state, and expectation of pain. Significant predictors of pain in childbirth as measured by the VAS shortly after delivery included postclass knowledge, anxiety state, chance locus of control, and expectation of confidence in ability to control pain.

Similar patterns of prediction appeared for both measures, as expected: the two were positively correlated (r ranging from 0.22 to 0.53). It is reasonable that the more knowledge and confidence a woman possessed, particularly after prenatal classes, the less pain she would subsequently report. The premise of most prenatal classes is to impart knowledge and to increase women's confidence in their ability to cope effectively with labor and delivery. The results of this study confirmed the assumption.

The women who participated in this study possessed a high level of confidence (mean 6.8 on the 10-cm visual analog scale) and expected to exercise a significant role in their own pain management. Actual confidence was predicted by expected confidence as measured before classes.

Finally, state anxiety was predicted by fears as measured before classes. Women with high levels of fear before classes subsequently reported less anxiety during childbirth. Fears as measured after classes did not predict anything about anxiety. Fears declined after classes, although the reduction was insignificant. The prenatal classes may have provided a setting for early disclosure and discussion of childbirth-related fears, thereby relieving these fears. When the sample was divided into subjects scoring high and low on knowledge, pain, and anxiety (see Fig. 1), mean differences of 7 to 10 points on MPQ total scores were found. These individual differences were clinically as well as statistically significant (10).

Limitations

One limitation of the study was the use of self-report measures, which are susceptible to numerous possible distortions. Behavioral measures such as the observational method of Bonnel and Boureau (19) would complement the present methods. In addition, the sample was small. Attrition posed a problem; several women had to be eliminated from the study because premature delivery prevented them from completing the classes. The mean length of time from the last class to delivery was 40 days. Possible extraneous influences could not be controlled for during this time, and it is possible that some subjects may have reviewed class material while others did not. Finally, the practice of employing a retrospective measure of labor pain has been criticized (11,20). Discrepancies have been found between the amount of actual pain reported during labor and the amount remembered by women two days postpartum.

CONCLUSION

Prenatal classes have been associated with reduced numbers of forceps deliveries, substantially decreased use of medication, and short labors (21). The components of classes we identified as predictive of a positive experience included knowledge of childbirth and confidence in ability to control pain. These two factors as measured after classes predicted a less painful childbirth experience. There were two unexpected findings: high levels of fear before classes predicted a less anxious childbirth, and a high level of anxiety after classes predicted a less painful childbirth. This is the portrait of the woman most likely to have a positive childbirth experience: anxious and fearful (perhaps realistically so), yet competent in her knowledge of the labor and delivery process and confident in her ability to control the pain associated with it.

ACKNOWLEDGEMENTS

The authors thank the following for their assistance at various stages of this research: Samuel Mikail, Barbara Calder, Deborah Lake, Myles Genest, and the prenatal instructors of the Saskatoon Childbirth Education Association, the Victorian Order of Nurses in Saskatoon, and the Saskatoon Community Health Unit. The suggestions of three anonymous reviewers for BIRTH are also acknowledged.

REFERENCES

1. Genest, M. Preparation for childbirth—evidence for efficacy: A review. *JOGN Nurs* 1981;10:82–85.
2. Humenick, S. S. Bugen, L. A. Mastery: The key to childbirth satisfaction? A study. *Birth Fam J.* 1981;8(2):84–90.
3. Willmuth, R., Weaver, L., Borenstein, J. Satisfaction with prepared childbirth and locus of control. *JOGN Nurs* 1978;3:33–37.
4. Cogan, R., Henneborn, W., Klopfer, F. Predictors of pain during prepared childbirth. *J. Psychosom Res* 1976;20:523–533.
5. Reading, A. E., Cox, D. N. Psychosocial predictors of labour pain. *Pain* 1985;22:309–315.
6. Bradley, C. F. Psychological consequences of intervention in the birth process. *Can J Behav Sci* 1983;15(4):422–438.
7. Walker, B., Erdman, A. Childbirth education programs: The relationship between confidence and knowledge. *Birth* 1985;11(2):103–108.
8. Knight, R. G., Thirkettle, J. A. The relationship between expectations of pregnancy and birth, and transient depression in the immediate post-partum period. *J. Psychosom Res* 1987;31(3):351–357.
9. Melzack, R. The McGill pain questionnaire: Major properties and scoring methods. *Pain* 1975;1:277–299.
10. Melzack, R., Taenzer, P., Feldman, P., Kinch, R. A. Labour is still painful after prepared childbirth training. *Can Med Assoc J* 1981;125:357–363.
11. Niven, C., Gijsbers, K. A study of labour pain using the McGill pain questionnaire. *Soc Sci Med* 1984;19:1347–1351.

12. Spielberger, C. D., Gorsuch, R. L., Lushene, R. E. *The State-Trait Anxiety Inventory*. Palo Alto: Consulting Psychologists Press, 1970.
13. Beck, N. C, Hall, D. Natural childbirth: A review and analysis. *Obstet Gynecol* 1978;52:371–379.
14. Schaefer, E. S, Manheimer, H. Dimensions of perinatal adjustment. Paper presented at the meeting of the Eastern Psychological Association, New York, 1960.
15. O'Connell, M. L. Locus of control specific to pregnancy. *J Obstet Gynecol Nurs* 1983;12:161–164.
16. Huskisson, E. C. Visual analogue scales. In: Melzack R, ed. *Pain Measurement and Assessment*. New York: Raven Press, 1983.
17. Klusman, L. E. Reduction of pain in childbirth by the alleviation of anxiety during pregnancy. *J. Consult Clin Psychol* 1975;43(2):162–165.
18. Wallach, H. S. Psychological and physiological childbirth related variables affecting pain of labour. Summary of master's degree thesis. Lakehead University, Thunder Bay, Ontario, 1982.
19. Bonnel, A. M., Boureau, F. Labour pain asssessment: Validity of a behavioral index. *Pain* 1985;22:81–90.
20. Norvell, K. T., Gaston-Johansson, F., Fridh, G. Remembrance of labor pain: How valid are retrospective measures? *Pain* 1987;31:77–86.
21. Charles, A. G, Norr, K. L, Block, C. R, Meyering, S., Meyers, E. Obstetric and psychologic effects of psychoprophylactic preparation for childbirth. *Am J Obstet Gynecol* 1978;131:44–52.

Feeding Baby: Nature and Nurture
Dori Stehlin

Parents of a new baby have a million things to do, but menu-planning isn't one of them. Until a baby is 4 to 6 months old, for breakfast, lunch and dinner—and, of course, the infamous middle-of-the-night feeding—the only items on the menu are either breast milk or infant formula.

Breast Milk Is Best

Usually a manufacturer won't announce that the competition's product is a better choice. But when the competition is breast milk, infant formula manufacturers concede—right on the label—that breast milk is best.

Human breast milk is the ideal nourishment for human babies. Its protein content is particularly suited to a baby's metabolism, and the fat content is more easily absorbed and digested than the fats in cow's milk.

Breast milk also may protect the infant against certain diseases, infections and allergies. A mother's milk contains cells from her immune system and antibodies against diseases to which she has been exposed. Antibodies she develops after the baby is born are also passed to the baby through the breast milk.

For example, if Mom catches the flu, she develops antibodies to that strain of flu virus. Richard Schanler, M.D., associate professor of pediatrics at Baylor College of Medicine, Houston, explains, "The baby will get some protection. [The baby] might not get the flu at all, or the case may be milder . . . than if he or she wasn't breast-fed to begin with."

However, risks of breast milk may outweigh advantages if a nursing mother takes certain medications or abuses drugs. The

251

quality and quantity of the mother's diet may affect the quality and quantity of breast milk. (See "Good Nutrition for Breast-Feeding Mothers" in the December 1986-January 1987 *FDA Consumer*.)

Breast-Feeding Success

"Learn about breast-feeding before the baby is born," says Julie Stock of the La Leche League, an international breast-feeding support and educational organization. "If you know a lot beforehand, you start to build a sense of confidence. Many attempts at breast-feeding fail because of wrong information."

Once the baby is born, breast-feeding as soon as possible after delivery and often is the first of three essential keys for success, says Stock.

The second key is no artificial nipples—that includes pacifiers as well as bottles of water or formula—during the first few weeks. Stock explains that some babies can become very confused by the different feel and the different way of sucking needed with a bottle or pacifier, and they may not be able to switch back to the breast.

Finally, it is important to make sure that the baby "latches on" to the mother's nipple correctly. "If [a mother] has those three things going for her, in general that will eliminate about 90 percent of the common problems that mothers have," says Stock.

The La Leche League has local chapter meetings throughout the country where expectant and new mothers can learn about breast-feeding, nutrition, and other aspects of child care. For the number of your local chapter, call the La Leche League at 1-708-455-7730 or write to La Leche League International, 9616 Minneapolis Ave., P.O. Box 1209, Franklin Park, Ill. 60131–8209.

Second Best

The composition of infant formula is similar to breast milk, but it isn't a perfect match. Further, the exact chemical makeup of breast milk is still unknown.

"We're always discovering things in human milk that are there in small quantities that hadn't been looked at before," says John C. Wallingford, Ph.D., an infant nutrition specialist with FDA's Center for Food Safety and Applied Nutrition. "But [infant formula] is increasingly close to breast milk, especially in the area of fatty acids and lipids."

More than half the calories in breast milk come from fat, and the same is true for today's infant formulas. This may be alarming to many American adults watching their intake of fat and cholesterol, especially when high saturated fats, such as coconut oil are used in formulas. (High saturated fats tend to increase blood cholesterol levels more than other fats or oils.) But the low-fat diet recommended for adults doesn't apply to infants.

"Infants have a very high energy requirement, and they have a restricted volume of food that they can digest," says Wallingford. "The only way to get the energy density of a food up is to increase the amount of fat."

Homemade Isn't Best

Homemade formulas should not be used, says Nick Duy, assistant to the director in FDA's division of regulatory guidance. Homemade formulas based on whole cows' milk don't meet all of an infant's vitamin and mineral needs. In addition, the high protein content of cow's milk makes it difficult for an infant to digest and may put a strain on the baby's immature kidneys. Substituting evaporated milk for whole milk may make the formula easier to digest, but it is still nutritionally

Reprinted from the *FDA Consumer*, September, 1990.

inadequate when compared to commercially prepared formula. Use of soy drinks as an infant formula can actually be life-threatening.

Commercially prepared formulas are regulated by the Food and Drug administration as a food for special dietary use. "Infant formulas are the most heavily regulated food that there is," says Wallingford.

FDA regulations specify exact nutrient level requirements for infant formulas, based on recommendations by the American Academy of Pediatrics Committee on Nutrition. The following must be included in all formulas:

- protein
- fat
- linoleic acid
- vitamin A
- vitamin D
- vitamin E
- vitamin K
- thiamine (vitamin B_1)
- riboflavin (vitamin B_2)
- vitamin B_6
- vitamin B_{12}
- niacin
- folic acid
- pantothenic acid
- vitamin C
- calcium
- phosphorus
- magnesium
- iron
- zinc
- manganese
- copper
- iodine
- sodium
- potassium
- chloride

In addition, formulas not made with cow's milk must include biotin, choline and inositol.

The safety of commercially prepared formula is also enhanced by strict quality control procedures that require manufacturers to ana-lyze each batch of formula for required nutrients, to test representative samples for stability over the shelf life of the product, to code containers to identify the batch, and to make all records available to FDA investigators.

Formula Choices

The most common sources of protein in infant formulas are either cow's milk or soybeans. "For term infants, soy formulas appear to be as nutritionally sound as milk-based formulas, and their use is unlikely to expose infants to nutritional risk," wrote pediatrician Samuel J. Foman in 1987 in the *American Journal of Clinical Nutrition*. Baylor's Schanler agrees, but says that there is some question about whether the minerals in soy-based formulas can be used by the infant's body as well as those from cow's milk formula.

For a healthy, full-term infant, "cow's milk formula would be the first choice," Schanler says. "The only indication that I see for soy formula is for babies with lactose intolerance."

Lactose, also known as milk sugar, is the main carbohydrate in milk. Infants who don't have enough of the enzyme lactase to digest the lactose may suffer from abdominal pain, diarrhea, gas, bloating, or cramps. There is no lactose in soy formula.

Schanler does not think soy formula is a good choice for infants with milk allergies, however. "If there is a real history of [milk] allergy in the family, the baby might be allergic to soy, too," he says. Instead of soy, Schanler recommends special cow's milk formulas known as protein hydrolysates, which won't cause allergic reactions because the proteins are already broken down. "That way the chance of a cross reaction with the soy protein is eliminated," he explains.

Both milk and soy formulas are available in powder, liquid concentrate, or ready-to-feed forms. The choice should depend on "whatever the parents find convenient and can afford," says Schanler.

Whatever form is chosen, proper preparation and refrigeration are essential. Opened cans of ready-to-feed and liquid concentrate must be refrigerated and used within the time specified on the can. Once the powder is mixed with water it should also be refrigerated, if it is not used right away. The exact amounts of water recommended on the label must be used. Under-diluted formula can cause problems for the infant's organs and digestive system. Over-diluted formula will not provide adequate nutrition, and the baby may fail to thrive and grow.

Warming the formula isn't necessary for proper nutrition, says William MacLean, M. D., a pediatrician at infant formula manufacturer Ross Laboratories. "There is nothing magical about having [the formula] warmed up to body temperature," he says. "But if it's cold, some babies may refuse it. It's the baby's preference."

Bottles should not be heated in microwave ovens because the ovens don't heat evenly, MacLean warns. "The drop a mother tests on her wrist could be fine," he says. But, he explains, undetected "hot spots" in the formula could seriously burn the baby.

The best way to warm a bottle of formula is by placing the bottle in a pot of water and heating the pot on the stove, according to Christine Watson, a nurse who specializes in maternal and newborn care at the Shady Grove Adventist Hospital in Gaithersburg, M. D. "You can also run hot tap water over the bottle, but that isn't very quick," she says.

Vitamin Supplements—Yes or No?

The American Academy of Pediatrics says "the normal breast-fed infant of the well-nourished mother has not been shown *conclusively* to need any specific vitamin and mineral supplement. Similarly, there is no evidence that supplementation is necessary for the full-term, formula-fed infant and for the properly nourished normal child."

Many physicians recommend supplements, nevertheless—especially for breast-fed infants. "There is definitely some controversy here," says Wallingford.

The controversy on supplements usually revolves around the following:

Iron. Although the amount of iron in breast milk is very low (0.3 milligrams of iron per liter), the infant absorbs almost half. In contrast, while iron-fortified formulas contain 10 to 12 mg per liter, babies absorb only about 4 percent, amounting to about 0.4 mg per liter to 0.5 mg per liter. In either case, those amounts of iron are adaquate for the first 4 to 6 months, according to the American Academy of Pediatrics.

In the past, there was concern that iron-fortified formulas could cause gastrointestinal problems such as colic, constipation, diarrhea, or vomiting. But, based on several studies over the last 10 years, the American Academy of Pediatrics does not believe there is any evidence connecting these problems to iron and recommends that iron-fortified formula be used for all formula-fed infants.

Vitamin D. Insufficient vitamin D can cause rickets, a disease that results in softening and bending of the bones. Althogh the amounts of vitamin D in breast milk are small, rickets is uncommon in the breast-fed term infant. This may be because, like the iron in breast milk, the vitamin D in breast milk is easily absorbed by the baby.

Sunlight is important for the formation of vitamin D, but probably as little as a few minutes exposure a day is all the baby needs, says Schanler, and exposure to the whole body isn't necessary—just the arms and face are enough.

Fluoride. No one knows for sure if giving fluoride during the first six months of life will result in fewer cavities. Reflecting the uncertainty surrounding fluoride supplements, the American Academy of Pediatrics recommends starting fluoride supplements shortly after birth in breast-fed infants, but also says that waiting up to six months is acceptable. Because there is no fluoride in infant formula, that twofold recommendation also applies when ready-to-feed formula is used or when the water used for powdered or concentrated formula has less than 0.3 parts per million of fluoride.

Solid Evidence

Sometime between a baby's 4-month and 6-month birthdays solid food can be introduced. Exactly when depends on several factors.

One factor involves the disappearance of the involuntary action called the extrusion reflex. Before this reflex disappears, feeding solids usually involves putting a spoonful in the mouth and scraping most of it off the baby's face as he or she spits it back out.

Also, babies should be able to sit up and turn their heads away. That way, Schanler explains, they can communicate that they're not ready for the next spoonful or just not hungry anymore.

Usually, the first food recommended is a single-grain, iron-fortified infant cereal. Starting with single-grain cereals makes it easier to pinpoint any allergic reactions. (For more information on introducing solids, see "Good Nutrition for the Highchair Set" in the September 1985 *FDA Consumer*.)

The biggest concern with feeding solids too early is that the solids will replace breast milk or formula in the baby's diet. "Solids vary nutritionally depending on the food," says Schanler. "None of them is as complete as formula or breast milk. You don't want to rob [the baby] of milk."

Feeding babies exclusively with breast milk or formula during the first few months is not only the best thing for the babies' health, it can also be a blessing for busy, overtired parents. Now if only the baby would sleep through the night.

Gender Roles, Social Support, and Postpartum Depressive Symptomatology
The Benefits of Caring

Judith A. Richman, Ph.D., Valerie D. Raskin, M.D., and Cheryl Gaines, M.D.

Although women are assumed to be particularly vulnerable to depressive symptomatology after childbirth, the extent to which this symptomatology predominates over that found in men at this life cycle stage has not been addressed. This study examined gender differences in postpartum depressive symptomatology and the link between postpartum symptomatology and gender roles and relationships in a sample obtained from childbirth preparation classes. The data show no gender difference in depressive symptomatology at 2 months after childbirth. Women manifested a decrease in depressive symptomatology and men showed a slight increase from the preparenthood point. We partially link women's equivalent rather than higher distress levels to the protective effects of their varied social supports. By contrast, men depended primarily on their spouses, but both genders experienced a decrease in spouse support after childbirth. Female lack of support was more strongly associated with symptomatology in homemakers compared with employed women or women on maternity leave. Within the context of gender role changes, the data highlight benefits of female bonding in contrast to the "costs of caring" depicted by other researchers.

Depression is more common in women than in men (Weissman and Klerman, 1977), and women are assumed to be especially vulnerable to depression after childbirth (Hopkins et al., 1984). However, virtually all research studies of postpartum depressive states have used samples comprised solely of women. Thus, the extent to which there is a gender difference in depressive symptomatology after childbirth and the adaptation to parenthood has not been empirically assessed. The study reported here addressed two questions: a) Does a gender difference in depressive mood exist in a sample of couples undergoing the transition of parenthood? and b) Is the social structuring of the postpartum period an etiological determinant of the relative distress levels experienced by the two sexes?

ETIOLOGY OF POSTPARTUM DEPRESSIVE STATES: DIFFERENTIAL ATTENTION ACCORDED TO BIOLOGICAL, PSYCHOLOGICAL, AND SOCIAL-STRUCTURAL FACTORS

The transition to parenthood has been depicted by social scientists as a life event requiring considerable adaptation for both men and women (Lewis and Cooper, 1988). However, the sizable literature addressing the etiology of postpartum depression and gradations of depressive symptoms has tended to emphasize female hormonal changes congruent with a biological model (Handley et al.,

1977) or female intrapsychic conflicts involving ambivalence regarding the maternal role (Deutsch, 1945). Although researchers have begun to examine the effect of environmental variables such as overall social supports, marital satisfaction, and other life events (Cutrona, 1984; O'Hara et al., 1983; Stemp et al., 1986), what has been virtually ignored is the social structuring of gender roles and relationships and their consequences for fathers as well as for mothers.

An important component in the social structuring of gender roles and relationships involves the exchange of emotional and instrumental resources. Whereas involvement in supportive relationships has consistently been linked with low-level depressive mood (Brown and Harris, 1978; Thoits, 1982) limited attention has been directed to gender differences in the nature and psychological consequences of social bonding (Antonucci and Akiyama, 1987; Vaux, 1985). However, a large gender socialization literature depicts a female advantage in the capacity for intimacy and emotional exchange (Chodorow, 1978; Gilligan, 1982). This capacity has particular salience for the postpartum period, a period in the life cycle that is centered on interpersonal attachment—that of bonding to a new family member.

Research examining gender differences in support and psychological distress in varied populations depicts women as experiencing higher levels of support, particularly emotional support, yet remaining higher in distress (Vaux, 1985). One explanation for women's relatively high distress levels, despite their apparent advantage in support, is that women's involvement in social networks also entails an emotional drain or "cost of caring" (Kessler and McLeod, 1984). However, not all research has demonstrated a female disadvantage in depressive symptomatology: under some social conditions, women do not differ from men in depressive symptoms (Aneshensel et al., 1981; Ross et al., 1985) or even manifest lower levels than men (Ro-

senfield, 1980). These social situations have been linked with an egalitarian familial division of labor and female labor force participation. However, the extent to which gender-linked support structures also contribute to women's relatively lower (or men's relatively higher) levels of depressive symptomatology under certain conditions or at particular life cycle stages has not been addressed.

SOCIAL STRUCTURING OF THE POSTPARTUM PERIOD, SOCIAL SUPPORT, AND DEPRESSIVE MOOD IN WOMEN AND MEN

Using an anthropological perspective, Stern and Kruckman (1983) argued that postpartum depression is a phenomenon primarily limited to Western societies. In contrast to traditional cultures, Western societies lack adequate social recognition and interpersonal support surrounding the transition to parenthood. This support, in traditional cultures, involves mandated rest, assistance in tasks, and social recognition through rituals and gifts marking the new status of mother.

Sociological perspectives on the transition to parenthood (again focusing primarily on motherhood) have similarly suggested that the support received by mothers in modern societies is limited (Rossi, 1968). This lack of support is partially linked to the relative isolation of the modern nuclear family and consequent limitations in the availability of support from extended family members. Consistent with this view, empirical studies of postpartum reactions in new mothers have highlighted feelings of social isolation (Leifer, 1977).

An alternative perspective on the social structuring of new motherhood and postpartum distress involves the effect of the varied gender role arrangements that currently exist in American society. In 1987, 50.8% of new mothers were employed in the occupational structure or actively seeking employment within a year of giving birth (United States

Census Bureau, 1988). Because the traditional female role in the home has been depicted as socially isolating (Gove and Geerken, 1977; Gove and Tudor, 1973) women who return to work relatively early after childbirth may continue to be more embedded in social relationships on a daily basis and, consequently, may be lower in distress compared with homemakers. However, given competing demands of home and work, employed women may experience less support from the work environment in contrast to employed men.

GENDER, SOURCES, OF SUPPORT, AND POSTPARTUM DEPRESSIVE MOOD

Studies of social support and distress in varied populations have addressed the effects of aggregate support from social networks as a whole or support from one primary confidant. However, few researchers have examined the relative salience of particular sources of support. Yet, the extent to which individuals depend on particular (role-related) support sources may have major consequences for satisfaction with support provided, particularly if a major source of support is experiencing a similar stressor.

During the transition to parenthood, it has been shown that marital satisfaction decreases (Feldman and Nash, 1984). Decreased marital satisfaction is also likely to be correlated with decreased support derived from the marital relationship. Thus, the relative extent to which new mothers and fathers depend on each other *vs.* on other relationships for support is likely to affect the overall quality of the support received. Research on gender differences in styles of interpersonal relating suggests that men are much more dependent on their spouses for emotional support than on other network members (Antonucci and Akiyama, 1987). By contrast, women are more likely to seek out friends in order to share feelings and problems, whereas male friendships center more on instrumental activities (Fox et al., 1985). Given the decrease in spouse support likely to be experienced during the transition to parenthood, women may be more advantaged in overall support by virtue of their capacity to obtain support from more diverse network sources.

One potential source of support for new parents is support from their own parents. While psychoanalysts focus primary attention on the internal representations of parents maintained by individuals undergoing the process of becoming parents (Benedek, 1959; Zayas, 1987), sociologically, these inner representations may also correspond to actual relationships maintained in adulthood with parents and corresponding emotional and tangible support or lack of support provided by parents. Social psychoanalytic explorations of gender differences in mother-daughter and father-son relationships have suggested that the traditionally primarily female involvement in parenting has given rise to intense mother-daughter bonding but weaker father-son bonding, given the relative absence of fathers from traditional parenting roles within the family (Chodorow, 1978). From this perspective, new mothers may continue in adulthood their more intimate relationships with their mothers and receive greater support from them compared with the support received by new fathers from their own fathers.

A final source of support derives from the work environment of employed individuals. As a result of changing gender roles, particularly the increasing percentage of mothers of young children attempting to combine employment outside the home with family roles, a major social policy issue has involved the extent to which occupational environments provide the flexibility necessary for mothers to successfully integrate work and family roles (Freidan, 1986; Hewlett, 1986). Thus, employed women may perceive their work environment as less supportive than em-

258

ployed men. However, women returning to work during the post-partum period may experience a greater sense of social integration in contrast to homemakers, who may experience greater feelings of isolation from remaining in the home.

The central hypothesis derived from the preceding literature was that new mothers in the sample surveyed would not manifest higher levels of depressive mood than new fathers as a consequence of both the socialization-based female advantage in the capacity to form social supports and the changing work roles of women involving greater social integration derived from adult employment roles. As a consequence of differential socialization, we hypothesized that women would be more intimately connected to a greater variety of potential sources of support, including spouse, mother, and friends, with men depending primarily on their (similarly stressed) wives. Thus, women were expected to receive greater support overall, with a resulting advantage in psychological well-being. However, because the traditional female role in the home has been depicted as structurally isolating on a daily basis, employed individuals were hypothesized to experience greater overall support. Moreover, whereas employment roles were expected to be associated with greater female overall social integration in contrast to homemaker roles, employed women were, nevertheless, expected to receive less support from the occupational setting than employed men.

METHODS

Sample

Respondents were recruited from childbirth preparation classes held in 1987 at several hospitals in the greater Chicago area. The authors presented the study to class participants and obtained names, addresses, and expected delivery dates from interested respondents. (Approximately 90% of eligible participants volunteered for the study.) Eligible participants were married couples who were at least 18 years of age, expecting their first child, and had no major health problems. The participants were mailed self-report questionnaires, which were filled out at two time points: at 6 weeks before the expected delivery date and 8 weeks after delivery. Although primary focus involved social factors associated with postpartum depressive mood, similar measures were included at both time points to assess changes over time associated with the transition to parenthood.[1]

The time 1 sample included 192 individuals: 95 couples and two individuals whose spouses did not return the questionnaire. The time 2 follow-up produced a final sample of 177 individuals, or 92% of the initial sample (86 couples and five individuals whose spouses dropped out). There was no significant difference in depressive symptomatology between completers and time 2 dropouts. Both the male and female respondents were disproportionately college educated (63.2%) and white (84.2%), congruent with previous analyses of the demographic factors influencing selection into childbirth preparation classes (McCraw, 1981). The mean age of respondents was 31.0 for men and 29.3 for women. At time 1, the majority of both male and female respondents were employed fulltime. At the time 2 point, the majority of men remained employed full time, whereas the largest proportion of women was on maternity leave (41.8%), with 22.0% employed full time and 28.6% defining themselves as homemakers.

Measures

The self-report questionnaires included sociodemographic data and psychosocial measures including social supports and depressive symptomatology[2] (at each time point).

Table 1. Gender Differences in Depressive Mood and Social Support at Times 1 and 2

Measure	Time 1			Time 2		
	Men	Women	F	Men	Women	F
Depressive mood	9.65 ± 6.78[a]	12.14 ± 7.03[a]	6.268**	10.31 ± 7.03[a]	10.67 ± 7.99[a]	.099
Overall support	4.95 ± .98	5.21 ± .91	3.408†	4.96 ± .94	5.29 ± .89	5.908
Support source						
Spouse	6.48 ± .69	6.54 ± .91	.346	6.34 ± .86	6.38 ± .80	.076
Mother	4.86 ± 1.54	5.53 ± 1.37	8.718**	4.94 ± 1.32	5.49 ± 1.30	7.129**
Father	4.55 ± 1.53	4.39 ± 1.66	.367	4.51 ± 1.41	4.41 ± 1.72	.155
Boss	3.37 ± 1.52	3.02 ± 1.47	1.886	2.96 ± 1.59	3.11 ± 1.55	.257
Other	5.16 ± 1.19	5.83 ± 1.24	12.457***	5.26 ± 1.24	5.90 ± 1.03	13.432***
Support type						
Intimacy	5.37 ± 1.10	5.33 ± 1.00	.049	5.21 ± 1.33	5.44 ± 1.08	1.665
Practical	4.61 ± 1.20	5.03 ± 1.03	6.278**	4.71 ± 1.23	5.03 ± 1.07	3.349†
Emotional	4.72 ± 1.24	5.07 ± 1.05	4.097*	4.82 ± 1.12	5.13 ± 1.19	3.148†
Reassurance	5.09 ± 1.38	5.42 ± 1.12	3.121†	5.12 ± 1.16	5.56 ± 1.10	6.864**
Depressive mood, adjusted for overall support	9.58	12.21	6.061**	9.92	11.05	1.026

[a] $\bar{X}$ ± SD.
†$p < .10$; *$p < .05$**; $p < .01$; ***$p < .001$.

Social supports were measured by a modified version of the Social Support Network Inventory (SSNI; Flaherty et al., 1983), an instrument assessing perceived emotional and instrumental support. Four questions from the SSNI were rewritten to focus specifically on support in relation to pregnancy/anticipated parenthood at time 1 and parenthood at time 2. These questions, scored on a 1 to 7-point scale, are: a) How comfortable are you discussing feelings or thoughts about your or your wife's pregnancy and anticipated parenthood (or experiences as a new parent) with this person? (intended to tap intimacy); b) To what extent does this person provide practical help (*e.g.,* material things, loaning things, practical advice)? (intended to tap practical support); c) To what extent does this person give you emotional support by listening, talking, consoling, or just being with you? (intended to tap emotional support); and d) Most people who are about to become new parents (who become new parents) experience occasional anxieties about their competence, ability or self-worth. To what extent has this person reassured you in this area or would do so if you needed it? (intended to specifically tap reassurance of self-worth). While the SSNI asks the respondent to choose five individuals to whom they are closest, we were interested in the amount and consequences of support provided by specific role-related individuals. Thus, respondents were asked to rate the following individuals: a) spouse, b) mother, c) father, d) boss at work for employed individuals, and e) one additional significant other (which, in most cases, turned out to be a friend). The instrument was scored to provide an overall mean measure of support, mean scores for each support provider, and mean scores across providers for each support type (intimacy, practical support, emotional support, and reassurance). The alpha coefficients for the overall scale were over .80 for both men and women at each time point. The alphas for the source of support subscales ranged from .58 to .95, with most of the alphas over .80. Although the main theoretical focus of this study is on support differences in terms of providers, we also present data for support types.

Depressive symptomatology was measured by the Center for Epidemiologic Studies Depression (CES-D) Scale, a 20-item self-report symptom rating scale designed to measure depressive mood in community populations (Radloff, 1977; Weissman et al., 1977). The symptoms comprising the scale were selected to represent the major symptoms in the clinical syndrome of depression, although it is most representative of dysphoric mood. The instrument provides for a possible range of scores from 0 to 60, taking into account both the prevalence and persistence of each symptom. The alpha coefficients for the CES-D were .85 at time 1 and .84 at time 2 for men and .91 at time 1 and .81 at time 2 for women.

ANALYSIS AND RESULTS

Analyses of variance[3] were used to assess gender differences in depressive symptomatology and each dimension of social support at the two time points (shown in Table 1). First, Table 1 indicates that although women manifested significantly higher levels of depressive symptomatology at time 1 ($p < .01$), there was, as hypothesized, no gender difference in depressive symptomatology at time 2. In addition, paired t-tests examining women's and men's changes in distress over time revealed that women's levels decreased at the trend level ($p < .10$) whereas men's levels increased slightly (not shown in Table 1). With regard to gender differences in social support, Table 1 shows that, as hypothesized, women manifested an advantage over men at both time points in perceived overall support ($p < .10$ at time 1, $p < .05$ at time 2) and in support from mothers ($p < .01$ at both points) and "other" source ($p < .001$ at both points). Women also manifested higher scores than men on perceived practical support, emotional support, and reassurance at each time point. When paired t-tests examining men's and women's changes in social support over time were calculated (not shown in Table 1),

the hypothesized decrease in perceived spouse support was apparent for both genders ($p < .10$ for men and $p < .05$ for women). The only other significant change was a perceived decrease in boss support by men ($p < .05$).

To directly test the hypothesis that the female advantage in social support accounts, at least in part, for the lack of a female predominance in postpartum depressive symptomatology, analysis of covariance was used. The bottom of Table 1 presents the male and female mean levels of depressed mood adjusted for the effect of overall social support. As expected, when social support was held constant, male symptomatology decreased and female symptomatology increased at both time points, although primarily at time 2. At time 2, the male mean was reduced by .39 whereas the female mean increased by .42. At the same time, however, the support advantage does not completely explain the lack of a female predominance in symptomatology insofar as the genders still did not significantly differ.

In summary, consistent with gender role perspectives on women's more extensive social bonds, women manifested significantly greater perceived support overall and from their mothers and "other" source (generally a friend) at both points in time. In addition, although the genders manifested similar levels of perceived support from their spouses, perceived spouse support decreased after childbirth. Finally, consistent with the initial hypothesis, when overall support was held constant, the mean differences between the genders in depressive symptomatology increased, with male levels decreasing and female levels increasing.

To explore the relative salience of particular sources of support for depressive symptomatology or well-being, Table 2 presents the correlations between overall support and each dimension (source and type) of social support and depressive symptomatology for men and women at each time period. First, overall social support did not correlate

Table 2. Social Support and Depressive Mood at Times 1 and 2: Pearson Correlations

Measure	Time 1		Time 2	
	Men	Women	Men	Women
Overall support	−.10	−.07	−.13	−.41***
Support source				
Spouse	−.19*	−.09	−.27**	−.52***
Mother	.06	−.01	−.04	−.31**
Father	.06	−.03	−.05	−.32**
Boss	−.13	.04	−.11	.02
Other	−.15†	−.19*	−.05	−.22*
Support type				
Intimacy	−.18*	−.09	−.01	−.31***
Practical	.04	−.06	−.18*	−.28**
Emotional	−.08	−.03	−.03	−.32***
Reassurance	−.10	−.05	−.20*	−.42***

†$p < .10$; $p < .05$; **$p < .01$; ***$p < .001$.

with depressive symptomatology for either gender at time 1, whereas overall support was negatively correlated with female symptomatology at time 2 (−.41, $p < .001$), but not with male time 2 symptomatology. Looking at the associations between source of support and symptomatology, at time 1, spouse support was inversely associated with symptomatology for men but not women (−.19, $p < .05$), whereas "other" support was inversely associated with symptomatology for both genders (−.19, $p < .05$ for women and −.15, $p < .10$ for men). However, at time 2, only the relationship with spouse was linked to depressive symptomatology for men (−.27, $p < .01$). By contrast, women's relationships with their spouse, mother, father, and other significant person were also significantly linked, in an inverse direction, to depressive symptomatology. We can also note that each dimension of support was inversely linked to depressive symptomatology in women at time 2, whereas only practical support and reassurance were inversely linked to time 2 depressive symptomatology in men.

In sum, congruent with the initial hypothesis regarding the role of women's more extensive intimate attachments for psychological well-being, female well-being after parenthood was linked with support from each parent and another individual (usually a friend) in addition to support from spouse. By contrast, only spouse support was linked with male psychological well-being. It is also interesting to note the greater salience of social support for both genders during the postpartum period in contrast to the preparenthood time point. Finally, support from the workplace was unrelated to distress in both sexes.

Shifting to the effect of female work status on depressive symptomatology and social support, Table 3 compares homemakers, full-time employed women, and women on maternity leave at the postpartum period.[4] First, Table 3 indicates no significant difference in depressive symptomatology, although it is interesting to note that full-time employed women were highest in distress and women on maternity leave lowest. There was a trend level ($p < .10$) difference in overall support, with homemakers highest and employed women lowest.[5] The three groups did not differ with regard to individual support sources, although, in the area of support types, homemakers perceived greater reassurance compared with employed women (with women on maternity leave in between). Finally, when we looked at the effect of employment status on depressive symptomatology, holding overall support level constant, the differences between the three groups remained insignificant. However, we can note a reversal in comparative levels of distress in contrast to the mean differences before controlling for support: now, homemakers appeared highest in depressive symptomatology instead of employed women. At the same time, women on maternity leave were lowest, with or without controlling for social supports.

In summary, the hypothesized greater perceived isolation of homemakers in contrast to employed women was disconfirmed. However, overall social support appears to be more strongly related to the well-being of homemakers to the extent that their distress

Table 3. Female Differences in Depressive Mood and Social Support at Time 2 as a Function of Time 2 Employment Status[a]

| Measure | Female Employment Status | | | |
	Homemaker (N = 26)	Employment full-time (N = 20)	On maternity leave (N = 38)	F
Depressive mood	10.69 ± 8.45[b]	12.60 ± 8.54[b]	9.42 ± 7.63 [b]	1.011
Overall support	5.54 ± .99	4.95 ± .86	5.26 ± .79	2.643†
Support source				
Spouse	6.26 ± .94	6.30 ± .94	6.48 ± .64	.656
Mother	5.61 ± 1.29	5.17 ± 1.20	5.66 ± 1.29	1.019
Father	4.39 ± 1.63	4.21 ± 1.73	4.40 ± 1.84	.075
Other	5.81 ± 1.12	5.96 ± .90	5.97 ± .95	.225
Support type				
Intimacy	5.68 ± 1.12	5.03 ± .90	5.42 ± 1.07	2.166
Practical	5.17 ± 1.22	4.81 ± .93	5.04 ± 1.03	.630
Emotional	5.34 ± 1.33	4.84 ± .96	5.11 ± 1.04	1.099
Reassurance	6.00 ± 1.08	5.10 ± 1.00	5.47 ± 1.06	4.209*
Depressive mood, adjusted for overall support	11.70	11.37	9.37	.901

[a]Where the overall analysis of variance is significant, the Duncan procedure is used to test for differences between groups at the .05 level.
[b]$\bar{X} \pm SD$.
†$p < .10$; *$p < .05$.

levels go up and those of employed women go down when social support is held constant.

Table 4 presents the psychological salience of different sources and types of support for homemakers, full-time employed women, and women on maternity leave. First, Table 4 indicates that overall support was strongly linked to low depressive symptomatology in homemakers ($-.75$, $p < .001$) but not significantly linked to symptomatology in employed women or women on maternity leave. In addition, each source of support as well as type of support significantly related to symptomatology in homemakers. By contrast, only support from spouse and father was significantly linked ($-.41$, $p < .05$; $-.49$, $p < .05$) to symptomatology in employed women and only spouse support ($-.59$, $p < .001$) and mother support ($-.23$, $p < .10$) were linked at a significant or trend level to depressive symptomatology in women on maternity leave.

In sum, overall social support as well as support from diverse sources was linked to symptomatology in homemakers but not in employed women or women on maternity leave. Thus, an interaction clearly existed between female employment status and social support. Although spouse support was important to all groups, support effects were most consistently significant and negative only for homemakers, suggesting that they were most vulnerable in its absence.

DISCUSSION

Given the widely held assumptions regarding women's particular vulnerability to depressed mood in the period after childbirth, the data reported here show that, in a sample of largely middle-class couples, women and men did not differ in depressive symptomatology at 2 months after the birth of their first child. This finding can be interpreted in varied ways. First, the characterization of depressive mood in the postpartum period as a predominantly "female problem" may constitute a social construction of reality inadequately subjected to empirical testing by means of gender comparisons. Alternatively,

Table 4. Social Support and Depressive Mood in Women at Time 2 as a Function of Time 2 Employment Status: Pearson Correlations

	Employment Status Group		
	Homemakers (N = 26)	Employed full time (N = 20)	On Maternity leave (N = 38)
Support measures			
Overall support	−.75***	−.22	−.19
Support source			
Spouse	−.67***	−.41*	−.59***
Mother	−.46**	−.02	−.23†
Father	−.59**	−.49*	−.04
Boss	—	.08	−.18
Other	−.54**	.09	−.07
Support type			
Intimacy	−.58***	−.21	−.13
Practical	−.53**	−.15	−.07
Emotional	−.64***	−.25	−.05
Reassurance	−.72***	−.19	−.33*

†$p<.10$; *$p<.05$; **$p<.01$; ***$p<.001$.

consistent with Srole and Fisher's (1980) argument regarding the changing cohort-based experiences of women apparent in the Midtown Manhattan study data, contemporary parental roles may be more advantageous for women entering parenthood now compared with earlier periods (and, conversely, more demanding for men). Lastly, women's predominance over men in postpartum depressive mood may be more likely to occur in working-class than in middle-class contexts (Brown and Harris, 1978). Future studies should examine gender differences across class as well as ethnic groups.

We partially linked the lack of a female predominance in depressive mood in our study population to the female advantage in interpersonal attachments. Overall, the data show that women's greater involvement in and capacity to receive support from a variety of significant individuals in their lives in contrast to men's primary reliance on their spouse for support contributed to women's equal rather than greater vulnerability to depressed mood after childbirth. In addition, female employment status was linked to social supports and depressive mood, but somewhat

differently than originally hypothesized. The expectation that homemakers (and perhaps women on leave from work) would receive more limited social support than employed women by virtue of their greater social isolation was not borne out. However, social support from varied sources was strongly linked in an inverse manner to depressive mood in homemakers but not in employed women or those on maternity leave. Thus, when social support was lacking, this deficit was much more problematical for women in more traditional, family-centered roles than for women whose identities encompass occupational roles (whether they are currently working or are on leave from work). In addition, contrary to what was hypothesized, employed women did not perceive more limited support from their bosses in contrast to men.

Given the associations previously established between parenthood and female depressive mood (Brown and Harris, 1978; Gove and Geerken, 1977), an important question involves the extent to which the general female predominance over men in depressive symptomatology may emerge at a future time point. Does the female advantage in social support after childbirth continue past the postpartum period? If support lessens subsequent to the "celebration" of the first child, the data from this study clearly suggest that homemakers are likely to experience increased depressive mood. By contrast, employed women may require less support focused on their familial roles because they derive their esteem from multiple roles both inside and outside the home. In particular, work roles within the public world are accorded greater importance and worth compared with "invisible work" within the home in modern societies (Daniels, 1987; Gove and Tudor, 1973). Alternatively, employed women may experience their work environments as flexible at first, but increasingly less supportive and more rigid as time goes by. In addition, the (sizable) group of women on maternity leave at 8 weeks after delivery may experience increased distress upon returning to work as a consequence of maternity-related losses in areas such as job security, job advancement, job responsibility, and sick benefits as well as difficulties in arranging child care (Ross and Mirowsky, 1988).

Finally, whereas Kessler and McLeod (1984) suggested that women's increased vulnerability to depressed mood may be a consequence of the costs of caring resulting from their (burdensome) interpersonal attachments, the data presented here suggest that there are some conditions under which women experience the benefits of caring and consequent levels of depressed mood equivalent to those of men. At a point in the life cycle when the marital dyad is particularly stressed by the challenges associated with the transition to parenthood, middle-class women are able to call on a broader network of support to compensate for the decreased support from their spouse. By contrast, men's supportive attachments center more narrowly on their spouse, rendering them more vulnerable to total loss of support in the face of their wife's decreased availability. In sum, during the transi-

tion to parenthood and accompanying challenges of bonding to a new family member, women's social networks within a middle-class context appear to provide benefits more than entailing costs.

CONCLUSION

The data from this study of predominantly middle-class husbands and wives undergoing the transition to parenthood failed to show a female predominance in depressive symptomatology at 2 months after childbirth. Women manifested a decrease in depressive symptoms and men showed a slight increase from the preparenthood point. The lack of a female predominance in postpartum depressive symptoms partially derived from the multiple sources of social support experienced by women. By contrast, men's support sources were more narrowly focused on their spouses, and both genders experienced a decrease in spouse support after childbirth. In addition, women's changing gender roles involving occupational identities in addition to those derived from family roles were protective to the extent that deficits in social support were more strongly linked to symptomatology in housewives than in employed women. Finally, although previous research has linked women's predominance in depressed mood to the "costs of caring" derived from burdensome social relationships, this study points to the benefits of caring as well as changes in gender roles for explaining gender equivalence in depressed mood in the early months of parenthood. However, research addressing these issues in the context of greater social class and ethnic diversity would be useful.

NOTES

1. The time 1 point represents the preparenthood point, although for women it also encompasses the stress and discomfort of pregnancy. The 8 weeks postdelivery time 2 point was chosen to maximize the number of

employed women who would have already returned to work while at the same time capturing a period in which women experiencing postpartum depressive symptomatology would have a high likelihood of remaining symptomatic (Hopkins et al., 1984).

2. In addition to measuring depressive symptoms, questions assessing the quantity and frequency of alcohol consumption were added to tap male styles of manifesting distress. However, the data showed no change in male drinking over time, so the focus of analysis here is solely on depressive mood.

3. Analysis of variance assumes the use of independent samples. Because the majority, although not all, of the respondents in this sample are married couples, the data were also examined using paired (couples) analyses. Because the bivariate correlations between husbands' and wives' scores on the variables of interest (depressive symptomatology and social supports) were statistically insignificant and because the bivariate paired *t*-test analyses produced results equivalent to the analyses of variance results, analysis of variance and analysis of covariance are used here for ease of overall analysis and presentation.

4. The number of women employed part-time was too small to study.

5. This finding partially reflects the fact that boss support, included in overall support for employed women, is rated lower than other sources of support by employed women and men.

References

Aneshensel, C. S., Frerichs R. R., Clark, V. A. (1981) Family roles and sex differences in depression. *J Health Soc Behav* 22:379–393.

Antonucci, T. C., Akiyama, H. (1987) An examination of sex differences in social support among older men and women. *Sex Roles* 17:737–749.

Benedek, T. (1959) Parenthood as a developmental phase. *J Am Psychoanal Assoc* 67:389–417.

Brown, G., Harris, T. (1978) *Social origins of depression: A study of psychiatric disorder in women*. New York: Free Press.

Chodorow, N. (1978) *The reproduction of mothering*. Berkeley: University of California Press.

Cutrona, C. E. (1984) Social support and stress in the transition to parenthood. *J Abnorm Psychol* 93:378–390.

Daniels, A. K. (1987) Invisible work. *Soc Problems* 34:403–415.

Deutsch, H. (1945) *Psychology of women* (Vol 2). New York: Grune & Stratton.

Feldman, S., Nash, S. C. (1984) The transition from expectancy to parenthood: Impact of the firstborn child on men and women. *Sex Roles* 1:61–79.

Flaherty, J. A., Gaviria, M., Pathak, D. (1983) The measurement of social support: The Social Support Network Inventory. *Compr Psychiatry* 24:521–529.

Friedan, B. (1986) *The second stage* (rev ed). New York: Summit.

Fox, M., Gibbs, M., Auerbach, D. (1985) Age and gender dimensions of friendship. *Psychol Women Q* 9:489–502.

Gilligan, C. (1982) *In a different voice*. Cambridge, MA: Harvard University Press.

Gove, W. R., Geerken, M. (1977) The effect of children and employment on the mental health of married men and women (pp. 51–73). *Soc Forces* 56:66–76.

Gove, W. R., Tudor, J. F. (1973) Adult sex roles and mental illness. In J Huber (Ed), *Changing women in a changing society*. Chicago: University of Chicago Press.

Handley, S. L., Dunn, T. L., Baker, J. M., et al (1977) Mood changes in puerperium and plasma tryptophan and cortical concentrations. *Br Med J* 2:18–22.

Hewlett, S. A. (1986) *A lesser life: The myth of women's liberation in America*. New York: Warner.

Hopkins, J., Marcus, M., Campbell, S. (1984) Postpartum depression: A critical review. *Psychol Bull* 95:498–515.

Kessler, R. C., McLeod, J. D. (1984) Sex differences in vulnerability to undesirable life events. *Am Sociol Rev* 49:620–631.

Leifer, M. (1977) Psychological changes accompanying pregnancy and motherhood. *Genet Psychol Monogr* 95:55–96.

Lewis, S. N. C., Cooper, C. L. (1988) The transition to parenthood in dual-earner couples. *Psychol Med* 18:477–486.

McCraw, R. K. (1981) *Attitudinal, personality and demographic factors in the selection of childbirth preparation classes and the effects of preparation*. Unpublished doctoral dissertation, University of South Florida, Tampa.

O'Hara, M., Rehm, L. P., Campbell, S. B. (1983) Postpartum depression: A role for social networks and life stress variables. *J Nerv Ment Dis* 171:336–341.

Radloff, L. S. (1977) The CES-D scale: A self-report depression scale for research in the general population. *Appl Psychol Meas* 1:385–401.

Rosenfield, S. (1980) Sex differences in depression: Do women always have higher rates? *J Health Soc Behav* 21:33–42.

Ross, C. E., Mirowsky, J. (1988) Child care and emotional adjustment to wives' employment. *J Health Soc Behav* 29:127–138.

Ross, C. E., Mirowsky, J., Huber, J. (1983) Dividing work, sharing work, and in-between: Marriage patterns and depression. *Am Sociol Rev* 48:809–823.

Rossi, A. (1968) Transition to parenthood. *J Marriage Fam* 30:26–39.

Srole, L., Fisher, A. K. (1980) The Midtown Manhattan longitudinal study *vs* "the mental paradise lost" doctrine. *Arch Gen Psychiatry* 37:209–221.

Stemp, P. S., Turner, R. J., Noh, S. (1986) Psychological distress in the postpartum period: The significance of social support. *J Marriage Fam* 48:271–277.

Stern, G., Kruckman, L. (1983) Multi-disciplinary perspectives on postpartum depression: An anthropological critique. *Soc Sci Med* 17:1027–1041.

Thoits, P. A. (1982) Conceptual, methodological and theoretical problems in studying social support as a buffer against life stress. *J Health Soc Behav* 23:145–159.

United States Census Bureau (1988, June 16) Fertility of American women: June 1987. In *The New York Times*, p. 12.

Vaux, A. (1985) Variations in social support associated with gender, ethnicity and age. *J Soc Issues* 41:89–110.

Weissman, M. M., Klerman, G. L. (1977) Sex differences and the epidemiology of depression. *Arch Gen Psychiatry* 34:98–111.

Weissman, M. M., Sholomskas, D., Pottenger, M., et al (1977) Assessing depressive symptoms in five psychiatric populations: A validation study. *Am J Epidemiol* 106:203–214.

Zayas, L. H. (1987) As son becomes father: Reflections of expectant fathers on their fathers in dreams. *Psychoanal Rev* 74:443–464.

Chapter 8

Infertility and Modern Reproductive Technology

Infertility. Even among women who have never faced this problem, the word elicits feelings of sorrow and sympathy. As noted by Robinson and Stewart in the previous chapter, motherhood is a fundamental part of our society's definition of woman. While most heterosexual women spend a good portion of their lives trying to prevent an unwanted or poorly-timed pregnancy, they expect that they *can* and *will* have children when the time is right. To reach "the right time" and not be able to bear a child is devastating.

Though women vary in their response to infertility, their experiences have in common certain reactions and emotions. As described by **Woods** and her colleagues in the first article, these include chronic sorrow and concerns about their identity as women. Because childbearing is so central to our notions of femininity, many infertile women feel incomplete or less feminine. They often feel "defective" and alienated from other women. Incorporating the concept of infertility into a woman's self-identify is a struggle which can damage her self-esteem. In addition, the intimate nature of the diagnosis and treatment of infertility makes it difficult for infertile women to receive the kind of social and emotional support that they might expect for other major medical problems. Woods and her colleagues suggest ways in which medical professionals, friends, and family can support a woman as she copes with infertility.

Women also differ in their choices of and responses to infertility treatments. In the last 15 years, medical technology has provided a wide variety of options for the treatment of infertility. **Holmes** describes and critiques the most publicized of these innovations, in vitro fertilization. Ova are "harvested" from the woman's ovaries after hormone stimulation. Fertilization, typically by sperm provided by the woman's husband, takes place in a laboratory with neither prospective parent present. The article by **Holbrook** discusses in vitro fertilization as well as other options, including the low-tech solution of adoption and more controversial options such as artificial insemination by donor and surrogate pregnancy.

The benefits and successes of most of these techniques have been touted by the media on a regular basis ever since the first "test-tube" baby was born in 1978. However, these dramatic accounts overlook the costs of such treatments. As all of the articles in this chapter point out, even for those who can afford the high financial costs associated with most infertility tests and treatments, there are tremendous physical and psychological costs for such treatments. Even "simple" infertility treatments involve detailed discussion of sexual practices with medical professionals, timed intercourse, and post-coital medical examinations which are not only discomforting but depersonalizing. With some of these techniques, including in vitro fertilization, the woman faces serious medical risks from the surgery and prolonged, intensive hormonal treatment. She and her partner lose time from their jobs, and they usually feel as though their lives are on hold. The pursuit of one or several possible treatments lengthens the battle and may create additional distress in those for whom the treatments do not work.

Lauritzen uses his personal experience with modern reproductive technology to discuss feminist objections to these techniques. He concludes that many of the arguments against the further development and use of such technologies are valid. For example, the pressure from friends, family, health care professionals and society in general to pursue every possible option can infringe upon individual freedoms. And the psychological needs of infertile individuals and their potential offspring are usually ignored. There are a number of other moral and ethical issues involved.

These issues are the reason why the messages of the last three articles are for everyone, not just infertile individuals considering their options. They are messages that we all must hear. Though reproductive technology allows some infertile women to have children, the solutions challenge our ethical and legal systems. The embryos and children become products of manufacturing rather than the result of an intimate act of love. Consumers of the "products" (potential parents as well as society in general) may demand that they be without flaw. Given the rapid advances in the field of genetics, reproductive technologies may soon be able to fix "faulty" embryos to meet consumer specifications. This highlights the need for public policy on these issues, because the implications for any less-than-perfect children and for society as a whole are frightening. If allowed to move ahead uncontrolled, without serious critical analysis and without well-formulated public and legal policies, the time may come when *all* potential parents will feel pressured to use technology so that their offspring can be perfect.

For many infertile women, modern reproductive technology is a blessing. It can be an important and rewarding way to deal with infertility, even if a child does not result. But the ethical issues and potential dangers of this technology require us to be alert as to its power and to control its direction, now.

REFERENCES AND SUGGESTED READING

Birke, L., Himmelweit, S., and Vines, G. (1990). *Tomorrow's child: Reproductive technologies in the 90s.* London: Virago Press.
Holmes, H. B., and Purdy, L. M. (1992). *Feminist perspectives in medical ethics.* Bloomington: Indiana University Press.

Raymond, J. G. (1990, November/December). Reproductive gifts and gift giving: The altruistic woman. *Hastings Center Report,* pp. 7–11.

Sandelowski, M. (1988). Without child: The world of infertile women. *Health Care for Women International, 9,* 147–161.

Sokoloff, B. Z. (1987). Alternative methods of reproduction. Effects on the child. *Clinical Pediatrics, 26,* 11–16.

Stewart, D. E., and Robinson, G. E. (1989). Infertility by choice or by nature. *Canadian Journal of Psychiatry, 34,* 866–871.

Infertility: Women's Experiences

Nancy Fugate Woods, FAAN, PhD, Ellen Olshansky, RNC, DNSc,
and Mary Ann Draye, MPH, ARNP

Recent scientific nursing literature and clinical practice yield important information regarding women's varied responses to the diagnosis and treatment of infertility, as well as the multiple pathways women take through the infertility experience. In this article, we examine infertility through women's eyes, explore the influence of the social context on women's infertility experiences, and present ideas for clinical approaches to working with infertile women. Three approaches for nursing practice are suggested: (a) preserving self-esteem, (b) promoting access to social resources, and (c) facilitating use of coping methods to reduce distress.

Infertility is a phenomenon that is much more complex than its medical definition, which refers to the inability to become pregnant and carry a pregnancy to viability after 1 year of intercourse without using contraception (Speroff, Glass, & Kase, 1983). Although a great deal is known about the diagnosis and treatment of infertility, less is understood of the human experience and responses to its diagnosis and treatment. In this article, we focus on women's perspectives on the experience of infertility to convey the varied responses women have to the diagnosis, treatment, and multiple pathways through the infertility experience. Information from recent nursing scientific literature, as well as from women who have shared their experiences of infertility in the context of our clinical practices, is presented. We first present

an overview of various emotional responses to infertility, examining women's responses to diagnosis and treatment and to the options available to them for becoming parents. Next, we explore the influence of the social context on women's infertility experiences. We conclude with suggestions for ways to support women throughout their infertility experiences.

INFERTILITY: WOMEN'S EXPERIENCES

Women's responses to infertility are not universal, nor do they follow a uniform progression. Nevertheless, there are some commonalities in this human experience. Despite the early infertility literature in which authors focused, through psychoanalytic or psychosomatic lenses, on women's emotions as causes of their infertility, there were early attempts to understand human responses to infertility.

Infertility and Grief

Barbara Menning (1977), a nurse and one of the earliest to study the human experience of infertility, analyzed the content of interviews with infertile women and men. She identified themes of stress and grief throughout her interviews. Generally, women expressed surprise at their infertility and subsequently experienced denial, anger, unworthiness or guilt, and depression. Menning distinguished the grief response of infertile women (and men) from the grief response associated with other

This article first appeared in *Health Care for Women International* (1991) 12: 179–190. Copyright © 1991, Hemisphere Publishing Corporation. Reprinted with permission.

losses. Infertility represented a potential loss rather than the loss of an actual child who had been born. Usually people experienced difficulty with or inability to discuss this potential loss. Moreover, infertility represented an uncertain loss, a probabilistic outcome rather than a deterministic one. Others often trivialized the loss—for example, by pointing out the woman's freedom associated with being child-free or by reminding her that she did not have some serious disease like cancer. Finally, there were no rituals of support to help women bear the loss associated with infertility. As a result of her own infertility experience, Barbara Menning founded an organization in 1973 to help others with their responses to infertility. On the basis of the grief model that helped her interpret the experiences of the women and men she had counseled, Menning named the organization RESOLVE. The model for RESOLVE counseling emphasized helping people accept their infertility, reaching resolution about whether they would pursue parenthood, and if so, how they would proceed.

Chronic Sorrow

Unruh and McGrath (1985) questioned the accuracy of the grief model in depicting human responses to infertility. Instead, they proposed a model of chronic sorrow, pointing out that sorrow experienced in infertility occurs not only for what is missing or perceived as lost, but also for what exists. Sorrow better reflects the painful emotions that are caused in part by therapies for infertility. The unusual, contrived procedures to produce the wanted child are unnatural, controlled by others, impersonal, and often painful and expensive. Moreover, emotional responses to infertility do not follow a sequential pattern, as is true for the grief response. An infertile woman may find her responses to infertility and its treatment intertwined and triggered by her menstrual period, pregnancies of other

women, insensitive comments from others, test results, treatment failures, frustrations with the health-care system, miscarriages, communication difficulties with a partner, and breakdown in her support network. Many women experience cyclic hope and despair corresponding to their menstrual cycles. Women who are most persistent in exploring treatment for their infertility become vulnerable to being labeled neurotic, dysfunctional, or maladjusted. Yet it is these persistent women who may experience chronic sorrow for extended periods and whose sorrow may actually increase in intensity through the long diagnostic and treatment period. Rapid acceptance of infertility is incompatible with participation in a demanding fertility investigation and its related treatment. Indeed, few women would continue in a fertility program without the hope that the treatment would be successful.

Given the dramatic changes in the assessment and treatment of infertility between the inception of RESOLVE in 1973 and Unruh and McGrath's work published in 1985, it seems reasonable that a model that accounted for women's experiences in the early 1970s would require modification in the 1990s.

Women's Responses to Infertility Treatment

There is great variability in women's experiences with infertility treatment, ranging from timing intercourse carefully and using clomiphene to induce ovulation to tubal surgery, sperm washing, artificial insemination, gamete intrafallopian transfer, and in vitro fertilization. Variability in treatment may be a function of the extensiveness of the problem producing the infertility and its resistance to self-correction or medical treatment. In other instances, the experience is influenced by the pacing of the diagnostic and treatment procedures a woman might choose. One woman might progress through the entire gamut of diagnostic tests and treatment options within 6 months, whereas others may require several years. Generally, the progression is from low-risk to high-risk diagnostic tests and from low-risk to high-risk treatment options. Usually, treatment starts with drugs, such as clomiphene, human chorionic gonadotropin, or follicle-stimulating hormone, and progresses to possible surgical intervention to correct an underlying problem or to in vitro fertilization or some variation of that procedure (Arditti, Klein, and Minden, 1984; Corea, 1985). Superimposed on that progression may be a pregnancy, pregnancy loss, decision making about adoption, and a reassessment of life values, including the importance of children in one's life. Responses to infertility and to infertility-related experiences with the health-care system become difficult, if not impossible, to disentangle (McCormick, 1980). It is not surprising that some women choose to take time out of a diagnostic and treatment program to reassess their feelings.

Infertility and Women's Identity

Olshansky's (1987a) 45 in-depth interviews, with 32 infertile persons and 13 couples, revealed that those who are distressed by their infertility take on an identity of self as infertile. That identity becomes central, pushing to the periphery other important identities. Olshansky (1987a) found that the process of taking on the identity of infertile involved symbolic rehearsals of being a parent and trying to become a parent, after which individuals take on an *informal identity* of themselves as infertile. Associated with this informal identity is informal fertility work in which they ''play probabilities'' by modifying their diets; changing positions and timing of sexual intercourse; and following suggestions from friends, literature, or media. When these strategies do not result in conception, the woman or couple seek clinical consultation,

taking on a *formal identity* as infertile. This formal identity can be specific, as in the case of a diagnosed cause of infertility, or general, as in unexplained infertility. After clinical confirmation, the couple undertake formal fertility work—the regimens of diagnostic tests, treatments, and surgeries. With greater commitment to fertility work, paradoxically, their infertility becomes all-encompassing as they work so hard at letting go of it. Eventually, infertile couples manage their identity of self as infertile by overcoming it, circumventing it, or reconciling their identity as infertile. Overcoming it occurs as people become pregnant as a result of, or in spite of, medical interventions. Circumventing the identity as infertile occurs through technological means, such as in vitro fertilization or artificial insemination, that allow them to bypass the underlying cause and become pregnant. Reconciling the identity of self as infertile happens through choosing alternatives such as adopting or choosing to be child-free. Although the underlying cause of infertility is not corrected and pregnancy is not achieved through technological means, people come to terms with their inability to bear children. The reconciliation allows the identity as infertile to diminish, becoming more peripheral in their lives. A different mode, remaining in limbo, does not successfully manage the identity as infertile, as couples continue to try to conceive without success.

Infertility as a Multidimensional Experience

Sandelowski and Pollock (1986) explored the experiences of 48 women seeking help at an infertility clinic. The researchers found that infertility was a multifaceted experience, more than merely failure to get pregnant. Women endured treatment for a problem that most women do not face. Common to women's experiences were themes of ambiguity, temporality, and otherness. Women experienced *ambiguity* about the reasons for their infertility, their health-care providers, life goals, pregnancy outcomes, diagnosis, treatment, past or future fertility, and control. Most striking was their uncertainty about their diagnosis and treatment and their love-hate feelings about their health-care providers. Treatment for them represented both a means of control and feeling out of control simultaneously. *Temporality* was reflected in women's comments about their consciousness of time and time limits. They spoke of time wasted; time running out; time-consuming rituals; menstrual cycle time; the cycle of planning, waiting, and reviewing delayed childbirth; and the slowing of time. Another dimension of time was the regimentation of sex and treatment. Women cycled between hope and despair with their menstrual cycles. They spoke of time running out, especially women in their 40s. *Otherness* referred to women's feelings of separation and deviance. They made social comparisons with other women, felt unfairly singled out, described themselves as not fitting in, being left out, not being understood, and feeling defective. They often felt alienated from their pregnant friends. Moreover, the otherness seemed to permeate their relationships with their partners, in that some women demanded support from their husbands, who were less interested in having children than they or who were reluctant to get treatment.

Thirty-nine women who were visiting an infertility clinic at a university hospital described the impact of infertility on their lives in five spheres: their person, their relationships with a life partner, their relationships with family and friends, their involvement in and commitment to work, and relationships with the health-care system (Draye, Woods, and Mitchell, 1988). Women indicated that infertility had a significant impact on their images of themselves, that they felt they were less feminine and incomplete as women, that they had let their partners down

by not having children, and that other life accomplishments seemed less important without children. Indeed, women appraised the effects of infertility as significantly more negative than did their partners. Women also reported significant problems in the area of work. Nearly half agreed that infertility had affected their career plans, such as committing themselves to a career. Sixty percent of the women who worked at home felt they needed to justify staying home because they had no children. Women also reported significant problems with the health-care system. These included feeling their privacy was invaded and that treatment was impersonal (Draye et al., 1988).

Few have traced the human experience of infertility over time. Draye, Mitchell, and Woods (in preparation) followed 24 women over an entire year, beginning at the first clinic visit, then 6 months later, and again at 1 year after the first clinic visit. Women completed questionnaires regarding their appraisals of problems related to infertility, personal resources, social resources, ways of coping, and depression. Women's sense of mastery over life decreased over the three time periods, as did self-esteem and support from a confidant, usually the spouse. Nevertheless, women's appraisals of infertility became less negative over the year, especially in the areas of family relationships and personal life. Three ways of coping—seeking social support, using problem-focused coping, and using avoidance and wishful thinking—declined over the year, with the most rapid rate of decline during the first 6 months. Over time, women used significantly fewer indirect coping behaviors such as avoidance and wishful thinking, but they also sought social support less. By the 12th month, women used more problem-focused coping. Depression declined slightly during the first 6 months and then increased slightly in the second half of the year, consistent with

Unruh and McGrath's (1985) concept of chronic sorrow.

At the first clinic visit and 1 year later, women were asked to describe the problem that was most stressful for them (Woods, Draye, and Mitchell, unpublished data). At the beginning of the study, women described a wide diversity of problems, spanning the areas of personal adjustment, marital relationship, relationships with family and friends, work, and the health-care system. Personal concerns included "feeling inadequate as a woman," "feeling I am almost too old for children" (at age 32), and "feeling sad regarding not having a pregnancy or a baby." Concerns related to relationships with a partner included "sex has become mechanical more and more," "feeling a child would make my marriage whole," and "quality of my marriage." Family and friends figured prominently in the concerns: "family and friends who have small children," "family and friends who are not aware of our desire for children," "other women treating having babies as the easiest thing in the world to do," and "all siblings and friends having babies but me." Problems related to work included "preoccupation with work," "treatment competes with work schedule," "coordinating other parts of my life with the unknown of having children," and "questioning whether to commit to a career or wait until I am pregnant or not." With respect to the health-care system, women described concerns such as "painful tests," "fearing death during surgery," "difficulty keeping appointments for diagnostic procedures," "negative, disease-model approach in the clinic," "lack of insurance coverage for infertility," and "lack of caring regarding this issue."

Many women described their total life as being on hold: "My life seems to be in limbo. I'm afraid to make plans for the future or to prioritize right now." One woman described her feelings of emptiness, lack of personal commitment in life, and "feelings which bordered on despair, especially with the beginning of a new menstrual period." By the end of the year, the dominant responses concerned their health, dealing with the health-care system, and their concerns about adoption. Women reported health-related experiences, such as "having had two miscarriages during the last 6 months," waiting and hoping for the results of tubal surgery, and worrying about secondary infertility after the birth of an infant conceived during infertility treatment. Women who were concerned about becoming parents reported "wondering about starting adoption procedures while continuing treatment," "plunging into adoption," "feeling confused about options—in vitro fertilization versus adoption." Others talked about the feelings of being in limbo that Olshansky (1987a) described: "feeling ambivalent about having children," "inability to throw myself into a career when I think I may be taking pregnancy leave soon," and "wanting a firm yes or no so I can get on with my life."

These findings are consistent with Olshansky's (1987b) study that revealed the profound effects that infertility has on women's career identities. Of interest is that at the beginning of the study women described the centrality of infertility in their lives, consistent with Olshansky's (1987a) descriptions of the identity as infertile, pushing everything else to the periphery. After a year of treatment, women had become pregnant (overcome), were working toward circumventing their infertility through treatment, or were reconciling themselves to infertility and exploring adoption or weighing child-free living, consistent with the trajectory presented by Olshansky (1987a).

INFERTILITY: THE SOCIAL CONTEXT

Social perspectives of women as childbearers influence the context and conditions under

276

which women experience infertility. Unruh and McGrath (1985) pointed out that women's right to control over their bodies is a feminist ideal not yet universally attained. Some women find that mutual participation in health-care decisions is undermined by professionals who withhold information; refuse to evaluate other professionals' competence; blame women for diagnostic and treatment problems; avoid questions, assertions, or emotions; minimize their concerns; and shield them from truthful but upsetting information. Still other women are denied the right to control their own bodies on the basis of social class; infertility treatment is inaccessible to many because of its costs and lack of insurance coverage.

Women experience infertility differently as a function of class. Sandelowski and Pollock (1986) found that women of middle socioeconomic status (SES) were goal oriented in their infertility treatment, emphasizing achievement of pregnancy, whereas lower SES women waited longer to get treatment. Middle SES women seemed to be fighting the infertility experience; lower SES women seemed more accepting of it. For many middle SES women, infertility represented their first experience with adversity, whereas for lower SES women, adversity had been part of life.

Unruh and McGrath (1985) also pointed out that women commonly have been blamed for the conditions that have caused them personal distress. Sandelowski (1986) suggested that infertility is intimately related to choice. Indeed, she used the metaphor of *Sophie's Choice* to illustrate the plight of the infertile woman. Whether choosing the problem or choosing the treatment, a woman feels culpable about the choice. It is not uncommon for women to feel guilty about and responsible for their infertility. Linking IUD use to tubal damage, birth control pills to ovulation disorders, abortions to cervical damage, and decisions to delay childbearing to lowered fertil-

ity indicts women for their life-styles while deflecting attention from iatrogenically induced problems.

Unruh and McGrath (1985) also pointed out that "women have been socialized to value themselves primarily through their childbearing roles." Thus, it is not surprising that many women who experience infertility question their self-worth (Draye et al., 1988) and take on an identity as infertile that becomes greater than life or their relationship with a life partner (Olshansky, 1987a).

Moreover, women experience greater distress than men and appraise the impact of infertility on their lives as more negative and more encompassing than do men. Comparing men and women who participated in their study, Draye et al. (1988) found that women had a lower sense of mastery in life and lower self-esteem than their male partners. Women also had more symptoms of depression and felt less supported than their partners. Nevertheless, they engaged in more of every type of coping activity: seeking social support, problem-focused coping, and avoidance and withdrawal.

Unruh and McGrath (1985) also showed that women have more in common with one another than their differences in fertility. Infertility is one end of a continuum. Choice seems to be the underlying dimension linking both unplanned pregnancy and the infertility experience. Avoiding pregnant women or women with children seems to reinforce the feelings of isolation and separateness among women. This separateness becomes problematic for women who experience infertility and subsequently become pregnant. They have unique concerns and are like both their infertile and fertile counterparts. Infertile women who become pregnant often respond with joy and ambivalence: joy over the desired conception and ambivalence due to the difficulty in getting pregnant or worries about the pregnancy. These women are likely to feel surprise and resent the delay in their life plans. They are likely to be reluctant to share the news with infertile friends and with fertile friends and family. They may worry about losing the baby and feel fearful of sharing the joyful feelings, even with their partner. As a result, they are likely to be isolated. Soon they are cut off from their supportive network of both infertile and fertile friends. Worry that pregnancy may be another disappointment is reinforced by their being labeled as *high risk* by their health-care providers. These women sometimes conceal their pregnancies and attend RESOLVE meetings, feeling more comfortable there than at childbirth groups (Rothman, 1986)! Women who miscarry may feel the same alienation from women who are mothers. They experience an emotional roller coaster, plummeting from excitement and joy to sadness and uncertainty. Feelings of surprise, fear, hope, anxiety, denial, frustration, self-blame, ambivalence, guilt, and betrayal are not uncommon (Borg and Lasker, 1981; Swanson-Kauffman, 1986).

THEORETICAL PERSPECTIVES FOR HELPING

Theoretical models for supporting women through the paths they choose to deal with infertility have begun to emerge. Understanding the social context of infertility experiences as a basis for providing support to women is central to the model we propose. Woods et al. (in preparation) found that infertile women who felt supported by their social network preserved their self-esteem and sense of mastery over life. In turn, these women appraised infertility as less negative than women who had lower self-esteem. The women with high self-esteem and mastery also used more problem-oriented coping and were less depressed than their counterparts. Women who appraised their infertility as negative used more avoidance and withdrawal coping strategies, wished the problem

would go away, sought social support less often, and were more depressed.

Looking back on their experiences with infertility over the past year, women were able to identify what helped them. Relationships with a supportive spouse and sensitive, supportive friends helped, as did sharing experiences with other infertile women. They named several other helpful resources: (a) having personal strengths, including patience and the ability to focus on the problem; (b) taking time out to put their problem in perspective; (c) taking action, such as applying for adoption; (d) investing in other spheres of life, such as work and other children; and (e) having faith in God (Woods, Draye, and Mitchell, unpublished data).

The results of this review suggest three primary approaches to helping infertile women:

1. Preserving their self esteem
2. Promoting access to social resources
3. Facilitating their use of coping methods that reduce distress.

These actions are presented in detail in Table 1.

CONCLUSION

We have presented an overview of women's varied responses to infertility, drawing from current nursing literature as well as from our clinical experiences of working with infertile women. Although much diversity exists in women's responses, common themes are apparent that suggest the theoretical foundation for suggested clinical nursing approaches to working with infertile women that we have presented.

BIBLIOGRAPHY

Arditti, R., Klein, R., and Minden, S. (Eds.). (1984). *Test tube women: What future for motherhood?* London: Pandora.
Borg, S., and Lasker, J. (1981). *When pregnancy fails.* Boston: Beacon Press.

Table 1. Three Primary Approaches to Helping Infertile Women

Preserving self-esteem can be fostered through:

1. Acknowledging the validity of women's experiences and emotional responses
2. Minimizing the interference of infertility treatment with other sources of esteem, such as work; and
3. Offering mutual participation and promoting control in the health-care system by offering choices, encouraging vacations, scheduling tests and treatments in a flexible fashion, sharing knowledge, and supporting a woman's decision to stop treatment

Promoting access to social resources reflects the importance of positive affect and affirmation in infertile women's lives. Social resources can be enhanced through:

1. Preserving emotional ties to family and friends by providing them with information about infertility, its treatment, and how to help
2. Helping infertile women share their experience with others, especially other women
3. Permitting and acknowledging that one's partner may be at a different place emotionally and may also need support in working through feelings related to infertility; and
4. Lobbying for health policies that include third-party payment for infertility services

Finally, facilitating the use of coping methods that reduce distress can occur through:

1. Balancing direct coping methods (such as problem solving) with indirect coping methods (such as avoidance and withdrawal)
2. Expanding support networks to include others experiencing infertility, such as through RESOLVE, to deflect support demands from spouses; and
3. Integrating attention to emotional care and physical care in infertility clinics

---

Corea, G. (1985). *The mother machine: Reproductive technologies from artificial insemination to artificial wombs.* New York: Harper & Row.

Draye, M., Woods, N., and Mitchell, E. (1988). Gender differences in the infertility experience. *Health Care for Women International, 9,* 163–175.

Draye, M., Mitchell, E., and Woods, N. (in preparation). Infertility: Women's experiences throughout the first year of treatment.

McCormick, T. (1980). Out of control: One aspect of infertility. *Journal of Obstetric, Gynecologic, and Neonatal Nursing, 9*(4), 205–206.

Menning, B. (1977). *Infertility: A guide for the childless couple.* Englewood Cliffs, NJ: Prentice-Hall.

Olshansky, E. F. (1987a). Identity of self as infertile: An example of theory generating research. *Advances in Nursing Science, 9*(2), 54–63.

Olshansky, E. F. (1987b). Infertility and its influence on women's career identities. *Health Care for Women International, 8*(2–3), 185–196.

Rothman, B. (1986). *The tentative pregnancy: Prenatal diagnosis and the future of motherhood.* New York: Penguin Books.

Sandelowski, M. (1986). Sophie's Choice: A metaphor for infertility. *Health Care for Women International, 7,* 439–453.

Sandelowski, M., and Pollock, C. (1986). Women's experience of infertility. *Image, 18*(4), 140–144.

Speroff, L., Glass, R., and Kase, N. (1983). *Clinical gynecologic endocrinology and infertility.* Baltimore: Williams & Wilkins.

Swanson-Kauffman, K. (1986). Caring in the instance of unexpected early pregnancy loss. *Topics in Clinical Nursing, 8*(2), 37–46.

Unruh, A., and McGrath, P. (1985). The psychology of female infertility: Toward a new perspective. *Health Care for Women International, 6,* 369–381.

Woods, N., Draye, M., and Mitchell, E. (unpublished data). Women's experiences with infertility: Problems and ways of coping.

Woods, N., Mitchell, E., and Draye, M. (in preparation). Personal and social resources, coping and depression in infertile couples. *Research in Nursing and Health.*

SUGGESTED ADDITIONAL READINGS

Bernstein, J., and Mattox, J. H. (1982). An overview of infertility. *Journal of Obstetric, Gynecologic, and Neonatal Nursing, 11*(5), 309–314.

Elstein, M. (1975). Effect of infertility on psychosexual function. *British Medical Journal, 3,* 296–299.

Friedman, B. M. (1981). Infertility workup. *American Journal of Nursing, 81*(11), 2040–2046.

Kraft, A. D., Palombo, M. A., Mitchell, D., Dean, C., Meyers, S., and Schmidt, A. W. (1980). The psychological dimensions of infertility. *Ameri-*

can *Journal of Orthopsychiatry, 50*(4), 618–628.

McCusker, M. R. (1982). The subfertile couple. *Journal of Obstetric, Gynecologic, and Neonatal Nursing, 11*(3), 157–162.

Rosenfeld, D. L., and Mitchell, E. (1979). Treating the emotional aspects of infertility: Counseling services in an infertility clinic. *American Journal of Obstetrics and Gynecology, 135*(2), 177–180.

Salzer, L. (1986). *Infertility: How couples can cope.* Boston: Hall.

Sandelowski, M. (1987). The color gray: Ambiguity and infertility. *Image, 19*(2), 70–74.

Shapiro, C. H. (1982). The impact of infertility on the marital relationship. *Social Casework: The Journal of Contemporary Social Work, 63*(7), 387–393.

Wiehe, V. (1976). Psychological reactions to infertility: Implications for nursing in resolving feelings of disappointment and inadequacy. *Journal of Obstetric, Gynecologic, and Neonatal Nursing, 5*(4), 28–32.

In Vitro Fertilization:
Reflections on the State of the Art

Helen Bequaert Holmes, Ph.D.

ABSTRACT: *Using data collected from in vitro fertilization/embryo transfer (IVF/ET) programs, which have mushroomed worldwide during the past eight years, I summarize current clinical practices and results with regard to success rates, patient selection, ovulation induction, oocyte retrieval, semen collection, laboratory fertilization, embryo transfer, and pregnancy outcome. Each step may entail risks, clinical problems, and/or ethical issues. Among concerns that arise from reflection on the practices and issues are risks to offspring, psychologic/emotional effects, use of women in experiments, possible overuse of IVF, financial issues, and proposed future extensions of reproductive engineering.*

As of June 1986 one-millionth of all people then living on earth had been conceived outside the human body (1). Tremendous amounts of time, effort, and high-level technical and clinical skills have been devoted to producing those babies. Now practically every major city where Western medicine is practiced has at least one in vitro fertilization/embryo transfer (IVF/ET) clinic; many university teaching hospitals have units; private hospitals, group practices, and corporate franchises run programs. Most obstetric and gynecological journals include a substantial number of papers on IVF, and at least two new journals are entirely devoted to this topic. Five world congresses on IVF/ET—three in Europe, one in Australia, one in the United States—have been held (2). Even those who believe that reproduction is a natural human process cannot ignore these developments.

Generally accepted as world leaders are the pioneer programs on three continents: Bourn Hall in Cambridge, England; Monash University in Melbourne, Australia; and the Jones Institute at Eastern Virginia Medical School in Norfolk, VA. These continue to enroll large numbers of patients; to have (except for occasional lapses) the best success rates, to introduce new variations, and to pursue aggressive experimentation; but dozens of other units run close on their heels. Programs dot the map in Australia, Great Britain, West Germany, France, Canada, and the United States. One or more active clinics can also be found in each of Ireland, Sweden, Finland, Denmark, Belgium, the Netherlands, Switzerland, Austria, Italy, Spain, Yugoslavia, Greece, Israel, Saudi Arabia, South Africa, India, Japan, Korea, Hong Kong, Taiwan, New Zealand, Colombia, and Brazil. According to the American Fertility Society, there are now 160 centers in the United States, about one-quarter of them privately run (3).

In less than 10 years IVF/ET seems to have changed from a promising innovation to a standard procedure, and has become an integral part of obstetrics/gynecology training. World-recognized IVF experts, such as Howard W. Jones, Jr., of Norfolk, claim that success with IVF/ET is almost equal to natural reproduction (4–7).

The typical description found in newspapers or popular magazines runs something like this. An infertile woman is given fertility drugs to stimulate the development of many eggs in her ovary. These eggs are aspirated in the operating room, and are fertilized in the laboratory with her husband's or a donor's sperm; after these divide and become pre-embryos, they are transferred to the future mother's uterus by a catheter inserted through the cervix. Such descriptions deceptively simplify the process for IVF/ET requires experts in reproductive endocrinology, pelvic reparative surgery, andrology, and tissue culture working together in finely tuned teamwork (8). Some insist that a nurse-coordinator is vital to their success. Clinics often "work out the bugs" on 50 or more patients before they succeed in producing their first live infant (9).

What is meant by "success" in IVF/ET? Most clinics report success percentages as "pregnancies per embryo transfer"; however, since embryo transfer is the sixth of seven steps, clearly failures in the first five steps are excluded by this approach. Some authors therefore have accused programs of massaging data, or misleading the public (9–11). Furthermore, the word "pregnancy" is used inconsistently in that some units include both preclinical and clinical pregnancies, whereas others count only clinical pregnancies (6,9). The preclinical pregnancy, more commonly called biochemical, is defined as a menstrual period delayed 14 days or less and a serum titer of 10 to 25 mIU/ml human chorionic gonadotropin (hCG) 11 to 13 days after oocyte retrieval (2,6,12–14). Clinical pregnancy is recorded when a gestational sac and heartbeat are detectable with ultrasound. "Clinical pregnancy," however, includes ectopic pregnancies, miscarriages before 12 weeks, spontaneous abortions at any time, preterm births, and stillbirths, as well as live term deliveries. A minority view is that the take-home baby per stimulation cycle rate is the only really useful statistic for a patient (9,10). This statistic would give a 4 to 5 percent success rate for 1985–1986 in the United States (3). Sher, of the Northern Nevada Fertility Center (NNFC), urges all centers to use the statistic he coined, the "probable birth rate," which is the number of pregnancies carried beyond three months per number of egg retrievals performed. Then the NNFC, according to an independent audit, has a 20 percent probable birth rate (3).

Some IVF practitioners now speak of "seven essential steps" of IVF (5,15) and predict that once scientific medicine perfects each step, laboratory baby conception will be more successful than in nature (5). Some suggest that everyone should then reproduce by IVF (16,17), and that genetic tests eventually could ensure the birth of few or no defective offspring (18–20).

I will describe IVF as it is practiced in early 1988 by examining each of those seven steps.

THE SEVEN STEPS OF IVF/ET

Step 1: Patient Selection

The original rationale for developing IVF/ET was to enable women with obstructed fallopian tubes to bear children (21). Soon it became extended to women infertile for other reasons, such as endometriosis, ovulation disorders that fail to respond to ovulation induction, adhesions, antisperm antibodies in cervical mucus or blood, and idiopathic infertility (9,11,17,21–23). More significantly, it was extended to subfertile men, that is, males with oligospermia, limited sperm motility, and antisperm antibodies (21,22,24). With azoospermic males, if artificial insemination by donor (AID) previously failed, AID plus IVF is used. Thus, a fertile woman may be exposed to the risks of IVF procedures because of her husband's subfertility or infertility (9,18). Statistics on success with IVF in various etiologies of infertility are difficult to interpret because of so many confounding variables, methods of categorizing patients, and ways of reporting results. In general, pregnancy success appears to be independent of the cause of infertility (2).

Other criteria for patient selection vary from program to program (23,25,26). Most clinics will not accept women over age 40 years (9,25–27). The NNFC accepts no woman with a uterus under 70 mm in length from ectocervix to fundus, and no male with fewer than 5×10^6 motile sperm per ml (26). Almost all units require previous extensive infertility work-ups of both male and female, including postcoital tests, hysterosalpingography, exploratory laparoscopy, and sperm analysis.

A few programs accept women without ovaries, and recruit donor ova from other patients, sisters, or candidates for tubal ligation (28–30). Still fewer units accept women without uteri and then search for fertile women to be gestators (31), although information on this is scanty due to the secrecy in which such procedures must be carried out. By May 1987 two successful term deliveries from such gestators were known (31,32); later the popular press covered a grandmother in South Africa who bore triplets for her daughter (33).

Psychologic screening is part of the pretreatment in some programs, but not all (25,26,34). In their screening process, the NNFC has eliminated 17 percent of applicants (26), but most programs screen only to identify couples who may require emotional support, or to encourage self-referral for psychiatric help (34).

A pretreatment interview, however, must determine whether the couple has adequate finances. Most countries with national health insurance now cover IVF; they often have long waiting lists and accept couples only if the wife will be under age 40 when she reaches the top of the list. In countries with fee-for-service medicine, waiting lists may be very short. Some insurance companies cover part or all of IVF—often around $5000 per attempt—sometimes for an extra premium. In the United States, Maryland, Massachusetts, Hawaii, and Texas are the first four states to require insurers to cover infertility treatments (35).

So far as I know, no program accepts lesbians or single women; many, however, accept unmarried couples "in a stable relationship" (23,27). Couples with children (with secondary infertility, or with children from a previous marriage or before a tubal ligation) are usually not excluded (27). Indeed, previous pregnancy correlates with a higher success rate (25–27). Moral gatekeeping, combined with financial considerations and the professionals' choice of acceptable clinical conditions, confuses any ethical analysis of patient selection. When a program accepts couples with less serious infertility problems, not only will its census and income increase, but so will its success rate (9,10).

Step 2: Induction of Ovulation

Since the one ovum per month normally produced by menstruating women is difficult to find surgically, and since accurate determination of the moment of ovulation is essential, IVF candidates are primed with fertility drugs to induce multiple ovulation at a predictable time. Furthermore, data over the past six years show clearly that the more embryos transferred, the higher the chance of pregnancy (36,37).

The protocol for administering fertility drugs varies from unit to unit, and there is no worldwide or even national agreement on what works "best." Many studies compare one regimen with another, but often these do not use randomized controls and/or do not correct for the number of embryos transferred (2). The most commonly used regimen before 1984 (38), also in use in 1987, calls for daily injections of 50 or 100 U of clomiphene citrate on days 5 through 9 of the menstrual cycle, followed by human menopausal gonadotropin (hMG) for several days; hMG (Pergonal) is about 50 percent luteinizing hormone (LH) and 50 percent follicle-stimulating hormone (FSH). One to three ampules are administered daily or every other day, equivalent to 75 to 225 IU FSH per day (38). Plasma estrogen is assayed daily (twice daily close to ovulation), and urine LH is monitored. Ultrasound examinations assess follicular size. When the leading follicle reaches a diameter of about 18 mm or an LH surge is anticipated, hMG is stopped for a day or two, and then human chorionic gonadotropin (hCG), 4,000 to 10,000 IU, is administered.

Oocyte retrieval is scheduled 30 to 36 hours after the hCG (38,39).

If the LH surge occurs too soon so that ova have already left the follicles, or if too few follicles ripen, the cycle is "cancelled." At established programs, 10 to 35 percent may be cancelled (9,40,41).

One recent attempt to prevent cancellation and to "perfect" ovulation induction is computer (instead of human) assessment of the ultrasound data and the hormone levels in blood and urine. A second gambit is to use oral contraceptive pills to synchronize the pre-IVF menstrual cycle in a group of candidates in an attempt both to standardize drug regimens for all patients and to make efficient use of the time of personnel (17,42).

A third strategy is apparently effective enough that it may soon become part of the standard regimen. A gonadotropin-releasing hormone (GnRH) agonist, applied several times a day as a nasal spray (or sometimes subcutaneously), is used to block endogenous production of FSH and LH on women who previously were "poor responders." Used during the preceding cycle, and/or in the retrieval cycle with Pergonal, this hormone analog suppresses the normal ovarian control functions of the pituitary (pharmacologic hypophysectomy) in women who have dominant follicle formation or premature LH surges (17,40,43–46). Buserelin is the GnRH analog used in Europe (17,40,44,46); leuprolide acetate is used in the United States because it is the only analog that has approval of the Food and Drug Administration for use in clinical experiments (43,45).

Risks and Issues

Clinicians are concerned to tread the fine line between superovulation and ovarian hyperstimulation syndrome. Some advise aspirating all enlarged follicles, even in cancelled cycles, to avoid ovarian cysts and hypertrophy (Belaisch-Allart J et al., poster displayed at the 5th World Congress on IVF and ET, Norfolk, VA, 5–10 April 1987). Probably, cases of premature menopause (47), ovarian hypertrophy (Karow WG et al., poster displayed at the 5th World Congress on IVF and ET, Norfolk, VA, 5–10 April 1987), ovarian cysts (Belaisch-Allart J et al., poster), and ovarian cancer (48,49) after fertility drug treatment are underreported because there is little follow-up of patients who undergo IVF. In one unit in Melbourne, two-thirds of 92 unsuccessful IVF candidates had endocrinologically abnormal menstrual cycles three months later (44). In a French survey, former patients reported increased menstrual irregularities (Belaisch-Allart J et al., poster). Irregular menstrual periods, erratic flow, and cramping may seem trivial, but they can be handicaps; women who must cope with such problems regularly may be able to accomplish little else. It is also reasonable to speculate that women treated with fertility drugs, especially repeatedly, will be at risk for endometrial, cervical, ovarian, and breast cancer for two or three decades.

The risk to both mother and fetus from ovulation induction that first comes to mind—multiple pregnancies—is discussed under Step 6. Possible risks to offspring of fertility drugs and ultrasound are discussed under Reflections.

Step 3: Oocyte Retrieval

Oocytes must be suctioned from follicles by puncturing each one with a double-channel aspirating needle. Laparoscopy is the classic method, for which women are given general anesthesia with endotracheal intubation, and pneumoperitoneum (pure CO_2 or a mixture of 5% O_2, 5% CO_2, and 90% N_2) (2,26,39,50). Three instruments are inserted in the abdomen: the laparoscope, the retrieving needle (left lower quadrant), and holding forceps (right lower quadrant) (39). The ovaries are turned and explored; each ripe follicle is punctured,

and its contents are aspirated and immediately examined microscopically for ova by an embryologist. Usually all accessible ripe follicles in both ovaries are punctured, except in some Roman Catholic hospitals where a maximum of three is the policy. Successful oocyte retrieval (i.e., one or more) was 82 percent in Australia in 1983 (41), with an average of 2.3 ova per successful laparoscopy; current figures are slightly higher.

Laparoscopy requires considerable technical support, however, and cannot be used if patients have extensive pelvic adhesions (2). Because of these drawbacks and morbidity from surgery and endotracheal intubation (one recorded death [51]), clinicians in Europe have invented and pioneered what they believe to be less traumatic methods of oocyte retrieval, using ultrasound to find ripe follicles (ultrasonically directed oocyte retrieval, UDOR, or ultrasonically guided aspiration, UGA). These methods have been accepted enthusiastically worldwide, and they may almost completely replace laparoscopic egg recovery (2,7,52). Three basic routes (and sometimes combinations) are used; transabdominal/transvesical; periurethral; and transvaginal. Patients may receive no anesthesia, local anesthesia at the site of needle puncture, light epidural, sedation (e.g., atropine, pethidine, and/or diazepam), or, in a few clinics, general anesthesia (53). The aspirating needle is guided to each follicle by tracking its movements on an ultrasound screen. Before 1985 ultrasound transducers were placed on the abdomen; a full bladder was required for visualization. In 1985 the vaginal transducer came on the market and is now the most popular with practitioners. Because the head of this transducer is only 15 to 30 mm from the ovary, follicles can be pictured clearly without a full bladder (54).

In 1982 in Copenhagen, Lenz developed the first method, transabdominal/transvesical retrieval (TUDOR) (53,55); Wikland in Gothenburg used it extensively (53,56). A patient's bladder is filled with sterile saline; the needle passes through the abdominal wall, into and out of the bladder, and into the ovary, with a separate puncture for each follicle. The procedure was popular in 1984–1985. In 1984 in London, Parsons pioneered periurethral retrieval (57). Here also the bladder must be filled with saline before a hollow tube, through which the retrieval needle passes, is inserted into the urethra. The needle moves into the bladder and punctures it near each ripe follicle in each ovary.

The third (transvaginal) UDOR method is now mostly widely used. First tried in Gothenburg with the transabdominal ultrasound transducer (53,56), it was refined by Dellenbach and his team in Strasbourg when the transvaginal transducer came into use (54). The aspirating needle passes through the wall of the posterolateral pouch of the vagina directly into the ovary, first on one side, then on the other. For best results, the vaginal transducer has a needle guide on its side; patients are sometimes given a paracervical block as local anesthesia (58).

Early users of UDOR did not recover as many oocytes as they had by laparoscopy, but the rates have since become comparable.

Risks and Issues

The rare complications of laparoscopy include misplacement of carbon dioxide from the pneumoperitoneum causing acidosis and cardiac arrest (59); air embolism (52,60); respiratory arrest from anesthesia (61), the cause of one death reported in the public press (51); stress hormone response (62); puncture of internal organs (52,60,61); hemorrhage (63); resurgence of pelvic inflammatory disease; and pelvic adhesions (64).

Supporters of UDOR point out that it avoids the dangers of anesthesia, is less expensive, requires fewer personnel, and as an outpatient procedure requires neither hospital nor operating room (7,52,55,65). In a study of UDOR at 20 centers over two years, one fatality was reported (66). Discomfort from the full bladder, pain when the ovary is penetrated, mild hematuria, and pain afterward have discouraged widespread adoption of TUDOR (7,9,53,55,67), or have led to using general anesthesia (61). The currently popular transvaginal method is followed by bleeding that varies from light spotting to moderate (67); it also risks injury to blood vessels, trauma to viscera, and infection by contamination from the vagina (68). However, patients who have experienced both transvaginal UDOR and laparoscopy greatly prefer UDOR (65,67).

In any outpatient procedure, patients are at risk if hospital services turn out to be required. Ashkenazi et al. (61) reported that 14 of 102 patients who underwent TUDOR were hospitalized one to six days with minor complications of cystitis, pyelonephritis, hemoperitoneum, hydrosalpinx, ovarian hyperstimulation, or exacerbation of previous pelvic inflammatory disease. Cohen et al. (58) hospitalized 2 of 177 patients for severe pain after transvaginal UDOR. Serious complications, such as bowel and blood vessel punctures, are rare but do occur (65–67). Finally, in private doctors' offices and in privately funded clinics, patients do not have the protection (such as it is) of ethics committees or of institutional review boards.

Step 4: Semen Collection

If oocytes are recovered, the husband or partner is asked to produce a semen sample. Masturbation under stress, especially if the man is the subfertile member of the couple, can be another hurdle. With oligospermic men, samples are often obtained before the day of oocyte retrieval to test appropriate methods of enhancing the semen (24). For example, evaluation of a split ejaculate (first fractions in one container, remainder in another) may demonstrate which fraction has more motile sperm. Collection directly into culture medium is useful when there is severe sperm agglutination, and aggregation of several sperm samples may help when the sperm count is very low (24). For azoospermic men or those whose sperm failed to fertilize in a previous IVF attempt, donor semen is used.

The semen sample is washed and centrifuged twice in culture medium, and the most active sperm then swim up to the top of a falcon tube (69,70).

Step 5: Fertilization and Cleavage

An embryologist or medical technician, or a team, takes over at this point. An aliquot of active, washed sperm is added to each oocyte; sometimes oocytes are held for a day or so first if they seem immature. The culture media vary from center to center: most programs use a standard, balanced salt solution with added buffers, pyruvate, amino acids, and antibiotics (2,38,71). As a source of protein, heat-inactivated blood serum—the patient's own, donor serum, or cord blood from placentas—is usually added; however, some units report success using bovine serum albumin or no protein supplement (2).

New IVF programs have low success with fertilization (50,71); therefore considerable experience with mouse IVF is recommended (50,71,72), and outside experts are often invited as consultants. For example, in the IVF-Australia franchise that is bringing the Australian procedure to the United States, the only Australian still working in this country is an embryologist (Battle-Mutter P; personal communication, 1987). In the best laboratories, in 90 to 95 percent of oocyte retrievals at least one egg is fertilized (11,15,73); of these zygotes about 90 percent develop further.

Step 6: Embryo Transfer

If one or more embryos progress to at least the 4-cell stage, usually about 48 hours after oocyte retrieval, they are placed in a stiff catheter and deposited through the patient's cervix near the top of the fundus equidistant from the cornua (74), usually with the woman in the knee-chest position (74). The transfer is usually done quickly without anesthesia; rarely it can be painful and difficult, especially if a tenaculum (long-handled forceps with hooks for grasping the cervix) is required. More and more units use ultrasound at this stage to ensure that the catheter does not scrape the endometrium.

To attempt to increase success by circumventing steps 5 and 6, Asch (75) of San Antonio, Texas, in 1984 invented and implemented the procedure known as gamete intrafallopian transfer (GIFT), also called tubal sperm-egg transfer (TSET). For this, a patient must have at least one functioning fallopian tube. Ovulation induction and oocyte retrieval by laparoscopy proceed as in standard IVF, but the semen sample is obtained prior to surgery. While the patient is still under anesthesia, the embryologist selects the best oocytes, puts them with culture medium and washed sperm in a catheter, and passes the catheter through the laparoscope. The contents are injected into the ampulla of the fallopian tube (75). If enough oocytes are collected, two or three per tube may be injected. In some Roman Catholic hospitals GIFT is accepted because the gametes make contact inside a woman's body (76).

With GIFT, extra oocytes often are fertilized in the laboratory, and may be used for regular ET in the same cycle, or, after freezing, in a later GIFT cycle. In 1987 both ET and GIFT are used in the same cycle in some clinics; each unit has its own policy about which method to choose if there are too few ova. For example, NNFC uses GIFT only if more than eight oocytes are obtained, and inserts two oocytes with sperm down each fallopian tube; remaining oocytes are fertilized in vitro and replaced in the same cycle (77). At the Women's Hospital of Texas, two or three oocytes are saved for IVF and the rest used with GIFT (Grunert GM et al., poster displayed at the 5th world congress on IVF and ET, Norfolk, VA, 5–10 April 1987).

Because most GIFT patients have idiopathic infertility, and because patient selection and clinical methods differ from center to center, it is hard to determine whether GIFT is more successful than IVF. One randomized, controlled clinical trial comparing GIFT and IVF/ET in couples with idiopathic or male infertility showed no significant difference in pregnancy rates (76).

Risks and Issues

One important issue for patients and physicians is how many embryos to transfer. The chances of pregnancy are higher if many are transferred, but then, so are the chances of a multiple pregnancy (2,36–38,73,74,78). Edwards thinks that multiple implantations occur more frequently than expected from the binomial distribution; he believes that a sort of synergism takes place, which he calls "helping," in which an embryo capable of implantation seems to help its siblings that otherwise are not; he speculates that decidualization or luteotrophic factors are involved (37,73). Multiple pregnancy introduces significant risks, jeopardizing mother and child with a higher incidence of morbidity from problems such as toxemia, gestational diabetes and hypertension, congenital anomalies, intrauterine growth retardation, and malpresentation (78–81), as well as social problems of caring for triplets and higher-order multiple offspring (82). From 1979 through 1986 in Australia, 22.2 percent of 1345 IVF pregnancies of at least 20 weeks' gestation were multiple (83); approximately 38 percent of the surviving babies are twins, triplets, or quadruplets (80,83).

A second issue is what to do with "spare" embryos. Before cryopreservation was possible, the choices were to discard, donate to another infertile couple, or donate for experimental uses. Now, if a clinic offers embryo freezing, most couples elect that. In April 1986 Ashwood-Smith estimated 20 normal births worldwide from frozen embryos (84), with the most experienced centers at Bourn Hall, Monash University, and the Béclère Hospital near Paris. The estimate one year later is 65 (17). Experimental data are still unclear about the best cryoprotectant, the best stage to freeze, and rapid versus slow freezing (84–86). An embryo is considered to have survived thawing if 50 percent or more of its blastomeres are still intact. Typical results are as follows: at Béclère, 62 percent survival of 2- to 9-cell embryos frozen in propanediol (87); at Monash, 57 percent survival of 8-cell embryos after slow freezing in dimethylsulfoxide (85); and at Bourn Hall, 52 percent survival of blastocysts after slow freezing in glycerol and fast thawing (84). Many advocates of embryo freezing believe that embryos have the best chance of implanting in a normal (unstimulated) cycle. In Melbourne, the first 27 surviving embryos gave a 22 percent pregnancy rate (85), about the same as the rate with fresh embryos. Since no further laparoscopy is needed, freezing of embryos does increase the rate of pregnancies per laparoscopy (85–87).

Banking of human embryos raises many ethical, social, and legal problems about storing human life, and questions about what to do if parents die, disagree about disposition of the embryos, never reclaim them, and so on (88). Therefore many units have attempted the very difficult process of freezing unfertilized human oocytes, working first with animals such as the mouse, rat, and rabbit (88). As of December 1986 three live births from frozen eggs had been reported: twins in Adelaide (89) and a singleton in Bonn (88).

Step 7: Establishment of Pregnancy

Although only 20 to 30 percent of embryo transfers result in pregnancy (38), making the

Table 1. Survey Results: Embryo Transfer Outcome in In Vitro Fertilization Programs*

Survey	Third World Congress (38)		National Perinatal Statistics Unit (83)		Fifth World Congress (90)		USA National Registry (91)	
Numbers of centers reporting	65 worldwide		16 Australasia		55 worldwide		41 USA	
Years covered	Through Jan. 84		1979–1986		Through Dec. 85		1985, 1986	
Number of embryo transfer cycles	7993		NR		NR		5253	
	#	%	#	%	#	%	#	%
Pregnancies	1700	[21.3]	2242			NR		NR
Biochemical pregnancies	285	16.8†	336	15.0†		NR		NR
Clinical pregnancies	1084	63.8†	1906	85.0†	2342	NR	822	[15.6]
Ectopic	19	1.8	104	5.5	122	5.2	42	5.1
Spontaneous abortion	324	29.9	454	23.8	616	26.3	291	35.4
Ongoing	572	52.8	NA		141?	6.0	NA	
Stillborn		NR	49	2.6		NR	9	1.1
Deliveries‡	523	24.4	1296	68.0	1463	62.5	480	58.4

* Based on voluntary reporting with no peer review of data submitted. Percentages refer to outcome per confirmed clinical pregnancy except these in brackets, which are per ET cycle.
† Percentage per all pregnancies.
‡ For Congress surveys, may include stillborn.
NR = not reported and not calculable from data given; NA = not applicable because report postdates all pregnancies.

sixth and seventh steps the most inefficient aspect of IVF/ET, many consider that this percentage is very close to the natural rate of implantation in fertile women (25%). With progress in medical science, they predict IVF/ET will become better than nature (5–7).

Rates of biochemical and ectopic pregnancies, spontaneous abortions, and preterm births seem to vary considerably from program to program, almost as if they were local phenomena. When data are pooled, however, the incidence of each of these turns out to be higher than in the general population. Table 1 shows data from the World Collaborative Study for the Third World Congress (38), the Study for the Fifth World Congress (90), the 1987 report from the National Perinatal Statistics Unit in Sydney, Australia (83), and the American Fertility Society 1988 register (91). Except perhaps for the Australian one, these surveys are of little value because clinics voluntarily decide whether to participate, and there is no peer review (3). For example, for the Fifth World Congress Study, only four Australian teams sent data because they were sending results to their own national registry. For the American Fertility Society register, no data came from the two programs in the United States that are estimated to have the second and third largest numbers of IVF pregnancies (3,91).

Using some sets of reasonably accurate data from the Australian Perinatal Statistics Unit (as in Table 1) (83), the first 100 deliveries at the Jones Institute (4), and the first 100 at Béclère Hospital in France (12), percentages of biochemical pregnancies are 15.0, 18.1, and 15.5; of ectopic pregnancies, 5.5, 1.3, and 2.1; and of spontaneous abortions, 23.8, 14.8, and 19.0, respectively.

Risks and Issues

Clinicians concerned about the low pregnancy rates have some evidence that hyperstimulation does not prepare the endometrium properly for implantation (92), and that ultrasound (93), fertility drugs (94), or punctures (95) may make it difficult for follicles to form functioning corpora lutea.

Patients are sometimes advised that, if they are not pregnant, their menstrual period may come up to seven days early (NNFC patient flow sheet, 1987). Some units try "luteal phase support," daily injections of progesterone or hCG starting at oocyte retrieval and continuing sometimes for several weeks (96). Of 72 teams that gave data on luteal phase support for the Third World Congress, 32 used progesterone, 20 used hCG, and 20 used nothing (38). In 1986 hCG was used after embryo transfer in 50.9 percent of all IVF pregnancies reported to the Australian Perinatal Statistics Unit (83). However, randomized clinical trials have shown that neither progesterone (94) nor hCG (97) improves pregnancy success rates.

Reflections

What About the Children?

The health of resulting children may be the most important assessment of IVF/ET. In the collaborative study for the Third World Congress, only nine birth defects were reported in 600 term deliveries (38). Recent data from 1697 IVF births in Australia, however, show 6.7 times the expected incidence of transposition of the great vessels, five times the expected cases of spina bifida, and 1.3 times the expected rate of hypospadias (83,98). Reliable information is underascertained because many women have their babies in hospitals not associated with their IVF unit (98).

The recent Australian study also reported that 21 percent of the IVF births occurred before 35 weeks; that 23.7 percent of all IVF pregnancies were multiple, with about 38 percent of the babies twins, triplets, and quadruplets (83,99); and that 36.4 percent of the live and stillborn infants weighed less than 2500 g. The perinatal death rate was 46.0 per 1000 births (83).

Children born from IVF seem to have little follow-up beyond the first year, yet there are good reasons to keep them under observation. Some conditions to consider include failure to thrive, neurological damage from the frequent ultrasound examinations during early pregnancy (100), and reproductive tract abnormalities, including compromised genitalia and adolescent cancers, from residual exogenous hormones in the mother's body during pregnancy (101). The children also may be at risk for emotional problems from being a "precious child," purchased at great price (11).

The "Roller-Coaster"

Some authors concerned about the psychological well-being of women who undergo IVF refer to the procedure's "roller-coaster effect" (3,11). When any of the seven steps succeeds, the patient and her partner have an emotional high—tremendous rejoicing that one more hurdle has been passed. When a step fails, there is a depressive low (11,15), even though, as is clear from the descriptions above, practically nothing the couple can do will influence the success of any step. In a survey of 29 Dutch women who had undergone treatment, a majority reported that the stress of waiting to see if they were pregnant was the most unpleasant part (102). One noted that, after the infertility tests she had had previously, the physical pain of IVF was nowhere near as miserable as the psychologic stress. Among 121 Australian couples who abandoned IVF after one attempt, the second most common reason for drop-out (after finances) was the associated stress, anxiety, and depression (103).

On the other hand, some enthusiastic participants seem almost addicted (11). One New Zealander wrote on an unpublished questionnaire in 1986, "I find IVF very exciting and hardly stressful at all. . . . I have had 7 successful cycles, a total of 16 embryos transferred and had 1 biochemical pregnancy. I will continue to have as many more cycles as I can get until my age becomes a problem." When surveyed, most candidates say that the technology has given them new hope (11,104). Even when they know about the low success rates, they still believe that the odds are in their favor (11,102,104).

Experimental Subjects

Another concern is that infertile women who seek IVF almost invariably end up as subjects in research. A male partner interviewed by Lasker and Borg (11) complained, ". . . pretty soon we realized those guys were only spending ten minutes with us if we were lucky . . . The whole process is so much black magic . . . You get the impression you're part of an experiment, just a little cog in their big machine."

The American Fertility Society requires members of its In Vitro Fertilization Special Interest Group to carry out research and submit papers to the annual meeting (8). Some researchers randomize incoming patients, some use patients as their own controls (previous treatment regimen vs current regimen), and some compile data retrospectively. Since any one variation in a treatment step may be no better than any other, one could argue that experimentation is harmless. However, I am concerned about 1) the treatment of women as guinea pigs, causing physicians who are sincerely sympathetic to the pain of infertility to lose sight of their patients as whole persons; 2) the difficulty for a women who is desperate for a child to say "no," that she will not participate in an experiment; 3) the tiny possibility of obtaining meaningful results from such experiments—each woman's physiology is different, the cause of her infertility is different, and the subfertility of her husband is different, and, although one may deliberately manipulate variables in one step of IVF, the chance variations within the other six steps remain uncontrolled; 4) the even tinier likelihood that results from these

experiments will actually influence treatment, for clinicians get into ruts (one example is luteal phase support, continued by most programs despite experimental data showing it does no good); and 5) the risks of mid- and long-term sequelae of experimental manipulations, even if it is assumed that short-term effects are adequately monitored in most IVF programs.

Enthusiastic research continues on "perfecting" each of the seven steps, often focusing on minutiae, as seen in the titles of papers presented at fertility society meetings worldwide. Hormone regimens are compared, methods of detecting follicle size are described, follicular fluid is analyzed, new methods for luteal phase support are devised, and so forth. In the United States and in the private clinics in Great Britain, patients often are financially supporting their physicians' research projects.

Treatment-Independent Pregnancy

Some women on IVF waiting lists become pregnant without treatment. At the Dalhousie University Fertility Centre in Nova Scotia, 61 percent of 437 pregnancies in 1145 infertile couples occurred independent of treatment (105). At McMaster University in Ontario, 3 of 12 patients who failed to become pregnant with IVF conceived naturally 10 to 12 months later (106). At the Ohio State University hospitals, of women without tubal blockage, 13.9 percent achieved pregnancies through IVF treatment while 11.3 percent became pregnant without (14). Therefore, couples who seek IVF may have as much success conceiving naturally as by virtue of IVF.

Finances and Resources

In the United States entrepreneurs are finding infertility a lucrative field. By one estimate, the procedures are a $30- to $40-million market (3). The director of clinical research at Serono Laboratories (Randolph, MA), the only U.S. producer of Pergonal, estimates that 6000 cycles of IVF were performed during 1986 (3). In the United States the IVF-Australia program, which directs some of its profits back to Monash University, has set up the first two of a chain of IVF clinics. Except when insurance covers some or all of the procedures, IVF is an option only to the wealthy, or to those who incur heavy debts or use up their savings (35). Financial burden is usually given as the main reason that couples drop out after one or more attempts (11,103).

When government health plans cover some or all of IVF/ET, the public costs are huge. Bartels, of the University of Sydney, calculated that from 1980 to 1984 the Australian government spent $32 million as direct Medicare payments to IVF candidates (roughly 70% of their costs), not including the public costs of neonatal intensive care for the resulting premature babies (99). To diminish some of their out-of-pocket expenses, Australian patients are not billed for IVF directly, but are asked to make a tax-deductible donation to their clinic's research program, for example, $500 to the Royal North Shore Hospital in Sydney (99).

Extension of IVF/ET to Wider Populations

The existence of IVF may have made some gynecologists more concerned about preserving women's fertility, about taking complaints of abdominal pain more seriously, and about using conservative surgery in ectopic pregnancies. Just as the category "high risk" in obstetrics expanded, however, so now has the category "infertile." Fertility drugs are being prescribed after shorter periods of trying to conceive. Combinations of drugs (e.g., GnRH and Pergonal) are being tried (17,40) and luteal phase support has become almost routine (38,93,96).

Clinicians have even suggested that everyone ought to reproduce by IVF; this in-cludes sterilizing all teenagers by tubal ligation; later, when ready to reproduce, they can contact their local IVF center (16,17,107). A variant of this proposal is to remove surgically slices of a teenager's ovary, to be frozen until she wants it to be stimulated by hormones to produce an oocyte for an IVF pregnancy (A Templeton, personal communication, 1985). Allegedly, the teenager would also benefit later in her mid-forties because, according to these theorists, the ovary would remain young.

Another push to make IVF/ET routine is contained in the proposal to test for genetic anomalies before a pregnancy starts (19,20,107). Researchers are already removing single cells from embryos at the 8-cell stage or later to test for chromosome number defects, for parts of chromosomes containing defective genes, and for genes that make defective enzymes (18,20). To date, DNA probes for the Y chromosome to detect sex have been successful (108).

Conclusion

The general public and perinatal caregivers have been led to believe that IVF/ET is a solution to infertility. Press stories from IVF centers are often headlined "Miracle Baby." The public controversies are ethical and social ones: should embryos be frozen, should they be used in experiments, and should surrogate wombs be permitted, and, if so, should the gestating mother be paid? These issues are not trivial, but they affect only a small percentage of the portion of IVF candidates who complete step 5 and get embryos. Larger issues are the risks to mothers and offspring, the misrepresentation of success, the pressure on infertile couples to keep trying, the increasing reliance on technologic solutions, and the diversion of money, resources, and physicians' talents away from pressing community health needs into a procedure that may create more morbidity than it cures.

REFERENCES

1. Hodgen GD. Infertility: year 2001. Presented at the second annual conference for IVF Nurse-Coordinators, Norfolk, VA, 3–5 April 1987.
2. Boyers SP, DeCherney AH. Human in vitro fertilization and embryo transfer: an overview. In: Mishell DR, Kirschbaum TH, Morrow CP, eds. *The Yearbook of Obstetrics and Gynecology*. Chicago: Year Book, 1987:413–459.
3. Raymond CA. In vitro fertilization enters stormy adolescence as experts debate the odds. *JAMA* 1988;259:464–465,469.
4. Andrews MC, Muasher SJ, Levy DL, et al. An analysis of the obstetric outcome of 125 consecutive pregnancies conceived in vitro and resulting in 100 deliveries. *Am J Obstet Gynecol* 1986;154:848–854.
5. Jones HW Jr. Keynote address. Presented at the second annual conference for IVF Nurse-Coordinators, Norfolk, VA, 3–5 April 1987.
6. Jones HW, Acosta AA, Andrews MC, et al. What is a pregnancy? A question for programs of in vitro fertilization. *Fertil Steril* 1983;40:728–733.
7. Schulman JD. Laparoscopy for in vitro fertilization: end of an era. *Fertil Steril* 1985;44:713.
8. American Fertility Society. In vitro fertilization special interest group application for membership. *Fertil Steril* 1986;42(suppl 1):90S–94S.
9. Corea G, Ince S. Report of a survey of IVF clinics in the US. In: Spallone P, Steinberg DL, eds. *Made to Order: The Myth of Reproductive and Genetic Progress*. London: Pergamon Press, 1987:133–145.
10. Blackwell RE, Carr BR, Chang RJ, et al. Are we exploiting the infertile couple? *Fertil Steril* 1987;48:735–739.
11. Lasker JN, Borg S. *In Search of Parenthood*. Boston: Beacon Press, 1987.
12. Frydman R, Belaisch-Allart J, Fries N, et al. An obstetric assessment of the first 100 births from the in vitro fertilization program at Clamart, France. *Am J Obstet Gynecol* 1986;154:550–555.
13. Roger M, Belaisch-Allart J, Del Pozo D, et al. Early detection of pregnancy and the concept of biochemical pregnancy after in vitro fertilization. In: Testart J, Frydman R, eds. *Human In Vitro Fertilization*. INSERM Symposium 24. Amsterdam: Elsevier, 1985:247–256.
14. Roh SI, Awadalla SG, Friedman CI, et al. In vitro fertilization and embryo transfer: treatment-dependent versus -independent pregnancies. *Fertil Steril* 1987;48:982–986.
15. Seibel MM, Levin S. A new era in reproductive technologies: the emotional stages of in vitro fertilization. *J In Vitro Fert Embryo Transfer* 1987;4:135–140.
16. Hellema H. Voortplanting zonder seks. *intermediair* 20 February 1987;pp. 47,49,51.
17. Laborie F. New reproductive technologies: news from France and elsewhere. *Reprod Genet Engin: J Int Feminist Anal* 1988;1:77–85.
18. Bartels D. Built-in obsolescence: women, embryo production and genetic engineering. *Reprod Genet Engin: J Int Feminist Anal* 1988;1(2):(in press).
19. Edwards RG. Potential of research on human embryos. In: Feichtinger W, Kemeter P, eds. *Future Aspects in Human In Vitro Fertilization*. Berlin: Springer-Verlag, 1987:245–250.
20. McLaren A. Can we diagnose genetic disease in pre-embryos? *New Scientist* 1987;10 Dec: 42–43,46–47.
21. Acosta AA, Chillik CF, Brugo S, et al. In vitro fertilization and the male factor. *Urology* 1986;28:1–9.
22. Ansari AH. Indications and screening of IVF patients. In: Fredericks CM, Paulson JD, DeCherney AH, eds. *Foundations of In Vitro Fertilization*. Washington, DC: Hemisphere, 1987:163–169.
23. Steptoe P. The selection of couples for *in vitro* fertilization. *Ann NY Acad Sci* 1985;442:487–489.
24. Cohen J, Edwards R, Fehilly C, et al. In vitro fertilization: a treatment for male infertility. *Fertil steril* 1985;43:422–432.
25. Johnston WIH, Oke K, Speirs A, et al. Patient selection for *in vitro* fertilization: physical and psychological aspects. *Ann NY Acad Sci* 1985;422:490–503.
26. Sher G, Knutzen V, Stratton C, et al. In vitro fertilization and embryo transfer: two-year experience. *Obstet Gynecol* 1986;67:309–315.
27. Clark A, Forbes-Smith P, Bycroft R, et al. Reproductive and social history of IVF patients with tubal infertility. *J In Vitro Fert Embryo Transfer* 1986;3:189.

28. Rosenwaks Z. Donor egg. Presented at the second annual conference for IVF Nurse-Coordinators, Norfolk, VA. 3–5 April 1987.

29. Rosenwaks Z. Donor eggs. In: Jones HW, Jones GS, Hodgen GD, Rosenwaks Z, eds. *In Vitro Fertilization Norfolk,* Baltimore, MD: Williams & Wilkins, 1986:270–278.

30. Trounson A, Leeton J, Besanko M, et al. Pregnancy established in an infertile patient after transfer of a donated embryo fertilised in vitro. *Br Med J* 1983;286:835–838.

31. Surrogacy standards set by Mt. Sinai. *CenterViews* (Center for Biomedical Ethics/Case Western Reserve University School of Medicine) 1987;2(2):1,3–4.

32. One story with a happy ending. *Life* July 1987, p. 42.

33. Levin E, Reid S. Motherly love works a miracle. *People* 19 October 1987, pp. 38–43.

34. Freeman EW, Boxer AS, Rickels K, et al. Psychological evaluation and support in a program of IVF and ET. *Fertil Steril* 1985;43:48–53.

35. Saltus R. In vitro method gives birth to new hopes. *Boston Sunday Globe* Nov. 15, 1987; pp. 1,53.

36. Gronow MJ, Martin MJ, McBain JC, et al. Aspects of multiple embryo transfer. *Ann NY Acad Sci* 1985;442:381–386.

37. Speirs AL, Lopata A, Gronow MJ, et al., Analysis of the benefits and risks of multiple embryo transfer. *Fertil Steril* 1983;39:468–471.

38. Seppälä M. The world collaborative report on *in vitro* fertilization and embryo replacement: current state of the art in January 1984. *Ann NY Acad Sci* 1985;442:558–563.

39. Steptoe P, Webster J. Laparoscopy for oocyte recovery. *Ann NY Acad Sci* 1985; 442:178–181.

40. Palermo R, Amodeo G, Navot D, et al. Concomitant gonadotropin-releasing hormone agonist and menotropin treatment for the synchronized induction of multiple follicles. *Fertil Steril* 1988;49:290–295.

41. Speirs AL, Trounson A, Warnes GM. Summary of results. In: Wood C, Trounson A, eds. *Clinical In Vitro Fertilization.* Berlin: Springer-Verlag, 1984:157–163.

42. Patton P, Burry K, Wolf DP, et al. The use of oral contraceptives to regulate oocyte retrieval. *Fertil Steril* 1988;49:716–718.

43. Awadalla SF, Friedman CI, Chin NOW, et al. Follicular stimulation for in vitro fertilization using pituitary suppression and human menopausal gonadotropins *Fertil Steril* 1987;48:811–815.

44. Healy DL. Lessons from using LH-RH analogs in IVF. Presented at the fifth world congress on in vitro fertilization and embryo transfer, Norfolk, VA, 5–10 April 1987.

45. Serafini P, Stone B, Kerin J, et al. An alternate approach to controlled ovarian hyperstimulation in "poor responders": pretreatment with a gonadotropin-releasing hormone analog. *Fertil Steril* 1988;49:90–95.

46. Weise HC, Fiedler K, Kato K. Buserelin suppression of endogenous gonadotropin secretion in infertile women with ovarian feedback disorders given human menopausal/human chorionic gonadotropin treatment. *Fertil Steril* 1988;49:399–403.

47. Hamberger L. Do continuous superovulation treatments damage the ovary? Discussion on clomiphene citrate. In: Edwards RG, Purdy JM, eds. *Human Conception In Vitro.* London: Academic Press, 1982:67–69.

48. Ben-Hur H, Dgani R, Lancet M, et al. Ovarian carcinoma masquerading as ovarian hyperstimulation syndrome. *Acta Obstet Gynecol Scand* 1986;65:813–814.

49. Carter ME, Joyce DN. Ovarian carcinoma in a patient hyperstimulated by gonadotropin therapy for in vitro fertilization: a case report. *J In Vitro Fertil Embryo Transfer* 1987;4:126–128.

50. Jones HW, Jones GS, Andrews MC, et al. The program for in vitro fertilization at Norfolk. *Fertil Steril* 1982;38:14–21.

51. Gomes dos Reis AR. In-vitro fertilization in Brazil: the story told by the newspapers. In: Spallone P, Steinberg DL, eds. *Made to Order: The Myth of Reproductive and Genetic Progress.* London: Pergamon Press, 1987.

52. Massey JB, Kort HI. Oocyte retrieval by laparoscopy. In: Fredericks CM, Paulson JD, DeCherney AH, eds. *Foundations of In Vitro Fertilization.* Washington, DC: Hemisphere, 1987:107–124.

53. Wikland M, Enk L, Hamberger L. Transvesical and transvaginal approaches for the aspiration of follicles by the use of ultrasound. *Ann NY Acad Sci* 1985;442:182–194.

54. Dellenbach P, Nisand I, Moreau L, et al. Transvaginal sonographically controlled follicle puncture for oocyte retrieval. *Fertil Steril* 1985;44:656–662.

55. Lenz S, Lauritsen JG. Ultrasonically guided percutaneous aspiration of human follicles

under local anesthesia: a new method of collecting oocytes for in vitro fertilization. *Fertil Steril* 1982;38:673–677.

56. Wikland M, Nilsson L, Hansson R, et al. Collection of human oocytes by the use of sonography. *Fertil Steril* 1983;39:603–608.

57. Parsons JH, Riddle A, Booker M, et al. Oocyte retrieval for in vitro fertilisation by ultrasonically guided needle aspiration via the urethra. *Lancet* 1985;1:1075–1076.

58. Cohen J, Debache C, Pez JP, et al. Transvaginal sonographically controlled ovarian puncture for oocyte retrieval for IVF. *J In Vitro Fert Embryo Transfer* 1986;3:309–313.

59. Dugan KA. Diagnostic laparoscopy under local anesthesia for evaluation of infertility. *JOGN Nurs* 1985;14:363–366.

60. Mintz M. Risks and prophylaxis in laparoscopy: a survey of 100,000 cases. *J Reprod Med* 1977;18:269–272.

61. Ashkenazi J, David MB, Feldberg D, et al. Abdominal complications following ultrasonically guided percutaneous transvesical collection of oocytes for in vitro fertilization. *J In Vitro Fert Embryo Transfer* 1987;4:316–318.

62. Lehtinen A-M, Laatikainen T, Koskimies AI, Horovoka J. Modifying effects of epidural analgesia or general anesthesia on the stress hormone response to laparoscopy for in vitro fertilization. *J In Vitro Fert Embryo Transfer* 1987;4:23–24.

63. Bergqvist D, Bergqvist A. Vascular injuries during gynecologic surgery. *Acta Obstet Gynecol Scand* 1987;66:19–23.

64. Ashkenazi J, Feldberg D, David B, et al. Ovum pickup for in vitro fertilization: a cause of mechanical infertility? *J In Vitro Fert Embryo Transfer* 1987;4(4):242–245.

65. Lavy G, Diamond MP, Nero F, et al. Transvaginal and transabdominal ultrasound for monitoring of follicular development in an in vitro fertilization and embryo transfer program: patient response. *J In Vitro Fert Embryo Transfer* 1987;4:293–295.

66. Wikland M. Oocyte retrieval under the guidance of a vaginal transducer. Presented at the fifth world congress on in vitro fertilization and embryo transfer, Norfolk, VA, 5–10 April 1987.

67. Honea KL. Ultrasound-guided transvaginal ovum retrieval. In: Fredericks CM, Paulson JD, DeCherney AH, eds. *Foundations of In Vitro Fertilization.* Washington, DC: Hemisphere, 1987.

68. Howe RS, Wheeler C, Mastroianni L. et al. Pelvic infection after transvaginal ultrasound-guided ovum retrieval. *Fertil Steril* 1988;49:726–728.

69. Makler A, Murillo O, Huszar G, et al. Improved techniques for collecting motile spermatozoa from human serum. I. A self-migratory method. *Int J Androl* 1984; 7:61–70.

70. Mahadevan M, Baker G. Assessment and preparation of semen for in vitro fertilization. In: Wood C, Trounson A, eds. *Clinical In Vitro Fertilization. New York: Springer-Verlag, 1984:83–97.*

71. Quinn P, Warnes GM, Kerin JF, Kirby C. Culture factors affecting the success rate of in vitro fertilization and embryo transfer. *Ann NY Acad Sci* 1985;442:195–204.

72. Veeck LL, Maloney M. Insemination and fertilization. In: Jones HW, Jones GS, Hodgen GD, Rosenwaks Z, eds. *In Vitro Fertilization Norfolk.* Baltimore, MD: Williams & Wilkins, 1986:168–200.

73. Edwards RG. In vitro fertilization and embryo replacement: opening lecture. *Ann NY Acad Sci* 1985;442:1–22.

74. Jones HW Jr. Embryo transfer. *Ann NY Acad Sci* 1985;442:375–380.

75. Asch RH, Balmeceda JP, Ellsworth LR, Wong PC. Gamete intra-fallopian transfer (GIFT): a new treatment for infertility. *Int J Fertil* 1985;30:41–45.

76. Leeton J, Rogers P, Caro C, et al. A controlled study between the use of gamete intrafallopian transfer (GIFT) and in vitro fertilization and embryo transfer in the management of idiopathic and male infertility. *Fertil Steril* 1987;48:605–607.

77. Marriage VA, Sher G, Knutzen VK. A combined procedure of GIFT and IVF/ET at the Northern Nevada Fertility Clinic. Presented at the second annual conference for IVF Nurse-Coordinators, Norfolk, VA, 3–5 April 1987.

78. Kerin J. Incidence of multiple pregnancy after in vitro fertilisation an embryo transfer. *Lancet* 1983;2:537–540.

79. Australian In Vitro Fertilisation Collaborative Group. High incidence of preterm births and early losses in pregnancy after in vitro fertilisation. *Br Med J* 1985;291:1160–1163.

80. Bartels D. High failure rates in in-vitro fertilization treatments. *Med J. Aust* 1987; 147:474–475.

81. Hays PM, Smeltzer JS. Multiple gestation. *Clin Obstet Gynecol* 1986;29:264–285.

82. Price FV. Risking high multiparity: multiple gestation and assisted reproduction. *Birth* 1988;15(3):157–163.

83. National Perinatal Statistics Unit, Fertility Society of Australia. *IVF and GIFT Pregnancies, Australia and New Zealand, 1986.* Sydney: NPSU, 1987.

84. Ashwood-Smith MJ, Simons R. The freezing of early human embryos and blastocysts. In: Feichtinger W, Kemeter P, eds. *Future Aspects in Human In Vitro Fertilization.* Berlin: Springer-Verlag, 1987:97–100.

85. Mohr LR, Trounson AO. Cryopreservation of human embryos. *Ann NY Acad Sci* 1985;442:536–543.

86. Testart J, Lassalle B, Belaisch-Allart J, et al. Human embryo freezing in an in vitro fertilization and embryo transfer program. In: Feichtinger W, Kemeter P, eds. *Future Aspects in Human In Vitro Fertilization.* Berlin: Springer-Verlag, 1987:91–96.

87. Testart J. Results of in vitro fertilization with embryo cryopreservation and a recommendation for uniform reporting. *Fertil Steril* 1988;49:156–158.

88. Diedrich K, Al-Hasani S, van der Ven H, Krebs D. Successful in vitro fertilization of frozen-thawed rabbit and human oocytes. In: Feichtinger W, Kemeter P, eds. *Future Aspects in Human In Vitro Fertilization.* Berlin: Springer-Verlag, 1987:50–57.

89. Chen C. Pregnancies after human oocyte cryopreservation. Presented at the fifth world congress on in vitro fertilization and embryo transfer, Norfolk, VA, 5–10 April 1987.

90. Cohen J, Mayaux MJ. IVF pregnancies: results of an international survey. Presented at the fifth world congress on in vitro fertilization and embryo transfer, Norfolk, VA, 5–10 April 1987.

91. Medical Research International. In vitro fertilization/embryo transfer in the United States: 1985 and 1986 results from the national IVF/ET Registry. *Fertil Steril* 1988;49:212–215.

92. Rönnberg L, Isotalo H, Kauppila A, et al. Clomiphene-induced changes in endometrial receptor kinetics on the day of ovum collection after ovarian stimulation: a study on cytosol and nuclear estrogen and progestin receptors and 17β-hydroxysteroid dehydrogenase. *Ann NY Acad Sci* 1985; 442:408–415.

93. Demoulin A, Bologne R, Hustin J, Lambotte R. Is ultrasound monitoring of follicular growth harmless? *Ann NY Acad Sci* 1985;442:146–152.

94. Hamberger L, Hahlin M, Hillensjo T, et al. Luteotrophic and luteolytic factors regulating human corpus luteum function. Presented at the fifth world congress on in vitro fertilization and embryo transfer, Norfolk, VA, 5–10 April 1987.

95. Garcia J, Jones GS, Acosta AA, Wright GC. Corpus luteum function after follicle aspiration for oocyte retrieval. *Fertil Steril* 1981;36:565–572.

96. Jones GS. Luteal phase in a program for in vitro fertilization. In: Jones HW, Jones GS, Hodgen GD, Rosenwaks Z, eds. *In Vitro Fertilization Norfolk.* Baltimore, MD: Williams & Wilkins, 1986:221–237.

97. Buvat J, Marcolin G, Herbaut J-C, et al. A randomized trial of human chorionic gonadotropin support following in vitro fertilization and embryo transfer. *Fertil Steril* 1988;49:458–461.

98. Lancaster PAL. Congenital malformations after in-vitro fertilisation. *Lancet* 1987; 2:1392–1393.

99. Bartels D. The public costs of IVF programs. Presented at the annual symposium of the Australian Academy of the Social Sciences, Melbourne, 11 November 1987.

100. Ellisman MH, Palmer DE, André MP. Diagnostic levels of ultrasound may disrupt myelination. *Exp Neurol* 1987;98:78–92.

101. Cunha GR, Taguchi O, Namikawa R, et al. Teratogenic effects of clomiphene, tamosifen, and diethylstilbestrol on the developing human female genital tract. *Hum Pathol* 1987;18:1132–1143.

102. Holmes HB, Tymstra Tj. In vitro fertilization in the Netherlands: experiences and opinions of Dutch women. *J In Vitro Fert Embryo Transfer* 1987;4:116–123.

103. Mao K, Wood C. Barriers to treatment of infertility by in vitro fertilization and embryo transfer. *Med J Aust* 1984;140:532–533.

104. Zoeten MJde, Tymstra Tj, Alberda ATh. The waiting-list for IVF. The motivation and expectations of women waiting for IVF treatment. *Hum Reprod* 1987;2:623–626.

105. Collins JA, Wrixon W, Janes LB, Wilson EH. Treatment-independent pregnancy among in-

fertile couples. *N Eng J Med* 1983;
309:1201–1206.

106. Jarrell J, Gwatkin R, Lumsden B, et al. An
in vitro fertilization and embryo transfer
pilot study: treatment-dependent and treatment-independent pregnancies. *Am J Obstet
Gynecol* 1986;154:231–235.

107. Chargaff E. Engineering a molecular night-
mare. *Nature* 1987;327:199–200.

108. West JD, Angell RR, Thatcher SS, et al.
Sexing the human pre-embryo by DNA-
DNA in-situ hybridisation. *Lancet* 1987;
1:1345–1347.

Adoption, Infertility, and
the New Reproductive Technologies:
Problems and Prospects for Social Work and Welfare Policy

Sarah M. Holbrook

*In this article, the author examines
the social and psychological issues
raised by infertility and addresses problems resulting from the increasing commercialization of children through
adoption practices as well as through
the proliferation of new reproductive
technologies. The author begins with
a discussion of infertility and considers some aspects of adoption, the traditional solution to infertility. Some
historical, technical, ethical, psychological, and social aspects of artificial insemination, along with newer
developments of surrogacy, such as in
vitro fertilization and frozen embryos,
also are discussed. Recommendations
are suggested for meeting the service
needs of people who have problems
associated with infertility. Finally, the
author stresses the importance of research along with the necessity for social workers to take a leadership role
in helping society both to understand
the ethical issues related to and to develop enlightened public policy on infertility, adoption, and the new reproductive technologies.*

Infertility is a growing social issue that has
encouraged the increasing commercialization
of children through nontraditional adoption
practices as well as through the proliferation
of reproductive technologies. Infertility can
be defined as the inability to conceive after a
year of unprotected intercourse or the inability to carry a pregnancy to term (Shapiro,
1988, p. xi). While there has been an increase
in infertility attributed to such factors as environmental toxicity and delayed childbearing, the supply of healthy babies available
for adoption has simultaneously diminished.
This decrease is due to the legalization of
abortion, the widespread use of birth control,
and the fact that many single women keep
their babies rather than surrender them for
adoption.

THE PROBLEM OF INFERTILITY

Although approximately 50 percent of infertile
couples eventually achieve conception, the goal
of having children is at least temporarily suspended
for these individuals, causing enormous

stress (McEwan, Costello, and Taylor, 1987). Because people grow up thinking that conception and giving birth are matters of choice, they experience infertility as an unanticipated crisis and usually react with shock to the discovery of their condition (Shapiro, 1982). Couples who suspect that they have a fertility problem become pre-occupied with conception and their fantasies and daily activities reflect this (Kraft et al., 1980). They often suffer depression with each onset of menstruation as hopes for pregnancy are dashed once again (Batterman, 1985). Thus, the quest for fertility becomes an obsession (Valentine, 1986). Many people who want a family and are threatened with the reality of being unable to conceive feel desperate and will go to great lengths to become parents.

ADOPTION:
THE TRADITIONAL OPTION

The traditional option for people who have difficulty with conception has been adoption. Historically, adoption took place on an informal basis within the extended family or community. For example, if a rich person wanted to adopt an heir, this could be handled through individualized legislation. In 1851, the first law to establish adoption procedures was passed to ensure the right of inheritance for informally adopted children.

In the nineteenth century, maternal mortality at childbirth coupled with the death of adults from infectious diseases (especially the poverty-stricken immigrants in the cities) produced a large urban population of orphans. Between 1853 and 1929, 90,000 youngsters from the eastern states went on "orphan trains" to the Midwest, where they were publicly displayed and selected by farm families to help them with the labor. As health care improved, the supply of orphans gradually decreased. Agencies that had been caring for orphans decided to expand their services. They began opening maternity homes—saving illegitimate children from what they considered morally repugnant situations—and began placing them for adoption in upstanding, deserving families (Chesler, 1989).

White clients received priority in terms of services. Black children, for the most part, continued to be adopted informally, or they languished in foster homes. Because white children, in general, have always been more in demand and easier to place than black children, discrimination continues despite the recent permanency planning thrust in child welfare. Ironically, neglect of this population has often resulted in more self-determination for black unmarried women, who have been freer to decide whether or not to keep a baby, than for white women, who have experienced enormous pressure from both agencies and the community at large to surrender their illegitimate babies. In addition, adopted children, especially white children placed through agencies, have suffered enormous deprivation of their right to access to information concerning their biological origins. Traditionally, many adopted children were never told about their adoption and often suffered great trauma when they found out by accident. Although parents are now discouraged from keeping adoption a secret from a child, adoptees still do not have the right in this country to learn the identity of their biological parents.

Adoption agencies oriented toward placing white children thrived until the early 1970s, when the supply of babies declined precipitously, due, in part, to the increased availability of safe abortions and to the fact that young women often decided to keep their babies rather than surrender them for adoption. Agencies had to suspend or drastically reduce the placement of babies, leaving infertile people to explore alternatives to the formal adoption system. The rate of independent adoptions (those not involving conventional channels) soared in states such as

New York, where this practice is legal. People flocked to lawyers and "baby brokers," who often charge exorbitant fees even though "baby selling" is illegal (Johnson, 1987). Couples began advertising in newspapers, particularly in small rural towns and on college campuses, offering to pay the medical expenses of the mother-to-be and describing their qualifications as parents. In addition, people further explored the possibilities of adopting a child from abroad. Between 1973 and 1983, the number of foreign adoptions in this country doubled (Rule, 1984). However, despite the proliferation of methods to procure children, the demand continued to exceed the supply of babies. This factor, along with various scientific developments, caused people to pursue vigorously both old and new reproductive technologies.

REPRODUCTIVE TECHNOLOGIES

Artificial Insemination

Approximately 250,000 children are conceived each year in the United States by artificial insemination by donor (often called "AID") (Zimmerman, 1982). This procedure, in which semen from a donor is injected by a doctor into the genital tract of the woman, is most often used when the husband is infertile but the wife can conceive. Recently, single women who want children have also used this process. Approximately 80 percent of women who attempt artificial insemination conceive, although many attempts may be necessary before conception occurs (Noble, 1987).

The practice of artificial insemination began in the United States during the 1880s. However, the procedure was kept relatively secret because of ethical concerns. At the same time, in Europe, Paolo Mantegazza recommended using sperm banks for veterinary and human purposes. He recommended that soldiers going off to war freeze their sperm so they would be able to sire a child if the were incapacitated or killed. However, techniques for freezing and thawing sperm remained relatively inadequate for almost a century. Then came a scientific breakthrough in the 1950s, which involved the development of a glycerol-based preservative that would keep the sperm intact during freezing and thawing (Robinson and Pizer, 1985). In 1953, at the University of Arkansas, three successful pregnancies resulted from frozen sperm. Since then, numerous children have been conceived using this process. Conception has occurred with human sperm frozen for as long as 2 1/2 years (Fletcher, 1988).

Approximately 30 sperm banks exist in the United States. None is listed in the phone book for fear of being the target of protestors. The largest sperm bank in the world, the Idant Sperm Bank in New York City, has over 30,000 specimens and has sired over 11,000 babies since 1971. Yet, despite advances in the freezing process, the majority of inseminations use fresh semen. This practice reflects many doctors' belief that conception occurs more readily with sperm that has not been frozen. However, this policy has become controversial because frozen (as opposed to fresh) sperm can be quarantined and guaranteed thereafter to be free of the acquired immune deficiency syndrome virus (Frank and Vogel, 1988).

Traditionally, the operations of sperm banks have been cloaked in secrecy. In part to ward off attempts at outside regulation, they have regulated themselves through the American Association of Tissue Banks (AATB). Of the 23 states regulating artificial insemination, only a few require prospective donors to have standard medical screenings. Historically, the majority of donors have been medical students who receive payment for each semen donation (Noble, 1987). Although in theory these students give consent to have their sperm disseminated, they are told nothing about the outcomes of their donations (Reamer, 1987). Little exploration has been done to examine the attitudes and feelings of these students with regard to this practice. However, one study described the fact that later in life some of these doctors have second thoughts about having sired numerous children, none of whom they will ever know. Some doctors living in less populated areas of the country worry that their own children might unknowingly marry one of their half-siblings (Baran and Pannor, 1989).

A major problem exists because most children conceived via artificial insemination have never been told about the circumstances surrounding their conception. Traditionally, most couples were advised by authorities not to tell anyone about the artificial insemination procedure, thus enabling these couples to keep the husband's infertility a secret. Also, the husband is not required by law to adopt the child. Consequently, hundreds of thousands of children (Noble, 1987) have been unknowingly deprived of the basic facts about their origins, an enormous violation of their rights. Another problem occurs when a person does learn about his or her origins via artificial insemination but cannot find biological information about the father if the donation was made through a sperm bank. Such a bank's records, if they exist at all, are normally not made available (Baran and Pannor, 1989).

Surrogacy

If in some respects artificial insemination involves adoption of a sperm, the practice of surrogacy has pursued a diametrically opposed approach that might be characterized as the adoption of an egg via ''rental'' of a womb. The term ''surrogacy'' is something of a misnomer, as historically the surrogate mother donates her egg and bears the child for another couple, making her the biological mother (Andrews, 1989). Surrogacy is used when the wife is unable to conceive or unable to carry a pregnancy to term. Her husband's sperm is used to artificially inseminate the surrogate mother.

Surrogate motherhood has occurred informally throughout the ages. As Field (1988) pointed out, in the Bible when ''Sarah, Rachael, and Leah were infertile, they gave their handmaids—Hagar, Bilhah, and Zilpah—to have babies for their husbands'' (Genesis 16:1–4, 15; 30:1–10, as quoted in Field, 1988). Over the years, people who could not have children persuaded friends, relatives, or strangers to carry babies for them. Then, in the mid-1970s, contract surrogacy emerged. By 1986, about 500 children had been born using this method (Field, 1988). As scientific techniques have become more sophisticated, new options have become available. For example, if a wife has viable eggs but is unable to carry a pregnancy to term, her cycle can be synchronized with that of the surrogate mother, after which doctors can retrieve her eggs, fertilize them with her husband's sperm, and then implant the embryo into the surrogate (Perloe and Christie, 1987). In this case, the surrogate mother becomes the gestational but not the biological mother.

Typically, surrogate mothers in recent years have been paid about $10,000 for their services (Liebmann-Smith, 1989). The fact that a mother receives money for conceiving a child intentionally to give the baby away has raised profound issues that society will have to work toward resolving. In terms of pay, baby selling is illegal in this country. However, proponents of paid surrogacy state that surrogate mothers are not paid for the baby but rather for the time, effort, and pain of bearing the child and that the child's own biological father is supplying the supportive payment (Kolbert, 1986). Many people feel that a woman has a right to determine what she wants to do with her own body, including renting the space in her womb (Freedberg, 1989). However, others such as Field

(1988) claim that fees for surrogacy could result in an underclass of breeder women (perhaps evoking visions of *1984* or *Brave New World*.) In terms of self-determination, one must ask whether women should be denied payment for surrogate services even if economic conditions in society prompt them to choose this line of work. (By contrast, it is interesting to note that few people in society have complained about the practice of paying male donors for their sperm.) At the time he heard the Baby M case, Judge Harvey Sorkow suggested that "The surrogate father's sperm is legally recognized in all states. The surrogate mother is not. If a man may offer the means for procreation, then a woman must equally be allowed to do so" (Andrews, 1989, p. 165). Another question that arises concerns the issue of who is liable if the "product" (the baby) is defective or does not meet the parents' expectations and who will take care of such a child (Noble, 1987).

Much of what has been written about paid surrogacy has focused on the rights and responsibilities of parents. More importantly, the implications of paid surrogacy must also be determined for the children involved. Some experts feel that the babies are the ultimate victims of this procedure. Speaking about these children, lawyer Sharon De Angelo stated that "Their very existence was prenegotiated, predesigned, and contracted for just like any other commercial transaction. The child is a product with his or her status indistinguishable from other manufactured goods" (Andrews, 1989, p. 261). Whatever the merits of this business analogy, professional social workers, along with society as a whole, will have to come to terms with the meaning of surrogacy for the child—whether that child is an offspring who is to be given away by his or her biological mother or whether that child is the sibling of a child who resides in the surrogate mother's household. In this connection, Chesler (1989) raised some important issues:

Who is a child's mother? The woman who gives birth to her? Or the woman married to the child's father? The woman who actually takes care of her? Or the woman who can offer her the most money? . . . Is a child's true mother really her father? Does a child need a biological mother, if her father wants to take exclusive care of her—without involving any women? . . . Are most biological mothers "unfit" or are they less fit than genetic fathers or adoptive mothers? Should biological motherhood be abolished in the "best interests" of the child? What is a "fit" mother? Who should decide? . . . Would each child be better off served by a minimum of four "mothers": she who donates the egg, she who incubates the fetus and gives birth, she who legally adopts the newborn, and she who is the child's primary caregiver? (p. 8)

Much research and careful thought are needed in this area. Meanwhile, in *The New Fertility and Conception,* Stangel (1988) advised that "surrogacy at this time represents a vast area of uncharted waters and any couple considering entering into such an agreement should do so with great caution, if at all" (p. 210).

In Vitro Fertilization

A more high-technology reproductive technology, in vitro fertilization, is also fraught with complexities and ethical problems, some of which pertain to its commercialization. In vitro fertilization refers to a process by which a doctor stimulates a woman's ovaries with medication, removes several eggs in a surgical procedure called a laparoscopy, and fertilizes them in a petri dish. The resulting embryos are then implanted into the womb. This technique became a reality in 1978 when Louise Brown was born after years of work by Dr. Robert Edwards and Dr. Patrick Steptoe in Oldham, England. In 1979, Howard and Georgeanna Jones brought in vitro fertilization to the United States and set up a clinic at the East Virginia Medical School (Perloe and Christie, 1987).

The average cost for in vitro fertilization is about $5,000 per attempt. Recently, variations of this procedure have become available—for example, gametic intrafallopian transfer, in which eggs are extracted, combined with sperm, and injected into the fallopian tube where, with luck, conception takes place. Although in vitro fertilization technology is impressive, the results have been less than impressive. Of approximately 200 clinics performing in vitro fertilization worldwide (Frank and Vogel, 1988), most have had little or no success. Nevertheless, about 5,500 in vitro babies have been born in the United States, and about 600 of those were born last year (Chartrand, 1989). However, controversy continues to plague the in vitro procedure, especially at clinics where misleading information concerning success rates (as well as other questionable practices) has been published recently. Also, many people worry that creating life outside the womb will upset the natural order of things or violate God's intent. Zimmerman (1982) described the issue as follows: "Scientists are presumptuous in believing that the natural system of genetic programming can be duplicated without disturbing or harming it when so little is known about how it works" (p. 238).

Frozen Embryos

A related area of controversy pertains to the freezing of embryos. This addresses a major problem created by in vitro fertilization; when several eggs are fertilized in the lab and then implanted, the mother risks multiple pregnancy, which can endanger her life as well as that of the fetuses. By freezing embryos, doctors can implant fewer at a time without having to repeat the extremely uncomfortable, expensive, and time-consuming process of retrieving and fertilizing new eggs (Godwin, 1989). However, problems arise with regard to what to do with the leftover embryos after pregnancy occurs. Ironically,

the process of using new technology to produce children has created embryonic orphans (Rothman, 1989). Recently, Lieber (1989) wrote about a related situation in an article entitled "A Piece of Yourself in the World":

> In 1981 Elsa and Mario Rios, a wealthy California couple who wanted to have a child, sought the services of the Queen Victoria Medical Center fertility clinic, in Melbourne, Australia. Each had had a child from a previous marriage, though Elsa's ten-year-old daughter had recently been killed while playing with a gun. Elsa, thirty-seven, was treated with fertility drugs, and three developing eggs, or oocytes, were surgically extracted from her ovaries. The eggs were combined in a petri dish with sperm from an anonymous donor (her fifty-four-year-old husband was infertile). One resulting embryo was placed in her uterus. The others underwent cryopreservation, a process of freezing in liquid nitrogen. After ten days Elsa spontaneously aborted. Distraught, she decided against becoming pregnant again soon. The Rioses were killed in a plane crash in 1983. They died without wills, leaving an estate of $8 million. Among the "survivors" were the two frozen embryos. (p. 76)

After much controversy, legislation was passed in Australia to allow these two embryos to be "adopted" and implanted in another woman if a suitable recipient became available. Currently, Mary Sue Davis and Junior Lewis Davis, a couple in the process of a divorce, are fighting over the custody of six frozen embryos:

> Mr. Davis maintains that the embryos, now in storage at the Fertility Center of Eastern Tennessee in Knoxville, are not alive and that the central issues are purely legal ones involving joint property of the marriage. His lawyer says the issue is simple: Mr. Davis does not want his wife to bear a child using the embryos after they are divorced . . . But that is exactly what Mrs. Davis wants to do. And she insists that the embryos are living and that the case

involves custody issues and questions related to a woman's right to choose whether to bring pregnancy to term.[1] (Smothers, 1989, p. 1)

This country has no national policy or laws regarding frozen embryos. In late 1985, Congress established a Biomedical Ethics Board to study some of these issues (Grobstein, 1988).

TOWARD THE FUTURE

As a profession, social work must work toward helping society cope with the many facets of the infertility crisis and with the problems and opportunities created by the new reproductive technologies. As reported by Lee and Morgan (1989), "The changing reproductive processes offer at once opportunities for liberation and for enslavement. The genesis and revelation of reproductive technology and its power biomedically to determine, manage, and control reproduction, has piloted medical science across a Rubicon for which there is no return ticket" (p. 2). Social workers must take a leadership role and approach these challenges on the levels of service and policy.

At the service level, people coping with infertility problems need many types of assistance. They need guidance on securing appropriate medical treatment, counseling with regard to the frightening and sometimes painful aspects of medical problems, assistance in explaining feelings about alternatives such as in vitro fertilization or artificial insemination, and help in coping with the failures as well as the successes of these attempts (Shapiro, 1986). Accepting a diagnosis of infertility can be an agonizing process, and people often need support in confronting their permanent inability to bear a child. Those considering adoption need services to help them evaluate their readiness, learn about the process, decide upon the type of adoption (for example, domestic versus foreign), deal with the legal aspects, sort out finances, and so on. Similarly, people considering surrogacy and pregnant women contemplating the surrender of their children for adoption need access to many services, including skilled counseling with regard to the options available, reliable legal advice, and medical help. Adoptees or offspring created by new reproductive technologies (especially those struggling with issues regarding their natural, biological, or adoptive parents) and biological parents (who may have surrendered their children long ago, given them up in surrogacy arrangements, or donated sperm to sperm banks) need access to counseling.

Because of these complexities as well as the growing need for services, social workers need to be trained in the fields of adoption, infertility, and the new reproductive technologies (Reid, 1977). Schools of social work should develop courses to train social workers and others such as lawyers and medical practitioners to deal with the range of adoption and infertility issues, with special emphasis on the ethical concerns raised by the new reproductive technologies. For example, Miall (1989) recently pointed out that extreme technological intervention encourages a system of values that devalues involuntary childlessness. In any case, perhaps a requirement for certification or licensing of people providing guidance in this field could improve services and make it easier for the public to find reliable professionals. In the future, many decisions will be made in society regarding such issues as surrogacy, the use of sperm banks, and providing adoptees and the offspring created by new reproductive technologies with identifying information. Research relating to the effects of these procedures on those involved (especially with

---

1. Since this article went to press, Circuit Court Judge W. Dale Young (Maryville, Tennessee) announced his decision that embryos are people rather than property and should go to their mothers. He also ruled that human life begins at conception.

regard to the children and their identity) needs to be done (Richardson, 1987). Schools of social work must become centers for some of this research.

The social work profession also needs to take a leadership role in making needed services available to all. For example, many adoption and infertility services are available to people with money but usually not to the poor (Morales, 1977). This inequality becomes more evident when one considers the high rate of infant mortality in this country, mostly among the minority poor ("Bad Luck Babies," 1990). To quote Frank and Vogel (1988), "While the health care system allows the wealthy to conjure up babies out of petri dishes, the same system affords little care to poor infants who have been conceived without medical intervention" (p. 125). Perhaps social workers should use some of the problems and opportunities caused by the new reproductive technologies not only to work toward resolving new issues but also to highlight and point the way toward ameliorating existing injustices.

As the profession that provides the bulk of counseling in this country, social work is in a good position to learn about the effects of infertility, adoption practices, and the new reproductive technologies on families and to contribute, through observation and research, to knowledge in these areas. Perhaps most importantly, social workers must use knowledge, experience, and commitment to meet the needs of humanity by helping to develop and to formulate a more enlightened public policy concerning the problems of infertility and the new reproductive technologies.

REFERENCES

Andrews, L. (1989). *Between strangers*. New York: Harper & Row.

Bad luck babies. (1990, March 29). *New York Times*, p. A22.

Baran, A., and Pannor, R. (1989). *Lethal secrets,* New York: Warner Books.

Batterman, R. (1985). A comprehensive approach to treating infertility. *Health and Social Work,* 10(1), 46–54.

Chartrand, S. (1989, April 11). Experts assess a decade of in vitro fertilization. *New York Times,* p. C5.

Chesler, P. (1989). *Sacred bond.* New York: Vintage Books.

Field, M. A. (1988). *Surrogate motherhood.* Cambridge, MA: Harvard University Press.

Fletcher, J. (1988). *The ethics of genetic control.* Buffalo, NY: Prometheus Books.

Frank, D., and Vogel, M. (1988). *The baby makers.* New York: Carroll & Graf.

Freedberg, S. (1989). Self-determination: Historical perspectives and effects on current practice. *Social Work,* 34, 33–38.

Godwin, P. (1989, March). The high cost of fighting infertility. *Changing Times,* pp. 73–78.

Grobstein, C. (1988). *Science and the unborn,* New York: Basic Books.

Johnson, J. (1987, October 29). Baby brokering: Desperate girl's case reveals shadowy world. *New York Times,* p. B1.

Kolbert, E. (1986, October 6). A dispute on Baby M. *New York Times,* p. B3.

Kraft, A. D., Palombo, J., Mitchell, D., Dean, C., Meyers, S., and Schmidt, A. W. (1980). The psychological dimensions of infertility. *American Journal of Orthopsychiatry,* 50, 618–627.

Lee, R., and Morgan, D. (1989). Is birth important? In R. Lee and D. Morgan (Eds.), *Birth-rights* (pp. 1–16). London, England: Routledge & Kegan Paul.

Lieber, J. (1989, June). A piece of yourself in the world. *The Atlantic Monthly,* pp. 76–80.

Liebmann-Smith, J. (1989). *In pursuit of pregnancy.* New York: Newmarket Press.

McEwan, K. L., Costello, C. G., and Taylor, P. J. (1987). Adjustment to infertility. *Journal of Abnormal Psychology,* 96, 108–116.

Miall, C. E. (1989). Reproductive technology vs. the stigma of involuntary childlessness. *Social Casework,* 70, 43–50.

Morales, A. (1977). Beyond traditional conceptual frameworks. *Social Work,* 22, 387–393.

Noble, E. (1987). *Having your baby by donor insemination.* Boston: Houghton Mifflin.

Perloe, M., and Christie, L. G. (1987). *Miracle babies.* New York: Penguin Books.

Reamer, F. G. (1987). Informed consent in social work. *Social Work,* 32, 425–428.

Reid, W. J. (1977). Social work for social problems. *Social Work,* 22, 374–381.

Richardson, J. W. (1987). The role of a psychiatric consultant to an artificial insemination by donor program. *Psychiatric Annals,* 17(2), 101–105.

Robinson, S., and Pizer, H. F. (1985). *Having a baby without a man.* New York: Simon & Schuster.

Rothman, B. K. (1989). *Recreating motherhood.* New York: W. W. Norton.

Rule, S. (1984, July 26). Couples taking unusual paths for adoptions. *New York Times,* pp. A1, B5.

Shapiro, C. H. (1982). The impact of infertility on the marital relationship. *Social Casework,* 63, 387–393.

Shapiro, C. H. (1986). Is pregnancy after infertility a dubious joy? *Social Casework,* 67, 306–312.

Shapiro, C. H. (1988). *Infertility and pregnancy loss.* San Francisco: Jossey-Bass.

Smothers, R. (1989, April 22). Divorcing couple fighting over embryos: Joint property or offspring? *New York Times,* p. A1.

Stangel, J. (1989). *The new fertility and conception.* New York: New American Library.

Valentine, D. D. (1986). Psychological impact of infertility: Identifying issues and needs. *Social Work in Health Care,* 11(4), 61–69.

Zimmerman, S. L. (1982). Alternatives in human reproduction for involuntary childless couples. *Family Relations,* 31, 233–241.

What Price Parenthood?
Paul Lauritzen

Current reproductive technology challenges us to think seriously about social values surrounding childbearing. Thoughtful discussion must combine careful attention to the experience of pursuing parenthood by technological means with principled reflection on the morality of this pursuit.

The ceremony goes as usual.

I lie on my back, fully clothed except for the healthy white cotton underdrawers. What I could see, if I were to open my eyes, would be the large white canopy of Serena Joy's outsized colonial-style four-poster bed, suspended like a sagging cloud above us. . . .

Above me, towards the head of the bed, Serena Joy is arranged, outspread. Her legs are apart, I lie between them, my head on her stomach, her pubic bone on the base of my skull, her thighs on either side of me. She too is fully clothed.

My arms are raised; she holds my hands, each of mine in each of hers. This is supposed to signify that we are one flesh, one being. What it really means is that she is in control, of the process and thus of the product . . .

My red skirt is hitched up to my waist, though no higher. Below it the Commander is fucking. What he is fucking is the lower part of my body. I do not say making love, because this is not what he's doing. Copulating too would be inaccurate, because it would imply two people and only one is involved. (Margaret Atwood, *The Handmaid's Tale*).

This chilling depiction of the process of reproduction in the fictional Republic of Gilead provides a vision of what many feminists believe will soon be reality if the new reproductive technologies (NRTs) proceed unchecked. Children will be thought of exclusively as products. Women will be valuable merely as breeders. Reproductive prostitution will emerge as women are forced to

Reprinted with permission of the Hastings Center from The Hastings Center Report, March/April, 1990, pp. 38–46.

sell wombs, ovaries, and eggs in reproductive brothels.[1] Men will be more fully in control than ever.

There was a time when I would have dismissed such claims as wildly alarmist. I still believe these worries to be overblown. Yet I have been haunted by this passage from *The Handmaid's Tale* as I have stood, month after month, holding my wife Lisa's hand as she, feet in stirrups, has received my sperm from the catheter that her doctor has maneuvered into her uterus. Indeed, once, when the nurse asked me to stand behind her to hold steady an uncooperative light, I wondered perversely whether I shouldn't, like Serena Joy, play my symbolic part by moving rhythmically as the nurse emptied the syringe.[2] Having experienced the world of reproductive medicine firsthand, I believe we need to take a closer look at feminist objections to NRTs.

Here, then, I will review objections that some feminists have raised to such technologies as *in vitro* fertilization (IVF), artificial insemination with donor sperm (AID), and surrogate motherhood, and relate these objections to my own experience. I take up feminist objections because, although there is no one "feminist" response to reproductive technology, some of the most forceful objections to this technology have come from writers who are self-consciously feminist and understand their opposition to the NRTs to be rooted in their feminism.[3] Moreover, the international feminist organization FINRRAGE (Feminist International Network of Resistance to Reproductive and Genetic Engineering) is committed to opposing the spread of reproductive technology, and it is from this group that we have the most sustained and systematic attack on NRTs in the literature.[4] I relate these objections to my own experience because, in my view, all serious moral reflection must attend to the concrete experience of particular individuals and thus inevitably involves a dialectical movement between general principles and our reactions to particular cases. The need to balance appeals to abstract rules and principles with attention to the affective responses of particular individuals has not always been sufficiently appreciated in moral theory or in medical ethics.[5] Yet such a balance is necessary if we are to understand both how moral decisions are actually made and how to act compassionately when faced with troubling moral situations.

My experience leads me to believe that there are some real dangers in pursuing these technologies, that individuals should resort to them only after much soul searching, and that society should resist efforts to expand their use in ways that would make them available as something other than a reproductive process of last resort. In the case of my wife and me, this soul searching is upon us. It now appears that artificial insemination with my sperm will not be successful. We are thus confronted with the decision of whether to pursue *in vitro* fertilization, artificial insemination with donor sperm, or adoption. This paper is one moment in that process of soul searching.

Like many couples of our generation and background, my wife and I delayed having children until we completed advanced degrees and began our jobs. With careful deliberation, we planned the best time to have children given our two careers, and were diligent in avoiding pregnancy until that time. What we had not planned on was the possibility that pregnancy would not follow quickly once we stopped using birth control. This had not been the experience of our friends whose equally carefully laid plans had all been realized. For them, birth control ended and pregnancy followed shortly thereafter. For us, a year of careful effort, including charting temperatures and cycles, yielded only frustration.

Because we had indeed been careful and deliberate in trying to conceive, we suspected early on that there might be a problem and we thus sought professional help. A post-coital examination by my wife's gynecologist revealed few, and rather immobile sperm. I was referred to a specialist for examination and diagnosed as having two unrelated problems: a varicocele and retrograde ejaculation. A varicocele is a varicose vein in the testicle that is sometimes associated with a reduction in both the numbers and quality of sperm. Retrograde ejaculation is a condition in which a muscle at the neck of the bladder does not contract sufficiently during ejaculation to prevent semen from entering the bladder. As a result, during intercourse semen is ejaculated into the bladder rather than into the vagina. Both conditions are treatable, in many cases. Indeed, the doctor's diagnosis was followed almost immediately by a presentation of possible "therapies," given roughly in the order of the doctor's preferences, all presented as points on the same therapeutic continuum. A varicocele can be repaired surgically. Retrograde ejaculation can sometimes be eliminated through the use of drugs and, failing that, can be circumvented by recovering sperm from urine and using it for artificial insemination. Should both these treatments fail, *in vitro* fertilization might be successful. And, if all else fails, donor insemination is always a possibility.

Since surgery for a varicocele is not always successful and since surgery is more invasive than either of the treatments for retrograde ejaculation, I tried these latter treatments first. Unfortunately, neither drug therapy - nor artificial insemination was of any avail. Possibly because of damage done to the sperm as the result of the varicocele, the numbers and quality of sperm recovered from urine for insemination were not such as to make conception likely. After trying artificial insemination (AIH) for six months, we decided to attempt to repair the varicocele. Following this surgery, there is generally a three to nine month period in which a patient can expect to see improvement in his sperm count. After nearly seven months, we have seen virtually no improvement. Although we have begun AIH once again, we do not have high hopes for success.

This is the bare chronicle of my infertility experience. A complete record would be too personal, too painful, and too long to present here. But something more should be said. For someone who loves children, who has always planned to have children, infertility is an agonizing experience. In a culture that defines virility so completely in phallocentric terms, infertility can also threaten male identity, for infertility is often confused with impotence. Infertility is damaging in other ways as well. The loss of intimacy as one's sex life is taken over by infertility specialists strains a relationship. More generally, the cycle of hope and then despair that repeats itself month after month in unsuccessful infertility treatment can become unbearable. Nor is the experience of infertility made easier by the unintended thoughtlessness or uncomfortable attempts at humor of others. It is hard to know which is worse: to endure a toast on Father's Day made with great fanfare by someone who knows full well your efforts to become a father or to suffer yet another comment about "shooting blanks."

With this as background, I would like to consider four interrelated, but distinct objections that have been raised to NRTs. According to feminist opponents, the new reproductive technologies are inescapably coercive; lead to the dismemberment of motherhood; treat women and children as products; and open the door to widespread genetic engineering.

THE TYRANNY OF TECHNOLOGY

Although opponents of reproductive technology do not generally distinguish types of coercion, there are typically two sorts of claims made about NRTs. The first is that the very existence (and availability) of these technologies constitutes a sort of coercive *offer;* the second, that the future of these technologies is likely to include coercive *threats* to women's reproductive choices.[6] The first claim is often a response to the standard reasons given for developing these technologies. Advocates of NRTs typically argue that these techniques are developed exclusively to help infertile couples, expanding the range of choices open to them.[7] Moreover, the medical community is portrayed as responding to the needs and interest of infertile patients to find technological means to produce pregnancy if the natural ones fail, IVF programs, for example, are almost always defended on the grounds that however experimental, painful, or dangerous they may be to women, women choose to participate in them. Thus, it is said, IVF increases choice.

Feminists who believe NRTs to be coercive claim that such a choice is illusory, because in a culture that so thoroughly defines a woman's identity in terms of motherhood, the fact that women agree to participate in IVF programs does not mean they are truly free not to participate. According to this view, we must not focus too quickly on the private decisions of individuals.[8] Individual choices are almost always embedded in social contexts, and the context in our culture is such that a childless woman is an unenviable social anomaly. To choose to be childless is still socially disapproved and to be childless in fact is to be stigmatized as selfish and uncaring. In such a situation, to offer the hope of becoming a mother to a childless woman is a coercive offer. Such a woman may well not wish to undergo the trauma of an *in vitro* procedure, but unwillingly do so.

Robyn Rowland has appreciated the significance of this social context for infertile women. "In an ideological context where childbearing is claimed to be necessary for women to fulfill themselves," she writes,

"whether this is reinforced by patriarchal structures or by feminist values, discovering that you are infertile is a devastating experience."[9] The response may be a desperate search to find any means of overcoming this infertility, a search that may render the idea of choice in this context largely meaningless.

Moreover, feminists insist, developing these technologies is not about increasing choice. They are not, by and large, available to single women—infertile or not—or to lesbian women. Further, if doctors were truly concerned for the suffering of infertile women, we would expect much greater effort to publicize and to prevent various causes of infertility, including physician-induced sterility, as well as to inform women more fully about the physical and emotional trauma that various types of fertility treatments involve.[10] This neglect became dramatically apparent to me when I discovered Lisa at home weeping quietly but uncontrollably after a "routine" salpingogram for which she was utterly unprepared by her doctor's description of the procedure.[11] I will return to this theme below but I hope the claim of feminist opponents of the NRTs is clear. If doctors were in fact concerned about the well-being of their infertile patients, they would treat them less as objects to be manipulated by technologies and more as persons. The fact that this is often not the case should reveal something about the underlying motivations.[12]

The second claim about the possibility of coercive threats is really a concern about the future. While we may debate whether a desperately infertile woman really is free to choose not to try *in vitro* fertilization, still, no one is forcing her to participate in an IVF program. But what about the future? This question is meant to point to how thoroughly medicine has encroached on the birth process. The use of ultrasound, amniocentesis, genetic testing and counseling, electronic fetal monitoring, and cesarean sections have all increased the medical community's control over the process of birth. Why should the process of conception by any different? If anything, a pattern suggests itself. What was originally introduced as a specialized treatment for a subclass of women quickly expanded to cover a far wider range of cases. What was originally an optional technology may quickly become the norm.[13]

Such interventions can be coercive not only in the sense that, once established as the norm they are difficult to avoid, but in the stricter sense that women may literally be forced to submit to them, as with court-ordered cesarean sections. Will compulsory treatment be true of the new technologies as well? Will the technology that allows for embryo flushing and transfer in surrogate cases be required in the future as part of a process of medical evaluation of the fetus? The concern that the answers to these questions is too likely to be ''yes'' stands behind some claims that the NRTs are dangerously coercive. The potential for a loss of control over one's reproductive destiny is increased with the development of these technologies. And the coercion that could follow such a loss of control is worrisome.

Have I experienced a loss of control or coercion? The answer is a qualified yes. I certainly have not felt coerced in the second sense. I have not been physically forced to undergo infertility treatment, nor has there been any threat, actual or implied, connected with the prospect of avoiding NRTs altogether. Still, I have experienced the existence of these technologies as coercive. And here the notion of a coercive offer is helpful. Although the inability to have children has not threatened my social identity in the same way it might were I a woman, nevertheless, the pressure is real. Having experienced this pressure, and having met others whose desperation to bear a child was almost palpable, I do not doubt that the offer of hope held out by available technologies, however slim and

unrealistic in some cases, is indeed a form of coercion.

The problem here might reasonably be called the tyranny of available technologies. This ''soft'' form of coercion arises from the very existence of technologies of control. Increased control by the medical profession over the birth process, for example, has not resulted because of a conspiracy to gain control, but rather because, once the technology of control exists, it is nearly impossible not to make use of it. If, as I believe, this pressure to make use of existing technologies is a type of coercion, I have experienced this coercion powerfully during my infertility treatment. If surgery might repair the problem, even if the chances are not great, how can I not have surgery? If surgery and artificial insemination have not worked, but some new technique might, how can I not try the new technique?

The very existence of the technology inevitably changes the experience of infertility in ways that are not salutary. One of the peculiar aspects of infertility is that it is a condition that a couple suffers. Individuals can have retrograde ejaculation or blocked tubes, but only couples can be infertile. As Leon Kass has noted, infertility is as much a relationship as a condition.[14] Yet infertility treatment leads us to view infertility individually, with unfortunate consequences. The reason is that couples will often not be seen together in infertility treatment, and, even when they are, they will receive individual workups and be presented with individual treatment options. Now it might be said that providing individuals with options increases agency rather than diminishes it. Yet with this agency comes a responsibility that may not itself be chosen and that reduces the prospects for genuine choice. For once an individual is presented with a treatment option, *not* to pursue it is, in effect, to choose childlessness and to accept responsibility for it. From a situation in which infertility is a relational problem for which no one is to blame, it becomes an individual problem for which a woman or man who refuses treatment is to blame.[15] Reproductive technology structures the alternatives such that a patient is "free" to pursue every available form of assisted reproduction or to choose to be childless.

This problem is compounded by the fact that infertility specialists simply assume that patients will pursue all available treatments and typically present the variety of treatment options as just different points on the same therapeutic spectrum, distinguished primarily by degree of invasiveness. In our case, taking relatively mild drugs in an effort to make an incontinent muscle more efficient lies at one end of the continuum, at the other end of which lies IVF. Surgery, I suppose, falls somewhere in the middle. At no time in my experience, however, has anyone suggested that treatments differ qualitatively. (The only exception to this was my urologist's opposition to an experimental treatment for male-factor infertility.) It has generally been assumed that if one therapy fails, we will simply move on to the next. And that is the problem. If the technology exists, the expectation is that it will be used. Again, if IVF might work, how can we not try it? The force of these questions covers us like a weight as we consider what to do next.

THE DISMEMBERMENT OF MOTHERHOOD

A second objection raised against the NRTs is that they question the very meaning of motherhood. The reality of oocyte donation, embryo flushing, and embryo transfer produces another possible reality: the creation of a child for whom there are three mothers: the genetic mother, the gestational mother, and the social mother.[16] In such a situation, who is the *real* mother? In the absence of a compelling answer, the claim of each of these three women to the child will be tenuous.

Maternity will be as much in dispute as paternity ever was. And whatever criteria are used to settle this issue, the result for women is that the reproductive experience may become discontinuous in much the way it has traditionally been for men. Just as paternity has been uncertain because the natural, biological relation between the father and child could always be questioned, so too might maternity become a sort of abstract idea rather than a concrete reality. Just as paternity has been a right rather than a natural relation, so too might maternity become.[17]

The significance of this can be seen if one takes seriously Mary O'Brien's claims that men's reproductive experience of discontinuity, that is, the inevitable uncertainty of genetic continuity, has contributed significantly to men's need to dominate. The problematic nature of paternity, O'Brien suggests, can account for the sense of isolation and separation so common in men, in part because for men the nature of paternity is such that the natural experiential relation of intimacy with another is missing.

Feminists' celebrations of motherhood have also made much of the biological continuity women have traditionally experienced with their children. Caroline Whitbeck and Nancy Hartsock, for example, have both discussed how the biological differences between men and women, especially as they are manifested in reproduction, account for some of the differences in how men and women experience the world.[18] Many women do not experience the sharp separation between self and others so common to male experience, Hartsock and Whitbeck note, a fact both explain by appeal to the way in which female physiology mediates female experience. In the case of women who are mothers, the experience of pregnancy, labor, childbirth, and nursing shape a way of responding to the world and to others. For a mother whose milk lets down at the sound of her

309

child's cry, a sense of deep connection and continuity is established.[19]

On this view, the danger of the new technologies of birth is precisely that they alienate women from procreation and thus rob them of one of the most significant sources of power and identity. It is precisely this realization that leads Connie Ramos, a character in Marge Piercy's *Woman on the Edge of Time*, to react with such horror at the division of motherhood envisioned by Piercy. In a world where gestation takes place in artificial wombs, where men as well as women nurse the young, women have lost something of tremendous value and men have gained something they always wanted: control of reproduction. Connie's response to seeing a breast feeding male poignantly expresses this point:

> She felt angry. Yes, how dare any man share that pleasure. These women thought they had won, but they had abandoned to men the last refuge of women. What was special about being a woman here? They had given it all up, they had let men steal from them the last remnants of ancient power, those sealed in blood and in milk.[20]

One of the gravest concerns raised about the new technologies of birth, then, is that they represent the culmination of a patriarchal imperative: to gain for men what they have always lacked, namely, the power to reproduce. The fear is that this desire is close to realization. Gena Corea has put this point forcefully:

> Now men are far beyond the stage at which they expressed their envy of woman's procreative power through couvade, transvestism, or subincision. They are beyond merely giving spiritual birth in their baptismal-font wombs, beyond giving physical birth with their electronic fetal monitors, their forceps, their knives. Now they have laboratories.[21]

Since this objection essentially focuses on the impact on women of the NRTs, my experience cannot speak directly to this issue.

Nevertheless, because part of what is at stake is the importance of the unity of genetic and social parenthood, as well as the unity of genetic and gestational parenthood, this is not a concern exclusively of women; it is a concern I have confronted in reflecting about donor insemination and adoption. One of the most striking aspects of my experience is how powerfully I have felt the pull of biological connection. Does this mean that genetic and social parenthood should never be separated or that parenthood should be defined strictly as a biological relation? I believe the answer to both questions is ''no,'' but my experience leads me to believe also that a unity of genetic, gestational, and social parenthood is an ideal that we ought to strive to maintain.

THE COMMODIFICATION OF REPRODUCTION

The third objection found in some of the feminist literature on NRTs is that they tend to treat human beings as products. Not only can these technologies divide up motherhood, they can divide up persons into parts. Even when they are used to treat infertility, it is often not men or women who are being treated, but testicles, sperm, ovaries, eggs, wombs, etc. While this is true to some extent of all treatment in the specialized world of modern medicine, it is acute in reproductive medicine. Robyn Rowland has described the situation as one in which women especially are treated as ''living laboratories'' in which body parts and systems are manipulated in dramatic fashion without knowledge about the consequences of such manipulation.[22] Clearly, this has been the case in the development of *in vitro* fertilization, where women have not been adequately informed about the experimental nature of the procedure, possible side effects, or poor success rates.

In addition, the language of reproductive medicine can also be dehumanizing.

Eggs are "harvested" as one might bring in a crop. Body parts are personified and thus attributed a sort of individuality and intentionality; cervical mucus is said to be "hostile," the cervix itself is said to be "incompetent," and the list could go on.

Yet as troubling as the langauge and practice surrounding this technology may be in treating persons like products, it is the application of this technology that treats persons *as* products that is completely objectionable. This has clearly happened with the development of a commercial surrogate industry and donor sperm banks, and it is the danger that attends the establishment of oocyte donor programs. Indeed, Corea's idea of a reproductive brothel seems inescapable. If there are not yet houses of ill repute where one can go to purchase embryos and women to gestate them, there are brochures available containing pictures and biographical information of women willing to sell their services. Nor can the development of commercial surrogacy arrangements be dismissed as the misguided and unintended application of reproductive techniques, an application of NRTs mistakenly and uncharacteristically driven by the profit motive. Treatment of infertility is big business, and the drive to develop reproductive technology is clearly fueled by financial incentives.[23]

Nothing perhaps illustrates this more clearly than the development of an embryo flushing technique by a team of physicians at Harbor-UCLA Medical Center. In April 1983, this team successfully flushed an embryo from one woman and transferred it to a second woman who carried the fetus to term. The project was funded by Fertility and Genetics Research, a for-profit company begun by two physicians who envisioned the establishment of a chain of embryo transfer clinics where infertile women could purchase embryos to gestate themselves. Indeed, to insure maximum profits for themselves, the Harbor-UCLA team sought to patent the equipment and the technique they developed.[24]

Not only do men and women get treated as products, so do children. The logic here is clear enough. If women are paying for embryos or being paid for eggs, the embryos and the eggs cannot but be understood as products. Because they are products, buyers will place demands on them. We will expect our products to meet certain standards and, if they fail, we will want to be compensated or to return the damaged goods. In a society that sells embryos and eggs for profit, children will inevitably be treated as property to be bought and sold, and just as inevitably it follows that different children will carry different price tags. As Barbara Katz Rothman puts it, "some will be rejects, not salable at any price: too damaged, or the wrong colour, or too old, too long on the shelf."[25]

My own experience leads me to believe that this tendency toward the commodification of reproduction is one of the most worrisome aspects of the NRTs.[26] In part, this tendency is troubling because it manifests itself not simply in commercial surrogacy transactions—transactions that many if not most people find morally problematic—but in applications of these technologies that almost no one questions. For example, few, I believe, would have qualms about the sort of artificial insemination that Lisa and I have undertaken and yet perhaps the most difficult part of AIH for us has been the struggle to maintain a degree of intimacy in the process of reproduction in the midst of a clinical environment designed to achieve results. As Katz Rothman has pointed out, the ideology of technology that fuels this commodification is not reducible to particular technological tools or to particular commercial transactions. Rather it is a way of thinking of ourselves and our world in "mechanical, industrial terms," terms that are incompatible with intimacy.[27] Interestingly, the Roman Catholic Church has rejected AIH precisely because it separates procreation from sexual intercourse and the expression of love manifest in the conjugal act.[28] While I reject the act-oriented natural law reasoning that stands behind this position, there is an insight here that should not be overlooked. Once procreation is separated from sexual intercourse, it is difficult not to treat the process of procreation as the production of an object to which one has a right as the producer. It is also difficult under these circumstances not to place the end above the means; effectiveness in accomplishing one's goal can easily become the sole criterion by which decisions are made.

This anyway, has been my experience. Although Lisa and I tried for a time to maintain a degree of intimacy during the process of AIH by remaining together during all phases of the procedure as well as after the insemination, we quickly abandoned this as a charade. The system neither encourages nor facilitates intimacy. It is concerned, as it probably should be, with results. And so we have become pragmatists too. We do not much enjoy the process of AIH, to say the least, but we also do not try to make it something it is not. A conception, if it takes place, will not be the result of an act of bodily lovemaking, but a result of technology. We have come to accept this. Yet, such acceptance comes at a price, for our experience of reproduction is discontinuous. A child conceived by this method is lovingly willed into existence, but it is not conceived through a loving, bodily act.

Having accepted the separation of sexual intercourse and procreation, however, it is difficult to resist any sort of technological manipulation of gametes that might result in conception. We have, so to speak, relinquished our gametes to the doctors and once this has been done, how can various technological manipulations be judged other than by criteria of likelihood of success? This is precisely the problem: once one has begun a process that inevitably treats procreation as the production of a product, the methods of production can only be evaluated by the end result.

REPRODUCTIVE TECHNOLOGIES AND GENETIC ENGINEERING

The fourth objection to NRTs is that their general acceptance and use is an inevitable route to widespread use of genetic engineering. It should be no mystery why this might be thought to be the case. Once the embryo, for example, is treated as a product to be bought and sold, there will be great pressure to produce the perfect product. The attraction of genetic engineering under such circumstances should be obvious. Genetic screening and therapy would be a sort of quality control mechanism by which to insure customer satisfaction.[29] Moreover, the greater access to embryos and to eggs provided by IVF and embryo flushing means that genetic manipulation of the eggs or the developing embryo is now more feasible than it once was. Even more importantly, however, this greater access to embryos and eggs, combined with the possibility of freezing and storing those not used to attempt a pregnancy, means that experimentation can go forward at a much faster rate. Scientists have experimented with the injection of genetic material into non-human eggs for some time, and a recent issue of *Cell* reported the introduction of foreign genetic material into mouse sperm.[30] It is not unreasonable to suppose that such manipulations will one day extend to human gametes. Indeed, one experimental technique being developed to treat forms of male infertility in which sperm is unable to penetrate the egg involves isolating a single sperm in order to introduce the sperm directly into the egg.[31] The obvious question is: How will this sperm be selected? The most likely answer will be: by a determination that it is not genetically abnormal.

Thus far, most genetic experimentation, manipulation, and screening has been defended by appeal to the goal of eliminating human suffering. If genetic abnormalities can be detected or even treated, much human suffering might either be avoided or alleviated. Yet, how does one distinguish between attempts to eliminate suffering and attempts at eugenics? The fact that it is so difficult to answer this question is one reason to be concerned about NRTs. Moreover, the equation of genetic abnormality or disability with suffering can be questioned. As Marsha Saxton has pointed out, we cannot simply assume that disabled people "suffer" from their physical conditions any more than any other group or category of individuals "suffer."[32] Indeed, decisions about bearing genetically damaged fetuses are generally made in relative ignorance of what sorts of lives potential offspring might actually have.[33] "Our exposure to disabled children," Saxton writes, "has been so limited by their isolation that most people have only stereotyped views which include telethons, [and] displays on drugstore counters depicting attractive 'crippled' youngsters soliciting our pity and loose change" (306).

If reproductive technology is developed because every person has a right to bear a child, does it not follow that every person has a right to bear a perfect child? Advocates of NRTs would not admit this, and yet it seems to be the logical conclusion of the commitment to produce a child, no matter the cost. To see the difficulties here, we need only ask how we are to define the perfect child, and whether a commitment to eliminate genetic abnormalities means that women will lose the freedom not to test for or to treat abnormalities.[34]

In my view, the concern here is a real one for, once one has begun to think in terms of producing a product, it becomes exceedingly difficult to distinguish between technological interventions except on the basis of the resulting product. And since the product one desires in this instance is a healthy baby, a technological intervention that helps to achieve this, even one that involves genetic manipulation, is likely to be both initially attractive and ultimately irresistible. My own reaction to the new technique of overcoming male infertility by isolating a single sperm and injecting it into an egg it would otherwise be unable to penetrate is instructive. My initial response was that of tremendous excitement. Here was a treatment that could clearly overcome our problem. That fact that I did not produce great numbers of sperm or that the ones I produced were not likely to be capable of penetrating an egg did not matter. In theory, very few sperm are required and the work of penetration is done for them. The fact that such a technique involves placing an extraordinary amount of control in the hands of the doctor who selects the single sperm from among the many millions that even a man with a low sperm count is likely to produce did not even occur to me. In fact, it was my doctor, who had moral reservations about this technique, who first pointed this out to me. What is perhaps more troubling, however, is that when the issue of control was pointed out to me, I found no immediately compelling reason to object. I had, after all, been routinely providing sperm for a lab to manipulate in an effort to produce a collection that was capable of penetrating my wife's egg. Was selecting a single sperm that could accomplish the goal really so different?

In light of these various objections and my own experience, then, my basic response is one of concern. I do not believe that the predominantly male medical profession is acting in bad faith in developing reproductive technologies, as some critics suggest. Much of the feminist literature on NRTs is cynical and deeply contemptuous of what is seen as a patriarchal and conspiratorial medical establishment. My own experience, however, does not bear this out. Although there is

313

much about my treatment for infertility that I have found frustrating, anxiety-producing, and distasteful, and although I have felt at turns coerced by the existence of the technologies themselves; angry at the loss of intimacy in my relationship with Lisa; and worried by my own near obsession with the goal of achieving a pregnancy, I have never had reason to doubt the sincerity of my doctor's care and concern. That my experience has been so negative despite treating with a doctor who is very much aware of the potentially dehumanizing aspects of infertility treatment is further evidence of how serious the problems with these technologies may be.

This is not to deny that infertility specialists are too concerned with technological fixes; in my view, they are. While there is no conspiracy to gain control of the process of reproduction, there is increased control. And if one theme joins the various objections to the new reproductive technologies, it is that they increase the medical profession's control over the process of reproduction and that such control has deleterious consequences. We have not, by and large, thought through the consequences of this sort of intervention and control. Neither infertile couples nor those who try to alleviate their suffering, nor indeed the community that is generally supportive of the desire to have children has really asked whether that desire should be met at all costs. Is the desire to have children a desire for a basic human good? Can it be met through adoption or only through biological offspring? Are there other, competing social goods that set limits on how far we, as a community, should go to meet this need? These are certainly questions that I had not addressed before my experience of infertility. Even now I am not certain how to answer all of them. I am certain, however, that my desire to have children is strong. I am also equally certain that we need to attend to these questions as a society. For anyone not blinded by self deception will admit that

wanting something does not always make it right.

REFERENCES

1. See Gena Corea, ''The Reproductive Brothel'' in *Man-Made Woman*, Gena Corea *et al.,* eds. (Bloomington: Indiana University Press, 1987), 38–51.
2. The medical profession has gone to some lengths to insure that artificial insemination is defined as a medical procedure, and thus controlled by doctors. Most of my wife's inseminations have been administered by doctors, even when this has been inconvenient for us. The two exceptions have been when Lisa ovulated on the weekend and then, apparently, insemination did not need to be performed by a doctor.
3. Although for convenience I will refer in this paper to ''feminist'' objections, I cannot stress enough that there is not one feminist response to reproductive technology, but several. Indeed, feminist responses range from enthusiastic support to moderate and cautious support to radical opposition. See Anne Donchin, ''The Future of Mothering: Reproductive Technology and Feminist Theory,'' *Hypatia* 1 (1986), 121–37.
4. Patricia Spallone and Deborah Lynn Steinberg, eds., Made to Order (Oxford: Pergamon Press, 1987).
5. But see Sidney Callahan, ''The Role of Emotion in Ethical Decisionmaking,'' *Hastings Center Report* 18:3 (1988), 9–14.
6. On the difference between coercive offers and coercive threats, see Virginia Held, ''Coercion and Coercive Offers,'' in *Coercion,* J. Roland Pennock and John Chapman, eds. (Chicago: Atherton, 1972), 49–62.
7. I use ''couples'' here intentionally. The justification for developing reproductive methods is almost always to help infertility within marriage. There is an irony in this: Although physicians tend to treat infertility as a problem for an individual, they insist that that individual be part of a heterosexual marriage. Thus it is not just infertility that is of concern, but infertility in certain types of situations.
8. For a discussion of the difficulty of providing an adequate account of free choice given the assumptions of modern liberalism, see Barbara Katz Rothman, *Recreating Motherhood* (New York: W. W. Norton, 1989), 62.

9. Robyn Rowland, "Of Woman Born, But for How Long?" in *Made to Order*, 70.

10. See Spallone and Steinberg, eds., *Made to Order*, 6–7.

11. The test involves injecting radiopaque dye into the uterine cavity after which x-rays are taken. The fallopian tubes are outlined wherever the dye has penetrated. Using this procedure, it is sometimes possible to determine whether a woman's tubes are blocked.

12. Here my experience and Lisa's differ dramatically. The infertility specialist I have seen could not be more sensitive or attentive to the human dimension of our difficulties. By contrast, Lisa's experience with the gynecologists involved with insemination has been almost entirely negative, in part because she has not been treated fully as a person by them.

13. Spallone and Steinberg, eds., *Made to Order*, 4–5.

14. Leon Kass, *Toward a More Natural Science* (New York: The Free Press, 1985), 45.

15. I am, in effect, suggesting that more choice is not always better. This is not a popular view in our culture, but it can be persuasively defended. For such a defense, see Gerald Dworkin, "Is More Choice Better than Less?," *Midwest Studies in Philosophy* 7, Peter A. French, Theodore E. Uehling, Jr., and Howard K. Wettstein, eds. (Minneapolis: University of Minnesota Press, 1982), 47–61.

16. Gena Corea, *The Mother Machine* (New York: Harper and Row, 1985), 290.

17. Mary O'Brien, *The Politics of Reproduction* (Boston: Routledge and Kegan Paul, 1981), 55.

18. See Nancy Hartsock, "The Feminist Standpoint: Developing the Ground for a Specifically Feminist Historical Materialism," in *Discovering Reality*, Sandra Harding and Merrill B. Hintikka, eds. (Dordrecht: D. Reidel, 1983), 283–310; and Caroline Whitbeck, "A Different Reality: Feminist Ontology," in *Beyond Domination*, Carol C. Gould, ed. (Totowa, NJ: Rowman and Allanheld, 1983). 64–88.

19. Emily Martin, *The Woman in the Body* (Boston: Beacon Press, 1987).

20. Marge Piercy, *Woman on the Edge of Time* (New York: Ballantine Books, 1976), 134.

21. Corea, *The Mother Machine*, 314.

22. Robyn Rowland, "Women as Living Laboratories: The New Reproductive Technologies," in *The Trapped Woman*, Josefina Figueira-McDonough and Rosemary Sarri, eds. (Newbury Park, CA: Sage Publications, 1987), 81–112.

23. According to the Office of Technology Assessment, $164 million is paid to close to 11,000 physicians every year for artificial inseminations alone. Add to this the variety of other infertility services provided every year to childless couples and the total cost is at least $1 billion (U.S. Congress, Office of Technology Assessment, *Artificial Insemination Practice in the U.S.: Summary of a 1987 Survey* [Washington: Government Printing Office, 1988]).

24. Although there are currently no franchised clinics in the U.S., the ovum transfer procedure using uterine lavage is commonplace. See Leonard Formigli, Graziella Formigli, and Carlo Roccio, "Donation of Fertilized Uterine Ova to Infertile Women," *Fertility and Sterility* 47:1 (1987), 162–65.

25. Barbara Katz Rothman, "The Products of Conception: The Social Context of Reproductive Choices," *Journal of Medical Ethics* 11 (1985), 191.

26. The tendency to treat children as commodities is not solely the product of developing NRTs, of course, but the culmination of a process begun with the old reproductive technology of contraception. Once the inexorable connection between sexual intercourse and procreation was broken, it became possible to choose when to have children. From that point on, it made sense to treat children in some ways as products, the purchase of which, so to speak, could be planned as one planned the purchase of other expensive items.

27. Katz Rothman, *Recreating Motherhood*, 49.

28. Sacred Congregation for the Doctrine of the Faith, *Instruction on Respect for Human Life in Its Origin and on the Dignity of Procreation*, in *Origins* 16 (March 1987), 697–711.

29. Katz Rothman, "The Products of Conception," 188.

30. For a discussion of the transgenic animals that result from the genetic manipulation of eggs, see V. G. Pursel *et al.*, "Genetic Engineering of Livestock," *Science* 244 (1989), 1281–88. Also see M. Lavitrano *et al.*, "Sperm Cells as Vectors for Introducing Foreign DNA into Eggs: Genetic Transformation of Mice," *Cell* 57:5 (1989), 717–24.

31. Actually, there are at least three different techniques being investigated. See Jon W. Gordon et al., "Fertilization of Human Oocytes by Sperm from Infertile Males After Zona Pellucida Drilling," *Fertility and Sterility* 50:1 (1988), 68–73.

32. Marsha Saxton, "Born and Unborn: The Implications of Reproductive Technologies for People with Disabilities," in *Test-Tube Women,* Rita Arditti, Renate Duelli Klein, and Shelley Minden, eds. (London: Pandora Press, 1984), 298–313.

33. Anne Finger, "Claiming All of Our Bodies: Reproductive Rights and Disabilities," in *Test-Tube Women,* 281–97.

34. See Ruth Hubbard, " 'Fetal Rights' and the New Eugenics," *Science for the People* (March/April 1984), 7–9, 27–29.

Chapter 9

Menopause— That Other Awkward Age

Menopause has negative connotations for most women. Many of our societal stereotypes combine to make this last transition of a woman's reproductive system a dreaded event. As the end of reproductive viability, menopause implies, for many women and men, the end of femininity. Intermingled with this is the cultural stigma attached to aging. Ours is a youth-worshiping society. We fight to preserve our looks and bodies, arguing that you're only as old as you feel. But, even the least age-conscious woman may find it difficult to ignore menopause as a sign that time, and youth, are passing.

The notion of menopause as an ending was once realistic. Although the age at which women experience menopause has increased over time, so has their expected life-span. In 1900, the average age at which a woman experienced menopause was 45 years. The average life expectancy of women at that time was 49 years. Today, women experience menopause at approximately 50 years of age, while the average life expectancy for women has increased to 75–80 years. On average, a woman will live one quarter of her life after menopause. Thus, as Ursula LeGuin (1976) suggested, it is better to look at menopause as a time of transition similar to puberty. Menopause should be a time when we evaluate our goals and achievements and adjust our course for the future.

Menopause is simply the cessation of menstrual periods due to a decline of ovarian hormone levels. As **Ginsburg** points out, science has not yet identified the cause of menopause, but there are a number of factors which may be involved in determining the age at which it occurs. There is no evidence of any relationship between the age of menopause and the age of menarche, however. Women who experience menarche earlier do not necessarily face an earlier menopause. Cigarette smoking, on the other hand, has been consistently associated with an earlier menopause. Women who smoke go through menopause as much as two years earlier than non-smokers.

Many of the fears about menopause are due to a lack of understanding of this physiological process. **Willis** provides a straight-forward explanation of the biological changes of menopause. Both Willis and **Should You Take Estrogen?** discuss the role of estrogen replacement therapy (ERT) in eliminating, delaying or attenuating some of the physical side-effects of decreased ovarian estrogen production. This treatment is not without risks and should not be used without careful analysis of those risks. Menopause is only one aspect of the overall aging process called the climacteric. Both women and men experience the climacteric; only women experience menopause. While ERT can prevent or reverse some of the symptoms caused by menopause, it cannot prevent or reverse aging.

Hunter provides evidence that the emotional well-being of climacteric women is not adversely affected by being postmenopausal. Most women do not regret the end of monthly menstrual periods. As is the case with the premenstruum, our stereotypes strongly associate emotional upheaval with the hormonal changes of menopause. No evidence for such a relationship exists. While women who are premenopausal predict negative experiences at menopause for themselves and for others, postmenopausal women have a much more positive view of this normal biological process.

REFERENCES AND ADDITIONAL SUGGESTED READINGS

Avis, N. E., and McKinlay, S. M. (1991). A longitudinal analysis of women's attitudes toward the menopause: Results from the Massachusetts Women's Health Study. *Maturitas* 13:65–79.

Doress, P. B., Siegal, D. L., and the Midlife and Older Women Book Project (1987). *Ourselves, Growing Older: Women Aging with Knowledge and Power*. New York: Simon and Schuster.

LeGuin, U. (1976, Summer). The space crone. *The CoEvolution Quarterly*.

Leiblum, S. R. (1990). Sexuality and the midlife woman. *Psychology of Women Quarterly* 14:495–508.

Mooradian, A. D., and Grieff, V. (1990) Sexuality in older women. *Archives of Internal Medicine* 150:1033–1038.

Peck, W. A. (1990). Estrogen therapy (ET) after menopause. *Journal of the American Medical Women Association* 45:87–90.

Ussher, J. M. (1989). Chapter 5. *The Psychology of the Female Body*. New York: Routledge.

What Determines the Age at the Menopause?

Jean Ginsburg

> The menstrual discharge ceases in most women about their fortieth year; but with those in whom it goes on longer it lasts even to the fiftieth year, and women of that age have been known to bear children. But beyond that age there is no case on record.[1]

Aristotle's assessment was similar to those of Hippocrates and also Roman authors, so it seems that 2000 years ago most women entered the menopause in their early 40s.[2] Mediaeval authors, however, gave the 50s as the age when menses ceased[3]—much closer to the timing for twentieth century women.

In the past 100 years data from schoolchildren have shown a steady fall in the age at menarche in industrialised communities.[4] Has there been a corresponding change in the age at the menopause? Unfortunately, reported surveys of the menopause have suffered from methodological defects. Retrospective interviews underestimate the age at the menopause, as does digit preference when women round up a recollected age to 40, 45, or 50 years. A mean also underestimates the age at the menopause; it would be more accurate to use the median. Even in prospective studies there is no agreement on whether the menopause begins with the last episode of bleeding or after amenorrhoea has been present for nine months or more.

Nevertheless, those studies least subject to bias show a striking agreement that the median age at the menopause is currently around 50 in Western industrialised societies.[5] In Britain it is 50.78,[5] in the United States 49.8,[6] and in white South Africans 48.7[7] with little apparent change over the past century. In non-European women, however, the menopause seems to occur earlier—in South Africa and the United States black women have an earlier menopause than white women.[8] [9]

What determines the age at which the menopause occurs? For most of the factors claimed to influence the timing the evidence is poor. For example, the common belief that women with an early menarche have a later menopause or the reverse has no factual basis.[5] Nutrition, however, is important. In New Guinea a group of women with severe prolonged malnutrition and low height and weight had a median age at the menopause of only 43.6 years whereas another group in the same region but with much better nutrition and correspondingly greater height and weight had a later menopause, at 47.3 years.[10]

Parity is linked with menopausal age: nulliparous women have an early menopause,[7] [11] while increased parity, particularly in the higher social classes, correlates with a later menopause.[5] [12] One surprising report is that mothers of twins enter the menopause about a year earlier than women who have had singleton infants[12]—why is not clear. A woman's age at the time of her last pregnancy has also been reported to influence her age at the menopause, women whose last pregnancy occurred before the age of 28 reputedly having an earlier menopause than those with their last pregnancy at a later age.[13] This could, however, be due to a longer fertile period in the women with later

This article first appeared in the *British Medical Journal* (1991) 302: 1288–1289. Copyright © 1991, British Medical Journal. Reprinted with permission.

pregnancies. There is also some evidence that blindness may lead to a later menopause.[14a]

Chronic systemic infections or localised disease of the reproductive system impair fertility, but neither systemic nor genital disease seems to influence the age at the menopause. With the exception of mumps oophoritis, pelvic or systemic infections rarely cause ovarian failure. A familial link associated with partial deletion of the long arm of the X chromosome has been found in a few cases but not in our series.[14b 14c]

One of the few well documented influences on the age at the menopause is tobacco smoking. Women who smoke enter the menopause up to two years earlier than those who do not.[15–18] The effect seems to be dose related and may be mediated partly through lowered oestrogen concentrations.[19–21] Studies in rodents have shown that benzpyrene destroys primordial oocytes. The rodent ovary contains an enzyme system metabolising polycyclic aromatic hydrocarbons to cytotoxic, potentially carcinogenic intermediates.[22] If the human ovary responds similarly this would explain the earlier menopause of cigarette smokers. The aromatic hydrocarbons of cigarette smoke might also accelerate aging of oocytes by increased oxidation of cell membranes as a result of combustion products such as nitrous oxide.[23]

The most important factor determining a woman's age at the menopause is the number of ovarian follicles. Human primordial germ cells separate from somatic cells at an early stage of embryogenesis. Some 1000–2000 migrate to the gonadal ridge, where they multiply rapidly to a maximum of between five million and seven million follicles around the fifth month of intrauterine life. Multiplication then stops. Thereafter there is a steady loss of primordial follicles from the fetal ovary, so that by the time the baby is born each ovary contains about one million follicles.[24 25]

This number continues to diminish after birth (independently of any cyclic hormonal change or the physiological state of the woman), but fewer than 0.01% are ovulated; the remainder degenerate. Little is known about the mechanisms responsible, although the observations that follicles fail to grow in anencephalic fetuses[26] and that in rodents hypophysectomy retards the rate of loss of primordial follicles[27] show the importance of the pituitary gland. Depletion of ovarian follicles occurs independently of physiological and environmental factors (with the exception of those that actually destroy follicles) until the perimenopausal phase is reached. The rate of loss of primordial follicles then accelerates, and the menopause occurs when the number of primordial follicles has fallen to a critical number.[28 29]

The accelerated loss of primordial follicles in the perimenopausal phase occurs in parallel with rising gonadotrophin concentrations. It is not known, however, whether the rate at which ovarian follicular reserve becomes depleted is regulated primarily by factors within the ovary itself or whether the accelerated follicular loss at this stage results from a primary change in the control of gonadotrophins. Nor is the trigger mechanism known, nor what determines the timing of any altered neuroendocrine activity, particularly in the perimenopausal phase. Clearly the timing of the phase of accelerated follicular loss and its speed will determine age at onset of the menopause. Is the date of the menopause genetically "programmed" for each woman or might it be influenced through the neuroendocrine control of gonadotrophin secretion? Could the time at which menopause occurs be altered—forwards or backwards?

Factors such as parity, nutrition, race, and smoking influence the age at the menopause by at most three years either side of the normal median age. Some women, however, have a premature menopause—before the age of 40; in a few it occurs below the

320

age of 30. Premature ovarian failure is probably much commoner than generally appreciated. In a series of 1001 women under the age of 40 presenting consecutively with amenorrhoea at an endocrine clinic 8% had never menstruated (primary amenorrhoea) (J Ginsburg *et al,* fifth international congress on the menopause, 1987). Of the remainder—that is, those with secondary amenorrhoea—9% had raised gonadotrophin concentrations and were considered to have premature ovarian failure. Seven per cent of this group had plentiful primordial follicles on ovarian biopsy, which suggests resistance to gonadotrophins—the resistant ovary syndrome. No ovarian follicles were found at laparoscopy in the remaining 93%. The cause of premature ovarian failure in the women without ovarian follicles was iatrogenic—the result of chemotherapy or radiotherapy—in 12% and autoimmune failure in 3%. But in most of those with premature ovarian failure no cause could be found for the absence of ovarian follicles.

In women with premature ovarian failure it is not clear whether fewer primordial germ cells migrate to the germinal ridge in fetal life, whether the rate of multiplication up to the fifth month of intrauterine life is reduced, whether the rate of follicular loss thereafter is greater than normal, or whether there is a combination of all three factors.

Almost all the factors reported to influence the age at the menopause accelerate its onset. Yet if we knew what determined follicular atresia and its accelerated onset in the perimenopausal phase could the process possibly be delayed and the potential store of viable primordial follicles be increased so that the menopause was delayed? Or is the limit set by natural aging processes in the reproductive system as a whole? Either way, knowledge of these factors and how they are integrated could have important implications for both regulating fertility and treating infertility.

NOTES

1. Aristotle: [*Historia Animalium*] Book VII trans R Creswell. London: George Bell and Sons, 1897. *c* 350 BC.
2. Amundsen DW, Diers CJ. The age of the menopause in classical Greece and Rome. *Hum Biol* 1970;**42**:79–86.
3. Amundsen DW, Diers CJ. The age of menopause in medieval Europe. *Hum Biol* 1973;**45**:605–12.
4. Tanner JM. The secular trend towards earlier physical maturation. *Tijdschrift voor Sociale Geneeskunde* 1966;**44**:524–39.
5. McKinlay S, Jefferys M, Thompson B. An investigation of the age at menopause. *J Biosoc Sci* 1972;**4**:161–73.
6. Treloar AE. Menarche, menopause and intervening fecundability. *Hum Biol* 1974;**46**:89–107.
7. Benjamin F. The age of the menarche and certain factors influencing these times. *S Afr Med J* 1960;**3**:316–20.
8. Frere G. Mean age at menopause and menarche in South Africa. *S Afr J Med Sci* 1971;**36**:21–4.
9. MacMahan B, Worcester J. Age at menopause: United States. In: *US Vital and Health Statistics 1960–62.* Washington DC: Government Printing Office, 1962. (Series I:No 19.)
10. Scragg RFR. Menopause and reproductive span in rural Niugini. *Annual Symposium of the Papua New Guinea Medical Society* 1973:126–31.
11. Hauser GA, Remen U, Valaer M, Erb H, Mueller T, Obiri J. Menarche and menopause in Israel. *Gynaecologia (Basel)* 1963;**155**:38–47.
12. Soberon J, Calderon JJ, Goldzieher JW. Relation of parity to age at menopause. *Am J Obstet Gynecol* 1966;**96**:96–100.
13. Brand PG, Lehert PL. A new way of looking at environmental variables that may affect the age at menopause. *Maturitas* 1978;**1**:121–32.
14a. Lehrer S. Fertility and menopause in blind women. *Fertil Steril* 1981;**36**:396–8.
14b. Skibsted L, Westh H, Niebuh RE. X long arm deletions: a review of non-mosaic cases studied with banding techniques. *Hum Genet* 1984;**67**:1–5.
14c. Krauss CM, Durksoy RN, Adkins L, *et al.* Familial premature ovarian failure due to an interstitial deletion of the long arm of the X chromosome. *N Engl J Med* 1987;**317**:125–31.

15. Jick H, Porter J. Relation between smoking and age of natural menopause. Report from the Boston collaborative drug surveillance program, Boston University Medical Center. *Lancet* 1977;i:1354–5.
16. Kaufman DW, Slone D, Rosenberg L, *et al.* Cigarette smoking and age at natural menopause. *Am J Public Health* 1980;**70**:420–2.
17. Andersen FS, Transbol I, Christiansen C. Is cigarette smoking a promoter of the menopause? *Acta Med Scand* 1982;**212**:137–9.
18. Adena MA, Gallagher HG. Cigarette smoking and the age at menopause. *Ann Hum Biol* 1982;**9**:121–30.
19. Baron JA, Adams P, Ward M. Cigarette smoking and other correlates of cytologic estrogen effect in post menopausal women. *Fertil Steril* 1988;**50**:766–71.
20. Khaw KT, Tazuke S, Barrett-Connor E. Cigarette smoking and levels of adrenal androgens in postmenopausal women. *N Engl J Med* 1988;**318**:1705–9.
21. Longcope C, Johnston CC. Androgen and estrogen dynamics in pre- and post-menopausal women: a comparison between smokers and non-smokers. *J Clin Endocrinol Metab* 1988;**67**:379–83.
22. Mattison DR, Thorgeirssom SS. Smoking and industrial pollution and their effects on menopause and ovarian cancer. *Lancet* 1978;i:187–8.
23. Tappel AL. Vitamin E and selenium protection from in vivo lipid peroxidation. *Ann NY Acad Sci* 1980;**355**:18–29.
24. Block E. Quantitative morphological investigations of the follicular system in women. *Acta Anat (Basel)* 1952;**14**:108–23.
25. Baker TG. A quantitative and cytological study of germ cells in human ovaries. *Proc R Soc Lond (Biol)* 1963;**158**:417–33.
26. Baker TG, Scrimgeour JB. Development of the gonad in normal and anencephalic human fetuses. *J Reprod Fertil* 1980; **60**: 193–9.
27. Jones EC, Krohn PL. The effect of hypophysectomy on age change in the ovaries of mice. *J Endocrinol* 1961;**21**:497–508.
28. Richardson SJ, Senikas V, Nelson JF. Follicular depletion during the menopausal transition; evidence for accelerated loss and ultimate exhaustion. *J Clin Endocrinol Metab* 1987;**65**:1231–7.
29. Richardson SJ, Nelson JF. Follicular depletion during the menopausal transition. *Ann NY Acad Sci* 1990;**592**:13–20.

Demystifying Menopause
Judith Willis

Generations past called it "change of life." Today we're more apt to call it what it is: menopause. Yet our understanding of this change in a woman's childbearing status may still be clouded by myth and mystification.

Natural menopause is the end of menstruation and childbearing capability that occurs in most women somewhere around age 50. Today women can expect to live about a third of their lives after menopause.

Technically, the term "menopause" refers to the actual cessation of menstrual periods. When a woman has not had a period for a year, then the date of her last menstrual period is retrospectively considered the date of her menopause. However, the term "menopause" has come to be used in a general sense in place of the more proper terms, "climacteric" or "peri-menopause," which

Reprinted from the *FDA Consumer*, July/August, 1988.

encompass the years immediately preceding and following the last menstrual period.

To cut through some of the myth and mystery surrounding the hormonal changes that accompany menopause, it is necessary first to understand what happens in the cycle of a normally menstruating woman.

The menstrual cycle, averaging 28 days, is divided into two phases. The first is called the follicular, or pre-ovulatory, phase and lasts 10 to 17 days. The second is the luteal, or post-ovulatory, phase lasting 13 to 15 days.

CHANGING CYCLE

Usually sometime in a woman's early to mid 40s—two to eight years before actual menopause—her menstrual cycle begins changing. Notably, levels of hormones such as estrogen, produced by the ovaries, decrease; ovulation (release of eggs from the ovaries) stops or becomes more infrequent; and the pattern of the menstrual cycle changes.

Initially this may mean heavier and/or more frequent periods. Later, periods may be scantier and less frequent. Lack of ovulation may cause some light bleeding or spotting between periods. However, not all women follow this pattern exactly. Some may experience simply a wide variability in the time and quantity of flow, and a few may have little or no change in menstrual cycle. For some women, the unpredictability of menstrual pattern changes is unsettling because social activities can no longer be planned around a specific cycle, and there is no period due date to help determine pregnancy status. And indeed, because most women continue to ovulate at least in some cycles, pregnancy is possible until a woman has actually passed menopause. In fact, in some cultures where women bear many children, it is not uncommon for a woman to give birth to her last child and never menstruate again.

In the vast majority of cases, menstrual irregularities in the years before menopause are simply manifestations of the normal transition in the woman's hormonal status. Sometimes, if these irregularities cause too many problems or if a woman's doctor suspects that the uterine lining is not being shed completely during menstruation as happens during a normal period, the doctor may suggest treatment with a synthetic progesterone, called a progestin, to make the cycle more regular. In cases of extremely heavy bleeding, the doctor may recommend surgery.

The age at which a woman has her last period is not known to be related to race, body size, or her age when she began to menstruate. The average age for menopause in American women is 50 to 52. But it is not abnormal for it to occur several years earlier or later. Some studies show that women who have had many children reach menopause earlier. And smokers may experience menopause an average of one to two years earlier than nonsmokers.

Even after menopause, women's bodies continue to produce estrogen, but far less of the hormone is made in the ovaries. Most postmenopausal estrogen is produced in a process in which the adrenal gland makes precursors of estrogen, which are then converted by stored fat to estrogen. However, far less estrogen is produced in this manner than is produced in the ovaries before menopause.

HOT FLASHES

The most common symptom of menopause, the hot flush or flash, may begin before a woman has stopped menstruating and may continue for a couple of years after menopause. Although it is known that the hot flash (or "vasomotor flush," as doctors sometimes call it) is related to decreased estrogen levels, exactly how this occurs is not completely understood.

Many women describe the hot flash as an intense feeling of heat. Some say it actually feels like the temperature in the room has risen. Most commonly the sensation starts in the face, neck or chest and may extend to other parts of the body. It is usually accompanied by perspiration and may last a few seconds to several minutes. Increased heart rate and finger temperature have been documented during hot flashes.

About half of the women who have hot flashes visibly blush or have a patchy reddish flush of the face, neck and chest. For some women, the feeling of heat is followed by a feeling of being chilled. The hot flash may be particularly disturbing when it occurs during sleep. This problem, often involving profuse sweating, can awaken the women and is credited for much of the insomnia sometimes associated with menopause.

Up to 75 percent to 85 percent of women have hot flashes, but less than half of all women experiencing a natural menopause have symptoms severe enough to warrant medication. Obese women tend to have a lower incidence of hot flashes, possibly because they have higher levels of estrogen, converted from stored fat.

Many women find they can cope with hot flashes by dressing in layers that can be removed, wearing natural fabrics, drinking cold rather than hot beverages, keeping rooms cooler, and sleeping with fewer blankets.

ESTROGEN REPLACEMENT

For women who cannot get sufficient relief without drugs, hormone replacement therapy may be prescribed. The length of time that a woman is advised to continue taking hormones may vary from several months to several years, depending on her symptoms.

Often abbreviated ERT, estrogen replacement therapy may relieve at least two other postmenopausal problems related to lower estrogen levels: urogenital atrophy and osteoporosis. The first of these involves both the vagina and bladder. The vagina becomes foreshortened, thins, and lubricates less efficiently. Itching, burning and dryness may result. Intercourse may become painful and vaginal infections more frequent. A similar tissue thinning occurs in the bladder, sometimes resulting in urinary discomfort, which may include the sudden and/or frequent need to urinate.

Osteoporosis involves loss of bone mass. It occurs in the elderly of both sexes, but is particularly common in fair-skinned, short, thin women. Smoking is an additional risk factor. It is estimated that 25 of every 100 white women over 60 suffer spinal fractures as a result of osteoporosis.

Although osteoporosis is by no means a universal outcome of menopause, some estimates say that 60 percent of untreated white women will develop some symptoms. In addition to ERT, weight-bearing exercise and sufficient calcium intake—particularly if begun years *before* menopause—may help prevent the bone loss associated with this condition.

Other symptoms experienced by some menopausal women that are probably related to lower estrogen levels in include joint pains and sensations of tingling, prickling or creeping of the skin.

Estrogen therapy can be taken in several different dosage forms: vaginal creams, oral tablets, transdermal patches (by which the drug is slowly absorbed through the skin), and intramuscular injection. The first three are the most common dosage forms. The vaginal cream is usually given to relieve local problems of the vagina and bladder.

Although many women report a lessening of symptoms such as headaches and depression when they take estrogen, studies have not consistently shown these to be related to hormone changes. Some believe that these symptoms may be more a byproduct of other factors, such as life changes that a woman may be going through around the age of 50, preconceived and possibly erroneous ideas of what menopause may be like, and a woman's response to society's undervaluation of aging women.

In any case, because of the rare but serious adverse effects associated with estrogen use, ERT would not be considered medically appropriate for other symptoms of lowered estrogen in the absence of hot flashes, urogenital atrophy, or the potential for osteoporosis.

ADDING PROGESTIN

The most serious adverse effect of non-contraceptive estrogen use is a higher risk of endometrial cancer (cancer of the inner lining of the uterus). For a number of years after this relationship was established in the mid-70s, ERT fell into some disfavor.

In the last few years, the use of ERT has again been on the rise, with doctors increasingly prescribing a progestin in the last 10 to 13 days of each estrogen cycle to prevent endometrial hyperplasia (abnormal increase in endometrial cells), a presumed precursor of cancer. It should be noted that FDA has not yet added this use to progestin labeling and is presently evaluating data about both progestin's possible protective effects against endometrial cancer and the possible but unknown cardiovascular risk, which may include an adverse effect on cholesterol.

Postmenopausal women who are on estrogen/progestin therapy may experience some menstrual-like bleeding (although it is usually far lighter than a normal menstrual period). For this reason, some women do not like to take progestins.

The weight of evidence from scientific studies is that there is not a higher incidence of breast cancer in women who take estrogen. However, women who have had breast cancer should not take ERT (except in cases where it is part of cancer treatment), because some tumors are dependent on estrogen for their growth. Others for whom estrogen is contraindicated are those who have a known or suspected estrogen-dependent tumor, may be pregnant, have undiagnosed abnormal genital bleeding, active thrombophlebitis (blood clots) or clotting disorders, or have previously had these when given estrogen.

Since there are some women with a variety of conditions for whom ERT may not be the best choice, the benefits and risks of ERT should be weighed carefully by each woman and her physician.

Less serious side effects of ERT include enlarged and tender breasts, nausea, skin discoloration, water retention, weight gain, headache, and heartburn.

A possibly beneficial side effect of estrogen is that it may raise the levels of the desirable kind of cholesterol known as high-density lipoproteins (HDLs). (See "Knowing Your LDLs from Your HDLs" in the November 1987 *FDA Consumer*.) Scientists think that postmenopausal women who take estrogens may have added protection against heart disease. However, when progestins are added, this effect may be canceled out.

The form of progestin most often prescribed for use with ERT, medroxyprogesterone (brand names Provera, Amen, Curretab and others), seems to only slightly lower HDL levels. ERT, both with and without added progestins, lowers total cholesterol. In contrast to oral contraceptives, which use a higher dose of hormones, ERT appears not to influence blood pressure in any significant way.

Some women who cannot take estrogens can receive a certain degree of relief from hot flashes by taking a progestin alone. But this hormone does not reverse urogenital atrophy, may increase inappropriate hair loss or gain, and may lead to abnormal bleeding.

If it is not advisable for a woman to take an estrogen or a progestin, a doctor may prescribe Bellergal-S, a combination of phenobarbital, ergotamine and belladonna alkaloids, which FDA has approved for relieving hot flashes. While not specifically approved for hot flashes, clonidine (Catapres and others), a heart drug, is sometimes prescribed for this purpose, and studies show that it gives some relief.

Doctors may also prescribe other drugs for relief of symptoms such as insomnia, headache and depression. FDA has noted that at least one product is being marketed over-the-counter for the relief of "tension, irritability, and stress headache during menopause." The agency is investigating the claims of this product, which contains acetaminophen (the active ingredient in Datril, Tylenol, Panadol and others) and an antihistamine (an ingredient approved for OTC use in allergy, cold, and sleep-aid preparations).

As the proportion of women nearing menopause increases with the advancing age of "baby boomers," it is likely that more attention will be paid to the interests of menopausal women. This focus may provide impetus for a more complete scientific unraveling of the mysteries surrounding this stage of life, so that women may deal with it on a factual basis and be free to live the latter third of their lives in the fullest manner possible.

TERMS YOUR DOCTOR MAY USE WHEN DISCUSSING MENOPAUSE

Arthralgia—pain in a joint; experienced by some women during climacteric.

Breakthrough bleeding—any visible blood when not expected.

Climacteric—the years leading up to and following the last menstrual period. Also called "peri-menopause."

DUB—dysfunctional uterine bleeding; excessive and/or unpredictable bleeding from the womb, not due to any abnormality, that frequently occurs in the few years before menopause.

Dyspareunia—difficult or painful sexual intercourse.

Endometrium—lining of the uterus (womb).

FSH—follicle-stimulating hormone; stimulates development of sacs that hold the eggs.

GnRH—gonadotropin-releasing hormone; stimulates the release of FSH and LH.

Hysterectomy—surgical removal of the uterus (womb).

LH—luteinizing hormone; stimulates the release of the egg from the sac.

Leiomyoma—also called a fibroid; a non-cancerous growth in the womb that occurs in 20 percent to 25 percent of women before menopause and causes no symptoms in most women.

Menorrhagia—heavy menstrual bleeding and excessively long periods.

Myomectomy—surgical removal of fibroids from the uterus.

Oligomenorrhea—infrequent menstruation with diminished flow.

Oophorectomy—surgical removal of the ovaries, sometimes called castration.

Paresthesia—sensation of tingling; prickling or creeping of the skin; experienced by some women during climacteric.

Withdrawal bleeding—"planned" bleeding while on a medication that occurs during the hormone-free period of a cycle or after progestin has been added to a continuous estrogen cycle.

Should You Take Estrogen?
A Report from the National Institutes of Health

During menopause, the amount of estrogen produced by the body declines. The loss of this female hormone may cause troublesome symptoms such as hot flashes (sudden warm flushes of the face, neck, and chest), excessive sweating (especially at night), and vaginal dryness. Although most women have little or no difficulty with these symptoms, some experience severe discomfort.

Estrogen loss is also the leading cause of osteoporosis in older women. Osteoporosis, a bone disease that produces fragile bones, affects 24 million Americans. A fall or minor accident can cause bones weakened by osteoporosis to break easily.

Although some degree of bone loss can be expected in the course of normal aging, some women are more likely than others to develop osteoporosis. Women at highest risk are those who have an early or artificial menopause (when both ovaries are surgically removed or caused not to function). White women, women who are extremely inactive, take corticosteroid medicines (drugs used to treat arthritis and other inflammatory diseases), or have a slight build also are at risk of developing osteoporosis. In addition, women who have a low intake of calcium in their diet, smoke cigarettes, drink an excess amount of alcohol, cannot absorb calcium, or have thyroid or kidney disease have an increased risk of developing this bone disease.

Some women take estrogen to replace the natural estrogen lost during and after menopause. Estrogen replacement therapy (ERT) may be given to women with severe menopausal symptoms and to those at high risk of developing osteoporosis. Although experts believe that estrogen is an effective treatment for osteoporosis, it is not recommended for all menopausal women. Each woman and her doctor must consider the benefits and risks of ERT.

About 10 percent of women who take ERT have side effects such as headaches, nausea, and vaginal discharge. Fluid retention, swollen breasts, and weight gain also may result from ERT.

Estrogen use has been linked to an increase in endometrial cancer (cancer of the lining of the uterus). This cancer has been found more often in women who use ERT containing estrogen as the only ingredient. Most women today take a combination of estrogen and progestin, another female hormone. This combined treatment appears to reduce or eliminate the risk of endometrial cancer. In addition, women who have had a hysterectomy (removal of the uterus) are in no danger of developing endometrial cancer.

Studies of a possible association between ERT and heart disease show contradictory findings. A Harvard Medical School report indicates that estrogen may reduce the risk of heart disease, while the Framingham Heart Study reports that heart attack and stroke are more common in women using estrogen. To resolve this controversy, the National Heart, Lung, and Blood Institute, the National Institute on Aging, and several other Institutes within the National Institutes of Health will soon study the effects of estrogen on the cardiovascular system.

Caution is warranted when considering ERT for women with high blood pressure, liver disease, diabetes, thrombophlebitis (blood clots in a vein), seizure disorders, migraine headaches, gallbladder disease, obesity, or cancer. Daughters of women who took diethylstilbestrol (DES) during pregnancy may have reproductive system changes that make the use of estrogens dangerous.

All women taking ERT should be examined once a year. This check-up should include a blood pressure reading, breast and pelvic exams, and a re-evaluation of the usefulness of ERT. Unusual vaginal bleeding should be reported to a doctor at once.

For women who cannot or choose not to take estrogen, there are other ways to deal with menopausal symptoms. For example, one simple way to lubricate the vagina is to apply water-soluble surgical jelly (*not* petroleum jelly).

Certain health habits can help strengthen bones, particularly when started early in life. All adult women should get 1,000 mg of calcium daily, and postmeno-pausal women not taking ERT should get 1,500 mg each day. Milk and dairy products are the best dietary sources of calcium. Other foods high in calcium include dark green leafy vegetables, salmon, and tofu (soybean curd).

Vitamin D is necessary for calcium absorption, and 400 international units of this vitamin are recommended daily. Brief, daily exposure to sunlight (which causes the body to manufacture vitamin D) and eating a balanced diet usually are enough to ensure an adequate intake of this vitamin. Finally, weight-bearing exercise—walking or jogging—strengthens bones and helps prevent osteoporosis.

Many menopausal and postmenopausal women benefit from ERT, but it is not for everyone. To learn whether this treatment might be effective for you, talk with your doctor.

Emotional Well-Being, Sexual Behaviour and Hormone Replacement Therapy
Myra S. Hunter

Improvements in the design of epidemiological studies of the climacteric and postmenopause have been made in the past 25 years. But more complex theoretical models are necessary if we are to give due emphasis to the influence of psychological, social, cultural and hormonal factors and their interactions. The majority of studies show that emotional problems are not more prevalent during the climacteric and postmenopause and that psychosocial factors, such as stressful life-events, are more likely causes of emotional distress during mid-life. Vaginal dryness increases in postmenopausal women but there are varied reasons for changes in other aspects of sexual behaviour which require further research. While estrogen may have a "mental tonic" effect when prescribed in high doses, HRT does not appear to have a significant effect upon mood or sexual behaviour over and above placebo effects and the relief from vasomotor and vaginal symptoms.

Reprinted with permission from *Maturitas* (1990) 12: 299–314. Copyright © 1990, Elsevier Scientific Publishers Ireland Ltd.

INTRODUCTION

The past 25 years has seen the development of the medical model of the menopause in Western societies: the menopause as an oestrogen deficiency disease which, if left untreated, might impair the health and well-being of climacteric and postmenopausal women. Symptoms such as irritability, tiredness, anxiety, sexual disinterest and lack of concentration are described as common climacteric problems. Hormone replacement therapy (HRT) is hailed by some doctors to be a treatment for "menopausal depression" and to play a role in improving the quality of life for postmenopausal women.

Cross-cultural research [1–3] provides clear evidence that the meaning ascribed to the menopause and hence its treatment is, to an extent, socially constructed. The degree to which women in general have been influenced by the medical model of the menopause is uncertain. In a recent North American study of women's attitudes, the majority felt that the menopause should be "viewed as a medical condition and treated as such". However, at the same time, they attributed emotional problems to stressful life changes rather than hormonal fluctuations, and they preferred natural treatment options (such as exercise and dietary changes) to HRT [4]. When the attitudes of women and family doctors were compared, Cowan and colleagues [5] found that doctors tend to regard the menopause as a more pathological process than women, perhaps because their impressions are derived from clinic samples—samples known to report high levels of distress [6]. After reviewing the available evidence and drawing upon the experiences of Manitoban women, Kaufert and Gilbert [7] concluded that the menopause has not been medicalised to any great extent especially when compared with other reproductive events, such as pregnancy and childbirth.

Health professionals tend to hold a variety of clinical models, depending upon their age, training, area of specialisation and pattern of medical practice. Women also have their own lay models of the menopause and will be differentially influenced by medical and non-medical (or psychosocial) models depending upon their exposure to information, their socioeconomic status, peer group values and existing health beliefs [8,9].

Women's well-being during the menopause, as during other times of life, is likely to be dependent upon the appropriateness of the explanatory models that they and their doctors use to understand their emotions and behaviour [10,11]. Fortunately, more complex models are beginning to be developed, which should provide a forum for discussing the influences of hormonal and psychosocial factors as well as their interactions [12].

During the past decade improvements have been made in the methodology and design of epidemiological studies of the climacteric and postmenopause. These are described in detail by Kaufert and Gilbert [13].

Several large-scale cross-sectional studies were set up in the 1980s, using broadly similar methodologies, in Manitoba [14], in Massachusetts [15], in Japan [3] in Norway [16] and in South East England [17]. Four of these projects have a prospective component—premenopausal women being followed for between three and five years until they become peri or postmenopausal. Drawing on data from these and other recent studies, the following questions will be considered:

(i) Is the menopause associated with changes in emotional well-being and sexual behaviour?

(ii) What factors are associated with emotional distress during mid-life?

(iii) What is the role of oestrogen?

(iv) Is HRT justified as a treatment for emotional and sexual problems?

The broad terms emotional well-being and emotional distress are used here to include depressed mood as well as clinical depression and non-psychotic psychiatric disorder. These categories are referred to separately where relevant. Research on sexual behaviour is included in the following sections as a topic in its own right, as well as providing an example of how hormonal changes can indirectly affect emotional well-being.

(i) Is the menopause associated with changes in emotional well-being and/or sexual behaviour?

While there is general consensus that hot flushes, night sweats and vaginal dryness increase during and after the menopause [18], the evidence from epidemiological studies pertaining to emotional symptoms and sexual behaviour has been equivocal. However, a clearer picture is emerging.

Emotional Well-Being

Of the cross-sectional studies carried out in the 60s and 70s, some have shown perimenopausal increases in the prevalence of psychological symptoms [19,20], while in others no changes were evident [21–23]. In subsequent cross-sectional studies, carried out during the 1980s, methodology continued to be refined. Several studies [13,24,25] included standardised instruments to measure emotional well-being and others a prospective component [13,16,24,26].

First, Holte set up the extensive Norwegian climacteric project which has a cross-sectional ($N = 2400$) and a 4-year prospective ($N = 200$) phase. The cross-sectional results show that psychological symptoms did not increase during the climacteric or postmenopause [27] and the prospective data are beginning to support these findings [16].

In Manitoba 2500 women, aged between 40 and 59 years, were included in a cross-sectional postal survey. Approximately

one fifth were then followed up, using 6 telephone interviews, for 3 years. There were no significant increases in emotional symptoms (assessed by symptom scales, the Bradburn index of well-being and the CES depression scale) in women of differing menopausal status in the cross-sectional phase nor in the prospective phases of this study [13,14]. In a similarly designed survey of over 8000 women living in Massachusetts, McKinlay and McKinlay [15] again found no changes in emotional symptoms with menopausal status. This was also the case when the first three prospective assessments were examined using a cross-sectional design [24]. In fact, it was the women who had undergone a surgical, rather than a natural, menopause who were more likely to be depressed.

In the cross-sectional and prospective phases of the South East England study symptoms, attitudes and help-seeking behaviour, were assessed [25,26]. The results of the two phases of the study were similar and showed that, for the majority of women, the menopause was not a major crisis and did not influence ratings of general health nor medical help-seeking behaviour. However, there was a small but significant increase in depressed mood (scale validated by comparison with 30-item General Health Questionnaire [28]) in peri and postmenopausal women, reflected in the items irritability and reduced enjoyment in activities. Possible explanations of this finding are discussed elsewhere [26] and in section (ii).

Finally, Lock [3] found that Japanese women who had stopped menstruating did not report any more emotional symptoms than the women who were still menstruating. For most women it was "konenki" (a self-defined gradual period of change associated with ageing) which was accompanied by symptomatology. It is interesting that few of these Japanese women reported having hot flushes. This study, together with that of Beyenne [1] and others, illustrates the relative nature of "climacteric symptoms" and the possible influence of cultural, psychological and possible physiological differences, such as health and diet, upon experience of symptoms.

In summary, there is a growing body of evidence, based on the results of recent well controlled epidemiological studies, that points to the conclusion that, for the majority of women, emotional well-being is not adversely affected by the climacteric or postmenopausal. There is a wide variation in women's experience of the menopause and, in some studies, increases in minor symptoms, particularly during the perimenopause, have been found. The possible reasons why some women might become depressed during the climacteric or postmenopausal are discussed in section (ii).

Psychiatric Disorder

The diagnosis of involutional melancholia is no longer considered to be appropriate [29]. In general, there is no conclusive evidence that psychiatric disorder is particularly prevalent during the climacteric and postmenopause [30,31]. The majority of studies, using psychiatric interviews or standardised assessments, have failed to demonstrate an increase in the incidence or prevalence of psychiatric disorder during the climacteric or postmenopause [32–34]. There was a slight exacerbation of existing symptoms in perimenopausal women in Hallstrom's study [33]. However, these women still had fewer symptoms than younger women who were premenopausal.

Ballinger's results are the exception [35]. Using the General Health Questionnaire (GHQ, [28]), in a survey of over 500 Scottish women, she did not find an increased prevalence of psychiatric cases during the perimenopause. However, the GHQ scores might have been inflated by items reflecting somatic and vasomotor symptoms. In a fur-

ther analysis of the data, hypochondriasis and insomnia were found to be more common in perimenopausal women—symptoms which could be associated with vasomotor changes.

Sexual Behaviour

Although sexual problems are commonly reported in clinic samples [36], there have been few well-designed studies of non-clinic populations.

Kinsey and colleagues [37] interviewed women throughout the life cycle and found a decline with age in incidence and frequency of marital coitus, and of coitus to the point of orgasm, but not a decline in women's solitary sexual activities, such as masturbation, until well after 60 years of age. Pfeiffer et al. [38] also found a gradual decrease in sexual interest and coital activity with age, particularly between 45 and 55, for both men and women. Similarly, in a more recent British study of both sexes [20], the men in the study reported greater sexual disinterest in their late 40s and early 50s than the women.

One of the most extensive studies of sexual behaviour was conducted by Hallstrom [33], who examined both age and menopausal status in over 800 Swedish women. He found a progressive decline in sexual interest across menopausal stages, over and above the effects of age, and a similar trend was evident for coital frequency and orgasm. The decline was associated with low social class and psychiatric disorder.

McCoy and Davidson [39] carried out the first longitudinal study of sexual behaviour in 16 women. Small but significant decreases in sexual activity, sexual thoughts and vaginal lubrication were found, but not in orgasmic frequency or sexual enjoyment. Questions were included about sexual interest, satisfaction and vaginal dryness in the cross-sectional and prospective studies carried out in S.E. England [25,26]. Approximately 70% of the sample of 474 women, aged between 45 and 56 years, reported being sexually active. While there were no differences between pre-, peri- and post-menopausal women (aged 45 to 54), fewer of the older postmenopausal women (55–65 years ($N = 179$)) were sexually active. Sexual interest did decrease stepwise across menopausal stages, when the effects of age were controlled, and vaginal dryness (causing discomfort with intercourse) was more prevalent in postmenopausal women. However, this latter symptom was not confined to the postmenopause—26% of pre- and perimenopausal women reported vaginal dryness compared with 40% of those who were postmenopausal. Despite these changes, over 80% of all the women felt satisfied with their sexual relationships. Sexual difficulties were associated with marital problems, stress and ill-health, as well as menopausal status.

A tentative conclusion is that, on average, there seems to be some reduction in sexual interest and/or behaviour during and after the menopause. However, certainly not all couples have sexual problems. Most studies suffer from methodological problems and require careful interpretation. For example, partner unavailability is an important issue for some women in this age group and clearly partners' sexual interest is relevant [40]. Factors such as marital conflict and a woman's sense of well-being, her level of stress, her attitudes towards the menopause, her experience of hot flushes, night sweats and particularly vaginal dryness and dyspareunia should also be considered. Painful intercourse can lead to secondary anxiety and sexual inhibition in both partners. On the other hand regular and continued sexual activity does appear to protect against vaginal dryness [41].

Further prospective research is needed to examine the relative importance of hormonal (central nervous system mechanisms as well as vaginal lubrication and blood flow), psychological and social factors. Sexual behavior is reviewed more fully elsewhere [42–44], and the hormonal influences upon sexual behaviour are discussed in section (iii).

(ii) What factors are associated with emotional distress during mid-life?

When approaching the menopause a woman brings with her certain expectations of the menopause and ageing, habitual ways of coping with stress, a level of physical health and emotional well-being and a complex social network offering varying degrees of stress and support. Her reaction to the menopause will be determined by an interaction of these social and psychological factors as well as her experience of symptoms such as hot flushes and vaginal dryness.

Life Stresses and Social Situation

Mid-life is commonly regarded as a time of psychosocial transition and readjustment. While some women might face widowhood, an "empty nest" and worries about elderly parents, these events are not necessarily temporally linked to the menopause, particularly now that there is greater variability in the timing of life stages.

A child leaving home is a life change which is not necessarily stressful. While there is some evidence from clinic samples that fewer menopausal symptoms are reported when children are still at home [45], the results of general population surveys suggest that those who have "emptied their nest" are not more prone to depression [46] and that this event is met with relief by many couples [47]. In general, it seems to be women of child rearing age, particularly those who have young children at home, who tend to report more emotional problems.

There is, however, a great deal of evidence indicating that stressful life events, in particular losses or bereavements, lead to emotional and somatic symptoms for women in general [48,49] and for women during the climacteric [50,51].

Greene and Cooke [50] carried out a detailed investigation of the impact of a range of stresses in climacteric and post-menopausal women. Stressful life events accounted for a greater proportion of the variation in psychological and somatic symptoms than did menopausal status, and it was life events including exits (people leaving the social network, for example, loss of parents) that were particularly associated with symptoms [51]. Similar conclusions were drawn by Holte [16] who, in the preliminary analysis of his longitudinal data, found that life events and previous symptoms were the major predictors of symptoms during the climacteric and postmenopause.

An interesting hypothesis—that life stress has a direct biochemical effect upon oestrogen levels—has been suggested [52]. However, there is only limited evidence so far. Firstly, Ballinger found that oestrogen levels increased as depression lifted in a sample of depressed patients [52]. Secondly, several epidemiological studies provide evidence that women who suffer from psychiatric disorder before the menopause might be more prone to vasomotor symptoms when they reach the menopause [17,33,34,53]. The impact of stress upon oestrogen levels, and hence vasomotor symptoms and the interactions between these variables, warrants further attention.

Studies of marital and employment status and social class have produced equivocal results, probably because these variables are complex and produce numerous interactions. An intimate confiding relationship can have a protective effect, or buffer, against other life stresses [48]; but clearly it is the quality of the relationship that is important for mental health [54]. In general, working class women tend to have more symptoms than middle class women, as do married women and those who are housewives with children at home, compared with single women or those without children [48,55,56]. In the S.E. England and Massachusetts studies [24,26] single women were found to be less likely to be depressed, followed by married women and those who were widowed, divorced or separated. In the latter study, there was an interaction between years of education and marital status, the less well-educated women who were widowed, divorced or separated being most likely to be depressed.

Employment can act as a stress buffer, but not necessarily—its effects will depend upon a woman's marital status, social class and the nature of her work [57]. Jennings and colleagues [58], reporting on the cross-sectional phase of the Massachusetts study, found that while unemployed women were least healthy, full-time home-makers were less healthy than employed women. The relationship between health and employment was stronger in women who had fewer years of education.

The difficult task of unraveling the effects of psychosocial variables is one which will continue. While it is clear that psychosocial factors, such as life stresses, are associated with reduced emotional well-being, there is no convincing evidence that mid-life is more stressful than other life stages, for example, early motherhood. When the relative impact of menopausal status and psychosocial factors has been examined, psychosocial factors account for much more of the variation in depression than menopausal status [13,24,26,59].

Coping Ability, Attitudes and Expectations

The way in which social transitions are experienced and whether symptoms are attributed to the menopause or not, will depend, among other things, upon an individual's coping strategies, beliefs and expectations. Coping ability has rarely been studied in the context of the menopause. Women who have a past history of emotional problems are, not surprisingly, also more likely to have such problems during the menopause [26,33,53].

Experience of menstruation and pregnancy have been thought to influence reactions to the menopause, but the evidence is insufficient and inconsistent to date. For example, in one study, distaste for menstruation and problems with pregnancy and delivery were associated with positive attitudes to the menopause [60], while in another, reports of past menstrual problems were one of the main predictors of psychological symptoms in climacteric women [59]. While a psychological explanation (that menstrual coping behaviour is learnt) seems plausible, a hormonal explanation is also possible. Some sort of hormonal vulnerability, leading women to have both menstrual and menopausal symptoms, has been proposed [61], but has not yet been systematically studied.

Attitudes and beliefs about the menopause have been investigated in the context of the cultural meaning ascribed to this life stage [60,62], and in terms of the attitudes held by individuals within a particular culture [17,63]. Negative stereotypes of menopausal women are prevalent in Western societies where the menopause is associated with decline of functions, ageing and reduced youth and beauty.

In one of the earliest studies of attitudes, Neugarten and co-workers [63] found that women individually do not hold such negative attitudes as might be expected, and that premenopausal women had more negative attitudes than women who had already experienced the menopause. More recently, McKinlay and McKinlay [15], found that between 70 and 80% of their sample associated the cessation of periods with relief.

Using a different approach, Boulet et al. [64] asked a large sample of Belgian women to rate the potential impact of the menopause upon their lives. They found that the menopause was perceived as being relatively unimportant compared to other life events.

Attitudes to the menopause are not one-dimensional. In a study of British women's attitudes, expectations and stereotypes, the menopause was regarded as an event which brought emotional and physical symptoms but which also brought relief from menstruation and pregnancy. In the prospective phase of this study stereotyped beliefs and expectations were included as possible predictors of later depression, together with other psychosocial and health variables. A stepwise regression analysis revealed that previous depression, holding negative stereotyped beliefs, together with not being employed and being working class—assessed before the menopause—accounted for approximately 50% of the variation in depressed mood in peri- and postmenopausal women [26].

So although depressed mood increased in peri and postmenopausal women in this study, menopausal status accounted for only a small percentage of the variation in depressed mood (2%), whereas the prospective results show that a considerably larger proportion of the variation (50%) can be explained by individual and social factors.

In the Norwegian cross-sectional study [59] personal expectations of the menopause were associated with emotional and somatic symptoms. The prospective phase of this study is in progress [16].

In summary, psychosocial factors—including life stresses, previous depression, and probably also beliefs about the menopause—play a more important role in determining a woman's emotional well-being than her menopausal status. Unfortunately few studies have had the resources to combine hormonal assessments in epidemiological surveys; the Norwegian study is the exception and should clarify this question further.

(iii) The role of oestrogen

From the biological perspective, psychological symptoms can be seen as direct or indirect consequences of decline in ovarian function. Various mechanisms have been proposed, including lowered levels of oestrogen and progesterone, raised levels of follicle stimulating hormone (FSH) or luteinising hormone (LH) or altered hypothalamic function. The indirect effects of hormonal changes include the impact of severe vasomotor symptoms and vaginal dryness upon emotional well-being and sexual relationships.

There is evidence from animal experiments and laboratory studies that oestrogen might activate and progesterone depress the central nervous system (CNS) [65,66]. Several mechanisms have been proposed to explain oestrogen's possible "mental tonic" action. For example, oestrogen may have a monoamine oxidase inhibitory effect leading to increased noradrenaline synthesis and increased CNS activation. Depression in menopausal women may then arise as a result of hypoestrogenisation and catecholamine depletion [67,68].

Another hypothesis is that oestrogens influence tryptophan release; oestrogen deficiency is associated with low concentrations of free plasma tryptophan and hence depression [69,70]. While there is some support for these theories [71,72], a direct relationship between depression and oestrogen levels is not generally supported by other studies [73].

The results of correlational studies have failed to demonstrate an association between hormone levels and psychological variables in menstruating women; for complex behaviour, such as mood and sexual behaviour, environmental factors and individual differences, account for most cyclic variations [74–76].

Few studies have been carried out to investigate hormone levels in non-clinic samples of menopausal women who are not taking HRT, but the available evidence points to a lack of association between mood and hormone levels. Coope [77] found that neither oestrogen nor FSH correlated with scores of postmenopausal women on the Beck depression scale [78]. In a more detailed study, Ballinger and colleagues [79] took four separate measures of oestradiol, progesterone, FSH and LH and testosterone in pre-, peri- and postmenopausal women. Eighty-five women took part and completed the General Health Questionnaire (GHQ, [28]). No significant associations between GHQ scores or ratings of depression and hormone levels were apparent, apart from the finding that for postmenopausal women raised GHQ scores were associated with high oestrogen levels.

Sexual interest and behaviour also appears to be relatively independent of oestrogen levels [80]. No significant correlations having been found between oestradiol and sexual interest [33,79,81], nor between testosterone and "loss of libido" [81,82]. However, vaginal dryness, leading to dyspareunia and discomfort for some women, is associated with lowered oestrogen levels [83] and appears to be the only aspect of sexual behaviour that clearly fits with an hormonal explanation.

Several studies were set up in the 1970s to assess symptoms before and after surgical menopause and then again in response to HRT or placebo. In the first of these, Utian [84] concluded that most symptoms, including depression and libido, were not associated with ovarian function. While general mood did improve with oestrogen treatment, mood change bore little relationship to the oophorectomy. He coined the phrase "mental tonic effect" to explain this lifting of mood with HRT.

In a similar study—but this time including a double-blind crossover design—Dennerstein and colleagues [61] compared several hormonal regimes, using the Hamilton depression scale and visual analogue scales. Hamilton scores improved with oestrogen treatment and to a lesser extent with progesterone and placebo. An analysis of covariance revealed that the improvement in mood could be partly explained by the "domino effect" (relief from hot flushes). Oestrogen, but not progesterone, also had a significant effect on sexual desire, enjoyment and orgasmic frequency, but not on coital frequency. Changes in sexual desire and mood were correlated.

Improvements in mood, assessed by the Multiple Adjective Checklist, were also found when intramuscular injections (oestrogen vs. testosterone vs. oestrogen plus testosterone vs. placebo) were given to women who had undergone hysterectomy and bilateral oophorectomy [85]. Depressed mood lifted in response to the hormonal treatments while anxiety did not. The relationship between mood and vasomotor symptoms was not assessed.

While this type of design enables causal relationships to be examined more clearly, the extent to which hormonal and emotional reactions to surgical menopause mirror the more gradual changes during the natural menopause is questionable. It is also difficult to see how placebo groups remained blind when such favourable relief from vasomotor symptoms was achieved.

The effects of HRT on naturally menopausal women have been studied in several double-blind cross-over designs in the past 20 years. Comparison between studies is difficult because of the varied and often unstandardised measures used.

In general, a strong placebo effect of psychological symptoms to any kind of medication has been found [86,87]. When treated and untreated groups were compared on standardised psychological tests, there were no differences between oestrogen therapy and placebo using the Beck depression scale [77,87,88], the Hamilton Rating Scale [89], nor the GHQ [86]. Conflicting results emerged using the Minnesota Multiphasic Personality Inventory (MMPI), Strickler et al. [90] finding no difference between oestrogen therapy and placebo, while Durst and Maoz [91] found reductions in scales reflecting depression. Some improvements in minor emotional symptoms, particularly emotional well-being, have been demonstrated with oestrogen therapy when unstandardised rating scales were used [86,91,92]. While in other studies [87,88] no improvements were found using such measures. Campbell and Whitehead [86] regarded the reduction of psychological symptoms in their study as largely due to the relief from hot flushes, a conclusion which is supported by Dennerstein and colleagues [93].

The use of high doses of oestrogens is controversial. There is limited evidence that mood in depressed patients might be improved under such regimes [68]. Montgomery and co-workers [94] assessed the impact of implants of oestradiol (50 mg), oestradiol plus testosterone (100 mg) and a placebo on psychological symptoms measured by the Kellner and Sheffield's self rating scale of distress (SRD30). Overall, there were no differences between treatment and placebo conditions. For perimenopausal women there was an initial improvement in the treated group (2 months after implantation), but between 2 and 4 months after implantation the placebo group improved, while the treatment groups did not. When postmenopausal women were considered there were no significant group differences at 2 or 4 months. Nevertheless the authors conclude that "climacteric depression responds well to hormone replacement therapy". But, even if oestrogens were shown to have a positive effect on mood, assumptions cannot then be made about the original causes of depression.

The role of hormones in treating sexual problems is also controversial. The particular benefit of oestrogen is the alleviation of vaginal dryness which can cause dyspareunia. However, testosterone has been recommended for women with low sexual desire

[95] and, while there is limited evidence suggesting that testosterone might increase sexual motivation [96] and/or sexual responsiveness [41,97], there is evidence which fails to show such an effect [98]. Increases in hostility have also been found with the use of testosterone [85]. Finally, when testosterone injections were compared with psychosexual counselling for problems of loss of libido, the latter treatment was shown to be superior [99].

Now that progestogens are generally prescribed with oestrogens, it is clearly important to evaluate the effects of both hormones. Dennerstein and colleagues [61,100], found that when a progestogen was added to oestrogen, the beneficial effects on mood and sexual functioning were reduced, a conclusion which is supported by others [101,102].

(iv) Is HRT justified as a treatment for emotional and sexual problems?

The following summaries of the preceding sections are relevant to this question:

(i) Emotional problems do not necessarily increase during the climacteric or post-menopause. While there is considerable individual variation in women's experience, the recent well-designed prospective studies show few overall changes as women progress through the menopause. Further research is needed to investigate individual differences, such as the impact of menstrual symptoms, irregularities, and hormonal fluctuations during the perimenopause, and the impact of premature and surgical menopause.

(ii) Psychosocial factors, in particular life stresses, account for much more of the variation in emotional well-being than does menopausal status. Interactions between emotional state and oestrogen levels warrant further investigation.

(iii) Holding unduly negative beliefs about the physical and emotional aspects of the menopause might lead women to experience greater distress when their menopause is reached. The "deficiency disease" view of the menopause is not appropriate for emotional problems experienced during the menopause, and might even reinforce negative beliefs about this life stage.

(iv) On balance, hormone replacement therapy does not appear to improve emotional well-being when standardised tests are used. A direct (CNS) effect of oestrogens upon mood, particularly when given in high doses, cannot be ruled out altogether but, given points (i) and (ii), such treatment would seem inappropriate.

It follows that HRT is not justified as a treatment for emotional problems. However, this is not to deny the secondary benefits from the relief of vasomotor and/or vaginal symptoms which HRT can bring to those who are distressed by such problems. For example, sleep problems and sexual difficulties might resolve and energy levels improve as a result. Further research is needed to disentangle the range of variables which influence sexual behaviour during this life stage. However, psychosexual counselling, together with hormonal treatment of vaginal dryness or dyspareunia if necessary, can help to alleviate sexual problems.

There are several approaches that can help women to find solutions to emotional problems. Obviously the first stage of problem-solving is to try to understand the reasons for distress. If emotional symptoms are inappropriately attributed to the menopause, then underlying problems, for example marital conflict or grief reactions, are likely to remain unresolved. Counselling, marital and psychosexual counselling, cognitive therapy, psychotherapy and support groups can then be considered [103,104].

There is also evidence that psychological approaches such as relaxation and stress reduction can alleviate vasomotor symptoms [105,106], and that exercise can promote feelings of well-being and possibly lead to reductions in symptoms associated with the menopause [107].

Whenever possible it would make sense for women to find solutions to emotional and social problems, and ways of coping with stress, before they reach the menopause. If they are well prepared (by being informed, having realistic expectations and a knowledge of the range of treatments and methods available to alleviate symptoms that might arise [108]) then they are likely to approach this life stage with a sense of personal control and mastery—factors which facilitate coping and are associated with emotional well-being.

REFERENCES

1. Beyenne Y. Cultural significance and physiological manifestations of menopause, a biocultural analysis. Cult Med Psychiat 1986; 10: 47–71.
2. Kaufert P. Anthropology and the menopause: the development of a theoretical framework. Maturitas 1982b; 4: 181–193.
3. Lock M. Ambiguities of aging: Japanese experience and perceptions of menopause. Cult Med Psychiat 1980; 10: 23–46.
4. Leiblum SR, Swartzman LS. Women's attitudes about the menopause: an update. Maturitas 1986; 81: 47–56.
5. Cowan G, Warren LW, Young JL. Medical perceptions of menopausal symptoms. Psych Women Quarterly 1985; 9(1): 3–14.
6. Ballinger S. Psychosocial stress and symptoms of menopause: a comparative study of menopause clinic patients and non-patients. Maturitas 1985; 7: 315–327.
7. Kaufert PA, Gilbert P. Women, menopause and medicalisation. Cult Med Psychiat 1986; 10: 7–21.
8. Rosenstock IM, Kirscht JP. Why do people seek health care? In: Stone GC, Adler NE, eds. Health psychology: a handbook. San Francisco: Jossey Bros, 1979.
9. Mechanic D. The experience and expression of distress: the study of illness behaviour and medical utilization. In: Mechanic D, ed. Handbook of health, health care and the health professions. New York: Free Press, 1983.
10. Watts FN. Attributional aspects of medicine. In: Antaki C, Brewin C, eds. Application of attribution theory to clinical and educational psychology. London: Academic Press, 1982.
11. Hewstone M. Attribution theory and common sense explanations: An introductory overview. In: M. Hewstone, ed. Attribution theory: social and functional extensions. Oxford: Basil Blackwell, 1983.
12. Greene JG. Psychosocial models of the climacteric. In: Zichella L, Whitehead M, Van Keep PA, eds. The climacteric and beyond. UK. USA: Parthenon, 1987; 155–167.
13. Kaufert PA, Gilbert P. Researching the symptoms of the menopause: an exercise in methodology. Maturitas 1988; 10(2): 117–131.
14. Kaufert PA. Women and their health in the middle years: a Manitoba project. Soc Sci Med 1984; 18(3):279–281.
15. McKinlay M, McKinlay JB. Health status and health care utilization by menopausal women. In: Notelovitz M, Van Keep PA, eds. The climacteric in perspective. Proceedings of the fourth int. congress on the menopause. Lancaster: MTP Press Ltd, 1986.
16. Holte A. The Norwegian menopausal project. Paper presented at the fifth int. congress on the menopause. International Menopause Society, 1987.
17. Hunter MS. Psychological and somatic experience of the climacteric and postmenopause: predicting individual differences and help-seeking behaviour. PhD thesis. University of London, 1988.
18. Studd JWW, Chakravarti S, Oram DH. The climacteric. Clinics in obstetrics and gynaecology 1977; 4(1): 3–29.
19. Jaszman ND, Van Lith ND, Zaat JCA. The peri-menopausal symptoms: the statistical analysis of a survey. Med Gynae Social 1969; 4(10): 268–277.
20. Bungay GT, Vessay MP, McPherson CK. Study of symptoms in middle life with special reference to the menopause. Br Med J 1980; ii: 181–183.
21. McKinlay SM, Jefferys M. The menopausal syndrome. Br J Prev Soc Med 1974; 28: 108–115.

22. Thompson B, Hart SA, Durno D. Menopausal age and symptomatology in a general practice. J Bio Soc Sci 1973; 5: 71–82.
23. Greene JG. A factor analytic study of climacteric symptoms. J of Psychosom Res 1976; 20: 425–430.
24. McKinlay JB, McKinlay SM, Brambrilla D. The relative contributions of endocrine changes and social circumstances to depression in mid-aged women. J Health Soc Beh 1987; 28: 345–363.
25. Hunter MS, Battersby R, Whitehead M. Relationships between psychological symptoms, somatic complaints and menopausal status. Maturitas 1986; 8: 217–228.
26. Hunter MS. Psychological and somatic experience of the menopause: A prospective study. Psychosom Med 1990; 52: 357–367.
27. Mikkelsen A. Holte A. A factor-analytic study of "climacteric" symptoms. Psychiat Soc Sci 1982; 2: 35–39.
28. Goldberg D. The detection of psychiatric illness by questionnaire. London: Oxford Univ Press, 1972.
29. Rosenthal SH. The involutional depressive syndrome. Am J Psychiat 1968; 124, 11: 21–35.
30. Winokur G. Depression in the menopause. Amer J Psychiat 1973; 130, 1: 92–93.
31. Weissman MM, Klerman GL. Sex differences and the epidemiology of depression. In: Bayes M, Howell E, eds. Women and mental health. New York: Basic Books Inc, 1981.
32. Hagnell O. Incidence and duration of episodes of mental illness in a total population. In: Hare EH, Wing JK, eds. Psychiatric epidemiology. London: Oxford Univ Press, 1970.
33. Hallstrom T. Mental disorder and sexuality in the climacteric: A study in psychiatric epidemiology. Goteborg: Scandinavian Univ Books, 1973.
34. Gath D, Osborn M, Bungay G, Iles S, Day A, Bond A, Passingham C. Psychiatric disorder and gynaecological symptoms in middle aged women; a community survey. Brit Med J 1987; 294: 213–218.
35. Ballinger CB. Psychiatric morbidity and the menopause; screening of general population sample. Br Med J 1975; 9: 344–346.
36. Sarrel PM, Whitehead M. Sex and menopause: defining the issues. Maturitas 1985; 7: 217–224.
37. Kinsey AC, Pomeroy WB, Martin CE, Gebhard DH. Sexual behaviour in the human female. Philadelphia: Saunders, 1953.
38. Pfeiffer E, Verwoerdt A, Davis GC. Sexual behaviour in middle life. Am J Psychiat 1972; 128: 1262–1267.
39. McCoy NL, Davidson JM. A longitudinal study of the effects of menopause on sexuality. Maturitas 1985; 7: 203–210.
40. Bachmann GA, Leiblum SR, Kemman E, Colburn DW, Swartzman L, Sheldon R. Sexual expression and its determinants in the postmenopausal woman. Maturitas 1984; 6: 19–29.
41. Leiblum SR, Bachmann GA, Kemman E, Colburn D, Swartzman L. Vaginal atrophy in the postmenopausal woman. J Am Med Ass 1983; 249: 2195–2198.
42. Davidson JM. Sexual behaviour and its relationship to ovarian hormones in the menopause. Maturitas 1985; 7: 193–201.
43. Dennerstein L. Sexuality in the climacteric years. Maturitas 1985; 7: 191–192.
44. Sarrel PM. Sexuality. In: Studd JWW, Whitehead MI, eds. The menopause. London: Blackwell Sci Publ, 1988.
45. Van Keep PA, Kellerhals JM. The impact of socio-cultural factors on symptom formation. Psychother Psychosom 1974; 23: 251–263.
46. Krystal S, Chiriboga DA. The empty nest process in mid-life men and women. Maturitas 1979; 1: 215–222.
47. Glenn MD. Psychological well-being in the post parent stage: some evidence from national surveys. J Marriage Family 1975; 37: 105–110.
48. Brown GW, Harris T. Social origins of depression. London: Tavistock Publications, 1978.
49. Paykel ES. Recent life events in the development of depressive disorders. In: Depue RA, ed. The psychobiology of depressive disorders. New York: Academic Press, 1978; 245–262.
50. Greene JG, Cooke DJ. Life stress and symptoms at the climacterium. Br J Psychiat 1980; 136: 486–491.
51. Cooke DJ, Greene JG. Types of life events in relation to symptoms at the climacterium. J. Psychosom Res 1981; 25: 5–11.
52. Ballinger S, Cobbin D, Krivanek J, Saunders D. Life stresses and depression in the menopause. Maturitas 1979; 1: 191–199.
53. McKinlay J, Brambilla DB. Do menopausal symptoms cause depression, or does depres-

sion cause more reported symptoms? Paper presented at the fifth int. congress on the menopause. International Menopause Society. Sorrento, Italy 1987.

54. Gove WR, Hughes M, Style CB. Does marriage have positive effects on the psychological well-being of the individual? J Health Soc Behav 1983; 24: 122–131.

55. Bebbington PE, Hurry J, Tennant C, Sturt E, Wing JK. The epidemiology of mental disorders in Camberwell. Psychol Med 1981; 11: 561–580.

56. Surtees PG, Dean C, Ingham JG, Kreitman NB, Miller PMcC, Sashidharan SP. Psychiatric disorder in women from an Edinburgh community: associations with demographic factors. Brit J Psychiat 1983; 142: 238–246.

57. Krause N. Employment outside the home and women's psychological well-being. Soc Psychiat 1984; 19: 41–48.

58. Jennings S, Mazaik C, McKinlay S. Women and work: an investigation of the association between health and employment status in middle-aged women. Soc Sci Med 1984; 4: 423–431.

59. Holte A, Mikkelsen A. Menstrual coping style, social background and climacteric symptoms. Psychiat Soc Sci 1982; 2: 41–45.

60. Maoz B, Dowty N, Antonovsky A, Wijsenbeek H. Female attitudes to the menopause. Soc Psychiat 1970; 5: 35–40.

61. Dennerstein L, Burrows GD, Hyman C, Sharpe K. Hormone therapy and affect. Maturitas 1979; 1: 247–259.

62. Flint M. The menopause: reward or punishment. Psychosomatics 1975; 16: 161–163.

63. Neugarten BL, Wood V, Kraines RJ, Loomis B. Women's attitudes towards the menopause. Vita Humana 1963; 6: 140–151.

64. Boulet M, Lehert PH, Riphagen FE. The menopause viewed in relation to other life events—a study performed in Belgium. Maturitas 1985; 10: 333–342.

65. Asso D. The real menstrual cycle. Avon: Wiley & Son, 1983.

66. Backstrom J. Oestrogen and progesterone in relation to different activities in the central nervous system. Acta Obs Gynaecol Scand. (Suppl.) 1977; 66: 1.

67. Klaiber EL, Broverman DM, Vogel W. The effects of oestrogen therapy on plasma MAO activity and EEG driving responses of depressed women. Am J Psychiat 1972; 128: 1429–1498.

68. Klaiber EL, Broverman DM, Vogel W, Korbayasti V. Oestrogen therapy for severe persistent depression in women. Arch Gen Psychiat 1979; 36: 550–554.

69. Aylward M, Maddock J. Plasma tryptophan levels in depression. Lancet 1973; 936.

70. Aylward M. Oestrogens, plasma tryptophan levels in peri-menopausal patients. In: Campbell S. ed. The Management of the menopause and post menopausal years. Baltimore: Univ Pak Press, 1976.

71. Coulam CB. Age, oestrogens and the psyche. Clin Obstet Gynae 1981; 24: 219–229.

72. Oppenheim G. Oestrogen in the treatment of depression: neuropharmacological mechanisms. Biol Psychiat 1983; 18 (6): 721–725.

73. Osborne M. Depression and the menopause. Br J Hosp Med 1984; 32: 126–129.

74. Parlee MB. Menstrual rhythms in sensory processes in vision, audition, taste and touch. Psych Bull 1983; 93 (3): 539–548.

75. Abplanalp JM, Rose RM, Donnelly AF, Livingstone-Vaughn C. Psychoendocrinology of the menstrual cycle: the relationship between enjoyment of activities, moods and reproductive hormones. Psychosom Med 1979; 14 (8): 605–615.

76. Strauss B, Appelt H. Psychological concomitants of the menstrual cycle: a prospective longitudinal approach. J Psychosom Obs Gynaecol 1983; 2–4: 215–219.

77. Coope J. Is oestrogen therapy effective in the treatment of menopausal depression? J Royal Coll Gen Pract 1981; 31: 134–140.

78. Beck AT, Ward CH, Mendelson M, Mock J, Erbaugh J. An inventory for measuring depression. Arch Gen Psychiat 1961; 4: 561–571.

79. Ballinger CB, Browning MCK, Smith AHW. Hormone profiles and psychological symptoms in peri-menopausal women. Maturitas 1987; 9: 235–251.

80. Bancroft J. Human sexuality and its problems. Edinburgh: Churchill Livingstone, 1983.

81. Bachman GA, Leiblum SR, Sandler B, Ainsley W, Narcessian R, Shelden R, Hymans, HN. Correlates of sexual desire in postmenopausal women. Maturitas 1985; 7: 221–216.

82. Studd JWW, Chakavarti S, Oram, DH. The climacteric. Clin Obstet Gynaecol 1977; 4(1): 3–29.

83. Hutton JD, Jacobs HS, James VHT. Steroid endocrinology after the menopause—a review. J R Soc Med 1979; 72: 835–841.

84. Utian WH. Definitive symptoms of post-menopause incorporating use of vaginal parabasal cell index. In: Van Keep PA, Lauritzen C, eds: Frontiers in hormone research: oestrogens in the post-menopause. Basel: Karger, 1975.

85. Sherwin BB, Gelfand MM. Sex steroids and affect in the surgical menopause: a double-blind, cross-over study. Psychoneuroendocrinology 1985; 10: 325–335.

86. Campbell S. Double blind psychometric studies on the effects of natural oestrogens on postmenopausal women. In: Campbell S, eds. The Management of the menopause and postmenopausal years. Lancaster: MTP Press, 1976.

87. Coope J, Thompson JM, Poller L. The effects of natural oestrogen therapy on menopausal symptoms and blood clotting. Br Med J 1975; iv: 139–143.

88. George GCW, Beaumont PJV, Beardwood CJ. Effects of exogenous oestrogens on minor psychiatric symptoms in postmenopausal women. S Afr Med J 1973; 47: 2387–2394.

89. Thompson J, Oswald I. Effect of oestrogen on the sleep, mood and anxiety of menopausal women. Br Med J 1977; 2: 1317–1319.

90. Stickler RC. The role of oestrogen replacement in the climacteric syndrome. Psychol Med 1977; 7: 631–637.

91. Durst N, Maoz B. Changes in psychological well-being during postmenopause as a result of oestrogen therapy. Maturitas 1979; 1: 301–315.

92. Gerdes LC, Sonnendecker EWW, Polakow ES. Psychological changes effected by oestrogen—progestogen and clonidine treatment in climacteric women. Am J Obs Gynaecol 1982; 142: 98–104.

93. Dennerstein L, Burrows GD. A review of studies of the psychological symptoms found at the menopause. Maturitas, 1978; 1: 55–64.

94. Montgomery JC, Appelby L, Brincat M, Versi E, Tapp A, Fenwick PBC, Studd JWW. Effect of oestrogen and testosterone implants on psychological disorders in the climacteric. The Lancet 1987; Feb 7: 297–299.

95. Studd J, Collins W, Chakravarti S, Newton J, Oram D, Parson A. Oestradiol and testosterone implants in the treatment of psychosexual problems in the postmenopausal woman. Brit J Obs Gynaecol 1977; 84: 314–315.

96. Sherwin BB, Gelfand MM. Differential symptom response to parenteral oestrogen and/or androgen administration in the surgical menopause. Amer J Obs Gynaecol 1985; 151: 153–160.

97. Carney A, Bancroft J, Mathews A. Combination of hormonal and psychological treatment for female sexual unresponsiveness: a comparative study. Br J Psychiat 1978; 132: 339–346.

98. Mathews A, Whitehead A, Kellett J. Psychological and hormonal factors in the treatment of female and sexual dysfunction. Psychol Med 1983; 13: 83–92.

99. Dow MGT, Gallagher J. A controlled study of combined hormonal and psychological treatment for sexual unresponsiveness in women. Br J Clin Psychol 1989; 28: 201–212.

100. Dennerstein L, Burrows GD, Wood C, Hyman G. Hormones and sexuality: effect of oestrogen and progestogen. Obs Gynae 1980; 56 (3): 316–322.

101. Holst J, Backstrom T, Hammarback S, van Schoultz B. Progestogen addition during oestrogen replacement therapy—effects on vasomotor symptoms and mood. Maturitas 1989; 11: 13–20.

102. Paterson MEL. A randomized, double-blind, cross-over study into the effect of sequential mestranol and norethisterone on climacteric symptoms and biochemical parameters. Maturitas 1982; 4: 83–94.

103. Green JG, Hart DM. The evaluation of a psychological treatment programme for menopausal women. Maturitas 1987; 9 (1):41–48.

104. Hunter MS. Psychological aspects of the climacteric and postmenopause. In: Studd JWW, Whitehead MI, eds. The menopause. London: Blackwell Sci Publ Ltd, 1988.

105. Germaine LM, Freedman RR, Behavioural treatment of menopausal hot flushes: evaluation by objective methods. J. Consul Clin Psychol 1985; 52 (6): 1072–1079.

106. Stevenson DW, Delprato DJ. Multiple component self control programme for menopausal hot flushes. J Behav Ther Exper Psychiat 1983; 14 (2): 137–140.

107. Gannon L. The potential role of exercise in the alleviation of menstrual disorders and menopausal symptoms: a theoretical synthesis of recent research. Women Health 1988; 14 (2): 105–127.

108. Hunter MS. Your menopause. London: Pandora Press, 1990.

Chapter 10

Women's Health and Wellness

In 1988, widespread publicity proclaimed a breakthrough in the prevention of one of the leading causes of death in the United States. The results of a large Federally-funded research project showed that the simple procedure of taking one aspirin a day reduced the risk of heart attacks and strokes. Recently, this same finding is again receiving widespread publicity, but for another reason. This scientific breakthrough was based on the study of 22,071 men and 0 women. Although women pay half the taxes in this country and cardiovascular disease is the second most common cause of death for women, no women were included in the study. This omission is not unique to the aspirin study. Many major drugs and medical treatments were and continue to be developed and tested predominantly or exclusively on men. For example, one major project is currently assessing whether aerobic exercise can reduce the incidence of cardiovascular disease and sleep disorders in the elderly. Both are common and serious problems for elderly men and women. Though the researchers had hoped to study both men and women, they were told by their funding agency to use only male subjects. The reason: inclusion of women was an "unnecessary and costly duplication".

Is that the case? Is it really necessary to use both male and female subjects in medical research? The answer is clearly "yes", for at least two reasons. One, many diseases appear to affect men and women differently. For example, the relationship between high blood cholesterols and heart disease may not be as strong in women as in men, suggesting that the risk factors for this disease differ for the two sexes. Yet a 1990 study investigating another possible risk factor for heart disease—heavy coffee consumption—concluded from examination of 45,589 men and no women that high coffee intake was not associated with stroke or heart attacks and therefore need not be a concern. The other major reason for including women as research subjects is the growing body of evidence showing that treatments and drugs developed on men may not work on women and in some cases may actually harm them. Very preliminary evidence suggests that over-the-counter diet pills containing phenylpropanolamine, which were tested primarily in young men, may have serious side effects when taken by women with high estrogen levels (a consequence of some oral contraceptives).

Why have women been largely excluded from these studies? The justifications most commonly given by researchers include: (1) women's hormonal/menstrual cycles "interfere"; (2) women don't get the particular disease being studied as often as men do or they get it much later in life; and (3) women participating in drug tests might become pregnant, with possible harmful effects on their fetuses leading to costly law suits.

Let's look more closely at these reasons. If women's menstrual cycles affect their responses to drugs, shouldn't physicians know what those effects are so that they can prescribe the drugs appropriately, perhaps varying the dosage at different times of the cycle? It has been known for years that the effectiveness of many drugs varies with the time of day when they are taken. Consequently, cancer chemotherapy treatments are often given at the time of day when they have the most effect against cancer cells and/or the fewest side effects. Second, women do experience some health problems less frequently than men. But the women who do develop so-called "male" diseases deserve adequate treatment. Since treatments developed for such problems are used for women as well as men, their effectiveness and safety should be determined for both sexes. Finally, the concern for the fetus in drug trials is exaggerated. The overwhelming majority of women in such trials do not become pregnant, and without much extra effort researchers could decrease this percentage even further. For example, if reproductive-aged women are needed for a particular study, researchers could recruit women who have been sterilized, women who have had hysterectomies, women with no current heterosexual partners and no current plans to become pregnant, etc. Such categories could provide more than enough women for such studies. Moreover, the Federal agency which oversees drug trials already requires that before companies can test new drugs on reproductive-aged women, they must first test the drugs on men and for birth defects in animals. Unfortunately, most companies never take the final step and test their products' effects on women.

Thus, there is clear evidence of gender bias in health research. On a positive note, this has now become a publicized and political issue, and several powerful members of Congress are committed to addressing it. A special office has been set up at the largest Federal funding agency to enforce previously ignored regulations about at least "considering" women research subjects. And, as more and more women choose to pursue careers in health research, inequities may slowly begin to disappear.

One of many health problems relatively ignored in women by both the mass media and the research community is AIDS (acquired immunodeficiency syndrome). As the article by **Campbell** points out, "far more attention has been given to women as infectors [of male sexual partners and of babies] than to the very real risks that they face as infectees." Yet, according to the World Health Organization, a healthy woman is 14 times more likely than a healthy man to be infected with the AIDS virus during heterosexual contact with an infected partner. Though infection with the AIDS virus is believed to be increasing more rapidly in women than in any other group, most researchers admit that the incidence of AIDS in women is significantly under-counted. There are several reasons for this. In general, there is less alertness to AIDS in women. Also, most cases of AIDS in women appear in poor and/or minority women with access to neither education nor health care. Finally, the AIDS disease manifests itself differently in women than in men. It often first appears in AIDS-infected women as gynecological disease (cervical cancer, vaginal infections, pelvic inflammatory disease). The "official" definition of AIDS, by the Centers for Disease Control, is based on the symptoms seen in gay men and male drug addicts. It fails to acknowledge these gynecological diseases so common among AIDS-infected women. When women with AIDS cannot get their diagnosis formally confirmed, they cannot receive disability benefits or participate in studies of experimental treatments. Fortunately, the re-definition of AIDS by the Centers for Disease Control in November, 1991, will partially correct for this problem.

Another major inequity in health research is the lack of attention paid to women's specific health issues. With the exception of studies on hormone replacement therapy, menopause remains largely ignored. Virtually nothing is known about chlamydia, an increasingly common sexually transmitted disease that results in sterility for thousands of women every year. The incidence of breast cancer in this country has doubled since 1960 to 1 in 10 women yet the amount of Federal research money allocated to breast cancer research remains appallingly low. Moreover, the type of large-scale, long-term studies oriented toward prevention that have been carried out for heart disease (which is seen as primarily a "male" disease) have typically not been funded for serious "female" diseases such as breast, cervical and ovarian cancers. Despite this relative lack of attention, some substantial progress has been made in the diagnosis and treatment of breast cancer, as outlined in the two articles by **Segal.**

The incidence of cervical cancer has also been increasing, especially in young women. Currently, the best way to detect cervical cancer is with the Pap test, a routine part of gynecological exams. As **Carter** describes, the Pap test also detects a precancerous condition called cervical dysplasia, which has been linked with HPV (human papillomavirus, or genital warts; a sexually-transmitted disease). Though there is some concern about the accuracy of the Pap test, it remains a valuable and important part of health care for women.

Other health problems of special concern to women include hysterectomy and depression. Hysterectomy (the removal of the uterus, sometimes accompanied by the removal of the ovaries and Fallopian tubes) is the second most common surgical procedure in this country (Cesarean section delivery of babies is the most common). About 90% of hysterectomies are performed for benign reasons (i.e., not related to cancer), and there are striking differences among women of different racial and educational backgrounds in how frequently it is performed. The incidence of this major surgery in essentially healthy women, with its high cost, lengthy recovery and serious side effects, remains scandalously high.

Though depression is not strictly a women's health issue, it is more than twice as common in women than in men. Unfortunately, it is also taken less seriously in women than in men. **Paykel** reviews a variety of explanations for why depression is more common in women, and concludes that multiple factors related to the biology and the social roles of women are involved. The importance of social factors is underscored by the repeated finding that the highest incidence of depression is in married women who are 20–40 years old and have children. In addition, studies of satisfaction with life consistently find that, on the whole, unmarried women and married men are more satisfied with their lives than married women and unmarried men. These factors no doubt play a role in the high incidence of depression among women.

REFERENCES AND SUGGESTED READING

Hufnagel, V. G. (1988). The conspiracy against the uterus. *Journal of Psychosomatic Obstetrics and Gynecology, 9,* 51–58.

Lewis, R. (1987, April). Pap smears: A closer look. *Health,* pp. 69–72.

Love, S. (1990). *Dr. Susan Love's breast book.* New York: Addison-Wesley.

Meilahn, E. N., Matthews, K. A., Egeland, G., and Kelsey, S. F. (1989). Characteristics of women with hysterectomy. *Maturitas, 11,* 319–329.

Notelovitz, M. (1990). Exercise and health maintenance in menopausal women. *Annals of the New York Academy of Sciences, 592,* 204–220.

Rehm, D. (1991, April). Is there gender bias in drug testing? *FDA Consumer,* pp. 9–13.

Richardson, D. (1988). *Women and AIDS.* New York: Routledge Press.

Solomon, A. (1991, May 14). The politics of breast cancer. *Village Voice.*

Spencer, P. (1988, March). The scary truth about the Pap. *Health,* pp. 70–78.

White, E. C. (1990). *The black women's health book.* Seattle: Seal Press.

Woodman, S., and Lange, D. (1990, September). Dangerous practices. *Mirabella,* pp. 150–154.

Women and AIDS
Carole A. Campbell

Abstract—This article describes the epidemiology of acquired immunodeficiency syndrome (AIDS) in women in the United States. Comparisons of female and male transmission categories are made and emphasis is placed on the heterosexual transmission and undetermined risk categories for women. Since its onset in 1981, AIDS has affected males predominantly and female AIDS cases have not received as much attention. AIDS education efforts have not targeted women as much as men, despite women's vulnerability to infection, especially through heterosexual transmission. AIDS tends to generate many issues that concern women's sexuality—contraception, pregnancy and abortion among them. Some of the special problems that women with AIDS face are discussed. Women's role as caregiver for persons with AIDS also is examined. Attention is directed to the ways in which AIDS is associated with the traditional female role.

INTRODUCTION

The first cases of acquired immunodeficiency syndrome (AIDS) in the United States were recognized and described in 1981. The appearance of AIDS in disparate groups, linked only by probable routes of transmission, was among the first pieces of evidence suggesting an infectious cause. AIDS was first described among homosexual men in 1981 [1]. In the following year it was recognized in intravenous (IV)-drug users [2] and Haitians [3]. Also in 1982 AIDS was reported in recipients of blood or blood products [4, 5], infants born to mothers at risk [6], and heterosexual partners of persons with AIDS [7]. Initially it was thought that the newly appearing female AIDS cases were the result of transmission through IV-drug usage. Soon it was realized that these women had become infected through heterosexual contact with an infected male. More female AIDS cases resulting from heterosexual transmission began to appear in 1983 and the percentage of female cases in that category has continued to increase yearly from that time. This trend in heterosexual transmission may serve as a good marker for future trends. AIDS in women also is of special interest because women with AIDS or with human immunodeficiency virus (HIV) infection are the major source of infection of infants with AIDS [8]. Trends in AIDS in women may help to determine future trends in pediatric cases.

This article describes the epidemiology of AIDS in women in the United States. Emphasis is given to the significant growth in the proportion of women with AIDS in the heterosexual transmission category from 1982 to 1988. Routes of perinatal transmission are described. AIDS tends to present critical fertility and reproductive issues for women. Some of these issues are examined in this article. The special problems that women with AIDS face are addressed. AIDS education efforts aimed at women are examined. Attention is directed to the way in which women's involvement in the AIDS epidemic is associated with the traditional female role.

Reprinted with permission from *Social Science and Medicine* (1990) 30: 407–415. Copyright © 1990, Pergamon Press plc.

Table 1. Adult AIDS cases in the United States, 2 January, 1989 [8]

Transmission category, adults/adolescents	Males		Females		Total	
	Cum. No.	(%)	Cum. No.	(%)	Cum. No.	(%)
Homosexual/bisexual	50,325	(68)			50,325	(62)
IV-drug	12,529	(17)	3622	(52)	16,151	(20)
Homosexual and IV-drug	5874	(8)			5874	(7)
Hemophilia/coagulation	751	(1)	22	(0)	773	(1)
Heterosexual	1516	(2)	2073	(30)	3589	(4)
Transfusion	1297	(2)	747	(11)	2044	(3)
Undetermined	2143	(3)	519	(7)	2662	(3)
Total (% of cases)	74,435	(91)	6983	(9)	81,418	(100)

AIDS CASES IN ADULTS IN THE UNITED STATES

As of 2 January, 1989, women comprised 9% or 6983 of the total 81,418 adult AIDS cases in the United States (Table 1). A large majority of these women are in their child-bearing years with 79% between ages 13 and 39 [9].

AIDS tends to affect minority women more than minority men since a greater percentage of men with AIDS are white. About half (52%) of the women with AIDS are black and 19% are Hispanic (Table 2). AIDS cases have occurred 14 times more frequently among black women and 9 times more frequently among Hispanic women than among white women [10].

The major transmission category for women with AIDS is IV-drug usage. Fifty-two percent of female cases fall in this category (Table 1). This category has been the major route of transmission for women since the onset of the disease. This transmission category is the principal link to other adult populations through heterosexual transmission and to children through perinatal transmission.

Heterosexual contact with an infected male is the second largest transmission category for women. Thirty percent of female cases fall in this category (Table 1). This category can include sexual contact with male IV-drug users, males infected by blood products and males who are bisexual. Female IV-drug users and sexual partners of male IV-drug users make up the largest number of HIV-infected women of child-bearing age. It is particularly noteworthy that in 1982, 14% of female cases were from heterosexual contact with an infected male [9]. The proportion of women with AIDS in the heterosexual transmission category has increased annually in the last 6 years. In comparison to female cases, a much smaller proportion (2%) of male AIDS cases are in the heterosexual transmission category (Table 1). Male cases have not shown such a significant increase in the heterosexual category over this time period. Men with AIDS outnumber women with AIDS in all transmission categories except heterosexual transmission.

Transmission from blood transfusions comprises 11% of female cases (Table 1). In comparison, 2% of male cases fall in the transfusion category. Although the male percentage is lower, the number of male cases exceeds the number of female cases in the transfusion category, in contrast to the heterosexual transmission category.

The final transmission category for women is that of undetermined risk. Seven percent of female cases fall in this category (Table 1). The undetermined risk category includes those persons for whom no specific risk is identified. It also includes persons for whom risk information is incomplete due to death or refusal to be interviewed. Persons who are lost in follow-up efforts are also in this category. The Centers for Disease Control does not separately tabulate persons who

Table 2. Adult AIDS cases in the United States by race and gender, 2 January, 1989 [8]

Race/ ethnicity	Gender				
	Males	(%)	Females	(%)	Total
White	45,359	(61)	1948	(28)	47,307
Black	17,618	(24)	3604	(52)	21,222
Hispanic	10,773	(14)	1360	(19)	12,133
Asian	440	(1)	42	(1)	482
American Indian	75	(0)	12	(0)	87
Unknown	170	(0)	17	(0)	187
Total	74,435	(100)	6983	(100)	81,418

Table 4. Adult male and female AIDS cases in the United States, 1981–1988 [8, 9]

	Males	Females	Total	(%) Female of total
1981*	196	6	202	3.0
1982	687	51	738	6.9
1983	2213	162	2375	6.8
1984	4384	302	4686	6.4
1985	8062	569	8631	6.6
1986	12,085	972	13,057	7.4
1987	19,387	1689	21,076	8.0
1988	28,498	3295	31,793	10.0

* Reporting began in late spring.

report only heterosexual contact with a prostitute or sex with multiple partners. Such persons are included in the undetermined risk category [8]. In comparison to female cases, a smaller proportion (3%) of male AIDS cases are in the undetermined risk category.

The percentage of total cases that the undetermined risk category comprises for both males and females has not fluctuated dramatically over the last 6 years. It should be emphasized though that the percentage of female cases in this category started at 14 in 1982 which is considerably larger than the male percentage at 2 (Table 3). The percentage of female cases of undetermined risk has remained consistently larger than the percentage of male cases over the last 6 years. In 1981 women comprised 3% of all AIDS cases (Table 4). Female AIDS cases now comprise 9% of the total number of cases and the male to female ratio of AIDS cases is 11:1 [8].

Table 3. Trends in heterosexual contact and undetermined risk, 1982–1988 [8, 9]

	Percentage of cases						
	1982	1983	1984	1985	1986	1987	1988
Heterosexual							
Males	0.2	0.1	0.3	0.3	0.4	2	2
Females	14	14	17	20	26	29	29
Undetermined							
Males	2	3	2	2	3	3	4
Females	14	12	12	11	10	9	8

At the present time a heterosexual woman in the United States faces a greater risk of becoming infected with HIV through sexual intercourse than does a heterosexual man. There is a larger pool of men infected by other means such as IV-drug use and homosexual contact. Since a greater proportion of men are infected, a woman is more likely than a man to encounter an infected partner. The relative efficiencies of male-to-female versus female-to-male transmission also may be relevant here.

HIV infection has occurred in a high percentage of women exposed only occasionally to semen from a single man. To date no cases of transmission through artificial insemination have occurred in the United States, but 4 of 8 Australian women who received semen from a single infected donor became infected [11]. Infected semen had been injected directly into the uterus through a catheter. In similar cases of only occasional exposure, 10 out of 17 women became infected through vaginal intercourse with one infected man [11].

PEDIATRIC AIDS CASES AND ROUTES OF PERINATAL TRANSMISSION

Pediatric AIDS cases follow a racial distribution similar to that of women since most are the result of perinatal transmission from infected mothers. These cases also follow a similar geographic distribution with the majority of both pediatric and female cases being in New York, New Jersey and Florida [8]. There is a strong overlap between geographic areas of IV-drug use among women and HIV prevalence among infants.

Between 1982 and 1986 the increase in the number of women with AIDS in the IV-drug, heterosexual and unidentified risk categories was closely paralleled by the increase in pediatric patients whose mothers were in those risk groups. A majority (78%) of pediatric AIDS cases are a result of perinatal transmission [8].

The frequency of transmission from an infected mother to her fetus or newborn infant ranges from 25 to 50% [11]. Uninfected as well as infected infants have been born to mothers who previously have given birth to an infected child. The actual rate of perinatal transmission is difficult to determine because there are no laboratory tests that reliably establish HIV infection in newborns. As is the case with other infections, newborns naturally carry antibodies passively acquired transplacentally from their mothers. They may test positive for HIV antibody but actually may not be infected themselves. There is no way to distinguish maternal antibodies from antibodies in an infant infected with HIV. It takes up to 15 months for maternal antibodies to disappear. Newborns produce a limited antibody response to HIV because of their physiologically depressed immune systems. Laboratory diagnosis of HIV in children aged under 15 months currently is based on virus isolation from lymphocyte cultures and on antigen capture in serum. Virus culture from blood or other tissues is an expensive and cumbersome technique and is not always reliable [12]. Antigen capture is not sufficiently sensitive and is not always reliable either [12]. In order for an infant's true HIV status to be determined, it is necessary to follow the infant during the first 15 months in order to detect the loss of maternal antibody and the development of serologic or virologic markers of infection.

Evidence for intrauterine transmission, as opposed to intrapartum transmission, comes from a case where an infected mother gave birth to an infected child in a cesarean delivery. Further evidence is found in the isolation of HIV from cord blood [13] and fetal tissues [10]. Facial malformation has been found in some infants, suggesting that infection occurred between the twelfth and sixteenth week of gestation [13].

Immunosuppression naturally accompanies pregnancy as a means to prevent the body from rejecting the fetus. Pregnancy, especially during the last 3 months, is a relatively immunosuppressed condition. It appears that increasing maternal immunosuppression facilitates perinatal transmission. Preliminary results from a large study in Zaire found an association between a low T-helper to T-suppressor ratio in the mother and early laboratory and clinical infection in the infant [14]. The development of AIDS or AIDS-related complex (ARC) in perinatally infected children is significantly associated with the presence of symptomatic HIV infection in their mothers [15], but perinatal transmission may occur in the absence of severe maternal disease.

The effect of pregnancy on existing HIV infection has not been clearly established though two studies have found a high frequency of AIDS and ARC among women during the months after delivery [16, 17]. The critical variable here is duration of infection and it is not known in most cases. Information on the effect of pregnancy on HIV infection would be highly valuable in terms of counseling women.

Data about the timing during pregnancy or the perinatal period of transmission of HIV to the fetus or newborn are not generally available. Moreover, it is not known whether intrapartum transmission occurs as it can with the herpes virus. Only intrauterine and postnatal transmission have been documented. It is not known whether cesarean delivery decreases or increases the risk of transmission. Such information would be helpful to infected women.

Three cases of transmission of HIV from mother to infant through breast milk have occurred [10]. The mothers contracted HIV through postpartum blood transfusions. In these cases the infants would not receive transplacental anti-HIV antibody before birth and breast feeding appears to be the most likely route of transmission. However, it should be stressed that transmission has not always occurred when infected mothers have breast fed their infants. The risk of transmission through breast milk appears to be small compared to the risk through intrauterine transmission. It could be the case that breast feeding after acquisition of HIV, as in the case of a postpartum transfusion, carries a higher risk of viral transmission.

Information on HIV antibody prevalence available from 27 studies of women in settings related to women's health and childbearing gives some sense of the current rate of infection among women of reproductive age [18]. These studies were conducted in 19 inner-city areas in 12 states. Rates from 11 to 30% were found among pregnant IV-drug users. For women who didn't use IV-drugs, prevalence rates ranged from a fraction of 1% in most areas to 2.6% in New York City. A study of newborns in Massachusetts using the newborn's blood as an indicator of the mother's serologic status found that 1 of every 476 or 2.1/1000 women giving birth in Massachusetts was positive for HIV antibody [19]. A study testing infants' cord blood in an inner-city hospital in Brooklyn found an even higher prevalence of HIV infection, a rate of 20/1000 [20]. A study of newborns' blood specimens conducted in New York state in late 1987 found the prevalence of infection outside the metropolitan area of New York City to be 1.3/1000 and the rate for New York City, 16.4/1000, or 1/61 infants [21].

The rate of HIV infection in women of reproductive age can serve as a good indicator of the course of the epidemic. Since these women became infected directly through IV-drug usage or indirectly through heterosexual contact with male IV-drug users or bisexual men, they serve as an important bridge group. In addition, perinatal acquisition of HIV by infants of infected mothers is associated with a high probability of infant morbidity and mortality. There is a high rate of disease progression in perinatally infected children during the first year of life [10].

AIDS AND REPRODUCTIVE ISSUES

AIDS presents some extremely complex fertility and reproductive decisions for women. Since the majority of children are infected perinatally, prenatal testing for HIV has been recommended as a means of preventing AIDS in children. Prenatal testing is complicated by the fact that not all pregnancies are planned. Women don't always have or take control over conception and many pregnancies happen more by default than intent. Prenatal testing will be effective only for those pregnancies that are planned. Even so, it's not clear that knowledge of antibody status will prevent women from having children. Childbearing for some women is such a strong cultural expectation that a 25–50% chance of having an infected child may be acceptable odds. Risk-taking and pregnancy can be compared to risk-taking and AIDS since neither fertilization nor infection are certain.

Many infected women, however, do not know that they are infected when they are pregnant. They may learn of their own infection only after they give birth to an infected child since pediatric AIDS cases become manifest early in life with about half appearing during the first year. Infected mothers often have to deal not only with the consequences of their own illness but also those of their child's at the same time.

Women undergoing artificial insemination need to be aware of the possible risk of infection they face. Most licensed sperm banks now test semen and the American Fertility Society has guidelines that exclude high risk men from donating. Some banks required that the donor be HIV negative both at the time of donation and 60 days later before his sperm will be used. Some sperm banks even test 90 days later. Some physicians prefer fresh semen because they claim that it results in impregnation more effectively. At present there really are not enough data to show whether fresh or frozen semen gives different pregnancy rates. Most artificial insemination is handled by private physicians with their own sources of sperm. These sources may not always test for HIV. The Congressional Office of Technology Assessment's 1988 study surveyed 1500 physicians and found that physicians who conduct the entire artificial insemination process themselves do not always check thoroughly for the AIDS virus or for genetic disorders [22]. Only about half the doctors performing the procedure test in advance for the AIDS virus or for genetic disorders. In 1987, 172,000 women sought pregnancy through artificial insemination and 65,000 babies were born through this process [22]. The Food and Drug Administration set voluntary testing guidelines for physicians in February of 1988 and now is considering implementing regulations. Some professionals in the insemination field feel that the study has blown the problem out of proportion and stress that there haven't been any cases of AIDS transmitted through artificial insemination in the United States.

Because AIDS has been so strongly linked with sex, it is hard for some women even to recognize a past insemination as a possible risk factor. Pregnancy is usually foremost on the minds of women undergoing artificial insemination, not risk of HIV infec-

tion. Even though pregnancy might not result from artificial insemination, HIV could be transmitted from infected sperm in this process nonetheless.

There are limits to the usefulness of amniocentesis since it cannot determine if a fetus is infected with HIV. It is not possible to tell if antibodies are the fetus's own or the mother's. But even if it were possible to detect HIV infection with certainty, transmission could occur at a later stage in pregnancy after amniocentesis had been conducted. Abortion at this stage may not be an option. Moreover, transmission possibly may take place at birth. Amniocentesis thus doesn't offer the same safeguards for HIV infection as it does for other diseases. The HIV maternal antibody test, as compared to other fetal tests such as amniocentesis, is not a good predictor of future infant health.

Reproductive rights of women surface again with the AIDS issue. A central issue is the right of an infected woman to be pregnant. The right to become pregnant and to maintain a pregnancy could be seen as part of a woman's right to control her body. However, as more child-bearing women become infected and give birth to infected children, childbearing could come under the surveillance of the state. Women of child-bearing age could be among the first groups to undergo mandatory testing as part of an attempt to control women's reproductive choices. The widespread practice of safe sex could serve to drastically reduce the birth rate.

Reproductive rights take on a new meaning when applied to AIDS and AIDS tends to turn the abortion issue on its head. The state traditionally has expressed an interest in preserving and protecting the rights of the fetus. This interest was most clearly demonstrated in the 1973 Roe v. Wade decision when the Supreme Court recognized a woman's right to choose an abortion. The court ruled that a woman's right to privacy must be weighed against the state's interest in protecting the future life of the fetus. The state's interest in fetal survival tends to diminish, however, when the mother is infected with HIV [23]. The state's duty to protect potential life tends to shift to the interest of protecting society from another person with AIDS. In this view, seropositive women do not have the right to become pregnant and should be sterilized automatically. Seropositive pregnant women do not have the right to maintain a pregnancy and should undergo abortions. Sterilization and abortion would be advocated for health reasons alone. Conservatives though might be opposed to this view on grounds that pregnant women should remain pregnant because every fetus, even a defective fetus, has the right to life and ultimately to an AIDS death. Abortion for HIV infections may be opposed on grounds that it is a step towards abortions for a wide range of defective fetuses [24].

Counseling given for abortions in AIDS pregnancies is quite different from counseling for abortions for other diseases such as Down's syndrome, since in an AIDS pregnancy the mother herself already is infected with the virus. She will need to take precautions in order to protect herself from further development of the virus. Moreover, should she decide to go forth with the pregnancy, she herself may not live to be able to raise the child. However, the situation of an infected woman is similar to that of a woman carrying a Down's syndrome child in one sense. Usually these women are seeking termination not of an unwanted pregnancy but of a wanted pregnancy that was actively sought until learning the possible outcomes.

SPECIAL PROBLEMS FACED BY WOMEN WITH AIDS AND AT RISK FOR AIDS

The rapid loss of health associated with AIDS has implications for both males and females afflicted with the disease. Correspond-ingly, loss of health often can bring on loss of employment and loss of employment in turn has implications for finances and health insurance.

Although little social class information on persons with AIDS exists, it probably could be safely inferred from data on race and AIDS that women with AIDS are more poor than men with AIDS since women are more likely to be black and Hispanic. These women often suffer from poverty and discrimination without the added weight of AIDS. They are not always able to control the nature and the quality of their health care.

Some inferences from data on IV-drug users as an AIDS patient group also could be made. IV-drug users usually develop more lethal opportunistic infections than other patient groups and thus have a shorter life expectancy [25]. Often these individuals have other complicating underlying conditions-tuberculosis, hepatitis and cirrhosis among them. Their immune systems are extremely suppressed because of these diseases and also because of the effect of the drugs themselves. Their conditions usually require hospitalization and cannot easily be treated on an outpatient basis. As a patient group, these individuals are usually unemployed and thus do not have group health insurance. As a result, they do not have a family physician and their first contact with the health care system is often in the emergency room. Their disease is usually in a fairly advanced state by the time it is even diagnosed. This patient group usually does not have access to experimental drug therapy. Moreover, these individuals lack equal access to home health care since many home care attendants are not willing to go into poor neighborhoods.

Demographic information on female IV-drug users indicates that these women are more likely to have young children and to be the sole support of these children [26]. The career of addicted women is different from that of addicted men. As compared to men, these women face a narrowing of life options, including fewer friendships and limited education and employment opportunities [27]. Fewer drug treatment programs exist for female IV-drug users than for male IV-drug users, both in absolute numbers and in proportion to need [26]. Most treatment centers will not house women who are pregnant or women with children.

HIV antibody prevalence is three to four times higher among prostitutes who acknowledge IV-drug use than among those who do not [18]. The lives of women who use drugs and who engage in prostitution may be complicated further by their illegal survival activity and incarceration. Prostitutes who use IV-drugs are often street prostitutes and are most often subject to arrest [28]. A large number of street prostitutes are black and Hispanic women. This is partly related to poverty but it is also due to racism which prevents these women from working in brothels, casinos, escort services, and massage parlors [29]. These agencies usually almost exclusively employ Anglo and Asian women [30]. Addicted street prostitutes may buy drugs rather than condoms with what little money they earn. They might not always remember to use condoms because of the drugs' effects. Moreover, they are not in a strong position to enforce condom use with customers. Prostitutes are at risk of becoming infected with HIV from their boyfriends or husbands who are sometimes IV-drug users and who generally do not use condoms [31].

Few resources exist for prostitutes who want to leave prostitution. Legislation for mandatory HIV antibody testing of women arrested for prostitution has been passed in several states. The actual intent of mandatory testing is to get women out of prostitution. Ironically though, the effect may be to limit their occupational mobility even more [32]. A prostitute who has been arrested already has a difficult time getting out of prostitution

because of the criminal record she acquires. Her criminal record is made worse because of the more serious criminal penalties associated with her HIV status.

With most illnesses, it is the mother who assumes the caregiver role in the family. But with AIDS, the mother herself may be ill since most pediatric cases are the result of perinatal transmission. She may have to plan for the welfare of her children after her own death. There is no inclusive coordinated care system in place for women who become ill. As compared to infected males, infected women who seek AIDS-related services usually seek services not only for themselves but for their children as well [33]. Currently adult residential or long-term care facilities are not able to handle pediatric cases and pediatric facilities cannot accommodate mothers of sick children. There is a pressing need for 'family' homes that would allow mothers and children to remain together.

Women with AIDS may find themselves dealing with institutions that respond in ways that reinforce the traditional role of women. The institution of welfare has been seen as instilling feelings of dependency, passivity, resignation, and powerlessness in women [34]. Similarly, physicians' diagnoses and treatments may reinforce the traditional sex role of women [35–37]. Sexism in the response from obstetrician-gynecologists also has been addressed [38, 39]. Since AIDS has affected men predominantly, women with AIDS may not find physicians especially responsive to their illness. Physicians may be slow to recognize the symptoms of AIDS in women and the disease may be in a fairly advanced stage before it is even diagnosed. The potential for misdiagnosis exists as well.

An AIDS diagnosis itself can further inculcate the female stereotype since it carries with it a great deal of powerlessness and uncertainty for women. Infected women may not have the same support system and sense of community as infected men. As a result, women with AIDS may feel isolated and alone and may keep their infection secret for fear of discrimination against them or their families. They may not have the support of an extended family like they may have in other health crises because of the stigma associated with AIDS. Mothers with infected babies may feel a tremendous sense of guilt and grief about infecting their children. Infected women who don't have children often must deal with the loss of their child-bearing potential.

Women's response to AIDS often places them in the traditional role of nurturer and caregiver. Even when the mother herself is not infected such as in the case of a son's homosexually transmitted AIDS, she is often the one to assume the family caregiver role. Women in the role of mothers, wives, sisters and daughters are usually the ones to provide care [33, 40]. Male family members are the most resistant to homosexually transmitted AIDS—fathers tend to be least supportive of all and brothers also may have negative reactions [41]. The stress of the disease is very often shifted onto women.

The demands of caregiving can be extremely isolating for women. Mothers are used to sharing their knowledge about childhood diseases but are not always able to do this with AIDS because of the stigma it carries. For some mothers, though, the caregiving role has been cathartic. Two mothers, for example, wrote books about their sons' struggles with AIDS [42, 43]. Mothers also have organized support groups for other mothers caring for children with AIDS. Women affected by AIDS tend to seek out therapy and support groups more than do men. The National Hemophiliac Foundation has found that few hemophiliac men with AIDS will go to therapy or attend support groups [44]. It's much more common for the wives of these men to be involved in such activities.

Many AIDS support services currently available arose out of gay men's health con-cerns and thus have a predominantly male focus. Some women may feel uncomfortable with discussing their concerns about AIDS in support groups with men. Mothers of grown children with AIDS are not always comfortable in mixed groups and sometimes have expressed a need to be only with other mothers [40].

The epidemiology of female AIDS cases brings together disparate groups of women—IV-drug users, transfusion recipients and sex partners of IV-drug users, transfusion recipients and hemophiliacs. Although what they all have in common is AIDS, their differences may be greater than this similarity. Not all women will find comfort in support groups. Women of different socio-economic backgrounds may vary in the amount of comfort they feel in group therapy settings. Poor women, in comparison to middle class women, are not always able to 'talk it out' endlessly and may not find much relief in this type of therapy [45].

Some of the special situations that AIDS presents for women have been discussed in this section. As the number of female cases continues to rise, an even greater strain may be placed on family social services. There may be more of a need for welfare services for mothers and children if these mothers are no longer able to work. There may be even more of a need for foster care for children whose mothers have died from AIDS. As the number of HIV-infected children continues to rise, there may be an additional need for special day care services.

AIDS EDUCATION EFFORTS AIMED AT WOMEN

The emphasis that has been placed on risk of transmission through IV-drug usage may be misleading. More recent attention has been given to female nonintravenous drug users, in particular, the heavy users of the refined form of cocaine known as 'crack' [46].

These women may exchange sexual favors for crack but since there is no monetary transaction, they may not consider themselves prostitutes. Yet, they face a risk of infection from the high number of unprotected sexual exposures they have. Since efforts toward prevention have aimed at IV-drug users and prostitutes, female cocaine users who do not see themselves as belonging to these groups may not protect themselves or modify their behavior. Because of the highly addictive nature of crack, these women who exchange sex for crack are seen as a new generation of prostitutes [47]. Moreover, as compared to heroin, crack heightens sexuality and makes users vulnerable to HIV infection [47].

Success of AIDS education efforts will depend first of all on whether outreach efforts reach women at risk. Women who use IV-drugs are among the most difficult to reach since their lifestyles are often transient, unstable and impoverished. These women often take risks in their day-to-day survival. They constantly face risks of overdose, poor health, and physical violence. AIDS then is just one risk among many for them. They may have other priorities and constraints in their lives. In order to be effective, educators must put AIDS in perspective in relation to these priorities and constraints.

A majority of female sex partners of male IV-drug users do not use drugs [48]. These women may not realize the risk they face through sexual relations with their partners. IV-drug users are usually identified when they seek treatment or when they're arrested but since these women do not use drugs, they don't come in contact with treatment centers or with the criminal justice system. Even if these women are reached with AIDS information, they may not be able to be assertive and insist on using condoms since they are already in a subordinate relationship and are especially vulnerable to physical abuse. Their insistence on using condoms could bring on a risk of physical violence. These women may be reluctant to introduce condoms because they are dependent on their male partners for economic support.

Condom use is a particularly sensitive issue among minorities. Using condoms sometimes threatens minority males' sense of masculinity [45]. The position of the Catholic church on condoms also has influenced some minority group members' views. In addition, condom use has been interpreted by some minorities as having genocidal implications [33, 45]. AIDS preventive education could be seen as feeding into racist agendas by promoting the message that blacks and Hispanics should stop having children altogether. It is therefore important that educational efforts be culturally sensitive.

AIDS prevention education must also recognize the impact of cultural attitudes toward gender roles. Male Hispanic adolescents, influenced by the role of 'Machismo', may feel that impregnating a woman is proof of virility and manhood. The female counterpart to Machismo, 'Marianismo', requires that young Hispanic females defer to these males [49]. This deference makes it difficult for these young women to introduce safe sex practices.

There are also gender-related misperceptions surrounding condom use. A survey of attitudes and sexual practices of adolescents in San Francisco [50] reflects these misperceptions. Females in the study were uncertain about males' views on using condoms, although males reported quite positive views about using them. Educational interventions will need to target these types of misperceptions in order to increase the use of condoms among young women. Unprotected anal sex is sometimes practiced by young women who want to remain virgins until marriage [51]. AIDS educational efforts will need to reach this group of women whose behavior is at risk.

Because AIDS has largely affected males, women with AIDS have been made to fit into a male profile. AIDS education efforts haven't targeted women as much as other persons at risk. Women are frequently absent in AIDS brochures. When the media have included women, they usually focus on white women, despite the fact that a vast majority of female cases are black and Hispanic [52]. Recent articles on heterosexual risk that have appeared in popular magazines target a white middle-class readership. Pictures that accompany these articles show mainly white women.

The distinction between women as 'infectors' and women as 'infectees' can be made and it becomes evident that far more attention has been given to women as infectors than to the very real risks that they face as infectees [52]. Initially there was a lack of attention to the problem of AIDS among women until there was concern that prostitutes were spreading the disease [53, 54]. Prostitutes seem to have gotten far more attention for their role in infecting customers than for the serious risk of infection they face [29, 30, 33]. Moreover, little attention has been given to the role the customer plays in the act of prostitution, although he is usually the initiator of the transaction. Mandatory testing of prostitutes could serve to protect the customer more than the prostitute since the prostitute may be antibody negative, but there is no assurance that the customer is [32].

Despite women's vulnerability to AIDS, there has been a general lack of attention to the seriousness of the problem of AIDS in women. Data on women and AIDS are not routinely collected or reported. For example, figures on the total number of women who are pregnant and who have AIDS or who have died from AIDS are not available. Nor is there much data on parity and AIDS. Health departments in some states collect data on pregnancy and parity of female AIDS cases, but no composite profile reflecting the total number of cases exists. These data would be valuable in assessing the future course of the epidemic. It also would be helpful to know more about the personal lives of female AIDS cases, including their family situations, resources, and the special problems they face.

Thus far clinical trials of the experimental drug, azidothymidine (AZT), largely have involved gay men. Hemophiliacs, IV-drug users and persons infected through heterosexual contact haven't been included in these trials. Little data exist about the effects of drug therapy on HIV infection in women.

Although women haven't been targeted with AIDS education as much as men, many health professionals see the hope of controlling the AIDS epidemic as relying a great deal on the effort of women. Women have been found to seek health care more readily than men [55, 56] and to take preventive health steps more than men [57]. There is some debate on this issue and some feminists have questioned the idea of directing AIDS preventive education at women since men are largely the ones doing the infecting [45]. AIDS prevention, just like birth control, is made a female responsibility and in this way, women are kept in the caregiver role. Targeting women with AIDS education is defended by some public health professionals who feel that women have a more sharply defined sense of the future and are more responsible about health issues than men [45]. These professionals tend to think that what success can be achieved against AIDS very much depends on women's response. Women also play an important role in the socialization of their children and in this role may be involved in educating their children about AIDS.

CONCLUSION

The debate over whether AIDS will explode into the heterosexual community as it did in the homosexual community seems more to be over whether AIDS will affect heterosexual men and women equally. The high rate of heterosexual transmission of HIV for women underscores the need for sexually active women to be aware of the risk they face from partners who they do not know well. The high rate of transmission from undetermined risk tends to suggest that women may not know about the past IV-drug or bisexual practices of their partners. Sexually active women with more than one lifetime partner are advised to reduce their risk of HIV infection by using condoms during intercourse. Celibacy of course will prevent infection but it is not a viable option for many women.

Prevention of HIV in women will require that women be assertive about condom use. It is projected that AIDS will move down in age and adolescents have been identified as a probable 'next' risk group for the disease. The high rate of teenage pregnancy in the United States tends to suggest that condoms are not being used consistently. It is therefore essential that young women especially be informed about condoms and be encouraged to use them if they are sexually active.

Since early 1987 the AIDS epidemic has leveled off among white gay men in Los Angeles County, San Francisco and New York City, the three cities hit earliest and hardest by the disease [58]. This leveling off in the number of new cases is believed to reflect the adoption of safer sex practices by white gay men in these cities. There has been an increase in AIDS cases among IV-drug users. This increase will have consequences for females who are themselves IV-drug users or the sexual partners of IV-drug users. Moreover, this increase among IV-drug users has relevance for future trends in pediatric AIDS cases resulting from perinatal transmission. The increase in AIDS cases among IV-drug users already is reflected in the number of pediatric AIDS cases. In fact, children comprise the fastest growing group of AIDS cases [59].

This article has described the ways in which AIDS is associated with the traditional feminine stereotype. As AIDS cases continue to increase, the burden of AIDS care will fall more and more on women if sex roles in AIDS care persist in patterns established so far.

Prevention of HIV infection in women will require that they not only take a more assertive role over their own health, but also a more assertive role in making public policy on AIDS. Although women are experienced in lobbying for other public health programs, they have been notably absent from the public health dialog on AIDS. The data on heterosexual risk for women highlight the need for women to organize and to take preventive steps.

REFERENCES

1. Centers for Disease Control. Pneumocystis pneumonia. *Morbid. Mortal. Wkly. Rep.* **30**, 250–252, 5 June, 1981.
2. Centers for Disease Control. Update on Kaposi's sarcoma and opportunistic infections in previously healthy persons—United States. *Morbid. Mortal. Wkly. Rep.* **31**, 294–301, 11 June, 1982.
3. Centers for Disease Control. Opportunistic infections and Kaposi's sarcoma among Haitians in the United States. *Morbid. Mortal. Wkly. Rep.* **31**, 353–361, 9 July, 1982.
4. Centers for Disease Control. Update on acquired immune deficiency syndrome (AIDS) among patients with hemophilia A. *Morbid. Mortal. Wkly. Rep.* **31**, 644–652, 16 July 1982.
5. Centers for Disease Control. Possible transfusion-associated acquired immune deficiency syndrome (AIDS)—California. *Morbid. Mortal. Wkly. Rep.* **31**, 652–654, 10 Dec., 1982.
6. Centers for Disease Control. Unexplained immunodeficiency and opportunistic infections in infants—New York, New Jersey, California. *Morbid. Mortal. Wkly. Rep.* **31**, 665–668, 17 Dec., 1982.
7. Centers for Disease Control. Immunodeficiency among female sexual partners of

males with acquired immune deficiency syndrome. (AIDS)—New York. *Morbid. Mortal. Wkly. Rep.* **31**, 697–698, 7 Jan., 1983.

8. Centers for Disease Control. *AIDS Weekly Surveillance Report—United States,* 2 Jan., 1989.

9. Guinan M. E. and Hardy A. Epidemiology of AIDS in women in the United States, 1981 through 1986. *J. Am. med. Ass.* **257**, 2039–2042, 17 April, 1987.

10. Curran J. W., Jaffe H. W., Hardy A. M., Morgan W. M., Selik R. M. and Dondero T. J. Epidemiology of HIV infection and AIDS in the United States. *Science* **239**, 610–616, 5 Feb., 1988.

11. Allen J. R. and Curran J. W. Prevention of AIDS and HIV infection: needs and priorities for epidemiologic research. *Am. J. publ. Hlth* **78**, 381–386, April 1988.

12. Amadori A., Giaquinto C., Zacchello F., DeRossi A., Faulkner-Valle G. and Chieco-Bianchi L. *In vitro*-production of HIV-specific antibody in children at risk of AIDS. *Lancet* **1**, 852–854, 16 April, 1988.

13. Friedland G. H. and Klein R. S. Transmission of human immunodeficiency virus. *New Engl. J. Med.* **317**, 1125–1135, 29 Oct., 1987.

14. Nzilambi, N., Ryder R. W. and Behets F. Perinatal transmission in two African hospitals. *Third International Conference on AIDS,* Washington, D.C., June 1987.

15. Mok J. Q., Giaquinto C., DeRossi A., Grosch-Worner I., Ades A. E. and Peckham C. S. Infants born to mothers seropositive for human immunodeficiency virus, preliminary findings from a multicentre European study. *Lancet* **1**, 1164–1168, 1987.

16. Minkoff H., Nanda D., Mendez R. and Fikrig S. Pregnancies resulting in infants with acquired immunodeficiency syndrome or AIDS-related complex: follow-up of mothers, children and subsequently born siblings. *Obstet. Gynec.* **69**, 288–291, 1987.

17. Scott G. B., Fischl M. A. and Klimas N. Mothers of infants with the acquired immunodeficiency syndrome, evidence for both symptomatic and asymptomatic carriers. *J. Am. med. Ass.* **253**, 363–366, 1985.

18. Centers for Disease Control. Human immunodeficiency virus infection in the United States: a review of current knowledge. *Morbid. Mortal. Wkly. Rep.* **36**, 1–48, 18 Dec., 1987.

19. Hoff R., Berardi V. P., Weiblen B. J., Mahoney-Trout B. S., Mitchell M. L. and Grady G. F. Seroprevalence of human immunodeficiency virus among childbearing women. *New Engl. J. Med.* **318**, 525–530, 3 March, 1988.

20. Landesman S., Minkoff H., Holman S., McCalla S. and Sijin O. Serosurvey of human immunodeficiency virus infection in parturients. *J. Am. med. Ass.* **258**, 2701–2703, 1987.

21. Lambert B. One in 61 babies in New York City has AIDS antibodies, study says. *The New York Times,* **1**, 13 Jan., 1988.

22. Lichtblau E. Artificial insemination data raises fears. *Los Angeles Times* **1**, 14, 10 Aug., 1988.

23. Franke K. Turning issues upside down. In *AIDS: The Women* (Edited by Rieder I. and Ruppelt P.), pp. 226–232. Cleis Press, San Francisco, Calif., 1988.

24. Murphy J. Women with AIDS. In *AIDS: Principles, Practices and Politics* (Edited by Corless I. B. and Pittman-Lindeman M.), p. 74. Hemisphere, New York, 1988.

25. Porter P. Minorities and HIV infection. In *The AIDS Epidemic* (Edited by O'Malley P.), pp. 371–379. Beacon Press, Boston, Mass., 1989.

26. Shaw N. and Paleo L. Women and AIDS. In *What To Do About AIDS* (Edited by McKusic L.), pp. 150–151. University of California Press, Berkeley, Calif., 1986.

27. Rosenbaum M. *Women on Heroin,* p. 132. Rutgers University Press, New Brunswick, N.J., 1981.

28. James J. Prostitution: arguments for change. In *Sexuality Today and Tomorrow* (Edited by Gordon S. and Libby R.), pp. 110–113. Duxbury Press, North Scituate, Mass., 1976.

29. Richardson D. *Women and AIDS,* pp. 43–44. Methuen, New York, 1988.

30. Leigh C. Further violations of our rights. In *AIDS: Cultural Analysis, Cultural Activism* (Edited by Crimp D.), pp. 177–181. MIT Press, Cambridge, Mass., 1988.

31. Centers for Disease Control. Antibody to human immunodeficiency virus in female prostitutes. *Morbid. Mortal. Wkly. Rep.* **36**, 157–161, 27 March, 1987.

32. Campbell C. Prostitution and AIDS. In *Behavioral Aspects of AIDS* (Edited by Ostrow D. G.). Plenum Press, New York. In press.

33. Stephens P. C. U.S. women and HIV infection. In *The AIDS Epidemic* (Edited by

O'Malley P.), pp. 381–401. Beacon Press, Boston, Mass., 1989.

34. Campbell C. Women, work and welfare. Unpublished MA thesis, University of Colorado, 1979.

35. Smith-Rosenberg C. and Rosenberg C. The female animal: medical and biological views of women and her role in the nineteenth century. *J. Am. Hist.* **60**, 332–341, 1973.

36. Barker-Benfield B. The spermatic economy: a nineteenth century view of sexuality. *Feminist Stud.* **1**, 45–74, 1972.

37. Wood G. D. The fashionable disease: women's complaints and their treatment in nineteenth century America. *J. Interdis. Hist.* **4**, 25–32, 1973.

38. Lambert H. Biology and equality: a perspective on sex differences. *Signs* **4**, 97–117, 1980.

39. Scully D. and Bart P. A funny thing happened on the way to the orifice. In *The Sociology of Health and Illness* (Edited by Conrad P. and Kern R.), pp. 350–355. St. Martin's Press, New York, 1981.

40. Richardson D. *Women and AIDS*, p. 34. Methuen, New York, 1988.

41. Brown B. Creative acceptance: an ethics for AIDS. In *AIDS: Principles, Practices and Politics* (Edited by Corless I. and Pittman-Lindeman M.), p. 230. Hemisphere, New York, 1988.

42. Peabody B. *The Screaming Room.* Oak Tree, San Diego, Calif., 1986.

43. Moffatt B. C. *When Someone You Love Has AIDS.* NAL Penguin, New York, 1986.

44. Norwood C. *Advice for Life. A Woman's Guide to AIDS Risks and Prevention,* pp. 139–140. Pantheon, New York, 1987.

45. Gross J. The bleak and lonely lives of women who carry AIDS. *The New York Times,* 27 Aug., 1987.

46. Sterk C. Cocaine and HIV seropositivity. *Lancet* **1**, 1052–1053, 7 May, 1988.

47. Bowser B. Crack and AIDS: an ethnographic impression. *Multicult. Inquiry Res. AIDS* **2**, 1–2, Spring 1988.

48. DesJarlais D. C. Heterosexual partners: a risk group for AIDS. *Lancet* **2**, 1346–1347, 1984.

49. Worth D. and Rodriquez R. Latina women and AIDS. *Rad. Am.* **20**, 63–67, 1987.

50. Kegeles S. M., Adler N. and Irwin C. E. Sexually active adolescents and condoms: changes over one year in knowledge, attitudes and use. *Am. J. publ. Hlth* **78**, 460–467, April 1988.

51. Kelly J. AIDS conference reports. *The National News* **4**, Sep./Oct. 1988.

52. Wofsy C. Human immunodeficiency virus infection in women. *J. Am. med. Ass.* **257**, 2074–2076, 17 April, 1987.

53. Patton C. *Sex and Germs,* p. 41. South End Press, Boston, Mass., 1985.

54. Treichler P. A. AIDS, gender and biomedical discourse: current contests for meaning. In *AIDS, The Burdens of History* (Edited by Fee E. and Fox D.), pp. 190–266. University of California Press, Berkeley, Calif., 1988.

55. Graham S. Socio-economic status, illness and the use of medical services. *Milbank Meml Fund Q.* **35**, 58–66, Jan. 1957.

56. Blackwell B. L. Upper middle class adult expectations about entering a sick role for physical and psychiatric dysfunctions. *J. Hlth Hum. Behav.* **8**, 83–95, June 1967.

57. Freeborn D. K., Pope C. R., Davis M. A. and Mullooley J. P. Health status, socioeconomic status and utilization of outpatient services for members of a prepaid group practice. *Med. Care* **15**, 115–128, Feb. 1977.

58. Steinbrook R. AIDS slowdown in three key cities seen. *Los Angeles Times* **1**, 26, 6 Dec., 1988.

59. Heyward W. L. and Curran J. W. The epidemiology of AIDS in the U.S. *Scient. Am.* **259**, 78, Oct. 1988.

Breast Cancer: Complacency the Enemy of Cure
Marian Segal

Nineteen years ago at the age of 43, Joyce Fine of Bethesda, Md., had a radical mastectomy to treat breast cancer. She didn't discuss her disease much with anyone then, except her husband.

Twenty years ago and more, Fine remembers, cancer was not talked about. "Everything was secretive then. Obituaries of people with cancer read that they died of 'a lingering illness.'" Fine thinks that her father's mother may have had breast cancer, but she's not sure. The impression came from a single conversation she happened to overhear.

A NEW ATTITUDE

There is today an unprecedented openness about breast cancer. Along with strides in diagnosis and treatment have come long overdue changes in attitudes and awareness about the disease. Happy Rockefeller, Betty Ford, Nancy Reagan, Jill Eikenberry, Shirley Temple Black, Gloria Steinem, and many other public figures have come forward in recent years to tell about their experiences, bringing breast cancer out of the closet and offering women hope and encouragement. But it's certainly not just because of the celebrities that breast cancer has captured the public's attention. For a disease that strikes 1 in about 10 American women (the American Cancer Society puts the figure at 1 in 9) it's almost become a rarity *not* to know someone who has had breast cancer.

Since the early 1970s, according to the National Cancer Institute (NCI), the incidence of breast cancer has increased about 1 percent a year. In 1970, there were about 69,000 newly diagnosed cases, compared with 150,000 in 1990. The number of deaths rose from 30,000 in 1970 to 44,000 in 1990.

Although researchers have identified several risk factors for breast cancer and are gathering data on possible others, one thing that's clear is that no woman can afford to be complacent. That fact came home to Ellen Weinberg of Chevy Chase, Md., when she was diagnosed last December.

"I had no risk factors at all," she says. "There was no family history. My son was born when I was 27. I did not start menstruating especially early. I grew up in a house where my dad was diabetic and a little overweight, so I've always had a low-fat diet. There was just nothing. The one mistake I made was that I didn't have a mammogram. I knew I should start having them at 40, but I was only 42, I was very healthy, I had no risk factors, and I felt no urgency. I just hadn't gotten around to it."

RISKS: THE KNOWN

Some risk factors for breast cancer are clearly established, as are some factors known to reduce the chance of developing the disease. Although the average lifetime risk of breast cancer for a woman is 1 in 10, the actual risk of getting it in any given year is less than 1 in 100. A woman's risk rises continuously with age, but never exceeds 1 percent a year.

Reprinted from the *FDA Consumer*, July/August, 1991.

Breast cancer is more common in women from North America and Northern Europe and in women of high socioeconomic status. In the United States, women of European Jewish descent also have an increased risk. Certain types of benign (noncancerous) breast disease, radiation exposure, and family history of the disease are also established risk factors. Also, among post-menopausal women, obesity is associated with an increase in risk.

Women whose mothers or sisters have had breast cancer have two to three times the usual risk of developing the disease. The risk is greatest if the relative developed breast cancer before menopause or if both breasts were involved. Nevertheless, only 10 to 15 percent of women with breast cancer have a family history of the disease. As NCI researcher Susan Bates, M.D., says, the statement that "There's no breast cancer in my family" should provide a woman no security whatsoever.

In the Nov. 30, 1990, issue of *Science,* Stephen H. Friend, M.D., Ph.D., of the Massachusetts General Hospital Cancer Center reported that certain alterations in a gene called p53 lead to increased susceptibility to breast and certain other cancers, all occurring at unusually young ages. About 100 families around the world have been identified with this rare syndrome, named Li-Fraumeni for the two scientists who first described it in 1969. Follow-up of the four families originally identified revealed 16 new cancer cases when only one would have been expected.

The p53 gene is one of a few tumor suppressor genes researchers have identified. These genes act to control normal cell processes, and cancer results when the gene is missing or damaged and other genetic changes occur. The p53 gene is transmitted through the father's side of the family as well as the mother's.

Another genetic trait associated with breast cancer is wet ear wax. The breasts and the glands that produce ear wax are both apocrine glands. According to NCI's *Breast Cancer Digest* women with wet ear wax are twice as likely to develop breast cancer as those with dry wax. Wet ear wax is a dominant genetic trait in the United States—85 percent of whites and virtually all blacks in this country have wet ear wax. In Asia, where wet ear wax is rare, breast cancer is also much less prevalent.

A link between radiation and breast cancer has been established from studies of survivors of Hiroshima and Nagasaki and from women who have undergone radiation therapy or had repeated fluoroscopy, used many years ago to treat tuberculosis. The interval between exposure and disease development varies, but, according to Bates, the average is 20 years.

Women who begin menstruating before age 12, become menopausal after age 50, delay childbearing until after age 30, or bear no children are also at higher risk. On the other hand, the risk is lower in women who have their first child before age 18 and in women who, because of surgical removal of the ovaries, become menopausal before age 35.

RISKS: THE UNKNOWN

Reserpine (a drug for high blood pressure), chemicals in hair dyes, alcohol consumption, dietary fat, use of birth control pills, and estrogen therapy have all been suggested as risk factors, but results from various studies have been contradictory, and their role in disease development remains controversial.

Some research has indicated that birth control pills might increase the risk of breast cancer, particularly in pre-menopausal women between the ages of 45 and 55, in women with a family history of breast cancer, or among young women who use them before the first pregnancy. One long-term study, however, reported that neither short-term nor long-term (more than 11 years) use

Breast Self-Examination (BSE)

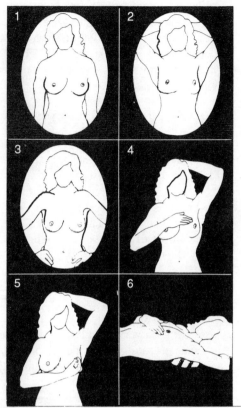

Breast self-examination should be done once a month so you become familiar with the usual appearance and feel of your breasts. Familiarity makes it easier to notice any changes in the breast from one month to another. Early discovery of a change from what is "normal" is the main idea behind BSE. If you menstruate, the best time to do BSE is two or three days after your period ends, when your breasts are least likely to be tender or swollen. If you no longer menstruate, pick a day, such as the first day of the month, to remind yourself it is time to do BSE.

1. Stand before a mirror. Inspect both breasts for anything unusual, such as any discharge from the nipples, puckering, dimpling, or scaling of the skin.

The next two steps are designed to emphasize any change in the shape or contour of your breast. As you do them you should be able to feel your chest muscles tighten.

2. Watching closely in the mirror, clasp hands behind your head and press hands forward.

3. Next, press hands firmly on hips and bow slightly toward your mirror as you pull your shoulders and elbows forward.

Some women do the next part of the exam in the shower. Fingers glide over soapy skin, making it easy to concentrate on the texture underneath.

4. Raise your left arm. Use three or four fingers of your right hand to explore your left breast firmly, carefully, and thoroughly. Beginning at the outer edge, press the flat part of your fingers in small circles, moving the circles slowly around the breast. Gradually work toward the nipple. Be sure to cover the entire breast. Pay special attention to the area between the breast and the armpit, including the armpit itself. Feel for any unusual lump or mass under the skin.

5. Gently squeeze the nipple and look for a discharge. Repeat the exam on your right breast.

6. Steps 4 and 5 should be repeated lying down. Lie flat on your back, left arm over your head and a pillow or folded towel under your left shoulder. This position flattens the breast and makes it easier to examine. Use the same circular motion described earlier. Repeat on your right breast.

Reprinted from the *FDA Consumer*, May, 1986.

appeared to increase risk, even in these groups of women. For now, the Food and Drug Administration requires that birth control pills carry a label indicating that the association between oral contraceptives and breast cancer is not clear.

Women who receive estrogen replacement therapy (ERT) may also be at increased risk. ERT is recommended for some menopausal women to counteract hot flashes and sweating and to slow bone thinning (osteoporosis). ERT may also confer protection from cardiovascular disease. A recently published study of 118,000 female nurses followed for 10 years found a "modest" increase in risk in current users—more so with increasing age, but not in past users, even if therapy had lasted more than 10 years. The researchers, led by Graham Colditz, M.B., B.S. (British equivalent of M.D.), of Brigham and Women's Hospital in Boston, concluded that, "Though this increase in risk will be counterbalanced by the cardiovascular benefits, [there is a] need for caution in the use of estrogens."

Of increasing interest is the possible relation of a high-fat diet to breast cancer. The death rate from breast cancer is highest in countries, including the United States, in which the intake of fat and animal protein is high. For instance, Japanese women historically have a low risk for breast cancer, but that risk has been rising dramatically, concurrent with a "Westernization" of eating habits; that is, from a low-fat to high-fat diet. Within Japan, the risk is 8.5 times higher for wealthier women, who eat meat daily, than among poorer women.

When large populations move from a low-incidence area to a high-incidence area and adopt the local lifestyle, they tend to take on the cancer risk patterns of their new homeland. Among immigrants from Asia to the United States, the incidence of breast cancer typically rises somewhat in the first generation, then continues to rise in subsequent generations until it approaches that of the United States.

A study involving nearly 57,000 women, published in the March 6, 1991, *Journal of the National Cancer Institute,* found an association between breast cancer and fat intake that, the authors say, "appears unlikely to have arisen by chance," even though the link is not strong and two previous studies contradict their results. It could be that the issue is muddled because the difference in fat content between the lower fat and higher fat diets of the women studied may not be great enough to influence breast cancer development. Americans typically consume 40 percent of their calories in fat. A reduction to 30 percent may not be significant in reducing breast cancer risk.

To examine the question further, NCI has approved funding for a 15-year trial that includes 24,000 women aged 50 to 69 who typically eat 38 percent of their calories from fat. Forty percent of the women will be taught how to follow a diet with only 20 percent of calories from fat, and the rest will follow their usual diet. The study will compare the incidence of breast cancer, colorectal cancer, heart disease, and overall mortality between the two groups.

Meanwhile, Bates advises that, "although there is not a definitive answer to the dietary fat hypothesis, the link seems to be plausible, and efforts to alter our diet would appear prudent."

THE ESTROGEN CONNECTION

These risk factors may appear unrelated, but a possible common thread may be estrogen. Estrogen causes breast cells to grow, and there may be times in a woman's life when the breast is more susceptible to cancer-causing substances in the environment.

"Most of the risk factors listed can in some way increase the exposure to estrogen," says Bates. "A longer menstrual history, the additional estrogens from birth control pills or from estrogen replacement at menopause, even a high-fat diet, alcohol, or just being overweight may increase the amount of estrogen in the bloodstream, or may increase the amount available to the woman's breast tissue."

An American Cancer Society study published in 1982 analyzed the contribution of 10 common risk factors by following more than 365,000 white women 30 to 84 years old for six years. One telling conclusion was that three-quarters of all breast cancer cannot yet be attributed to any known specific cause. "From the point of view of the clinician," the authors state, "all women should be treated as being at appreciable risk for breast cancer."

Nevertheless, it is important to remember that having one or more risk factors does not mean that a woman is certain, or even likely, to develop breast cancer. It means only that she may be at statistically greater risk than another woman.

Despite the continuing rise in the incidence of breast cancer, the death rate has remained fairly stable over the past 50 years. This can be attributed largely to earlier detection. (See accompanying article, "Mammography Saves Lives.")

Anatomy of a Disease

The breast is a gland designed to produce milk. Milk ducts leading to the nipple originate from lobules inside 15 or 20 lobes arranged like spokes around a wheel. The spaces around and between the milk-producing lobes are filled with fat. Ninety percent of breast cancers arise from the milk ducts. When ductal carcinoma, as it is called, remains confined to the duct, it is called *in situ,* or intraductal, cancer. When the cells penetrate the walls of the duct and invade surrounding tissue, it is called invasive ductal cancer. About 5 percent of breast cancers are lobular carcinomas, which originate in the lobules.

Two atypical kinds of breast cancers are inflammatory breast carcinoma and Paget's disease. Whereas most breast cancers are slow growing and painless, inflammatory breast carcinoma progresses very rapidly and is painful, with symptoms resembling an infection. The breast is warm and reddened, and the skin may appear pitted like an orange peel. In Paget's disease the nipple becomes crusted; cancer cells grow upward along the ducts from a malignancy deeper in the breast.

When an abnormality is detected in the breast by mammography, the doctor may recommend a biopsy. If a lump is found by palpation (feeling the mass), a biopsy is almost always necessary, regardless of the results of mammography. Exceptions may be certain lumps found in women who have histories of lumpy or cystic breasts.

The biopsy—surgical removal of all or part of the lump or suspicious area—allows a pathologist to examine the tissue and determine with certainty whether or not the lesion

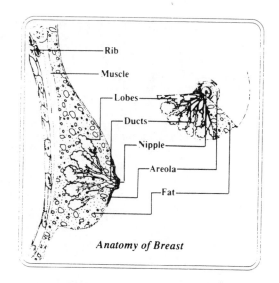

Anatomy of Breast

is cancerous. Eighty percent of palpable lumps are benign (not cancerous).

Biopsy does not always require hospitalization. It can be done as an outpatient procedure. Also, some biopsies are done by fine needle aspiration, using a local anesthetic. The doctor inserts a needle into the lump and tries to withdraw fluid. If it is a cyst, it will collapse when the fluid is removed. If it is solid, the doctor may remove some cells with the needle to send to the laboratory for analysis.

The common practice nowadays is to do a biopsy first and then schedule surgery, if necessary, within the next few weeks. Some women may still opt for the one-step procedure that was routine when Joyce Fine had her mastectomy. (Until the late 1970s, it was standard procedure for the patient having a biopsy to sign a consent form permitting the surgeon to remove the breast at the same time if the tumor was found to be cancerous.)

The interval with the two-step procedure, however, allows the woman time to find out about and choose among her treatment options, get a second opinion, and prepare for her hospital stay. The brief delay in treatment does not reduce the chances for a successful outcome. Some states have passed

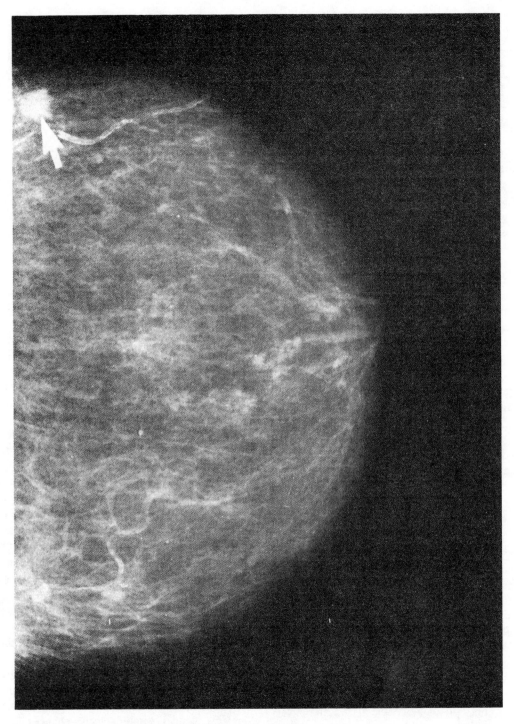

Mammogram of a woman's breast. Arrow shows location of a lump.

laws requiring that women be told a two-step procedure is their legal right and, in some cases, that they be given specific information about their options.

MAMMOGRAPHY SAVES LIVES

Widespread screening programs for women 50 and over can reduce breast cancer death rates by 30 percent. A new analysis of a study by the Health Insurance Plan of Greater New York published by the National Cancer Institute (NCI) in 1988 showed that mammographic screening can also reduce breast cancer death by 24 percent in women 40 to 49.

Mammography is the best method available for detecting tumors in their early stages. It can detect 85 to 90 percent of breast cancers in women over 50 and can discover a tumor up to two years before a doctor or patient would otherwise know it's there.

It appears that government and health organization programs encouraging women to get mammograms are beginning to pay off. A recent survey of 980 women conducted by the Jacobs Institute of Women's Health and NCI showed that 64 percent of women 40 and over have had at least one mammogram, up from 37 percent in 1987.

Twelve medical organizations—including NCI, the American Cancer Society, and the American Medical Association—recommend that women between the ages of 40 and 49 have their breasts examined by their doctors yearly and get a mammogram every one to two years. Starting at age 50, the mammogram should also be done yearly. These guidelines apply to women who have no symptoms of breast cancer, such as a lump or other change in the breast. A woman with symptoms should see her doctor immediately. And, for some women who have no symptoms but may be at higher risk for the disease, a physician may recommend more frequent mammograms.

Even though more women are getting mammograms, only 31 percent are following the guidelines, and, according to a report in the Centers for Disease Control's *Morbidity and Mortality Weekly Report* of Sept. 14, 1990, "if death rates are to be decreased, mammography use rates must continue to increase, and women must return for repeat mammograms at recommended intervals."

Nearly three-fourths of women in the Jacobs Institute survey who had had a mammogram did so because their doctors recommended it. Almost half the women (45 percent) who had never had a mammogram said their doctors never recommended it.

Of the women who had never had a mammogram, reasons cited were that they had no family history or that they were not at risk, usually meaning they thought mammograms were important only for women who feel a lump or have other symptoms of breast cancer. Many said that mammograms cost too much. Another reason given was fear of radiation.

Of the women who had one mammogram but did not follow the recommended guidelines, 35 percent stopped because the first mammogram was negative and therefore they felt they didn't need any more. Some women cited cost, a lack of family history of the disease, and fear of radiation as reasons for not continuing care.

The expense of mammograms is being addressed by local efforts to reduce cost and by legislation in a growing number of states. As of July 1990, 29 states required insurance companies to provide some level of coverage for mammography screening.

Mammography quality has improved significantly in the last six years. Results of state surveys supported by FDA found that the average score of images produced by the machines climbed from 7.8 in 1985 to 9.9 in 1990. (The range of scores is 0 to 16, with a score of 8 considered acceptable.) The survey results were reported in the November 1990 issue of the journal *Radiology*. The authors,

Fred G. Reuter, D.Sc., and other scientists from FDA's Center for Devices and Radiological Health, attributed the better image quality now achieved partly to use of equipment dedicated to mammography rather than general x-ray use, improved techniques and film processing, and the development of more sensitive screen and film systems.

The improved images necessitated only a slight increase in radiation to the patient, and the radiation levels remained well within generally accepted safety guidelines. In fact, the levels were about two-thirds lower than those found in a 1979 survey. According to the researchers, the benefits of improved image quality far outweigh the slight increase in radiation. FDA is conducting research on ways to further improve mammography, and it plans to support state radiation control agencies on their survey of mammography equipment and practices in 1992.

When selecting a mammography facility, women should find out if it is accredited by the American College of Radiology (ACR). The ACR accredits facilities based on evaluation of equipment, film processing, and the credentials and experience of the technologists who take the mammograms and the radiologists who interpret them. Women who have breast implants should ask the facility if they use special mammography techniques designed for women with breast implants. To find an accredited facility or to get other information on mammography, call the NCI Cancer Information Service toll-free at 1–800–4–CANCER or a local chapter of the American Cancer Society.

Breast Cancer
Woman Is Partner in Choosing Treatment
Marian Segal

In a recent talk on breast cancer, Susan Bates, M.D., remarked, "It has been said that a woman must know more about her disease in breast cancer than a physician. With the array of choices currently facing a woman diagnosed with breast cancer this is more true now than ever before."

The choices that Bates, a researcher at the National Cancer Institute (NCI), refers to were not available to Joyce Fine of Bethesda, Md., 19 years ago when, at 43, she underwent a Halsted radical mastectomy—removal of her entire breast, the underlying chest muscles, all the axillary (underarm) lymph nodes, and some additional fat and muscle. Fine's surgeon did not discuss with her possible treatment alternatives. The Halsted radical was the standard treatment for breast cancer in 1972.

"There was no discussion," Fine recalls. "He convinced me I had to have the tumor out as soon as possible and that I should sign a release that if they find at biopsy that it's cancerous, they should remove it right away."

Reprinted from the *FDA Consumer*, September, 1991.

The surgeon acknowledged that Fine could have a two-step procedure, in which only a biopsy would be done at first, and surgery, if the tumor proved malignant, would be scheduled later. (See "Breast Cancer: Complacency the Enemy of Cure" in the July–August 1991 *FDA Consumer* for more on breast biopsy and the two-step procedure.) "But he said that if I go that way, it would metastasize [spread] and I couldn't be put under anesthesia again soon," she says. "It would be a waiting period of a couple weeks, and I was so frightened I said I'd do it in one procedure. He made me feel as though if I didn't, I might be dead in two weeks."

And so, like so many women with breast cancer then, Fine went into surgery not knowing if she would leave the hospital physically the same as she entered, or minus one breast as the result of extensive, disfiguring surgery.

"Beginning in the 1940s, studies were suggesting that so much surgery was not necessary," says Bates. "In Europe, by 1971, smaller operations were accepted, but in the United States, change was slow in coming. Surgeons were reluctant to abandon the Halsted radical mastectomy for fear of giving inadequate treatment."

TREATING EARLY-STAGE DISEASE

Both the surgery and the process Fine experienced now belong to medical history. Surgical treatment now emphasizes breast conservation—preserving the breast when possible. Lumpectomy (also called segmental mastectomy or tylectomy), in which only the tumor and a margin of surrounding tissue is removed, is light years away from the Halsted radical, both in its physical and psychological effects.

Radical mastectomy was based on the rationale that breast cancer started with a tumor in the breast and, over time, spread in an orderly fashion to the lymph glands under the arms and then, through the lymph and blood, to other parts of the body—usually the lungs, liver, bone, or brain. Halsted's procedure was designed to remove the avenues of possible spread.

By the late 1970s, experts had determined that the Halsted radical mastectomy was not necessary. As Bates says, "It was a consensus that less is more."

This conclusion was based on research that changed the concept of how breast cancer progresses. It is now understood that very early in the disease (although exactly how early is not known), breast cancer cells travel through the blood and lymph to other parts of the body. In this process, called micrometastasis, the cancer is so small it can't even be detected with a microscope. Treatment now emphasizes removing the tumor while sparing the breast and controlling metastasis with the use of additional therapy that may include radiation, chemotherapy (using drugs that kill cancer cells), hormone therapy, or a combination.

As new approaches to surgical and medical treatment have been tried, each method has had its supporters and dissenters. In 1957, NCI organized the National Surgical Adjuvant Breast Project to create a pool of data gathered from research on breast cancer treatments. In the late 1970s, scientists reviewed study results and determined that simple, or total, mastectomy, in which only the breast was removed, was as effective as the Halsted radical.

Then, in 1990, at a National Institutes of Health consensus development conference on treatment of early-stage breast cancer, a panel of experts agreed that still less-extensive surgery, lumpectomy, gave the same results if radiation followed surgery to kill any remaining cancer cells. The lymph nodes are also removed for examination during this procedure.

The panel concluded that breast conservation treatment is not only appropriate for most women with early-stage disease, but also "is preferable because it provides survival equivalent to total mastectomy and also preserves the breast. Total mastectomy remains an appropriate primary therapy when breast conservation is not indicated or selected."

"Despite nearly 20 years of studies showing that survival with lumpectomy and radiation is equivalent to that of mastectomy, only one-fifth of women eligible for lumpectomy have the procedure. This may be due in part to the slowness of some surgeons to accept and offer, without subtle or explicit bias, the newer procedure," says Bates.

Wendy Schain, Ed.D., a participant at the NIH conference and psychosocial director of adult oncology at the Memorial Cancer Institute in Long Beach, Calif., says that of the 14 most recent studies examining the psychosocial consequences of breast surgery, all showed that patients with breast conservation therapy had significantly improved body images compared with patients who underwent mastectomy.

"For most of the kinds of psychological symptoms we measure, there are not vast differences in magnitude between the two treatment groups," she says. "But the issues underlying the different symptoms are very dissimilar. The depression in mastectomy patients is due primarily to feelings of disfigurement and concern about the impact on intimate relationships, whereas the underlying reasons for depression in breast conservation are fatigue and loss of vitality.

"Chemotherapy, whether following mastectomy or lumpectomy, is the single most psychologically undermining course of treatment," says Schain. "It pervades all areas of well-being, both physical and psychological, ranging from feelings of lowered self-esteem to energy drain and other physical distresses."

Schain says that some patients with lumpectomy seem to have some increased anxiety about recurrence, but that the studies on this are "pretty much split and should not be interpreted to mean that the cosmetic benefits gained from breast conservation would be offset by increased fear of recurrence."

Many factors govern the patient's reaction, she says, and much depends on the individual's psychological defenses and interpretation of treatment outcome. For example, for one woman, treatment with lumpectomy helps minimize her concern about the disease because she is reassured by the less-extensive surgery. The continued presence of her breast increases her comfort and reduces her fear. But another woman may react to the preserved breast with a concern over whether or not "they got it all."

Women who have multicentric breast cancer (cancers that develop at several locations within a single breast), or whose tumors are large relative to breast size and therefore would not have a good cosmetic result, are among those who may not be candidates for breast conservation.

No single procedure can be recommended as ideal for all patients. Women and their surgeons must base their decisions on the patient's medical status and her particular concerns. Her choice may be influenced by emotional considerations, finances, access to care, body image, and personal beliefs.

ADJUVANT THERAPY

Following either mastectomy or lumpectomy with radiation, additional (adjuvant) therapy is given to most women whose cancer has spread to the lymph nodes. This may be chemotherapy or hormone therapy, or both. A current controversy in treatment concerns whether or not to treat node-negative breast cancer patients (patients in whom the disease has not spread to the lymph nodes) with adjuvant therapy. Seven of 10 node-negative women will never have a recurrence of disease. Of the remaining three, standard adjuvant therapy will prevent recurrence in one. Unfortunately, there is no way yet to predict which three will have a recurrence, nor which one of those will be helped by adjuvant treatment. The dilemma, says NCI's Bates, is, "Do we treat 10 to help one, and potentially three, if our treatments can improve?"

The NIH consensus panel concluded that, "The decision to use adjuvant treatment [in node-negative patients] should follow a thorough discussion with the patient regarding the approximate risk of relapse without adjuvant therapy, toxicities of therapy, and its impact on quality of life." They further agreed that, except for patients in clinical trials, "it is reasonable not to employ adjuvant therapy in patients with tumors 1 centimeter or smaller because their chance of recurrence is less than 10 percent in 10 years." For pa-

tients with larger tumors, other predictors of recurrence should be considered.

Drug Therapy

Many drugs have been tried alone and in combination to find the best regimen to treat breast cancer. Cancer drugs can have serious side effects. They are designed to kill cancer cells, but they also affect other rapidly growing cells, such as blood-forming cells and those that line the digestive tract. As a result, they may lower resistance to infection, sap energy, and cause bruising or bleeding, nausea, vomiting, mouth sores, loss of appetite, hair loss, and other side effects. Premenopausal women may also experience hot flashes, vaginal dryness, painful intercourse, and irregular menstrual periods.

For 42-year-old Ellen Weinberg of Chevy Chase, Md., the choice of treatment came with the chemotherapy, not surgery. (Because her cancer was multicentric, Weinberg had a total mastectomy.) She saw two oncologists about adjuvant therapy and got two different opinions.

"That's really where I was hoping there would be no discrepancy—that both would say the same thing. But of course they didn't," she says. One recommended CMF—a combination of cyclophosphamide (Cytoxan), methotrexate, and 5-fluorouracil. The second oncologist told her about CMF and another regimen, CAF, which uses doxorubicin hydrochloride (Adriamycin) instead of methotrexate. "He said that CMF would be fine for me and that CAF was a more aggressive treatment—that I would probably have more severe side effects with it, but he described adriamycin as having a very good track record."

Weinberg chose the CAF. "I knew I was buying myself a whole lot of trouble short-term and I didn't know if the result was going to be any different long-term. And everyone said the prognosis was real good anyway. It was a sort of agony, but I came to that decision and I felt very comfortable with it.''

Side effects of chemotherapy vary with each patient, according to the treatment given and the individual's reaction. Weinberg, who has had three of six treatments so far, says that for her, it is like being very sick with the flu. ''You feel hot, cold, very lethargic, you get strange tingles and pains. Some people get achy. I feel toxic. I can't describe it any other way.'' She also had severe vomiting after the first treatment, but less so with the second, when she was given Marinol (oral marijuana derivative) to help reduce the vomiting. With the third treatment, Weinberg was given ondansetron hydrochloride (Zofran), which FDA had just approved (in March 1991) to combat nausea and vomiting associated with cancer chemotherapy. With Zofran, she didn't vomit at all, but the other side effects remained.

Hormone therapy, usually in the form of a drug called tamoxifen (Nolvadex), is most often given to women whose cancer cells are estrogen-receptor positive. Tamoxifen blocks estrogen from binding to the cell's receptors for that hormone, thus keeping the cells from getting the hormones they need to grow. Originally approved by FDA in 1977 for patients with advanced breast cancer and subsequently for patients with less severe disease, tamoxifen was approved for use in node-negative patients in June 1990. Hormone therapy can also produce a number of side effects, but they are usually not severe. They may include symptoms of menopause, such as hot flashes, missed periods, and vaginal dryness.

Tamoxifen is also being studied in England as a preventive agent for breast cancer, and a similar study is planned in the United States. NCI is funding a study by the National Surgical Adjuvant Breast Project, which will be designed to test the effectiveness of this drug in preventing a first occurrence of breast cancer. The study will eventually include about 16,000 women at high risk for the disease.

Treating Advanced Disease

Breast cancer that has advanced to Stage III or IV (see ''Determining Therapy'') requires chemotherapy or hormone therapy, or both, to treat its spread. Treatment may also include surgery or radiation therapy, or both, to control the breast tumor. Hormone therapy may be accomplished with drugs such as tamoxifen or, in pre-menopausal women, by removing the hormone-producing ovaries. Women whose cancer has spread beyond the breast to other parts of the body usually have less extensive breast surgery, but receive hormonal therapy or more aggressive chemotherapy directed to treating both local and metastatic disease. If necessary, radiation may be used for local control.

Most tumors eventually develop drug resistance. New treatments under study for patients with advanced breast cancer involve removing some of the patient's bone marrow and administering high-dose chemotherapy to overcome drug resistance. This is followed by reinfusing the bone marrow to prevent life-threatening drug toxicity. This therapy is also being tried in patients at high risk of disease recurrence.

Other means of reversing drug resistance with various agents are under study. One such agent, verapamil (approved for treating high blood pressure), has been shown in laboratory studies to block a cell surface protein that pumps chemotherapy drugs out of a cell, thereby making it drug resistant.

Fortunately, most breast cancers are now detected at the earlier, more treatable stages. (See ''Determining Therapy.'') Seventy-five to 80 percent of women diagnosed with breast cancer in 1990 had small, localized tumors, and about two-thirds of those had no lymph node involvement. According to the American Cancer Society, the five-year survival rate for localized breast cancer has risen from 78 percent in the 1940s to 91 percent today.

Scientists are continually researching more effective treatments for both early and advanced breast cancer. It is important to remember that cancer risk and survival statistics are averages based on large numbers of people. The chance of developing breast cancer is unique to each individual, as is the chance of recovery of any given patient.

NCI's Bates sums up: "For the medical community, the direction is clear—research. For women, the direction is also clear—take charge. Eat right, avoid a diet and a lifestyle that might increase your risk of cancer. At the age of 40 begin to get mammograms and get them on schedule."

DETERMINING THERAPY

Treatment is based on the extent of the disease and the biology of the specific tumor. Evaluation of these factors guides the approach to surgery and, if needed, adjuvant therapy. In addition, a woman's age and menopausal status are significant. Breast cancer tends to be more aggressive in younger, pre-menopausal women.

First, based on tumor size and degree of metastasis, the disease is classified into one of the following stages:

- **Carcinoma *in situ:*** Very early breast cancer that has not invaded nearby tissues.
- **Stage I:** The tumor is localized and no larger than 2 centimeters (about 1 inch).
- **Stage II:** The tumor is no larger than 2 cm, but the cancer has spread to the underarm lymph nodes, *or* the cancer is between 2 and 5 cm (about 2 inches) and may or may not have spread to the lymph nodes, *or* the cancer is bigger than 5 cm, but has not spread to the lymph nodes.

- **Stage III:** The tumor is larger than 5 cm and has spread to underarm lymph nodes, *or* the tumor is smaller than 5 cm and the underarm lymph nodes have grown into each other or into other tissues, *or* the tumor has spread to tissues near the breast (such as the chest muscles and ribs) or to lymph nodes near the collarbone, *or* it is inflammatory breast cancer. (Inflammatory breast cancer is fast-progressing with infection-like symptoms in which the skin is warm and reddened and may appear pitted.)
- **Stage IV:** The cancer has spread to other organs of the body, usually the lungs, liver, bone, or brain.

Carcinoma *in situ* has a cure rate approaching 100 percent with surgery alone. Tumors of 1 cm or less also carry a particularly good prognosis—less than 10 percent recurrence in 10 years. In general, the risk of recurrence rises with increasing tumor size and lymph node involvement.

Breast tumor tissue can be examined for important "markers" that give clues to the aggressiveness of the disease and can, therefore, help guide therapy. Some of these markers are:

- **Estrogen and progesterone receptors.** Patients whose cancer cells have proteins (receptors) to which these hormones bind have a better prognosis because the cells can be treated with hormone therapy.
- **Histologic type.** Breast cancers vary in their cell type. For example, invasive ductal cancers can sometimes be categorized into further subtypes, such as mucinous, tubular and medullary. Lobular cancers are another cell type. The various types have different rates of growth and metastasis.
- **DNA studies.** The degree of disruption of DNA in the cell nucleus correlates with the disease aggressiveness. The more disarrayed the DNA, the greater the risk of

relapse. Also, cells that divide more rapidly carry a poorer prognosis.

- **HER-2 oncogene.** This gene is sometimes found in tumors of patients whose cancer has spread. Detected early, it could predict metastasis and identify patients who would benefit from more aggressive treatment.
- **Cathepsin D.** High levels of this protein are associated with a poorer prognosis. Secreted by the cancer cells, cathepsin D may aid their spread to other parts of the body.

RECONSTRUCTION OPTIONS

Breast reconstruction after mastectomy used to be very complex, and the results were often disappointing. So, as recently as the 1960s, few women chose to have it done. Many were not aware it was a possibility. Since then, however, advances in plastic surgery have made breast reconstruction easier, more successful, and more popular.

Not every woman who has had a mastectomy chooses reconstruction. Some women decide against it because they don't want to have any more surgery or they feel the risks outweigh the benefits or for other reasons. Many women prefer to wear breast forms (prostheses).

For women who desire reconstruction, however, the option is now available with few limitations. Even women who have had radical surgery or whose skin has been grafted, damaged by radiation therapy, or is otherwise thin or tight can have successful reconstructive surgery.

Although some women have breast reconstruction during the same surgery as their mastectomy, many surgeons recommend waiting three to six months. This allows time to complete radiation or chemotherapy and for the mastectomy incision to heal.

There are three major types of breast reconstruction. "Simple" reconstruction uses a silicone gel breast implant. It is usually done in patients who have healthy chest muscles to support the reconstructed breast and enough good skin to cover the implant. "Latissimus dorsi" and "rectus abdominus" are used in patients with more extensive loss of muscle and skin. This situation is less common with the trend to less radical surgeries.

"Simple" Implant Placement

This operation takes one to two hours. It is usually done under general anesthesia, but local anesthesia is sometimes used and it can be done as outpatient surgery. A small incision is made along the lower portion of the breast near the mastectomy scar, and the implant is inserted in the pocket created under the chest muscle. A drain may be inserted temporarily to remove excess fluid. If the surgeon is able to make the reconstruction incision in the original mastectomy scar, there will be no additional scarring. In fact, the appearance of the mastectomy scar can be improved, but not eliminated, during this operation.

Silicone breast implants have been in use since the 1960s. As of 1989, about 2 million women have had them implanted—about one-fourth for reconstruction after mastectomy. (The rest have been for cosmetic surgery to augment or change the shape of the woman's natural breast.)

Many women have been highly satisfied with the appearance, size, and softness of their reconstructed breasts and have reported a number of psychological benefits. Some women, however, have had problems with the implants, prompting concern about their safety.

The most common problem associated with breast implants is capsular contracture. This occurs when scar tissue shrinks around the implant, making it feel hard and sometimes misshaping it. Other known health risks include false mammography results, infection, silicone leakage and migration to other parts of the body, and implant rupture. There have also been questions raised about the possibility of long-term risks that may include some immune reactions and carcinogenicity (ability to cause cancer). Experts are divided on these questions.

Silicone gel implants have been marketed under a "grandfather" clause in the Medical Device Amendments of 1976, which exempted them from standard pre-market approval. Because of the safety issues, FDA in June 1988 classified the implants into Class III—giving the agency authority to request safety and effectiveness data after 30 months. In April 1991, FDA published a final regulation requiring submission of the data.

The agency has received 1,200 comments about the benefits and risks of the devices and, although the comments varied, a significant number of women proposed that the implants remain available as long as consumers are fully informed of the potential risks.

Women who are considering breast reconstruction with silicone gel implants should discuss any concerns they may have with their plastic surgeons and possibly other health professionals, consumer groups, and women who have had the surgery. They can also ask the plastic surgeon for the printed information that comes in the implant package.

Latissimus Dorsi

"Latissimus dorsi" reconstruction gets its name from the broad flat back muscle that the surgeon moves to the chest to take the place of muscles that have been removed during the mastectomy. The surgeon also transfers skin and other tissue from the patient's back to the mastectomy site. An implant is then placed under the new muscle, and drains may be inserted temporarily. This operation takes longer and requires longer hospitalization than simple reconstruction. It leaves a scar on the back in addition to the mastectomy scar on the chest.

Rectus Abdominus

In this procedure, the surgeon transfers one of the two rectus abdominus muscles (the parallel vertical abdominal muscles) to the breast area, along with skin and fat from the abdomen. The surgeon shapes this flap of muscle, skin and fat into the contour of a breast. If there is enough abdominal tissue available, no implant is needed. One of the "side effects" of this procedure, which some might consider a benefit, is a tightening of the stomach, colloquially called a "tummy tuck." This procedure leaves a horizontal scar across the lower abdomen in addition to the mastectomy scar.

Nipple and Areola Construction

Breast reconstruction fashions the shape of the breast but does not always include a reconstructed nipple and areola (the dark skin around the nipple). Some women, who wish primarily to improve their appearance in clothing, choose not to have the additional one- to two-hour operation to reconstruct the nipple and areola. During this operation, the areola is most commonly fabricated from skin on the upper thigh or from behind the ear, and the nipple is created either from tissue from the newly created breast mound or from the other nipple. Skin from the vaginal lips can also be used to reconstruct the nipple and areola. If the reconstructed areola is not dark enough, ultraviolet light can be used to darken the skin.

Although breast reconstruction offers a more normal appearance both in and out of clothes, women should be aware that if there are scars from these operations they are permanent and that reconstruction does not restore lost sensation.

Dangerous Lesions
Zoé F. Carter

For most college-age women, cancer is an abstraction. But a precancerous condition called dysplasia of the cervix, detectable by a Pap test, is on the rise among women in their late teens and early twenties. Dysplasia is easy to treat and rarely recurs if caught early. But left untreated, approximately 30 percent of moderate or severe cases eventually develop into cervical cancer, usually when a woman is in her thirties or forties. In 1990 approximately 13,500 women in this country were diagnosed with cervical cancer; about 6,000 died of it. In response to this trend, the University of North Carolina at Chapel Hill set up a special dysplasia clinic four years ago after the percentage of abnormal Paps at UNC jumped from 3 percent to 12 percent in two years.

Here's what every college woman needs to know about protecting herself against cervical cancer.

Precursor to Cancer

Dysplasia is a condition in which the cells of the cervix (the narrow canal that links the lower part of the uterus with the vagina) change in either size or shape. The medical term for dysplasia is *cervical intra-epithelial neoplasia* (CIN). CIN-I is a mild cell abnormality that will, in some cases, regress without treatment. CIN-II is a more extensive abnormality, and CIN-III is a premalignant lesion, also sometimes referred to as carcinoma *in situ* (confined to the site of origin). Considered a precancerous condition, CIN-III is virtually 100 percent curable. "Deaths from cervical cancer are preventable and shouldn't occur," says Stephen Wyatt, D.M.D., M.P.H., the acting chief of the cancer prevention and control branch of the Centers for Disease Control.

If CIN-III lesions are not treated, invasive cancer—in which abnormal cells spread from the site of origin deeper into the cervix—can develop from six months to 10 years later. This is the stage when most women first exhibit symptoms (bleeding between periods or after intercourse). It is also when most deaths occur.

The HPV Link

According to an American College Health Association study, one in 10 college women is infected with HPV—the human papillomavirus—one of the country's fastest growing sexually transmitted diseases (STDs). Several of HPV's many different strains cause genital warts or lesions that have been linked to both dysplasia and cancer.

"The increase of dysplasia in young women is probably due to HPV," says George Malkasian, M.D., a senior consultant to the Mayo Clinic's Department of Obstetrics and Gynecology. "And 40 to 90 percent of cervical cancers are related to HPV infections."

Although medication can control its symptoms, there is no cure for HPV. But not every woman who is infected develops dysplasia or cancer, and some doctors believe that HPV is so common among sexually active women that it is part of the normal vagi-

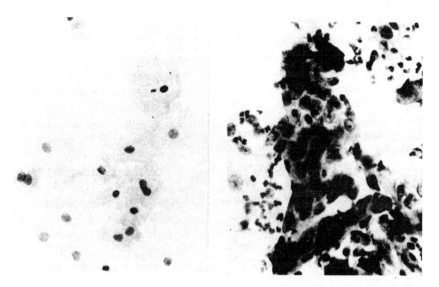

PAP smear of normal uterine cervix cells (left) and markedly dysplastic cells (right), magnified 500 times. The normal cells have smaller nuclei (dark stain) and abundant cytoplasm, compared with the abnormal cells. From the *FDA Consumer*, September, 1989.

nal flora. "Cervical cancer is a multifactorial disease," says Carolyn Runowicz, M.D., the director of the division of gynecologic oncology at Albert Einstein College of Medicine, Montefiore Medical Center, in New York. "HPV is a factor, but there has to be more than one factor for the cells to change and become cancerous."

Still, since most doctors believe that the majority of patients with dysplasia have been exposed to HPV, it makes sense for sexually active women to minimize their risk of getting the STD by practicing safer sex. This means using condoms and spermicide—even if another method of birth control such as the Pill is already being used.

Factoring Risk

Having sex before age 18 or having more than three sexual partners in a lifetime increases a woman's likelihood of contracting HPV and cervical cancer.

Smoking has also been linked to increased risk for cervical cancer. Questions remain, but some researchers believe that nicotine triggers cell changes in the cervix similar to those it effects in the lungs, since both organs are covered by squamous (scaly) cells. Other experts theorize that smoking may suppress the body's immune function, allowing HPV infections to thrive. "If you want to protect your reproductive health, don't light up," Runowicz says.

All About the Pap

The Pap smear—a quick, painless test that involves collecting a small number of cervical cells and examining them for abnormalities—may be a woman's best protection against cervical cancer. "Early diagnosis is the key to survival with any cancer," Wyatt says.

Even the Pap test is far from perfect. It has a high rate of false negatives (10 to 15 percent), and it is possible for a woman with dysplasia to have a normal Pap result. Still, young sexually active women should get a Pap test every year. Despite the Pap's imperfections, the screening test has helped to cut the death rate for cervical cancer by 60 percent in the past 30 years.

An abnormal Pap could indicate an infection, like vaginitis or HPV, or cellular changes. If cellular changes have occurred, the lab will indicate whether the squamous intra-epithelial lesion (SIL) is high or low grade. A low-grade SIL includes HPV infections and CIN-I, or mild dysplasia. A high-grade SIL signals moderate or severe dysplasia. According to Henry W. Buck, M.D., the chief of gynecology at the student health service at the University of Kansas in Lawrence, "an HPV infection and CIN-I are often present together."

Treating the Problem

If a Pap smear indicates an SIL, doctors usually do a colposcopy, an exam of the cervix using a special magnifier to visually examine the cells. The exam is painless and takes approximately 20 minutes. Sometimes the doctor will also perform biopsies—the removal of small pieces of tissue that are then examined under a microscope. Most women experience discomfort during biopsy and light bleeding afterward.

When the diagnosis is dysplasia, the most common treatment is cryosurgery, which kills the abnormal cells by freezing them. This procedure is performed in a gynecologists's office and takes less than 10 minutes. Most patients have some cramping during the procedure and a watery discharge for several days or weeks afterward.

Laser surgery, which vaporizes or heats away the diseased tissue, is another option. It is often the treatment of choice in the case of more advanced lesions. Women may experience a burning sensation during this in-office

---

One Woman's Story

Jane Martin,* 22, had just graduated from college. While visiting her family in New York, she had a routine checkup with her mother's gynecologist. "My mother called and told me the doctor found something funny about my Pap test," she says.

It turned out that Martin had three precancerous lesions on her cervix, a condition that was probably related to HPV. "There was only one man with whom I didn't use condoms," she says. "I really regret that now."

Martin had laser surgery that she says was "painful but only lasted five minutes." Her three-month follow-up exam found her to be healing well. "But I am more careful about my body and other people's bodies now, and I try to get all my friends to use condoms," Martin says. "I wouldn't want anyone I know to have to go through this."

*Not her real name.

---

procedure, which is usually performed under a local anesthesia.

For advanced lesions, repeat abnormalities, or lesions that can't be adequately seen by a colposcope, doctors perform conizations, surgical or laser removals of a cone-shaped section of the cervix.

Although none of these treatments compromises a woman's fertility, extensive conization can make it difficult for a woman to bring a pregnancy to term.

Once treated, dysplasia usually doesn't recur. "Only 5 to 10 percent of the women we treat for dysplasia require additional treatment," says James Lindblade, M.D., the director of the women's health clinic at the University of Wisconsin–Madison.

Many gynecologists recommend that the partners of women treated for HPV infection or dysplasia see a doctor as well. "We don't know what the risk is for cancer in men because penile cancer develops at a later age. But HPV is definitely an equal-opportunity disease," Buck says. "Sixty percent of the partners of the women we see have lesions." Early detection may be difficult—lesions may not be visible to the human eye and HPV is often asymptomatic—but it is crucial.

The Emotional Side

Some women who feel guilty and embarrassed about having an HPV infection or dysplasia believe they are a punishment for having "too much" sex. But these conditions are common and can occur in women with very little sexual experience. "I've seen CIN-III in 18-year-olds," Buck says. "One had been sexually active for only about six months." Talking to other women who have been diagnosed and treated or to a counselor at the college health service can help a woman come to terms with her feelings.

Depression in Women
E. S. Paykel

Depression in treated samples shows an approximately 2 : 1 female predominance. The sex ratio is not due simply to more help-seeking behaviour in women, for it applies equally in studies of community prevalence. Differential acknowledgement and direction of distress may be a partial explanation, supported by male predominance of alcoholism and completed suicide, and by a possible recent increase in depression in young men. Biological mechanisms acting through hormonal effects on the brain are plausible, but hard to test. Epidemiological studies indicate that much of the excess occurs in married women aged 25–45 years with children. This strongly suggests social causation and highlights the vulnerable situation of young mothers. The full explanations for the sex difference are not yet clear, but are likely to combine factors related to expression of distress, biology and social situation.

Depression is the most prevalent disorder in psychiatry. It is also a condition in which illness shades imperceptibly through subclinical distress to a normal mood which is part of universal human experience. Defining thresholds for the disorder and trying to think separately about disorder and normal mood has therefore been important, even if abrupt dis-

Reprinted with permission from the *British Journal of Psychiatry* (1991) 158 (suppl. 10), 22–29. Copyright © 1991, The Royal College of Psychiatrists.

tinctions are artificial. Community prevalence studies indicate that 5% of the population satisfy the criteria of the Present State Examination (PSE; Wing *et al.* 1974) or DSM-III (American Psychiatric Association, 1980) criteria for defined psychiatric depression in a six month period.

Perhaps the most striking fact about depression is its differential sex incidence, with more women affected than men. This paper examines in detail the differential sex ratio and considers alternative explanations for it. It is not possible to point to one single explanation, or indeed to many firm conclusions, but in my view the evidence is gradually making up a consistent story.

Sex Ratios

Table 1 shows sex ratios in treated cases of depression in some representative studies in Western cultures between 1942 and 1973, reviewed by Weissman and Klerman (1977). There are many other studies, and more recent ones, but they also show a female predominance. The average female : male ratio in these studies was around 2.1 : 1 and all showed female predominance. In the literature as a whole there are some exceptions, but not many.

A number of broad explanations for this difference have been advanced. The first suggests that perhaps it is entirely an artefact: women may simply seek help more for the depression which both sexes have equally. A second obvious set of explanations has to do with biological make-up: there may be genetic differences due to the different chromosomal makeup of the sexes, or female sex hormones may have an effect in some way. A more popular line of explanation lies in social effects of life stress, of social vulnerability factors and absence of support, and of women's role in society more widely. A fourth explanation is that the two sexes may differ in the way distress gets ac-

Table 1. Sex ratios in some studies of treated depression (from Weissman & Kerman, 1977)

Study	female : male ratio
USA	
Cooper et al, 1942	2.0
Wechsler, 1961	2.5
Gardner et al, 1963	2.1
Rosen et al, 1964	1.5
Duvall et al, 1966	2.3
Tarnower & Humphries, 1969	2.4
Lehmann, 1971	1.7
Paykel et al, 1970	3.0
Pederson et al, 1972	1.5
Cannon & Redick, 1973	2.1
Europe	
Kielholz, 1959	1.5
Essen-Moller & Hagnell, 1961	1.8
Juel-Nielsen et al, 1961	3.0
Odegaard, 1961	1.4
Adelstein et al, 1964	1.9
Grewel, 1967	2.6
Lehmann, 1971 (England)	1.6–1.9
Mean	2.1

knowledged and directed: into depression in females, in other ways and disorders in males. This explanation lies somewhere between and involves aspects of all the other three.

The remainder of this paper will examine detailed evidence for each of these broad explanatory hypotheses.

Help-Seeking Behaviour

Conclusive answers from the literature can only be given to the first explanation: the differential sex ratio is not simply due to differences in help-seeking behaviour. There are some well documented differences in the extent to which the two sexes tend to use medical services in general. Most studies of attendance at doctors for physical or psychiatric complaints, show women attending more. For instance, Hinkle *et al* (1960), in their study of telephone employees in New York aged over 20 years, found women had more visits to the doctor and were away from work for health reasons more frequently than men.

These differences were almost all accounted for by minor illnesses: men had more life-threatening illnesses and had higher death rates. Higher consulting rates do not necessarily mean a greater readiness to consult: they might simply mean more illness. Kessler *et al* (1981) analysed data for psychiatric symptoms from four large-scale community surveys. Women did report more psychiatric distress but also showed a greater readiness to consult at the same level of morbidity: this appeared to be due to a greater readiness to translate non-specific feelings of distress into a recognition that they had an emotional problem.

However, for specific depressive symptoms and anxiety the female predominance in treated samples is found to an equal or greater extent in community samples. It is useful to make a distinction in these between studies using questionnaires, which report symptoms, but not necessarily of sufficient severity to reach the level of disorder, and studies employing definitions for psychiatric disorder, which usually give lower rates.

With regard to depressive symptoms, Boyd and Weissman (1982) reviewed the point prevalence in some community studies. These gave relatively high rates of 13%–20% overall. Table 2 summarises the sex ratios. From these data a mean sex ratio of 1.9 can

Table 3. Prevalence rates for depressive disorders in recent community surveys employing psychiatric definitions for major depression–PSE/ID/CATEGO and DSM-III/RDC

	Rates per 100		
	Men	Women	Total
PSE/ID/CATEGO (1 month)			
Henderson *et al*, 1979	2.6	6.7	4.1
Bebbington *et al*, 1981	4.8	9.0	7.0
Dean *et al*, 1983		5.9	
Mavreas *et al*, 1978	4.3	10.1	7.4
DSM-III/RDC (6 month)			
Weissman & Myers, 1978*b*	3.2	5.2	4.3
Dean *et al*, 1983		7.0	
Myers *et al*, 1984	1.7	4.0	3.0
Canino *et al*, 1987	2.4	3.3	3.0
Mean	3.2	6.4	4.8

be calculated, which is virtually the same as that for treated depression.

Studies employing psychiatric definitions give lower total rates, as might be expected from more stringent criteria. Here, the recent large-scale epidemiological studies employing DSM-III/Research Diagnostic Criteria (RDC; Spitzer *et al*, 1978) or PSE criteria, including the US Epidemiological Catchment Area (ECA) studies, provide the best evidence. Table 3 summarises six-month prevalences for major depression in some of these studies. Calculating average sex ratios gives a figure of 2.0—again virtually identical to that for treated depression.

The female predominance of depression is therefore not an artefact of treatment seeking. In the US ECA studies, women with psychiatric disorders were a little more likely to consult a doctor than men, although, if they sought help, men were more likely to turn to a specialist. The overall difference was small, around 10%–20% (Shapiro *et al*, 1984), and this was for disorder irrespective of diagnosis. There is relatively little direct evidence specific to depression of clinical intensity as to who seeks help.

Table 2. Sex ratios of point prevalence of depressive symptoms in some community samples (from Boyd & Weissman, 1982)

Study	Female : male ratio
Martin *et al*, 1957	2.4
Warheit *et al*, 1973	1.8
Mellinger *et al*, 1974	1.8
Blumenthal, 1975	2.7
Comstock & Helsing, 1976	
Missouri	1.4
Maryland	1.8
Weissman & Myers, 1978*a*	
1967 survey	1.3
1969 survey	1.8
Mean	1.9

Biological Causes

Given that the difference is real, what is the likely explanation? Here we are on less certain grounds regarding conclusions. Part of the problem has been the absence of tough-minded research directly aimed at resolving the questions; part is that the right kinds of studies, comparing the two sexes, are not easy.

Biological explanations have centered around genes or hormones. Regarding the former, there is clear evidence from twin studies of a genetic element in affective disorders. This is most marked for bipolar disorder but fairly clear, although less in magnitude, for unipolar psychotic depression (McGuffin & Katz, 1986). For unipolar neurotic depression, although there is also a familial element, twin studies are far less conclusive as to whether its origin is genetic or environmental. Even for bipolar disorder, the genetic evidence now suggests multiple genes rather than single ones.

If a disorder is X-linked, with a gene on the X chromosome, differential sex incidence will be found. X-linked dominant disorders will be more common in women. An X-linked recessive condition, such as haemophilia, almost solely occurs in men but can be transmitted to offspring only via women.

There is some evidence of X linkage in bipolar disorder. This evidence depended initially on linkage studies using phenotypic markers, but there are now more recent studies using markers localised to the distal portion of the long arm of the X chromosome which show X linkage (Mendlewicz et al, 1987). If it does occur, it is only in some families rather than in all. However, this is unlikely to explain the sex incidence. The biggest problem lies in the sex incidence of bipolar disorder, which is approximately equal. Here there are some good studies of incidence, which, where possible, is more illuminating than prevalence since it is not affected by differential prognosis. In some Danish annual incidence studies quoted by Boyd & Weissman (1982) the female : male ratios were 1.1, 1.3, 0.5, 1.3, averaging, in this unrepresentative series, at 0.9. These studies are not exhaustive but others, including prevalence figures in the American ECA studies, show similar trends. There is no good evidence for X linkage in unipolar disorders.

This difference between bipolar disorder and the other affective disorders in sex incidence is important and has not received enough comment. It reinforces the evidence that bipolar disorder is a separate disorder. It also appears more biological in origin than other forms of depression: perhaps this hints that the female predominance in unipolar disorders is more psychosocial in origin.

The more obvious biological possibility lies in the important hormonal differences between women and men, the former having exposure to oestrogens and progestogens rather than predominantly to androgens, and to cycling of gonadotrophins and sex hormones. Here it is virtually impossible to make useful direct female : male comparisons at present—such comparisons show the obvious, but in most circumstances are totally confounded by other sex and gender differences.

Indirect inferences can be attempted from some possibly hormone-related phenomena. Pre-menstrual tension appears to be a real phenomenon, which includes depression among other feelings such as tension and irritability. Occasionally women show virtually a clinical depression pre-menstrually, particularly, in my clinical experience, when relapsing into a depressive episode. Unfortunately, however, the specific hormonal change responsible for pre-menstrual tension remains obscure.

The remaining lines of evidence are rather negative. Oral contraceptives were blamed for depression at one time: studies are at best equivocal and several placebo-controlled studies do not show any increase in depressed mood (Weissman & Slaby,

1973). The effect, if present, is a small one: clinical major depression rarely appears related to use of oral contraceptives.

Childbirth is undoubtedly associated with an increase in onsets of major psychosis and hospital admissions in the first post-partum month (Kendell et al, 1987), and is a time of massive hormonal change. Increased onset of bipolar disorder does seem to occur at this time, but many post-partum psychoses are not affective. Recent evidence indicates that such psychoses are not related to recent life stress, making hormonal aetiology more plausible (Martin et al, 1989; Brockington et al, 1990; Dowlatshahi & Paykel, 1990).

Milder post-partum depression at the general practice or subclinical level is common, but recent studies (Cox et al, 1989) making comparisons with age-matched non-postpartum women suggest that rates are not very dramatically raised: depression is common in married women in the childbearing era. Such milder depression appears to be highly related to life events and social stress (Paykel et al, 1980; Watson et al, 1984; Cooper & Stein, 1989).

However, the excess of depression in women is by no means confined to the period shortly after childbirth. Onsets at this time cannot explain more than a very small proportion of the total.

The fourth possibility, the biological menopause, does not make a contribution. At least three studies have failed to show any peak in major depressive disorder at the biological menopause (Winokur, 1973; McKinley & Jeffries, 1974; Hallstrom, 1973), although psychosocial changes and life events occurring around this time in the life cycle may be important.

This leaves little solid to depend on. Nevertheless, it is hard to ignore the possible contribution of hormones. This need not be directly in adulthood. The developing male and female brains in utero, in the neonatal period and in infancy are exposed to differ-

ent hormonal environments, resulting in such effects as later hormonal cycling. Differences in brain function related to level of emotionality or particular mood states cannot be ruled out, at least until brain function is better studied.

Social Causes

Social causes have been the focus of more research. Stronger links are emerging, although the evidence is not as strong as some of the claims. Much of the research, for instance that on social vulnerability factors, has been confined to female samples. Before conclusions about their contribution to the sex ratio can be drawn, we need to have similar studies in men.

Social explanations have generally concerned life events, social support, or women's roles and status. Regarding the first, there is now a large and conclusive volume of research showing that clinical depressions are preceded by elevated rates of the more threatening classes of life events (Paykel & Cooper, 1991). Women do not appear to experience more life events than men. Studies in the community which have looked at the question suggest equal event rates, but that women react with higher symptom intensities to the same stress (Uhlenhuth & Paykel, 1973). Also the two sexes, when asked to rate the stressfulness of different events, weight them similarly (Paykel et al, 1971). The answer appears to lie in a greater vulnerability to the effects of life events, rather than more life-event stress. Such vulnerability might be genetic or environmental, biological or social.

Social vulnerability studies have laid particular emphasis on social support. They include the seminal studies of women by Brown and Harris (Brown & Harris, 1978; Brown & Prudo, 1981; Brown et al, 1986) implicating, most clearly, the absence of a confidant, and less consistently, the presence of young children at home, being of lower social class, not working, and early loss of mother. Although there has been much debate about these, the evidence from other studies seems quite good for the first two or three. For work outside the home there has been less replication, and studies suggest more complex effects. For instance, Parry (1986) found that, in the case of working-class women, working outside the home was associated with less depression where there was good social support; where there was not good support, however, it was associated with more depression. Important factors seem to be whether a woman chooses to work or is driven to it by necessity and whether it leaves no gap at home or produces a situation where problems with growing children are worsened. All these need testing in men. The available evidence suggests that not working because of unemployment is generally very bad for them.

The third set of social explanations concerns the psychosocial disadvantages of women's roles and status. Such hypotheses suggest that particularly the housewife role is associated with low social status. Social discrimination makes it difficult to achieve mastery by direct action and assertion, inequities lead to legal and economic helplessness, dependency on others, chronically low self-esteem, and low aspirations. Learned helplessness is induced, starting from childhood socialization, self-images and expectations. Again, Brown's work has contributed in relation to depression by a recent focus on low self-esteem and its antecedents (Brown et al, 1986): again the way forward would also seem to lie in comparative studies of the two sexes.

Epidemiological Studies

Epidemiological studies are starting to provide some answers concerning the interactions of sex with age, marital status and having children.

Jorm (1987) carried out combined analyses of a large number of studies of sex and age in depression. He looked at sex ratio with age and found a curvilinear relationship. The female predominance is absent in childhood, most marked in middle age, and weak in old age. In a complicated regression analysis looking at rates of depression rather than just ratios, there was a high rate for women in their 20s which declined slowly as they got older. The rise in rate reached its peak well after puberty in females, and the decline started well before the menopause and showed no acceleration then: these are difficult to explain on endocrine hypotheses.

For marital status there is a somewhat consistent trend, as was pointed out in the 1970s by Gove, an American sociologist (e.g. Gove & Tudor, 1973). He noted that high rates of many mental illnesses for women are particularly accounted for by married women: single women have lower rates, although for those divorced, separated and widowed, rates are often high. For men the ratio is reversed: those who are single have higher rates than those who are married. For men marriage appears to be protective, for women detrimental. This result was also found in the Camberwell survey (Bebbington et al, 1981), although not all studies support it (Romans-Clarkson et al, 1988). Bebbington (1987), reviewing first admission statistics for depression, found lower rates for the married than the single in both sexes, but again the effect was much more marked in men than in women.

With regard to age, sex and marital status, there are some old findings which have never achieved the prominence they deserve. Grad de Alarcon and colleagues set up a case register to compare services in Chichester and Salisbury, around 1960. Later, they reported specific referral rates for psychiatric treatment by age, sex, marital status and diagnosis (Grad de Alarcon et al, 1975). For depression there was the expected excess of women over men in middle age, and this was found for married women in particular. They also found an excess of neurotic depression for married women aged 25–44 years. There was in fact a later peak for psychotic depression, in unmarried women aged 35–65 years, but this was smaller and less convincing. Other studies, not altogether consistently, suggest similar results.

The last piece of evidence concerns having children. Gater *et al* (1989) found that first admission rates for affective psychosis for the North West Region were higher in women. Detailed breakdown of the results showed the excess was accounted for by women who had had one or more children. Marital status and parity are closely associated, but looking respectively at unmarried women with children and those married but without children, the excess appeared to be accounted for by having children. Unfortunately, these latter conclusions were of necessity based on rather low numbers. Once you have a child, of course, you have the social consequences for a long time. Bebbington *et al* (1991), using data for prevalence of minor affective illness, obtained similar findings, although in their data it was less clear whether having children rather than marital status was responsible.

These findings point in a consistent direction. There is a particular peak of depression in women aged 20–40 years who are married and have children. It is difficult to reconcile these findings with any endocrine hypothesis, easy to do so with hypotheses of social causation pointing to the particular problems of young mothers in developed Western societies, where families are nuclear and geographically mobile, extended family support is uncommon, and a woman with children is particularly dependent on the quality of relationships with her partner. In our own studies of life events and depression, marital arguments and break-up have been among the most common antecedent events (Paykel, 1974).

Differential Acknowledgement and Direction of Distress

A final possible explanation for the differential rates lies in a difference in acknowledgement and direction of distress. It is commonplace that women in our society cry more readily than men. It is accepted as normal that a woman should weep on receiving very bad news but it is regarded as dubious for men to do so. This is usually explained as a matter of social acceptance in our culture, and undoubtedly much of it is. Some of it could be biological: higher emotionality might be a concomitant of greater sensitivity in interpersonal relationships and perceptiveness of the needs of others, something which might have biological value in differentiated childbearing.

This concerns normal mood but might carry over to pathological disorder. Some other problems are more common in men, particularly alcoholism and crime. Crime does not bear any great relationship to mood disorder, and in most cases it is not psychiatric. Alcoholism does have a relationship to mood disorder. Winokur (1979) described 'depressive-spectrum' disease in which women tend to have depression, while male family members have alcoholism and antisocial personality. It could be that men disguise their depression by drinking, or, at a deeper level, distress is directed into other disorders. Men have a higher rate of suicide than women, so perhaps the depression is there. There might be other explanations for this difference, however: more women unsuccessfully attempt suicide, and the choice of method may determine outcome, since men tend to use violent methods of high lethality, women to use less lethal overdoses.

It might therefore be that, irrespective of help seeking, women are more prepared to acknowledge their depression and to report it in surveys. Briscoe (1982) found women more willing to acknowledge feelings, both positive and negative. Angst & Dobler-Mikola (1984), in a community survey in a Zurich canton, found one-year prevalences for depression to be higher in women than men, but little difference between the sexes for prevalence in the last three months. They suggested the most likely explanation to be that men tended to forget. This seems more relevant to identification of mild cases in the community than to severe treated disorder.

A valuable approach in confirming this lies in studies of other cultures where such factors might operate differently. The Old Order Amish of Pennsylvania, a fundamentalist religious group, are a subculture in the US who lead a 19th-century life, with strong prohibitions on drink and antisocial behaviour. They appear to have high rates of affective disorder. Among them unipolar disorder, as well as bipolar, shows an approximately equal sex incidence (Egeland & Hotstetter, 1983).

More distant cultures would be informative. Weissman & Klerman (1977) reviewed a number of studies from Guinea, India and Papua, where the Western sex ratio appeared to be reversed to a male predominance. Unfortunately they were all studies of treated samples. In many of these cultures women lead a life which is relatively enclosed in the family, and they might not have access to help-seeking to the same extent as men. More community studies are needed, and are starting to appear. Such studies will have to contend with methodological difficulties of non-Western ways of expressing depression, and also to look at factors which might change the rates, such as better extended family support.

A final piece of evidence is provided by Western temporal trends. There is suggestive evidence that reported Western rates of depression, as detected in community surveys, are increasing, particulary for young men, and that the sex ratios are becoming more equal. The ECA studies in the US have been inferred to show this (Klerman, 1988), as has a similar study in Christchurch, New Zealand (Joyce et al, 1990). Care is needed in interpretation: the conclusion depends on reported lifetime rates being higher in the young than would be expected from lifetime rates in the old, but the instrument, the Diagnostic Interview Schedule, may well be unreliable for lifetime recollection (Parker, 1987), and the elderly might simply forget.

More persuasively, Murphy (1986) has reviewed four community studies, two in the USA, one in Canada and one in Sweden, repeated 10–20 years apart. They showed a trend for sex ratios to equalise. There have been considerable societal changes towards less gender-role differentiation, especially in Scandinavia, which might both change the acknowledgement and the social stress. Perhaps men are starting to acknowledge their depression. Sex ratios for depression appear to be more equal in university students (Wilhelm & Parker, 1989), and Jenkins (1985) found no major sex differences in rates in civil service executive officers.

Conclusions

The explanations for a differential sex incidence of depression are still only tentative. The most plausible conclusion is that there are multiple factors at work in the same direction.

Help-seeking behaviour may make a small contribution to treated rates, but only a small one. Biological factors cannot be discounted, at least not those based more on the effects of hormonal environment on brain biology than on an abnormal gene on the X chromosome. There is a particular vulnerability to depression in married women aged 20–40 years with children. This strongly suggests a social explanation. Differential acknowledgement may also be important, and may be changing. More research is needed which, in illuminating this specific problem, is likely in addition to reveal much that is of central importance for the genesis of depression in general.

REFERENCES

Adelstein, A. M., Downham, D. Y., Stein, Z., et al (1964) The epidemiology of mental illness in an English city: inceptions recognised by Salford Psychiatric Services. *Social Psychiatry*, **3**, 445–468.

American Psychiatric Association (1980) *Diagnostic and Statistical Manual for Mental Disorders* (3rd edn) (DSM–III). Washington, DC: APA.

Angst, J. & Dobler-Mikola, A. (1984) The definition of depression. *Journal of Psychiatric Research*, **18**, 401–406.

Bebbington, P. E. (1987) Marital status and depression: a study of English national admission statistics. *Acta Psychiatrica Scandinavica*, **75**, 640–650.

——. Hurry, J., Tennant, C., et al (1981) Epidemiology of mental disorders in Camberwell. *Psychological Medicine*, **11**, 561–579.

——. Dean, C., Der, G., et al (1991) Gender, parity and the prevalence of minor affective disorder. *British Journal of Psychiatry*, **158**, 40–45.

Blumenthal, M. D. (1975) Measuring depressive symptomatology in a general population. *Archives of General Psychiatry*, **32**, 971–978.

Boyd, J. H. and Weissman, M. M. (1982) Epidemiology. In *Handbook of Affective Disorders*, (ed. E. S. Paykel) Edinburgh: Churchill Livingstone.

Briscoe, M. (1982) Sex differences in psychological well-being. In *Psychological Medicine* (monograph suppl. 1). Cambridge: Cambridge University Press.

Brockington, I. F., Martin, C., Brown, G. W., et al (1990) Stress and puerperal psychosis. *British Journal of Psychiatry*, **157**, 319–326.

Brown, G. W. and Harris, T. O. (1978) *Social Origins of Depression. A Study of Psychiatric Disorder in Women.* London: Tavistock.

—— and Prudo, R. (1981) Psychiatric disorder in a rural and an urban population: I. Aetiology of depression. *Psychological Medicine*, **11**, 581–599.

——, Andrews, B., Harris, T., et al (1986) Social support, self-esteem and depression. *Psychological Medicine*, **16**, 813–831.

Canino, G. J., Bird, H. R., Shrout, P. E., et al (1987) The prevalence of specific psychiatric disorders in Puerto Rico. *Archives of General Psychiatry*, **44**, 727–735.

Cannon, M. and Redick, R. (1973) *Differential Utilisation of Psychiatric Facilities by Men and Women: US 1970.* Statistical note 81, June 1973. Washington, DC: Surveys and Reports Section, US Department of Health, Education and Welfare.

Comstock, G. W. and Helsing, K. J. (1976) Symptoms of depression in two communities. *Psychological Medicine*, **6**, 551–563.

Cooper, M., Lemkau, P. and Tietze, C. (1942) Complaint of nervousness and the psychoneuroses: an epidemiological viewpoint. *American Journal of Orthopsychiatry*, **12**, 214–223.

Cooper, P. J. and Stein, A. (1989) Life events and postnatal depression: the Oxford study. In *Current Approaches: Childbirth as a Life Event* (eds J. L. Cox, E. S. Paykel and M. L. Page). Southampton: Duphar Medical Relations.

Cox, J. L., Paykel, E. S. and Page, M. L. (eds) (1989) *Current Approaches: Childbirth as a Life Event.* Southampton: Duphar Medical Relations.

Dean, C., Surtees, P. G. and Sashidharan, S. P. (1983) Comparison of research diagnostic systems in an Edinburgh community sample. *British Journal of Psychiatry*, **142**, 247–256.

Dowlatshahi, D. and Paykel, E. S. (1990) Life events and social stress in puerperal psychoses: absence of effect. *Psychological Medicine* **20**, 655–662.

Duval, H. J., Kramer, M. and Locke, B. Z. (1966) Psychoneuroses among first admissions to psychiatric facilities in Ohio, 1958–1961. *Community Mental Health Journal*, **2**, 237–243.

Egeland, J. A. and Hostetter, A. M. (1983) Amish study: I: Affective disorders among the Amish, 1976–1980. *American Journal of Psychiatry*, **140**, 56–61.

Essen-Moller, E. and Hagnell, O. (1961) The frequency and risk of depression within a rural population in Scandinavia. *Acta Psychiatrica Scandinavica*, **162**, (suppl.), 28–32.

Gardner, E. A., Bahn, A. K., Miles, H. C., et al (1963) All psychiatric experience in a community. *Archives of General Psychiatry*, **9**, 365–378.

Gater, R. A., Dean, C. and Morris, J. (1989) The contribution of childbearing to the sex difference in first admission rates for affective psychosis. *Psychological Medicine,* **19,** 719–724.

Gove, W. R. and Tudor, J. R. (1973) Adult sex roles and mental illness. *American Journal of Sociology,* **78,** 812–835.

Grad De Alarcon, J., Sainsbury, P. and Costain, W. R. (1975) Incidence of referred mental illness in Chichester and Salisbury. *Psychological Medicine,* **5,** 32–54.

Grewel, F. (1967) Psychiatric differences in Ashkenazim and Sephardim. *Psychiatry, Neurology and Neurochir,* **70,** 339–347.

Hallstrom, T. (1973) *Mental Disorder and Sexuality in the Climacteric.* Goteberg, Sweden: Ortadius Biktryckeri A.B.

Henderson, S., Duncan-Jones, P., Byrne, D. G., *et al* (1979) Psychiatric disorder in Canberra. A standardised study of prevalence. *Acta Psychiatrica Scandinavica,* **60,** 355–374.

Hinckle, L. E., Redmont, R., Plummer, N., *et al* (1960) II. An explanation of the relation between symptoms, disability, and serious illness in two homogeneous groups of men and women. *Journal of Public Health,* **50,** 1327–1336.

Jenkins, R. (1985) Sex differences in minor psychiatric morbidity. In *Psychological Medicine* (monograph suppl. 7). Cambridge: Cambridge University Press.

Jorm, A. F. (1987) Sex and age differences in depression: a quantitative synthesis of published research. *Australian and New Zealand Journal of Psychiatry,* **21,** 46–53.

Joyce, P. R., Oakley-Browne, M. A., Wells, J. E., *et al* (1990) Birth cohort trends in major depression: increasing rates and earlier onset in New Zealand. *Journal of Affective Disorders,* **18,** 83–89.

Juel-Nielsen, N., Bille, M., Flygenring, J., *et al* (1961) Frequency of depressive states within geographically delimited population groups. *Acta Psychiatrica Scandinavica,* **162,** 69–80.

Kendell, R. E., Chalmers, J. C. and Platz, C. (1987) Epidemiology of puerperal psychoses. *British Journal of Psychiatry,* **150,** 662–673.

Kessler, R. C., Brown, R. L. and Broman, C. L. (1981) Sex differences in psychiatric help-seeking: evidence from four large-scale surveys. *Journal of Health and Social Behavior,* **22,** 49–64.

Kielholz, P. (1959) Drug treatment of depressive states. *Canadian Psychiatric Association Journal,* **45,** 129–137.

Klerman, G. L. (1988) The current age of youthful melancholia. Evidence for increase in depression among adolescents and young adults. *British Journal of Psychiatry,* **152,** 4–14.

Lehmann, H. E. (1971) The epidemiology of depressive disorders. In *Depression in the 70s* (ed. R. R. Fieve). The Hague: Excerpta Medica.

Martin, C. J., Brown, G. W., Goldberg, D. P., *et al* (1989) Psychosocial stress and puerperal depression. *Journal of Affective Disorders,* **16,** 283–293.

Martin, F. M., Brotherston, J. H. F. and Chave, S. P. W. (1957) Incidence of neurosis in a new housing estate. *British Journal of Preventive and Social Medicine,* **11,** 196–202.

Mavreas, V. G., Beis, A., Mouyias, A., *et al* (1978) Psychiatric disorders in Athens. A community study. *Social Psychiatry,* **21,** 172–181.

McGuffin, P. and Katz, R. (1986) Nature, nurture and affective disorder. In *The Biology of Depression* (ed. J. F. W. Deakin). London: Royal College of Psychiatrists/Gaskell.

McKinley, S. M. and Jeffries, M. (1974) The menopausal syndrome. *British Journal of Preventive and Social Medicine,* **28,** 108–115.

Mellinger, G. D., Balter, M. B., Parry, H. J., *et al* (1974) An overview of psychotherapeutic drug use in the United States. In *Drug Use: Epidemiological and Sociological Approaches,* (eds E. Josephson and E. E. Carrol), pp. 333–336. New York: Hemisphere Publishing.

Mendelwicz, J., Simon, P., Sevy, S., *et al* (1987) Polymorphic DNA markers on X chromosome and manic-depression. *Lancet, i,* 1230–1231.

Murphy, J. M. (1986) Trends in depression and anxiety: men and women. *Acta Psychiatrica Scandinavica,* **73,** 113–127.

Myers, J. K., Weissman, M. M., Tischler, G. L., *et al* (1984) Six-month prevalence of psychiatric disorders in three communities: 1980–1982. *Archives of General Psychiatry,* **41,** 959–967.

Odegaard, O. (1961) The epidemiology of depressive psychoses. *Acta Psychiatrica Scandinavica,* **162,** 33–38.

Parker, G. (1987) Are lifetime prevalence estimates in the ECA study accurate? *Psychological Medicine,* **17,** 275–282.

Parry, G. (1986) Paid employment, life events, social support and mental health in working class mothers. *Journal of Health and Social Behaviour,* **27,** 193–208.

Paykel, E. S. (1974) Recent life events and clinical depression. In *Life Stress and Illness* (eds E. K. E. Gunderson & R. H. Rahe). Springfield, Illinois: Charles C. Thomas.

—— and Cooper, Z. (1991) Life events and social stress. In *Handbook of Affective Disorders*

(2nd edn) (ed. E. S. Paykel). Edinburgh: Churchill Livingstone (in press).

——, Emms, E. M., Fletcher, J., et al (1980) Life events and social support in puerperal depression. *British Journal of Psychiatry*, **136**, 339–346.

——, Klerman, G. L. and Prusoff, B. A. (1970) Treatment setting and clinical depression. *Archives of General Psychiatry*, **22**, 11–21.

——, Prusoff, B. A. and Uhlenhuth, E. H. (1971) Scaling of life events. *Archives of General Psychiatry*, **25**, 340–347.

Pedersen, A. M., Barry, D. J. and Babigian, H. M. (1972) Epidemiological considerations of psychotic depression. *Archives of General Psychiatry*, **27**, 193–197.

Romans-Clarkson, S. E., Walton, V. A., Herbison, G. P., et al (1988) Marriage, motherhood and psychiatric morbidity in New Zealand. *Psychological Medicine* **18**, 983–990.

Rosen, B. F., Bahn, A. K. and Kramer, M. (1964) Demographic and diagnostic characteristics of psychiatric clinic outpatients in the USA, 1961. *American Journal of Orthopsychiatry*, **34**, 445–468.

Shapiro, S., Skinner, E. A., Kessler, L. G., et al (1984) Utilization of health and mental health services. Three epidemiologic catchment area sites. *Archives of General Psychiatry*, **41**, 971–978.

Spitzer, R. L., Endicott, J. and Robins, E. (1978) Research Diagnostic Criteria: rationale and reliability. *Archives of General Psychiatry*, **35**, 773–782.

Tarnower, S. M. and Humphries, M. (1969) Depression: a recurring, genetic illness more common in females. *Diseases of the Nervous System*, **30**, 601–604.

Uhlenhuth, E. H. and Paykel, E. S. (1973) Symptom intensity and life events. *Archives of General Psychiatry*, **28**, 473–477.

Warheit, G. J., Holzer III, C. E. and Schwab, J. J. (1973) An analysis of social class and racial differences in depressive symptomatology: a community study. *Journal of Health and Social Behaviour*, **14**, 291–299.

Watson, J. P., Elliott, S. A., Rugg, A. J., et al (1984) Psychiatric disorder in pregnancy and the first postnatal year. *British Journal of Psychiatry*, **144**, 453–462.

Wechsler, H. (1961) Community growth, depressive disorders, and suicide. *American Journal of Sociology*, **67**, 9–16.

Weissman, M. M. and Klerman, G. L. (1977) Sex differences and the epidemiology of depression. *Archives of General Psychiatry*, **34**, 98–111.

—— and Myers, J. K. (1978a) Rates and risks of depressive symptoms in a United States urban community. *Acta Psychiatrica Scandinavica*, **57**, 129–231.

—— and —— (1978b) Affective disorders in a US urban community. The use of Research Diagnostic Criteria in an epidemiological survey. *Archives of General Psychiatry*, **35**, 1304–1311.

—— and Slaby, A. E. (1973) Oral contraceptives and psychiatric disturbance: evidence from research. *British Journal of Psychiatry*, **123**, 513–518.

Wilhelm, K. and Parker, G. (1989) Is sex necessarily a risk factor to depression? *Psychological Medicine* **19**, 401–413.

Wing, J. K. and Sturt, E. (1978) *The PSE-ID-CATEGO System: Supplementary Manual*. London: MRC Social Psychiatry Unit.

——, Cooper, J. E. and Sartorius, N. (1974) *Measurement and Classification of Psychiatric Symptoms: an Instruction Manual for the PSE and Catego Program*. London: Cambridge University Press.

Winokur, G. (1973) Depression in the menopause. *American Journal of Psychiatry*, **130**, 92–93.

—— (1979) Unipolar depression. Is it divisible into autonomous subtypes? *Archives of General Psychiatry*, **36**, 47–52.

Glossary

Abortifacient A substance which will trigger an abortion.

Adhesions Fibrous, scar-like tissue attached to the surface of other tissues.

Adjuvant Additional, assisting.

Adrenal gland A hormone-producing gland sitting just above the kidney.

Affect State of the emotions.

Affective disorder A disease characterized by changes in mood; depression, for example.

AIDS Acquired immunodeficiency syndrome.

Amenorrhea (amenorrhoea) Cessation of menstrual periods. Primary amenorrhea: never having had a menstrual period. Secondary amenorrhea: cessation of menstrual periods after having had them in the past.

Amniocentesis A technique for prenatally diagnosing genetic and other disorders in a fetus, by examining cells from the amniotic fluid surrounding the fetus.

Amniotic Refers to the fluid, or the sac containing that fluid, which surround the fetus in the womb.

Androgens The group of steroids to which testosterone belongs. Present in both men and women, though in greater amounts in men. Can be converted by fat tissue to estrogen.

Anencephalic Marked defect in fetal development, in which most of the brain fails to develop.

Anorexia nervosa An eating disorder most common in adolescents and characterized by obsession with food and sharply decreased eating.

Anovulatory Lack of ovulation.

Anterior pituitary See pituitary.

Areola The pigment surrounding the nipple of the breast.

Atonic colon An intestine lacking normal muscle tone and contractions.

Autosexual Referring to sexual pleasure provided by one's self.

Axillary Refers to the armpit

Azoospermic Absence of living sperm.

Bartholin's glands Glands in the labia majora and the lower part of the vagina which secrete mucous.

Basal body temperature Body temperature upon awakening, which is usually lower than at other times of the day. One method of monitoring fertility.

Biopsy Surgical removal of tissue in order to examine it.

Bipolar depressive disorder A psychological disorder in which person alternates between periods of severe depression and periods of upbeat, energized hyper-activity.

Blastocyst The term used to describe an embryo at a particular early stage of development.

Blastomere One of the cells into which the egg divides after its fertilization.

Bleeding diathesis Spontaneous bleeding.

Breakthrough bleeding Non-menstrual bleeding that often occurs in women using progesterone-based contraceptives.

Breech presentation When a baby is positioned for birth so that its head and shoulders are not born first.

Bulimia Also called the binge-and-purge syndrome. An eating disorder most common in women in which large amounts of food are eaten, followed by vomiting or excessive use of laxatives.

BUN Abbreviation for blood urea nitrogen (a blood gas).

Candida The organism responsible for vaginal yeast infections.

Capacitation A change that sperm undergo in the vagina that makes them capable of fertilizing an egg.

Carcinogenicity Ability to cause cancer.

Cardiac arrhythmia A disruption of the normal beating rhythm of the heart.

Catecholamine A group of substances that are used by nerve cells to communicate with each other.

Cathartic A laxative, causing movement of the bowels.

Catheter A tube.

Caudal anesthesia Anesthesia from approximately the waist down, produced by injecting a pain-killing drug into the fluid around the spinal cord.

Cephalopelvic disproportion When the pelvis is too small for the baby's head.

Cerebral palsy Defective control and coordination of the muscles, resulting from brain damage.

Cervical cap A rubber cap similar to a diaphragm which is covered with spermicide and then placed against the cervix, for contraception.

Cervical dysplasia Another term for cervical intraepithelial neoplasia.

Cervical intraepithelial neoplasia (cervical dysplasia) Abnormalities in the number or shape of cells in the cervix. Considered a precancerous condition.

Cervical os The mouth of the cervix, just above the vagina.

Cervical stenosis Narrowing of the cervix.

Cervicitis Inflammation of the membranes of the cervix.

Cervix The lower, narrow, part of the uterus, which extends to the vagina.

Cesarean section (C section) Delivery of a baby through an opening made surgically in the mother's abdomen and uterus.

Chlamydia A sexually transmitted disease that is often symptomless in women and that can result in infertility.

Chorionic villi Hairlike projections of the membrane that surrounds the fetus early in the pregnancy; it eventually develops into the placenta.

Chorionic villus sampling (CVS) A technique for prenatally diagnosing chromosomal and genetic disorders in a fetus, by examining cells taken from the placenta.

Cirrhosis A progressive liver disease, often associated with alcoholism.

Climacteric The years immediately preceding and following menopause.

Clitoris A small structure above the urinary opening of women. Develops from the same embryological tissue as the penis. It erects during sexual excitement.

Clomiphene A drug used to induce ovulation.

Coitus Sexual intercourse.

Coitus interruptus During sexual intercourse, the withdrawal of the penis before ejaculation occurs.

Colposcopy An examination of the cervix, using a special magnifier to visually examine the cells.

Congenital heart disease Heart disease present from birth. May be hereditary or due to some influence during prenatal development.

Conization Surgical or laser removal of a cone-shaped section of the cervix. Sometimes also called a cone biopsy.

Conjunctival hemorrhage Bleeding that results when blood vessels rupture in the mucous membrane covering the eye.

Contraceptive sponge A spermicide-containing sponge which is placed against the cervix, for contraception.

Corpus luteum The structure that develops from the ruptured ovarian follicle after ovulation. It secretes hormones that are necessary to maintain pregnancy.

Cryopreservation The preservation of tissue by freezing it.

Cryosurgery Killing tissue by freezing it.

Culpotomy (colpotomy) A cutting operation in the vagina, or cervix.

Cystic fibrosis A disease characterized by excessive production of mucus, particularly in the lungs.

Cystitis Inflammation of the bladder.

Cystocele/rectocele Hernia of the bladder or rectum. (A hernia is a rupture or protrusion of some organ.)

Decidualization The shedding of the endometrial tissue during menses.

Deep-vein thrombosis Blood clots in the major veins deep in the body.

Diabetes mellitus A disease caused by a deficiency of the hormone insulin, accompanied by abnormally high sugar in the urine.

Diethylstilbestrol (DES) A synthetic estrogen taken in the past to prevent miscarriages. Associated with the development of vaginal cancer in the women's daughters.

Dizygotic twins A pair of twins that have developed from two separate eggs.

Douching Projecting fluid into the vagina, to wash it out.

DSM-III-R The most recent version of the diagnostic manual devised by the American Psychiatric Association. Very widely used to diagnose psychological and mental disorders.

Ductal carcinoma A type of breast cancer, located in the milk ducts.

Dysmenorrhea Painful menstruation, cramps.

Dyspareunia Pain during sexual intercourse.

Dysplasia See cervical intra-epithelial neoplasia.

Dystocia Difficult labor.

Ectopic pregnancy An embryo or fetus that is developing in the abdominal cavity but outside of the uterus.

Edema Accumulation of fluids in tissues, leading to swelling.

Electroencephalogram (EEG) A recording of the brain's electrical activity (brain "waves").

Encephalitis Inflammation of the brain.

Endogenous Originating or produced from within the organism.

Endometrial hyperplasia An abnormal increase in the number of endometrial (uterine lining) cells. A presumed precursor of cancer.

Endometriosis The presence of endometrial (uterine lining) tissue outside of the uterus, which may bleed in synchrony with the uterine endometrium.

Endometrium The cells lining the uterus.

Epidemiology The study of the spread and prevalence of a disorder.

Episiotomy A surgical incision made at the entrance to the vagina during delivery, to facilitate delivery and minimize tearing of the mother's tissue.

ERT Estrogen replacement therapy.

Erythematous buccal mucosa Red and sometimes bleeding gums.

Estradiol One type of estrogen; produced by the ovary in women.

Estrogen A hormone produced primarily by the ovaries, but also by the placenta, adrenal gland cortex, and in fat tissue. Also present in men.

Estrogen replacement therapy Use of estrogen to treatment symptoms of menopause, primarily hot flashes, urogenital/vaginal atrophy and osteoporosis.

Estrous cycle The sexual cycle of higher animals other than humans.

Extocervix The lower or outer portions of the cervix.

Fecundity Fertility.

Fetal alcohol syndrome A syndrome observed in the babies of women who heavily used alcohol during pregnancy.

Fetal monitor Any device placed on a fetus to measure its activity and functioning. Example: a heart rate monitor.

Fetal scalp monitoring Monitoring of the fetal heart rate during labor and delivery, through a monitor implanted on the fetal scalp.

Fibroadenoma A benign tumor derived from glandular tissue.

Fibrocyst A cyst in connective tissue.

Fibroids A tumor resembling fibers or connective tissue.

Fluoroscopy Examination of the inner parts of the body through the use of X-rays and opaque solutions.

Follicle stimulating hormone (FSH) A hormone secreted by the pituitary gland which stimulates the development of ovarian follicles and is involved in ovulation.

Follicles See ovarian follicles.

Follicular phase Also called the pre-ovulatory phase. The first half of the menstrual cycle, lasting 10–17 days.

Fundus The main body of the uterus, above the cervix.

Gamete intrafallopian transfer (GIFT) Transfer of sperm and eggs into the fallopian tubes. Also called tubal sperm-egg transfer.

Gonad The organ that produces the sex cells: ovaries in women and testes in men.

Gonadotropin-releasing hormone (GRH, GnRH) A hormone secreted by the hypothalamus which influences the release of FSH and LH by the pituitary.

Gonorrhea A sexually transmitted disease.

Halsted radical Another term for radical mastectomy.

Hematoma Localized bleeding under the skin; a bruise.

Hematuria Blood in the urine.

Hemoglobin The oxygen-carrying pigment of red blood cells.

Hemoperitoneum Bleeding into the peritoneal (abdominal) cavity.

Hemophilia An inherited blood disorder in which the blood does not coagulate.

Hemoptysis Bleeding in the lungs; spitting up blood.

Herpes A sexually transmitted viral disease.

HIV Human immunodeficiency virus; the cause of AIDS.

Hot flush or flash The most common symptom associated with menopause. An intense feeling of heat usually accompanied by perspiration.

HPV See human papillomavirus.

HRT Hormone replacement therapy.

Human chorionic gonadotropin A hormone produced by the placenta during pregnancy.

Human menopausal gonadotropin A hormone found in the urine of menopausal women; used to induce ovulation.

Human papillomavirus A sexually transmitted disease that often causes genital warts or sores and that has been linked to cervical dysplasia and cancer.

Hydrosalpinx An accumulation of fluid in the Fallopian tube.

Hypertension High blood pressure.

Hypocalcemia Low calcium.

Hypochloremia Low chloride.

Hypoestrogenisation Low estrogen levels.

Hypokalemia Low potassium.

Hypomagnesemia Low magnesium.

Hyponatremia Low sodium.

Hypophysectomy Removal or inactivation of the pituitary gland.

Hypospadias A defect in which parts of the urethra are open on the under side of the penis; abnormal urethral orifices.

Hypothalamus A part of the brain that regulates many basic functions and that secretes hormones influencing the pituitary gland.

Hypothyroidism A condition in which the thyroid gland is inactive or secretes too little thyroid hormone.

Hysterectomy Removal of the uterus.

Hysterosalpingography A technique based on injection of radio-opaque materials that allow the uterus and fallopian tubes to be visualized.

Idiopathic infertility Infertility of unidentifiable cause.

IM Within or into muscle.

Infibulation The most extreme form of female genital circumcision. The clitoris and labia minora are removed. The labia majora are then sewn together, leaving a single small hole for urine and menstrual flow.

Inflammatory breast disease A type of breast cancer with symptoms resembling an infection; it progresses very rapidly.

In utero In the uterus.

In vitro fertilization Fertilization of an egg by sperm, outside of the woman.

Involutional melancholia Depression associated with menopause.

IUD (intra-uterine device) A type of contraception in which a small metal or plastic object is placed inside the uterus.

IVF/ET See in vitro fertilization.

Keloidal formations Scar-like tissue.

Ketones Chemical byproducts that result from the breakdown of proteins.

Labia majora The outermost and largest round folds of tissue surrounding the urinary and vaginal openings.

Labia minora Folds of tissue surrounding the clitoris and the urinary and vaginal openings; inside the labia majora.

Lactation Producing milk from the breasts; breastfeeding.

Lamaze preparation A type of childbirth preparation designed to facilitate birth, reduce pain and increase the parents' emotional enjoyment of delivery.

Lanuga A fine downy hair that may cover the arms, legs and face of someone with anorexia nervosa.

Laparoscopy Examination of the contents of the abdominal cavity by inserting an electrically lighted tube through the abdominal wall.

Laparotomy A small incision made through the abdominal wall.

Late luteal phase dysphoric disorder The most recent medical term for premenstrual syndrome (PMS).

Libido   Sexual desire or drive.

Ligation   Tightly tying a thread or wire around an organ or tissue.

Lipoproteins   Fatty substances that circulate in the blood.

Lumpectomy   Removal of a breast tumor plus a small amount of the surrounding tissue.

Lupus   A disorder of the immune system.

Luteal phase   Also called the post-ovulatory phase. The second half of the menstrual cycle, lasting 14 ± 2 days.

Luteinizing hormone (LH)   A hormone secreted by the pituitary gland which has multiple actions during a woman's monthly cycle.

Luteotrophic   Stimulating the development and function of the corpus luteum.

Malpresentation   When the position of a baby during delivery is other than head and shoulders first.

Mammogram/mammography   The use of X-rays to examine breast tissue for lumps and other problems. The best way to detect early breast cancer.

Maternal serum alphafetoprotein test   A test of a mother's blood, performed in the 16th week of pregnancy, which can detect certain defects in her fetus's developing nervous system.

Menarche   The occurrence of the first menstrual period.

Menopause   The cessation of menses. When a woman has not had a menstrual period for a year, then the date of her last one is considered the date of her menopause.

Menorrhagia   Excessive amount or duration of menstruation.

Menses   Menstrual bleeding.

Menstrual synchrony   The tendency for women to have synchronized menstrual cycles; that is, they menstruate at approximately the same time.

Metastasis (metastasize)   The spreading of a disease from its tissue of origin.

Micro-metastasis   The traveling of cancer cells very early in the disease to other parts of the body. The parent cancer site is still extremely small.

Mittelschmerz   Pain that occurs as the result of ovulation.

Monoamine oxidase   An enzyme important in the chemistry of the brain.

Monozygotic twins   A twin pair that has developed from the same egg.

Mons veneris   The pubic mound; the prominence caused by a pad of fatty tissue over the joint between the pubic bones in women.

Morbidity   A disease state.

Mood lability   Mood instability; quickly changing moods.

MSAFP   See maternal serum alphafetoprotein.

Mucus method   A method of fertility awareness based on cyclic changes in the cervical mucus.

Multiparous (multipara)   Has given birth more than once.

Mumps oophoritis   Infection of the ovaries associated with the mumps.

Myocardial infarction   Heart attack.

Neural tube defect   A type of defect in the developing nervous system.

Node-negative   Adjective for cancer that has not yet spread to the lymph nodes.

Noradrenaline (norepinephrine)   One of many substances used by nerve cells to communicate with each other.

Norplant   A recently introduced long-acting method of contraception in which capsules containing progesterone are implanted under the skin of the upper arm.

Nulliparous (nullipara)   Has never given birth.

Oestradiol   Alternate spelling of estradiol.

Oestrogen   Alternate spelling of estrogen.

Oestrous   Alternate spelling of estrous.

Oligospermia   Less than normal amounts of sperm in the ejaculate.

Oophorectomy   Another term for ovariectomy.

Oocyte(s)   Another term for ovum (ova).

Osteoporosis   Loss of bone mass. Associated with decreased estrogen levels, as in menopause.

Ovarian follicles   The cells and sac surrounding the developing ovum in an ovary.

Ovarian hypertrophy   Overgrowth or overstimulation of the ovaries.

Ovariectomy   Removal of the ovaries.

Ovulation   The release of an egg from an ovary.

Ovum   The egg in the ovaries. Plural: ova.

Paget's disease   A type of breast cancer.

Pap test/smears   A routine gynecological test in which tissue samples taken from the cervix are examined, to detect cervical cancer.

Palpation   Examination by means of the hands; touching, feeling.

Parity   Refers to whether a woman has given birth or not. See nulliparous, primiparous, multiparous.

Parotid glands   One set of salivary glands.

Pediatric   Referring to children.

Pelvic inflammatory disease (PID)   Infection of the pelvic cavity.

Perinatal   Around the time of birth.

Peritoneal cavity   The abdominal cavity in the body.

Pharonic circumcision   See infibulation.

Phenylketonuria   A serious disorder in which a particular amino acid cannot be properly used by the body.

Pheromone   A chemical substance used by an organism to communicate with another member of the same species.

PID   See pelvic inflammatory disease.

Pineal gland   A gland near the top of the brain whose hormones are involved in reproduction and biological rhythms.

Pituitary   A gland at the base of the brain that secretes hormones regulating the growth and activity of other glands.

PKU   See phenylketonuria.

Placebo   Any inactive substance given in place of a drug.

Placenta previa   The placenta is located in the lower part of the cervix, blocking the cervical os.

Plasma lipids   The fats circulating in the blood.

Polyp   A mass of tissue that bulges outward from the normal tissue surface.

Posterior fornix   A recess at the top of the vagina, lying close by the cervix.

Post-ovulatory phase   See luteal phase.

Postpartum   The period following childbirth and delivery.

Pre-ovulatory phase   See follicular phase.

Primiparous (primigravida, primipara)   Having given birth just once.

Primordial follicles   The developmental precursors to ovarian follicles.

Primordial germ cells   The developmental precursors to sperm and ova.

Progesterone   A hormone secreted primarily by the corpus luteum, which makes the uterine lining more favorable for implantation of a fertilized egg.

Progestin   Synthetic progesterone.

Prognosis   The probable outcome of a disease.

Prolapsed cord   When part of the umbilical cord is delivered before the fetus.

Psychosis   Any major psychological disorder which seriously hampers a person's ability to function.

Puerperium   The period from childbirth until return of the uterus to its normal size; usually about 42 days.

Purdah   Being in seclusion or hidden from view; refers to women, as during menstruation or pregnancy.

Pyelonephritis   A type of bacterial infection of the kidney.

Quickening   The signs of life felt by the mother, caused by the movements of her fetus.

Radical mastectomy   Removal of the entire breast, the underlying chest muscles, the underarm lymph nodes and some additional fat and muscle.

Regional enteritis   Also called Crohn's disease. A type of inflammation of the intestine.

Renal disorder   Any disorder of the kidneys.

Retrograde ejaculation   A condition in which semen enters the man's bladder during ejaculation.

Rh factor   One characteristic used to divide individuals into blood groups.

Rubella   German measles.

Scrotum   The sac containing the testes in men.

Segmental mastectomy   A partial mastectomy, in which the breast tumor is removed, along with a wedge of normal tissue surrounding it, including some skin and part of the muscle below the tumor.

Semen   The fluid containing sperm, nutrients and other substances.

Sepsis   Infection.

Seropositive The term used whenever a person's blood tests positive for some disease or disorder. Often used to refer to infection with the AIDS virus.

Sperm agglutination Clumping of the sperm in the ejaculate; may cause male infertility.

Sperm granuloma A small cyst which develops around sperm.

Sperm washing The treatment of sperm after being collected from a man's ejaculate and before being introduced artificially into a woman.

Spermicide A substance which is capable of killing sperm.

Spina bifida A type of birth defect, in which the spinal column is defective.

Squamous intra-epithelial lesion An abnormality of certain types of cells in the cervix.

STD Sexually transmitted disease, such as herpes or gonorrhea.

Suction curettage Using suction to remove tissue or materials from the inside of a cavity, such as the uterus.

Symphysis pubis The cartilage joining the two pubic bones.

Symptothermal method A method of fertility awareness based on monitoring changes in cervical shape, al mucous, basal body temperature and ovulatory sensations.

sexually transmitted disease.

Teratogenic Capable of causing birth defects.

Testosterone One type of androgen.

Theoretic effectiveness The maximal effectiveness of a contraceptive method when it is used precisely as prescribed or advised by the manufacturer.

Thrombophlebitis Blood clots.

Thyrotoxicosis The state caused by excessive amounts of thyroid hormone.

Toxemia During pregnancy, any metabolic problem that results in high blood pressure, fluid buildup and swelling in tissues, and elevated protein in the urine.

Toxic shock syndrome A serious type of infection by "staph" bacteria, historically associated with the use of certain kinds of tampons.

Transplacental Across the placenta.

Trichomonas A sexually transmitted disease.

Tryptophan An essential amino acid that is a component of many proteins.

Tubal ligation Tying off or cutting the Fallopian tubes; a means of sterilization in women.

Tylectomy Another term for lumpectomy.

Ulceration The formation of an ulcer, or wound, in tissue.

Ulcerative colitis Inflammation of the intestine, accompanied by ulcers.

Ultrasound Using ultrasonic waves to locate, measure or visualizing deep body structures of a fetus.

Unipolar depression Standard, "common", depression which may be mild to severe.

Uremia Excessive amounts of urea and other wastes in the blood.

Urogenital atrophy Thinning of the vaginal and bladder tissues, resulting in dryness and irritation. A result of decreased estrogen, as in menopause.

Use effectiveness The effectiveness of a contraceptive as it is actually used by people.

Uterine evacuation Emptying the uterus of tissue or material.

Vaginal atrophy See urogenital atrophy.

Vaginal barrel The main portion of the vagina.

Vaginal pessary A device introduced into the vagina, to support tissue or to deliver medication of some kind, such as spermicide.

Vaginitis Inflammation or infection of the vagina.

Varicocele A varicose vein in a testicle.

Vas deferens The duct through which sperm travel from the testes to the penis.

Vasectomy Tying off or cutting the vas deferens; a means of sterilization in men.

Vasocongestion Pooling of the blood in a tissue.

Vasomotor flush or response See hot flash or flush.

Withdrawal bleeding Occurs in women using oral contraceptive pills on a 28 day cycle, in which she takes no hormones for the last 7 days of the cycle and consequently has a "menstrual period".